Also by Charles E. Silberman

Criminal Violence, Criminal Justice
Crisis in the Classroom
Crisis in Black and White
The Open Classroom Reader
The Myths of Automation

A CERTAIN PEOPLE

SUMMIT BOOKS
NEW YORK

American Jews and Their Lives Today

CHARLES E. SILBERMAN

Published by SUMMIT BOOKS
A Division of Simon & Schuster, Inc.
Simon & Schuster Building
1230 Avenue of the Americas
New York, New York 10020
SUMMIT BOOKS and colophon are trademarks of Simon & Schuster, Inc.
Designed by Edith Fowler
Manufactured in the United States of America

10 9 8 7 6 5 4 3 2 1
First Edition

Library of Congress Cataloging in Publication Data

Silberman, Charles E., date.
A certain people.

Includes index.
1. Jews—United States—Social conditions.
2. Social mobility—United States. 3. United States—
Civilization—Jewish influences. 4. Judaism—
United States. 5. Jews—United States—Identity.
6. United States—Ethnic relations. I. Title.
E184.J5S496 1985 305.8'924'073 85-12593
ISBN 0-671-44761-0

To my grandson, Matthew Josef Silberman,
the first member of the fifth generation
and to the grandchildren who,
with God's grace, will follow

"Behold, our children are our guarantors."

ACKNOWLEDGMENTS

My first debt—for the title—is to the author of the biblical Book of Esther and to the editors of The Jewish Publication Society of America translation. The phrase "a certain people" comes from chapter 3, verse 8: "Haman then said to King Ahasuerus, 'There is a certain people [the Hebrew phrase *am-echad,* might also be translated "a singular people"] scattered and dispersed among the other peoples in all the provinces of your realm, whose laws are different from those of any other people and who do not obey the king's laws; and it is not in Your Majesty's interest to tolerate them.' "

For nearly two millennia that progression—from the fact of group difference to the innuendo of subversion and thence to the need to outlaw and destroy—was one of the realities of Jewish life; as recently as my own childhood, to be different was to be considered alien and unassimilable and sometimes suspect. But one of the glories of American society is its ever-increasing ability to regard group differences as sources of vitality and strength rather than of weakness. There is a striking parallel, therefore, between the Book of Esther's legend of salvation—the capital city of Shushan (Susa) rejoices when Haman is hanged and Mordecai succeeds him as prime minister—and the post-

World War II experience of American Jews, who have moved from the periphery of American society into its mainstream.

My other debts are many and profound. That there is a book at all is due to the wisdom and imagination of my longtime editor and publisher James H. Silberman, who knew better than I what would excite my interest. He proposed the book and patiently nurtured it and me through barren as well as fertile years, encouraging me when I needed encouragement and prodding me when I needed prodding. His insightful and tactful editing has made this a far better book than it otherwise would have been.

I could not have written a book of this scope without the financial support I received from a number of individuals and foundations, support that made it possible for me to study Jewish communities in every section of the country, engage a series of talented part-time research associates, and turn over much of the time-consuming typing, duplicating, and record keeping to a succession of able and cheerful part-time secretaries.

My primary debt is to the Lilly Endowment, Inc., of Indianapolis, whose generous grant in March of 1980 paid for a substantial part of my research budget, and to Dr. Robert Wood Lynn, the endowment's senior vice-president for religion. A faithful reader and critic of every draft, Dr. Lynn provided continuous intellectual and moral support, and his endless flow of letters expressing the endowment's deep interest in my research encouraged others to look favorably on my applications for funds.

I am indebted as well to a devoted friend, Richard F. Kaufman, of Muskegon, Michigan, who provided several unsolicited grants; to Samuel J. Silberman (no relation), of New York, and the matching grants from the Gulf & Western Foundation; Edith and Henry Everett, of New York; Micha Taubman, of the Emet Foundation, in Larkspur, California; the Jacob and Hilda Blaustein Foundation, of Baltimore, and its vice-president, David Hirschorn; Nathan Appleman and Kenneth B. Smilen, of New York; the Ethel and Philip Klutznick Charitable Trusts, of Chicago; and Amy Macht Gross, executive director of the Martin and Sophia Macht Foundation, of Baltimore.

I owe debts of a different kind to Arnold Forster, Steven Shaw, and Dr. Louis Kaplan, good friends who served as remarkably effective *shtadlanim*, or intermediaries, on my behalf, and to the Honorable Philip M. Klutznick, chairman of the Memorial Foundation for Jewish Culture, on whose recommendation the foundation received and administered most of the grants for me. I am grateful, as well, to Dr. Norman E. Frimer, former executive director of the foundation, who provided warm encouragement and sage advice; Dr. Jerry Hochbaum, the current director; and Mr. David Goldman, controller of the foundation. I am also grateful to the Radius Institute and its director, Steven Shaw, for administering one of the grants for me.

Special tribute is due the late Albert S. Kahn, of Boston, the deus ex machina who rescued me in the spring of 1983 when most of the grants acknowledged above had expired. In the course of conversations on another, largely unrelated matter, Dr. John R. Silber, president of Boston University, had told Mr. Kahn of my research and shown him a description of it that I had written as part of an unsuccessful application for a fellowship from another agency. On his own initiative, and without any solicitation on my part, Mr. Kahn decided to supply the fellowship himself—for two years instead of one, so that I could concentrate on finishing the book without the interruptions and distractions that seeking additional aid would have entailed. I am grateful to Dr. Silber for having brought my need to Mr. Kahn's attention as well as for arranging for Boston University to administer the grant without any charge for overhead; to Leonard Fein, editor and publisher of *Moment* magazine, who encouraged Mr. Kahn to proceed; and most of all to Albert Kahn himself, the memory of whose quiet generosity will stay with me always. I hope that this book will serve as my monument to him. To paraphrase Isaiah, whose promise is read in synagogue on Yom Kippur morning, "His righteousness shall go before him, the glory of the Lord will be his rear guard."

An unusually talented group of journalists and scholars provided me at various times with extra eyes, ears, legs, and minds; their research added depth and breadth to the book in ways not always visible to them. (Because their research has been filtered through my own consciousness and, in some instances, used for conclusions they did not reach or for arguments they did not make, I have merged their voices with mine; in addition to this general expression of gratitude, therefore, I have acknowledged their specific contributions in the Notes on Sources in the rear of the book.) Shulamit Magnus, now director of the Department of Modern Civilization of the Reconstructionist Rabbinical College, applied a historian's knowledge and approach to my journalistic needs; in particular, her analysis of the ways in which their different histories have shaped and continue to shape the American and the European Jewish communities and her insightful history of Israel-Diaspora relations provided much of the background on which Chapter Two is based. Dr. Steven J. Zipperstein, now a lecturer in modern Jewish history at Oxford University, made a penetrating study of the evolution of Orthodox Judaism in the United States, which informs my discussion of Orthodoxy in Chapters Six and Seven. Diane Winston, now the religion reporter for the Raleigh, North Carolina, *News and Observer*, conducted interviews on subjects ranging from the Protestant clergy's attitude toward Jews to the future of Jewish women's organizations. Chapter Three is based in part on the probing interviews with Jewish corporate executives, lawyers, and financiers conducted by Myra Alperson, now associate editor of *Columbia College Today;* Ms. Alperson also tracked down arcane references for me. Mordecai Newman and Robin Reif provided useful research on the past and present role of Jews in the entertainment industry, referred to in Chapter Four.

Most important of all, Steven Silberman, now a reporter for the Memphis, Tennessee, *Commercial Appeal*, helped shape both the substance and the arguments of Chapters Three and Four through his penetrating memoranda on the role of Jews in TV and print journalism, science, academic life, and real estate development; his extraordinarily revealing interviews with key people in each of these fields; and his thoughtful discussions of each of the issues involved. Nor was Steve's role limited to the long summer in which he worked considerably more than full time. A devoted son as well as a gifted journalist, he has affected the shape and tone of the entire book through his sensitive and detailed comments on every draft of every chapter. "A wise son brings joy to his father," the Book of Proverbs declares; "the father of a righteous man will exult."

I am grateful to David McCune, Susan Watt, and Constance Thornton, graduate students, who transcribed tape-recorded interviews; typed lectures, speeches, and the early drafts of the first few chapters; kept careful track of the expenditure of funds transmitted to me by the Memorial Foundation for Jewish Culture; and prepared meticulously accurate quarterly financial reports. Jeffrey Benson of The Computer Studio made it possible for me to shift from typewriter to word processor with ease, and without losing time or copy. An even larger debt is owed to Doris Preisick, who spent countless nights and weekends entering earlier drafts into my belatedly acquired computer; duplicating, collating, and binding each of several "final" printed drafts of every chapter; and, as she had done on an earlier book, calling my attention to mistakes in my typing, spelling, and syntax as well as to the mysterious glitches wrought by a normally docile but occasionally recalcitrant word processor.

To thank everyone who shared time and knowledge with me and my research associates would require a separate chapter, but there are some whose contributions were too important to go unacknowledged here. My largest debts by far are to Professor Steven M. Cohen, of Queens College and The Hebrew University, Professor Charles S.

Liebman, of Bar-Ilan University, and Milton Himmelfarb, of The American Jewish Committee. Professor Cohen generously shared, before publication, the fruits of his innovative and often trailblazing research on the demography, attitudes, and behavior of American Jews; provided special tabulations and cross-tabulations of his data; and commented on each draft. Professor Liebman, the most astute student of Jewish religious life in the United States and Israel, shared his knowledge with me in several day-long meetings and frequent telephone conversations and through his telling criticisms of the manuscript. His encouragement and support, proffered despite serious disagreement with the principal argument of Part Two of the book, helped teach me the meaning of friendship as well as of disinterested scholarship. Mr. Himmelfarb put his encyclopedic memory and profound knowledge of Jewish history and contemporary Jewish life at my disposal, answering frequent questions and providing much needed sources and quotations. He also served as an unpaid editor, correcting innumerable errors of fact, syntax, and spelling and providing sage advice on matters of substance and style.

I am grateful as well to Professor Bruce A. Phillips, of Hebrew Union College-Jewish Institute of Religion in Los Angeles, who gave me access to his demographic studies of a number of Jewish communities before publication and provided special tabulations on a number of crucial points; to Professor Calvin Goldscheider, of Brown University, who shared the manuscript of his own book on American Jewish life before publication and gave me the benefit of his expertise on the technical questions involved in the study of fertility and intermarriage; to Professor Jonathan Woocher, of Brandeis, who provided invaluable insights into Jewish communal life; to Geraldine Rosenfield, of The American Jewish Committee, who shared her unparalleled knowledge of survey data on the American public's attitudes toward Israel and toward American Jews; and to Professor Abraham J. Karp, of the University of Rochester, who gave me access to his all-encompassing knowledge of American Jewish history, as well as to the first draft of his own manuscript on the subject.

A debt of a different sort is due the staff of the Blaustein Library of The American Jewish Committee—in particular, to Cyma Horowitz, the library director, and assistant librarians Michelle Anish and Esther Eidensohn, who served, in effect, as an unpaid research staff, tracking down and checking countless references and citations, calling my attention to sources I otherwise would have missed, photocopying journal articles for my use, and bending the library's own rules to accommodate the time pressure under which I was operating. I am grateful also to Morton Yarmon, director of public relations for The

American Jewish Committee, who gave me full access to the committee's resources and helped in other ways, too numerous to mention.

The analysis of trends in intermarriage and fertility provided in Chapter Seven benefited immeasurably from the advice and data I received from Professor Bernard Lazerwitz of Bar-Ilan University, Barry Schrage, assistant director of the Jewish Community Federation of Cleveland, Professor William Yancey of Temple University, Professor Morton Weinfeld of McGill University, Professor Paul Ritterband of the City University of New York, Professor Gary Tobin of Brandeis University, Dr. Barbara Shamir of Washington University, in St. Louis, and Professor Sergio DellaPergola of The Hebrew University of Jerusalem. I am grateful also to Irving Bernstein, Maurice Cerrier, Dr. Gerson D. Cohen, Dr. Saul B. Cohen, Theodore Comet, Rachel and Paul Cowan, Leonard Fein, Darrell D. Friedman, Professor Herbert J. Gans, Rabbi Laura Geller, Bernard D. Fischman, Bertram H. Gold, David S. Gottesman, Blu Greenberg, Dr. Irving Greenberg, Stanley Horowitz, Rabbi Wolfe Kelman, Professor Seymour Martin Lipset, Professor Deborah E. Lipstadt, Professor Deborah Dash Moore, William Novak, Nathan Perlmutter, Edward I. Riegelhaupt, Daniel Rose, Yehuda Rosenman, Dr. John Ruskay, Arthur Samuelson, Dr. Carl Scheingold, Rabbi Alexander Schindler, Carmi Schwartz, Steven Shaw, Henry Siegman, Sidney J. Silberman, Professor Marshall Sklare, Mark Talisman, Av Westin, and Kenneth Wollack.

I have been privileged to have the support of my four sons. The contribution of my youngest son, Steven Silberman, has been acknowledged above. I am also grateful to David Silberman for his lengthy, probing, and caring comments on every draft; to Rick Silberman, an attentive and thoughtful reader, who called my attention to many books and articles I otherwise would have missed; and to Jeff Silberman, my West Coast clipping service.

As she has with everything I have written, my wife, Arlene Silberman, served as my editor of first resort, commenting on every version of every draft, including many that mercifully never saw the light of day. The book is shorter, kinder, and more lucid because of her gentle but probing questioning, her intolerance of cant and jargon, and her uncanny ability to detect (or elicit from me) what it was that I was really trying to say. My debts to her, however, transcend her contribution as editor; I experience her love anew each day.

Standing under the *chuppah*, or wedding canopy, nearly thirty-seven years ago, my wife and I were too young and too preoccupied with our own new-found love to comprehend what my cousin, the late Rabbi Joseph H. Lookstein, meant when he spoke to us of continuity. I understood more when each of our four sons was born, but it was not until I saw our son Jeff holding *his* son—our first grandchild, Matthew Josef Silberman—that I could fully comprehend Rabbi Lookstein's homily. That comprehension deepened eight days later at Matt's *brit milah*, or ritual circumcision, that awesome and sacred ceremony that symbolizes the unbroken chain of Jewish continuity.

Nor did the symbolism end there. In the Torah portion we read in synagogue the next day, the dying Jacob blesses his son Joseph, placing his hands on the heads of Joseph's sons, Ephraim and Menassah, and invoking the names of his own grandfather and father, Abraham and Isaac; thus Jacob's famous blessing, repeated each Sabbath eve in traditional Jewish homes, spans five generations. With Matt's birth my life has encompassed the same span, for my grandson, now an enchanting three-and-a-half-year-old, is the fifth generation of Silbermans to live in the United States. This book is dedicated to him—and to the grandchildren who, with God's grace, will follow.

It is appropriate to end at the beginning by acknowledging my profound indebtedness to my parents of blessed memory, the late Cel L. and Seppy I. Silberman. I feel their presence always but never so palpably as at this season, when my wife and I are preparing our home for Passover; I am writing this on Sunday, March 24, which is the second day of the Jewish month of Nisan. In the Prophetic portion read in synagogue yesterday, Ezekiel declares that "if the prince gives a gift unto any of his sons, it is his inheritance." My parents were princes in the literal or etymological sense: first among their fellow human beings; and "the crown of a good name," as the Talmud tells us—the crown they wore so effortlessly—"transcends them all." Their gifts were many: their quiet piety and integrity; their abundant and unquestioning devotion to each other and to their children; the love they showered on countless relatives and friends; their reverence for learning; their gentle inability to say a harsh word to or about anyone; and most important in this context, their profound faith in and devotion to their God and their people. All these are my inheritance and an unerring guide to daily conduct; I should like to think that this book reflects and transmits something of their commitment to *netzakh Yisrael*, the eternity of Israel.

C.E.S.

New York City
March 24, 1985
The Second of Nisan, 5745

CONTENTS

PART ONE

An American Success Story

CHAPTER ONE

INTRODUCTION: THE GREAT TRANSFORMATION

"We live in the description of a place and not in the place itself," Wallace Stevens wrote, in a poet's formulation of a sociological truth. But how do people live when the place itself is changing, and when those presumed to be adept at description cannot agree on where it is, or whether it still exists at all?

The question is anything but academic; it confronts American Jews, as well as Italian-, Polish-, and other hyphenated Americans who think of themselves as inhabiting both a particular ethnic/religious and a general American place. Since the end of World War II, ethnic Americans (and we are all ethnics) have been buffeted by wildly differing descriptions of the place they occupy in American society.

It is not surprising that this should be so. Take the case of American Jews, who provide the subject matter of this book. American Jews are going through a period of extraordinary ferment—in the careers they select and the neighborhoods and sections of the country in which they live; the mates they choose and the number of children they have; the nature and intensity of religious observance; the shape of communal life and leadership; the patterns of political authority and influence; whether or not they identify themselves as Jews and, if so, the ways in which they express that identification; the means by which they resolve the tension between their concern with Jewish survival and their desire to be fully integrated into American life; how they perceive non-Jews, as well as the ways in which they perceive themselves and their position in American society. The trends are anything but clear-cut; serious observers disagree over what they are and, equally important, what they portend.

This book is the result of one person's attempt to understand what is happening; it is addressed to Jews and Gentiles alike. My goal is to help explain American Jews to themselves and to their non-Jewish neighbors.

The need is great—on both sides. The ferment and confusion grow out of a profound change that has occurred in the position of Jews in American society since the end of World War II, and especially since 1960—a change that makes the environment of American Jewish life today wholly unlike anything that any Jewish community has ever encountered before. Change has been so rapid, in fact, that American Jews in their twenties and thirties inhabit a completely different world from that in which their parents grew up.

The essence of the change is that American society has broken open to Jews, as well as to members of other ethnic and religious groups, in ways that were not expected—indeed, in ways that could not even have been imagined—a generation ago. The new openness of American society means that American Jews today confront an extraordinary range of options, options that simply were not available in my own childhood and that I and every other Jew assumed never would (or could) be open to us. When I was growing up in New York in the 1930s, for example, brown-shirted members of the German-American Bund used to sell their virulently anti-Semitic newspaper just a few blocks from where I now live; the synagogue my family attended was frequently defaced with swastikas and crosses; an elementary school classmate who ventured onto alien turf had a swastika cut into his hand with a penknife.

It would be an exaggeration to call such incidents routine; my life was reasonably happy and uneventful, and the world I inhabited did not seem particularly hostile. It was, nonetheless, a world of informal but firm quotas and restricted opportunities, one in which Jews saw themselves (and were seen by others) as outsiders. Where we lived, where we worked and at what occupation or profession, even where we played (for the ball fields in New York City's Central Park were divided into Jewish and non-Jewish turf) were affected, and often determined, by what "they" (non-Jews) would allow. At the two Ivy League universities I attended, the number of Jewish students was not allowed to exceed 20 or 25 percent, and contact with non-Jews was limited to the classroom; Jews and Gentiles shared very little social life. Contact was even less frequent in the world of work. Some professions, such as engineering, were virtually closed to Jews, and access to others, such as medicine, journalism, and academic life, was severely limited. It was fruitless, moreover, for a Jew interested in a business career to seek a job with a large corporation; not even the telephone company knowingly employed Jews.

All this we accepted as the way of the world, however much we may have chafed against it or tried to create a society free of prejudice. As an old saying reminded us—if, indeed, anyone could forget—"It is hard to be a Jew." The Great Depression of the 1930s made it even harder, for the scarcity of jobs seemed to exacerbate the anti-Semitism that had been growing in the United States since the late nineteenth century. "For the Jew, the primary need of earning a livelihood is beset with humiliating obstacles," Mordecai M. Kaplan, one of the seminal Jewish thinkers of the century, reported in 1934. Kaplan likened the status of American Jews to that of Sisyphus. "Brought to the point where they see the chance of bettering their condition, of attaining social standing and a relative degree of security," he wrote, "they are told these things are not for them . . . the prospect of the Jew's attaining social and economic equality is . . . remote . . ."

How different it has been for my children and the generation of which they are a part! Their decisions about where to go to school, where to work and at what, where to live, and with whom to be friendly have been totally unaffected, in the negative sense, by the fact that they are Jews. My oldest son, for example, attended Harvard Law School at a time when its dean and half its faculty were Jewish; after law school he clerked for a Jewish Chief Judge of a prestigious Court of Appeals and for a black Associate Justice of the United States Supreme Court.

For my children and for the other members of their generation equality is a fact, not just an aspiration. They face no quotas—except, perhaps, at country clubs they would not care to join—and opportunities appear limitless; the only meaningful constraints are those of energy and talent. Although pockets of discrimination remain here and there, virtually every occupation and almost every position in American society is now open to American Jews, from chairman and chief executive officer of the Du Pont Corporation and president of Columbia University (or, for that matter, Dartmouth) to secretary of state. In short, American Jews now live in a freer, more open society than that of any Diaspora community in which Jews have ever lived before. I will describe this transformation in the next three chapters.

And yet American Jews, at least those of my generation or older, are afflicted with a grave sense of unease. They worry that anti-Semitism is on the increase, and they fear that their own success and newfound prominence are a source of danger—that they will awaken dormant pools of envy and resentment and revive traditional anti-Semitic suspicions of a Jewish conspiracy to control the country, if not the whole world. American Jews wonder, therefore, whether they are as safe as they once had thought; they suspect that their position is eroding and that the United States may be less hospitable to Jews in the future than it has been in the recent past. The alternation of periods of prosperity and acceptance with times of poverty and persecution is, after all, one of the recurrent themes of Jewish history.

And yet American Jews also worry that things may be too *good*—that the very freedom and openness of American society may pose a mortal threat to the survival of American Judaism. Since the beginnings of Jewish Emancipation in the eighteenth century, Jews have feared an open society as much as they have welcomed and, indeed, fought for it. Consciously or unconsciously, Jews suspect that it has been anti-Semitism that has kept them a people and that the relative absence of anti-Semitism in the United States will dissolve their will to survive as a distinct group. As Leonard Fein, editor and publisher of *Moment* magazine, wryly puts it, "It is seduction, not rape, that [American Jews] fear the most." Or as Professor Jacob Neusner of Brown has written, "The central issue facing Judaism in our day is whether a long-beleaguered faith can endure the conclusion of its perilous siege."

In short, the position of Jews in American society has changed so dramatically, and with such bewildering speed, that American Jews are confused about who they are and anxious about how they fit into the society. One of my goals, therefore, is to help American Jews understand where they have been, where they now are, and where they are (or seem to be) heading.

They are not heading for a fall. For one thing, America really *is* different—different in kind, not just in degree—from any other society in which Jews have lived. The critical difference is not that Gentile Americans like Jews more or dislike them less than Gentile Germans, Frenchmen, or Englishmen do (although an important strain of philo-Semitism has always been present in American life), it is that in the United States anti-Semitism never has been an instrument of governmental or church policy. On the contrary, powerful forces built into the marrow of American society confine anti-Jewish attitudes to the private domain, thereby preventing anti-Semitism from becoming the official policy of the government or of the other major institutions in

American life. Those forces are stronger now than they were; a genuinely multiethnic, multireligious society, such as the United States has become in the last quarter-century, cannot permit anti-Semitism to intrude into its public life. Short of changes so profound as to transform the entire society, it is hard to imagine American Jews being pushed out of the positions they now occupy, individually and collectively.

Nor is Judaism seriously threatened by the new openness of American society. After five and a half years of research that have taken me the length and breadth of the United States, I am persuaded that a lachrymose view of American Jewish life is unfounded. It is true that an open society makes it easier for Jews to abandon their Jewishness, but it also reduces the temptation to try, for Jewishness is no longer perceived as a burden, still less as an embarrassment, as it was in my youth. Then, young Jews often rebelled against their Jewishness, and a considerable number sought to abandon it in the hope of gaining acceptance in the non-Jewish world. Today, by contrast, young Jews are comfortable with their Jewishness, whether they express it in religious or secular terms. Those who stop identifying themselves as Jews do so out of indifference rather than rebellion, and many of them reclaim their Jewishness when their children are born.

In short, the end is *not* at hand; for all the talk about intermarriage and assimilation, Judaism is not about to disappear in the United States. On the contrary, as I will demonstrate in Part Two of this book, the overwhelming majority of American Jews are choosing to remain Jews—some kind of Jews, if not necessarily the kind their grandparents or great-grandparents were. There is a tendency to equate the erosion of certain forms of Jewishness, such as the use of Yiddish or the observance of the dietary laws, with the disappearance of Judaism itself. But new forms are emerging and old ones are reviving as American Jews seek to express their Jewishness without inhibiting their full participation in American life. The new ways include lobbying for increased aid to Israel and demonstrating on behalf of Soviet Jewry; the old ones comprehend such rituals as lighting Chanukah candles and attending a Passover seder—both of these observances more widely practiced now than a generation ago—and a growing tendency to give children biblical or Israeli rather than "American" names. In some segments of the American Jewish community, moreover, generational change is now accompanied by an intensification, not a diminution, of religious observance. We are, in fact, in the early stages of a major revitalization of Jewish religious, intellectual, and cultural life—one that is likely to transform as well as strengthen American Judaism.

I have a second goal as well—to explain American Jews to their

Gentile neighbors, for the breaking open of American society has transformed relations between the two groups. Christians to whom, in the past, Jews were an obscure and ancient sect, written about in the Bible but invisible in the contemporary world, now find themselves in daily contact with Jews—as coworkers, employers, or employees; as customers or suppliers; as patients or clients; as business allies or competitors; as fellow members of the boards of civic and cultural organizations; as an organized and increasingly aggressive political-interest group; as neighbors, classmates, friends, or lovers; and, increasingly, as husbands, wives, and in-laws.

It is all very puzzling. Who are these people, Christians wonder, who have moved so rapidly from obscurity to positions of prominence, even influence, in American society—people who so closely resemble other Americans in some ways and who are so stubbornly different in others? Why, for example, do Jews seem to stick together so much? And why the strange insistence on remaining Jewish by people who have no visible Jewish identity? How to understand the apparent paradox that people who ignore or even reject the Jewish religion continue to call themselves Jews?

Nor are these the only questions. What accounts for the upward mobility American Jews have displayed and the extraordinary occupational success they now enjoy? Why the concentration in business, science, academic life, and the professions? Why are Jews so actively engaged in civic, philanthropic, and political activity, and why are they so obsessed with Israel's well-being? And, why, in the face of their success and acceptance, do Jews worry so much about anti-Semitism? Or as a journalist friend asked me, how long will it be before American Jews begin to relax?

In suggesting answers to these questions I hope to achieve a third and final goal: to illuminate the nature of American pluralism. "Out of many, one" has always been the American ideal, but the reality has often been less than that, if more than any other society has achieved. Since the end of World War II, however, the gap between ideal and reality has been substantially narrowed, and for some groups almost completely closed, for, to repeat, the United States has become a genuinely multiethnic, multireligious, and, increasingly, a multiracial society.

This change is fraught with uncertainty over the kind of "one" we are becoming and with disagreement over the kind we *should* become. Can we be one and still remain many—and can we remain many and still be one? Is membership in a separate and distinctive ethnic group compatible with loyalty to the larger society? How does the desire for full integration in American life affect an individual's commitment to his or her ethnic group? And what is the proper relation between the individual and the group or between individual rights and group rights? I cannot claim to have answered these questions definitively, but I believe the answers can be inferred from my analysis of the ways in which the members of one distinctive (and in some ways unique) group have sought—and gained—full membership in American society without abandoning their group identity.

My use of the first-person singular is deliberate; few literary conventions seem more pointless to me, or more misleading, than the substitution of "we" or "this writer" for the pronoun "I." Writing is nothing if not an assertion of self, an "act of saying I," as Joan Didion has put it, "of saying listen to me, see it my way." Thus all writing is political. As the central character in Tom Stoppard's play *The Real Thing* remarks, "If you get the right [words] in the right order, you can nudge the world a little," or at least change the readers' ideas of what the world is, or ought to be, like.

Readers are entitled to know who is speaking to them and from what perspective—all the more so because the questions any writer asks, and thus the answers he or she finds, are shaped by the writer's values and life experience. I write as an American and as a Jew, as one who revels in both identities and who believes that each enriches the other. There are times, of course, when the claims of my Jewishness come into conflict with the claims of my Americanness, but that is true of all the other identities that define me as a human being. I am, after all, both a husband and a father, just as I once was a husband and a son; I am also a parent and a grandparent, a relative and a friend, a writer and a husband. It is not always easy to reconcile the claims arising from each of these identities; no nonwriter (or nonspouse of a writer) can fully appreciate the frequency with which the demands of that lonely vocation come into conflict with every other obligation. Yet life would be infinitely poorer if we each paid allegiance to only one identity. In a sense, therefore, this book is about the various ways in which American Jews have come to terms with these two poles of their being.

CHAPTER TWO

"...AND SOME ARE BORN JEWS"

To be a Jew in the twentieth century
Is to be offered a gift. If you refuse,
Wishing to be invisible, you choose
Death of the spirit, the stone insanity.
Accepting, take full life, full agonies . . .
Daring to live for the impossible.

MURIEL RUKEYSER

1

"Before the beginning of the nineteenth century, all Jews regarded Judaism as a privilege," Mordecai M. Kaplan wrote in 1934 in the opening sentence of his magnum opus, *Judaism as a Civilization;* "since then, most Jews have come to regard it as a burden."

More than a burden: for many Jews their Jewishness was a source of embarrassment, even shame. When he was growing up in the 1920s, Henry Morgenthau III, a Boston writer and television producer and scion of one of the most distinguished American Jewish families, recalls, "being Jewish was something that was never discussed in front of the children."* Jewishness "promised no secret delights or dark

* Morgenthau's grandfather was brought to the United States from Germany in 1865 at the age of ten. He became a highly successful real estate broker and developer and served as ambassador to Turkey and to Mexico during Woodrow Wilson's administrations. Morgenthau's father, a Dutchess County neighbor of the Roosevelts, was FDR's secretary of the treasury, the first Jew to hold that cabinet rank; after Roosevelt's death he became the first general chairman of the United Jewish Appeal (1945–1950) and the first chairman of Bonds for Israel (1950–1954).

pleasures. It was instead a kind of birth defect that could not be eradicated but (with proper treatment) could be overcome, if not in this generation, then in the next. The cure was to be achieved through a vigorous lifelong exercise of one's Americanism."

This message was conveyed in a variety of ways. When he was five, Morgenthau writes, he told his mother that a friend had asked him his religion; his mother's response was pained silence. "What is my religion, Mother?" the puzzled child asked. "If anyone ever asks you that again, just tell them you're an American," his mother firmly replied. "The conversation was over, never to be reopened," Morgenthau adds. "As though sealed in a vacuum it remains photographed in my memory to this day, long after many seemingly more important occurrences have faded."

The acculturated middle-class Orthodox world in which I grew up a decade later was light years away from the Morgenthaus' assimilated upper-class milieu; we *knew* we were Jewish and would have answered accordingly if asked. And yet we felt some of the same discomfort and embarrassment, albeit mixed with pride. Indeed, the fundamental rule on which my generation of American Jews was raised was "Shah!"—Be quiet!—Do not call attention to yourself. It would have been inconceivable for anyone, rabbi or layman, to wear a yarmulke (skullcap) in public, notwithstanding the Orthodox injunction to keep the head covered as a sign of respect for God. (When they were out of doors, rabbis and particularly devout laymen wore fedoras, in keeping with the style of the day.) A prominent Orthodox rabbi a few years my junior recalls the admonition his mother gave him during his student days, when he began wearing a yarmulke outside the home. "It's not nice," she told him.

Most of the time we did not have to be told to be "nice"—that is, inconspicuous. In talking about a Jewish subject in public we lowered our voices automatically, and we were careful never to read a Hebrew book or magazine or an English publication on a Jewish subject when riding on a subway or bus. Our goal was to fade into the crowd; like most Jews, we went to great lengths and at times engaged in complex circumlocutions to avoid calling attention to ourselves or to our strange rituals and customs.

ITEM: Early in his career the tenor Jan Peerce was invited to dinner with the Rockefellers. In the atmosphere of that ancient period, Peerce told his biographer, he was too uncomfortable to explain to his hosts that he observed the Jewish dietary laws and so would have to eat fish instead of meat; instead he cast about wildly to find some plausible excuse to decline the invitation altogether.

The fear of being conspicuous continues to guide members of my own and earlier generations.

ITEM: A few weeks after a neighbor's father moved in with her, members of the block association came to call—not to welcome the elderly gentleman but to protest his habit of sitting on the front lawn quietly reading his Yiddish newspaper while he caught the afternoon sun. "It's not nice," they complained, by which they meant that they were embarrassed by his public display of Jewishness. Had the eighty-two-year-old man read a French paper, the block association members would have been delighted with the touch of class he added to the neighborhood.

ITEM: The funeral had been uplifting as well as moving. The dead woman, who had died in her eightieth year, had been filled with vitality until the end, and in his eulogy the rabbi had evoked her presence with warmth and humor. Reluctant to break the spell, the mourners stood outside for a while reminiscing. Finally I started to leave, but a cousin came running after me. "Mother has something she wants to tell you," she said with a glint in her eye. "Take your yarmulke off, darling," my pious eighty-two-year-old aunt said as I returned. "You're outside; it's not nice."

One can laugh now, but in my childhood and youth, to be "nice" was not just a matter of etiquette; it was a sacred canon. "The Jews are probably the only people in the world to whom it has been promised that their historic destiny is—to be nice," Maurice Samuel wrote in 1932 in *Jews on Approval*, a scathing critique of American Jewish life. "This singular concept has played such an important role in recent Jewish history that it almost characterizes an epoch." The obsession with being nice, in Samuel's view, reflected the belief that anti-Semitism was "the result of a lack of niceness in the Jews. If the Jews would only temper their voices, their table manners and their ties, if they would be discreet and tidy in their enthusiasms, unobtrusive in their comings and goings, and above all reticent about their Jewishness, they would get along very well."

But not *too* well; for there was no way to escape the stigma that Jewishness entailed and that condemned its victims to a subordinate, even marginal, role. "There are certain problems of life for which no solution is possible," Harry Austryn Wolfson, the first Jew to hold a chair in Judaic studies at Harvard, wrote in 1922, and Jewishness was one of them. "Because of our Judaism we must be prepared to give up some of the world's goods even as we must be prepared to make sacrifices because of other disadvantages with which we may happen to be born," Wolfson continued. "All men are not born equal. Some are born blind, some deaf, some lame, and some are born Jews." Just as those who are blind, deaf, and lame "have to forego many a good thing of life," so "to be isolated, to be deprived of many social goods and advantages, is our common lot as Jews." Wolfson concluded his dour pamphlet, addressed to Jewish college students, with a plea to "submit to fate" rather than "foolishly struggle against it."

This view of Judaism was not limited to American Jews, nor was Wolfson's metaphor of Jewishness as physical disability original with him; as he acknowledged, it was coined a century earlier by the great German Jewish writer Heinrich Heine. "Those who would say that Judaism is a religion would say that being a hunchback is a religion," Heine wrote. "Judaism is not a religion but a misfortune."

It is hard now to recall how widespread that attitude was and how deeply rooted, for with the breaking open of American society and the entry of Jews into the mainstream of economic, social, and political life, the old burden has been lifted. Being Jewish no longer is a misfortune, except, perhaps, for social climbers or those who would like to be president. And yet the attitudes that grew out of that sense of burden are fixed indelibly in the consciousness of older Jews, who find it hard to believe that their newfound acceptance is real or, if real, that it can endure. One cannot comprehend the magnitude of the change that has occurred in the position of Jews in American society, still less the ways in which that transformation is affecting Jewish religious and communal life, without understanding why the stigma developed or how it shaped the consciousness and behavior of American Jews. And since most adult American Jews are only a generation or two removed from their European roots, that in turn requires some knowledge of the peculiar relationship that once existed between European Jews and the countries in which they lived.

For most of its history European Jewry constituted a pariah group. As an authoritative sixteenth-century theological dictionary declared, "To be a Jew is an offense"—an offense that was often punished by mass murder or expulsion. (Both the Sabbath and the Yom Kippur liturgies commemorate the martyrs of the Middle Ages.) At one time or another almost every European city or state expelled its Jewish population: England in 1290 (from then until 1650 a royal edict forbade Jews even to visit England), France in 1306, Spain in 1492, Vienna in 1670, and Prague in 1744, to name just a few. Wherever Jews resided, it was by sufferance of the monarch and only so long as they served some state purpose; Jews did not begin to become citizens until the late eighteenth century in France, and later elsewhere.

In general, Jews were confined to designated neighborhoods—

usually behind ghetto walls—and limited to a handful of specified occupations, such as moneylending and trade, that no one else wanted (or was able) to engage in. There were exceptions, of course, especially in pre-Inquisition Spain and Portugal, where Jews occupied high government positions, but in most of Europe, Jews lived out their lives within the confines of their own isolated and self-contained communities. They were separate and unequal—a people dwelling apart, with a culture and set of mores at variance with those of the peoples among whom they dwelt.

They were also a people despised. When Europeans began debating whether or not to admit Jews as citizens, the question was not whether Jews were crude, boorish, and morally and culturally inferior; everyone, friend and foe alike, agreed that they were. The issue, rather, was whether those moral and cultural defects could be overcome and Jews thereby turned into useful members of society. Thus the Royal Academy of Arts and Sciences in the French city of Metz announced in 1785 that it would award a prize two years later for the best essay explaining whether, or how, Jews could be turned into useful citizens.*

In one form or another the question was debated throughout Europe. Those opposed to Emancipation argued that the Jews could not change, that these "implacable enemies of the human race," as Voltaire called them, were congenitally immoral and parasitical, and that their religion made it impossible for them to be loyal to the state.

Those who favored Emancipation, on the other hand, insisted that the Jews' nasty habits were the product of their environment rather than their genes and that their behavior would improve if that environment were changed. "Let us concede that the Jews may be more morally corrupt than other nations," Christian Wilhelm von Dohm, the principal Prussian advocate of Emancipation, wrote in 1781. One could hardly expect anything else, Dohm explained, given "the oppressed condition in which they have been living for centuries." Indeed, "everything the Jews are blamed for is caused by the political conditions under which they now live, and any other group of men, under such conditions, would be guilty of identical errors." It followed, therefore, that gradually freeing Jews from the restrictions placed on them would make them "better men and useful citizens."†

* The subject for the essay contest of the preceding year was whether illegitimate children could be turned into productive citizens.

† Removing the restrictions had to be a gradual process, Dohm conceded, for the Jews were not yet ready for full equality. It would take two generations, for example, before their greed was reduced to the point at which they could be entrusted with public office.

In the words of one of the winners of the Metz essay contest, society ought to strive "to raise the Jews to the level of educated and civilized peoples."

That the Jews were not yet at the level of civilized people was taken as a given, as was the need for them to shed their most loathsome habits. One of the most despised of these was the use of their vernacular language, Yiddish—a "nasal, duck-like quack," Goethe called it, that in his view served to preserve "disgusting values and habits." Abandonment of Yiddish was explicitly called for in the Edict of Tolerance, issued to the Jews of Vienna by the Austrian Emperor Joseph II in January of 1782. This was necessary, the emperor declared, if his goal of making the Jews "useful and serviceable to the state" was to be realized.

The message was driven home in a variety of ways. When the philosopher Moses Mendelssohn, the preeminent figure of eighteenth-century Jewish Enlightenment, wanted to move to Berlin, he asked a friend to intercede with Frederick the Great on his behalf. (Jews could not live in Berlin without the emperor's permission.) The Marquis d'Argens, Frederick's cultural adviser, wrote him as follows: "An intellectual who is a bad Catholic begs an intellectual who is a bad Protestant to grant the privilege [of residence in Berlin] to an intellectual who is a bad Jew." As the historian-essayist Milton Himmelfarb has remarked, "Mendelssohn was not really so bad a Jew as that, but to be allowed—grudgingly—to live in Berlin, he had to be thought a bad Jew. This, then, was the first lesson that modern Jews learned: if you want to be admitted to the delights and excitements of modern culture, do not be a good Jew."

To some Jews the message was, Do not be a Jew at all. "I lack the strength to wear a beard, to let them call 'Ikey Mo' after me on the street," Heinrich Heine declared. "I haven't even the strength to eat matzoh." Wishing to shed the "misfortune" he had declared Judaism to be and believing that "the baptismal certificate is the ticket of admission to Western culture," Heine became a Lutheran in 1825. He made no pretense about his motivation, which was to advance his career. The credit (or blame) for his baptism, Heine quipped, should go to Napoleon's geography teacher, "who did not tell him that Moscow winters are very cold," for if Napoleon had retained his empire, he would have emancipated the Jews of Germany as well as those of France.

Thousands of Jews followed Heine's example. Moses Mendelssohn's son Abraham raised his own children as Christians, he explained to his composer son Felix, because it was the religion "most accepted by the majority of civilized people. Eventually, I myself adopted Christianity, because I felt it my duty to do for myself that which I recognized as best for you."

The great philologist and historian Daniel Chwolson was even blunter in explaining why he joined the Russian Orthodox Church. (In that age, Jews who converted to Christianity almost invariably chose the branch that was dominant in their particular country.) He was baptized out of conviction, Chwolson said, the conviction that "it was better to be a professor in St. Petersburg than a melammed [a lowly teacher of elementary Hebrew] in Eyshishok" (the Lithuanian shtetl—village—from which he came).

For most converts to Christianity, however—Chwolson was a notable exception—baptism provided a ticket of admission only to the sideshow of Western civilization, not to the main event. Heine, for example, never received a university or civil service appointment, as he had hoped, and he came to realize that Prussia would always remain his "little stepfather land," that those he considered his fellow countrymen would always see him as an outsider. In general, Jews who converted to Christianity discovered that in the eyes of the rest of the world they were still Jews, with all the stigma attached to that label. "What would I gain by this change?" an aspiring contemporary of Heine's asked a Christian friend who had urged him to become a Protestant in order to advance his career. The writer knew whereof he spoke; a few years earlier, when conversion of Jews appeared to be increasing, the great Protestant theologian Friedrich Schleiermacher had warned that if the trend were to continue, it would bring about that most dreadful of prospects, the Judaization of the church.

Most Jews, of course, did not convert to Christianity, but it was almost impossible for them not to experience some failure of nerve or feeling of inadequacy as they confronted the Gentile world. Earlier in history, to be sure, Jews had been treated with even greater contempt, but they had not been traumatized by it; secure in their faith, they had seen themselves as a holy nation, one chosen by God to redeem the world. Feeling superior to their Gentile persecutors, they had been content to live apart. But the same intellectual currents that tore down the ghetto walls also weakened, and for many, shattered the ancestral faith. Now eager for acceptance in the dazzling Gentile world that was beginning to open to them, enlightened Jews did not doubt the Gentile view of their own moral and cultural inferiority, for Western life and thought and culture seemed to them superior in almost every way.

That it was *different* could hardly be denied. "Be a Jew at home and a person in the streets," the poet Yehudah Leib Gordon advised his coreligionists, in a line that became the great maxim of nineteenth-century European Jewish enlightenment. Gordon's formula was not simply a call to Jews to restrict their religion to the private sphere—itself a profound move away from the traditional view of Judaism as encompassing all aspects of life—it was, as well, an unconscious expression of self-hatred, a statement that to be a Jew was something less (or at least other) than to be a person. And it was a succinct reminder that if Jews were to make their way outside their community, they would have to acquire a whole new set of manners—which is to say a whole new way of relating to others.

Thus to enter the Gentile world Jews had to cross a wide abyss, leaving their intensely intimate and expressive traditional community—one that the anthropologists Mark Zborowski and Elizabeth Herzog have characterized as "life is with people"—for a highly impersonal modern society—"life is with strangers." To make that journey Jews had to learn to suppress the spontaneity and blunt directness of their native culture, in which reticence—what we think of as "manners"—was not (and to some degree still is not) a virtue. "Having love," Irving Howe has explained, Jews "had no need of politeness."

ITEM: My next-door neighbor was devoted to her Yiddish-speaking father and invariably understanding of his idiosyncrasies. One morning, however, her patience wore thin. "Just once, Poppa," she pleaded, "couldn't you say 'please' or 'thank you'?" "What happened?" the old gentleman responded. "All of a sudden you're a stranger?"

This view of interpersonal relations extended beyond the family, for in the traditional Jewish world no Jew was a stranger to any other Jew; the community was conceived of as an extended family.

ITEM: During her childhood in Eastern Europe the psychoanalyst Helene Deutsch, one of Freud's disciples, was at home alone one day, reading in her bathrobe, when the local wood dealer barged in without knocking. "I jumped up and demanded angrily, 'Mr. Stein, couldn't you knock first?' " Deutsch wrote. "The answer was: 'Why? Isn't this a Jewish house?' "

Learning Gentile manners was no easy matter; the sociologist John Murray Cuddihy has called the process "the ordeal of civility." And ordeal it was. "The politeness which I practice every day," Freud wrote, "is . . . dissimulation"—the dissimulation, he explained, which people adopt when they have to accommodate themselves to another person's overwhelming power. In Cuddihy's persuasive view, Freud's whole theory of the unconscious may be understood as an intellectual acting-out of the ordeal of civility. The id that has to be "civilized" by the ego is really "the Yid"—*dos pintele Yid*, to use the familiar Yiddish term—"the little Jew" that, in Jewish folklore, exists inside every Jew, no matter how assimilated, and whose earthiness the assimilating Jew had to learn to repress.

Some Jews made little effort toward repression; those whose lives continued to be centered in the Jewish community simply learned to affect a different set of manners when they were in public. A story Freud told illustrates how thin the veneer was and the relief with which traditional Jews reverted to their own direct ways when they were with other Jews. "A Galician Jew was traveling in a train," Freud wrote in his *Jokes and Their Relation to the Unconscious*.

> He had made himself really comfortable, had unbuttoned his coat and put his feet up on the seat. Just then a gentleman in modern dress entered the compartment. The Jew promptly pulled himself together and took up a proper pose. The stranger fingered through the pages of a notebook, made some calculations, reflected for a moment, and then suddenly asked the Jew: "Excuse me, when is Yom Kippur?" "Oho!" said the Jew, and put his feet up on the seat again before answering.

Those who wanted to be part of the larger society had a harder time. Seeing Gentile manners as superior, they had to struggle constantly to destroy what they considered the vulgar little Jew within them; they lived in constant fear that Gentiles would associate them with other Jews—those they saw as loud or pushy or acquisitive and who were responsible, in their view, for anti-Semitism.

Intellectuals were particularly susceptible to this kind of self-hatred, Jean-Paul Sartre explained in 1946, in *Anti-Semite and Jew*, because for them becoming an intellectual was not just an occupation or vocation; it was "an avenue of flight"—indeed, "the royal road of flight"—from the taint of being Jewish. "The rationalism of the Jews is a passion—the passion for the universal," Sartre elaborated.

> If they have chosen this rather than something else, it is in order to fight the particularist conceptions that set them apart. Of all things in the world, reason is the most widely shared; it belongs to everybody and to nobody; it is the same to all. If reason exists, then there is no French truth or German truth; there is no Negro truth or Jewish truth. There is only one Truth. . . . The best way to feel oneself no longer a Jew is to reason, for reasoning is valid for all and can be retraced by all.

But reason was of no avail; the revival of anti-Semitism in the late nineteenth and early twentieth centuries persuaded Jews of this sort that their stain was indelible. The result was a new wave of virulent self-hatred. "Do you know how it feels to curse the soil on which one lives?" the philosopher Theodor Lessing asked in 1930. "To draw poison from one's roots instead of nourishment? . . . to hate, senselessly and for an entire lifetime, your father, your mother, your teachers and all those others who have bred and shaped you in their own disgusting image?"

For some, suicide offered the only escape; as one such intellectual wrote: "It is there all the time, it is within me: this knowledge about my descent. Just as a leper or a person sick with cancer carries his repulsive disease hidden under his dress and yet knows about it himself every moment, so I carry the shame and disgrace, the metaphysical guilt of my being a Jew. What are all the sufferings and disappointments and inhibitions which come from the outside in comparison with this hell within? To have to be what one despises!" For with the rise of Hitler, the escape hatches were closed. "There exists today hardly a more tragic fate than that of those few who have truly fought themselves free from their Jewish ancestry and who now discovered that people do not believe them, do not want to believe them," this despairing writer added. "Where, where can we go?" And yet he did not blame the Nazis; the fault lay with "that cursed breed of men whose poisonous self-blood" threatened to destroy the purity of the German nation. "Germans, your walls must remain secure against penetration," he concluded. "Remain hard! Remain hard! Have no mercy! Not even with me!"

This degree of self-hatred was unusual, except among intellectuals of a certain stripe, but it was the rare Jew who escaped some measure of self-hatred or feeling of inferiority altogether. In confronting the modern Western world, there was an almost universal failure of nerve. No segment of Jewry was exempt from it, not even those who continued to believe that God had chosen the Jews for His own transcendent purpose and who were therefore deeply committed to Jewish survival. At one end of the religious spectrum, for example, important leaders of Orthodoxy tried to rebuild the ghetto walls. Since contact with the Gentile world would inevitably persuade Jews to surrender their Judaism, they reasoned, the preservation of Judaism depended on keeping that contact to an absolute minimum and on insulating the faithful against any Gentile influences that might filter through.

To do this required a radical break with the reality, if not necessarily the theory, of traditional Judaism. Over the preceding 2500 years, as the historian Gerson D. Cohen, chancellor of the Jewish Theological Seminary of America, has argued, Judaism survived, and often flourished, because of its ability to incorporate elements of the surrounding culture without losing its essential continuity with the past; the most creative periods of Jewish religious and cultural life, in fact, had been those of great cultural assimilation and cross-fertilization. In the late eighteenth and early nineteenth centuries, however, change, *any* change—indeed, the very *idea* of change—came to be seen as the enemy. As Rabbi Moses Sofer, the principal ideologist of Orthodox fundamentalism, decreed, "All that is new is forbidden by the Torah," that is, by divine law.

At the other end of the religious spectrum, early- and mid-nineteenth-century German Jewish reformers tried to redefine Judaism to fit Protestant categories. They expurgated the national and ethnic aspects of Judaism, dropped Hebrew as the language of prayer, prayed with uncovered heads, and introduced sermons, organ, choir, and other changes designed to make worship in the synagogue resemble a Protestant service as much as possible. Reform Judaism was in a sense the mirror image of Orthodox fundamentalism; to exaggerate just a bit, the reformers tended to see change—almost any change—as desirable. More precisely, they saw modernity as the norm to which Judaism would have to be adapted. It was not just that reformers dropped any part of Jewish tradition that seemed out of keeping with the spirit of the age. They went further, putting the burden of proof, so to speak, on the tradition: rituals and practices were to be dropped unless one could demonstrate their contemporary relevance.

In the late nineteenth and twentieth centuries, meanwhile, secular Zionists accepted the notion that anti-Semitism was the inevitable if unfortunate by-product of the fact that Jews were different and thus resented by the host peoples among whom they resided. The solution to "the Jewish problem," therefore, was what Zionists called the "normalization" of Jewish life. If Jews were allowed to create their own state, they would become *k'chol ha-goyim*, a nation like every other nation. Those who wanted to remain Jews would move to the Jewish state, while those who remained in the Diaspora would disappear through assimilation—a phenomenon devoutly to be hoped for, because, as one Zionist theorist wrote, "The Judaism of the Galut [Diaspora] is not worthy of survival."

To most Zionists, in fact, the preceding eighteen centuries of Jewish history had been an aberration and a waste. As Yudka, the central character in a short story by the Israeli writer Haim Hazaz, declares: "We have no history at all. . . . Because we didn't make our own history, the goyim made it for us . . . and we took it from them as it came. But it's not ours, it's not ours at all! Because we didn't make it, we would have made it differently, we didn't want it to be like that, it was only others who wanted it that way and they forced it on us, whether we like it or not . . ." And so Yudka would forbid the teaching of Jewish history. The message he would give schoolchildren is, "Boys, from the day we were driven out from our land we've been a people without a history."

To secular Zionists, in short, creation of a Jewish state would enable Jews to start all over again, to recreate themselves into a new and more likable people. "Was the Jew really so insensitive, so dead to the world, as not even to realize how much more beautiful and rich was the Gentile's life than his own?" asked the novelist Joseph Brenner, an early twentieth-century Zionist leader. "No, this is impossible!" he answered. "Our function now is to recognize and admit our meanness since the beginning of history to the present day, all the faults in our character, and then to rise and start all over again."

There is, of course, an element of caricature in my characterization of the Jewish response to modernity. Fundamentalism was only one strain within Orthodoxy; some important Orthodox leaders sought an accommodation between Judaism and modern European culture, most notably the influential Samson Raphael Hirsch, who argued that to fulfill his mission the Jew would have to extend his Judaism to "areas never imagined by his father." For, as Hirsch put it, the authentic Jew "will not be a stranger to anything which is good, true, and beautiful in art and in science, in civilization and in learning." Reform Judaism, moreover, was far more than just an attempt to make Judaism acceptable to the Gentiles, nor was it merely a watering down of tradition; as conceived by its leading figures, it was an alternative expression of that tradition. Specifically, Reform was a new formulation of Jewish Messianism, one that emphasized the universalist dimension of Judaism, which the preceding centuries of persecution had tended to suppress.

Neither was Zionism merely an expression of Jewish self-hatred; even more than Reform Judaism, it transformed the meaning of Jewish Messianism. Instead of waiting for God to bring about the Messianic Age in His own way and time, as Orthodoxy believed, and instead of serving as witnesses to the inevitable triumph of monotheism, as Reform proposed, the Zionists insisted that Jews had to go to work to bring about their own redemption; thus Zionism brought about the reentry of Jews into the political world.

The failure of nerve was there, nonetheless, and was an important animating force. Indeed, the failure was inevitable, given the terms on which Jews were admitted to citizenship: in return for Emancipation, Jews had to surrender an essential part of their self-definition—that they were a people as well as a religious community.* "To the Jews as a nation, nothing; to the Jews as individuals, everything," a leading

* For an explanation of the interrelationship of religion and ethnicity in Judaism, see Section 4 below, especially pp. 70–73.

French advocate of Emancipation had declared when the French National Assembly was debating citizenship for the Jews. And in greater or lesser degree, French (and after them, German) Jews accepted the formulation.

2

When they crossed the Atlantic, Jews found a far more hospitable environment. True, some of the early colonists would have preferred to keep Jews out, but the continent was too vast and the need for settlers (especially settlers with the skills some of the early Jewish merchants and international traders brought with them) too great for anti-Jewish sentiment to prevail. For the most part, therefore, Jews did not have to wage a battle to be included, and Gentile Americans did not have to debate the question of whether or on what terms Jews should be granted citizenship.*

Almost from the beginning, moreover, Americans developed a tradition of tolerance unlike anything Europe had known—a by-product of the nature of the religions the early settlers had brought with them. The first Europeans to arrive were members of dissenting sects who came here in search of religious freedom. Each group wanted freedom only for its own sect, of course, but the multiplicity of denominations made it impossible for any one group to impose its beliefs and practices on others. Bit by bit, American religious groups gave up the notion of using state power to enforce religious conformity; they came to see themselves as voluntary associations whose religious claims were binding only upon their own members.

In this new world Judaism was accepted as simply one more religious denomination, and Jews participated in the life of the larger community to a degree that would have been inconceivable in Europe. For example, in an account of the parade in Philadelphia celebrating the ratification of the Constitution, a newspaper described "the clergy of the different Christian denominations with the rabbi of the Jews walking arm in arm"—not a scene one could have encountered, or even imagined, in any European city of that (or a considerably later) era. Understandably, Jews saw America as different.

ITEM: "You cannot know what a wonderful country this is for the common man," a Jewish resident of Virginia wrote to her European parents in 1791. "One can live here peacefully"—that is, without being

* A few colonies debated whether Jews should be permitted to hold public office; Maryland, for example, did not grant Jews the prerogative until 1826.

burdened by anti-Semitism. The writer went on to describe the amicable relations between Jew and Gentile.

The leaders of the new republic, meanwhile, took pride in the openness of American society. "The citizens of the United States of America have a right to applaud themselves for having given to mankind examples of an enlarged and liberal policy, a policy worthy of imitation," George Washington wrote to the Jews of Newport, Rhode Island, in response to their letter of congratulations on his election as president. "It is now no more that toleration is spoken of, as if it was by the indulgence of one class of people that another enjoyed the exercise of their inherent natural rights. For happily the government of the United States, which gives to bigotry no sanction, to persecution no assistance, requires only that they who live under its protection should demean themselves as good citizens in giving it on all occasions their effectual support."

Acceptance was made easier by the fact that until the middle of the nineteenth century there were not enough Jews to create a visible Jewish presence. Equally important, perhaps, the first Jews to come here had left the ghetto long before their arrival. An urbane and cosmopolitan group of merchants and international traders, these Spanish and Portuguese Jews—"the first modern Jews," as the historian Yosef Yerushalmi has called them—had been on the move for some time. Most were descendants of Marranos, Jews who had publicly converted to Catholicism to avoid being burned at the stake but who had continued their allegiance to Judaism in private. When the Inquisition turned its attention to the Marranos and began ferreting them out, those who could do so fled the Iberian Peninsula, moving first to England or Holland and then, in some cases, to Brazil, Curaçao, Jamaica, and the Virgin Islands. Some of the latter in turn settled in what was to become the United States, where they were joined by a handful of Marranos and other Jews who came here directly from Spain and Portugal.

In the New World the Marranos resumed their lives as Jews, but in a new way: their Judaism combined an unquestioning (and often uninformed) Orthodoxy within the synagogue with relaxed observance and substantial assimilation outside. American Jews "are not identifiable by their beards and costumes, as is the case with the Jews who live among us," a Hessian soldier who fought in the Revolutionary War wrote home with some bewilderment. "Jewish women have their hair dressed and wear French finery like the women of other faiths," while the men "are dressed like other citizens, shave regularly, and also eat pork." Anticipating Y. L. Gordon's formulation, they were Jews at home and "people" outside.

This practice continued for some time despite a change in the nature of Jewish immigration. By the early eighteenth century the Sephardim, as the Spanish and Portuguese Jews were called, began to be outnumbered by far more traditional Ashkenazi Jews, who trickled in from England and the German-speaking areas of Western and Central Europe and, from time to time, Poland; but the Sephardim maintained religious and cultural ascendancy nonetheless. Despite occasional tensions between the two groups, the Ashkenazim stood in awe of the already Americanized and rather aristocratic Sephardim who had preceded them and quickly adopted the Sephardic practices of speaking English and following American styles of dress, appearance, and deportment. By the time the republic was established, therefore, American Jews were a highly acculturated middle-class group, largely indistinguishable from other Americans, with whom they intermarried with considerable frequency.

All this changed when the pace of Jewish immigration accelerated. During the first three centuries of American history Jewish immigration had been sporadic and individual, with just a few people coming at any one time. During the 1820s, 1830s, and 1840s, however, a severe slump in trade in Germany and the Austro-Hungarian Empire combined with increasingly virulent anti-Semitism to push Jews out of Central Europe en masse. With entire families and groups of families from a single locality coming here, the Jewish population of the United States jumped from an estimated 3000 in 1818 to 15,000 in 1840; it more than tripled, to 50,000, in the next ten years, and tripled again, to 150,000, during the 1850s. The largest single group came from Bavaria and other parts of what ultimately became the German Reich, but there were significant numbers from Vienna, Posen (a section of Poland under German rule), Alsace, and other areas of Central and East Central Europe, whose Jews spoke German and were strongly influenced by German culture.

These "German Jews," to use the catchall term, changed the religious and cultural tenor (and as we will see below, the geography) of American Jewish life. As a group they were far less cosmopolitan than their predecessors; many were poorly educated but religiously observant Orthodox Jews who were shocked by the religious laxity they encountered here. Since they were opposed to religious change of any sort, their initial impulse was to reproduce the Orthodox synagogues they had left behind—to use the same melodies, the same order of service, the same rites and rituals they had known in their little towns in Germany and Poland.

The established congregations, however, wanted no part of the new immigrants, whom they considered boorish and uncouth and as threatening to their status as the German Jews would later find Eastern European immigrants to be. "Situated as our Congregation at present is and with prospects . . . of future wealth and a respectability and standing of which its members may well feel proud," the membership committee of New York's Shearith Israel declared in 1835, "it becomes its imperious duty to cherish and protect its resources by the introduction of laws rendering the admission of improper persons as members more difficult than it has heretofore been."

This haughty reaction was understandable, for the German Jewish immigrants were a boisterous and earthy lot; in their unabashed expressiveness they closely resembled the later immigrants from Eastern Europe, to whom, later in the century, they would show the same disdain. Emotions were perilously close to the surface and erupted with ease; frequent and intense disagreements over small matters of religious ritual often ended in fist fights. "Blows passed in a certain synagogue in New York on Kol Nidre evening [the holiest night of the year] because the one party insisted that at the close of the Service the *Adon Olam* be sung first and then the *Yigdal*, while the other insisted on the opposite," Rabbi Isaac Mayer Wise, the principal religious leader of the German Jews, recalled in his memoirs. Earlier in his career Wise had been a combatant himself: standing before the open ark of his Albany congregation on Rosh Hashanah, 1850, he received a punch in the nose from the synagogue president. (The president had fired Wise, who led the service nonetheless.) In the melee that followed, Wise gleefully recalled, the battling congregants fought off the sheriff and his posse, who had come to restore order.

It did not take long, however, before the unruly immigrants began to adapt to American ways. There was no greater advocate of acculturation, in fact, than Wise himself after his move to Cincinnati, which he turned into the religious center of the German Jews. "The Jew must become an American in order to gain the proud self-consciousness of the free-born man," Wise declared, and so he himself "began to Americanize with all [his] might." "We must be not only American citizens," Wise explained, but "Americans through and through outside the synagogue."

Acculturation was made easier by the fact that the German Jewish immigrants dispersed throughout the country. Lacking the capital and international connections that the Sephardim possessed, the German Jews were fortunate to arrive when the United States was expanding geographically as well as economically. Hence they followed the routes of expansion, fanning out as peddlers throughout the East, Midwest, Far West and South. Peddling required little capital and no particular skill, but it filled a vital economic need; before the invention of the mail-order catalog it was the principal means by which city-made goods found their way into the countryside.

It was also a difficult life, whose loneliness, insecurity, and back-breaking work the Jewish peddlers hated. "It is hard, very hard indeed to make a living this way," Abraham Kohn, a Bavarian Jewish immigrant, wrote in his diary in 1842. "I must stop this business, the sooner the better." And stop he did; like that of most Jewish immigrants, Kohn's goal was to settle down at the first opportunity and establish a store or other business. Within five years he had opened a small clothing store in Chicago and had helped organize the first synagogue; by 1860 Kohn had become a major political figure as well, presenting his friend President-elect Abraham Lincoln with an American flag in his capacity as Chicago's city clerk.

There were many similar success stories. "How wonderfully, how very beneficially conditions have changed since 1837," a German-language paper edited by Wise noted in 1860. "Many, very many of these beggarly-poor emigrants are nowadays at the head of business concerns that own enormous property, command unlimited credit and amass each year great fortunes. . . . The signs of their enterprises blaze in all the big commercial cities of the Union, such as New York, Philadelphia, Cincinnati, St. Louis, New Orleans." Most immigrants, of course, did not amass great fortunes; some remained abjectly poor. As a group, however, the German Jewish immigrants managed to move into the commercial middle class with extraordinary rapidity, in cities and towns of every size and in every part of the country.

By 1860 there were no fewer than 160 identifiable Jewish communities in the United States and a Jewish traveler could find a synagogue almost everywhere he went—in places such as Albany, Utica, and Buffalo, New York; Cincinnati, St. Louis, Chicago, and Detroit; Wheeling, West Virginia; Mobile, Alabama, and Galveston, Texas; and as far west as San Francisco.

The Civil War accelerated the process of acculturation. Jews served in the army and helped in the war effort in other ways, and for the first time rabbis served as army chaplains—a dramatic demonstration of the equal position Jews enjoyed in America; in Europe the army had always been a prime locus of anti-Semitism. Thus immigrants who had thought of themselves as Germans came to see themselves not only as Americans but as Americans who belonged.

That feeling was intensified after the Civil War as industrialization, urbanization, and rapid economic growth propelled the German Jewish immigrants into the middle and upper-middle class. They were not alone in moving up: this was the golden age of entrepreneurship in the United States, and fortunes were being amassed on a scale undreamed of before. Even for this period, however, the Jewish ascent was remarkable; as the historian John Higham has written, no other immigrant group "has ever risen so rapidly from rags to riches." Onetime peddlers became millionaires, among them investment bankers such as Joseph Seligman, Mayer Lehman, Marcus Goldman, and Solomon Loeb; retailers such as Benjamin Bloomingdale and Lazarus Straus; clothing manufacturers such as Levi Strauss and Philip Heidelbach; real estate brokers and developers such as Henry Morgenthau, Sr.; and the mining magnate Meyer Guggenheim. And affluence was not limited to this small elite; an 1890 Census Bureau survey of 10,000 Jewish families, most of them German immigrants, found that seven families in ten had at least one servant.

As the Gilded Age began, Jews were confident that they could be fully integrated into American life without surrendering their Jewishness; this was, after all, a period of unbounded faith in progress and confidence in the ultimate triumph of reason. That confidence seemed to be vindicated in 1867, when Wise and his friend Rabbi Max Lillienthal were invited to address the first meeting of the new Free Religious Association in Boston. As Leon Jick dryly remarks: "Wise, who had been assaulted on the pulpit of an impoverished Albany congregation in 1850, shared the rostrum in Boston with Emerson in 1867 and declared his conviction that reason could lead man to perfection."

The combination of affluence and optimism was transforming American religion. "Everywhere there were signs of expansion and prosperity in churches," the historian Clifton E. Olmstead wrote. "Where once there was a simple frame meeting house, there now stood a magnificent edifice testifying to the affluence of its congregation. Robed choirs, strengthened by professional singers, marched with dignity to their stations . . . and ministers . . . devoted more attention to conducting their services 'decently and in order' . . ."

Jews too felt the need not only to demonstrate their faith but to announce their arrival—to say, in effect, "We are here." They were moving into homes in "better" neighborhoods, as befitted their affluence, and they wanted synagogues to match. "The honor of Judaism in Cincinnati and throughout the West," Isaac Mayer Wise declared, required that his congregation "come out of Lodge Street into the broad daylight of a more suitable locality." The ornate new Plum Street Temple, opened in 1868 at a cost of $263,525, could accommodate 2000 worshipers; as a local newspaper remarked, "Cincinnati never before had seen so much grandeur pressed into so small a space."

There was even more grandeur in New York, where Temple Emanu-El, which had become the congregation of the German Jewish investment bankers and merchant princes, dedicated an imposing new building at Fifth Avenue and Forty-third Street. At the first meeting of the congregation, in 1845, the impoverished German immigrants had raised a grand total of $28.25 among them; just twenty-three years later the sale of pews for the new building netted $708,575.

Construction of temples, as the new synagogues were grandly called, was accompanied by a radical change in liturgy and style of worship.* Before the Civil War, as Leon Jick has demonstrated in his history of the origins of Reform Judaism in America, religious reforms had been modest and accompanied by considerable ambivalence; the goal was to make the Sabbath service more intelligible and appealing to congregants no longer fluent in Hebrew without sacrificing tradition. After the war the ambivalence disappeared, and laymen and rabbis, with the former in the lead, pursued Reform with a capital "R."

In one congregation after another, changes of a far-reaching sort were introduced: the length of the service was sharply curtailed; the traditional prayers for the return to Zion and restoration of the Temple and of the Davidic monarchy were dropped; references to the resurrection of the dead were eliminated; organ music was introduced; English replaced Hebrew as the primary language of prayer; the traditional segregation of the sexes was abolished, so that men and women sat together in family pews; and regulations were passed prohibiting male worshipers from wearing prayer shawls and hats. This last was often the final break with tradition and the most important symbolically, since it eliminated the principal visual difference between Jewish and Protestant worship.

Nothing epitomized the new mood so dramatically as the famous "trefa [nonkosher] banquet" at Cincinnati's Highland House on July 11, 1883. At this dinner, given to honor the first graduating class of Hebrew Union College, the first American rabbinic training school, the menu included littleneck clams, soft-shelled crabs, oysters (a particularly high-status dish at that time), and shrimp—all foods prohibited under the Jewish dietary laws. When the clams were served as the first course at what was supposed to have been a kosher dinner, the Orthodox rabbis present rushed from the room, thereby shattering Isaac Mayer Wise's dream of presiding over a united American Jewish community. The decision to serve the forbidden foods had been made by the wealthy Cincinnati businessmen who underwrote the cost of the

* The change in nomenclature was no mere rhetorical device; it reflected the reformers' conviction that America was the promised land and that it was therefore no longer appropriate to pray for the restoration of the Temple in Jerusalem.

dinner; eager for social acceptance, they wanted to demonstrate how fully American they were.

3

The wistful yearning for social acceptance was never fully realized. For the upwardly mobile German-American Jews the Gilded Age had already begun to tarnish, as Isaac Leeser, Wise's principal rival for leadership of the American Jewish community, had warned. "In most large cities Jewish people occupy some of the finest residences," Leeser had written in 1865 in an editorial expressing the traditional Jewish fear that visibility would lead to anti-Semitism. "Now, if nothing else will cause prejudice, this circumstance will do so to a certainty. While we are poor and unsightly, we may be tolerated; but let us only look up, and become the social equal of our neighbors, and their ire will be at once roused."

As indeed it was, although not for the reason Leeser had thought. What happened, in essence, was that the new captains of industry, snubbed as parvenus by the old elite, tried to elevate their own social standing by excluding Jews from the hotels and clubs they frequented. The event that symbolized the emergence of a new social anti-Semitism was the so-called "Second Battle of Saratoga" in the summer of 1877, when Joseph Seligman, the investment banker, was denied the accommodations he had reserved at the Grand Hotel in Saratoga Springs, New York, where he and his family had stayed a number of times before. "No Israelites shall be permitted in the future to stop at this hotel," its new manager, Judge Henry Hilton, declared.*

Hilton's decision unleashed a storm of criticism from such people as Henry Ward Beecher, William Cullen Bryant, and the partners of Drexel, Morgan & Company, as well as a number of newspaper edi-

* Hilton had become the manager of the Grand Hotel because he was executor of the estate of its owner, the merchant prince Alexander T. Stewart, who had died the year before. Hilton's decision to exclude Seligman had been motivated by personal animus as well as a desire to improve the social standing of the hotel, which had seen better days. For one thing, Seligman was a member of the Committee of Seventy, a group of prominent New Yorkers who sought to destroy the power of the Tweed Ring, of which Hilton was a prominent member. To make matters worse, Seligman had been offered—and had turned down—a cabinet post in U. S. Grant's administration as well as a nomination to run for mayor of New York—and Hilton had desperately craved both offices. Hilton was miffed too because he had not been invited to a dinner Seligman and his brother gave for Grant when he left the presidency.

torial writers. The controversy was front-page news during the entire summer, for Seligman was no ordinary Jew. Some of the new Jewish millionaires may have been less than fully polished, but not Seligman. Like most of the Jewish investment bankers of the period, Seligman had started out as a peddler; unlike his peers, he was a graduate of a German university, an adviser to President Rutherford B. Hayes and a close friend and confidant of former President Ulysses S. Grant. (Incidentally, Seligman employed Horatio Alger as a tutor for his children.)

The protests were to no avail; the tide was running the other way. A year after Seligman was turned away in Saratoga Springs the New York City Bar Association blackballed a Jewish applicant—the first of a long series of moves designed to restrict Jews to the lower rungs of the legal profession. That same year the Greek-letter fraternities at New York's City College decided to exclude Jewish members, and the year after that Austin Corbin, president of the Manhattan Beach Company, announced his determination to bar Jews from his hotel in Brooklyn's Coney Island, on the ground that "they are driving away the class of people who are beginning to make Coney Island the most fashionable and magnificent watering place in the world." "We must have a good place for society to patronize," Corbin told a reporter for the New York *Herald*. "We cannot do so and have Jews. They are a detestable and vulgar people."

It did not take long for members of the old elite to rival the parvenus in their hatred of Jews. Feeling displaced by the growing materialism of American life, which was making wealth rather than ancestry the primary source of social status, they directed their resentment against the Jews rather than against the captains of industry who were elbowing them aside. Of these socially displaced aristocrats none was more resentful, or more obsessed with Jews, than Henry Adams. "I am myself more than ever at odds with my time. I detest it, and everything that belongs to it, and live only in the wish to see the end of it, with all its infernal Jewry," Adams wrote to a friend in 1896. Indeed, Adams longed for a Götterdämmerung in which "men of our kind might have some chance of being honorably killed in battle"—the only way to escape the growing enslavement by "the Jew," who "makes me creep." "We are in the hands of the Jews. They can do what they please with their values."

Aristocratic fear of displacement was exacerbated by mass immigration of Italians, Poles, Slovaks, and Jews—especially Jews—which was making the United States a far more polyglot nation than it had been. In 1870, when migration of Eastern European Jews was just beginning, there had been only about 170,000 Jews in the United States, a mere 0.4 percent of the population. In the next ten years some 70,000 Eastern European Jews arrived, my paternal grandfather among them—and then the floodgates opened. By 1900 more than 20 percent of the immigrants coming to the United States were Jews. Severe economic dislocation had already forced Russian and Polish Jews out of their traditional occupations, turning them into an impoverished proletariat, when the assassination of the liberal czar Alexander II in 1881 touched off a wave of bloody pogroms.

This combination of forces produced the largest migration in Jewish history. In the half century following the czar's assassination half the Jewish population of Eastern Europe moved to the United States—some two and a half million people in all. "America was in everybody's mouth," Mary Antin, who came here in 1891, wrote in her autobiography; even the "children played at emigrating." By 1900 the American Jewish population had passed the one million mark; by the mid-1920s, when new immigration exclusion legislation went into effect, there were more than four million Jews in the United States—3.5 percent of the total population.

In the large cities of the East and Midwest the proportion was considerably higher, for the new immigrants came to the United States when urbanization and industrialization were at their peak. Too poor even to become peddlers—the Jews who arrived in 1900, for example, had only $9 with them, on average, compared to $15 for immigrants as a whole—they took the jobs that were available, most often in the clothing factories and other light industries that were springing up to produce items that before urbanization had been manufactured at home.

And so the Eastern European Jews poured into the old "areas of first settlement" in Boston, New York, Philadelphia, Cleveland, Chicago, Detroit, and other cities, producing something new to American life—large, densely packed Jewish slums that were appalling even by the standards of that age. "I suppose there are and have been worse conditions of life, but if I stopped short of savage life, I found it hard to imagine them," William Dean Howells, the dean of American letters, wrote in 1896 after a trip to New York's Lower East Side. "Nowhere in the world are so many people crowded together on a square mile as here," Jacob Riis reported six years later; the density was double that of the worst slums in London. In a typical tenement apartment with two tiny rooms, Riis elaborated, lived a family of father and mother, twelve children, and six boarders. (Almost every family had boarders—who often had to sleep in shifts—for without them immigrant families could not afford to pay the five-dollar monthly rent.) And conditions were no better in Boston, Cleveland, Chicago, or any of the other cities to which Jewish immigrants moved.

It was not just a question of numbers; the Eastern European Jews came from a different world, many of whose forms they reproduced here. With their profusion of synagogues, kosher butcher shops, restaurants and bakeries, public baths, bookstores, Yiddish newspapers, dance halls and theaters, not to mention the rows of pushcarts and barrels that made the streets almost impassable, the new Jewish neighborhoods had an exotic vibrancy and intensity that enthralled such journalists as Lincoln Steffens and Hutchins Hapgood. But that same intensity and drive repelled the aristocratic Henry Adams and the fastidious Henry James and terrified the "uptown Jews," as the assimilated German Jews came to be called. To the insecure German Jews, Nathan Glazer has written, the Eastern Europeans were "a frightening apparition. Their poverty was more desperate than German Jewish poverty, their piety more intense than German Jewish piety, their irreligion more violent than German Jewish irreligion, their radicalism more extreme than German-Jewish radicalism."

Notwithstanding their distaste for the "wild Asiatics" and their "un-American ways," and despite an initial desire to see the immigration stopped, the German Jews quickly came to the newcomers' aid. Recognizing that their own fate was now tied to that of the Eastern European Jews, and accepting the ancient principle that *kol Yisrael arevim zeh bazeh*—each Jew is responsible for every other Jew—the "uptowners" created and financed an extraordinary network of philanthropic agencies. There were immigrant-aid societies, settlement houses and "Y"s, family service agencies, free loan societies, orphanages, and a host of other institutions designed to find homes and jobs for the immigrants, to teach them and their children the English language and American ways, care for abandoned wives and children, rescue young women from prostitution and divert young men from delinquency, and in a wide variety of ways "uplift" and Americanize the Eastern European Jews and speed their integration into American society.

No immigrant group had ever been quite so eager to be "uplifted." Most non-Jewish immigrants retained a close attachment to the countries or villages from which they came; among some groups as many as two thirds returned to the mother country. This initial ambivalence about American life meant that acculturation occurred fairly slowly. To Jewish immigrants, on the other hand, the United States was the only place they could call home. However much they may have missed the close communal life they had left behind, they were delighted to be free from the fear of pogroms and the official anti-

Semitism of Russia and Poland. Thus almost none of the Jews who came here from Eastern Europe returned.

For most Jewish immigrants, in fact, life in America was a second birth; unencumbered by nostalgia for "the old country," they approached the process of "becoming American" with the same intensity and determination they applied to every other aspect of life.

ITEM: ". . . it was a second birth they were witnessing, an experience which they had once gone through themselves and which was one of the greatest events of their lives," says the protagonist of *The Rise of David Levinsky*, Abraham Cahan's epic novel of Eastern European Jewish immigrant life, recalling his first day in America.

ITEM: "Once I live in America, I want to *know* that I live in America!" the central character in Cahan's novella, *Yekl*, shouts at his determinedly old-world wife when she objects to his shaving his beard and sideburns. (The novella was the basis for the film *Hester Street.*)

For reasons I will explore in Chapter Four, the Eastern European Jews climbed out of the working class with extraordinary speed, many of them in the course of a single generation. In contrast to the German and Sephardic Jews, who had stuck to business as their primary means of earning a living, a small but ever growing minority of the children of Eastern European immigrants sought higher education and entry to the professions. In the second decade of this century Jewish students began entering Ivy League colleges and professional schools in significant numbers; by 1932 more than 20 percent of Harvard's undergraduates were Jews, as were 15 percent or more of the students at its law and medical schools.

Their welcome was less than enthusiastic. An occasional Jewish student was one thing, especially if he came from an assimilated, upper-middle-class home, but numbers of Jewish students were something else again—especially the ambitious and hardworking children of immigrants from Eastern Europe. Raised in traditional (and often Yiddish-speaking) homes, these new Jewish students had difficulty understanding the "canons of genteel intercourse," as Thorstein Veblen called them, by which elite universities were governed—canons that placed a higher value on athletics and manners and what was generally called "character" than on academic ability. "Oh, Harvard's run by millionaires," fraternity brothers sang,

And Yale is run by booze,
Cornell is run by farmer's sons,
Columbia's run by Jews.

So give a cheer for Baxter Street
Another one for Pell
And when the little sheenies die,
Their souls will go to hell.

Columbia tried to defend itself against the canard. "One of the commonest references that one hears with regard to Columbia is that its position at the gateway of European immigration makes it socially uninviting to students who come from homes of refinement," Dean Frederick Keppel wrote in 1914. "The form which inquiry takes in these days of slowly dying race prejudice is, 'Isn't Columbia overrun with European Jews who are most unpleasant persons socially?' " Understandable as the question may have been, Keppel explained, it missed the point: "What most people regard as a racial problem is really a social problem. The Jews who have had the advantage of decent social surroundings for a generation or two are entirely satisfactory companions."

There were, of course, "Jewish students of another type who have not had the advantages of their more fortunate fellows," Keppel conceded. "Often they come from an environment which in any stock less fired with ambition would have put the idea of higher education entirely out of the question. Some of them are not particularly pleasant companions, but the total number is not large, and every reputable institution aspiring to public service must stand ready to give to those of probity and good moral character the benefits which they are making great sacrifices to obtain."

Even so, there was a limit to Keppel's genuine nobiesse oblige, for he was eager to halt the loss of students from "homes of refinement," who increasingly were choosing colleges such as Amherst and Williams, which had virtually no Jews enrolled. To restore Columbia's social standing, both Keppel and his successor, Herbert Hawkes, decided that it was necessary to reduce and thereafter to limit the number of Jewish students. This they succeeded in doing: the proportion of Jews enrolled dropped from about 40 percent in 1914 to 21 percent four years later, and to 15–16 percent during the 1920s. Most other elite institutions followed suit. "We must put a ban on the Jews," Dean Frederick S. Jones of Yale told a meeting of the Association of New England Deans in 1918, because their academic success was discouraging Gentile students. Undergraduates were unwilling to compete for "first honors," Jones explained, since they did "not care to be a minority in a group of men of higher scholarship record, most of whom are Jews."

The methods by which this reduction was accomplished are significant, for they help explain why America continued to be different even in the face of rampant anti-Semitism and why Jews were able to move up so rapidly after World War II, when the barriers crumbled. Much as Keppel, Hawkes, and their counterparts at other universities wanted to limit the number of Jews, they shied away from formal quotas, as the authors of the restrictive immigration acts of the 1920s did also. To incorporate anti-Semitism in federal law or formal university regulations violated American notions of fairness and thus went beyond the temper of even that bigoted age. The college deans and presidents resorted instead to a variety of subterfuges to put their informal quotas into effect. They sought "geographic balance" in the student body—which meant limiting the number of students from the Northeast; this automatically reduced the number of Jewish students.

The administrators also introduced various tests of "character" and other desired nonacademic traits. Dean Hawkes, for example, enlisted E. L. Thorndike of Teachers College, one of the founders of psychological testing, to develop a series of tests for admission. "Most Jews, especially those of the more objectionable type, have not had the home experiences which enable them to pass these tests as successfully as the average native American boy," Hawkes said, explaining the results. There were those, of course, who saw the tests as something less than objective; Yale's admissions director reported to the university's Committee on Limitation on Numbers that the Columbia tests could "be arbitrarily made to serve the end desired."*

Lest there be any doubt as to what end was desired, Columbia, along with Yale and most other private colleges and universities, began asking questions not only about religion and national origin but also about the maiden names of the applicants' mothers. Some Jewish applicants (or their fathers) were now anglicizing their last names to mask their Jewishness, but the practice was too recent to have affected the mother's family name. As a further precautionary measure, an applicant was also required to submit a photograph, so that one's physiognomy could be scrutinized for Jewish characteristics. (These requirements were still in effect when I applied for admission in January 1941.)

* Some of the founders of the so-called science of mental testing provided an apparent scientific basis for anti-Semitism; the most notable was Henry Goddard, whose statue stands in front of the headquarters of the Educational Testing Service in Princeton, New Jersey. In 1912 Goddard administered the Binet IQ test and other standardized tests to a representative sample of immigrants passing through Ellis Island; 83 percent of the Jews, Goddard reported, were "feeble-minded."

The great Charles Eliot, who had converted Harvard from a provincial denominational college into a great national university during his forty-year tenure (1869–1909), had welcomed Jews as both students and faculty. To fulfill its role, Eliot had argued, Harvard must be open to all, regardless of "class, caste, race, sect, or political party." "It is doubtless true that Jews are better off at Harvard than at any other American college," Eliot had added, "and they are, therefore, likely to resort to it"—as indeed they did.

That was precisely the problem in the view of President A. Lawrence Lowell, Eliot's successor, but he wanted to avoid the surreptitious measures used by other colleges and universities in their admissions procedures. "During the earlier period of our country, and indeed to some extent so long as there was a broad area of frontier life to the westward, newcomers from other lands were easily assimilated," he told the class of 1922 in his commencement address. But "now that our population has become more dense, and huge numbers of strangers newly come from overseas are massed together in industrial centers, the problem of assimilation has become more difficult." Lowell had been opposed to large-scale immigration of "alien races" for some time, on the ground that "no democracy could be successful unless it was tolerably homogeneous," and Harvard's homogeneity, in his view, was now threatened by the growing number of first- and second-generation Jewish students, whose very presence evoked anti-Semitism on the part of the rest of the student body. "To shut the eyes to an actual problem of this kind and to ignore its existence," he told the graduating class, "or to refuse to grapple with it courageously, would be unworthy of a university."

The courageous course, in Lowell's view, was to impose a clear-cut quota. "It is the duty of Harvard to receive just as many boys who have come, or whose parents have come, to this country without our background as it can effectively educate," Lowell wrote to Judge Julian W. Mack of the U.S. Court of Appeals, the first Jewish member of Harvard's Board of Overseers. "Experience seems to place that proportion at about 15%"—a figure that included Chinese and Irish-Americans as well as Jews. After a long and bitter controversy in which ninety-year-old Eliot led the opposition to Lowell's proposal, the Harvard faculty voted for measures similar to those Columbia had adopted, that is, to seek a student body representative of the American population as a whole. The end result was the same: Jewish enrollment at Harvard was cut from 21 percent to 10 percent.

The debate over the "Harvard Plan," as the faculty solution came to be called, received national attention and was as traumatic for that generation of Jews as the "Second Battle of Saratoga" had been nearly a half century earlier.* Although Harvard's Jewish students had initially believed that the call for quotas "came from dislike of certain Jews," as Harry Starr, president of the Harvard Menorah Society, wrote, they quickly "learned that it was numbers that mattered; bad or good, *too many* Jews were not liked. Rich or poor, brilliant or dull, polished or crude—*too many Jews* turned out to be the ailment for which there was only one cure [emphasis in original]."

"Too many Jews" were a problem everywhere, because Jews had come to be seen as an alien, virtually unassimilable group—unassimilable not through lack of receptivity on the part of Gentiles but because the stubborn Jews refused to surrender their "foreign" ways. "More than half the difficulty would be overcome," Lowell told a member of the Harvard Department of Religion, if, when admitted, Jews would "be overcome with an oblivion of the fact that they were Jews, even though all the Gentiles were perfectly aware that they were Jews." In other words, so long as Jews remained Jews, there was no way for them to become full members of American society.

Even those most favorably disposed toward Jews saw "the Jewish problem" this way. In 1936, for example, the editors of *Fortune* devoted their entire February issue to "Jews in America"; their goal was to defend Jews against the charge that they controlled American business. Analyzing the economy industry by industry, *Fortune* demonstrated that this simply was not the case; Jews were almost wholly absent from commercial banking and insurance; automobile, steel, petroleum, and chemicals production; advertising and journalism; and, indeed, most other industries to which power adhered. Far from controlling the economy, American Jews were confined to a few, mostly minor, sectors.

But this fact was itself cause for concern, in *Fortune*'s view, for it led to undue visibility. "What is remarkable about the Jews in America," the editors wrote, "is not their industrial power but their curious industrial distribution, their tendency to crowd together in particular squares of the checkerboard. The reason for their crowding must be found in their most pronounced psychological trait—their clannishness, their tribal inclination."

To be sure, Jews were concentrated in a handful of occupations and industries because they had been excluded from the rest, the editors explained. But however unjust those barriers were, the fact remained that Jews did tend "to inundate a field where other Jews have made entrance." The end result was "that wherever the Jews may be,

* It was in an effort to soften the pain that Harry Wolfson wrote the pamphlet in which he urged Jews to accept their Jewishness in the same way that blind, deaf, and lame people accepted their handicaps.

industrially or culturally or professionally or merely geographically, they are always present in numbers and they are almost always present as Jews."

And that in turn made solution of "the Jewish problem" unlikely. "Can this universal stranger be absorbed in the country which has absorbed every other European stock?" the editors asked. Probably not, they answered. "The other immigrant groups accept the culture of the country into which they come," whereas "the Jews for centuries have refused to accept it and are now, in many cases, unable to accept it when they would. The habit of pride . . . is too strong in them. Even many of those who have deserted the traditions of their people and accepted in every detail the dress and speech and life of the non-Jewish majority are still subtly but recognizably different."

And to be different, in those days, was to give offense. "The practices of the Orthodox Jewish faith, by emphasizing the different culture of the Jew, enhance anti-Semitism," J. F. Brown, chief research psychologist of the Menninger Clinic, explained in 1942 in a paper, "The Origin of the Anti-Semitic Attitude." "The costumes of the rabbis; the celebration of the chief feasts, especially the Sabbath, on other dates than those of the Christian culture; prohibitions regarding diet; the façades of synagogues—all mark the Jew out." The "only way" to counter anti-Semitism, Brown concluded, would be for Jews to surrender their religion, their customs, and anything else that marked them off from others and disappear into the crowd. "Responsible" Jewish leaders, he added, should not only urge "immediate cultural and final racial assimilation" but also do what they could "to discourage the entrance of Jews into those businesses and professions which are now 'over-populated' with Jews, and distribute them . . . into others which are 'under-populated.' "

Brown's essay, interestingly enough, was one of sixteen in a landmark volume, *Jews in a Gentile World*, in which some of the country's leading social scientists turned their attention to the causes and remedies of American anti-Semitism. In another essay in the volume Talcott Parsons of Harvard, who was to become the most influential American sociologist of our time, explained that a major reason for anti-Semitism was the "over-sensitiveness to criticism" and " 'abnormal' aggressiveness and self-assertion" that American Jews displayed. "The 'chosen people' idea held by the Jews is another source of friction," Parsons went on to say. "Gentiles usually resent the arrogance of the claim that a group who are in a sense 'guests' in their country claim a higher status than the 'host' people." What is significant here is not Parsons' dislike of the concept of chosenness which I will discuss later, but the way he defined the position of Jews in American society: they were guests in *his* country and would be well advised to behave like guests instead of acting as if they belonged here.

This, it should be noted, was the advice Jews were getting from sympathetic friends—liberal scholars who were using the latest insights of psychology, sociology, history, anthropology, and political science to try to solve "the Jewish problem." As Talcott Parsons put it, "The amount of discrimination which actually exists is far too great to be compatible with the author's own personal ideals." How much discrimination would have been compatible with his personal ideals he neglected to say, but he did call for "reduction of most of the present forms of discrimination and the complete elimination of a good many of them." "While anti-Semitism cannot be eliminated completely, cut off at its very roots, it can be considerably reduced."

Parsons was vague about how this could be brought about; he was more concerned with specifying what Jews should *not* do if they wanted to avoid provoking greater anti-Semitism. "Generally speaking, any policy which tends to make Jews as Jews more conspicuous . . . would tend to be an invitation to anti-Semitic reaction," he argued. And nothing would make Jews more conspicuous than to press for legislation outlawing discrimination—a view that J. F. Brown echoed. "The mere attempt might in itself create additional anti-Semitism," Brown explained.

In fairness to Parsons, Brown, and Company, their strictures were well intentioned; this was a time of widespread animosity toward Jews. Two years earlier a public-opinion survey had found that 63 percent of Americans believed that Jews, as a group, had "objectionable traits"; a majority believed that German Jews were wholly or partly to blame for the Nazis' persecution of them. Moreover, a series of polls conducted between 1940 and 1945 indicated that a third to a half of the American public would have sympathized with or actively supported an anti-Semitic political campaign; no more than 30 percent would have opposed it. And anti-Semitic sentiment increased as World War II progressed: the proportion viewing Jews as "a menace to America" rose from 17 percent in 1940 to 24 percent in 1944; in that latter year the proportions viewing German- and Japanese-Americans as a menace were only 6 percent and 9 percent, respectively.

4

No wonder the operative principle on which my generation of American Jews was raised was "Shah!" and that our Jewishness was a source of anxiety and discomfort. We were, after all, in a no-win situation: if we tried to assimilate, we were pushy, and if we kept to ourselves, we were alien and tribal. The sociologist Robert K. Merton has called this the "damned-if-you-do-and-damned-if-you-don't" approach to intergroup relations. "Through a faultlessly bisymmetrical prejudice, ethnic and racial out-groups get it coming and going," Merton wrote in 1948 in a now classic paper, "The Self-Fulfilling Prophecy." "The systematic condemnation of the out-grouper continues largely *irrespective of what he does.*" Indeed, "the victim is punished for the crime [emphasis in original]."

This happens, according to Merton, through a kind of "moral alchemy," whereby the in-group "transmutes virtue into vice and vice into virtue, as the occasion may demand." The same actions are evaluated differently, that is to say, according to who performs them. "Did Lincoln work far into the night? This testifies that he was industrious, resolute, perseverant, and eager to realize his capacities to the full," Merton explains.

> Do the out-group Jews or Japanese keep these same hours? This only bears witness to their sweatshop mentality, their ruthless undercutting of American standards, their unfair competitive practices. Is the in-group hero frugal, thrifty and sparing? Then the out-group villain is stingy, miserly, and penny-pinching. . . . Did the indomitable Lincoln refuse to remain content with a life of work with the hands? Did he prefer to make use of his brain? Then, all praise for his plucky climb up the shaky ladder of opportunity. But, of course, the eschewing of manual work for brain work among the merchants and lawyers of the out-group deserves nothing but censure for a parasitic way of life. Was Abe Lincoln eager to learn the accumulated wisdom of the ages by unending study? The trouble with the Jew is that he's a greasy grind, with his head always in a book, while decent people are going to a show or ball game.

Virtues are virtues only when confined to the proper group; the right activity by the wrong people is cause for contempt rather than praise. This double standard is highly functional for those who impose it; it is one of the most effective means by which members of a social or economic elite maintain their power and prestige.

For members of the out-group, on the other hand, the double standard has a bizarre effect: achievements become cause for concern rather than (or as well as) for pride. "If the Jew is condemned for his educational or professional or scientific or economic success," Merton explains, "then, understandably enough, many Jews will come to feel that these accomplishments must be minimized in simple self-defense."

Hence the curious spectacle to which Merton pointed: Jewish defense agencies "busily engaged in assuring the powerful in-group that they have not, in fact, been guilty of inordinate contributions to science, the professions, the arts, the government, and the economy. . . . In a culture which consistently judges the professionals higher in social value than even the most skilled hewers of wood and drawers of water, the out-group finds itself in the anomalous position of pointing with defensive relief to the large number of Jewish painters and paper hangers, plasterers and electricians, plumbers and sheet-metal workers."

One consequence was a self-consciousness in public. When he began his doctoral studies at Harvard in the 1950s, Rabbi Irving Greenberg, now president of the National Jewish Resource Center and a distinguished Orthodox rabbi, could not bring himself to wear a yarmulke in public. Harvard was "their" turf, not his; he wore a hat when he went out doors but remained bareheaded in the library and classroom buildings. It was not until the end of his third year of studies that Greenberg began to see Harvard as *his* turf too and so felt comfortable enough to wear his yarmulke at all times. (During the early stages of their courtship his wife, the writer Blu Greenberg, felt a mixture of pride and acute discomfort over the yarmulke perched on her date's head; his six-foot-six height made it conspicuous even when they were sitting in a theater or concert hall.)

Among older Jews the sense of discomfort remains. "I know I look like a rabbi, but I just can't wear a yarmulke when I go into Bullock's Wilshire," the rabbi of a Beverly Hills congregation told me. "I feel too conspicuous."

When I was growing up it was not just a question of avoiding the embarrassment that arose from being conspicuous; the message Jews received was that to be accepted they had to stop being Jewish—or at least *visibly* Jewish. Hence the popularity of the "nose job," a surgical procedure designed to transform the aquiline "Jewish nose" into an upturned organ that would make its owner—so it was devoutly hoped—look like an Anglo-Saxon. (The "nose job" did not begin to lose its popularity until Barbra Streisand's rise to fame in the 1960s.)

Anglicizing one's name was widespread. In the late 1940s and early 1950s, when name changing was at a peak, some 50,000 Americans filed petitions with state courts each year seeking permission to change their family names; 80 percent of them were Jews. At times, of course, the reason was clearly a practical one. Shortly before World War II a cousin of mine who had trained to be an airline pilot was turned down repeatedly for a job after he had received his license. He changed his name from Levy to Leeds and was promptly hired. Shortly after the war an acquaintance who had been unable to get a clerical job with the

New York Telephone Company was hired when she reapplied after having changed her name from Prenowitz to Prentice.

Frequently, however, the motivation had less to do with career needs than with a wistful desire for acceptance. After my cousin had changed his name to Leeds, several uncles and cousins who were in the "rag trade," as the women's clothing business was affectionately known, followed his example; yet a non-Jewish name conferred no economic advantage in that predominantly Jewish industry. Frequently, moreover, it was the old who urged the young to change their names. I can remember as if it were yesterday a well-to-do aunt taking my brother and me aside without our parents' knowledge to urge us to abandon the name Silberman for one more likely to assist our rise out of genteel poverty. She was enraged when we demurred. We owed it to our parents to "be successful," my aunt insisted, and it was incumbent on us to choose a name "they" would find acceptable.*

No one was more careful to expunge his or her Jewishness than Jews who were in the public eye, and of these none did it more systematically than actors and comedians. Curiously enough, the moguls who built the movie industry–people such as Harry Cohn, Samuel Goldwyn, Louis B. Mayer, Adolph Zukor, Carl Laemmle, A. J. Balaban, and the Warner brothers–retained their Jewish names. But, sensitive to attacks on Jewish control of the movies, they were determined to avoid any hint of Jewishness in the films they created, and they insisted that Jewish actors and actresses assume Anglo-Saxon names–a demand to which the would-be stars happily acceded. Thus Bernard Schwartz became Tony Curtis, Issur Danielovich became Kirk Douglas, Julius Garfinkle became John Garfield, Laszlo Lowenstein became Peter Lorre, Jill Oppenheim became Jill St. John, Betty Joan Perske became Lauren Bacall, Muni Weisenfreund became Paul Muni, Theodosia Goodman turned into Theda Bara, and Samile Diane Friessen was reborn as Dyan Cannon.

Moreover, comedians such as Jack Benny (né Benjamin Kubelsky), Eddie Cantor (Israel Iskowitz), George Burns (Nathan Birnbaum), and Ed Wynn (Isaiah Leopold) created public personae with no Jewish–indeed, no ethnic–identity whatsoever. There were excep-

* There was an element of black humor about the conversation, since Silberman had not been the original family name. After several years as a peddler in rural Iowa during the 1870s my paternal grandfather, whose name was Zarkey, settled in Des Moines. To make his way in America, friends told him, he would have to choose an American name. Still unfamiliar with American usage, he walked up and down the main shopping street looking for an American name. He saw the name Silberman on the window of a haberdashery shop. Liking its sound, and not having heard it in Kovno, his Lithuanian hometown, he chose it as his new name.

tions, of course, such as Fanny Brice and Sophie Tucker, but for the most part, Jewish entertainers of that era acknowledged their Jewishness only in subtle ways, evident to other Jews but invisible to Gentiles.

Jews who wanted to enter the upper reaches of American society had to go further still. "One of the longest journeys in the world is the journey from Brooklyn to Manhattan—or at least from certain neighborhoods in Brooklyn to certain parts of Manhattan," Norman Podhoretz wrote in the opening sentence of *Making It,* the first of his two autobiographical volumes.

> I have made that journey, but it is not from the experience of having made it that I know how very great the distance is, for I started on the road many years before I realized what I was doing, and by the time I did realize it I was for all practical purposes already there. . . . It appalls me to think what an immense transformation I had to work on myself in order to become what I have become: if I had known what I was doing I would surely not have wanted to. No wonder the choice had to be blind; there was a kind of treason in it: treason toward my family, treason toward my friends. In choosing the road I chose, I was pronouncing a judgment upon them, and the fact that they themselves concurred in the judgment made the whole thing sadder but no less cruel.

There may be a selective filter to Podhoretz's memory: it is hard to believe that he was as wholly ignorant of what he was doing as he recalls. Nor did every American Jew who made it into the upper middle class turn his back on his family and his origins as thoroughly as Podhoretz describes himself as having done.

And yet for American Jews growing up in the 1920s, 1930s, and 1940s, certain kinds of success did involve what Podhoretz calls "the brutal bargain." "Making it" in the world of high culture, academia, government, corporate enterprise, and the learned professions often required estrangement from one's roots. The requirement was no less firm for being masked. "The demand being made on me as a student of Western Culture . . . was seductively abstract and idealized: 'Become a gentleman, a man of enlightened and gracious mind!' " Podhoretz wrote of his undergraduate years at Columbia College. "It is not that Columbia was being dishonest in failing to mention that this also meant, 'Become a facsimile WASP!' In taking this corollary for granted, the college was simply being true to its own ethnic and class origins; and in nothing did this fidelity show itself more clearly than in the bland unconsciousness that accompanied it."

The "brutal bargain" was not restricted to American Jews; it was demanded of the members of every ethnic group whose culture diverged significantly from that of mainstream Protestant America. "We soon got the idea that 'Italian' meant something inferior, and a barrier was erected between children of Italian origin and their parents," Leonard Covello, the first Italian-American to become principal of a New York City high school, wrote in his autobiography, referring to his own school experience. "This was the accepted process of Americanization. We were becoming Americans by learning how to be ashamed of our parents."

What made Jews different from other groups was, in part, the degree to which Jewish parents accepted—indeed, encouraged—the process. Because of the intensity of their desire to see their children rise above their own social and economic status, some parents were even willing to withstand humiliation if they thought it would contribute to their children's upward mobility.

ITEM: Nearly half a century later a successful corporate lawyer recalls with startling clarity his admissions interview for Phillips Academy in Andover, Massachusetts. He and his father were scheduled to meet the interviewer, an Andover alumnus, at the latter's club. When they arrived, the alumnus met them outside the door and explained apologetically that he had forgotten that the club did not admit Jews to its premises. The boy wanted to leave, but his father, convinced that attending Andover would open doors that otherwise would be closed, insisted on remaining; the interview was conducted with the three of them standing at the curb. (My friend was admitted and hated every minute he was there—with what passion he had not fully appreciated until 1980, when George Bush, campaigning for the Republican presidential nomination, called to solicit a contribution from his fellow alumnus.)

The self-abasement inherent in this kind of upward mobility made Jewishness a "persistent torment," as Joseph Proskauer, adviser to Governor Alfred E. Smith and longtime president of the American Jewish Committee, put it. "There were matters one never talked about but always thought about," Felix Frankfurter remarked: "one was your height, another was your Jewishness." (After her first meeting with Frankfurter, Eleanor Roosevelt, who had not yet learned to overcome the anti-Semitism of her upbringing, described him as "an interesting little man but very Jew.")

In many upwardly mobile Jews, self-abasement turned into self-hatred; as Heine's biographer, S. S. Prawer, put it, emancipated Jews "frequently took a self-torturing and prophylactic pleasure in applying to themselves the stereotypes evolved by their enemies"—and none more so than the greatest journalist of the century, Walter Lippmann.

As Franz Kafka once said of Heine, Lippmann's "conflict with Jewry" was "exactly what makes him so typically Jewish." "I do not regard the Jews as innocent victims. They hand on unconsciously and uncritically from one generation to another many distressing personal and social habits," Lippmann wrote in 1922 in a letter supporting President Lowell's call to Harvard to reduce the "excessive" number of Jews there. In the clash of cultures that a large Jewish presence at Harvard made inevitable, Lippmann explained, "my sympathies are with the non-Jew. His personal manners and physical habits are . . . distinctly superior to the prevailing manners and habits of the Jews."

To be sure, Lippmann wanted the number of Jews at Harvard reduced by indirect means, such as seeking a national geographic balance among the student body, rather than by a formal quota. When Lowell followed the latter course, Lippmann attacked him in biting prose that provided a rare glimpse of the wounds that underlay his lifelong attempt to escape his Jewishness: "Harvard, with the prejudices of a summer hotel; Harvard, with the standards of a country club, is not the Harvard of her greatest sons."

Lippmann's self-hatred stemmed from more than the hurt of early rejection; he was accepted into the circles of the mighty and into most of their clubs as well. But the great journalist seems to have been perennially fearful that acceptance would turn into rejection if he were to be tagged with the label "Jew." His parents, after all, had been part of that generation of German-American Jews who had thought that financial success would bring them social acceptance, only to find themselves excluded from the "better" resorts and clubs.

Their only child did not want to expose himself to that kind of snub. Walter Lippmann avoided identification as a Jew, his biographer, Ronald Steel, explains, "by the fact that he did not 'look Jewish,' and by immersing himself—through his marriages, his social life, his professional contacts—into the dominant white Protestant culture." (Both his marriages were to non-Jews.) Thus Lippmann refused to belong to Jewish organizations or even to lecture to them, going so far as to turn down an award from the Jewish Academy of Arts and Sciences. He avoided identification as a Jew so successfully, in fact, that some of his closest friends did not know that he was Jewish; those who did know the terrible secret were careful never to mention it.

ITEM: For his seventieth birthday a group of Lippmann's admirers prepared a book of essays in his honor. One of those invited to contribute to this Festschrift was Carl Binger, an eminent psychiatrist and childhood friend of Lippmann's, who was asked to write about Lippmann's early years. Binger agreed but emphasized that he could not refer to Lippmann's Jewishness without destroying their friendship; indeed, he believed the journalist would never speak to him again if he mentioned it. Binger got around the problem by noting in passing that Lippmann had attended Dr. Sachs's School for Boys, the private school in which members of "Our Crowd" enrolled their sons.

For Lippmann the cardinal sin was to be "conspicuous," meaning noticeable as a Jew. "The Jews are fairly distinct in their physical appearance and in the spelling of their names from the run of the American people," Lippmann declared in 1922 in his only published writing on the subject. "They are, therefore, conspicuous," and this conspicuousness was the heart of the Jewish problem. (Lippmann's essay "Public Opinion and the American Jew" was a contribution to a special issue of the *American Hebrew*, devoted to "The Better Understanding Between Jew and Non-Jew in America.") Although Jews might not be "more blatantly vulgar" than other groups, Lippmann went on to explain, "sharp trading and blatant vulgarity are more conspicuous in the Jew because he himself is more conspicuous"—hence behavior that is tolerable in others is inexcusable when engaged in by Jews. "For that reason," Lippmann continued, "the rich and vulgar and pretentious Jews of our big cities are perhaps the greatest misfortune that has ever befallen the Jewish people. They are the real fountain of anti-Semitism."*

The great journalist tried so hard to keep his Jewishness inconspicuous, in fact, that he never referred in print to the Holocaust, which some might consider an even greater misfortune to the Jewish people than the vulgarity that so offended Lippmann. In a column of May 1933, written after the Nazis had burned books written by Jews, Lippmann did take note of Hitler's anti-Semitism, only to defend it as one of the factors that kept German aggression in check. "By satisfying the lust of the Nazis who feel they must conquer somebody and the cupidity of those Nazis who want jobs," Lippmann wrote, "[persecution of the Jews] is a kind of lightning rod which protects Europe."

Hitler's treatment of the Jews did amount to "ruthless injustice," Lippmann conceded a week later, but the injustice was not something about which fair-minded people ought to be concerned. "We have heard once more, through the fog and din, the hysteria and the animal passions of a great revolution, the authentic voice of a genuinely civilized people," Lippmann wrote, referring to a conciliatory speech Hitler had made. Germans should not be judged by their anti-Semites, any

* The editors of the *American Hebrew* hailed Lippmann's article as "not only admirably presented but valid." Two years later, in a special issue, "Who's Who in American Jewry," they described Lippmann as "a whole man and a perfect critic."

more than the French should be judged by the Reign of Terror, the Catholic Church by the Inquisition, Protestantism by the Ku Klux Klan, or "the Jews by their parvenus."

Lippmann was far from unique. His contemporary Robert Moses, who transformed the New York metropolitan area with his highways, bridges, housing projects, and parks, always denied that he was Jewish; Moses even threatened to sue the editors of the *Jewish Encyclopedia* for libel if they included his biography. And Lippmann's two rival pundits, David Lawrence and Arthur Krock, were also uncomfortable with their Jewishness. Krock hid his, and during his tenure as chief of *The New York Times*'s Washington Bureau he was careful to avoid hiring Jewish reporters. When one of his proteges told him that members of the bureau thought he was anti-Semitic, Krock replied, "Well, maybe I am." Lawrence, on the other hand, did not deny that he was Jewish, but he protested bitterly when he learned that a *Time* profile of him was going to mention that he was the son of a cantor; such a description would be anti-Semitic, he told the *Time* editor.

In the United States, in short, no less than in Europe, Jewish intellectuals were particularly prone to self-hatred, for all the reasons Sartre specified. As Lippmann's friend Bernard Berenson, the well-known art connoisseur and esthete, wrote, "We Jews tend to think of ourselves as prejudice paints us." For much of his life the Lithuanian-born Berenson tried hard *not* to think of himself as a Jew; he referred to himself as an Anglo-Saxon and spoke of "our Puritan forebears." As the art historian Meyer Schapiro bitingly remarked, Berenson's ancestors must have been "rabbis on the Mayflower."

In fact they were rabbis in Lithuania. Berenson's parents came to the United States in 1875, when he was ten; his father was a Boston street peddler and his mother cooked for boarders. The ambitious young Bernhard (he later dropped the "h") gained admission first to Boston University, then to Harvard, where he was considered a prodigy, and then to the salons of the Back Bay, whose proprietors financed his graduate study in Europe and the beginnings of his career as adviser to art collectors, curators, and dealers.

Determined to live as an elegant gentleman, Berenson decided to ease his path in the European manner: he was baptized an Episcopalian at twenty and adopted the patronizing anti-Semitism of the upper class of that day.* "It is only by a study of Jewish institutions and literature that we shall begin to understand the puzzling character of the Jews," Berenson wrote in 1888, when he was twenty-three. "Begin to under-

* When he settled in Italy in the 1890s Berenson realized that being an Episcopalian was not quite the asset it had been in Back Bay; he discovered an affinity for Catholicism and was baptized in that faith.

stand, I say, for comprehend them we never shall. Their character and interests are too vitally opposed to our own to permit the existence of that intelligent sympathy between them and us which is necessary for comprehension . . ."

If Berenson, Lippmann, and their generation of Jewish intellectuals hated Jews because they were so different from other Americans, members of the next generation of intellectuals—American-born children of Eastern European immigrants—were angry that Jews had become so much *like* everyone else. "No people on earth are more correct, more staid, more provincial, more commonplace, more inexperienced," the art critic Clement Greenberg wrote; "none observe more strictly the letter of every code that is respectable; no people do so completely and habitually what is expected of them . . ."

Greenberg's essay was part of "A Symposium on American Literature and the Younger Generation of American Jews—a generation that was just beginning to make its literary presence felt. Although a few contributors spoke warmly of their Jewishness, most saw it as irrelevant to their lives or their work. Unlike the Catholic writer "who has been inwardly lacerated by religious doubts," *Time* drama critic Louis Kronenberger wrote, the Jewish writer "has merely had to cut loose from something, not cut a part of himself away." "I cannot discover anything in my professional intellectual life which I can specifically trace back to my Jewish rearing," said Lionel Trilling. "I should resent it if a critic of my work were to discover in it either faults or virtues which he called Jewish."* "Modern Jewish religion at its best may indeed be intelligent and soaked in university knowledge," Trilling added, "but out of it there has not come a single voice with the note of authority—of philosophical, or poetic, or even of rhetorical, let alone of religious authority," thereby dismissing with a stroke of the pen the work of scholars such as Franz Rosenzweig, Martin Buber, Hermann Cohen, Mordecai Kaplan, Harry Wolfson, Salo Baron, and Gershom Scholem.

The contributors to a 1961 *Commentary* symposium "Jewishness and Younger Intellectuals" were even more disdainful of American Jews for being so conspicuously middle-class; most were irritated as well by *Commentary*'s implied suggestion that Jewishness played any role in their lives. "I am nothing if I am not an individual," Alfred G. Aronowitz, then a reporter for the *New York Post*, declared. "Actually, there is nothing less important than being a Jew." Jason Epstein, of Random House, found *Commentary*'s questions about Jewishness "remote and a little bizarre." "I represent a biological phenomenon

* For a portrait of the way in which Trilling's Jewishness affected his academic career, see Chap. Three, pp. 98–99.

whose value on earth is much to be doubted," he explained. "That I am also a Jew seems relatively unimportant"—all the more so because "the traditional human groupings are on the way out."*

But of course the traditional human groupings were on their way back in as Epstein wrote. Fueled in part by the civil rights movement and, in larger measure, by the growing openness of American society, the 1960s and 1970s were to see an explosive increase in ethnic identity. Among Jews, moreover, that identity had never really weakened; indeed, the intractability of Jewish self-hatred is a direct consequence of the extraordinary durability Jewish group identity has always shown. As Aronowitz complained in his contribution to the *Commentary* symposium, "The trouble with being a Jew has always been the trouble others go through to remind you of it."

Until recently, in fact, Jews who wanted to escape their Jewishness found it virtually impossible to do so. No matter how much or what they changed—whether their names, their noses, their manners, or their friends—Jews learned that they were no more acceptable afterward than they had been before. Berenson, for example, never lost his sense of being an outsider: "at times I seem to myself to be a typical Talmud Jew," he confided to his diary in his eighty-eighth year. The rise of Nazism had confirmed his suspicion that once a Jew, always a Jew, and he began to recognize that for all the prime ministers, presidents, and kings who had come to dine with him at I Tatti, his Renaissance estate outside Florence, for all the real friendship and acceptance he had gained in some circles, there were others in which he had (in the words of one biographer) "been endlessly snubbed, insulted, and mocked, or accepted with reservations," because of his status "as an outsider and a Jew."

In his waning years, therefore, Berenson acknowledged his Jewishness, at least to himself and to such of his friends as Isaiah Berlin and Lewis Namier, with whom he exchanged Yiddish jokes. It was wonderful, he wrote, to "drop the mask of being *goyim* and return to Yiddish reminiscences, and Yiddish stories and witticisms! After all, it has been an effort . . . to act as if one were a mere Englishman or Frenchman or American . . ."

Even so, Berenson would not discuss his origins with his Gentile friends; and he was racked with guilt over his lifelong attempt to pass.

* Epstein was equally detached from the thirteen-year-old state of Israel—"an admirable experiment about which I know little." "I doubt [the experiment] will work," he added. "It is too much a creature of will and not enough the result of long, slow organic history. Like Totoland, or for that matter Disneyland, its foundations are too visible for its future to seem secure."

ITEM: The year after his graduation from Harvard, Berenson published a short story that provided a metaphor for his entire life. In the story Israel Koppel, a young Lithuanian Jew of twenty-two—Berenson's age—returns to his shtetl from the big city, where he has spent four years studying and immersing himself in the culture of the Gentiles. The young man falls ill suddenly, is pronounced dead, and is promptly buried, in accordance with Jewish law. That night Koppel's father is awakened by recurrent nightmares in which he dreams he is confined in a close space, smothered with darkness and unable to move. In the nightmares father and son fuse into one: "Since he had begun the study of Gentile lore, these Jewish superstitions had seemed something to laugh at," the father/son reflects. "Were they true after all? Had the Lord slain him in the bloom of his youth for his disbelief? . . . He surely was not perfect, judged by any law; and, according to Jewish beliefs, he had been guilty of unspeakable sins . . ." The father awakens, convinced he has received a desperate message from his son. He opens the grave and discovers the worst; his son's distorted, anguished face and contorted limbs reveal the fact that he had been buried alive.

One need not be a psychiatrist or literary critic to grasp the symbolism of Berenson's story: one who abandons his origins will be crushed by the weight of either his people's retribution or his own guilt. Since he had tried to bury his past, Berenson's biographer, Meryle Sechrest, writes, "his sense of guilt guaranteed that he would never be able to lay it to rest." In the story, she notes, Israel Koppel does not try to fight his way out of the grave; he concedes the justice of his sentence, burial being an appropriate punishment for having committed "unspeakable sins." "A day scarcely passes without my feeling deeply penitential about my life," Berenson wrote in his diary shortly before his death. (Out of respect for the feelings of his long-time secretary and lover, Nicky Mariano, who had nursed him with great care and devotion, Berenson received the last rites of the Catholic Church, but in deference to Jewish tradition he was buried in a shroud.)

A heavy burden of guilt was the common fate of Jews who tried to pass. "If you refuse" Jewishness, "wishing to be invisible," the poet Muriel Rukeyser wrote, "you choose / Death of the spirit, the stone insanity." For it is not only Gentiles who see Jewishness as immutable and who therefore regard Jewish converts to Christianity as Jews; this is how Jews themselves have always viewed the *meshummad*, or willing convert.

ITEM: The elegant and dashing Otto Kahn, a noted investment banker (Kuhn, Loeb & Company) and controlling stockholder in the Metropolitan Opera Company, was strolling along Fifth Avenue with the humorist Marshall Wilder, who was a hunchback. Kahn pointed out the church to which he belonged and asked, "Marshall, did you know that I once was a Jew?" "Yes, Otto," Wilder replied, "and I once was a hunchback." The story is striking for the way in which it turns Heine's metaphor back upon itself.

The ineradicability of the *meshummad*'s Jewishness is a staple subject of Jewish humor.

ITEM: A Jew converts to Christianity and is asked to preach the sermon in church the following Sunday. He ascends the pulpit proudly and begins, "Fellow goyim . . ."

In part, this attitude toward apostasy is a response to the hostile environment in which Jews have so often lived. In societies in which Jews were ostracized and persecuted, to convert to Christianity was, in effect, to join the enemy's camp. Thus conversion was seen as an act of abandonment and betrayal—an attitude that is shared by most religious and ethnic groups that have suffered persecution. American blacks tend to be contemptuous of those who pass for white, and Irish Catholics of those who pass for WASP. "For a colonized people such as the Irish," John Murray Cuddihy has written, "even soft-pedaling the Faith, let alone apostasy, was invariably construed as social climbing, as an act of ingratiation with the Anglo-Protestant Ascendancy. And perhaps it was."

The visceral reaction continues today, in less intense form, among American Jews. As the jokes they tell reveal, Jews still regard conversion to Christianity with suspicion, and they view converts as people motivated by opportunism rather than religious conviction.

ITEM: Three Jews who had recently been converted to Episcopalianism were having a drink together in a posh country club. They started talking about the reasons for their conversions.

"I converted out of love," the first one said. Seeing the dubious looks on his friends' faces, he added, "Not for Christianity but for a Christian girl. As you know, my wealthy wife insisted that I convert."

"And I converted in order to succeed in the law," the second one said. "I never would have been appointed a federal judge if I hadn't become an Episcopalian."

"I converted because I think that the teachings of Christianity are superior to those of Judaism," the third one said.

"Whom are you trying to kid?" the first man answered with considerable heat. "What do you take us for—a couple of goyim?"

The belief that converts to Christianity (or any other religion) remain Jews is far more than an expression of distaste for social climbers; it is an inescapable by-product of the way Judaism defines itself—has always defined itself. Indeed, the fact that there is no way to stop being Jewish is the largest, and certainly the most puzzling, difference between Judaism and Christianity. In the Jewish self-definition, belief and practice determine whether one is a *good* Jew or a *bad* Jew but not whether one *is* a Jew; to be a Jew is an indelible status, from which there is no exit.

The reason, quite simply, is that Judaism defines itself not as a voluntary community of faith but as an involuntary community of fate. According to the central myth of Judaism, every generation of Jews—past, present, and future, men, women, and children—was present at Mount Sinai when the covenant between God and the Jewish people was established through the giving and receiving of the law. By virtue of being born into the community, a Jew is bound by the covenant; for male children, circumcision, performed on the eighth day after birth, is the visible symbol of that covenant, of membership in an involuntary community of fate. (Because the covenant so clearly includes women as well as men, modern Orthodox Jews, who continue to differentiate male and female roles, are joining Reconstructionist, Conservative, and Reform Jews in creating new ceremonies to celebrate the entry of a newborn daughter into the covenant.) There is nothing passive about belonging to that community, to be sure; to be bound by the covenant is to be bound by an enormous set of obligations. But whether one accepts or rejects those obligations (and whether one fulfills or ignores them), one remains a Jew.

There is an important element of voluntarism nonetheless: one can become a Jew by choice, and religious law prohibits Jews from making any distinction at all between those who are Jewish by birth and those who have chosen to be Jewish and have undergone rites of conversion. Moreover, the children of a woman converted to Judaism are automatically considered Jews by birth. "What was decision in one generation," as Rabbi Eugene B. Borowitz puts it, "is biology in the next." In practice, to be sure, Jews often view converts to Judaism (but *not* their children) with suspicion and/or patronization; it would be disingenuous to deny the strong current of exclusivity in Jewish life and thought. But this folk attitude runs counter to the dominant rabbinic tradition, which strongly rejects the notion of racial exclusivity; the messiah, after all, will be a descendant of King David, who was himself the great-grandson of the most famous of all converts to Judaism, Ruth the Moabite.

By the same token, there is great significance in Ruth's famous statement of conversion: "Your people shall be my people, and your God my God." Converts to Judaism do not simply commit themselves to follow Jewish religious rituals and beliefs; they commit themselves to the Jewish people as well, and they are formally adopted into the covenantal community. Membership in the community is symbolized by assuming a Hebrew name as the son or daughter of the patriarch Abraham. (In Hebrew nomenclature, one is known as So-and-so, the son or daughter of So-and-so.) As metaphoric descendants of Abraham, Jews by choice are able to participate in the central myths of Judaism: they and their descendants may (and should) regard themselves as having been present at Sinai and, during the Passover seder, as having been enslaved in Egypt and then freed.

Thus conversion to Judaism involves a change in ethnic as well as religious status, for Judaism never has distinguished the religious from the ethnic, national, and cultural aspects of identity; they are all inseparably intertwined. This in turn leads to the deeply rooted notion that Jewishness is indelible. To repeat, one may be a good Jew or a bad Jew, a religious Jew or a secular Jew; one may even stop identifying oneself as a Jew; but one never stops *being* a Jew—even after conversion to another religion.

ITEM: "I've always considered myself a Jew. I was born Jewish and so I remain," says Jean-Marie Cardinal Lustiger, the Catholic archbishop of Paris. Born in Paris to Polish Jewish immigrants, Aaron Lustiger, as he was then called (he added "Jean-Marie" but retains "Aaron" on his passport), was converted to Catholicism at thirteen. "I'm not stopping being Jewish, just the opposite," he recalls telling his angry parents. "I'm discovering a way of living it." "For me, the vocation of Israel is bringing light to the goyim," Cardinal Lustiger now explains. "I believe that Christianity is the means for achieving it."

Because they are still Jews, apostates who want to return to Judaism need not undergo conversion; all that is required is evidence that their intent is serious. For much the same reason those who turn away from Jewishness at one stage of their lives generally return at another. In their study of "religious dropouts" among American college students in the 1960s, David Caplovitz and the late Fred Sherrow found that although Jewish-born students were a bit more likely to identify themselves as having no religion than were students reared as Protestants and Catholics, the Jewish dropouts were far more likely to return to Judaism after they had left college. Three years after graduation nearly half the Jewish apostates again identified themselves as Jews, and four years later the proportion had reached 70 percent; over that same time span only a fifth of the Catholic and a little more than a third of the Protestant apostates had returned to the fold.

The degree to which Jewishness represents a communal and ethnic rather than a purely religious identity was evident in another of Caplovitz and Sherrow's findings. Among those who identified themselves as Catholics, nine out of ten described themselves as religious, as did four out of five Protestants; by contrast, fewer than half of those who called themselves Jews said they were religious.

This last fact puzzles Christians who take their Christianity seriously. "Most Christians would agree that there is something of the mystery of God in the continuation of living Judaism," a Lutheran theologian known for his sympathy to Judaism told me. To him Jewish survival is the embodiment of "some divine intent." But for that very reason, the theologian added, many Christians have difficulty understanding why nonreligious and even antireligious Jews continue to call themselves Jews. "If they are *religious* Jews, they have a good reason for not being Christians," he explained. "But if they're not *religious* Jews, if they have no *religious* reason for being Jewish, if they don't believe anything that in Christian terms is distinctive of religion–if they don't adhere to a creed or set of doctrines–then they're simply unbelievers."

A senior member of the faculty of a Presbyterian theological seminary put it more succinctly: "Many people *say* they're Jews, but they're not Jewish by virtue of their faith in God," he told me. "Why, I have seen folks who are no more Jewish than I am celebrate Passover!" The minister is even more puzzled by people who call themselves nonpracticing Jews. "What does it mean to be a Jew if you're not practicing?" he asked me in genuine bewilderment.

The confusion is rooted in the difference between the Jewish and Christian understandings of religion. Being a Jew is not the same as being a Presbyterian, Lutheran, Baptist, Episcopalian, or Roman Catholic, although the differences between Catholicism and Judaism are smaller than those between Judaism and Protestantism. The various Protestant denominations define themselves as more or less voluntary communities of faith; one is a Methodist, Congregationalist, Lutheran, Presbyterian, Episcopalian, and so on, by virtue of one's adherence to the beliefs and practices that distinguish one denomination from another.* But because Judaism defines itself as an involuntary community

* Because of the emphasis on belief and practice, one can also withdraw from one denomination and join another with relative ease. To stop believing and/or practicing the Lutheran (or Presbyterian or Baptist or any other) creed is to cease being a member of that denomination.

or fate, one is a Jew by virtue of one's birth, not one's beliefs or practices. Thus it is that Protestants speak of *joining* a particular church and Catholics of *becoming* a Catholic, whereas Jews speak of *being* Jewish; for Jewishness is an existential fact.

5

For all the discomfort, even self-hatred, American Jews have experienced, it would be profoundly misleading to suggest that they have seen their Jewishness solely, or even predominantly, in negative terms. Jewishness used to be a burden, to be sure, and Jews would have been less than human had they not wished to reduce it, or on occasion be rid of it altogether. Most of the time, however, most Jews have taken perverse pride in the fact that "it is not easy to be a Jew"; in the recesses of their souls they have felt that to be Jewish is a privilege as well as a burden.

There is no other way to account for the extraordinary (some would say stubborn) insistence on remaining Jewish that American Jews have shown—an insistence described in detail in Chapter Five. Most American Jews continue to identify themselves as Jews whether they live as Jews or not. "Today most Jews no longer obey God's injunctions, yet they still obey the call of some mysterious destiny," the Israeli historian Saul Friedlander has written. "Why this fidelity? In the name of what?"

It is a question others have asked as well; one cannot understand Jews or Judaism without apprehending the mystery of Jewish survival—and mystery there is in the ability of Jews to survive as a discrete and recognizable group. "The Egyptians, the Babylonians, and the Persians rose, filled the planet with sound and fury; then faded to dream-stuff and passed away," Mark Twain wrote in 1897; "the Greeks and Romans followed and made a vast noise, and they are gone; other peoples have sprung up and held their torch for a time but it burned out, and they sit in twilight now, or have vanished. . . . All things are mortal but the Jew; all other forces pass, but he remains. What is the secret of his immortality?"

What Twain called "immortality"—the persistence of the Jews in retaining their individual and collective identity in the face of political and social pressures that made other peoples disappear—has fascinated some observers and irritated others. Modern historians such as Arnold Toynbee have expressed annoyance over the "unnatural perseverance" of the Jews after they lost political independence in A.D. 70 and were "scattered and dispersed among the other peoples" of Europe, North Africa, and Asia Minor.

Throughout the ages both well-wishers and antagonists have urged Jews to give up their stubbornly separate ways and "normalize" their existence; most Jews have ignored the advice. For seventeen hundred years, in fact, Jews maintained their separate identity and, indeed, their separate communal existence in periods of tolerance and prosperity and times of poverty and persecution alike. Over the last two centuries of modernization, Jews willingly surrendered communal autonomy in exchange for citizenship and political equality, but they have continued to maintain a separate ethnic-religious identity. Most American Jews are highly acculturated members of American society; on a wide range of attitudes and behaviors they are indistinguishable from other Americans with similar occupations, incomes, and educational backgrounds. Important differences remain, nonetheless, and American Jews continue to be a distinct and identifiable ethnic-religious group.

There is a large element of irony, even paradox, in that fact. When they were struggling to break down the barriers against full participation in American life, Jews used to insist that they were just like everybody else, only more so, and that any seeming differences between them and others were either illusory or irrelevant. In their day-to-day lives, however, as I will discuss in Chapter Five, Jews—sometimes thoughtfully, often quite unconsciously—have insisted on being different, on retaining their group identity, religion, and culture.

ITEM: At a suburban dinner party my wife and I attended, our determinedly atheistic (and politically radical) host and hostess heatedly denied that they were Jewish. Judaism was a religion, they insisted, and since they did not believe in religion—*any* religion—they could not be classified as Jews. When someone suggested that they were Jewish nonetheless, since Judaism has an ethnic and cultural as well as a religious dimension, the couple demurred. They were individuals—citizens of the world—for whom such obsolete parochial attachments had no meaning.

The argument was settled unexpectedly the next evening when the couple stopped by our house to return an ice bucket they had borrowed. "We're starving!" they exclaimed as they entered. "What do you have to eat?" Asked why they were so famished, our erstwhile hostess explained, "We've been to a real goyish cocktail party." With feigned innocence my wife asked what she meant. "You know what I mean," our friend replied. "Lots of liquor and nothing to eat." Realizing the contradiction between that statement and her argument of the night before, our friend dissolved in laughter.

Attitudes about food and eating are among the most important and most enduring symbols of any culture, which is why the "trefa banquet" of 1883 was such a turning point in the history of Reform Judaism in America and why "ethnic foods" have played such a prominent role in the contemporary revival of ethnicity. It is not surprising, therefore, that assimilated American Jews whose cuisine is otherwise indistinguishable from that of Protestant New Englanders or midwesterners continue to display a different attitude to the *quantity* of food they serve. Among Jews, as among blacks and Italian Americans and members of other once-persecuted or impoverished groups, abundance is highly prized, for food symbolizes—indeed, is almost synonymous with—love and friendship.

ITEM: "Food is always good, always good for people, always a token of good feeling," the anthropologists Mark Zborowski and Elizabeth Herzog write in *Life Is with People*, a description of the Eastern European shtetl. "To give food symbolizes not only maternal love but also the friendliness of the household to its visitors. Not to offer a guest 'honor' in the form of food . . . would be the equivalent of a rebuff."

Indeed, it would be rude and unfriendly *not* to press food on a visitor. Even now American Jews two and three generations removed from the shtetl are surprised by what seems to them the austerity of the White Anglo-Saxon Protestant approach to eating and entertaining.

The most important manifestation of Jewishness, however—and to non-Jews the most striking way in which Jews differ from other Americans—is the almost primordial tie Jews feel for one another. "Judaism has always been a form of consciousness," Leon Wieseltier writes, and that consciousness has always involved a powerful sense of connection with other Jews. "It seems impossible to lay a finger on anything tangible and measurable in the Jew's Jewishness," according to the historian J. L. Talmon; "yet an ailing, all-devouring self-consciousness comes like a film between him and the world . . . I believe the links holding Jews together . . . to be as invisible and as strong as the heaviest chains."

ITEM: "I was always an unbeliever, raised without religion . . . And I always tried to suppress nationalistic ardor . . . as something pernicious and unjust," Sigmund Freud wrote in 1926. But when publication of his shocking views on human sexuality in the 1890s led to his ostracism by Viennese society, Freud joined the Vienna lodge of B'nai B'rith, the international Jewish fraternal order, to find people who would "receive me with friendliness." Despite his rejection of Jewish religious and ethnic particularism, he told the members in a speech written for the seventieth-birthday celebration of the lodge, "there remained enough other things to make the attraction of Judaism and Jews irresistible—many dark emotional forces, all the more potent for being so hard to grasp in words, as well as the clear consciousness of an inner identity, the intimacy that comes from the same psychic structure."

American Jews are still bound by "the intimacy that comes from the same psychic structure." "To be a Jew," as the theologian Eugene Borowitz puts it, "means to have a bond with every other Jew—and somehow to know how to find him." When they were young, my children used to marvel at my ability to identify who was Jewish in whatever restaurant, theater, or other public place we happened to be; now they have the same talent.* "I walk with this sign as a frontlet between my eyes, and it is as visible to some secret others as their sign is to me," the sociologist Daniel Bell of Harvard has written, referring to what he calls "the double burden and the double pleasure of my self-consciousness, the outward life of an American and the inward secret of the Jew."

It is not surprising, therefore, that most American Jews continue to feel more comfortable in the company of other Jews. In one recent survey, for example, 61 percent of the respondents reported that "all," "almost all," or "most" of their friends were Jewish. This "clannishness," as it appears to others, is rooted in the sense of destiny that Jews the world over share with one another—a destiny that has some transcendent (and transcendental) significance. The Jewish sense of destiny in turn grows out of the ancient and still powerful belief in a mysterious and awesome relationship between God and the Jewish people—a conviction that, in some incomprehensible way, what happens to the Jewish people affects the fate of the world. "Each Jew knows how thoroughly ordinary he is," writes Milton Himmelfarb; "yet taken together, we seem caught up in things great and inexplicable." The total number of Jews in the world is smaller than a small statistical error in the Chinese census, Himmelfarb elaborates, yet the world remains obsessed with the Jews, and "big things seem to happen around us and to us."

It has been difficult for Christians to comprehend this Jewish sense of destiny because of the historical asymmetry between the two religions. Having grown out of Judaism, Christianity defined itself as the

* Members of the youth culture of the 1960s felt a similar mystical bond. Sitting in a theater one night, my wife and I were unable to gauge whether a long-haired youngster a few rows in front of us was male or female; the son who was with us promptly identified the youth as male. When we asked how he knew, he replied, "The same way you can tell whether someone is Jewish or not."

logical (and necessary) fulfillment of the earlier religion's messianic promise. Given this self-definition, as Rabbi Henry Siegman, executive director of the American Jewish Congress, puts it, "Judaism should have fallen away like the spent first stage of a multi-stage missile heading . . . toward heaven." That it did not do so was hard for believing Christians to accept, let alone understand. For the "scandal" of Jewish survival, as it was called, seemed to contradict what was thought to be the central notion of Christianity: that the old covenant between God and Israel had been replaced by a new one, that divine election had passed from the "old" to the "new" Israel, that is, to the church.

In the past two or three decades Christian theologians and historians have come to a new understanding of both the ancient and the continuing relationship between Judaism and Christianity. As Paul van Buren of Temple University, one of the most influential contemporary Protestant theologians, has written, the Holocaust and the creation of the state of Israel has forced Christians to recognize "that the Jews have been around all along and that they have continued their long walk through history . . . still praying to and praising their God, the Lord of Israel." This recognition, van Buren argues, provides grounds "for questioning whether in fact God has cast them off" and "for seeing that our millennia-long conversation, by assuming the rejection of the Jews, is involved in a contradiction." For "if God is not faithful to His people, if He does not stand by His covenant with Israel, why should we think that He will be any more faithful to His Gentile church?"

This new acceptance of the continuing validity of the "old" covenant between God and Israel means a new understanding of the nature of both Judaism and Christianity, one in which the Jews are seen as "God's elect people" and the Christians as "God's elect church." Both Jews and Christians have always worshiped the same God, van Buren argues—"the One designated in the Scriptures as the Holy One of Israel and the God of Abraham, Isaac, and Jacob," and "the One Jesus of Nazareth called Abba, Father." The difference is that Christians "have been called to walk the way of Israel's God in a new way." In short, Christianity does not displace Judaism; it is, rather, Christians' own way to the God of Israel. "For us Gentiles in the Way, then, Jesus is not the Lord but our Lord, the one Jew who has given us access to the God of the Jews."

Because Judaism has always defined itself as a people rather than as a church, covenant has been more than just a theological concept; it has been a living force in Jewish life. In a sense the theology of the Jews has shaped their history and their sociology. Indeed, Jews could not have survived two millennia of persecutions and pogroms had they not believed that their survival mattered—that they were, in the late Abraham Joshua Heschel's phrase, "God's stake in human history."

Most American Jews no longer believe in a God active (or undemocratic) enough to choose one particular people, yet they continue to believe in their own specialness—in their own destiny as Jews. And this in turn serves to keep Jewishness alive even in those who have abandoned any semblance of a Jewish way of life. Describing his return from youthful universalism, the novelist Herbert Gold has written:

> I thought to be a Jew because I was so named by others. I learned by being one that Jew is more than epithet. The content of tenuous community, risk, and history makes me feel immortal even though I'm not. No matter what happens to me, I am continuous with a past which was worthy of better than me; a present when others died to be Jews; a future constructed equally of fate and intention . . . I am a part of history, not merely a kid on a street corner or a man making out okay . . . I'm not sure what my destiny as a Jew means—or what the destiny of the Jews means—except that it is a unique fate, a peculiar devotion to world and spirit wrapped together.

"Whatever most diaspora Jews believe, they consider themselves primarily a distinctive religio-ethnic group rather than a community with a common creed," Richard Rubenstein states. "Far more Jews today accept the unity of Jewish destiny than the unity of Jewish belief."

Given this sense of destiny, Jews would have been less than human had they eschewed any notion of superiority whatsoever. Initially, to be sure, there was nothing invidious about the distinction between Israel and other nations; in the ancient Near East every nation had its own god, with whom it had a unique relationship. To the authors of Deuteronomy, moreover, Israel's election had nothing to do with merit or desert; it was the mysterious product of God's love.* Indeed, the prophets chastised the Israelites for thinking that God's concern was exclusive.† Nor is the idea of chosenness uniquely Jewish or Christian; "behind all ethnic diversities," Max Weber wrote, "there is somehow naturally the notion of the 'chosen people' . . ."

Inevitably, however, the experience of exile and persecution affected the way Jews interpreted the concept of chosenness. After the

* "Not because you are more numerous than all the other peoples has God embraced you and chosen you, for you are the fewest among the peoples, but because of God's love for you, and his keeping of the oath which he swore to your fathers . . . [Deuteronomy 7:7–8]."

† " 'To me, O Israelites, you are just like the Ethiopians,' declared the Lord [Amos 9:7]."

destruction of the First and Second Temples, Jews found consolation by interpreting election as a mark of distinction: whatever the reason God initially chose the Jews, their possession of the Torah made them morally superior to those who rejected it. Even so, the rabbis of the Talmud (the first through sixth centuries of the Christian era) kept exclusivity in check by emphasizing the dialectical tension between particularism and universalism that is central to Jewish thought.

The balance was altered by the renewal of persecution during the late Middle Ages, when Jews were subjected to mass expulsions, conversions and autos-da-fé. This great age of Jewish martyrdom, in which whole communities of Jews chose death over conversion to Christianity, inspired hatred against Christianity, as well as against the Christians who denied the Jews their right to exist. Medieval rabbinic leaders responded to the church's insistence that Jews were eternally damned for having rejected Christianity by reinterpreting the doctrine of Israel's election, attributing it to what they came to consider the innate spiritual superiority of the Jews. To medieval Jewish thinkers the difference between the Jewish way of life and that of the other nations was not the result of Israel's acceptance of the Torah, as the dominant tradition had argued until then; on the contrary, the new view held, Israel's acceptance of the Torah (hence its election) was the result of its unique–and superior–spiritual makeup. Being herded into ghettos only intensified this view. "The more the Jew was forced to close in on himself, the more he tended to emphasize Israel's difference from the cruel Gentile without," the author of the *Encyclopedia Judaica* article on chosenness has written. "Only thus did his suffering become intelligible and bearable."

The Holocaust–the most traumatic event in Jewish history since the destruction of the Second Temple–has had a similar effect. The fact that the rest of the world either sat passively by or cheered the Nazis on has contributed to a sense of moral superiority and lent credence to the ancient Jewish belief that "scratch a goy deep enough and you'll find an anti-Semite." Because the trauma was (and still is) so intense, Jews tend to see the Holocaust as a uniquely Jewish tragedy and thus almost to denigrate the loss of non-Jewish lives. The result is what the historian Ismar Schorsch of the Jewish Theological Seminary of America calls "a distasteful secular version of chosenness," in which it is Jews' monopoly on suffering that sets them apart from and makes them morally superior to others.

All this is quite unconscious. On the conscious level, American Jews reject any notion of innate superiority. Their religious leaders generally have tried to reinterpret the doctrine of Israel's election in nonexclusive and nonpejorative terms, when they have not ignored it or, as Mordecai Kaplan proposed, abandoned it altogether. Except for a handful of Orthodox extremists, moreover, American Jews are enthusiastic proponents of American religious pluralism, and they accept its fundamental tenets: no religion can claim exclusive truth; in public, at least, each religion will forgo any assertion of superiority. As Abraham Joshua Heschel put it, "God is either the Father of all men or of no man." "It seems to be the will of God," Heschel added, "that there be more than one religion."

And yet it is extraordinarily difficult for American Jews to expunge the sense of superiority altogether, however much they may try to suppress it. "We Jews have a remarkable history. In some respects we have been more preoccupied than other peoples with the belief in God and . . . with problems of life's meaning and how best to achieve life's purposes," writes Rabbi Ira Eisenstein, founder and former president of the Reconstructionist Rabbinical College, who advocates the elimination of the concept of chosenness from Jewish liturgy and thought. "*But we should not boast about it.* Humility is more befitting a people of such high aspirations. We ought not to say that God gave the Torah to us and nobody else . . . We should be old enough and mature enough as a people to accept our history with dignity, without resort to comparisons which are generally odious [emphasis added]."

Rank-and-file American Jews, especially those of the first and second generations, are likely to be less reticent—at least within the confines of family and friends. "Can't you grasp something of the principle of equality, God damn it!" Philip Roth's rebellious antihero Alexander Portnoy exclaims at the age of fourteen.

> We all haven't been lucky to be born Jews, you know. So a little *rachmones* [pity] on the less fortunate, okay? Because I am sick and tired of *goyische* this and *goyische* that! If it's bad it's the *goyim,* if it's good it's the Jews! Can't you see, my dear parents, from whose loins I somehow leaped, that such thinking is a trifle barbaric? That all you are expressing is your *fear?* The very first distinction I learned from you, I'm sure, was not night and day, or hot and cold, but *goyische* and Jewish! [Emphasis in original.]

As he grows up, however, Portnoy begins to appreciate the distinction. "The outrage, the disgust inspired in my parents by the Gentiles, was beginning to make some sense: the *goyim* pretended to be something special, while *we* were actually *their* moral superiors," Portnoy recalls, referring to his high school years. "And what made us superior was precisely the hatred and disrespect they lavished so willingly upon us!" [Emphasis in original.]

Through the concept of chosenness, Jews have fashioned an effective defense against the self-hatred that anti-Semitism engendered. The attributes and values that Jews developed through centuries of powerlessness—a distaste for physical combat, for example, and a preference for academic over athletic prowess—were endowed with moral superiority. At high school football games, Portnoy recalls, there was "a certain comic detachment experienced on our side of the field, grounded in the belief that this was precisely the kind of talent that only a *goy* would think to develop in the first place . . . We were Jews—and not only were we not inferior to the *goyim* who beat us at football, but . . . because we could not commit our hearts to victory in such a thuggish game, we were superior. We were Jews—*and we were superior* [emphasis in original]." Indeed, the only character in *Portnoy's Complaint* who is crippled by feelings of inadequacy is that rebel against Jewish particularism, Alexander Portnoy himself.

It would be disingenuous to imply that the "antigoyism" against which Alexander Portnoy (and Philip Roth) rail is only a response to anti-Semitism and nothing more. The Jewish sense of superiority serves other functions as well. It is a powerful inducement to achievement—one of the engines of the astonishing upward mobility American Jews have shown. In the secularized world in which most American Jews live, what an American Jewish child inherits is "no body of law, no body of learning and no language, and finally, no Lord," Roth has argued, but "a psychology . . . and the psychology can be translated into three words: 'Jews are better.' " The consequences are profound, for the psychology American Jews inherit forces them to validate their sense of superiority. "There was a sense of specialness and from then on it was up to you to invent your specialness, to invent, as it were, your betterness . . ."

This sense of superiority also serves to perpetuate group identity in the face of rapid acculturation. There are a number of reasons for "this almost unique desire for survival," according to Marshall Sklare, the most distinguished sociologist of American Jewish life, but among the most important "is the fact that Jews still possess a feeling of superiority, although more in the moral and intellectual realms now than in the area of spiritual affairs. While the feeling of superiority is a factor that has received comparatively little attention from students of the problem, it is of crucial importance because it operates to retard assimilation. Leaving the group becomes a psychological threat: such a move is viewed not as an advancement but as cutting oneself off from a claim to superiority."

CHAPTER THREE

"A GUY NAMED SHAPIRO"

1*

In *Pete 'n Tillie,* a comic film popular a few years ago, the character played by Walter Matthau was asked why he always called himself a Jew when he was three quarters Lutheran. Matthau's answer was as direct as it was revealing: "I'm a social climber."

There was irony of course in Matthau's response, but the line could not have evoked so much laughter had it been only that. Matthau's remark was funny precisely because it mixed irony with prescient social commentary. In the new lexicon of American ethnicity Jews no longer constitute a minority group, notwithstanding the fact that they represent only 2.5 percent of the American population. Minority status is now limited to those who continue to be handicapped by past or present discrimination. On these criteria, Jews now belong to the advantaged majority.

It would be feckless to suggest that no disabilities remain. Jews are still excluded from some elite clubs and neighborhoods and, in New

* This chapter is based, in part, on research by Steven Silberman and Myra Alperson.

York City, a number of cooperative apartment houses. Among some segments of the population, moreover, a significant residue of anti-Semitism remains; depending on what questions are asked in public-opinion surveys, responses from a fifth to a third of American adults still show anti-Jewish attitudes.

And yet it is clear that the old burden has been lifted. Along with members of other once-despised and discriminated-against ethnic and religious groups, American Jews have taken their place in the mainstream of American life, and a number of them have been accepted as part of the so-called Establishment.

Nothing has symbolized the changing position of Jews in American society so dramatically as the December 1973 election of Irving S. Shapiro as chairman and chief executive officer of that bluest of blue-chip corporations E. I. du Pont de Nemours and Company. True, Shapiro was not the first Jew to head a major American corporation, but none of those who preceded him were regarded as pioneers ushering in a new era in American life. Gerard Swope, who served as president of General Electric from 1922 to 1940, went to great pains to hide his Jewish origins; his closest associates at GE assumed that, like his wife, Swope was a Protestant. And although Philip Sporn, longtime head of American Electric Power (1947–61), always took pride in his Jewishness ("I was a fairly proficient Talmudic scholar," he told an interviewer in 1960), his appointment as president of the nation's largest public utility did not set any bells ringing. Perhaps because his name was not identifiable as such, few people realized that Sporn was Jewish. And since American Electric Power was hardly a household name—except to investors and to utility industry experts—the fact that Sporn served as its president drew no notice from the Jewish, let alone the business or general press.

Irving Shapiro's appointment as chairman of Du Pont was something else again; it was reported on the front pages of *The New York Times* and the *Wall Street Journal*, among other papers, and was the occasion for full-scale profiles in *Fortune* and other business journals. Du Pont, after all, was no ordinary corporation; its hundred-and-seventy-five-year history made it the oldest major firm in the country as well as one of the largest (number three in the *Fortune* 500) and best known. It was also one of the most aristocratic and inbred; until 1970, when Shapiro's immediate predecessor, Charles B. McCoy, became chairman, no nonmember of the Du Pont family had ever held that post. In a sense, Du Pont chairmen had been less appointed than anointed, in a manner that resembled royal succession more than the usual process of managerial selection.

Thus Shapiro's selection as Du Pont's chief executive hit his own family "like an absolute bombshell," as his son Stuart, a partner in a large New York law firm, put it. It hit most other observers, Jews and Gentiles alike, the same way. As Stuart Shapiro explained, "A lawyer doesn't become chairman of Du Pont, a Jew doesn't become chairman of Du Pont." (Shapiro was also the first Du Pont chairman who was neither a chemist nor an engineer.) Or as the U.S. ambassador to Great Britain told the Anglo-Jewish leader Lord Sieff of Brimpton on the day after Shapiro's appointment, "I could understand a Jew becoming President of the United States, but not chief executive officer of Du Pont."

Shapiro himself believes that his 1976 election as chairman of the two-hundred-and-twenty-member Business Roundtable, the preeminent organization of corporate chief executives, was even more significant. "Du Pont is just one company," he told me; "the Business Roundtable is *all* companies—and they asked a guy named Shapiro to be chairman." From the moment he became chief executive of Du Pont, in fact, "American industry opened its hand and said 'welcome'; I became a hot property on corporate boards." (Although now retired as Du Pont's chairman, he continues to sit on the Du Pont board, as well as on the boards of IBM, Citicorp, and the Bechtel Group, among others.) "I have no doubt that a few people cringed when I became chairman," Shapiro adds, "but I never heard about it or knew who they were. The key leaders of American industry made it damn clear that I was welcome in their club."

Part of the charm of this unassuming, Yiddish-speaking son of a Lithuanian-born pants presser is that he was not willing to join every club that wanted to make him welcome. When the most socially prestigious (and most restricted) country club in Wilmington asked the new chairman of Du Pont to become its first Jewish member, he turned them down. "I told them that it just would not be comfortable for my wife and me to socialize there," Shapiro told me. The club leaders were stunned by the rejection. "It never occurred to them that I might say no," he said with a smile. Shapiro hesitated briefly before making the decision because he knew it would embarrass the friends who had engineered the invitation, "but I just could not abide being in that setting for social purposes." It's different when a club is for business purposes: "then you do what you have to do." (Shapiro joined a previously restricted downtown club to make it easier to hold business lunches and dinners, but he also helped start a new club with an explicit nondiscriminatory policy.)

Shapiro's career is worth dwelling on because of the kind of man—and the kind of Jew—he is, as well as because of the position he attained. Specifically, the fact that a man as comfortable with his Jewishness as Shapiro is could become chairman of Du Pont is evidence that "the brutal bargain" is no more, that Jews no longer have to suppress or abandon their Jewishness to gain acceptance. "I accomplished all this by my deliberate decision to be myself," Shapiro told me with fierce but quiet pride. "I am what I am, and I can never change."

One of the aspects of his being that Shapiro refused to change was his name, for which he paid a heavy price early in his career. Although he finished fourth in his class at the University of Minnesota Law School and was an editor of its law review, he could not even get an interview, let alone a job offer, from a Minneapolis law firm. At that time—1941—Minneapolis was considered the most anti-Semitic city in the country; not even the Automobile Club would accept Jews as members. Understandably, Shapiro's professors, as well as a number of Jewish lawyer friends, urged him to change his name; "nothing will happen with a name like Shapiro," they told him. He considered the idea briefly and decided against it. "My parents had really struggled to put me through school, and the first thing I do is reject their name?" he recalled, his voice rising in passion. "No, I decided, that can't be. You've got to live by principles; you can't be opportunistic. And besides, I could not conceive of facing my father, who was a very proud man, and telling him his name was not suitable for me. So it really was not a tough call. It just was not the way I wanted to live." In retrospect Shapiro believes that keeping his name was one of the best decisions he ever made, "because it was clear who I was at all times."

Shapiro made it clear who he was in other ways as well; in the language of the nineteenth century, he has been "a Jew in the streets" as well as at home. From the beginning of his stay at Du Pont headquarters in Wilmington, Delaware, Shapiro has been active in Jewish communal affairs, serving as president (and, most recently, campaign chairman) of the Jewish Federation of Delaware, president of the Kutz Home for the Aged, and trustee of the Jewish Community Center of Wilmington, among other positions. Shapiro has affirmed his Jewishness in more personal ways as well. Not long after he joined the Du Pont legal department, for example, he invited his superiors to his son's bar mitzvah—the first time any of them had been inside a synagogue. ("I never realized there were rabbis who did not have beards," several executives told him.) And in the late 1970s, when his good friend George Shultz, then head of the Bechtel Corporation, invited him to visit Saudi Arabia, Shapiro accepted—on condition that he and Shultz visit Israel together on the same trip. (Saudi Arabia does not normally provide a visa to anyone coming from or going to Israel.) It proved to be Shultz's first visit to Israel.

Unlike many who make it to the top, Shapiro has neither forgotten nor turned his back on his humble origins; his life, in fact, is a classic Horatio Alger story. Shapiro's father, Sam, found work as a pants presser when he settled in Minneapolis, and his mother worked in a garment industry sweatshop; after their marriage the elder Shapiros took in four boarders to help pay the bills. When Irving Shapiro was eight his father borrowed five hundred dollars to open a small dry-cleaning store, which Jonas Shapiro, Irving's youngest brother, still runs; all three sons worked in the shop after school, walking the five miles each way from and to home to save the nickel carfare. When his father became ill, the teenaged Irving ran the business. "I dreaded it," he recalls, and "ducked out as soon as I could." Ducking out was no problem: Sam Shapiro was determined that his oldest son become a lawyer, and although Irving leaned toward accounting, he acceded to his father's wishes, helping to pay for his undergraduate and professional education through a combination of loans, odd jobs, and winnings at poker.

Shapiro's legal career began inauspiciously enough; he started out as a solo practitioner, renting space from another lawyer, which he paid for in kind—legal research, drawing up contracts, and so on. When the United States entered World War II, Shapiro, who had been rejected by the army—he had had severe asthma as a child—went to Washington to work for the Office of Price Administration. Two years later he transferred to the Criminal Division of the Justice Department, where he quickly won a reputation as a brilliant trial lawyer and writer of appellate briefs.*

A series of coincidences led Shapiro to Du Pont. In late 1950 he was in New York, arguing the government's case in the appeal of the conviction of the Communist party leaders. Shapiro's former boss at Justice, Oscar Provost, who was a senior attorney with Du Pont, happened to be in New York the next morning, when *The New York Times* carried a long account of Shapiro's argument. Provost called him and suggested that he join the Du Pont legal staff. The timing was fortunate. Shapiro had concluded that, lacking political connections, he had gone as far as he could go at Justice; he was glad to consider another job, and this one "looked like very interesting work." (Du Pont was expanding its legal staff to fight an antitrust suit, in which the antitrust division of the Justice Department was suing to force the company to sell its controlling 23 percent interest in General

* One measure of how endemic anti-Semitism used to be is that Shapiro's name was not always attached to the briefs he wrote. Tom Clark, who was assistant attorney general in charge of the Criminal Division during part of Shapiro's tenure there, was unhappy about having so many Jews working for him and frequently left their names off their briefs.

Motors.) Despite the advice of friends—Du Pont had a reputation for anti-Semitism—Shapiro accepted the offer.

At Du Pont, Shapiro was quickly thrust into a classic Jewish role, that of middleman—in this instance, between the Du Pont lawyers and members of top management. He had a rare talent for explaining the legal technicalities of the case to Du Pont executives and for communicating their concerns to the lawyers, most of whom the executives never saw. "The contact we always had on my level was Irv Shapiro," says Crawford Greenwalt, a former Du Pont president and chairman (and Du Pont in-law). "A great many people at the executive level got to know him."

They got to respect his ability and judgment as well. Although Du Pont lost the antitrust suit, the terms of settlement that Shapiro worked out and helped sell to Congress (special legislation was required) saved the Du Pont shareholders an estimated $1 billion in taxes. Increasingly, therefore, Du Pont executives began seeking Shapiro's advice on a broad range of business as well as legal questions. It was not simply that Shapiro was the kind of lawyer who helped his clients find ways to achieve their objectives, instead of simply putting up legal obstacles. He also had the ability to cut to the heart of a complex question and state the alternatives clearly. And by making a practice of sitting in on meetings of the sales and executive staffs, he came to know the various Du Pont businesses well. In 1965 Shapiro became assistant general counsel, jumping over several people who were senior to him; his influence in the company was considerably greater than his formal position implied.

Even so, as late as 1970 Shapiro's ambition was simply to become vice-president and general counsel of Du Pont. His horizon broadened suddenly in the fall of that year when the new chairman, Charles B. McCoy, told him, "It's about time you stopped being a lawyer and became a manager; I'd like you on the executive committee." "It didn't take long for me to say, 'If you want me, you've got me,' " Shapiro recalls. In one fell swoop he became a senior vice-president, director, and member of the executive committee.

The rest is history. In July of 1973 Shapiro became vice-chairman, a new position created for him as a way of testing the waters. The waters were calm, and when McCoy retired six months later, Shapiro succeeded him as chairman and chief executive officer. He reached the mandatory retirement age in 1981 and is now a partner in the booming law firm of Skadden Arps Slate Meagher & Flom. He heads the Wilmington office of the law partnership but continues to play an active role at Du Pont as a director and chairman of the finance committee.

The question of course is whether Shapiro's career represents simply one man's success story or the beginning of a major trend—a parable, if you will, of American (and American Jewish) life. Shapiro believes that his move to the top was a genuine breakthrough that marked the end of anti-Semitism as a significant factor in corporate life. "I am absolutely convinced that the situation has turned around completely," he told me. "Jewishness is simply not a relevant factor any more in most corporations." "Jewishness does not weigh against you any longer," he added. "In some companies, it might even be a positive factor; they want to demonstrate that they are operating on the merits, and promoting a Jew is a signal that they are no longer prejudiced."

Others are more skeptical. In the opinion of some, Shapiro's elevation was a fluke rather than a genuine breakthrough—the result of special circumstances (the antitrust suit against Du Pont) not likely to be repeated—and in the future Du Pont and other such companies will draw their chief executives from the usual WASP pool. Still others grant that Shapiro's appointment was part of a larger pattern but doubt that corporate anti-Semitism is now as insignificant as Shapiro suggests. In their 1982 study *Jews in the Protestant Establishment* Richard L. Zweigenhaft and G. William Domhoff point out that, like Shapiro, some of the most prominent Jewish chief executives did not follow the usual routes to the top. The Jewish-born W. Michael Blumenthal, for example, became president of Bendix after prominent service in the Kennedy administration and moved to the chairmanship of Burroughs after being secretary of the treasury under Jimmy Carter. Similarly, Richard Gelb, chief executive of Bristol-Meyers, started there as a vice-president after the drug firm had acquired Clairol, the family-owned company of which he had been president. "The careers of men such as Blumenthal, Gelb, and Shapiro suggest that non-Jewish business leaders are willing to promote Jewish executives within their corporations once these men have proven themselves," Zweigenhaft and Domhoff state. "However, it also seems to be the case that few Jews have been able to start at the bottom and prove themselves in the usual way. *Climbing the corporate ladder still remains problematical for Jews* [emphasis added]."

The argument will not hold; had Jews been required to climb the corporate ladder in the usual manner, the breakthroughs would not have come as early as they did. Although a few large corporations dropped their anti-Semitic barriers during or after World War II, it was not until the 1960s and 1970s that they began to employ Jewish college and business school graduates in significant numbers. Before then corporate recruiters rarely offered jobs to Jewish college and business school graduates, and when they did, Jewish students were often reluctant to accept for fear they would run into anti-Semitism on the job or bump up against an early ceiling.

ITEM: "Jews go where they can make a good living," Walter Shorenstein, an enormously successful San Francisco real estate developer, told me by way of explaining why he had chosen that particular field. "Where were they going to go forty years ago—the phone company? We lived in a closed society then; there were very few places on the corporate ladder where Jews could be coequal."*

For the most part, upwardly mobile Jews have shown a preference for professions and businesses in which one can be one's own boss. Temperament also played a role. "Corporate life is Mickey Mouse," Bernard Mendik, another real estate developer on the *Forbes* 400 list, told me. "It's like being in the army." More important, however, to be self-employed meant to be free of dependence on others, especially those others, the Gentiles, who could be expected to discriminate against Jews. "I was supposed to be a doctor—the family expected it," says Av Westin, vice-president for program development at ABC News; and in fact he was a premed student during his first three years of college. Westin's ambition changed when he spent the summer as a copy boy at CBS News; when he was offered a job there after college, Westin's family tried to persuade him to refuse it. "They don't like Jews out there," his uncle told him, "but you can always earn a living as a doctor, because Jews always get sick."

Jews who went into business, moreover, were drawn to fields in which their performances would be judged by an impersonal marketplace rather than bureaucratic superiors.

ITEM: "Elegant manners and fine breeding are of no help in a chess game," says Daniel Rose, an elegantly mannered and classically educated New York real estate developer, "and real estate development is an unending series of chess games, each one different from the others." (The fifty-six-year-old Rose took his undergraduate degree at Yale and studied philosophy at the Sorbonne before joining the family real estate firm started by his father and uncle.) Much the same is true of fields such as stock and commodities trading, which have also attracted a great many Jews.

* Shorenstein went where he could make a very good living indeed. When he got out of the service at the end of World War II his wife was pregnant and he needed an apartment as well as a job. He went to work selling real estate and became a partner in the firm in 1951 and its sole owner in 1960. Today he owns property in Kansas City, Houston, and Los Angeles as well as San Francisco and has a net worth of $300 million, according to the *Forbes* list of the 400 richest Americans.

These attitudes are disappearing now as Jews find that they are welcome in the executive suite and are judged objectively, but the old mind-set served to slow the Jewish move into corporate management. It is only in the last few years, therefore, that significant numbers of Jews who started at the bottom have reached the senior management level and thus have been eligible for promotion to the top.

And they *are* being promoted! Morris Tanenbaum, the fifty-six-year-old son of an immigrant delicatessen owner, went to work for the Bell System in 1952; he is now executive vice-president of American Telephone and Telegraph Company in charge of financial management and strategic planning and is considered the most likely person to succeed AT&T's current chief executive officer when the latter retires in 1986. A former Hebrew-school teacher, Tanenbaum grew up in Huntington, West Virginnia, and speaks Yiddish with a slight southern drawl. When a visitor observes that he looks Jewish in addition to having a clearly Jewish name Tanenbaum grins in agreement. Like Irving Shapiro, Tanenbaum's parents wanted him to become a lawyer. "It's very interesting and very nice, but how are you going to make a living?" they asked when he told them he was going to major in chemistry at Johns Hopkins.

It was an understandable question. "We know perfectly well that names ending in 'berg' or 'stein' have to be skipped by the board of selection of students for scholarships in chemistry," Albert Sprague Coolidge, chairman of the Harvard chemistry department, had told a Massachusetts legislative committee in 1946. It was pointless to accept Jews, Coolidge explained, because there simply were no jobs for Jewish chemists; the chemical industry had long been closed to Jews. "I wasn't offered any jobs, while the non-Jewish boys were all snapped up by the various chemical companies," Nobel Laureate Isidor I. Rabi has said, recalling his experience after receiving his undergraduate degree in chemistry at Cornell a quarter of a century earlier. "It was really terrible." It was less terrible when Tanenbaum was in college; the invention of the transistor and the development of polymers and synthetics had turned chemistry into a rapidly growing as well as intellectually exciting field. After graduating second in his class at Johns Hopkins, Tanenbaum went on to take a Ph.D. in physical chemistry at Princeton. He joined the research staff of Bell Labs immediately after receiving his degree.

Tanenbaum's mother worried nonetheless. (His father had died a few years earlier.) "I'd been told that the Bell System was anti-Semitic," Tanenbaum told me, "and I'd heard that there were no Jews at Bell Labs before World War II; it could be true." It *had* been true; nor was the absence of Jews coincidental. Philip Sporn, who had regarded anti-Semitism as simply one more obstacle to be overcome, could not get past the barrier at Bell Labs when he received his electrical engineering degree from Columbia in 1917; a job offer he had received was withdrawn when Sporn answered "I'm Jewish" to a question about his "church affiliation." Bell Labs still would not hire Jews in 1935 when Emanuel Piore received his Ph.D. in physics. The Lithuanian-born Piore, who went on to become chief scientist of the United States Navy and then vice-president, chief scientist, and a director of IBM, took a job with RCA–one of only two large corporations (GE was the other) whose research labs hired Jews. (It may not have been coincidental that the two firms willing to hire Jews in their research divisions each had Jewish chief executives–Swope at GE and David Sarnoff at RCA.)

During World War II, however, the need for scientific talent forced Bell Labs and other firms to substitute meritocratic considerations for the ones that previously had prevailed, and the postwar expansion of the American economy created the same need for managerial talent in the rest of the Bell System. Tanenbaum was just young enough, therefore, to have missed the barriers that handicapped others. "As far as I can judge," he told me, "being Jewish didn't play any role at all in my career." Nor did he worry that his Jewishness would put him at a disadvantage: "I felt I could perform well enough and that I'd be judged that way"–as clearly he was.

Although he moved up rapidly, Tanenbaum felt that he was not a good enough scientist to remain in research and therefore left the laboratory for management in 1964, moving to Western Electric as director of Research and Development. Seven years and two promotions later Tanenbaum became vice-president in charge of engineering, and then of manufacturing. He went back to Bell Labs in 1975 as executive vice-president, and he became a vice-president of AT&T a year later. Tanenbaum then spent two years as president of an operating company (New Jersey Bell)–the usual Bell System means of grooming people for top management–before returning to AT&T as an executive vice-president. He became chairman and chief executive officer of the newly created AT&T Communications, the second-largest subsidiary (118,000 employees and $30 billion in sales) of the reconstituted AT&T, in 1983, and was promoted to his present post in January of 1985. In short, Tanenbaum has followed the traditional route to the top.

Others have done the same–at AT&T and at a host of other corporations, both large and small.

ITEM: "He is going to be one of the great business leaders in the world before he is through," says former U.S. Representative Martha

W. Griffiths, a member of the Chrysler Corporation board of directors. The "he" in question is forty-nine-year-old Gerald Greenwald, Chrysler's vice-chairman and heir apparent. The son of immigrants (and, on his mother's side, the grandson of a cantor), Greenwald grew up in St. Louis, where his father was a wholesale produce dealer. "We were never hungry and the roof didn't leak, but there never was any extra money," Greenwald told me. An outstanding student and athlete—he was captain of his high school football team—Greenwald went to Princeton on a full scholarship. He became interested in labor economics during his junior year and initially planned to be a union organizer; he changed his mind, however, after an abortive three-week stint organizing garment workers in St. Louis.

Like his boss, Chrysler chairman Lee Iacocca, Greenwald has spent most of his career at Ford Motor Company, starting there in 1957 after receiving his B.A. from Princeton. "People I knew asked, 'What's a nice Jewish boy doing in a company like that?'" Greenwald recalls, referring to the pall that still hung over the company because of the anti-Semitic activities engaged in by Henry Ford, Sr., during the 1920s and 1930s.* But Henry Ford II, who had taken control twelve years earlier, had made a number of gestures, such as buying Israel Bonds, to signal the fact that a new era had begun. The result, Greenwald says, is that "by the time I arrived, Ford had become a meritocracy."

That, certainly, was the way it worked for him. In 1967, after seven promotions in nine years, Greenwald became controller of Ford's Brazilian subsidiary. He returned to Detroit in 1970, then moved on to managerial positions in Paris and London. Greenwald became president of Ford of Venezuela in 1976 at forty-one. Under his management, Ford's market share in Venezuela was the highest of any Ford subsidiary. When Iacocca signed on as chairman of Chrysler, he asked Greenwald to join him. "Jerry has the talent and the know-how of the entrepreneur who can analyze a problem and then move to solve it," Iacocca has written. Henry Ford II tried to persuade Greenwald to remain at Ford, but Greenwald explained that "he just couldn't pass up the excitement Chrysler represented." He became Chrysler's vice-president and controller in May of 1979; four months later he was pro-

* Ford's *Dearborn Independent* gave mass circulation to the "Protocols of the Elders of Zion," an anti-Semitic literary hoax purporting to be the creation of an international Jewish conspiracy bent on controlling the Western world. The "Protocols" had been concocted by an agent of the Russian secret police near the end of the nineteenth century. In the *Dearborn Independent*'s version, published under the title "The Jewish Peril," Lenin was the leader of the conspiracy and the investment banker Jacob Schiff its chief financier.

moted to executive vice-president for finance, and in April of 1981 he became vice-chairman—the highest position a Jew has ever attained in the auto industry, whose managements used to be even more homogeneous and ingrown than most. Until Greenwald's appointment "no Jew had ever reached the top ranks of the Big Three automakers," says Iacocca, adding, "I find it a little hard to believe that none of them was qualified."

That the change at Chrysler is more than cosmetic is evident from the fact that Greenwald is not the only Jew in the company's top management. Stephan Sharf—"one of those guys who had been kept under a bushel basket" during his years at Chrysler, as Iacocca describes him—is executive vice-president in charge of manufacturing, and Frederick Zuckerman, whom Iacocca hired away from IBM, is vice-president and treasurer.

ITEM: Reuben Mark, the forty-five-year-old chairman and chief executive officer of Colgate-Palmolive Company, has never worked for any other company. Mark started with Colgate in 1963 after receiving his M.B.A. from Harvard Business School. He moved up rapidly, becoming president of Colgate-Palmolive of Venezuela in 1972, vice-president and general manager of Colgate's Far East division in 1974, group vice-president in charge of domestic operations in 1979, and executive vice-president in 1981. Mark was appointed president and chief operating officer in 1983, and became chairman and chief executive officer a year later.

It may not be entirely coincidental that both Greenwald and Mark enjoyed meteoric rises in their companies' foreign operations. In the past, established industries and occupations often were closed to Jews, who were, in any case, reluctant to compete head-on with members of the dominant group for fear of provoking an anti-Semitic backlash. As a result, Jews traditionally have gravitated toward new industries and occupations. Because they had to take their opportunities where they could find them and because they were often marginal to the societies in which they lived, Jews became particularly adept at spotting new opportunities and capitalizing on them. As Sir Isaiah Berlin has written, centuries of experience have produced a "fantastic overdevelopment of [Jews'] faculties for detecting trends, and [for] discriminating the shades and hues of changing individual and social situations, often before they have been noticed anywhere else."

Something of the sort may have been at work in Greenwald's and Mark's careers. They went to work for Chrysler and Colgate-Palmolive at a time when those companies, like a great many others, were transforming themselves from domestic to multinational corporations. In a sense, overseas operations were a new industry and managing those operations a new occupation. It is also probable that Jews were more acceptable as managers of foreign than of domestic operations; as Greenwald has delicately put it, "With a big automobile company like Ford, the farther you get from headquarters, the more individual responsibility you have."

Whatever the routes they take, it is now becoming routine for Jews to move into top management—so much so that appointments of Jews no longer attract particular notice. This is not to suggest that anti-Semitism has disappeared in the executive suite; it was too deeply rooted for that to have happened overnight. Changes of the magnitude I am describing rarely occur all at once; they begin in a few places and then spread—slowly at first, and then at an accelerating pace as mores change or as prejudiced old-timers retire or die. "Tom Watson, Jr., doesn't have a prejudiced bone in his body," Emanuel Piore, who was the first Jewish vice-president of IBM, told me. But the younger Watson was not free to abandon IBM's all-WASP tradition until he was out from under his father's domination.*

What happened at IBM has happened at most other companies and, indeed, in the country as a whole; among most segments of the American population anti-Semitism and other forms of prejudice decline significantly from one generation to the next. As a new generation of stockholders, directors, and managers takes over, therefore, corporate anti-Semitism is rapidly becoming a thing of the past, as Richard Zweigenhaft, coauthor of *Jews in the Protestant Establishment*, now concludes. In 1983, just a year after that skeptical volume had been published, Zweigenhaft surveyed a sample of seventy-five Harvard Business School alumni in a study sponsored by the American Jewish Committee. Virtually all the non-Jewish and most of the Jewish respondents reported that being Jewish was now either a minor impediment or none at all to Jews' corporate careers. "Things have improved considerably for Jews in the corporate world over the last decade," Zweigenhaft concluded. Or as one of his Gentile respondents put it, "I think we're beyond [anti-Semitism]. It's not really relevant any more.

* Piore's experience with New York City's previously restricted University Club illustrates the impact an executive of Watson's stature can have on social as well as economic discrimination. An American Jewish Committee task force had been trying unsuccessfully for several years to persuade the club to admit Jews. They were eager to do so, the club's leaders told the task force members, but the process would take time because of the long waiting list. The waiting list shrank remarkably when Watson placed a phone call to say that he wanted Piore admitted; the restrictions against other Jews disappeared soon afterward.

Talking to a Goldberg or a Witherington—it just doesn't make any difference."

Most Jewish respondents drew the same conclusion, despite the fact that many of them had encountered anti-Semitism earlier in their careers.

ITEM: When he finished Harvard Business School in 1965, one respondent told Zweigenhaft, he went to work for a company that had a reputation as not being "a place for a Jewish boy." The reputation was deserved. "They were anti-Jewish, anti-black, anti-women—they were just bigoted people," he says, and he left after a few years. In his view, companies of that sort are a vanishing breed. "The prejudice . . . that did exist—and I think it was real—is virtually nonexistent; it certainly is for me. . . . I'm Jewish. I belong to a temple. I encountered bias in the late 1960s, and I believe it's virtually gone [now]" except, perhaps, he adds, in commercial and investment banking, where he suspects that social credentials may still be important. In his own field, management consulting, there has been a complete transformation. "Up to the mid-1960s they still emphasized such things as skin color and squareness of jaw," he says, "but about fifteen years ago they passed from the old-boy network to a real meritocracy. *People who deliver make it* [emphasis added]."

2

People who deliver now make it in virtually every area of American life. Take the practice of corporate law, where social breeding used to be more important than intellectual ability. "Brilliant intellectual powers are not essential," Paul D. Cravath, one of the deans of the corporate bar, told Harvard Law School students in 1920. "Too much imagination, too much wit, too great cleverness, too facile fluency . . . are quite as likely to impede success as to promote it. The best clients are apt to be afraid of those qualities."

To put those fears to rest, the "best lawyers" made certain not to hire the strange and irritating people who put so much stock in intellectual brilliance; if they could have had their way, they would have excluded Jews not only from their firms but from the bar itself. "I do not want anybody to come to the bar . . . who has not any conception of the moral qualities that underlie our free American institutions," Elihu Root, Jr., the most respected corporate lawyer of the day, declared in 1922, "and they are coming, today, by the tens of thousands."

Henry Taft worried that the bar would lose its influence if it continued to admit lawyers whose "gestures are unwholesome and overcommercialized" and whose "historical derivation" made it "impossible" for them to "appreciate what we understand as professional spirit."

It proved to be impossible to prevent Jews from becoming lawyers, but for the most part Jewish lawyers were confined to the least prestigious (and least rewarding) kinds of legal work, such as bill collecting, criminal law, petty negligence suits, bankruptcy cases, small real estate closings, and the like. The handful of Jewish firms with a corporate practice served only Jewish-owned businesses and thus were too small to hire even the best Jewish law school graduates. In the spring of 1936, when eight Jewish editors of the *Harvard Law Review* had not yet found jobs, Felix Frankfurter, who earlier had waxed poetic about the opportunities Harvard Law School offered Jewish students, wondered bitterly "whether this School shouldn't tell Jewish students that they go through . . . at their own risk of ever having opportunity of entering the best law offices."

Today the law may well be the most religiously and ethnically, if not yet racially integrated profession. "What can I tell you? It's changed," says Joseph Flom of Skadden Arps Slate Meagher & Flom, one of the most successful corporate lawyers in the United States. The son of an Eastern European immigrant turned manufacturer of shoulder pads, Brooklyn-born Flom earns well over $1 million a year as adviser to some of the country's leading corporations and investment banking firms. Flom's particular expertise is in proxy fights and contested tender offers and mergers, activities that first became respectable "or at least a little less déclassé" in the early 1970s but that now almost dominate the business news. (Skadden Arps, which had forty lawyers then, has well over three hundred now.) Because Jews tend to gravitate to new fields, where the opportunities are greatest, this newest and fastest growing legal specialty is largely dominated by Jewish lawyers: after Flom the most prominent takeover specialists are Martin Lipton, of Wachtell, Lipton, Rosen & Katz, and Arthur Fleischer, Jr., of Fried, Frank, Harris, Shriver & Jacobson. "Nobody makes a move without consulting one of those three," the head of the corporate department of a major law firm told me with a sigh of resignation.

Something similar happened earlier in the postwar period, when labor and tax law came into their own—that is, when corporations discovered that they needed lawyers who could negotiate with trade unions and guide them through the thickets of the Internal Revenue Code and other government regulations. These were skills that the "white-shoe" lawyers did not possess but that Jews had in abundance.

Barred from the corporate bar during the 1930s, the ablest Jewish law school graduates had flocked to Washington to take advantage of the opportunities the New Deal had created. After World War II, Jewish and Gentile lawyers who had known each other in government formed new and ethnically neutral firms, such as Arnold Fortas & Porter, in Washington, and Paul, Weiss, Rifkind, Wharton & Garrison, in New York, which attracted a share of the "best clients."

For a time the old-line firms resisted change. They did hire a few Jewish associates early in the postwar period to relieve the shortage of lawyers that the wartime draft had created. But when the Jewish associates came up for partnership in the early 1950s, they were usually blackballed by the old-timers. Within a relatively few years, however—the turning point varied from city to city and firm to firm—the all-WASP firms found themselves falling behind on what had become a very fast track. It was not simply that they lacked expertise in the new and growing fields of tax and labor law or that their younger litigators and corporate lawyers were not always up to the mark in an increasingly competitive corporate and legal environment.

Equally important, lawyer-client relations were undergoing a radical change. In the past, corporate law firms had "owned" their clients; that is to say, a single firm would do all the legal work for major corporate clients, whom they represented year in and year out. As the business environment became more and more complex, however, the corporate demand for legal services increased at an explosive rate, and with their legal bills mushrooming, many large corporations decided that the old arrangement served their law firms more effectively than it served them. To hold costs down, they set up their own legal departments to handle much of the work previously done by their outside counsel; Bank of America, for example, now has 350 lawyers on its staff, which makes its legal department one of the largest "law firms" in the country.

As corporations developed their own legal expertise, their allegiance to their traditional law firms dwindled even more; when they needed knowledge and skills of a sort lacked by their own staffs, they began turning to the best lawyers they could find, hiring one firm to represent them in an antitrust matter, another in a merger, a third in a proxy battle, and so on, without regard to the religious composition of the firms or the social backgrounds of the lawyers. Far from being afraid of intellectual brilliance, the "best clients" were determined to find it and put it to their own use. Today, as a result, the client lists of Jewish and Gentile firms are virtually interchangeable, and the distinction between the two groups of firms is becoming less and less meaningful; both Jewish and Gentile firms now hire and promote on the basis of merit alone, without regard to religious or ethnic background.

The transformation of academic life has been every bit as dramatic. American universities were virtually *Judenrein* until after World War II; "Dartmouth is a Christian college founded for the Christianization of its students," Dartmouth president Ernest M. Hopkins declared in 1945. Nor was Dartmouth sui generis. As Talcott Parsons observed in 1942, "Jewish representation in the academic field and in some of the other professions, like engineering, is entirely negligible."

It was so negligible, in fact, that when Isidor Rabi finished his graduate studies in Europe in 1929 he assumed that his career as a physicist was over. "Anti-Semitism was unbelievably rife in the universities and elsewhere," Rabi has recalled. "I had no hope of getting a job." Indeed, he did not even bother to apply for one. "I thought I would go back to New York and see what would happen and maybe, if worst came to worst, join my father in real estate." And, Rabi adds, "I didn't feel terrible about it; I had wanted to know physics and I had had a tremendous experience. I thought, O.K., if you can do better, fine—if not, not."

He did a lot better. Even in that bigoted age anti-Semitism could give way to genius, which the future Nobel laureate possessed in abundance. Before he left for home Rabi received a cable from Columbia University offering him a teaching job. Columbia had consulted the German physicist Werner Heisenberg, under whom Rabi had studied; despite his Nazi sympathies, Heisenberg had recommended Rabi as the best man for the job. Even so, Rabi would not have been hired had not the dean of the Columbia graduate faculty, George Baxter Pegram, been freer from prejudice than his peers.

In general, Jews required a patron—in addition to exceptional determination and drive—to obtain an academic appointment, for in those days the university was a citadel of established values, especially in a gentlemanly field such as English literature. "When I decided to go into academic life, my friends thought me naïve to the point of absurdity," the literary critic Lionel Trilling wrote in 1966. "Nor were they wholly wrong—my appointment to an instructorship in Columbia College was pretty openly regarded as an experiment, and for some time my career in the College was complicated by my being Jewish." When his appointment was up for renewal, in fact, Trilling was told that he would be "more comfortable" elsewhere; it was due to the intervention of the university's powerful and conservative president, Nicholas Murray Butler—who told the English department chairman, "At Columbia, sir, we recognize merit, not race"—that he became the first Jewish member of that department.* Even so, his widow, Diana Trilling, doubts that he could have been appointed had he borne his mother's family name of Cohen rather than his father's name. "I still remember Lionel's grin," Diana Trilling wrote, "the day he came home to report: 'We hired a new English instructor today. His name is Hyman Kleinman.' "

The dramatic change in the academic world began immediately after the war, when the boom in college enrollments created a geometric increase in the demand for faculty members; by 1969 Jews constituted 9 percent of the faculty of American colleges and universities as a whole and 20 percent of the faculties of the elite institutions. In some academic fields, such as sociology, anthropology, psychology, biochemistry, medicine, and law, the proportions are even higher; at the elite law schools, for example, Jews made up 38 percent of the faculty.

For a time university administration lagged behind. "It is almost impossible for a Jew to be appointed to an administrative position at any university not sponsored by Jews," the theologian Richard Rubenstein wrote in 1965 in a review of Digby Baltzell's *The Protestant Establishment*. A year later, in his annual report as president of the American Jewish Committee, Morris B. Abram noted that although approximately a thousand presidents of publicly supported colleges and universities had been appointed in the preceding seventeen years, not a single Jew had been among them and that in the 775 leading colleges and universities only 45 of the 1720 deans were Jewish. As Rubenstein heatedly commented, "The Protestant caste system remains as rigidly operative in the universities as it does in most business corporations."

But that system was being dismantled even as Rubenstein wrote. In 1962 Edwin H. Levi, the grandson of a distinguished Reform rabbi, became provost of the University of Chicago after twelve years as dean of its law school; in 1968 Levi became the university's president. And then the dam broke, especially in the Ivy League. Over the next three years Martin Meyerson, who had been president of the State University of New York at Buffalo, became president of the University of Pennsylvania; John G. Kemeny, who had come to the United States from Hungary in 1940 at fourteen, became president of "Christian" Dartmouth; Jerome Wiesner became president of MIT. Nor was that all: in 1970 Paul Marks became dean of Columbia's College of Physicians

* After Trilling's appointment his mentor, Emery Neff, came to call on him to say, as Diana Trilling recalls, "that now that Lionel was a member of the department, he hoped he would not use it as a wedge to open the English department to more Jews."

and Surgeons and Michael Sovern, now the university's president, became dean of its law school; Abraham Goldstein, whose father had been a peddler, was named dean of Yale Law School, and in 1971 Albert Sacks succeeded Derek Bok as dean of Harvard Law School.

The change was so rapid that it frightened some Jews whose mindset remained that of an earlier time.

ITEM: A few months after Sacks's appointment my host at a large dinner party brought me over to meet the guest of honor, one of the most distinguished American jurists of the time. We joined a small group surrounding the judge, who was telling the other guests how terribly upset he was that a Jew had been appointed dean of Harvard Law School. Assuming that the judge was joking—he was Jewish himself, after all, and had attended Harvard Law at a time when there was a quota of one on the number of Jewish faculty members (after Felix Frankfurter's appointment in 1914 Harvard Law School did not appoint another Jew for twenty-five years)—one of the guests jocularly remarked that he understood the Harvard trustees had been willing to appoint a WASP but couldn't find one who was qualified. The judge was not amused; he had been speaking in dead seriousness. Sacks's appointment, he explained, meant that the deans of the law schools at Harvard, Yale, Columbia, Penn, Berkeley, and UCLA were all Jewish, and it was dangerous for Jews to be exposed in that way; if problems arose, the Jews would be blamed.

But the United States has changed in ways that make this old fear obsolete. "I have known people who did not like Jews, but I have not encountered anti-Semitism," says Henry Rosovsky of Harvard, referring to the eleven years (1973–84) he spent as dean of the Faculty of Arts and Sciences, Harvard's second-most-powerful administrative post. Rosovsky knows how to recognize anti-Semitism; he grew up in Nazi Germany and fled to the United States with his family in 1940, when he was thirteen. "The United States really is different," Rosovsky says. "I was received warmly and with respect by Harvard alumni in every part of the country, and they could hardly have had any doubt about my Jewish identity."

ITEM: Had there been any doubt, it would have been resolved on September 16, 1979, when Rosovsky, carrying a Torah scroll in his arms, led a procession of students and faculty across Harvard Yard, past the stone statue of John Harvard, to dedicate the new home of the Harvard-Radcliffe Hillel Society. "This is an occasion of great joy for the Jewish community and for individual Jews at Harvard," Rosovsky told the group when they arrived at the new building. "Today Hillel is moving from the periphery of the campus to its very center." "Let it be said that Harvard welcomed us with open arms, as students and teachers," Rosovsky said of the university during the post–World War II era. "What is perhaps more remarkable is that we have succeeded in transforming ourselves from a group of individuals into a community; that is really what is being celebrated here today . . . But we should also thank the University, because it accommodated itself generously to our needs as a group."

Like Irving Shapiro, Rosovsky is active in Jewish communal life, serving as senior vice-president of the American Jewish Congress, among other posts. When President Bok offered him the deanship, Rosovsky told Bok that he was unwilling to give up his Jewish communal work and that if those activities would embarrass Bok or the university, he would prefer not to be dean. Bok "couldn't have cared less."

The trustees of Yale apparently felt the same way in 1978, for they offered Rosovsky the presidency of that university. Rosovsky's Israeli-born wife thought he should accept the offer because of the symbolism involved in a Jew's being president of Yale, but Rosovsky disagreed. "I felt we were beyond that," he told me. "Twenty years earlier that would have been a compelling argument, but not now," and so he turned the offer down. "The invitation came at the wrong time for me."* One measure of how much the United States has changed is that when Rosovsky declined the presidency, the aristocratic Yale trustees turned instead to the half-WASP, half-Italian-American, A. Bartlett Giamatti.

The new climate of acceptance has transformed the Jewish role in American politics as well. Jews have always been active as voters and as contributors to political campaigns, but until quite recently they shied away from elective office, except in districts with large Jewish populations. In the Ninety-third Congress, for example, which took office in 1975, there were twelve Jewish members of the House of Representatives, compared to thirty today; seven of them were from New York, and most of the remainder were from heavily Jewish districts in Chicago and a few other large cities. Jews played such a minor role in elective politics, in fact, that in his pioneering 1974 study *Jews and*

* Rosovsky was not certain that he liked administrative work well enough to spend the rest of his career as a university president; he also felt uncomfortable about leaving Harvard before a major curriculum reform that he had proposed and fought for had been implemented.

American Politics, Stephen D. Isaacs relegated his discussion of that subject to the twelfth chapter, in which he explained why the number of Jews serving in Congress was bound to decline.

One reason Jews avoided running for office, of course, was the traditional Jewish fear of visibility—the concern that if Jews were too prominent, they would be blamed for whatever went wrong. That fear had gained credence during the 1930s, when the publicity given to the Jewish members of Franklin D. Roosevelt's "brains trust" led Roosevelt haters to refer to the New Deal as the "Jew Deal." Both Jewish and non-Jewish politicians were convinced that since non-Jews would refuse to vote for Jewish candidates, Jews could not get elected in predominantly non-Jewish jurisdictions.

ITEM: When he left the White House in 1965, Myer Feldman, who had been Counsel to Presidents John F. Kennedy and Lyndon Johnson, was offered the Democratic nomination for district attorney in his hometown, Philadelphia, as a prelude to a race for U.S. Senator. Convinced that he could never win the latter post, Feldman turned down the invitation. A Jew "has an enormous handicap running for office in a state where you have such a small minority of Jews," he told Stephen Isaacs. "It would have to be a very unusual race and an unusual constituency to have a Jew run for public office. . . . I know Howard [Metzenbaum] and what he's told me about it; I know [Milton] Shapp and what he's told me about it."

If what he really wanted was elective office rather than a lucrative career as a Washington lawyer, Feldman made the wrong decision; Milton Shapp has served as governor of Pennsylvania, and Howard Metzenbaum is now in his second term as a senator from Ohio. "Anti-Semitism is not a problem anymore," Metzenbaum told me, then added a slight qualification: "It is not nearly as big a factor as it used to be."*

In most instances it is not a factor at all. "I have encountered some anti-Semitism but not a great deal; I've run into a lot more pro-Semitism," Senator Carl Levin of Michigan told me. ("I'm gonna vote for you because you're Jewish," a constituent confided to Levin the first time he ran for office. "You Jews are smart.") When opponents

* Metzenbaum is still bitter about his unsuccessful campaign for the Senate in 1970, which he lost by 35,000 votes. Metzenbaum is convinced that his Jewishness became an issue only after his opponent made a statement just a week before the election denouncing the injection of anti-Semitism into the campaign. "I don't accuse my opponent of having injected the issue," he says, "but the fact is, the more he spoke about it *not* being an issue, the more it *was* an issue."

do try to make an issue of a candidate's Jewishness, as happened to Representative Sam Gejdenson of Connecticut during his first race, the effort usually backfires. "Voters do not tolerate such tactics," Gejdenson, who was born in a displaced-persons camp in Germany in 1948, told me. "They violate some of the central rules of American politics." "Only bigots and Jews care that I'm Jewish," he added. "Most people are more concerned with how I vote." (There are fewer than 5000 Jews in Gejdenson's district of 538,000 people.)

In short, Jewishness no longer is a significant handicap in running for any office except that of president and, perhaps, vice-president. Although fear of anti-Semitism makes it unlikely that a Jew could gain the Republican or Democratic presidential nomination in the near future, some younger politicians believe that that barrier too will fall. Survey data provide support for their belief: the proportion saying that they would not vote for a qualified Jew for president has dropped from 46 percent in 1937 and 23 percent in 1961 to only 7 percent in 1983. What Americans would do in the privacy of the voting booth is another question of course, but it surely is significant that in responding to surveys, more people say they would not vote for a Mormon than would not vote for a Jew. A California poll taken in October of 1982 is even more revealing: 4 percent of the California electorate said they would not vote for a Jew, compared to 5 percent who would not vote for a black and 12 percent who would not vote for an Armenian. Three weeks later George Deukmejian, an Armenian-American, won the California governorship, narrowly defeating Tom Bradley, the black mayor of Los Angeles.

The fact is that Jews are being elected to every kind of position by every kind of constituency in every part of the country. In the Ninety-ninth Congress, which took office in January 1985, eight Jews serve in the Senate and thirty in the House of Representatives. Four of the eight senators—Rudy Boschwitz of Minnesota, Chic Hecht of Nevada, Edward Zorinsky of Nebraska, and Warren Rudman of New Hampshire—come from states in which Jews constitute less than 1 percent of the electorate. (The other senators are Arlen Specter of Pennsylvania and Frank Lautenberg of New Jersey, in addition to Levin and Metzenbaum.)

Much the same is true in the House of Representatives. "The wraps are coming off now," says Representative Barney Frank of Massachusetts. "Jews are getting elected from every kind of district; there's no longer any district that's 'bad' for Jews." Indeed, younger politicians see the world as completely open to them. "People my age do not see being Jewish as a barrier to accomplishing anything we work hard enough for and are bright enough to do," Representative

Martin Frost of Texas told me. "I guess that's a generational difference with our parents." (The first Jew elected to Congress from Texas in more than a century, Frost represents a district in which Jews comprise fewer than two-hundredths of 1 percent of the population.) Most Jews in state and local government feel the same way.

What has changed, moreover, is not just the number but the kind of Jews holding public office, and the environment in which they serve. In the past, Jews in government, like Jews everywhere, tended to be self-conscious about their Jewishness; they were usually reluctant to identify themselves with Jewish issues or causes. While the Holocaust was going on, for example, Jews such as Samuel Rosenman and Felix Frankfurter, who were among Franklin Roosevelt's most trusted advisers, made no attempt to persuade the president to try to rescue European Jewry or halt the slaughter. Indeed, Rosenman opposed creation of a rescue agency, watered down a statement on war crimes to eliminate "excessive emphasis on the Jews," and worried that any government assistance to European Jews would increase anti-Semitism in the United States. And Representative Sol Bloom of New York, chairman of the House Foreign Affairs Committee, who was disparagingly referred to as "the State Department's Jew," was putty in the hands of the virulently anti-Semitic Breckinridge Long, Assistant Secretary of State for special problems. (The one notable exception was Treasury Secretary Henry Morgenthau, Jr.)

Today most Jews serving in the executive branch are perfectly comfortable with their Jewishness. When he was assistant to the president for domestic affairs and director of the Domestic Policy Staff in the Carter White House, for example, Stuart Eizenstat always left the office early on Friday in order to be home for the Sabbath. He was also the host of an annual fund-raising brunch for the United Jewish Appeal and chairperson of the UJA fund-raising drive in the executive branch—something that would have been unthinkable in an earlier age. "I was the first practicing [that is, religiously observant] Jew on the White House staff," the forty-two-year-old Eizenstat told me with evident pride.

There is a new breed of Jew in the Congress as well. During the 1983 National Gathering of Holocaust Survivors in Washington, Sam Gejdenson addressed the survivors in Yiddish from the steps of the Capitol—hardly a gesture his self-conscious predecessors would have been comfortable making. The day I called on Martin Frost he had sponsored Rabbi Barton Lee, Hillel director at Arizona State University, as the House chaplain of the day. Frost and Lee have been friends since their high school years, when both were officers of the National Federation of Temple Youth.

With only a few exceptions, moreover, Jewish representatives, senators, and other officials feel no inhibitions about pushing issues of particular interest to Jews. "People are very accepting of it, comfortable with it," Barney Frank says, referring to the Jewish representatives' concern for Israel. "We kid about it, we make Jewish jokes about it." They also go to great pains to avoid creating the impression that they care *only* about Jewish interests, even refusing to organize a formal Jewish caucus. "It would be counterproductive," Metzenbaum told me. "I do not want to be known as 'the Jewish Senator.'" But in the new atmosphere of acceptance, it is taken for granted that minority group members will assert their ethnic or other group interest, as well as the interests of their constituency as a whole. "If you're a black congressman, you have your normal constituency that you represent, but on top of that you have the black community," Gejdenson says. "If you're a woman in Congress, you have some extra responsibility on women's issues. If you're a Jewish congressman, you have all your normal constituencies plus an extra responsibility. *That's what makes our system of government work* [emphasis added]."

Because they lack the self-consciousness of an earlier generation, members of the new breed of Jewish politician and officeholder are also far more relaxed in their relations with non-Jews.

ITEM: For all his unabashed ethnicity and espousal of Jewish interests, New York City Mayor Edward I. Koch's preoccupation with anti-Semitism and his suspiciousness of the Gentile world indelibly mark him as a member of the old school. "When we get together, we always talk about Israel and anti-Semitism," Koch told a Gentile dinner companion. "What do you people talk about?" A few weeks later, I suggested to this dinner companion that perhaps because Koch is only a second-generation American Jew he has not fully assimilated the magnitude of the change in American society. "He may be second-generation," my friend gently replied, "but he lives in his father's generation."

Members of the new breed live in their own generation. "I did not grow up in fear, and I'm not the type who sees anti-Semites under every bed," S. Ariel Weiss, the thirty-three-year-old executive director of the House Democratic Steering and Policy Committee, told me. "My parents gave me a sense of security about being Jewish; they also communicated a sense of being engaged with a world that is *not* Jewish"—a world in which "Ari" Weiss, a devout and practicing Orthodox Jew, is fully comfortable. (Weiss feels that his Orthodoxy has drawn him closer to his boss, House Majority Leader "Tip" O'Neill, a devout Catholic, who respects his young aide's religious commitment.) Being at ease does not mean that Weiss is oblivious to the world around him. "I've heard people in a fit of anger make some anti-Semitic remark to me or about me, but I don't see it as pernicious," Weiss told me. "It's just fallible human nature. There is no damaging or aggressive anti-Semitism here."

None of this is meant to suggest that anti-Semitism has disappeared entirely; it emerges just often enough to make it hard for Jews to drop their guard altogether. Even in the United States of the 1980s no Jew is immune to anti-Semitism, no matter how high a position he or she may have reached.

ITEM: Laurence A. Tisch, chief executive officer (and with his brother, Preston Robert Tisch, controlling stockholder) of Loews ($4.7 billion in sales, $11.5 billion in assets), is one of the most respected corporate executives in the United States. He is also one of the wealthiest Americans; he and his brother share a fortune that *Forbes* estimates at $1.1 billion. But when Tisch's son Andrew, who is president of Bulova Watch Company, tried to buy an apartment at 765 Park Avenue, he was turned down by the co-op board. A prominent lawyer had a similar experience with an apartment in a fashionable building on Fifth Avenue. "We already have a Jewish tenant," a member of the co-op board explained. (There are a dozen or so buildings in New York that continue to exclude Jews.)

ITEM: As vice-chairman of the New York Times Company and close aide to *Times* chairman and publisher Arthur Ochs Sulzberger, Sidney Gruson is one of the most powerful figures in the publishing industry. The Dublin-born Gruson happens to be an avid and able golfer as well, and in 1981 some of his Gentile golfing companions suggested that he join the Shinnecock Hills Golf Club in Southampton, Long Island. Gruson was dubious about his prospects, but when his friends assured him that restrictions against Jews were a thing of the past, he agreed to apply. "They never actually turned me down," Gruson told me two years later. "They just didn't bother to respond; I've never heard from them one way or another."

Nor are these isolated examples. Palm Beach, Florida, a leading watering hole of the rich, now has a number of Jewish residents, who have become increasingly prominent in social activities revolving around philanthropy. Far from easing their restrictions against Jews, however, the exclusive Bath and Tennis, Beach, and Everglades clubs have tightened up, forbidding their members even to have a Jewish guest for lunch or dinner. In one club a member was asked to leave in the middle of a tennis game because her partner was a Jew; in another, one of the most prominent socialites in the country received a formal reprimand because she had brought Estée Lauder to lunch.

Although it would be a mistake to ignore these incidents, neither should we make too much of them. For the people involved they are certainly no more than petty irritants. Estée Lauder has no shortage of places to have lunch with her friends; Sidney Gruson continues to play golf at the Sands Point Golf Club, to which he has belonged for some time; and Andrew Tisch had a wide range of apartments to choose from, as did the lawyer mentioned above. Moreover, the co-op board that rejected him subsequently approved the sale of the apartment to a prominent Jewish corporate executive.

More to the point, the clubs and co-ops that continue to exclude Jews are the vestigial remains of an era that is largely gone. Rejecting Larry Tisch's son was the act of "a group of upper-class WASPs who have lost their special status," Richard Ravitch, former chairman of New York's Metropolitan Transit Authority and a close friend of the Tisches, told me. "They have a lot of resentment, especially against Jews, but they really are a passing phenomenon." "They're not evil," a member of one of the restricted Palm Beach clubs told Suzanne Garment of the *Wall Street Journal* about his fellow members, "they're just scared." "The discrimination that remains is carried on by people who are less than stars and who think that you can't be somebody unless you exclude others," Irving Shapiro said, commenting on "the searing experience" one of his partners had had with a co-op he wanted to buy. Equally important, Shapiro added, anti-Semitism today is personal rather than institutional. "The issue is largely gone in an institutional sense."

One of the harsh lessons of history, of course, is that so long as "personal" anti-Semitism exists, some element of risk remains; under the "right" conditions, private attitudes could turn into public behavior. But that risk is far smaller than it used to be because of the continuing decline in "personal" as well as "institutional" anti-Semitism.

The change in attitudes has occurred in two stages. The first was brief and sudden. After reaching a historic peak during World War II—at least as measured by public-opinion surveys—anti-Semitism declined abruptly right after the war. Thus the proportion of Americans who considered Jews a "menace to America" dropped from 24 percent in 1944 to only 5 percent in 1950; the proportion reporting that it had "heard any criticism or talk against the Jews in the last six months" fell from 64 percent in 1946 to 24 percent in 1950 and to 11 percent six years later. The change was greatest among younger and more prosperous Americans, but anti-Semitism declined in every segment of the population.

Although other factors may have been involved, such as the camaraderie that military service entailed, it is hard to understand such a rapid and massive shift in public opinion except as a response to the Holocaust. Having seen where anti-Semitism can lead, Americans suddenly turned away from it; in the more sophisticated segments of the populace, in particular, it was no longer respectable to voice anti-Semitic attitudes in public, whatever one's private opinion. The new mood was exemplified (and also stimulated) by the popularity of Laura Z. Hobson's 1947 novel *Gentlemen's Agreement* and of the film made from it, which starred Gregory Peck. Some skeptics, to be sure, argued that the change was more apparent than real—that sophisticated Americans were simply reluctant to reveal their true feelings about Jews and that the polls therefore understated the amount of anti-Semitism that remained. But even if that were true—if anti-Semitism had merely been driven underground—it would have been a significant achievement. If anti-Semites now thought it gauche to express their anti-Semitism, that in itself would have been a profound change—one that inevitably affected their behavior.

In fact, the change was more than skin deep, which the growing acceptance of Jews demonstrates. As restrictions against Jews were dropped, animosity toward them fell; changing attitudes in turn led to further lessening of anti-Semitic behavior, which reinforced the shift in attitudes, and so on as the process fed upon itself. Other factors intervened as well, the creation of the state of Israel being among the most important; Israeli military daring and prowess transformed the Gentile image of the Jew, especially in the formerly anti-Semitic Bible Belt, as well as Jews' image of themselves.

Acceptance of Jews was made easier by their apparent willingness to define themselves as a religious rather than an ethnic group; Americans have always been more comfortable with religious than with ethnic differences. According to the doctrine of the triple melting pot, which gained a powerful hold on the American imagination during the early 1950s, immigrants and their descendants were expected to hold onto their identities as Protestants, Catholics, or Jews, while surrendering their ethnic distinctiveness.

In the new, benign atmosphere, in fact, Judaism emerged as one of America's "three great faiths," a formulation that enormously increased the standing of the Jews; public ceremonials now routinely included benedictions by a rabbi as well as a Protestant minister and Catholic priest. "In America, religious pluralism is . . . not merely a historical and political fact," Will Herberg wrote in 1955 in his influential *Protestant-Catholic-Jew*, "it is . . . the primordial condition of things, an essential aspect of the American Way of Life." This was so much of a truism, in fact, that Herberg felt no need to comment on, let alone explain, the drop in anti-Semitism or, for that matter, the equally impressive decline in anti-Catholicism, which has played an even larger role in American political developments.

Five years later John F. Kennedy was elected president—an event that symbolized the transformation of the United States from an essentially Protestant to a religiously pluralistic society. Since that time there has been a steady decline in prejudice of every sort, and Jews, among others, have been the beneficiaries. The reduction in hostility toward Jews has been accompanied, in fact, by a growth in positive attitudes. In 1940, for example, 63 percent of Americans said that Jews as a group had "objectionable traits"; by 1981, when a Gallup poll asked Americans to rate Jews on a ten-point scale, 81 percent had favorable and only 8 percent unfavorable opinions. The extremes were even more striking: 40 percent of the respondents said they had a "highly favorable" and 2 percent a "highly unfavorable" opinion of American Jews. Demographic factors make it likely that this trend will continue; except among black Americans, the younger and better educated people are, the less anti-Semitism they express. It is not surprising that this should be so: younger Americans have grown up in an open, pluralistic society in which anti-Semitism is frowned upon, and those who have gone to college have experienced the most open, pluralistic society of all.

3

To understand the transformation in the position of Jews in American society, we cannot look only at what has happened to Jews; the breakthroughs they have achieved are simply one manifestation of a far larger change. Since the end of World War II, and at an accelerating pace since 1960, the United States has become an increasingly open, pluralistic, and meritocratic society, in which position depends on what one can do rather than on who one is; and Jews are far from being the only beneficiaries.

Consider the explosive increase in opportunities available to younger women, who now compete with men on more or less equal terms. In Zweigenhaft's study of Harvard Business School alumni, only 13 percent of the female respondents reported that women were at a disadvantage in being hired by their companies; 43 percent said that being a woman was an advantage, and the same proportion indicated that the sex of the prospective employee did not matter.* And members of other previously discriminated-against groups are coming into their own too; as Talcott Parsons wrote in 1978 in a posthumously published postscript to his 1942 essay, "the Jews no longer stand out as *the* relatively successful, non-WASP minority group [emphasis in original]."

For few groups has the change been so striking as for Italian-Americans, who are moving into professional and managerial positions with extraordinary speed. When he returned to the United States after twenty years in Europe, says Avis president Joseph V. Vittoria, he "was almost overwhelmed by the growth of Italian influence. There was a tremendous increase in the Italian presence here."

ITEM: "The change is more than cosmetic; it's fundamental–and there is no turning back," says Angelo Costanza, the first Italian-American to head a major bank in New York State. The son of a Sicilian immigrant who never learned to read or write–his father went to work in a sulphur mine when he was seven and ran away to the United States at sixteen, when a cousin sent him the necessary seventeen dollars for the steerage fare–Costanza grew up in Rochester, New York, at a time when the dominant employer, Eastman Kodak, did not hire Italians, blacks, or Jews. Like Morris Tanenbaum, Irving Shapiro, and other Jewish chief executives, however, "Ange" Costanza never felt that he was at any great disadvantage. "I didn't know I was underprivileged until I took sociology my freshman year in college," he told me. "And I never thought I couldn't compete because of the barriers." When he was in law school in the early 1950s Costanza ignored the warnings from friends and relatives that there would be no opportunities for an Italian-American. "I believed that they would recognize ability," he said, "and that the discrimination that was there would not be a terrible obstacle."

It wasn't. While working as a summer intern at Central Trust, one of Rochester's largest banks, Costanza caught the eye of the bank chairman, who offered him a job after his law school graduation. With the chairman's blessing, Costanza went to work instead for the bank's law firm, where he spent seven years, mostly handling bank business. He moved over to Central Trust in 1963, and became president in 1965, at the age of thirty-seven–"I was the youngest bank president in town," he says with quiet pride–and chief executive officer a year

* Whether the barriers have fallen completely is another question; 30 percent of the female (and 22 percent of the male) respondents felt that women are promoted less rapidly than men. On the other hand, 61 percent of the women felt that there was no difference in promotions between men and women, and 9 percent felt that women were at an advantage.

later. He retired from the bank in 1984 to devote himself to a number of business ventures in partnership with a son, daughter, and son-in-law, but he is still an active member of the boards of the University of Rochester (chairman of its executive committee), Strong Memorial Hospital, and the Rochester Philharmonic, among others.

There are, in fact, striking parallels between the Italian and Jewish experiences in this country. Like Jews, Italian-Americans bore a heavy burden of embarrassment because of their origins. Ange Costanza still resents the elementary school teachers who taught him to be ashamed of his parents and to think of himself as other than American, and Chrysler chairman Lee Iacocca still bristles at the memory of elementary school classmates who called him a "dumb wop" and laughed at him for mentioning that he had had a pizza party for his birthday. "What kind of dumb dago word is that?" they asked him. For Jack Valenti, president of the Motion Picture Association of America and former White House aide to Lyndon Johnson, being an Italian-American in Texas was like having "a high squeaky voice."

Like Jews, upwardly mobile Italian-Americans faced a "brutal bargain" of their own, in which suppressing or abandoning their ethnic identity often appeared to be the price of "success" in the larger society. New York Governor Mario Cuomo, who spoke only Italian until he was eight but finished first in his law school class, was told by his professors that he would have to anglicize his vowel-laden names if he wanted to get ahead. For a time it looked as though the professors were right. After law school Cuomo spent two years clerking for Judge Adrian Burke of the New York State Court of Appeals, a coveted position that normally leads to job offers from the leading law firms in the state. Cuomo, however, heard from only one of the hundred or so firms to which he sent his résumé. (He ultimately joined a small and relatively obscure firm with offices in Brooklyn and Long Island.)

As is also true of Jews, success does not make Italian-Americans immune to the prejudice that remains. During the early years of his presidency of Central Trust, Ange Costanza was dogged by rumors that he was the banker for the Mafia and that he had gotten his job as a result of their support. Nor could Lee Iacocca escape a similar taint. He is convinced that one of the sources of the tension between him and Henry Ford II—tension that led to Iacocca's being fired as president of Ford Motor Company—was Ford's belief that Iacocca had mob connections. (Ford ordered the firm's law firm to conduct an extensive investigation of Iacocca's personal and business affairs; the investigation, which cost the auto company nearly $2 million, found nothing adverse.) Not long after Iacocca was fired, a Detroit newspaper quoted a Ford "family spokesman" as saying that Iacocca had been dismissed because he "lacked grace" and was too "pushy." "The son of an Italian immigrant born in Allentown, Pennsylvania," the "spokesman" added, "is a long way from Grosse Pointe."

There are other parallels as well. No matter how successful they are, older Italian-Americans, like older Jews, find it hard to lose the sense that they are "guests" in someone else's country. In social situations that include the WASP elite, a highly placed Italian-American told me, he still feels "different." "Not inferior," he explained, "just different. I still bear in my unconscious the notion that I'm not really an 'American.' "

Younger Italian-Americans do not bear that burden of self-consciousness; like younger Jews, they see themselves as full-fledged Americans and so are free to take pride in their ethnic identity. The change was driven home to William D'Antonio, executive officer of the American Sociological Association, when he visited his two daughters at their colleges a couple of years ago. On the first weekend his daughter Raissa, a student at the University of Vermont, told D'Antonio about a paper she had had to do for a psychology course, entitled "Five Things I Like About Myself"; one of the things she liked was being Italian. A week later D'Antonio visited his daughter Laura at Yale. "I'm the only 100 percent Italian in my dorm," she told him, "but I know at least a dozen people who *wish* they were Italian." When he was at Yale forty years ago, D'Antonio told a *New York Times Magazine* writer, "I would not have been able to admit that I was Italian, much less imagine any dozen people who *wished* they were Italian. It really does signify a change in how we think about ourselves."

How did so profound a change come about?

For one thing, the potential has always been there. From the beginning, as we saw in Chapter Two, the United States was different; a tradition of tolerance had grown out of the nature of the religions the early settlers brought with them. In Seymour Martin Lipset's telling phrase, the United States was "the first new nation"—the first to define itself as a religiously pluralistic society—and in fact early European visitors were struck both by the multiplicity of religious sects and by the harmony that prevailed among them. To be sure, the denominations were overwhelmingly Protestant, but as Tocqueville pointed out, the separation of church and state gave other religions a freedom and acceptance unknown in Europe.* In a sense, therefore, what has hap-

* The deism to which the Founding Fathers subscribed also helped. In his first address as president, for example, George Washington referred not to God or Christ but to the "Almighty Being," "Great Author," and "Parent of the Human Race," and during their presidencies Adams, Jefferson, Madi-

pened in recent years is simply that the United States has redeemed its own promise.

In another sense, however, the United States has created a new promise, or, more precisely, it has redefined the old one to make explicit the notion of ethnic and racial as well as religious pluralism. As already noted, Americans, especially white Protestant Americans, have always been more comfortable with religious than with ethnic or racial differences. During the early years of the republic, after all, blacks had no rights of citizenship whatsoever–indeed, they were categorized as property, not citizens–and thus the religious harmony that impressed European observers existed within the framework of what we would consider a remarkably homogeneous society. When the Constitution was signed, eight white Americans in ten were of British descent, and most of the remainder were from France or Germany. Many would have liked to keep it that way. Some of the Founding Fathers were concerned that too much diversity would lead to political or social divisiveness; others simply disliked people who were different from them and wanted to restrict American citizenship to people of Anglo-Saxon or at least Western European descent.

The country's origins made it impossible to do so. The United States, after all, had been created by an act of secession from the motherland; to the extent to which Americans shared a common language and cultural tradition, it was that of the nation they had rebelled against. To have defined American nationality in the traditional way thus would have obviated the creation of a distinctive American identity. From the beginning, therefore, American identity has been inclusive rather than exclusive; it has been defined by a set of ideas about freedom, equality, and diversity rather than by possession of a particular language or culture. In principle, at least, American nationality was open to anyone (anyone, that is to say, with a white skin) who wanted to become an American–anyone who was willing to accept the American covenant. Although practice often fell short of principle, the principle was always there, shaping Americans' sense of what ought to be and leading them to accept, however grudgingly, "the wretched refuse" of the earth.

Since the end of World War II that principle has come into play more powerfully than ever before. For one thing, the war itself dissolved some of the barriers that had kept Americans apart. Although anti-Semitism and other forms of prejudice reached a peak in the early 1940s in the nation at large, the armed forces were another matter.

---

son, and Monroe followed the same approach. In eschewing Christological language, the first presidents created a tradition of ecumenism in public discourse that made it much easier for Catholics and Jews to feel at home.

With ten million men in uniform, people of all religions and nationalities were living, fighting, and sometimes dying together—except, again, for black Americans, who continued to be segregated in separate units and assigned for the most part to menial roles. Although service in the armed forces occasionally reinforced people's prejudices, the reverse was more often the case: soldiers, sailors, and marines discovered that the similarities between themselves and members of other ethnic and religious groups were far greater than the differences and that at least some of their preconceptions were just plain wrong.

ITEM: I still recall the incredulity of a fellow crew member forty-one years ago when he learned that I was Jewish. "But you don't have horns!" the Indiana-born and -bred sailor exclaimed. I was the first Jew he had ever met, and he was astonished to discover that my appearance was not so different from that of anyone else on our tiny minesweeper.*

For minority-group members the war altered aspirations as well as perceptions. Roughly one million black Americans were in uniform by the time the war ended; the indignities visited on them in the name of the "Four Freedoms" served to increase their already ample store of anger and hate. That anger often exploded into violence—sometimes in riots, sometimes in formal revolts (news of which was suppressed; War Department files were classified to prevent dissemination), most often in individual acts of rebellion (casualties were unusually heavy among white officers who led black troops into battle). Discovering their own power to intimidate, black soldiers lost the fear of white authority that had helped keep the system of segregation in place; it is not coincidental that the civil rights movement took on a new shape and vitality in the postwar period.

Members of white ethnic groups were affected in analogous ways. Service in the army or navy took millions of first-, second-, and even third-generation Americans out of their urban ghettos and gave them, for the first time, a sense of the larger society and of the possibilities that might be open to them. "The army gave me my first exposure to the world beyond the Bronx, and it made me want to see more of that

* The folk belief that Jews have horns stems in part from the long association of Jews with the devil and in part from an ancient mistranslation of a Hebrew idiom used to describe Moses' appearance. When he came down from Mount Sinai, the biblical text (Exodus 34:29) reports, Moses' face "was radiant"—literally, "sent forth beams." When the Bible was translated into Latin in the second century, the Hebrew verb *karan* ("was radiant") was confused with the noun *keren* ("horn")—hence the Latin translation that Moses' face "was horned" (*cornuta esset*). The mistranslation is perpetuated in marble in Michelangelo's magnificent statue of Moses, in which two horns protrude from his head.

world," says Jerome Shapiro, chairman of the venerable Wall Street law firm of Hughes Hubbard & Reed. (The "Hughes" in the firm's name refers to Charles Evans Hughes, Chief Justice of the United States from 1930 to 1941.) After finishing first in his class at New York University, Shapiro went on to Harvard Law School. He did not apply to Yale Law School because the application form asked students to list the names of lawyers they knew, "and I didn't know any." An outstanding student at Harvard too, Shapiro was hired by Hughes Hubbard & Reed in 1949 and became its first Jewish partner (one of the first in any Wall Street firm) eight years later; he has been the firm's chief executive officer since 1975.

ITEM: Before *his* army service Henry Kissinger had hoped to become an accountant; he worked in a shaving-brush factory during the day and attended New York's City College at night. Drafted into the infantry, Kissinger was transferred to the Counterintelligence Corps because of his knowledge of German. He started as a translator, became an interrogator, and then, after the German surrender, was made an administrator in the military government. That experience, plus the guidance of a superior officer who became his mentor and patron—"Gentlemen do not go to the City College of New York," the officer is reported to have told Kissinger—led the future secretary of state to Harvard and a career light-years away from accounting.

Mobilization raised civilian aspirations as well—in particular, those of women. The shortage of male labor meant that women were actively recruited for factory and other "male" jobs previously closed to them; "Rosie the Riveter" became a prime symbol of the war effort. Although sex roles had been changing for some time, the mass movement of women into the labor force during the war transformed their perception of themselves and their place in society. After the war, to be sure, women returned (or were pushed back) into their traditional roles, but the consciousness that had been raised could not be denied; the women's movement of the 1960s was born out of the frustration women felt over the conflict between their new aspirations and the constraints imposed on them by what Betty Friedan called "the feminine mystique."

The economic boom that followed the end of World War II dramatically altered American life, erasing much of the old difference between blue-collar and white-collar life-styles. With auto and steel workers vacationing in Florida or Hawaii and sending their suburban-raised children to college, America had become a predominantly middle-class society. One consequence, largely unnoticed at the time, was that ethnicity lost its invidious association with immigrant poverty.

Growing up "American," the grandchildren of immigrants no longer felt they had to drop their ethnicity to get ahead. As time went on, they began to assert the ethnic heritage their parents had tried to forge.

The country changed in other ways as well. The increasing complexity of a growing economy, the rapidly expanding role of professional and technical knowledge, the new interdependence of America and the rest of the world, the increasingly intimate relation between science and technology, the omnipresence of government, the intricacies of the labyrinthian tax code and its importance in business decision making all put a new and heavy premium on expertise and talent rather than on social background, on having people who could perform, whether they wore "Topsiders" or not. The result, as we have seen, was that the United States became a more cosmopolitan and meritocratic society.

Understandably enough, the change has been traumatic for some white Protestants of Anglo-Saxon descent; for much of American history, after all, they had been the majority group. Even when they became a numerical minority, moreover, white Protestants retained their dominance of economic and cultural life—so much so, in fact, that they had little consciousness of belonging to a distinct ethnic group; their values appeared to be synonymous with American values and their culture with American culture. Since 1960, however, white Anglo-Saxon Protestants have had to learn to see themselves as members of a minority group—more precisely, as simply one minority group among many. And the psychic shock inherent in this change has been compounded by the realization that the ethnic groups to whom the so-called WASPs have given way often use the acronym as a term of opprobrium. It should not be surprising that a handful of upper-class WASPs have resented the change or that they have tried to restrict their apartment houses and clubs to people like themselves.

What is remarkable, in fact, is not that the new order is sometimes resented but that it has so often been accepted—at times, encouraged, even led—by those with the most to lose. "When you look at Harvard and Yale and see how the established aristocracies have changed those institutions, you *have* to believe that America is different," Henry Rosovsky told me in an observation that applies equally well to business, politics, and every other area of American life. "Some of them surely preferred it the old way; a few may still feel that Jews lack manners or are too careerist; but they believed that their responsibility went beyond being comfortable. They recognized that the university would become a dinosaur if it stayed closed, and so they opened it up. Their values transcended their solidarity with their class."

CHAPTER FOUR

HORATIO ALGER AND THE JEWS

1*

Most American Jews, of course, are neither corporation chairmen nor university deans. They live ordinary lives—many, to be sure, as doctors, lawyers, corporate executives, and university professors, but far larger numbers as real estate brokers, insurance salesmen, social workers, secretaries, bookkeepers and accountants, retail sales clerks and store owners, public-school teachers, garment and textile manufacturers and salesmen, pharmacists, dentists, engineers, journalists, and a host of other mostly white-collar occupations. (A small and declining number work as painters, electricians, plumbers, tailors, cab drivers, and mechanics.) Neighborhoods with heavy concentrations of Jews, such as Forest Hills–Rego Park in Queens and Flatbush in Brooklyn (12 percent of American Jews live in those two New York City boroughs), Pikesville in Baltimore, and Cleveland Heights, are quintessential middle-class areas. Like other Americans, most Jews struggle to meet their mortgage payments and pay their children's college tuition bills;

* This chapter is based in part on research by Steven Silberman.

a significant minority—perhaps as many as 15 percent, most of them elderly people—live in poverty or straitened economic circumstances.

But if the stereotype of Jews as uniformly wealthy is wide of the mark, they are nonetheless better off on average than members of most other ethnic and religious groups. In 1984, for example, fewer than one American Jewish family in six had an income of less than $20,000, compared to one in two among non-Hispanic whites. At the other end of the income pyramid, 41 percent of Jewish households had incomes of $50,000 or more—four times the proportion among non-Hispanic whites.*

One reason for this differential is that Jews are better educated than other Americans. Three Jewish men in five are college graduates—nearly three times the proportion among non-Hispanic whites; one in three have graduate or professional degrees—three and a half times the proportion in the population at large. Much the same disparities exist among Jewish and non-Jewish women: the former are twice as likely as the latter to have college degrees and four times as likely to have graduate or professional degrees. Today, moreover, college attendance is almost universal among young Jews. A 1980 national survey of male and female high school students found that 83 percent of the Jewish students planned to go to college and fully half expected to go on to graduate or professional schools; among white non-Jewish students, half were planning on college and fewer than one fifth expected to go to graduate or professional schools.

The difference is qualitative as well as quantitative: Jews not only receive more schooling, they get a better education. As we saw in Chapter Two, Jews began gravitating to Ivy League colleges and graduate schools in the beginning of the century. "It is doubtless true that Jews are better off at Harvard than at any other American college," Charles Eliot, who had opened that university to Jews, declared in 1901, "and they are, therefore, likely to resort to it." Jews may no longer be better off at Harvard than elsewhere, but they still resort to it, as well as to Yale and Princeton (both now have kosher dining fa-

* Because the U.S. Census is prohibited from asking questions about religion, there are no governmental statistics on incomes, occupations, educational attainment, or other characteristics of Jews or members of other religious or ethnic groups. A statistical portrait of American Jewry has to be pieced together from a variety of sources: demographic surveys sponsored by Jewish federations in a number of metropolitan areas; national surveys of high school and college students; public-opinion surveys, especially those directed by Professor Steven M. Cohen for the American Jewish Committee; and the fifteen-year-old National Jewish Population Study sponsored by the Council of Jewish Federations.

cilities) and most other elite schools. Since the 1950s or 1960s, when Ivy League institutions shifted to meritocratic admissions policies, Jews have made up about a third of the undergraduate student population and about the same in law and medicine.

ITEM: "Nobody came to my office screaming for more Jews," says R. Inslee Clark, who transformed Yale's admissions policies during his tenure as dean of undergraduate admissions (1965–70). "It was just a matter of natural selection." "When we were picking that first class in 1965," Clark adds, "no one counted Jews, but I knew that it was going up. It had to." In the early seventies, in fact, a popular "in" joke at Yale was that the Yeshiva of Flatbush was the only prep school in the country able to get all its Yale applicants accepted. (There were two a year from the Yeshiva.)

Elsewhere in the country, of course, Jews tend to be somewhat more diffused, but they still choose the more distinguished institutions. In 1971, for example, Jews made up 3.6 percent of all first-year college students but 17 percent of those enrolled at private universities. This concentration is the result of a number of factors: Jewish students set higher sights for themselves, receive higher grades, are willing to go farther from home to attend college, and are more confident about their own drive and ability. (Asked to rate themselves on academic ability and "drive to achieve," nearly twice as many Jewish as non-Jewish students put themselves in the top 10 percent.)

These differences in education inevitably affect the careers Jews choose and the jobs they hold. In the Boston metropolitan area, which contains the most carefully studied American Jewish community, two Jewish men in five and well over a third of Jewish women held professional jobs in 1975–twice the proportion among non-Jews. More than a quarter of the Jewish men, moreover and a fifth of the women were business managers or proprietors; the comparable figures among non-Jews were 16 percent and 6 percent, respectively.*

With its concentration of universities, medical schools, research labs, and "high tech" electronics firms, Boston offers more professional opportunities than most metropolitan areas, but it is far from unique; the proportion of Jews holding professional jobs is as high, or even higher, in Rochester, Nashville, Cleveland, and Seattle–to name cities in different parts of the country. Nationwide, at least a third of the Jewish labor force is working in professional occupations–twice the ratio in the labor force as a whole–with the specific proportion vary-

* I am indebted to Professor Calvin Goldscheider of Brown University for sharing his analysis of the Boston data with me before its publication.

ing from one metropolitan area to another according to the nature of the local economy and, equally important, the age of the Jewish population.

Since the end of World War II, in fact, there has been an extraordinary movement of Jews into the professions and a corresponding reduction in the number operating their own businesses. The magnitude of this change can be seen by contrasting the occupations of older and younger Jewish men. (Here again the 1975 Boston demographic study is particularly useful.) Men who were sixty years of age or older in 1975 were for the most part either immigrants or the children of immigrants, who had entered the labor force during the 1920s and 1930s and had come to maturity just before or during World War II. Their occupations still reflected the career choices they had made in that earlier period, when the labor force had a different structure and anti-Semitism limited the opportunities that were available. As a result, members of this age group were more heavily engaged in business than in the professions: 35 percent were business managers or proprietors, compared to 22 percent in professional occupations.* A small but significant minority—15 percent—were blue-collar workers, and 28 percent had clerical or sales jobs, half of them in real estate or insurance.

Jews thirty to thirty-nine years old, on the other hand, were far removed from the immigrant experience; most were third-generation Americans. They were also the first generation to grow up in a completely open society; by the time they were ready for college or graduate school, quotas had largely disappeared, and by the late sixties or early seventies, when their occupations were mostly set, the remaining barriers were being removed.

As might be expected, these younger men had chosen different careers from those of their elders. Fully 60 percent of them, in fact, were professionals—nearly three times the proportion among older Jews and two and a half times the proportion among non-Jewish men in their thirties. Fewer than one in five of the younger Jews, on the other hand, were managers and proprietors, a decline of 50 percent from the sixty-and-older group. Blue-collar employment had virtually disappeared, accounting for less than 3 percent of the group; by comparison, half the non-Jewish thirty-to-thirty-nine-year-olds in Boston were blue-collar workers.

The shift into the professions is even more striking when one compares the occupations Boston Jews had in 1975 with those their fathers had had. It was rare for the sons of businessmen to follow in their

* The latter figure, interestingly enough, was about double the proportion in that age group in 1965, when an earlier survey was taken. Clearly, Jews began choosing professional careers well before the recent breakthroughs.

fathers' footsteps: only 15 percent of those sons were businessmen themselves, whereas half had chosen a professional occupation.

ITEM: The late Samuel J. Bernstein of Boston, proprietor of a successful beauty-supplies business, was atypical in having a son who attained the prominence of his oldest child, the composer-conductor Leonard Bernstein, but he was representative in his intense desire to have his children come into the business with him and in his disappointment over their refusal to do so. (The family was typical in another way: Jennie Bernstein encouraged her son's musical career despite her husband's vehement objections.) As Leonard Bernstein's younger brother, Burton, a staff writer for *The New Yorker,* has recalled, their father "wanted only the best for Lenny, and the best meant a secure, comfortable life." "For years after Lenny's initial success, Sam harbored doubts about the stability of his son's career. He worried that it would all come tumbling down . . . [and] secretly wished that Lenny would one day return to Boston and the beauty-supplies business." (Sam Bernstein had the same wish for Burton and for the middle child, Shirley, who became a New York City television producer and literary agent.)

There is a certain poetic justice in the rejection by second-generation American Jews of their parents' occupations, for in coming to America the immigrants had often rejected the desires and values of their own parents. "It's a big disappointment to me that none of you kids wanted to take over the business and live in Boston," Sam Bernstein told one of them when he was negotiating the sale of the business he viewed as a fourth child. "But when I think about it, all the younger generations in the Bernstein family went against their parents' wishes. . . . I ran away from the *shtetl* to be a businessman in America. Now my own kids won't have anything to do with my work and my life. We're a funny family that way."

So too with a great many other American Jewish families. "The story of Jews in the South," Eli Evans has written, in a formulation that applies equally well to the North, "is the story of fathers who built businesses to give to their sons who didn't want them." Evans' own father had hoped he would take over the family-owned department store in Durham, North Carolina, but Evans went off to Yale Law School after college, worked for a time as a gubernatorial and presidential speech writer, and now heads a large charitable foundation.

Jews who were blue-collar workers, on the other hand, wanted nothing quite so much as that their sons should *not* follow in their footsteps. The sons obliged: nearly two thirds of the Bostonians whose fathers had been blue-collar workers had moved into a professional occupation. In professional families, by contrast, inheritance of the father's occupation was commonplace; three quarters of those whose fathers were professionals had followed in their fathers' footsteps.

I have been focusing on men so far, not to slight women but because in the recent past it was uncommon for Jewish women to pursue full-time careers. This had not been the case in Eastern Europe, where most women worked and some were their family's principal support. My maternal great-grandmother ran a butcher shop so that her husband could devote himself to full-time religious study. Arrangements of this sort were rare in the United States, but it was not at all uncommon for immigrant women to work—at least until their husbands were "on their feet," as the saying went, at which time it became a matter of pride for them to leave the labor force and devote themselves to their husbands and children—especially their children. This pattern continued for a long time; as recently as the mid-1970s the mothers of Jewish elementary school students were far less likely to be working full time than the mothers of non-Jewish students.

What a difference a generation makes! Jewish women now show the same preference for professional occupations as Jewish men; in Boston in 1975 nearly half the thirty-to-thirty-nine-year-old Jewish women had a professional occupation, compared to less than a fifth of those sixty and older. This change was not just a by-product of the new roles that women play in American society, for the growth in professional occupations among younger Jewish women was nearly five times that among non-Jews.*

This is not to suggest that Jewish women have yet gained occupational or educational parity with Jewish men; it is only to say that they have made rapid strides in that direction. When the Boston survey was taken, in fact, women were just beginning to enter traditionally male preserves; more recent data from other cities show an even larger break with the past.

ITEM: A 1982 survey in Cleveland asked eighteen-to-twenty-nine-year-old Jews about their parents' occupations and their own careers or career plans. Only one woman in twenty expected to be a full-time housewife; among their mothers the figure was nearly eight in twenty. The daughters of working mothers also expected to abandon their

* The movement of Jewish women into professional jobs was the result of an exodus from clerical and sales jobs rather than from business management; only 10 percent of older Jewish women and 9 percent of the younger age group were managers or proprietors. Among Gentile women the most striking change was a move out of blue-collar and into clerical and sales jobs—a shift that occurred among Jewish women during the 1930s, 1940s, and 1950s.

mothers' low-status occupations: more than 15 percent of the mothers, for example, but only 2 percent of the daughters held clerical jobs. The daughters were setting their sights a lot higher; more than half were planning careers in some profession. One of the most striking changes involved the law: 6 percent of the daughters were or planned to be lawyers—thirty times the number in the preceding generation.

Among younger Jewish women, in fact, the law is becoming the most popular profession: a 1980 national survey of first-year college students taken by the American Council on Education found that 9 percent of the Jewish women were planning to be lawyers—up from 2 percent in 1969. The proportion planning a career in business management increased by the same amount, and the number planning to be doctors tripled, from 2 to 6 percent. In this same period the number of Jewish women planning to be elementary school teachers dropped to two thirds, from 18 percent in 1969 to 6 percent in 1980; those choosing secondary school teaching plummeted from 12 percent to only 1 percent.

And aspirations keep rising; a 1980 national survey of high school sophomores and seniors found that two thirds of Jewish girls were anticipating a professional career—the same proportion as among Jewish boys.* There is a certain symbolism, perhaps, in the fact that the first Jew to become an astronaut is a woman engineer, Judith A. Resnick. The granddaughter of a *schochet*, or ritual slaughterer, Resnick has a Ph.D. in electrical engineering. Before becoming an astronaut in 1978 she was a design engineer for RCA and did research on the physiology of sight at the National Institutes of Health.

The exodus of Jews away from business and into the professions could not have occurred without both the abolition of quotas and changes in the American economy that have led to an expanding demand for professional services of all sorts. The growth in the number of Jewish doctors illustrates how opportunity and desire have combined to propel Jews into high-status occupations. Jewish parents have long regarded medicine as an ideal career choice for their sons; it appears to offer the autonomy and freedom from dependence on Gentiles that Jews have long sought, along with a social status—*yikhus*, in Yiddish—that businessmen have never been able to acquire in the Jewish community.

It took a while, however, before this reverence for doctors could be translated into a career choice. At the turn of the century most

* Some differences remained—the boys were somewhat more concentrated in higher-status professions—but the differences were relatively small.

Jewish immigrants were simply too poor to afford a medical (or for that matter, a high school or college) education for their children; and in any case, educational opportunities were limited. Until 1903, for example, New York City required only four years of schooling; there were no public high schools at all, and the handful of elementary schools could accommodate only a fraction of the children who were supposed to be there. (In 1894 a single elementary school on the Lower East Side turned away nearly a thousand children for lack of room.) During the first wave of Eastern European immigration, therefore, education provided a significant means of upward mobility for only a relative handful.

That changed rapidly as educational opportunities broadened and Jews began moving into the middle class; by the mid-1930s half the students applying to American medical schools were Jews. In no branch of higher education, however, was anti-Semitism quite so virulent or restrictive quotas so high; as a result, Jews constituted only 17 percent of those admitted to American medical schools. Those who could afford to do so attended medical school in Europe (ironically, Jews were more welcome in the medical schools of Mussolini's Italy than in the United States). But nearly six out of seven Jewish applicants had to abandon their ambition, and untold others did not bother to apply to medical schools at all; some became pharmacists or dentists instead. In Stamford, Connecticut, in 1938, for example, there were as many Jewish dentists as there were doctors; Jews of that era used to joke that "D.D.S." after one's name stood for "disappointed doctor or surgeon."

There are a lot more Jewish doctors today. In Boston in 1975 an astonishing 16 percent of Jewish males in their thirties were doctors, compared to only 1.3 percent of the sixty-and-over group and 8 percent of the male labor force as a whole. Because of its extraordinary concentration of hospitals and medical schools, Boston attracts more than its share of physicians, but even in business-oriented Jewish communities such as Minneapolis and St. Louis, the number of doctors is remarkably high–6 percent or more of the male Jewish labor force. In the American labor force as a whole, fewer than 1 percent of non-Jewish men are doctors; all told, about one American doctor in five is now Jewish.

What has changed, moreover, is not simply the number of Jewish doctors but the locus of their practice. In the past, Jewish doctors were confined for the most part to Jewish-sponsored hospitals; medical schools and research centers simply did not appoint Jews to their faculties or staffs. But when the barriers came down, Jews gravitated to medical education and research. By 1969 nearly a quarter of medical school faculty members were Jewish, and the proportion is higher in the more prominent institutions.

2

Jews are not the only beneficiaries of the opportunities American society has provided, but they have used those opportunities more effectively than most other immigrant groups. "The rise in socio-economic status of the Eastern European Jews and their descendants," the sociologist Milton M. Gordon wrote in 1963 in a landmark study of American ethnic groups, is "the greatest collective Horatio Alger story in American immigration history."

Gordon erred in only one respect: the ascent of the mid-nineteenth-century German Jewish immigrants was even more rapid than that of the Eastern European Jews. Indeed, Horatio Alger became a wealthy man himself because of the beneficence and financial acumen of Joseph Seligman, the immigrant peddler-turned-investment banker, who hired Alger to be a live-in tutor for his children; as one of the fringe benefits, Seligman invested Alger's book royalties for him.

It is nonetheless the ascent of the Eastern European Jews, who came here en masse after 1881, that needs to be explained, for it is from them that the overwhelming majority of contemporary American Jews are descended. Unlike the German Jewish immigrants, who fanned out as peddlers throughout the country, the poverty-stricken Eastern European Jews settled in the large cities of the East and Midwest, going to work in textile mills, clothing factories, and other light industries when they could not afford to set themselves up in trade. In 1900 three out of five were blue-collar workers, half of them employed in clothing manufacture; 5 percent were peddlers, many of them selling food or dry goods from barrels set out in the street; 10 percent had their own retail businesses—some of them junkyards, most of them tiny "mom and pop" grocery, clothing, or stationery stores, behind (or over) which they and their families lived. Only 10 percent worked in clerical or professional occupations.

It did not take long for these immigrants to begin climbing the occupational ladder; as a federal commission reported in 1900, "economic advancement comes to these poverty-stricken Hebrews with surprising rapidity." Half or more of them, in fact, moved into the middle class—in Boston within ten years' time, and in New York in fifteen to twenty-five years. Jewish immigrants "begin as helpers and advance to full-fledged mechanics," the great labor economist John R. Commons wrote in 1891 in a report on the New York clothing industry. "After they have worked for some time and have learned the trade, they open contractors' shops. They can begin with a capital of $50. From that they go into the wholesale manufacture of clothing."

The specific routes varied, but the goal was almost always the same—to go into business for oneself.

ITEM: When he arrived in New York in 1908 at sixteen, Samuel Bernstein found a job cleaning fish in the Fulton Fish Market—twelve hours a day, six days a week, for a wage of five dollars, out of which he saved a dollar. Four years later he moved to Hartford, where he worked in a barbershop his uncle had established, sweeping the floor, sterilizing combs and scissors, and performing other menial tasks. When a barber- and beauty-supplies salesman mentioned that his firm needed a stock boy in its Boston office, Bernstein jumped at the opportunity. By 1919 he had become manager of the Boston office, and in 1923 he opened his own firm; by 1927 Sam Bernstein had acquired the exclusive New England franchise for a new and enormously popular permanent wave machine, and his firm had become a large and profitable business.

ITEM: When Louis Borgenicht, the father of a childhood friend of my mother's, arrived in New York in 1888, he sold herring out of a barrel on a Lower East Side street corner. With the profits he bought a pushcart, from which he sold bananas, crockery, socks, notebooks, and anything else he could buy for a nickel and sell for a dime. Dissatisfied with what he was earning, Borgenicht wandered around the Lower East Side studying what people were wearing and the stores were selling. Noticing a young immigrant girl wearing an apron popular in Central Europe, from which he had come, Borgenicht bought 150 yards of material and with his wife's help made forty aprons, which he sold door-to-door for a profit of $2.60. Two years later Borgenicht gave up peddling to concentrate on the manufacture of children's dresses; by 1915 he had fifteen hundred employees and was known as "the king of the children's dress trade."

Although Borgenicht and Bernstein were more successful than most, the routes they traveled were typical of large numbers of Jewish immigrants; and yet a large Jewish working class remained for some time. Until immigration was cut off in the mid-1920s, those who made it into the middle class were replaced by those who had just arrived; and a third or more of the immigrants continued in their blue-collar occupations throughout their lives. "It puzzled me greatly when I came to read in books that Jews are a shrewd people particularly given to commerce and banking, for the Jews I knew had managed to be an exception to that rule," Alfred Kazin, the distinguished literary critic, wrote in *A Walker in the City*, a memoir of his childhood in the Brownsville section of Brooklyn. "I grew up with the belief that the natural condition of a Jew was to be a propertyless worker like my painter father and my dressmaker mother and my dressmaker uncles and cousins in Brownsville—workers, kin to all the workers of the world, dependent entirely on the work of their hands. All happiness in our house was measured by the length of a job." But if the immigrants could not always escape the working class themselves, their children almost invariably did.

In their eagerness to move up, some first- and second-generation Jews—far more than the selective filter of group memory allows present-day Jews to recall—followed the route which, at one point or another, every ethnic group has taken: crime. True enough, Jews were statistically "underrepresented" in criminal dockets, relative to other immigrant groups, even in the pre-World War I period, when Jewish crime and delinquency were at their peak. But the Jewish contribution to crime cannot be measured in numbers alone; as they did in law, medicine, and academic life, Jews moved to the top of the criminal "profession" too. During the late nineteenth and early twentieth centuries Jews dominated prostitution (Polly Adler was only one of a number of notable Jewish madams) and the so-called white slave trade, along with pickpocketing, fencing, and confidence games—criminal activities that depended on wit or dexterity rather than on physical strength and in which Jews had had considerable experience in Europe.

After World War I there was a significant drop in the number of Jewish criminals, as Jews moved, en masse, out of the old areas of first settlement as well as out of the working class itself. On Chicago's West Side, a principal spawning ground of crime, the Jewish population dropped by more than 50 percent between 1914 and 1920; in the ten-year period 1905 to 1915, two thirds of the Jews living in New York's Lower East Side—home of some of the best-known Jewish gangs—abandoned that Gehenna, as worried parents called it, for less congested and more suburblike neighborhoods in Brooklyn, Manhattan, and the Bronx. The change was reflected in criminal court statistics. In Manhattan just before World War I, for example, Jews accounted for nearly one felony arrest in four; by the eve of World War II the proportion was down to 7.5 percent.

In the 1920s and 1930s, however, a new group of Jewish criminals transformed the underworld by branching out into new fields of criminal activity.

ITEM: In much the same way that first- and second-generation Jews such as Harry Warner, Marcus Loew, Louis B. Mayer, Carl Laemmle, Jesse Lasky, and Harry Cohn created the motion picture industry by integrating film production and distribution with theater ownership, the legendary Arnold ("The Brain") Rothstein transformed crime from a haphazard, small-scale activity into a well-organized and well-financed business operation.* For Rothstein crime was a challenge rather than a way out of poverty. The proverbial "bad seed," he grew up on Manhattan's Upper West Side, the son of a successful garment manufacturer and Orthodox religious leader, and his good looks and polished charm enabled him to move with ease in New York society, where he was known as "the king of gamblers." Attacked in the press and in Henry Ford's *Dearborn Independent* as the mastermind behind the 1919 "Black Sox" scandal, Rothstein announced his retirement from gambling; in the future, he said, he would concentrate on his racing stable and real estate investments.

Instead, with the advent of Prohibition in 1920, Rothstein organized and financed the first large-scale bootlegging operation, complete with corporate and communications headquarters in a Times Square office building; he then turned his attention to the narcotics trade, which was even more profitable, and to underwriting the criminal activities of others. The "Morgan of the underworld," as one historian has called him, Rothstein, who was assassinated in 1928, was, in effect, the inventor of organized crime. "In his own way," Irving Howe wrote, "he was still another Jewish boy who made good."†

There were many others who "made good" in that way—men such as Morris Dalitz and his cohorts in the Cleveland Four, Isadore "Kid Cann" Blumenthal of Minneapolis, Solomon "Cutcher-Head-Off" Weissman of Kansas City, Harry and Louis Fleisher of Detroit's Purple Gang, Abe "Kid Twist" Reles, Louis "Lepke" Buchalter, and Jacob "Gurrah" Shapiro of Brooklyn's Murder Incorporated, Arthur "Dutch Schultz" Flegenheimer of the Bronx, and Samuel "the Greener" Jacobson of Chicago's Twentieth Ward Group—to name just a few. In contrast to their predecessors, Jewish gangsters of the twenties and thirties were every bit as violent and ruthless as their Gentile colleagues and competitors. They had to be, to secure a firm foothold in bootlegging and other rackets.

* Rothstein was the model for Jay Gatsby's mysterious business associate Meyer Wolfsheim in F. Scott Fitzgerald's *The Great Gatsby*.

† The scant attention Howe paid to Jewish crime in *World of Our Fathers*, his magisterial history of the Lower East Side, is a good example of the amnesia American Jews show about this part of their history.

The principal Jewish contribution to organized crime was not violence, however, but perfecting the rational business approach that Arnold Rothstein had originated. They did so in part by transcending the narrow boundaries of traditional ethnic-based crime; theirs was truly an ecumenical spirit, for they worked closely with the new generation of Italian-American crime leaders, such as Al Capone and Lucky Luciano. Most important of all, perhaps, these Jewish ecumenists blurred, and at times erased, the old distinction between crime and legitimate business.

ITEM: Moses Annenberg laid the foundations for one of the great American fortunes by capitalizing on the mania for horse race betting that swept the country during the 1920s. Using the strong-arm methods he had learned in the violent Chicago newspaper circulation wars and the business knowledge he had acquired as publisher of the New York *Daily Mirror* and director of circulation for the entire Hearst newspaper and magazine chain, Annenberg built the *Daily Racing Form,* which he bought for $400,000 in 1922, into the bettors' bible, one without any significant competition. Soon after acquiring the *Racing Form,* Annenberg also took control of the company that had been supplying racing results to bookmakers and racing papers; with the help of underworld friends—"I always thought of Annenberg as my kind of guy," Lucky Luciano said—he soon had a national monopoly on the supply of racing information.*

ITEM: It was Meyer Lansky of New York who, more than anyone else, "grasped the emergent possibilities of gangster capitalism," as Albert Fried has put it in his history of Jewish gangsters—thereby moving organized crime to a new stage of development. During the late 1920s leaders of the underworld had tried to reduce the endless internecine gang wars by forming a cartel in which each gang was guaranteed its existing share of the illegal liquor market. Lansky recognized that the criminal status quo could not survive the end of Prohibition, and he led the redeployment of gangster capital into new investment

* Like most Jewish racketeers (but unlike a number of those connected with the Teamsters Union), Annenberg kept his children away from any contact with his criminal activities. Knowing how devoted Annenberg was to his son, Walter, federal prosecutors pressing an income tax evasion case against Annenberg, whose income was said to be $6 million a year, threatened to indict Walter too unless the senior Annenberg pleaded guilty. To spare Walter, Moses complied, although he had a good chance of gaining an acquittal. Walter Annenberg went on to enlarge the family fortune greatly through his ownership of *TV Guide* and other magazines and newspapers, and to become a good friend of several Republican presidents, serving as ambassador to Great Britain in the Nixon administration.

outlets: the ownership of Florida racetracks, hotels, and real estate; lavish new gambling casinos in places such as Hot Springs, Arkansas, and Havana, Cuba; wide distribution of slot machines; and consolidation of bookmaking and numbers operations, among others. By making himself useful to almost everyone, Lansky raised the level of coordination and long-range planning; he was, as well, the first to anticipate the post–World War II boom and to see the enormous returns that development of Las Vegas and the Florida "Gold Coast" could provide. Most important of all, perhaps, Lansky understood the need to "launder" the profits from organized crime as a protection against prosecution, and he established the network of Swiss and Bahamian banking connections that made it possible to invest criminal earnings in real estate and other legitimate activities.

That chapter in American Jewish history is now largely over. A few elderly figures from the past are still around, such as Moe Dalitz, who manages the opulent Teamsters Union-owned LaCosta resort near San Diego, and Sidney Korshak, a Los Angeles lawyer who reportedly got his start working for Al Capone and who subsequently helped channel Teamsters pension fund money into Las Vegas casinos and other businesses. Some younger men too—most of them the sons of old-time Cleveland and Chicago racketeers—are still actively involved with Teamsters Union affairs, the most notable being Teamsters president Jackie Presser. But the numbers are few and dwindling; there are simply too many completely honest and legitimate ways of making money for more than an occasional Jewish deviant to be attracted to the underworld.

As a group, in fact, Jews abandoned crime early; the speed of their own ascent gave them too much of a stake in society to be attracted by illegal enterprise. By the mid-1920s American Jews had already become a middle-class community; and during the Great Depression of the 1930s, despite fears that they were being pushed back into the working class—"Jewish youth is turning again to the factory," an economist warned in 1941—they remained solidly entrenched in white-collar occupations. In Detroit in 1935, for example, only one Jew in four was a blue-collar worker; two in five held clerical or sales jobs, and a quarter were business managers or proprietors. And in Stamford, Connecticut, a smaller and more prosperous community, a 1938 survey found that one Jew in three was self-employed; only 12 percent were blue-collar workers. (The professions had not yet attracted many Jews: in Stamford only 6 percent held professional jobs, and in Detroit, 7.6 percent.)

And so it went, in greater or lesser degree, throughout the United

States. As the Depression waned, Jews resumed their upward climb. "The most striking fact" about American Jews, Talcott Parsons wrote in his 1942 essay, "is the comparative rapidity with which they gain economic and social status. It is a remarkable feat of social climbing."

3

What accounts for that "feat"?

One reason is that Jews were better equipped to use the opportunities that were available in America. To begin with, they were less traumatized by the process of adjustment to American society than, say, Italian and Polish immigrants, who had to make the painful transition from majority to minority status—from being at home to being despised strangers. Most immigrants, moreover, came here to seek temporary employment rather than to stay; men often came alone, with the expectation of returning home when they had saved enough to marry or to purchase a small farm. In the early years of the century, in fact, more than two fifths of non-Jewish immigrants returned to their native lands; among Italian immigrants the ratio was considerably higher, running above 70 percent. Some of those who went back to Italy ultimately returned here, but their strong ties to their native land made the adjustment to American culture slow and painful.

Jews, on the other hand, were more likely to be married and to bring their families with them; women and children made up a larger proportion of Jewish than of non-Jewish immigration. And although some Jews did return, especially in the late nineteenth century, most came here to stay; they were fleeing persecution, after all, as well as the poverty that was the major impetus for the move. "They pushed me into America," one immigrant wrote in his diary; "a powerful storm-wind ripped us out of our place and carried us to America," another wrote. To be sure, Jewish immigrants sometimes expressed regret over having left *di heim*, but this was nostalgia for home and family, not a longing for place; after the Kishinev pogrom of 1903 no more than 7 percent returned, many of them pious Jews who could not adjust to the secular nature of American society. In a sense, Jewish immigrants had no native country; they had been a pariah group, denied membership in the larger society of their native countries. For Jews, therefore, the move to America meant a rise in status, not a fall; however hard life was here, and it *was* hard, they were freer than they had ever been and so had a far more optimistic sense of what life in America could be.

Because of their history Jewish immigrants had a different set of aptitudes as well, aptitudes that made it easier for them to make their way in American society. For one thing, they were more familiar with urban life than most other immigrants; most Eastern European Jews came either from cities or from *miestechkos*, as the Russian census called them—towns and villages that were commercial or industrial centers for the surrounding countryside. And despite their poverty, two thirds of the Jewish immigrants had some occupational skill—as tailors, dressmakers, shoemakers, carpenters, and so on; by contrast, three quarters of the Italian immigrants had been unskilled laborers. Many of the Jewish craftsmen, moreover, had had some experience with trade; barred from the guilds, they had been forced to sell the wares they made in shops or market stalls of their own. Still others, like Louis Borgenicht, had worked as clerks in other people's shops. Jewish male immigrants were more likely to be literate as well—in Hebrew, Yiddish and Russian or Polish.

There was another difference, one that profoundly affected the way Jews perceived their situation. Unlike most other immigrants, whose families had been peasants or laborers for as long as anyone could recall, the Jews who came here were the children or grandchildren of merchants or petty traders, albeit merchants or traders who had been pushed down into the working class. Against the broad perspective of Jewish history, Nathan Glazer suggests, what needs explanation is less the speed with which Jews moved into the middle class in the United States than the speed with which they had been forced out of their traditional middle-class occupations in Eastern Europe and turned into an impoverished proletariat. For the Jews who came here, as Glazer has written, "business and education were . . . not a remote and almost foreign possibility, but a near and familiar one. They, or their friends or relatives, had the necessary experience or knowledge." Hence Jewish workers could "turn their minds to ways and means of improving themselves that were quite beyond the imagination of their fellow workers."

All the more so because Jews had had long practice in utilizing whatever opportunities happened to be at hand. "In order to make a living one tries his hand at anything and often at a number of things," Mark Zborowski and Elizabeth Herzog wrote in *Life Is with People*, their classic if somewhat romanticized portrait of the Eastern European shtetl. "So few are able to support themselves by a single occupation that it is common for a person to have several, which he carries on simultaneously or successively." "My father was a plasterer by trade," one of Zborowski and Herzog's informants told them, "but that was no way to make an entire living, so he dealt in flax, too. . . . And in the summer [he] built small wooden houses for the peasants." Because it was so hard to earn a living, Zborowski and Herzog go on to explain, "you never refuse a job, even if it requires a technique you have not mastered. If you don't know how, then you learn by doing. Somehow you will 'worry it out.' "

This tradition stood Jews in good stead in the New World, where opportunities were plentiful. Mass migration from more or less self-sufficient farms or country towns to city houses and apartments meant that people were now consumers rather than producers and so had to purchase food, clothing, and other items they once had made or grown at home. Industrialization drastically lowered costs, making it easier to meet the new and rapidly growing demand for consumer goods. Recognizing this, the earlier German Jewish immigrants had already moved into clothing manufacture in considerable numbers, and the new immigrants, a third of whom had worked in clothing production in Russia, provided a ready-made labor force for them. From there it was a natural transition for many of the newcomers to go into business for themselves.

There were other opportunities as well. Urbanization and industrialization required a vast expansion of retail and wholesale trade—occupations with which Jews had had long experience—and an even larger growth in the housing stock. That growth, and the frequency with which city dwellers, especially Jews, moved from one neighborhood to another, created opportunities for Jewish carpenters, painters, electricians, plumbers, plasterers, masons, and tinsmiths, and for real estate developers as well. Land values were skyrocketing; the rush from the Lower East Side to Brownsville early in the century, for example, raised the price of a lot from $50 to $3000 in two years. By the 1920s, 40 percent of New York City builders and developers were Jewish. Some had been carpenters or painters, others storekeepers or garment manufacturers who had invested their small savings to buy first one tenement, then another, ultimately graduating to construction on their own. The founder of the Tishman real estate empire owned a tiny dry goods store in Newburgh, New York, and the founder of the Rudin empire started with a grocery store on the Lower East Side; Richard Ravitch's grandfather had a small shop in which he made iron sidewalk gratings, and the first Uris fabricated steel fittings.

Many began even more modestly by taking in boarders. As her reputation for cooking spread, one woman has recalled, others asked if they too could take their meals with her: "Suddenly I'm having a restaurant—six or seven people eating at my table. Sometimes I had to serve in shifts." The woman also worked as a midwife, and her husband had a job in a clothing factory—hence they were able to save a little each week. In 1911, eight years after they had arrived in New

York, the husband suggested that they use their savings to buy a small building. "Me, with a building? I couldn't believe it. In the old country Jews didn't own. So I said, 'Sam, buy it. We're in America, everything is different here, everything possible.'" As indeed it was: buying one small property after another, "by the twenties we were already rich."

The same process occurred elsewhere; in a 1915 study of Boston immigrants, a group of Harvard and MIT scholars reported that Jews had "an abnormal hunger to acquire real estate." Nor was it only the upwardly mobile who displayed that hunger. His grandfather was "stone poor" his entire life, the journalist Theodore H. White has written, "and his pride was the wooden-frame house on Erie Street [in Boston] that he had bought in 1912 for $2,000," and in which White was born three years later. It was, as White adds, "the first home, the first piece of land, owned by any one of his family, for in their centuries of East European life, most Jews were either forbidden to buy land or too frightened to do so." Even when they could own property, moreover, Eastern European Jews had usually refrained from doing so or from having fixed investments of any sort; in a world in which they had to be prepared to flee at any time, they preferred to keep their capital as liquid as possible.

That preference still shapes Jewish behavior, even among those who have forgotten why; group memory is not easily erased. One reason Jews are so attracted to the professions is that they can carry their capital in their heads; and Jewish businessmen gravitate toward fields in which capital requirements are low and turnover rapid. The quest for liquidity is particularly strong among those who fled Hitler. Felix Rohatyn, the investment banker who played a major role in saving New York City from bankruptcy in the 1970s, vividly recalls his family's escape from France on foot across the Pyrenees. Rohatyn spent the evening before they left opening toothpaste tubes from the bottom and stuffing them with small gold coins—all that was left of the family fortune. "That experience has left me with a refugee's theory of wealth," Rohatyn has told several interviewers. "What is real to me is what I can put in the back of a toothpaste tube, or what I carry around in my head."

ITEM: Rohatyn's mentor, the late André Meyer, became one of the most influential investment bankers in the United States, but he lived, so to speak, with his bags packed, residing only in hotels. "He wanted to be able to go downstairs on any day and check out and leave," Rohatyn explains—"to just shut the door, turn in the key, pick up his airplane ticket, and go." Meyer took a similar approach to his firm's investments, often selling a lot sooner than his partners thought advisable. "André wanted to make sure he could sell it," one such partner explained. "And how did he make sure? He sold it."

Despite their historic avoidance of fixed investments, Jewish immigrants and their descendants have been drawn to real estate. Concentrated as they were in rapidly growing cities, they found it was an obvious way of making money on what was close at hand. Because so many fields had been closed to them in the past, says Richard Ravitch, the former head of a New York construction firm, "Jews had to be smart, quick, and facile, with a head for numbers—and that's real estate." Equally important, real estate was not closed to Jews by the social barriers that existed in other industries; the field was wide open, as Walter Shorenstein, a San Francisco developer, suggests, "because it does not lend itself to the corporate entity." It is, in fact, an intensely entrepreneurial activity—one with great risks ("if we make a mistake," Alan Tishman says, "we can't tear it down") as well as great rewards and one in which, in Shorenstein's formulation, "the individual is key." "Jews," he adds, "like to take a chance on the self." Or as New York real estate developer Bernard Mendik puts it, a successful real estate developer "needs wits and brains and lots of balls; you have to have the guts to put yourself on the line—literally to sign your life away."

Most important of all, perhaps, real estate development was—and still is—an easy field to enter; since developers operate largely on borrowed funds, they need very little capital of their own. "You don't need a factory, you don't need a product, you don't have to invest in inventory, and you don't have to go to school for eight or ten years," Shorenstein says. "All you need is a desk, a telephone, and maybe a secretary." And an idea and the capacity to carry it out, for "money flows to people with capacity."

ITEM: To buy his first piece of property in 1936, seventy-two-year-old Peter Feinberg of Palm Beach, Florida, told me, he needed $4300. He had no money himself; born in Poland, he had put himself through college and law school (and supported his parents as well) through his winnings at poker and crapshooting. Feinberg approached a more affluent friend at the real estate firm where both were working. "I said to him, 'You put up $3300 and I'll put up $1000 and we'll go fifty-fifty—only you have to lend me the $1000,'" Feinberg recalls. "He did, and we're still friends." That first investment led to another, and then another, until Feinberg started his own firm. With properties in Denver, Atlanta, Florida, and New York, he is now worth more than

$100 million, according to *Forbes*'s list of the four hundred richest Americans.

What is in short supply, in other words, is not money—contemporary developers all say there are plenty of investors around looking for places to put their money—but ideas. According to Larry A. Silverstein, another developer who made the *Forbes* list, a developer has to see something in a building that others have missed (Silverstein specializes in upgrading older office buildings) or have an idea for the use of a parcel of land that no one else has thought of. "That is the heart of development."

ITEM: Melvin Simon of Indianapolis went to work as a rental agent for a shopping center in the early 1950s, drawing $100 a week against commissions. Simon, the son of a New York garment worker, realized that attracting motion picture theaters to a shopping center would provide a use at night for the parking spaces, which comprise the bulk of the land on which shopping centers are built. Simon went into business for himself in 1959; now, at fifty-eight, he owns more than 120 shopping centers in 23 states, and has a net worth that *Forbes* puts at $225 million.

Seeing things others have missed is a talent that Jews, because of their marginality, have honed over a long period; as an English banking journal remarked in 1888, "The Jews have shown a marked excellence in what can be called the commerce of imperceptibles."

For first- and second-generation American Jews, however, real estate was more than just a business; they rushed to purchase property earlier in the century as a way of announcing that they were here to stay, that they had left their old fears behind. "My grandfather was making a statement when he bought his first piece of property," Alan V. Tishman, president of Tishman Management and Leasing Corporation, told me. "He was proclaiming that America was different, that it was a safe harbor." Real estate development also gives city dwellers the same psychic rewards that farming gives to others. "Building is the most creative part of the business world," Richard Ravitch says, for it involves "changing the face of the earth." "There is great pride in creating something," Alan Tishman adds. "You sweat it out, work it through, and there it is. We can walk around the city and see our buildings—and each building is the blood, sweat, and tears of creation."

The growth of Jewish-owned businesses, whether in real estate, trade, or manufacturing, was a source of upward mobility for others besides the proprietors themselves; it created employment opportunities for Jewish lawyers, accountants, and architects as well as for bookkeepers, secretaries, retail sales clerks, textile and garment salesmen, real estate brokers, insurance agents, rent and bill collectors, and building superintendents, not to mention painters, carpenters, plumbers, electricians, and other craftsmen. Reluctant to risk the anti-Semitism that might inhibit their chances in large corporations, Jews were able to find jobs working for other Jews; and if they were ready to go into business for themselves, they could often finance the venture through credit extended by Jewish suppliers as well as through their own savings.

The Jewish penchant for saving was a characteristic that many observers noted, often with disapproval. "Thrift is the watchword of Jewtown, as of its people the world over," Jacob Riis wrote in *How the Other Half Lives*. "It is at once its strength and fatal weakness, its cardinal virtue and its foul disgrace. Become an overmastering passion with these people who come here in droves from Eastern Europe to escape persecution . . . it has enslaved them in bondage worse than that from which they fled . . . over and over again I have met with instances of these Polish or Russian Jews deliberately starving themselves to the point of physical exhaustion . . . to save a little money."

Riis's observations were accurate enough, but he failed to grasp the meaning of what he saw. Saving was not an end in itself; it was, rather, a means to another end: to go into business for oneself, or to enable one's children to go into business or to spend the long years of study needed to enter a profession. As early as 1908, when Jews constituted 2 percent of the American population, they made up 13 percent of all law students, 18 percent of those preparing to be pharmacists, and 6 percent of dental students.

The emphasis on education and saving grew out of another characteristic that distinguished Jews from most other immigrants: the degree to which they were oriented toward the future—toward a future, moreover, that they expected to be better than the present. This orientation was encouraged by the Jewish religious world view with its strong Messianic emphasis and its belief that redemption occurs within rather than outside history. In Judaism, as the late Gershom Scholem wrote, "the Messianic idea has compelled a *life lived in deferment* [emphasis in original]." In contrast to the fatalism that characterized the culture of some other immigrant groups, Jews have always seen the world as susceptible to human control. In Jewish religious thought there is no divine jealousy of human activity and no inhibition against interfering with the forces of nature; on the contrary, God and man are viewed as partners in the work of creation.

These attitudes in turn contributed to parents' willingness to sacrifice their own comfort and well-being to advance their children's prospects. It is impossible to understand Jewish mobility and success without considering the distinctive nature of the parent-child relationship. Jewish parents traditionally have seen their children as extensions of themselves rather than as separate, still less subordinate, creatures; in the Eastern European Jewish formulation, children are their parents' *nachas*—a hard-to-translate term that means that children provide their parents with honor and fulfillment as well as with joy. Specifically, the child's success and achievement becomes the parent's success and achievement—and the child's failure the parents' failure. He understood why he was so driven to succeed, Alfred Kazin has written, when he "realized how little my parents thought of their own lives. *It was not for myself alone that I was expected to shine, but for them—to redeem the constant anxiety of their existence* [emphasis added]."

Nor was Kazin's case unique. "I'm what he lives for," Alexander Portnoy says of his father in *Portnoy's Complaint.* "He . . . saw in me the family's opportunity to be 'as good as anybody,' our chance to win honor and respect." "In that ferocious and self-annihilating way in which so many Jewish men of his generation served their families," Portnoy adds, "my father served my mother, my sister Hannah, but particularly me. Where he had been imprisoned, I would fly: that was his dream."

And so parents invested a large part of themselves in their children's—more precisely, their sons'—careers. (I am focusing on the parent-son relationship because until recently, family aspirations were centered almost entirely on the male offspring.) "My father lived vicariously through me to a distressing extent," Jerome Shapiro of Hughes Hubbard & Reed told me. "He enjoyed everything I did and every success I had." The same was true of my own father; concerned that he might forget to call my attention to an article he thought would interest me or to ask my opinion on news events since my last visit, he would keep notes on little three-by-five file cards, which he would rip out of his shirt pocket before I had a chance to take off my overcoat.

From infancy on, Jewish sons tended to be the focus of family life. "When I am not being punished, Doctor," Portnoy tells his psychiatrist, "I am being carried around that house like the Pope through the streets of Rome." "I was always asked to sit at the table and listen to my uncles and grandparents argue about politics," Av Westin of ABC-TV recalls. "If I said anything at all in my squeaky voice, they would stop and say, 'Isn't it wonderful he's paying attention.' " "I still wake up, pinch myself, and say, 'My God, those conversations I used to have with my father have worked out,' " says Eugene Eidenberg, who has had a successful career in academic life (vice-chancellor of the University of Illinois), politics (deputy mayor of Minneapolis, Assistant to the President for Intergovernmental Affairs in the Carter White House, director of the Democratic National Committee), and business (senior vice-president of MCI).

ITEM: Each day after school, Nobel Laureate Isidor Rabi has recalled, his mother would greet him with "Did you ask any good questions in school today?"

Sons not only were treated as special, they were told over and over again that they *were* special—the smartest and best-looking children in the world. "I can't help it that I'm so beautiful they stop Mother when she is wheeling me in my carriage so as to get a good look at my gorgeous *punim* [face]," Portnoy explains. "Of me," he adds, "my mother would say, with characteristic restraint, 'This *bonditt?* He doesn't even have to open a book—A in everything. Albert Einstein the Second.' "

To the outside world it appeared that Jewish parents spoiled their children, a charge to which the parents freely pleaded guilty. "Jewish mothers seemed singularly unconcerned with 'discipline' and 'independence training,' " the sociologist Zena Smith Blau has written of first- and second-generation Eastern European Jewish mothers. "They allowed their children a greater degree of latitude in acting out at home than was customary among Gentiles, and readily acknowledged that their children were *zelosen,* that is, pampered, demanding, spoiled"; for children were seen as fragile creatures who needed to be protected, through adolescence at the very least. And the fact that children were their parents' *nachas* gave them a certain power over their parents; Gentiles reared in the Anglo-American tradition interpret Jewish permissiveness as "spoiling" because they are less dependent on their children, hence less vulnerable to the children's demands. In the opinion of the political sociologist Charles Liebman, parents were not so much spoiling their children as bribing them to achieve in the desired manner.

Whether bribed or spoiled, children were certainly indulged—but not in the sense of being free to follow their own whims. On the contrary, indulgence was accompanied by high expectations and rigorous standards, for parents were anything but modest in their ambitions for their children. Not that the parents necessarily agreed on what their children should be. Fathers who had their own businesses usually wanted their sons to follow in their footsteps and were often impatient with, even contemptuous of the years "wasted" in college. I can remember the fathers of friends insisting that their sons would learn far more in "the business" than they could in college.

Mothers, on the other hand, usually wanted their sons to "better themselves" by becoming doctors or lawyers or professionals of some sort, and they saw higher education as the means by which their sons could climb above them. More often than not the mothers prevailed. "Jewish mothers were demanding, determined women who spared neither themselves nor their husbands and children," Blau writes. "They insisted on 'the best' whether they were shopping for food or selecting a doctor"—or judging their children's performance in school or elsewhere. "When her son began to make the first feeble sounds on his violin a Jewish mother already envisioned another Elman or Heifetz. If he showed scientific proficiency she foresaw another Einstein." Einsteins or not, mothers bragged shamelessly to others about their sons' achievements, if only to defend themselves against the bragging of their friends; *not* to boast was, in effect, to acknowledge that one's child was deficient.

ITEM: When he was first appointed a vice-president of Du Pont, Irving Shapiro told me, his mother could not wait to get to the swimming pool in her largely Jewish apartment complex to tell her friends. Her boasting was to no avail. "Your son is only a vice-president," one friend told her. "My son is a president; he has grocery stores all over Minneapolis."

The other side of the coin, of course, was that nothing but "the best" was acceptable. "At any signs of flagging effort," Blau writes, the mother "would inquire with withering contempt, 'So what [do] you want? To be a nothing?'" To mothers such as these, a B+ grade was cause for asking, "Why not an A−?," and for an A−, "Why not an A?"

Some sons paid (and still pay) a heavy price for this parental devotion: they became "*nachas*-producing machines" whose sole function was to "give their parents pleasure." In such homes children were loved not for themselves but for their accomplishments; those who could not measure up felt unworthy and unloved. Even accomplished youngsters sometimes felt that no matter what they did, their achievements were never large enough to meet their parents' expectations or to repay parents for their sacrifices. Alexander Portnoy is a case in point. "What *was* it with these Jewish parents, *what*," he asks his analyst, "that they were able to make us little Jewish boys believe ourselves to be princes on the one hand, unique as unicorns on the one hand, geniuses and brilliant like nobody has ever been brilliant and beautiful before in the history of childhood—saviors and sheer perfection on the one hand, and such bumbling, incompetent, thoughtless, helpless, selfish, evil little shits, little *ingrates*, on the other!"

It would be hard to imagine a family structure better suited to encourage achievement. Even the angry, neurotic Portnoy is a superachiever. "Mother, I'm thirty-three!" he shouts at one point. "I am the Assistant Commissioner of Human Opportunity for the City of New York! I graduated first in my law school class! Remember? I have graduated first from every class I've ever *been* in!" Portnoy has, in fact, provided his parents with precisely the kind of achievement they want and revere. "Whenever my name now appears in a news story in the *Times*, they bombard every living relative with a copy of the clipping," Portnoy grudgingly acknowledges. "Half my father's retirement pay goes down the drain in postage, and my mother is on the phone for days at a stretch and has to be fed intravenously, her mouth is going at such a rate about her Alex. In fact, it is exactly as it has always been: they can't get over what a success and a genius I am, my name in the paper, an associate now of the glamorous new Mayor . . ."

Obviously, not every Jewish son was first in his class or assistant to a glamorous mayor—but neither was every son as emotionally crippled as Portnoy. Studies of mental health and illness in several metropolitan areas indicate that although Jews have a somewhat higher rate of "mild" and "moderate" neuroses than Protestants or Catholics, they have a significantly lower rate of serious, disabling mental illness. The differential is so large, in fact, that the sociologist Leo Srole, director of the largest such study, concluded that there must be a "survival-insurance process rooted in the Jewish family and religious tradition. . . . The Jewish group historically can be viewed . . . as a culture mobilized for the prevention and, that failing, for the healing of the ailments of body and mind." One consequence is that Jews consult psychiatrists, as well as physicians, far more often than Protestants or Catholics do. (According to some researchers, the high proportion of Jews classified as neurotic is a by-product of their greater readiness to seek psychiatric help.)

In Zena Smith Blau's view, the much-maligned Jewish mother is responsible for this comparative mental health. Every child-rearing method entails some risk, she argues, but the risks of too much love and nurture are smaller (and the consequences more benign) than those of too little. If some sons were smothered by maternal devotion—"a Jewish man with parents alive is a fifteen-year-old boy, and will remain a fifteen-year-old boy till *they die!*" Portnoy exclaims—most developed a strong enough ego to succeed in school and in their own careers.

In fact, Jewish college students show considerably more self-confidence than Gentile students. A significantly larger proportion of Jewish than of non-Jewish freshmen, for example, rate themselves "above average" in academic ability, leadership ability, originality, and popularity with the opposite sex. (In one of the American Council on

Education's continuing surveys, Jewish students also rated themselves more highly on athletic ability.) As Geraldine Rosenfield of the American Jewish Committee has pointed out, these data contradict the stereotype of Jews as ridden with anxiety. "Jewish self-confidence, if not actual brashness . . . [results] from the eagerness of Jewish parents . . . to admire the remarkable qualities and achievements of their remarkable children." Or as Blau wryly put it, "Second-generation Jews lost a good many skirmishes with their mothers, but ultimately they won the war, just as their mothers intended."

It is not surprising that this should be so: precisely because children are their parents' *nachas*—because parents live vicariously through their children's achievements—it is the former who are dependent and vulnerable and the latter who are independent. Because so much is riding on their success, children are free—or driven—to seek the best business or professional opportunity, no matter how far away from their parents that opportunity may be, physically or psychologically, and to do so without feeling guilty about abandoning their family or community. Hence the extraordinary geographic as well as socioeconomic mobility American Jews display; in Rhode Island—an extreme example—70 percent of Jewish children move out of the state when they establish their careers; in Cleveland, 49 percent of the grown children move somewhere else. The process begins early, and with parental encouragement—witness the fact that Jewish students are far more likely than Gentile students to attend a college away from home and that the colleges they choose are farther away.

For all the talk of "smother love," therefore, Jewish sons appear to be emotionally freer and more independent of their parents than, say, Italian-Americans, who have a far more powerful sense of obligation. In Jewish culture, as the anthropologist Natalie F. Joffe has pointed out, giving almost always flows downward—from parents to children, rich to poor, learned to ignorant, old to young—and the obligations that result are complementary rather than reciprocal. Thus children are expected to repay their parents by showering love and "advantages" on their own children, not by taking care of their parents when the latter become old. It is not at all uncommon, in fact, for elderly parents to be virtually abandoned by their "successful" children; whole neighborhoods in South Miami Beach, Florida, Venice, California, and New York's Lower East Side are filled with such parents, who were portrayed movingly in Barbara Myerhoff's book and film *Number Our Days*. That this abandonment is not peculiar to affluent American Jews is evident from the *mayses* (folk tales) and Yiddish proverbs that elderly immigrants tell one another. "When a father helps a son, both smile," one Yiddish proverb has it; "when a son helps his father, both cry." "One parent can support ten children," another proverb goes, "but ten children can't support one parent."

4

A mystery remains nonetheless: Jews have not simply moved into the middle class or into professional occupations; in almost every field they have entered, be it crime or medicine, scientific research or real estate development, journalism or commodities trading, Jews have gravitated to the top.

ITEM: According to a study of the ethnic and racial backgrounds of people listed in the 1974–75 edition of *Who's Who in America*, Jews were two and a half times more likely to be included than members of the population at large. Relative to population, moreover, there were more than twice as many Jews as there were people of English heritage, the group that once dominated the American elite. The change over the preceding half century was striking: in 1924–25, people of English descent were nearly two and a half times as likely to be listed as American Jews.

ITEM: In a 1971–72 analysis of a much smaller group of leaders in some eight fields of endeavor, the sociologists Richard D. Alba and Gwen Moore found an even greater concentration. Of the 545 people studied, 11.3 percent were Jews—four times their proportion in the population as a whole.*

Because Jews are not distributed evenly across the occupational spectrum, overall figures such as these understate the impact Jews have had in the fields they do enter. Take business, for example, where Jewish representation in the elite is relatively modest—6.9 percent in Alba and Moore's group, which consists primarily of chief executive officers of the largest American corporations. Until recently, however, Jews with a talent for business have tended to go into business for themselves—in part because opportunities were limited in corporate management and in part because many preferred a more freewheeling style. Thus the Jewish representation among successful entrepreneurs is considerably higher than among corporate chief executives: some 23 percent of the people on the *Forbes* 1984 list of the four hundred rich-

* The phenomenon is not limited to the United States. Jews make up about 1 percent of the population of Great Britain, but 6 to 10 percent of the British elite; in Australia, where Jews are 0.5 percent of the population, they constitute 5 percent of the elite.

est Americans were Jews.* (If the *Forbes* 400 included only those who had built their own fortunes, the Jewish proportion would be closer to one third; Jewish mass immigration to the United States is so recent that there are no Jewish counterparts to the Du Pont family, 20 of whom (out of 1700 descendants) were worth enough in their own right ($150 million or more) to make the 1984 *Forbes* list, or the Rockefellers and Mellons (13 and 7 descendants, respectively).

It is in intellectual and cultural life, however, rather than in business that the ability of Jews to move to the top is most evident. Consider, for example, the composition of the American intellectual elite, which the sociologist Charles Kadushin of the City University of New York analyzed as part of a larger study of American leaders. Kadushin surveyed a group of leading intellectuals and asked them to identify the people who most influenced their thinking and, in their view, the thinking of their intellectual peers. Basing his conclusions on these "votes" as well as on an elaborate statistical count of articles and book reviews in the most influential intellectual magazines and journals, Kadushin defined the American intellectual elite as a group of 200 academicians, journalists, editors, novelists, and poets; half were Jews. Nor was this purely a function of New York City's preponderant role in American literary and intellectual life; the Jewish proportion was equally high among intellectuals living elsewhere. As a further refinement, Kadushin asked those he interviewed to rank the 200 in order of prestige and influence; of the 21 most eminent intellectuals, 15 were Jews.

Whatever the precise proportion (and one person's elite is another's coterie) there can be no doubt that Jews play a large role in American intellectual life. In 1975, for example, Jews constituted 10 percent of all faculty members but 20 percent of those teaching at elite universities; nearly half of the Jewish professors—compared to 24 percent of Episcopal and 17 percent of Catholic professors—were teaching at the top-ranked institutions. Jewish professors are also far more likely to publish articles in scholarly journals than their non-Jewish peers; thus Jews make up 24 percent of the academic elite—those who have published twenty or more articles.

Jews are equally prominent outside the academy. The thinking of the educated public is strongly affected, for example, by a relatively small number of literary and intellectual magazines and journals. Al-

* The precise proportion varies somewhat from year to year. In 1982, the first year the *Forbes* 400 was published, 105 of the group, or 26 percent, were Jews. The number dropped to 98 (25 percent) in 1983, when a stock market boom catapulted a number of newcomers onto the list, and 93 (23 percent) in 1984.

though there are some notable exceptions, such as William F. Buckley of the *National Review* and William Whitworth of the *Atlantic*, most of these publications are edited by Jews—William Shawn of *The New Yorker*, Robert Silvers and Barbara Epstein of *The New York Review of Books*, Irving Kristol and Nathan Glazer of *The Public Interest*, Stephen Graubard of *Daedalus*, Mitchell Levitas of *The New York Times Book Review*, Martin Peretz of the *New Republic*, Norman Podhoretz of *Commentary*, and Irving Howe and Michael Walzer of *Dissent*, to name just a few. Jews are almost as prominent in book publishing as well—an industry that was predominantly WASP in 1936, when *Fortune* examined it as part of its special issue, "Jews in America."

Nor is Jewish influence limited to the older of "the two cultures," to use the late C. P. Snow's term; 30 percent of American Nobel laureates in science have been Jews, and in the last fifteen or twenty years the proportion has been about 40 percent. Jews also account for a comparable proportion of the winners of other prizes and of the membership of the National Academy of Sciences. (In Great Britain, where Jews total 1 percent of the population, they make up 7 percent of the membership of the Royal Academy of Science.)

This preeminence has long fascinated students of intellectual life. In 1919, in a famous essay on the subject, Thorstein Veblen wrote:

> It is a fact which must strike any dispassionate observer that the Jewish people have contributed much more than an even share to the intellectual life of modern Europe. . . . It is not only that men of Jewish extraction . . . supply more than a proportionate quota to the rank and file engaged in scientific and scholarly work, but a disproportionate number of the men to whom modern science and scholarship look for guidance and leadership are of the same derivation. [Most important of all, Jews] count particularly among the vanguard, the pioneers, the uneasy guild of pathfinders and iconoclasts, in science, scholarship, and institutional change and growth.

In post-World War II America, certainly, Jewish scientists have tended to choose the branches of science that are on the cutting edge of intellectual discovery. Few Jews were attracted to astronomy, for example, until about twenty years ago, when the field suddenly exploded; now perhaps half the leading figures are Jewish. Much the same happened when biology, once concerned largely with classification, erupted with breakthroughs in microbiology, biophysics, biochemistry, and the like.

The explanation, Veblen argued, lies neither in the genes nor in Jewish culture, for it is "only when the gifted Jew escapes from the cultural environment created and fed by the particular genius of his own people, only when he falls into the alien lines of gentile inquiry and becomes a naturalised, though hyphenate, citizen in the gentile republic of learning, that he comes into his own as a creative leader in the world's intellectual interprise." The Jews who played the largest role in science and scholarship, that is to say, seemed to fall between two worlds: they had left the traditional Jewish community but had never been fully accepted in the Gentile world. It was this marginality, Veblen concluded, that accounted for their creativity: truly creative and enduring scholarship required both "exemption from hard-and-fast preconceptions" and "a skeptical animus"—and having abandoned one culture, with its preconceptions, without quite acquiring another, Jews had these qualities in greater abundance than those who were more rooted.

There is much to be said for Veblen's argument. Until recently Jewish intellectuals did tend to be "renegade Jews," as Veblen termed them; consider the portraits of Heinrich Heine, Bernard Berenson, and Walter Lippmann presented in Chapter Two. Even now, moreover, Jewish intellectuals often retain their sense of "otherness"—of feeling that they are not true insiders. But in contemporary America it is no longer accurate to argue, as Veblen did, that "it is by loss of allegiance . . . to the people of his origin that [the intellectual] finds himself in the vanguard of modern inquiry." Witness a Nobel laureate such as Rosalyn Sussman Yalow—"a Madame Curie from the Bronx," as *The New York Times* called her—who keeps a kosher home, or the growing number of intellectuals who are firmly rooted in and committed to Jewish tradition.

If they have not completely lost their sense of marginality—that is not likely to go until anti-Semitism disappears—most intellectuals, like most ordinary Jews, are now fully at home in both Jewish and American culture. Despite a widespread assumption that Jewish academicians are alienated from Judaism, for example, Steven M. Cohen's analysis of data from the 1975 Boston demographic study indicates that Jewish college professors are somewhat more likely to observe religious rituals than Jewish businessmen or salaried white-collar workers. And yet full acceptance has not (or not yet) diminished the intellectual achievements of Jews; as we have seen, their preeminence in intellectual and scientific life has grown in recent years, not declined.

Nor does Veblen's hypothesis account for the role Jews play in popular, as opposed to "high" culture, with one exception—comedy, where marginality and/or alienation does help explain the success Jews (and, more recently, blacks) have had. Comedy aside, most forms of popular entertainment would seem to require considerable empathy for mainstream thought and behavior, and Jews are as preeminent in theater, film, and television entertainment as they are in science and intellectual life.

ITEM: The Broadway musical, generally considered the most characteristically American theatrical form, has been largely an American Jewish creation. With a handful of notable exceptions, such as George M. Cohan and Cole Porter, the composers and lyricists who have given the Broadway musical its distinctive shape have almost all been Jews—people such as Jerome Kern, George and Ira Gershwin, Richard Rodgers and Lorenz Hart, Rodgers and Oscar Hammerstein, and, more recently, Alan Jay Lerner and Frederick Loewe, Marvin Hamlisch, and Stephen Sondheim. Even the exceptions have to be qualified to some degree: Cole Porter, who came from an upper-class WASP family, was powerfully drawn to Jewish liturgical music; "the secret of my success," he once told Richard Rodgers, "is that I write Jewish tunes."*

ITEM: The motion picture industry was largely a Jewish invention, and it remains a predominantly (although not exclusively) Jewish industry. In a study of the most influential writers, producers, and executives, the political scientists Stanley Rothman and S. Robert Lichter found that more than three out of five members of the "movie elite" are Jews. Not surprisingly, since television entertainment is in good measure an outgrowth of film production and is still closely connected with it, Jews make up almost as large a proportion of the "TV elite."

Marginality has contributed to their success, but in a way different from Veblen's conception. The principal consequence of Jewish marginality, the great Anglo-Jewish political philosopher and historian Sir Isaiah Berlin suggests, is not alienation but an intense desire for acceptance, which has led Jews to study their neighbors with almost obsessive care. Berlin likens the Jews of Europe to a group of travelers who have taken up residence among a tribe with whose customs they are not familiar. Since they are uncertain of their welcome—the "strangers" in Berlin's myth suspect that the host tribe may be as likely to expel as to accept them—they feel obliged to learn everything they can

* The composers of rock music, on the other hand, do *not* write "Jewish tunes," and Jews have played a much smaller role in that burgeoning field. More specifically, the historian E. Anthony Rotundo has suggested, words are unimportant in rock, whereas in the popular music Jews write, words are crucial, for the songs tell a story—and Jews tend to be storytellers. Jews also tend to be uncomfortable with the kind of raw and uncontrolled emotions and sensuality that are central to rock.

about how their hosts think and act. In the process the (Jewish) strangers

> become primary authorities on the natives; they codify their language and customs, they compose the tribe's dictionaries and encyclopedias, they interpret the native society to the outside world. . . . Hence the fantastic over-development of their faculties for detecting trends, and discriminating the shades and hues of changing individual and social situations, often before they have been noticed anywhere else. Hence, too, their celebrated critical acumen, their astonishingly sharp eye for the analysis of the past, the present, and sometimes the future also—in short, their well-known genius for observation and classification, and explanation—above all for *reportage* in its sharpest and finest forms. [Emphasis in original.]

To increase his understanding of what the host "tribe" wanted, in fact, Samuel Goldwyn, one of the greatest of the early movie moguls, used to sit in the front of a movie theater with his back to the screen, watching the audience's reactions to the film rather than the film itself. "If the audience don't like a picture, they have a good reason," he explained. "The public is never wrong."

It was, of course, more complicated than that; had Goldwyn and his contemporaries merely given the public what it already wanted, they would not have created an entire industry—one that transformed as well as reflected mass tastes. They were able to do so because of "their faculties for detecting trends, and discriminating the shades and hues of changing . . . social situations," to use Berlin's phrasing. The Jews who built the movie industry started out modestly enough, installing nickelodeons in saloons and other working-class haunts—a new business that required little capital to enter—and then graduating to distribution of the new "moving pictures." By the first decade of the century a number of them simultaneously recognized that the seedy environment in which films were shown would never attract the rapidly expanding middle class or the even larger upwardly mobile working class.

ITEM: Marcus Loew, a fur-factory worker turned nickelodeon owner, refurnished his Brooklyn amusement parlor and called it The Royal instead of Cozy Corner. In Chicago, Carl Laemmle, a former clothing salesman who owned a chain of nickelodeons, transformed his theaters into lavish White Fronts; and A. J. Balaban of Chicago displayed on the marquee of his theater a letter from Jane Addams of Hull-House attesting to the capacity of movies to educate.

It was not long before the new entrepreneurs began building "movie palaces" designed to appeal to rich and poor alike—more precisely, perhaps, designed to make the masses feel that they were rubbing elbows with (or at least getting the same treatment as) the rich. In New York, for example, William Fox, a former garment cutter, transformed the notorious Haymarket Saloon into a Greek temple-like movie house. These new theaters, with their uniformed ushers, lush carpets, and sweeping staircases, were so successful that films were soon in short supply; the Jewish entrepreneurs had to start producing their own films to keep their theaters operating. It did not take long for them to decide to change the product itself; by hiring Broadway stars to act in films that resembled plays, the new producers gave the movies a more cosmopolitan aura, completing the process of converting a lower-class medium of entertainment into one that appealed to all groups.

It was only after the fact, however, that all this seemed self-evident; established bankers were unwilling to lend to this new and rather disreputable industry, and the new film-makers had to turn to other sources of funds, such as A. H. Giannini's Bank of Italy (now known as the Bank of America, the nation's second largest) and the German Jewish partners of Kuhn, Loeb & Company. The growth of the movie industry was a classic instance of the ability of Jews to spot a trend invisible to others.

The growth of Jewish influence in journalism is a more complicated story. It is a highly sensitive subject as well, for anti-Semites traditionally have been as obsessed with Jewish "domination" of the mass media as with the Jewish role in international banking. According to his good friend Secretary of State John Hay, Henry Adams was "clean daft" on the subject of Jews and the press; to Adams, Hay remarked, "the Jews are all the press . . . I was amazed to see so sensible a man so wild." Henry Ford was equally daft; in his view, Jews "absolutely control the circulation of publications throughout the country," spreading "poisonous infections of revolutionary doctrines." More recently, Spiro Agnew complained that a "Jewish cabal" in control of the mass media was responsible for tilting American foreign policy toward Israel, and public figures as disparate as the Reverend Jesse Jackson and General George Brown, former chairman of the Joint Chiefs of Staff, have attacked Jewish "control" of the press.

Despite their prominent role in pre-World War II Austria, Hungary, and Germany, American Jews until recently were notable mainly for their absence from journalism. True enough, the three best-known political pundits of the prewar period—Walter Lippmann, David Lawrence, and Arthur Krock—were Jews, and so were the flamboyant and influential reporter and editor Herbert Bayard Swope, brother of Gerard Swope of General Electric, and reporters such as Ben Hecht and A. J. Liebling. But these men were exceptions to the rule. "Granted the great power of the movies in the influencing of modern society and the great influence of Jews in the movies," the editors of *Fortune* wrote in 1936, "it still remains true that the Jewish interest in journalism and advertising is extraordinarily small." When Leo Rosten surveyed the Washington press corps a year later in a pioneering study of the way the press shapes public opinion, only 4 of the 127 leading correspondents were Jews. (Although no data are available for the national press corps as a whole, it is doubtful that the Jewish representation came to more than 1 or 2 percent.)

In contrast to the situation in law, medicine, and academic life, moreover, Jews were not beating on the doors, trying to enter, for journalism, as Reuven Frank, retired president of NBC News, puts it, "was a scruffy occupation." "Going into journalism in those days was like going into the theater," says Richard Clurman, former chief of the Time-Life News Service. "It just wasn't respectable. It was not the kind of profession my grandparents would have sought for their children."

Understandably so, for journalism was not a profession at all; it was at best a craft, and a poorly paid one at that. It was also a largely dead-end occupation, with little intellectual challenge or satisfaction. Newspapers were concerned almost exclusively with local news—crimes, fires, riots, municipal politics, local scandals, and the like; by contemporary standards, even prestigious big-city papers such as *The New York Times* and the New York *World* carried remarkably little national or international reporting. Reporters, moreover, were precisely that—people who reported the facts of an event (the correct spelling of the names of the victims of a crime and the extent of their injuries or losses) to a rewrite man, who then wrote the story. Little education was required, and a college degree was often considered a handicap; reporters came from and for the most part remained firmly entrenched in the working class. As the syndicated columnist Joseph Kraft has written, "Nobody could have been attracted by the thought of becoming rich, or important, or powerful. Fame was not the spur."

For some, to be sure, journalism had a certain raffish appeal—witness the popularity of shows such as Ben Hecht and Charles MacArthur's 1930s hit *The Front Page*. The stage directions for that play, however, make abundantly clear why journalism was not a vocation to which upwardly mobile Jews were drawn. Hecht and MacArthur describe the pressroom in which the action occurs as "a bare, disordered room, peopled by newspaper men in need of shaves, pants pressing and small change. Hither reporters are drawn by an irresistible lure, the privilege of telephoning free. . . . Here is the rendezvous of some of the most able and amiable bums in the newspaper business; here they meet to gossip, play cards, sleep off jags and date up waitresses between such murders, fires, riots and other public events as concern them." They were, in fact, a hard-drinking, seedy, philandering crew for whom "scruffy" might almost be a compliment.

This was not the kind of life Jewish parents wanted for their children. "My parents told me that journalism was only for a bunch of drunks, and Jews are not drunks," says Mel Elfin, the fifty-six-year-old former chief of *Newsweek*'s Washington bureau. "Journalism was not an accepted vocation for a smart Jewish boy from Brooklyn." Parents also feared that journalism would not provide the independence that came from being a "professional." When Av Westin was adamant about taking a job with CBS Radio instead of going on to medical school, his family begged him to take a degree in engineering first. "That, at least, is a profession," they told him.

ITEM: But if some immigrants were opposed to their children's becoming journalists, other, more innocent parents were simply puzzled by the whole thing. "My Nathan is in the pen line," Nathan Glazer's mother told her friends in 1945 when her twenty-two-year-old son, now a sociology professor at Harvard, joined the editorial staff of *Commentary* magazine. She had no other way of explaining to her friends what it was that her son did for a living.

Parents know now what journalists do, for journalism has turned into a high-status profession. "This has been the best generation of all in which to have lived as a journalist in this country," Eric Sevareid said in his final broadcast as a CBS radio and television commentator. "We are no longer starvelings and we sit above the salt." Some sit higher than that. Journalists who work for "the imperial media," to use Joseph Kraft's term—the three networks, the public broadcasting service, the three largest newsmagazines, and the leading newspapers—have undergone "a startling transformation." "We have been among the principal beneficiaries of American life," Kraft explains. "We have enjoyed a huge rise in income, in status, and in power. . . . We have not merely been upwardly mobile, as the cant phrase goes. We have been shot from cannons. We have advanced almost overnight from the bottom to the top; from the scum of the earth . . . to the seats of the high and mighty. We have become a kind of *lumpen* aristocracy, affiliated, as priests at least, with the celebrity culture."

Some have become celebrities in their own right. There is no better measure of how far journalists have come, in fact, than the social distance that separates the "amiable bums" of Hecht and MacArthur's *The Front Page* from the heroic reporters portrayed in the film version of Robert Woodward and Carl Bernstein's best seller *All the President's Men,* in which Robert Redford played Woodward, Dustin Hoffman played Carl Bernstein, and Jason Robards played Ben Bradlee.

The catalyst for this change was World War II, which turned journalism into a growth industry and radically altered journalists' understanding of what constituted news. Suddenly what happened abroad mattered–mattered deeply–to Americans, who were glued to their radio sets when Edward R. Murrow was broadcasting from London. The number of reporters covering foreign and/or war news increased (fifteenfold, according to one informed estimate), and there was a qualitative change as well. The rise of Nazism and fascism made foreign reporting far more complex than it had been, turning journalism into an occupation that required a level of education and sophistication far beyond that possessed by the swashbuckling foreign correspondents of an earlier age.

The process accelerated in the postwar era. With the United States now the dominant world power, foreign news became increasingly important and complex, and the steadily expanding size and role of the federal government gave national affairs a journalistic weight they had never had before. The result was that journalism was transformed from an essentially provincial occupation into a cosmopolitan one, as newspapers devoted more and more of their space to national and international news.

This shift in the journalistic center of gravity was greatly accelerated by the emergence of the television networks as the dominant news medium. Because they aim for the largest possible national audience, the network news programs of necessity focus on national and international rather than local news, reserving the latter for occasional features, such as Charles Kuralt's *On the Road* series. (The reverse is true, interestingly enough, of local television news; in their preoccupation with crimes, fires, and other local disasters, the local TV stations have taken over the role once played by daily newspapers.)

All told, the once-scruffy vocation has become an intellectually exciting, reasonably well-paid, prestigious profession in which Jews play an increasingly important role. In 1982, for example, Jews made up a little less than 6 percent of the national press corps as a whole but 25 to 30 percent of the "media elite"–those working for *The New York Times*, the *Washington Post*, and the *Wall Street Journal;* for *Time*, *Newsweek*, and *U.S. News & World Report;* and for the news divisions of CBS, NBC, ABC, and the Public Broadcasting System and its leading stations. (A 1971 study put the number of Jews in the media elite at 26 percent.)

When one looks at the key decision-making positions, the Jewish role appears to be even larger.

ITEM: At *The New York Times,* the country's "newspaper of record" and probably its most influential, Jews now hold all seven of the top editorial positions listed on the paper's masthead. To be sure, the *Times* is a Jewish-owned paper, but until the late 1960s it was harder for Jews to rise to the top at the *Times* than at almost any other paper; the proprietors deliberately avoided putting Jews in positions of editorial leadership for fear of being labeled a "Jewish paper." "We have never put a Jew in the showcase," Arthur Hays Sulzberger, then the *Times*'s publisher (and son-in-law of its owner), told Arthur Krock in 1937 when Krock protested the fact that John Finley rather than Krock himself had been appointed editor of the editorial page. Sulzberger's son, Arthur Ochs Sulzberger, who became publisher in 1963, consciously abandoned his family's policy a few years later. In 1976, "Punch" Sulzberger, as he is known, appointed A. M. Rosenthal executive editor—the paper's top editorial position—and made Max Frankel editor of the editorial page.* "Dad was more concerned with the perception [of the *Times* as a Jewish paper] than I am," Sulzberger told me. "It's a different world now, and this is a different company." "Punch is enormously comfortable in his own skin," a senior executive told me. "He doesn't have his father's hang-ups."

ITEM: The Wall Street Journal, flagship of the Dow-Jones Company, is anything but Jewish-owned; it is, however, the largest daily newspaper and in some ways the best. Three of the *Journal*'s four top executives are Jews: Warren Phillips, the chief executive officer; Associate Publisher Peter Kann; and Managing Editor Norman Perlstine. Of the three leading papers only the *Washington Post* has a non-Jew, Benjamin Bradlee, as editorial chief; but there is no shortage of Jews in the top ranks of the *Post.*

ITEM: Jews are equally influential, if less well known, in the management of television news. It is the network correspondents, of course, who have become household names, among them Jews such as Mike Wallace, Morley Safer, Bernard Goldberg, and Morton Dean of CBS; Marvin Kalb and Irving R. Levine of NBC; and Herbert Kaplow,

* Rosenthal's use of initials instead of his first name, Abraham, is a relic of the earlier regime's self-consciousness. Rosenthal sounded Jewish enough in its own right, *Times* editors felt, without compounding the problem by using "Abraham" in a by-line.

Barbara Walters, and Ted Koppel of ABC. The greatest concentration of Jews, however, is at the producer level—and it is the producers who decide which stories will go on the air, and how long, and in what order they will run. In 1982, before a shift in assignments, the executive producers of all three evening newscasts were Jewish, as were the executive producers of CBS's *60 Minutes* and ABC's *20/20*. And Jews are almost equally prominent at the "senior producer" and "broadcast producer" levels as well as in senior management. When Reuven Frank stepped down as president of NBC News in 1984, for example, he was replaced by Lawrence Grossman, who left the presidency of PBS to take the position.

Sir Isaiah Berlin's myth about the perennially curious and anxious "strangers" is a useful starting point in understanding how Jews moved from being journalistic outsiders to insiders. Because they are *supposed* to be detached—journalists pride themselves on their "objectivity"—some Jews, at least, start with an edge, growing out of their residual sense of marginality. As Richard Cohen, a columnist for the *Washington Post*, puts it, "Jews are foreign correspondents in their own country." Cohen had not felt that way, interestingly enough, when he was a political correspondent for the *Post*, but when he began writing his column, he discovered that his readers saw him not as a journalist but as a *Jewish* journalist. "If I wrote about baseball," Cohen told me, "people would say I was writing from a Jewish perspective."

For most Jewish journalists, however, journalism has been the royal road to acceptance.

ITEM: "One thing happened to me when I became a journalist," says Hal Bruno, a veteran newspaper and newsmagazine reporter who now directs political coverage for ABC News. "I broke out of the ghetto." "Journalism had great appeal to me as a means of entering the larger world," Max Frankel of *The New York Times* told me. "You can be interviewing ambassadors in five years and presidents in ten." The German-born Frankel, who came to the United States in 1940 when he was ten, started working for the *Times* while still in college and became the paper's Moscow correspondent before his thirtieth birthday; he has served as White House and State Department correspondent as well as Washington bureau chief.

ITEM: "The great and near-great have all spoken here," Mel Elfin of *Newsweek* told a forum at the Women's National Democratic Club in Washington in introducing the main speaker, Marvin Kalb of NBC-TV. "This room reeks of history, and we have a Melvin from

Brooklyn introducing a Marvin from Washington Heights. That's what democracy is all about."

There are other attractions as well. "*Yikhus* [prestige], *tzedakah* [good deeds], and a yenta [gossip] quality explain it best," says Elfin. Journalists, that is to say, are gossips and storytellers at heart; they are eager to improve the world (surveys show this to be a major reason students are attracted to journalism), and they enjoy hobnobbing with famous and powerful figures. (The wholly unpretentious Elfin was pleased when Henry Kissinger called to congratulate him on his son's bar mitzvah.) "Journalism is history on the run," is the way Richard Cohen puts it. "It's a great way of seeing events, of being there, of being part of history." "I am not a distant spectator to history," said Lawrence Meyer, a *Washington Post* reporter. "I'm involved in it." And journalists are involved in a way that is particularly appealing to Jews, who have often seen themselves as the passive objects of history; journalism involves something of a reversal of roles, since journalists are writing about events instead of being the ones written about.

Journalism's appeal was enhanced by the fact that entry was so easy: precisely because journalism was such a low-status occupation, media owners had never erected the kinds of barriers that existed in such prestigious fields as law, medicine, and academic life. And whatever residual prejudice there may have been was offset by the need for talent; as Marvin Kalb puts it, "You can't say no to quality."

Entry was easiest of all in television news. "TV had a tough time getting people from radio," Reuven Frank, who came to NBC-TV in 1950 from the *Newark Evening News*, explains. "People didn't think TV would last." Understandably so, for television's cumbersome technology made it appear ill suited to the demands of daily journalism. Because of the enormous size and weight of the early equipment, it was hard to get to the scene of a news event, and because live coverage required days of advance planning, stories were usually shot on 16-millimeter film, which had to be shipped to New York to be developed, a process that often took several days. And so the nightly newscasts initially were produced as a sop to the Federal Communications Commission; the networks did not take the programs seriously until the middle 1950s, and it was not until 1963 that CBS and NBC expanded their newscasts to thirty minutes. (ABC waited until 1968.)

In those early years, therefore, it was relatively easy to get hired and even easier to move up, for there were as yet no conventions about who was qualified or even what the qualifications were. "No one would be hired today with the qualifications I had," Reuven Frank told me with a smile; or, as Av Westin put it, "I was the first kid on the block." Because staffs were small, moreover, and unions had not yet insisted on precise job descriptions for each position, the "first kids" handled almost every job, inventing the techniques as they went along. Don Hewitt, who took charge of the CBS evening news in 1950 at age twenty-five, developed many of the techniques that turned television news into a distinctive journalistic form; before Hewitt's innovations, TV newscasts resembled the old movie newsreels. Others, if not quite as precocious, had similar careers: Reuven Frank became executive producer of NBC nightly news in 1954, four years after he had joined the network, and Westin moved up almost as rapidly. "When I started," Westin explains, "it was a free ball; I was lucky to ricochet around."

PART TWO

A Jewish Success Story

CHAPTER FIVE

"I HAD NOT KNOWN HOW DEEPLY JEWISH I WAS."

1

Clearly, the transformation of American society has been good for American Jews, who have flourished as never before. Indeed, the opportunities that American society provides have attracted Jewish immigrants from Israel, as well as from virulently anti-Semitic countries such as the Soviet Union and Iran, and countries such as South Africa, where Jews fear that their currently comfortable position may be short-lived.

But what about the well-being of *Judaism?* Can the religion and culture of American Jews flourish as well as the Jews themselves, or will the openness of American society mean Judaism's gradual (or even rapid) withering away? Will Jews continue to be Jews if they have another choice?

The answer is far from self-evident. In the past, Jews remained Jews for one of three basic reasons: because they believed that was what God demanded of them; because they were born into an organic community with powerful sanctions and rewards; or because anti-Semites would not permit them to become anything else.

None of these factors can be relied upon today. Although American Jews are keenly aware of anti-Semitism, there no longer is enough of it to hold the community together; in the 1970–71 National Jewish Population Survey, only a little more than one respondent in ten agreed with the statement that "being Jewish is forced on Jewish people mainly by what non-Jews think and do." Nor is being Jewish forced upon Jews by their own community; because membership is voluntary, the Jewish community can exert no sanctions over those who leave. And leaving is now easy: the openness of American society means that Jews can simply drift away into the larger community—a dramatic reversal of the situation in the past, when Jews had to take some decisive action in order to stop being Jewish. Today, in contrast, Jews have to act in order to remain Jewish, for being Jewish is simply one choice among many. Even in the seemingly closed communities that Hasidic Jews have created in the Williamsburg, Crown Heights, and Boro Park sections of Brooklyn, a different life-style is only a haircut, a shave, and a subway ride away.

Except for those who live in Boro Park and its counterparts elsewhere, moreover, relatively few American Jews still believe in a God who makes demands on them; even fewer regard those demands as binding. On the contrary, most Jews, including a good many Orthodox Jews, are highly selective about the religious laws they obey, choosing to observe some while ignoring others. It is difficult to live in the modern world without exercising *some* selectivity. What distinguishes one Jew from another, therefore, is less the exercise of choice than the degree of selectivity they exercise—the number and range of the religious obligations they choose to fulfill—and the consequent guilt (or lack of guilt) they feel.

In this regard Jews are no different from members of other religious groups, every one of which has had to grapple with the consequences of living in a religiously pluralistic society. The essence of modernity, as the sociologist Peter L. Berger has pointed out, is that it brings about "a near-inconceivable expansion of the area of human life open to choices." In traditional societies people inherited their occupations, their status, their residences, their religions, and, more often than not, their husbands and wives; in the modern world all of these, and more, are matters of individual choice. In the past, Berger argues, heresy—from the Greek word meaning "to choose"—was a possibility; in the modern world it is a necessity. "Modernity creates a new situation in which picking and choosing becomes an imperative."

The movement from fate to choice—"the heretical imperative," as Berger calls it—has plunged every religion into crisis, but Judaism more so than most; for a world in which choice is inescapable threatens

Judaism's definition of itself. "It was, indeed, not quite of their own free will that [the children of] Israel declared themselves ready to accept the Torah," a Talmudic midrash (legend) about the giving of the Ten Commandments declares, "for when the whole nation approached Sinai, God lifted up this mountain and held it over the heads of the people, saying to them: 'If you accept the Torah, it is well; otherwise you will find your grave under this mountain.' "

There is no more mountain overhead, nor are there hosts of angels with crowns of fire, ready to hurl them at Jews who do not choose to remain Jews; the ancient covenant is now voluntary. American Jews inhabit a freer, more open society than any Diaspora Jews have ever lived in before; those under the age of forty or thereabouts belong to the first generation in history for whom Judaism appears to be an option rather than a burden or fate—the first generation able to choose whether or not to be Jewish "of their own free will."

What choice are they making?

As I will demonstrate in this chapter and the two that follow, most Jews are choosing to remain Jews—some kind of Jews, if not necessarily the kind their parents or grandparents were. To read the American Jewish press, however, or to hear the speeches at most meetings of most Jewish organizations, one would think that American Jews are choosing to abandon their Jewishness, that Judaism is in danger of disappearing in the United States. A "disaster is in the making," Elihu Bergman, then assistant director of the Harvard Center for Population Studies, wrote in 1977; by the year 2076, Bergman predicted, there would be no more than 944,000 Jews in the United States—down from 5.7 million—and there might be as few as 10,420. Despite the fact that the demographers whose projections Bergman used disavowed his forecast—their own prediction was that the American Jewish population would be stable for the rest of this century and then would decline gradually to a total of 3 to 4 million in 2076—American Jewish leaders have embraced Bergman's dour vision as if it had been carved in granite.*

In part, to be sure, this sort of pessimism is rooted in the Jewish

* "I am unaware of any convincing refutation of Leibenstein and Lieberman's procedures or their conclusions," a distinguished biblical scholar wrote in the Aug./Sept. 1982 issue of *Midstream*, referring to Harvey Leibenstein and Samuel Lieberman, the demographers whom Bergman had cited in his 1977 article. In fact, the refutation had come from Lieberman himself, along with a colleague, Morton Weinfeld, in their 1978 *Midstream* article. The projections Bergman used, Lieberman and Weinfeld explained, had been an arithmetic exercise, designed to organize discussion of the issues involved; the projections had been based on a host of unrealistic or, in some cases, demonstrably incorrect assumptions.

temperament; the tendency to look on the gloomy side is satirized in a famous line from the Yiddish play *The Dybbuk*, in which a character remarks, "Let's talk about happier things–how is the cholera epidemic in Kiev?" Among American Jews still close to their Eastern European roots, as among a number of other immigrant groups, there is a deep-rooted, if unconscious, belief that good fortune is always precarious. To mention it, therefore–to speak of one's own (or a friend's) good health, say–is an act of hubris that may invite retaliation by the omnipresent evil spirits. To prevent that intervention, many first- and second-generation American Jews will not offer a compliment or mention good fortune without adding the phrase *kayn aynhorá* (or *kineahora*), a contraction of the Yiddish words meaning "no evil eye"; more acculturated Jews "knock wood" instead, acting out the ancient (and universal) belief that noise will frighten evil spirits away. (Americans of all ethnic groups use noisemakers on New Year's Eve, when the spirits are supposed to be particularly rampant.)

But fear of disappearing is not just a vestige of an old and rapidly disappearing folk culture; it grows out of the Jewish historical experience. "The world makes many images of Israel," the great historian Simon Rawidowicz wrote, "but Israel makes only one image of itself–that of a being constantly on the verge of ceasing to be, of disappearing." Indeed, Rawidowicz referred to the Jews as "the ever-dying people," for "there was hardly a generation in the Diaspora period which did not consider itself the final link in Israel's chain."

Until the late eighteenth century, pessimism about the future was primarily a response to the hostility that Judaism so often evoked–an understandable fear that conquest, persecution, poverty, inquisitions, and pogroms would take their toll and that those who survived the ordeal of the moment would find it too difficult to continue as Jews. The obsession with disappearance, Rawidowicz suggested, served as a protective device: because Jews were always anticipating the end, "no catastrophe could ever take this end-fearing people by surprise . . . still less to obliterate it–as if Israel's incessant preparation for the end made this very end absolutely impossible."

With Emancipation the locus of fear shifted: the threat to Jewish survival seemed to come not from oppression but from its absence. When the ghetto walls were breached and European Jews began to enter the modern world–as we saw in Chapter Two–Western thought and culture appeared superior to Judaism in almost every respect. The result was a massive and almost universal failure of nerve; no important segment of Jewry was exempt from the fear that in free and open competition with Western, Christian culture, Judaism would be bound to lose. At times the fear seemed to be well grounded. In late eighteenth- and early nineteenth-century Germany, for example, where baptism was the ticket of admission to society, many upwardly mobile Jews were willing, even eager, to pay the price. "With every day that passes, we see how religion declines among our co-religionists," Saul Ascher, a Berlin journalist, observed in 1792. "Every day we see the number of apostates increasing."

In France, where Jews had gained political equality much earlier than in Germany, Jews also appeared to be abandoning Judaism—not for Christianity but for one or another of the new secular faiths. "The grandfather believes, the father doubts, and the son denies," an observer named Ben Levi wrote in 1840 in the earliest formulation of the "three-generations hypothesis"—the notion that members of a minority group are likely to lose their group identity over the course of three generations. "The grandfather prays in Hebrew, the father reads the prayer in French, and the son does not pray at all," Ben Levi continued. "The grandfather observes all festivals, the father observes Yom Kippur, the son does not observe any. The grandfather is still a Jew, the father has become an Israelite, and the son is simply a deist . . . unless he is an atheist, a Fourrierist, or a Saint-Simonist."

In the United States apostasy never was a significant phenomenon; Jews had tickets of admission to American society without having to be baptized. But the same openness that made baptism unnecessary made assimilation easy; the trend was so advanced, Joseph Lyons, of Savannah, Georgia, declared in 1820, that "certainly a synagogue will not be found in the United States fifty years hence."

Lyons, of course, did not anticipate the mass migration of initially devout German Jews, which increased the Jewish population of the United States from approximately 3000 in 1820 to 50,000 in 1850 and 150,000 a decade later. "Synagogues are springing up as if by magic," Isaac Leeser of Philadelphia, the religious and intellectual leader of the older Jewish community, reported in 1848; "the country is filling up with Jews." But as we saw in Chapter Two, it did not take long for the immigrants to shed their religious observances; the speed with which the German Jews assimilated made the three-generations hypothesis seem eminently reasonable once again. "Within fifty years," one commentator wrote in 1872, "the grandchildren at the latest will be indistinguishable from the mass of humanity which surrounds them. . . . Of that ancient people only the history of their perils and their sufferings will remain, and the story of the change which came over them in an enlightened age."

Others painted a similar picture. "Since the downfall of the Jewish monarchy there has been no age and no country in which the Israelites were more degenerate and more indifferent toward their religion than in our age and our country," Rabbi Bernard Illowy, one of the first Orthodox rabbis to come to the United States, declared in 1862. "Yes, run through the streets of all our large congregations and seek whether you can find ten men . . . who still adhere faithfully to the faith of their fathers."

Pessimism about the future was not limited to the Orthodox rabbinate. "You sit back, resting on your laurels, and are unaware of the disaster that is threatening you and your descendants," Rabbi Judah Magnes told the members of New York's Temple Emanu-El in 1910 in a sermon that led to his resignation as rabbi of the congregation. "For we have no youth, no young Jews and Jewesses, to take the place of the elders. Let each family of the congregation ask itself where the young are, and the answer will be, not within the congregation, but outside of it, indifferent to it; and faithless and disloyal to Judaism."

Nor did staying within the congregation ensure survival; with Sabbath services shifted to Sunday in many temples and conducted entirely in English in almost all of them, Reform Judaism seemed to be moving toward a merger with liberal Protestantism. "A prominent Christian lawyer of another city has told how he entered this building at the beginning of a service on a Sunday morning and did not discover that he was in Synagogue until a chance remark of the preacher betrayed it," Magnes told his congregants. "The old tree that brought forth many beauteous blossoms is almost stripped of its foliage, and one by one the golden autumn leaves are falling as the older men and women . . . pass to their rest."

But the old tree was blossoming again as a result of the infusion of a new group of Jews—this time from Eastern Europe. Indeed, the mass immigration of Eastern European Jews gave American Jewish life an intensity it had never had before. But the new immigrants applied the same intensity to the process of acculturation, and it did not take long for new forecasts of doom to be heard. To strict traditionalists any change was threatening, even the tendency of younger rabbis to preach sermons in English rather than in Yiddish. English sermons, the eminent Rabbi Jacob David Willowsky declared, "simply make the Jewish people like the rest of the nations. If these practices will not cease, there is no hope for the continuation of the Jewish religion."

Others had more realistic fears as the young seemed to drift away from their religion and culture. In 1924, using language remarkably similar to that in the French newspaper of 1840, a Yiddish newspaper in New York lamented the loss of religious commitment among Eastern European Jews. During the recent High Holiday season, the editors remarked, "Three generations rejoiced: The old—over the Torah;

the middle-aged—over the business page in the newspaper; the young—over the sports page."

Today the fear is more intense. "For all that we are preoccupied by the damage once done us by our enemies, we are still more concerned by the curse of friendship we now encounter," Leonard Fein, editor and publisher of *Moment* magazine, told the Conference of Jewish Communal Service in 1980 in a speech from which I quoted in Chapter One. "Deep down—and sometimes not so very deep—we still believe that we depended on the pogroms and persecutions to keep us a people, that we have not the fiber to withstand the lures of a genuinely open society. It is seduction, not rape, that we fear the most, and nowhere is the seducer more blatant, less devious, than here in America."

Far more is involved than just the failure of nerve that Fein satirizes; the fact is that an open society poses more of a challenge to Judaism than to other "ethnic churches." For example, first- and second-generation Norwegian or German-American Lutherans may be upset, even scandalized, when their children or grandchildren choose to worship in English rather than in Norwegian or German or when they drop other old-country customs, but Lutheranism itself is not affected—at least not in any fundamental way. The Lutheran Church (or the Italian or Polish Catholic Church) can withstand the weakening, perhaps even the disappearance of the ethnic identities of its members, for the connection between religion and ethnicity is coincidental rather than intrinsic.

Not so with Judaism, which, as we have seen, has never distinguished the religious from the ethnic and cultural realms. This fact insulates Judaism against a loss of religious faith—Jews remain Jews whether they accept the Jewish religion or not—but it makes Judaism far more vulnerable to cultural assimilation. Because there can be no Judaism without Jews, anything that reduces the number of Jews or weakens their attachment to their Jewishness poses a threat to Jewish survival; hence the intense and ancient Jewish fear of intermarriage and assimilation.

It is not surprising, therefore, that when the barriers that had kept Jews separate disappeared, the old fear of Judaism's demise intensified. In the two centuries since Emancipation began, the historian Arthur Hertzberg has written, "a generational clock has ticked away over and over again in the open society. Whether in New York and Philadelphia in 1840, in Paris and Bordeaux in the 1850s, in Budapest around the turn of the century, in Berlin and Vienna in the 1920s, and now in the United States . . . it tells the same frightening time. The third generation in the open society intermarries and erodes out of Judaism at a rate of one in three."

And by the fourth and fifth generations the falling away occurs at a massive rate, making American Jewry an endangered species. Judaism has survived until now, Hertzberg argues, only because the generation-by-generation erosion was offset from time to time by the arrival of a new group of religious immigrants, who set the "generational clock" ticking all over again, or by an outbreak of anti-Semitism, which led to a temporary intensification of Jewish identity among native-born Jews.

Neither remedy is available any longer: there is not enough anti-Semitism left to keep Jews Jewish, and it is hard to imagine an increase large enough to do so. More important, in Hertzberg's view, Hitler's "Final Solution" foreclosed the possibility of any new stream of immigration capable of breathing new life into American Judaism; the Jewish communities of Poland and Hungary no longer exist, and after sixty-five years of Soviet rule, Russian Jews are largely ignorant of Jewish religious ritual and practice. To the question "Will the Jews continue to exist in America?" Hertzberg says, "the answer must be in the negative. History, sociology, and the emptiness of contemporary Jewish religion all point in the same direction."

Hertzberg's apocalyptic answer is, of course, part of the tradition Rawidowicz described, in which forecasts of Judaism's imminent disappearance are intended to persuade Jews to return to the fold. Hertzberg is a rabbi and communal leader as well as a historian, and he wears all three hats when he assesses the Jewish future.

And yet the question he raises cannot be dismissed out of hand; it is, in fact, part of a larger scholarly debate over the role of ethnicity in American life. For thirty years or more scholars have differed over the strength and durability of ethnic groups—over whether their distinctive mores can withstand the lures of the dominant culture and whether American society is richer or poorer for the presence of these groups.

During the 1950s, for example, scholars announced the disappearance of ethnicity as a significant factor in American life. In his enormously influential book *Protestant-Catholic-Jew*, published in 1955 (see Chapter Three, pp. 108–109), Will Herberg argued that religion had replaced ethnicity as the locus of group identity. In Herberg's scheme of things, ethnicity was a brief and transitory stage through which immigrants and their descendants passed on their way to becoming Americans of the Protestant, Catholic, or Jewish persuasion. In accordance with what has come to be called straight-line theory, assimilation was seen as an inexorable historical trend that proceeds, generation by generation, until each ethnic group is fully absorbed into the larger society. Herberg recognized, of course, that American Jews were something of a special case—that is, they were both a religious and an ethnic group. But he argued that the ethnic factor was receding—that, like Italian and Polish Catholics, Jews were abandoning their distinctively ethnic ways and becoming a community whose members differed from other Americans only in the religion they professed.

Like the reports of Mark Twain's death, Herberg's obituary for ethnicity was greatly exaggerated; less than a decade later Nathan Glazer and Daniel P. Moynihan surveyed the field and announced that ethnicity was alive and well and flourishing in New York. "The point about the melting pot," they wrote, with only partial exaggeration, "is that it did not happen." True, the assimilating power of American society profoundly changed the cultures immigrants brought with them, but the fact that ethnic cultures had been transformed into something other than what they had been in the old country did not make them any less distinctive or identifiable—or any less significant to those adhering to them.

The result was a new appreciation of the complexity of the relation between acculturation and ethnic survival. A principal weakness of straight-line theory, one of its advocates, the sociologist Herbert Gans, acknowledges, is that it ignores the fact that immigrants brought two kinds of ethnic cultures with them—secular and sacred; they were Catholics as well as Italians or Poles, or in the case of Jewish immigrants, Jews in both a religious and an ethnic cultural sense. Although acculturation and assimilation have affected both sacred and secular cultures, their impact has been greater on the latter than on the former.

Most important of all, perhaps, the proponents of straight-line theory ignore the fact that ethnicity may remain, even though the original European heritage disappears; after five generations in the United States, Gans concedes, German, Irish, and Scandinavian Americans have retained a distinctive ethnic identity. One reason is that the United States has become increasingly hospitable to ethnic differences. "The changes that the immigrants and their descendants wrought in America now make it unnecessary for ethnics to surrender their ethnicity to gain upward mobility," Gans has written. "At the same time, the larger society also seems to offer some benefits for being ethnic. Americans increasingly perceive themselves as undergoing cultural homogenization, and whether or not this perception is justified, they are constantly looking for new ways to establish their differences from each other." Indeed, "now that it is respectable and no longer a major cause of conflict," ethnicity seems "to be ideally suited to serve as a distinguishing characteristic."

The result is something of a paradox: Americans retain their ethnic identities even as they lose the culture on which it was once based. Instead of returning to the ways of their grandparents or great-grandparents, younger "ethnics" are adopting what Gans calls "symbolic ethnicity"—ways of identifying with the group that do not interfere with full participation in American society. Members of the third and fourth generation are less interested in *being* ethnic, Gans suggests, than in *feeling* ethnic; the old concern with ethnic organization—with membership in the group—is being replaced by a new emphasis on identity.

Stripped of its polemics—whether contemporary ethnicity is "symbolic" or "real" is more a semantic than a substantive issue—Gans's position substantially narrows the terms of the debate. The question at issue is not whether acculturation and assimilation are going on; of course they are. Nor is it whether these processes affect ethnic cultures; of course they do. It is impossible to live in a society without adopting some of its mores and values.

The issue, in short, is not *whether* but *how:* in what ways acculturation and assimilation are affecting American Jews, Judaism (the religion of the Jews), and Jewishness (their ethnic culture), and what the significance of these changes may be for the future of Jewish life in America. For questions such as these, straight-line theory turns out to be an inadequate and in some ways misleading guide to what is happening.

To begin with, ethnic vitality does not require isolation, nor does assimilation necessarily mean disintegration or loss of élan. On the contrary, the most creative periods in Jewish history generally have been those in which Jews have had close and prolonged contact with other cultures.

ITEM: The Talmud—after the Bible, Judaism's most sacred document—was the creation of highly acculturated Babylonian Jews, who lived in a Diaspora analogous in many respects to the American one. Samuel, one of the two most influential Talmudic rabbis, was noted for his knowledge of medicine and astronomy, the two most highly regarded sciences in Babylonian society. For the most part, Babylonian Jews lived in close and constant contact with non-Jews, whose language and customs they adopted.

ITEM: Moses Maimonides (1135–1204), the greatest religious authority of the post-Talmudic period, was personal physician to the sultan of Egypt and a medical educator of great renown; translated from the original Arabic into Latin, his medical texts and treatises were used in European medical schools until the seventeenth century. Maimonides was a distinguished philosopher as well; his *Guide of the Perplexed*, in which he tried to reconcile traditional Jewish thought with the dominant Aristotelianism of the Middle Ages, influenced Catholic thinkers such as Thomas Aquinas, as well as all subsequent generations of Jewish scholars.

Taking everything together, the history of Judaism, as Jacob Neusner has put it, is "the history of the assimilation by the Jews of the cultural, social and religious traits characteristic of their neighbors." Indeed, it is precisely because of their ability to adopt the mores of the societies in which they have lived without losing essential continuity with the past that Jews have been able to maintain their identity as a separate and distinct group. In some periods, to be sure, assimilation has weakened or even threatened the community, but over the long sweep of Jewish history, as Gerson Cohen, chancellor of The Jewish Theological Seminary of America, has argued, assimilation has been the key to Jewish survival.

2

Let us turn, then, to the question at hand: in what ways are American Jews assimilating, and what are the consequences for the future? Specifically, is American Jewry an endangered species, as Hertzberg and others suggest?

My answer is no. Implicit in Hertzberg's (and most other) forecasts of inevitable decline is the notion that the present represents a fall from some prior state of grace. It does not—not because third- and fourth-generation American Jews are paragons of religious virtue, but because members of the first and second generation were not. In fact, the Eastern European immigrants were less observant and considerably less committed to traditional Orthodox ways than our highly romanticized picture of them suggests. There were exceptions, of course, but in general, the Jews who came to the United States were the least religious members of their communities. They had to be, to withstand the imprecations of their rabbis, who warned them not to leave home for a godless and trefa (impure) land.

ITEM: In *The Rise of David Levinsky*, Abraham Cahan's epic novel of adjustment to American life, the protagonist, a student of Talmud in Eastern Europe, describes the scene when he tells his *rebbe* (teacher) that he is thinking of leaving for the United States. "To America!" the rabbi shouts. "Lord of the World! But one becomes a Gentile there."

For many immigrants, including Cahan's fictional hero, attachment to Orthodox law had weakened well before they set out for the New World. "My former interest in the Talmud was gone," David Levinsky says, recalling the time just before his journey to America. "The spell was broken irretrievably. . . . Then it was that the word America first caught my fancy."

In short, the stereotype of Eastern European Jews as living in a time capsule, immune to modern secular culture, is wide of the mark. As Nathan Glazer has written: ". . . socialism, Zionism, and other radical secular political movements flourished among the East European Jews, particularly among those who moved to the cities from the small towns. There were Zionist socialists who wanted to set up a socialist state in Palestine; national socialists who wanted socialism with minority rights for the Jews in eastern Europe; and antinational socialists who simply wanted socialism and assumed, following Marx, that the Jews . . . would disappear once socialism was established." Nor did that exhaust the range of secular movements in which Jews were caught up. Among other groups, Diaspora nationalists wanted to become a separate nation within Eastern Europe, territorialists wanted a separate state elsewhere, and assimilationists simply wanted to disappear as Jews.

Economic pressures, meanwhile, forced many Jews to leave their homes and seek a living elsewhere, a process that also loosened ties to tradition. Before settling in New York, my wife's maternal grandfather spent several years as a seaman on a merchant vessel; David Toback, grandfather of the writer Carole Malkin, spent ten years traveling through Bessarabia and the Ukraine, working on the land and as a forester, pants presser, shopkeeper, and scribe, among other trades, before moving to New York.

By the time they arrived here, therefore, many, perhaps most immigrants were ready to give up their religious observances, if they had not done so already. For some the first step was to shave their beards and sideburns and adopt American styles of dress—a seemingly trivial change with enormous emotional resonance.

ITEM: "It was as though the hair-cut and the American clothes had changed my identity," David Levinsky recalls, of the end of his first day in New York. It was, in fact, more than just a change in identity; "it was a second birth," one that represented the culmination of the estrangement from tradition that had begun while he was still in Europe. (The symbolism involved in this change can be appreciated if we recall the intense emotions that were aroused during the 1960s when members of the youth culture took to wearing blue jeans and long hair.)

Superficial changes seemed important, moreover, because the beleaguered Eastern European rabbinate often failed to distinguish between folkways, such as the long black coat that Hasidic Jews still wear, and the requirements of Jewish law. Guided by the dictum that "all that is new is forbidden by the Torah," the rabbis spoke as though the slightest deviation from tradition was a lapse into heresy. This often persuaded immigrants that if they dropped one practice, they might as well abandon the rest—all the more so because most had learned only the practices of Judaism, not its theology or rationale. Orthodoxy "is absolutely inflexible," David Levinsky remarks in explaining why a change in dress had such a large impact on his religious beliefs. "If you are a Jew of the type to which I belonged when I came to New York and you attempt to bend your religion to the spirit of your surroundings, it breaks. . . . The very clothes I wore and the very food I ate had a fatal effect on my religious habits."

"Jews lost their faith so easily," Nathan Glazer explains, "because they had no faith to lose: that is, they had no doctrine, no collection of dogmas to which they could cling and with which they could resist argument. All they had, surrounding them like an armor, was a complete set of practices, each presumably as holy as the next." But once the armor was pierced, the immigrants were left unprotected.

And some changes in behavior were anything but trivial. The injunction to "remember the Sabbath day, to keep it holy" is one of the foundation stones on which Judaism is built; more than almost any other religious practice, the fact that Jews abstained from work on Saturday helped them retain their separate identity. ("More than the Jews kept the Sabbath," the early-twentieth-century essayist Ahad Ha-Am declared, "the Sabbath kept the Jews.") In the ghettos of Eastern Europe it had been easy to observe the Sabbath, for the whole world seemed to shut down at sundown on Friday. America, however, imposed a heavy economic penalty on Sabbath observance; with the six-day work week universal, Jews often had to choose between working on the Sabbath and earning less than a living wage or in some cases forgoing a job altogether.

Whatever else the "world of our fathers" may have been, therefore, it was not a golden age of Jewish religious life. Nor was it simply a matter of having to work on the Sabbath; in their eagerness to see their children take advantage of the opportunities the public schools afforded, the immigrants, who often had had only a rudimentary Jewish education themselves, did not attach a high priority to their children's religious education. In 1909, when immigration from Eastern Europe was at flood tide and New York Jewry was a predominantly first-generation community, only 25 percent of Jewish elementary school-age children were receiving any Jewish education at all—hardly signifying a religiously committed community, given the traditional Jewish emphasis on religious education and study. Twenty-five years later, during my own childhood, the proportion was no higher. Indeed, the synagogue my family and I attended—the largest and most prestigious Orthodox congregation in the country (its senior rabbi was the unofficial "chief rabbi" of New York)—offered no religious schooling at all; my frequently unemployed father engaged private tutors to instruct my brother and me.

Not surprisingly, young Jews of my generation tended to be indifferent to Judaism, as well as uninformed about it; according to a 1935 survey of fifteen-to-twenty-five-year-olds, most of them the children of immigrants, fully three quarters had not attended any religious service at all during the preceding twelve months. Today, by way of comparison, only 40 percent of young Jews report that they never go to synagogue; and one Jewish child in two receives at least some Jewish education.

How, then, did the stereotype of the pious Eastern European immigrants arise?

The answer lies in the complex relation between religion and ethnicity in Eastern European immigrant culture. In Western Europe the prospect of emancipation had led Jews to redefine themselves as a religion rather than as a nationality; they saw themselves as Frenchmen or Germans whose religion happened to be Judaism. In Eastern Europe, by contrast, emancipation was not a possibility—hence Jews defined themselves as Jews who happened to be living under Russian or Austro-Hungarian rule. In this they were no different from members of other national/cultural/linguistic minorities, such as Ukrainians, Poles, Slovaks, or Georgians, for whom religion was an intrinsic part of their ethnic identity.

This is not to suggest that Jewish immigrants were indifferent to religion as such. There were some, to be sure, who opposed religion on principle—those who had been caught up in one of the socialist or secular Zionist movements in Eastern Europe. But most immigrants tended to observe a number of traditional religious rituals: in 1917, for example, two thirds of New York city's Jewish families patronized kosher butcher shops. Even nonbelievers often lit Sabbath candles, bought kosher meat, and went to synagogue on the High Holidays and the anniversary of a parent's death, doing so out of habit rather than conviction.

As soon as they arrived, moreover, the immigrants formed their own synagogues, as much to meet their social as their religious needs; in Eastern Europe, after all, the synagogue had been a house of assembly as well as of prayer and study. Indeed, the sheer number of synagogues that were formed indicates that the impulse was more social and cultural than religious. Often meeting in a tenement room, these tiny congregations gave people from the same town or big-city neighborhood a place to gather, reminisce, and help each other in time of grief or need. As Irving Howe wrote in *World of Our Fathers:*

> In the communal life of the immigrants the synagogue, or *shul*, remained the single institution everyone took for granted. Despite the rise of secularist ideologies and the spread of a weary indifference among the masses, few could envisage a time when the *shul* would cease to be the center of Jewish life. God could easily be neglected in New York, it was probably not His favorite city, yet He was not at all forgotten. While only a minority continued to follow the rituals with literal exactness, the aura of faith, which is also to say, the particulars of old-world Jewish culture, remained strong in the nostrils of the immigrants.

It was that old-world Jewish culture, or Yiddishkeit (Jewishness), as it was called, that was primary; religious observances grew out of an ethnic and cultural far more than a religious impulse, although this was not a distinction the immigrants would have made or even understood. Buying kosher meat, lighting Sabbath candles, eating matzoh during Passover, reading a Yiddish newspaper or attending a Yiddish play, belonging to the Arbeiter Ring (Workmen's Circle) or some other fraternal order were all manifestations of Yiddishkeit, ways of maintaining one's identity as Jews. Even anti-religious immigrants, an observer remarked around the turn of the century, "relax their atheism on Yom Kippur."*

In short, irreligious and anti-religious, no less than religious immigrants lived in an intensely Jewish ambiance. Vivian Gornick of *The Village Voice* conveys this atmosphere in her description of the East Bronx neighborhood of her childhood.

> Although my parents were working-class socialists [and thus ideologically opposed to religion], the dominating character-

* Much the same is true in contemporary Israel: the secularists who throng to the beaches on Rosh Hashanah stay home or go to synagogue on Yom Kippur.

istic of the streets on which I grew up was Jewishness in all its rich variety. Down the street were Orthodox Jews, up the street were Zionists, in the middle of the street were shtetl Jews, get-rich-quick Jews, European humanist Jews. Jewishness was the great leveler. On *Pesach* [Passover] and Yom Kippur we did not have to be "observing" Jews to know that we were Jews. The whole world shut down, every one dressed immaculately, and a sense of awe thickened the very air we breathed; the organic quality of the atmosphere told us who we were, gave us boundary and idiomatic reference, shaped the face of the culture in which each one of us assumed a vital, albeit primitive, sense of identity.

That kind of Jewishness could never have survived the disappearance of the immigrant milieu on which it was based, all the more so because there was such an enormous educational gulf between parents and children. "It was in the very nature of the life" she led as a child, Gornick observes, "that even while one was being nourished by it, one was straining to separate from it," to become part of the larger, American world. As we have seen in the preceding chapter, the separation began early, with the parents' acquiescence, and even encouragement, when children first went to school. Irving Howe recalls:

> At the age of five I really knew Yiddish better than English. I attended my first day of kindergarten as if it were a visit to a new country. The teacher asked the children to identify various common objects. When my turn came she held up a fork and without hesitation I called out its Yiddish name, a *goopel.* The whole class burst out laughing at me with that special cruelty children can have. That afternoon I told my parents I had made up my mind never to speak Yiddish to them again, though I would not give any reason.

The gulf became almost impassable when children went off to college. Philip Roth's Alexander Portnoy tells his analyst:

> Back in my freshman year in college, when I was even more the son struggling to make the father understand, I remember that I tore the subscription blank out of one of those intellectual journals I had myself just begun to discover in the college library, filled in his name and our home address, and sent off an anonymous gift subscription. But when I came sullenly home at Christmas to visit and condemn, the *Partisan Review* was nowhere to be found. *Collier's, Hygeia, Look,* but where was his *Partisan Review?* Thrown out unopened—I thought in my arrogance and heartbreak—discarded unread, considered *junk*-mail by this schmuck, this moron, this Philistine father of mine!

Nor was it simply the arrogance of college freshmen that created a distance between parents and children; those who entered the professions inevitably became strangers to their parents. ". . . often in later years—after I had become a writer and an editor and was living only a subway ride away but in a style that was foreign to her and among people by whom she was intimidated," Norman Podhoretz has written, his mother "would gaze wistfully at this strange creature, her son, and murmur, 'I should have made him for a dentist.' " The fact that the parents had encouraged their children's mobility did not make the process any less poignant. "The father had pride in his American-born son that by its very nature could not be reciprocated," the novelist Anne Roiphe has written of her psychiatrist husband's father. "His victory was that his son was a stranger."

But if the old-world Jewish culture was disappearing, Jewishness was not. On the contrary, generation-by-generation changes in Judaism or Jewishness are not all of a piece; they sometimes move in opposite directions. By focusing on a few measures of religiosity or ethnicity, such as the use of Yiddish or observance of the dietary laws, one can produce a picture of straight-line decline. But to look *only* at these and to ignore the increased observance of other rituals or the emergence of new ways by which American Jews express their Jewishness is to provide a distorted picture of what is happening.

For all their determination to live in "good"—middle-class—neighborhoods, members of the second generation also preferred to live with other Jews; even those who were uncomfortable with their identity were reluctant to abandon it altogether. "The second-generation community, located in the better neighborhoods of the city, emulated the structure of the general community," Judith R. Kramer and Seymour Leventman wrote in *Jews of the Gilded Ghetto*, a study of generational change in Minneapolis (or "North City," as they called it). "Yet it retained its fundamentally ethnic character. It was, in effect, a gilded ghetto whose social life was carried on exclusively with Jews of appropriate status. The institutions were all middle-class, but the participants were all Jewish. Thus Jews organized their own Boy Scout and Girl Scout troops for the children; and if Gentile adults joined the American Legion or the Rotary or Kiwanis clubs, Jews joined the Jewish War Veterans association and organized business lodges of B'nai B'rith."

In some large cities, moreover, the new neighborhoods where second-generation Jews settled had even higher concentrations of Jews than the ones they had left. In 1920, for example—the beginning of a decade of extraordinary geographic mobility—a little more than half of New York's Jews lived in neighborhoods that were at least

40 percent Jewish; by 1930 nearly three quarters lived in neighborhoods with that degree of concentration. "Participation in the myriad aspects of New York culture did not mark the decline of Jewish life—as some had feared and others had hoped," Deborah Dash Moore writes in *At Home in America,* her history of second-generation New York Jews. "Rather, as they became middle-class New Yorkers, second-generation Jews created the framework for their persistence as an ethnic group. . . . they tailored their physical and institutional environment to make possible an ethnic communal alternative to assimilation. In doing so, they used acculturation to serve survivalist ends."

The result was something of a paradox: Jewishness flourished, while Judaism tended to wither, especially after the first blush of enthusiasm had worn off. When the new neighborhoods were built during the 1920s, synagogues went up as well—many of them "synagogue centers" designed to lure the young with swimming pools, gymnasiums, and social programs. With rare exceptions, however, only the older people came, and before long they too were staying away; synagogue membership hit a historic low during the 1930s, when only one family in four had any formal affiliation.

Jewishness, however, was in the air people breathed. Compared to most Jewish neighborhoods of the 1930s, Manhattan's Upper West Side, where I grew up, was a highly assimilated community, yet it had a palpable Jewish ambience. All but three or four of my elementary school classmates were Jewish—even the Gentile students stayed home on the major Jewish holidays—and there was no mistaking the clientele the local businesses were set up to serve. The restaurants were Jewish restaurants, the bakeries were Jewish bakeries, and the appetizing stores sold Jewish delicacies; even the shops whose wares had no ethnic character were mostly owned by Jews. (My favorite was the local tailor, whose sign read "J. Teitelbaum, French Cleaner.")

In such an atmosphere most Jews did not worry about Jewish continuity and so felt little need to belong to a synagogue or to provide their children with more than a rudimentary Jewish education, if that. To the extent to which people thought about Jewishness, their concern was not how to ensure its survival but how to escape its all-embracing grasp. The result, as Nathan Glazer has written, was that "one could live a completely Jewish life from a sociological point of view and yet have no connection with any Jewish institution, religious or non-religious. It was here, in other words, that one could have only Jewish friends, eat Jewish foods, follow Jewish mores and culture patterns, and yet have little consciousness of being a Jew."

That was not the case in the suburbs, to which Jews flocked after the end of World War II; there the consciousness of being a Jew suddenly came to the fore as Jews found themselves living in predominantly Gentile communities and neighborhoods. More was involved than just a shift from being part of the majority to being a tiny minority, for the Gentiles were usually different from those with whom Jews had had contact before. There had been non-Jews in the old neighborhoods, to be sure, but with rare exceptions they had been fellow "ethnics"—working-class Irish, Italian, and Polish Catholics who were as much outsiders as the Jews. In the immigrant Bronx neighborhood in which she grew up, Kate Simon has written, "Italians were really sort of Jewish." In other neighborhoods Gentiles may have been feared in a physical sense; my nose was broken as a child when my friends and I tried to flee the tougher, more physical Irish gang that "raided" us once a year to establish the fact that the streets belonged to them and that we played hockey and stickball only on their sufferance. But because the Gentiles occupied a lower position on the social ladder, Jews usually were not concerned with gaining their approval.

Suddenly, however, the Gentile neighbors were "Americans"—white Protestants rather than fellow ethnics; they were insiders in an age in which Jews still felt themselves to be outsiders, and they occupied the same if not a higher social class. In this environment Jews felt awkward and ill at ease, and they were eager—in fact, anxious—to gain their neighbors' approval. Studying the Jewish community of Park Forest, Illinois, one of the first (and largest) of the new postwar suburban housing tracts, in the early 1950s, Herbert Gans found that Jews almost invariably described themselves as "sticking out" in the "mixed community," as they described it, to which they had moved. (Jews made up no more than 10 percent of the total Park Forest population.)

Instead of atrophying, Jewishness was strengthened, for it was redefined along far more self-conscious—and far more religious—lines. Jews who had never thought about their Jewishness or who had done so only to reject it, Jews who were anti-religious on principle, Jews who had not been inside a synagogue in years—all such Jews suddenly found themselves joining and even organizing synagogues, which sprang up wherever Jews moved. Harry Gersh, a former trade union official turned Jewish communal executive, recalls in a 1954 essay that in the socialist, highly secularized milieu in which he had been raised, going to synagogue was a monumental act of nonconformity. But in the suburbs to which he and his friends had moved, *not* going to synagogue, or at least not *belonging* to one, had become the deviant act. "The synagogue symbolizes the most important change in the move to Suburbia," Gersh writes, "a change in our concept of ourselves as Jews."

The change was as profound as it was unexpected. "In moving from city to suburb, we had, if only subconsciously, a vision of a less 'Jewish' existence," Gersh says. This was not, in his view, a running away from Jewishness; it was an attempt to escape the ghetto and its particularism and to enter the larger, more universal world. But "here [in the suburbs], there are fewer of us. We are a measurable, countable quantity. Perhaps we feel the return of a fear we thought we had lost, or, if not quite that, then a certain anxiety." And so the new suburbanites sought the company of other Jews, who were most easily found in the synagogues and Jewish community centers that, often to their surprise, they found themselves joining. "In seeking a less 'Jewish' existence, no matter how subtly expressed," Gersh wryly concludes, "we find in Suburbia a more 'Jewish' existence."

The reasons were complex and varied. Had the Jews of suburbia merely wanted the company of other Jews, they might have built Jewish community centers, but not synagogues; in fact, they built both synagogues and community centers. One reason was that this was what the Gentiles expected of them, or what the Jews felt they had to do to win the respect of the Gentiles; Americans, to repeat, are more accepting (and more understanding) of religious than of ethnic differences. Building a synagogue was also a socially acceptable way for Jews to announce—to themselves, no less than to the rest of the world—that they had arrived. "We need a synagogue so they'll have more respect for us, to show that we have arrived, that we're not merely a bunch of individuals," the leader of the first effort to build a synagogue in Park Forest told Herbert Gans.

The result was not just a boom in synagogue construction; the buildings that were erected were often on a grander scale than those of the recent past, as Jews turned to architecture to express their new status in American life. In the 1920s, for example, when Jews had begun moving to Highland Park, a predominantly upper-class WASP suburb of Chicago, they organized a Reform congregation; reluctant to call attention to themselves, they built a modest sanctuary in an inconspicuous location. In the early 1960s, by which time there were four other synagogues in Highland Park, the congregation had outgrown its building and decided to erect a new sanctuary more in keeping with its sense of itself. They hired a nationally known architect, who designed what the sociologist Marshall Sklare describes as "a building of cathedral-like proportions," on the grounds of what had been a magnificent lake-front estate. The new synagogue, which became a tourist attraction for visitors in the Chicago area, was, as Sklare says, "the antithesis of its predecessor. While the old building was unobtrusive," Sklare explains, "the new one cannot be ignored.

The statement it conveys is that Jews no longer need to act as a fearful minority, afraid to display their wealth and achievements. By proclaiming the existence of the Jewish community to the community-at-large, the new building signifies that the Jews on the Heights have come out of the closet. The statement it makes is that Jews must now be accepted as equals."

More was involved, however, than just an attempt to impress the Gentiles or to gain their approval; geometric increases in synagogue membership were registered in new but predominantly Jewish suburbs, such as the Kew Gardens, Forest Hills, and Rego Park sections of Queens and Baltimore's Pikesville, as well as in predominantly Gentile areas, such as Highland Park. "Unlike sections of Nassau and Suffolk counties, which lie to the east beyond the city's limits, there is little of the frontier about Queens; except, perhaps, in one respect," Morris Freedman, a *Commentary* editor, wrote in 1955. "For many families, settling here seems to have involved a new adventure in Jewishness, expressing itself in formal affiliation, for the first time in their lives, with a Jewish community institution."

The impulse, again, was less religious than ethnic and national. The new suburbanites desperately wanted to be full members of American society, but it was not until that desire began to be realized that they discovered how much they wanted to remain Jews as well. Most important of all, they discovered how much they wanted their children to be Jewish, and they realized that this was not something they could take for granted, still less leave to chance. "When your street, counting both sides, has twenty houses, twenty families, and only one other than your own is Jewish, you wonder and worry," Harry Gersh writes in his 1954 essay. "How will the child know that he is Jewish and what it is to be a Jew? So we look about the house and take inventory. My wife doesn't *bench licht* [recite the blessings over the Sabbath candles] and I don't own a *tallis* [prayer shawl]. The *mezuzah* is gone from the door. (In the city there was always one left from tenant to tenant.) So outside our telling him so, and the occasional Jewish *meichel* [food], how will he know?"

It was a question most Jewish parents asked. The answer was usually the same—to enroll the children in Sunday school or afternoon Hebrew school; and given the way fees were usually structured, that meant joining a synagogue as well. In Park Forest in the early 1950s, 85–90 percent of the eligible Jewish children were enrolled; enrollments were substantial, if not quite that high, in predominantly Jewish neighborhoods as well. As Gersh remarks, "Most parents' knowledge of Judaism is nine parts feeling and one part fact." That feeling could not easily be transmitted to the children, for it was the unconscious product of the old extended family system, as well as of the old ethnic neighborhoods. When I was growing up, for example, we lived within walking distance of seven of my mother's eight brothers and sisters and all four of my father's siblings. It was taken for granted that Saturday afternoons would be spent visiting grandparents, great-aunts and -uncles, and assorted other relatives. By the time my children were born, however, family members were scattered throughout the New York metropolitan area. In short, the extended family system and the old neighborhoods disappeared together as family members began to go their separate ways in a social and psychological, as well as a geographic, sense.

Because suburban parents had had little or no religious education themselves, they usually were too ignorant of Judaism to answer their children's questions or to offer explanations before the questions arose; they turned to rabbis, teachers, and other professionals to make certain that the children "knew they were Jewish." But not *too* Jewish; parents were often at great pains to explain to the rabbi or religious-school principal that they did not want their children's religious education impinging on their own lives.

What the parents wanted, in other words, was not that their children should be religious but that they should be Jews—that they should think of themselves as Jews and, most important, that they should marry other Jews, so that the chain of Jewish peoplehood would not come to an end. Quite apart from religious school, therefore, children were caught up in a web of social activities designed to keep them in contact with other Jews and thus (or so it was hoped) reduce the likelihood of their marrying non-Jews later on. "Intellectually, many of us will maintain that the religion of the girl our son brings home is of minor importance. (It's of greater importance in the boy our daughter brings home)," Harry Gersh writes. "But this is not an intellectual business. Our inheritance from *Bube* and *Zeide* [Grandma and Grandpa] outweighs liberal logic. Common interests, common backgrounds, chances of conflict—whatever rationalizations we use—we prefer that our children marry Jews. This you do not leave to chance."

The result was an upturn in religious observance that surprised the participants themselves as well as most observers. The same concern that persuaded parents to enroll their children in religious schools and in synagogues and community-center social programs led them to adopt at least some religious rituals at home. The most popular rituals were those connected with Passover and Chanukah, which had long been the most child-centered Jewish festivals, but there was some increase too in the number of Jews lighting Sabbath candles on Friday nights. "I don't believe in it myself," parents would say while lighting

Sabbath candles or preparing a Passover seder, "but I want it for the children." Judaism, Nathan Glazer remarked in 1957, was "being re-created for the children."

3

The phenomenon that Glazer observed was the ultimate vindication of Mordecai Kaplan's once controversial notion of the centrality of Jewish peoplehood. In the traditional view, Judaism is primary: the Jewish people exists—indeed, was called into being—to serve its religion—to carry out God's will. In what he called "a Copernican revolution in [his] understanding of Judaism," Kaplan argued that, in reality, the relationship ran the other way. To Kaplan, peoplehood was primary; since Judaism was the creation—the religious civilization—of the Jewish people, "the Jewish religion existed for the Jewish people and not the Jewish people for the Jewish religion."

This, in any event, was how American Jews were behaving. Without having heard of Kaplan, they were acting out his thesis, adopting and adapting their religion to serve the ends of Jewish survival—of Jewish peoplehood. The old forms of Jewishness, after all—what the immigrant generation called Yiddishkeit—were on their way out, where they had not disappeared completely, for all the reasons discussed above. "And if these forms of being a Jew were no longer possible," Nathan Glazer asked, "what was left but religion? If, that is, one wanted to be a Jew."

And that, in fact, was what most Jews wanted—for themselves, they discovered to their surprise, as well as for their children. The catalytic event was the Six-Day War of June 1967 and, even more, the four weeks that preceded it, when it looked as if Israel was about to be destroyed. Indeed, it would be hard to exaggerate the impact these events had on Jewish consciousness. Because they were such a watershed in the development of Judaism and Jewishness, a brief chronology is in order before turning to the response itself.

• Although tensions had been building for several months, the crisis formally began on May 15, 1967, when Egypt mobilized its army. Two days later Egyptian President Gamal Abdul Nasser ordered the United Nations to withdraw its troops from the Sinai, where they had patrolled the Egyptian-Israeli border, and from the Straits of Tiran, where their job had been to ensure the free passage of ships to and from Israel. U.N. Secretary General U Thant quickly complied with Nasser's demand, despite the fact that the United Nations Emergency

Force, as it was called, had come into being in 1956 as part of the agreement by which Israel had withdrawn its troops from the Sinai peninsula. (In the same agreement the United States had joined with the other "Great Powers" to guarantee Israel's right to free passage through the Straits of Tiran.)

• By May 20 Egypt had massed some 100,000 troops and more than 1000 tanks along its borders with Israel; two days later the Straits of Tiran were closed to all ships going to and from Israel.

• On May 26 Nasser proclaimed that his goal was nothing less than the total destruction of the Jewish state; other Arab leaders announced their support of what some called a "holy war." "When the Arabs take Israel, the surviving Jews will be helped to return to their native countries," Ahmed Shukairy, head of what was then called the Palestine Liberation Army, declared, "but I figure there will be very few survivors."

• On May 30 King Hussein of Jordan flew to Cairo and signed a formal treaty placing Jordanian troops under Egyptian command. Iraq quickly followed suit, moving its troops into Jordan; Syria mobilized its army; Saudi Arabia offered financial and moral support; and troop contingents arrived in Egypt from countries as far away as Kuwait and Algeria. By June 2 or 3 Israel was surrounded on all three sides by Arab armies totaling 250,000 troops, 2000 tanks, and 700 bombers and fighter planes.

While all this was happening—while Arab leaders were massing their armies and promising "to drive the Jews into the sea"—Western political and religious leaders were silent, when they did not appear to be cheering the Arabs on. Warning Israel against taking military action, French President Charles de Gaulle imposed an embargo on the shipment of arms to the Middle East; since France until then had been Israel's principal supplier of weapons, and the Soviet Union had given Nasser almost a blank check for weapons purchases, de Gaulle's "even-handed" action hurt only Israel. Israel's attempts to solve the crisis through diplomatic measures were met with stony silence. In the United States, as in most other Western countries, individual religious leaders issued strong statements in support of Israel, but the churches themselves remained neutral, refusing to distinguish between Israel's claim to a right to exist and Arab claims to the right to destroy her.

To American Jews—indeed, to Jews everywhere—it appeared as though another Holocaust was in the making; equally important, it looked and felt as though once again the world would sit idly by while Jews marched to their death. Before 1967 American Jews had paid little attention to the Holocaust of the 1940s. Some, perhaps, felt guilty over their inability to prevent the dreadful event or, failing that, to rescue more than a handful of people; others needed the healing balm of time before they could come to terms with what had happened; most were simply too caught up in their own lives and in the exciting move from the margins of American society to its mainstream.

Whatever the reasons, the Holocaust was rarely mentioned; nor did American Jews display any interest in reading or teaching their children about the dread events. Before Elie Wiesel's searing memoir of his life at Auschwitz, *Night,* was published in the United States in 1960, more than a half dozen publishers had rejected the manuscript; although the book had already been published to critical acclaim in France, American publishers doubted that it would find an audience in the United States. (*Night* has subsequently sold more than a million copies and is now widely used as a text in Jewish religious schools.) And although the Eichmann trial in 1961, which turned the Holocaust into front-page news in American newspapers, had made it impossible for Jews to repress the events altogether, discussion of the Holocaust remained desultory even among theologians, who, with a few notable exceptions, ignored the subject or included it under the traditional rubric of "the problem of evil." When *Commentary* conducted a symposium on "the condition of Jewish belief" in 1966, for example, its editors did not so much as mention the Holocaust in the five long questions it sent to the participating rabbis and theologians, nor did more than a handful of the thirty-eight respondents raise the question on their own.

In May and June of 1967, however, the Holocaust was on almost every American Jew's mind; the result was an outpouring of emotion unlike anything they had ever experienced. "At first, anxiety and tension were commonplace," the historian Lucy Dawidowicz wrote in 1968 in an essay on the reaction to the war. "As the crisis deepened, irritability and nervousness became more marked." Glued to their television sets at home and transistor radios in the streets, Jews found it hard to think about anything else. When the war itself began—Israel launched a preemptive attack on June 5, virtually wiping out the Arab air forces in three hours—the hunger for news became insatiable. "The volume of transistor radios on New York's streets, rattling off news reports and bulletins, seemed sometimes almost to drown out the city's habitual noises," Dawidowicz wrote.

Nor was this simply a matter of intellectual curiosity; Jews were emotionally involved in a way they would not have thought possible a few months earlier. "In those days many of us felt that our own lives were in the balance," the late Abraham Joshua Heschel wrote shortly after the war had ended, "and not only the [lives] of those who dwelt in the land; that indeed all of the Bible, all of Jewish history was at stake. . . . The world that was silent while six million died was silent again, save for individual friends. The anxiety was grueling, the isolation was dreadful. . . . *I had not known how deeply Jewish I was* [emphasis is added]."

"I had not known how deeply Jewish I was!" This was the response, not of some newcomer to Judaism or casual devotee but of the man whom many, myself included, consider the greatest Jewish spiritual leader of our time. Others made the same discovery about themselves. "I must confess surprise over the depth of my own feelings," Rabbi Richard Rubenstein, another distinguished theologian, wrote. "There are unconscious depths to the phenomenon of Jewishness which even those of us who have spent our lives in its study cannot fathom."

Most Jews experienced the same surprise. "As soon as the Arab armies began to mass on the borders of Israel during the third week in May, 1967, the mood of the American Jewish community underwent an abrupt, radical, and possibly permanent change," Arthur Hertzberg wrote in the August 1967 issue of *Commentary*. ". . . the immediate reaction of American Jewry to the crisis was far more intense and widespread than anyone could have foreseen. Many Jews would never have believed that grave danger to Israel could dominate their thoughts and emotions to the exclusion of everything else; many were surprised by the depth of their anger at those of their friends who carried on as usual, untouched by fear for Israeli survival and the instinctive involvement they themselves felt.

"This outpouring of feeling and commitment appears to contradict all the predictions about the evaporating Jewishness of the American Jews," Hertzberg concluded, forgetting in his excitement that one of the gloomiest predictions had come from his own pen. (Hertzberg had first set forth the version of straight-line theory presented above in an essay published in 1964.)

American Jews were surprised by their own reaction because before 1967 they had seen Israel as an object of charity rather (or more) than as an integral component of their own identity. Judging by the 1966 *Commentary* symposium, for example, Israel's creation had had as little effect on theologians as the Holocaust. Despite the fact that for nearly two thousand years Jews had built their synagogues to face toward Jerusalem, and pious Jews had prayed for the restoration of Zion six times a day (in morning, afternoon, and evening prayers and in the grace recited after each meal), *Commentary*'s editors did not ask whether or how the creation of a Jewish state had affected Jewish belief; nor did the respondents—not even the six who subsequently settled in Israel—raise the question on their own. As Nathan Glazer had written in 1957 in the first edition of his *American Judaism*, "The two greatest events in modern Jewish history, the murder of six million Jews by Hitler and the creation of the Jewish state in Palestine, have had remarkably slight effects on the inner life of American Jewry."

In 1967 the effects were profound: American Jews felt as if their own fate was bound up with that of Israel, and they responded accordingly. The "outpouring of feeling and commitment" that resulted took a number of forms, the most unexpected, perhaps, being a turn to visible political action. Until then American Jews had been guided for the most part by the old Eastern European Jewish dictum, "Never criticize the czar." Fearful of evoking an anti-Semitic backlash, they had usually eschewed public demonstrations and protests, preferring to work quietly behind the scenes; after the creation of the state of Israel in 1948 American Jews had been careful to avoid any charge of "dual loyalty." In May and June they threw caution to the wind, turning into "a passionate, turbulent, clamorous multitude," as Lucy Dawidowicz put it. "We lost our cool completely," Leonard Fein wrote. "We begged, we pleaded, we demanded, we insulted, we threatened, we promised, we were aggressive, petulant, temperamental."

Jews responded in more traditional ways as well. When the war began they flocked to the synagogues—less to pray, however, than to be together with other Jews and to contribute money in support of Israel. "It seemed as if there was nothing American Jews could do except give money. This they did on a sacrificial level," Lucy Dawidowicz wrote, with some rhetorical exaggeration. For the 50 percent or so who gave to the Israel Emergency Fund of the United Jewish Appeal, giving money was not simply an act of charity, it was a way of enlisting in Israel's struggle for survival, of becoming a participant instead of a passive spectator. Large numbers of people, in fact, brought their contributions to the campaign offices in person, as if mailing a check was too easy; by coming themselves, they seemed to feel, they were participating in a physical way. Between May 22 and June 10, $100 million was collected, most of it in cash rather than in pledges; for the year as a whole, American Jews contributed $317.5 million to the joint campaign conducted by the UJA and local federations—nearly two and a half times the amount collected the year before. Of that total the UJA received $241 million—nearly four times its 1966 allocation—and another $190 million was raised through sales of Israel bonds. "The UJA didn't raise money," Herbert Friedman, its executive head, remarked, "it took it in."

The UJA was able to "take it in" on this scale because an extraordinarily effective fund-raising apparatus was in place already, one whose techniques had been honed over the preceding quarter of a century. The United Jewish Appeal had been created in 1939 in response to the crisis posed by the Nazi persecution of German Jews. Until then the Joint Distribution Committee and the United Palestine Appeal, the largest organizations providing assistance to Jews outside the United States, had conducted separate fund-raising appeals each year, competing bitterly with each other; attempts to create a united Jewish appeal had failed repeatedly because of animosity between the two groups.* But after the infamous Kristallnacht (night of broken glass) of November 10, 1938, when Nazi thugs burned synagogues and smashed the windows of Jewish-owned stores throughout Germany, and Hermann Göring's subsequent demand that German Jews pay the government an "indemnification" of more than seven billion marks, American Jewish communal leaders decided that only a united fund-raising campaign could raise the amount of money needed to assist European Jewry.

The pressure to eliminate the fund-raising competition came from the heads of local Jewish federations, which already had revolutionized fund-raising in their own communities. In a growing number of cities, federations had organized a single, united campaign to replace the separate fund-raising drives conducted each year by Jewish hospitals, community centers, family service agencies, old people's homes, and other Jewish-sponsored health and welfare agencies. Creation of joint campaigns had significantly lowered fund-raising costs and increased total revenues while saving large contributors the annoyance of being solicited by a number of different organizations. In the process, federations were becoming the dominant force on the local scene, for their control over fund raising had given them increasing power over the allocation of funds and thus over communal planning.

* The American Jewish Joint Distribution Committee (JDC), the larger of the two, had been established during World War I to provide assistance to European Jews, who suffered terrible dislocations during and after the war. The United Palestine Appeal (UPA) had been established in the early 1920s to help the tiny but growing Jewish community in Palestine. The competition between the two organizations was more than financial; there was a vast social and ideological gulf between the UPA, dominated by ardently pro-Zionist *Yidn*—first- and second-generation Eastern European Jews—and the Joint Distribution Committee, the favored organization of the non- and anti-Zionist *Yahudim*—the highly acculturated (and far more affluent) third- and fourth-generation German Jews. In the early 1930s the latter had also established a third UJA beneficiary, the National Coordinating Committee for Aid to Refugees and Emigrants Coming from Germany (NCCR), whose name was later changed to the National Refugee Service.

Formation of the Council of Jewish Federations and Welfare Funds in 1932 had stimulated the growth of federations—by 1939 there were approximately 135 in existence, compared to 50 in 1932 (there are some 225 today)—and made the federation heads a force to be reckoned with on the national scene; the CJF's General Assembly became a kind of annual summit meeting of communal leaders. A month before Kristallnacht, in fact, the CJF leaders had urged the Joint Distribution Committee, United Palestine Appeal, and National Refugee Service to join with them in creating a new kind of Jewish Welfare Fund drive, whereby the federations would raise money for overseas as well as for local needs, allocating the total take according to a formula agreed upon beforehand. After Kristallnacht the need to find havens for Jewish refugees from Germany made the ideological divisions between Zionists and non-Zionists seem less pressing; the latter agreed that Palestine would have to be developed as a refuge for Jews who could find no haven elsewhere, and the former reluctantly accepted the need to settle refugees in any country that would accept them.

The result, in early 1939, was the creation, on a one-year trial basis, of the United Jewish Appeal for Refugee and Overseas Needs. The trial was successful—in 1939 the UJA raised nearly $15 million, twice as much as had been collected by the separate campaigns the year before—but the agreement fell apart in late 1940 when the UPA refused to accept the same allocation (23 percent) for the 1941 campaign. Under pressure from CJF leaders, who recognized that support for the upbuilding of Palestine was a prerequisite for a successful campaign, the three relief agencies agreed to a "reconstituted" United Jewish Appeal in March of 1941, with a higher quota for UPA. The agency has continued ever since; by the end of World War II the joint campaigns had raised over $250 million, $124 million of it for the UJA.*

It was in the early postwar period, however, that the UJA became a powerful force in Jewish communal life. Meeting in Atlantic City in mid-December of 1945, the fifteen hundred delegates attending a national conference of the United Jewish Appeal for Refugees, Overseas Needs and Palestine, as it was now called, voted unanimously to mount a campaign to raise $100 million for UJA in 1946—more than triple the amount raised in 1945.

When Henry Montor, the executive head of both the UJA and the UPA, had first proposed a $100 million campaign, lay and profes-

* In New York City the ideological gap between Zionists and non-Zionists could not be bridged; the federation and the UJA conducted separate campaigns until the Yom Kippur War of 1973.

sional leaders thought he had taken leave of his senses, but, as one of his successors observed, Montor possessed the two qualities essential to successful fund raising—"vision and chutzpa" (brazenness). Before announcing his proposal Montor had persuaded William Rosenwald, son of the late Julius Rosenwald, the philanthropist who had built Sears, Roebuck into the nation's largest retailer, to go along with him. When serious doubts about the possibility of raising so large a sum were raised at the Atlantic City meeting, Rosenwald announced that he and the other members of his family would contribute one million dollars. "From then on," Abraham J. Karp has written in his history of the UJA, "everybody took the $100 million goal for granted."

In fact, the UJA received $103 million in 1946—nearly 80 percent of the $131 million raised in the joint campaign—and another $125 million in 1947. In 1948, the year the Jewish state was established, the joint campaign raised a little more than $200 million, $150 million of it for the UJA—the high-water mark until the Six-Day War. (The American Red Cross and United Way campaigns, which appeal to the entire American population, raised $72.5 million and $186 million, respectively, in 1948.)

To raise these sums Montor invented some new fund-raising techniques and perfected others that had been in use for some time. He launched the 1946 campaign, for example, with a national "big gifts" meeting in Washington in February. Those invited were told in advance that no gift of less than $10,000 would be accepted; some 350 people came. The meeting began with a speech by Bernard Baruch, then at the height of his fame. Baruch, who previously had rejected appeals from Jewish philanthropies on the grounds that he was "an American, not a hyphenate," had been inveigled into coming—and contributing $100,000—by his good friend Herbert Bayard Swope, retired editor of the New York *World*, who was on the UJA's payroll (at $50,000 a year) as a public relations consultant. After Baruch's speech the chairman, Edmund I. Kaufman, head of the national retail chain of Kay Stores, pledged $250,000 and then proceeded to call the name of each person present, asking for a pledge for 1946. Similar meetings were held to start off the campaign in each large city.

To understand this approach, which to outsiders seems to combine invasion of privacy with ostentatious display, one has to start with the fact that Judaism has no real counterpart for the Christian concept of charity. As the etymology of that term (from the Latin root *caritas*, or "love") implies, charity is a voluntary act of love by one person for another. The analogous Hebrew term *tzedakah* (from a root meaning "to be just") has an altogether different connotation: *tzedakah* is an obligation rather than a voluntary act of grace, an obligation inherent in one's membership in the community. Although benevolence (*khesed*, in Hebrew) and acts of loving-kindness (*gemilut khasadim*) are valued, Jewish tradition holds that the poor should not be dependent on them; as human beings they have the right to a decent life—hence the non-poor are expected to help, in accordance with their means. As Jacob Neusner puts it: "The Jew no more 'gives' tzedekah than the citizen 'gives' income taxes to the government. You pay your taxes because you must." And in the organic communities in which Jews lived before Emancipation, *tzedakah* was collected in much the same way as taxes.*

In a voluntary community, however, leaders have no sanctions at their disposal. How, then, enforce the obligation of *tzedakah?* The solution, devised in the 1920s by Joseph Willen, who directed the New York federation's fund-raising drives for nearly half a century, was to combine peer-group pressure with the psychic rewards that come from recognition by one's peers. Since, Willen believed, lawyers were more likely to respond to an appeal from their fellow lawyers, jewelry manufacturers from their fellow jewelry manufacturers, and so on, he began to organize a separate fund-raising campaign in each industry, trade, and profession. As Jews moved into new businesses and professions during the postwar period, the number of fund-raising divisions multiplied accordingly; in New York, for example, there are 92 separate divisions, ranging from obscure trades, such as tire dealers and pleaters and stitchers (about $50,000), Lighting, Wiring Devices, Distributors and Portable Lamp Division ($618,000 in 1983) and Garages and Parking Division ($525,000 in 1983), to the Wall Street division, which raises upwards of $11 million a year. In businesses with large numbers of Jews the divisions are broken down into subdivisions. Thus the women's industry has separate units for better apparel, popular-priced dresses, knitwear, intimate apparel, and coats and suits.

Willen's second and equally inspired invention was the testimonial "card-calling" luncheon or dinner—one for each industry, trade, and professional group. The very rich had always been able to gain recognition for their philanthropies by having buildings named after them; the multiplicity of testimonial lunches and dinners each year made it

* "In every city where Israelites reside, the inhabitants must appoint from among themselves well-known and trustworthy persons to act as *tzedakah* collectors, who collect from the people every Friday," Maimonides wrote in the *Mishne Torah*, his classic commentary on the Talmud. The collectors "should demand from each person what is proper for [that person] to give or what [that person] has been assessed for; and should distribute the money every Friday, giving each poor person enough for seven days. This is what is called 'the alms fund.' . . . We have never seen nor heard of an Israelite community that does not have an alms fund."

possible to extend recognition to much larger numbers of people, who could recall their moment of glory by means of the bronze plaque invariably awarded them. (Fund-raisers like to tell a perhaps apocryphal story about a guest of honor who insisted on supervising the most minute details of his dinner, down to the speech praising him, which he wrote himself. When the chairman read the text of the tribute the guest of honor burst into tears.)

The testimonial dinners serve other functions as well. If the person being honored is a businessman—until recently women were confined to a separate women's division—he usually can be counted on to pressure his suppliers, as well as his family, friends, and colleagues, to attend the event and to contribute an appropriate amount. (Clothing retailers, for example, invite the manufacturers from whom they buy.)* To reach people not captured through one of the trade or professional divisions there are testimonial brunches or other meals in synagogues and country clubs. In small communities the dinner may be organized on a community-wide basis, and in communities large and small the campaign usually is launched with a "big donors' kickoff dinner."

After an emotional appeal for funds (if the group is important enough, the speaker may be an Israeli general or government official) and one or more tributes to the guest of honor, the chairman gets down to the business at hand. Using file cards containing the necessary information—there is a separate card for everyone present—he calls the names one by one, announcing what each person had contributed the preceding year (Montor was insistent on this) and asking for his pledge for the new campaign. To fail to exceed or at least match one's gift of the previous year is to risk giving the impression that one has suffered business reverses. (Without card-calling, Montor argued, there is "no pressure on the prospect," and that made it too easy for contributors to "dodge their full burden.")

The process is less spontaneous than it seems. To create the right atmosphere, the chairman calls first on people he knows will make a large contribution, for the dinner is preceded by face-to-face solicitation of the honoree and other major contributors. The person being solicited usually is visited by two of his peers, just as Maimonides de-

* In the last ten years or so women have come to play an increasingly important role in most federations, serving as presidents of a number of large-city federations—for example, in Los Angeles and New York; in November 1984 the Council of Jewish Federations elected its first woman president, Shoshana Cardin, of Baltimore. The national UJA organization, however, remains an almost exclusively male preserve, with only two women holding national office. Segregation by sex continues even among the young, with the UJA maintaining separate male and female Young Leadership cabinets.

creed, for it is harder to say no to two acquaintances than to one. Before making their call the people doing the soliciting have briefed themselves on the prospect. "The more you know about your customer beforehand, the better your chance to make a sale," says Aryeh Nesher, an Israeli who is the UJA's most successful professional fund-raiser. And the most important thing to know is "how much to ask for," because "unless you mention a specific sum of money, it doesn't happen." Knowing how much to request requires considerable information not only about the prospect's financial status but about his Jewish background and commitment, as well as about his other philanthropies. "Your job may end up being to get him to change his priorities," Nesher explains. In any event, "seventy-five percent of the thing is decided before you even meet."

Successful solicitation also requires great psychological acuity; the solicitor has to know not only what approach to take but when and how to "close the sale." Hence volunteer fund-raisers have their skills refined in training sessions; in recent years videotapes of successful and unsuccessful solicitations have been used to good advantage.

ITEM: According to one perhaps apocryphal story, Nesher, who likes to meet his prospects in a restaurant because it is neutral turf, once tore up a check for $25,000, saying, "Lunch already has been paid for." The prospect promptly wrote another check for $50,000. Other men, of course, might have left without making any gift at all; the solicitor has to know when to accept a pledge as well as when to reject it.

For large contributors a softer sell is sometimes used; they may be invited to a "parlor meeting"—usually a dinner for ten or twelve people—at the home of some particularly prestigious donor. The guest list is usually put together with great care, and after the guests have had a chance to get to know one another and have had an hour or so of discussion about Israel's needs, the plight of Soviet Jewry (or Iranian or Ethiopian or some other group of endangered Jews), and the needs of local Jewish institutions, the host or chairman turns to the business at hand. "Unlike our regular fund-raising meetings, he didn't call on someone and say 'Joe, what are you going to do?,' " Bram Goldsmith, chairman of the City National Bank of Beverly Hills, has written, describing the parlor meetings held during his tenure as president of the Jewish Federation Council of Greater Los Angeles. "Instead, he would turn to one of the invitees very casually, seemingly at random, and say, 'How do you feel about what you've heard tonight, Joe?' . . . Now, we knew whom we were going to ask first, and invariably the person called upon would take a few minutes to talk about his concern and his interest in the campaign, and he'd always of course conclude by announcing his gift. The campaign leader would then turn to the next person, again casually, and go through the same process."

To set the right noncommercial tone campaign leaders would use the word "commitment" instead of "gift," "contribution," or "pledge" when announcing their gift. Rather than state, "I pledge $25,000," Goldsmith recalls, they would announce, " 'My commitment to Jewish survival is $35,000,' or 'My commitment to help people throughout the world is $25,000.' " (In 1970, 612 people attended the 53 parlor meetings that were held; they contributed a total of $2,950,000—which was 60 percent more than the same people had given in 1969.)

The desire for social acceptance is harnessed in other ways. Many Jewish country clubs, for example, make it clear to new applicants that a certain minimum gift to the local UJA/federation campaign is a prerequisite for admission. (More subtle but nonetheless real pressures are exerted after people have become members.)

The ritual of solicitation—and it is a ritual—can be seen in its most intense form at the annual retreat of the three hundred or so members of the UJA's national Young Leadership Cabinet. Divided into groups of six to nine, the young leaders—mostly affluent twenty-five-to-forty-year-old businessmen and professionals, although a few academicians have been added in recent years—practice what they call "total disclosure." Each member is expected to disclose his complete financial status—income, assets, and any expected inheritance—before indicating what he expects to contribute that year to his community's UJA/federation campaign. If the others are dissatisfied with the amount, they question (or challenge) him, and the final pledge is not determined until everyone present agrees that the amount is appropriate to the donor's means.

The Young Leadership Cabinet is a small, elite group whose members spend as many as eighty days a year away from home, soliciting others or training them in fund-raising techniques. But although this degree of dedication is rare, at least 50,000 people (and perhaps as many as 75,000) are actively involved with one or another aspect of local and national UJA/federation campaigns.

ITEM: Nationwide, some 3000 to 3500 twenty-five-to-forty-year-olds are involved in the leadership development programs run by most federations. These programs vary widely from city to city: some are little more than singles groups, with a smattering of Jewish education and fund-raising thrown in; others involve intense programs of study and of exposure to UJA and to the local institutions supported by the federation. (Perhaps a third of the LD members, as they are usually known, are actively involved in the annual compaign.)

ITEM: The Cleveland federation is widely regarded as a model for other communities because of both the number and size of the contributions it receives ("involvement with federation is the real religion here," one official told me) and the long list of national lay and professional leaders it has produced. The key to success, according to its retired executive head, Henry Zucker, is that by involving so many people in year-round activities, "the community has come to see Federation as a service organization, not a once-a-year dunning process." In fact, some 1200 people serve on the federation's fifty committees; including the committee members, between 2500 and 3000 people are involved in the annual federation/UJA campaign—in a metropolitan area containing 70,000 Jews, 37,000 of them between the ages of twenty-three and sixty-four.

ITEM: In January 1984, 38,000 volunteers in 135 separate communities made telephone calls or participated in some other way in UJA's "Super Sunday" program. (To extend the reach of its campaign, in 1981 the UJA originated "Super Sunday"—in most communities, the Sunday after the Super Bowl football game. Volunteers, who have been trained in advance, take turns at specially installed telephone banks calling every small donor whose pledge for the year has not yet been recorded.)

Given all this volunteer activity, it is not surprising that a large plurality of American Jews contribute to the annual UJA/federation campaign—30–40 percent of all households in ordinary years and perhaps as many as 50 percent when Israel is under attack. The ratio varies widely, however, from one community to another. In the New York metropolitan area, which contains 30 percent of American Jewry, no more than one household in five contributes in most years. By contrast, in small communities, where most Jews tend to know one another, it can be difficult to avoid making a contribution: in Des Moines, Iowa, for example, which has 900–1000 Jewish families, 75–80 percent contribute, and in Richmond, Virginia, with 8,000 Jews, the participation rate is 60 percent. There is a strong sense of community too in cities with much larger Jewish populations: in Cleveland (70,000 Jews), Milwaukee (30,000), and Minneapolis (22,000), for example, half to three quarters of the households contribute to the annual campaign.

What is remarkable about the whole process, of course, is that it is completely voluntary: except for the guest of honor's suppliers at an industry dinner (and for them it usually is a one-shot affair) no one *has* to submit to these pressures—certainly not year after year. Those who contribute do so because, consciously or not, they accept the concept of *tzedakah* on which the process is built.

Even so, the annual campaign depends heavily on the generosity of a handful of large contributors. "In every city," says Henry Zucker, "the top fifty gifts determine the campaign"—in part because they account for a large proportion of the total raised and in part because the amounts the largest donors give directly affect the size of gifts from other wealthy contributors. Nationwide, 1 percent of the donors (the 7000 or so people who give $10,000 or more) account for 60 percent of the funds raised, and the 19 percent who contribute between $1000 and $10,000 provide another 20 percent of the total. Thus the 80 percent of donors who give $1000 or less account for only 20 percent of the funds raised.

This pattern is not peculiar to Jewish life; in virtually every philanthropy a handful of donors account for the bulk of the money raised. The economics of fund raising tends to perpetuate this imbalance. Since the number of lay and professional fund-raisers is always limited, relative to the number of potential contributors, they tend to focus on large givers and on those who have the potential to become large givers. It requires less effort to persuade a wealthy nongiver to contribute $10,000, or a $10,000 giver to give $20,000, than to inveigle twenty $500 donors into doubling their gifts. What distinguishes the UJA/federation campaigns, therefore, is not their concentration on large givers but the number and size of the large gifts they receive, the techniques used to extract those gifts, and the intense emotional commitment (or in some cases resentment) that the campaigns evoke.

Not even the Six-Day War changed this dependence on large contributors. Yet in every community there were stories about people who had never contributed before but who, caught up in the fever, stepped forward this time.

ITEM: Six months after the war had ended, Marshall Sklare returned to "Lakeville," the pseudonym he had given Highland Park, Illinois, when he studied its Jewish community ten years earlier. Sklare was struck by the impact the Six-Day War had had on even the most assimilated Jews, as evidenced by the fact that several members of the anti-Zionist American Council for Judaism—people who had refused to contribute in the past on ideological grounds—had made gifts to UJA's Israel Emergency Fund. The gifts were small in dollar amount, Sklare wrote, but large in symbolic meaning.

ITEM: In New York, where penetration had always been low—competition between the separate UJA and federation appeals having reduced the effectiveness of each—the number of UJA contributors more than doubled. In Los Angeles, by contrast, notwithstanding a $500,000 gift from a man who had never given to the UJA/federation campaign before, there was no increase at all in the number of donors. And in Cleveland the number of contributors actually declined—in part because family members who previously had made separate contributions joined together in a single large gift and in part because fund-raisers were so busy appealing to large contributors that they did not have time to go after the fringe donors.

Taking everything together, therefore, the principal impact of the war was less to broaden the base of contributors (although some broadening did occur) than to increase the number of large contributors and, even more, to move them to new heights of giving.*

ITEM: In New York the first 74 gifts totaled $9.7 million—more than four and a half times as much as the same people had given the year before.

ITEM: In Columbus, Ohio, one businessman, whose annual gift had risen from $600 in 1961 to $3200 in 1966, gave $14,800 in 1967; another donor, whose 1966 contribution had been $750, gave $3200.

And every community had similar stories to tell. The result was that although contributions dropped in 1968, it was to a level far above the prewar figure. The Columbus donor who had given $3200 in 1966 gave $12,500 in 1968; the man whose prewar gift had been $750 gave $2800. For the country as a whole, 1968 contributions were 25 percent below those of 1967 but 70 percent higher than those of 1966. The threshold had changed, and by 1971 contributions reached $360 million—13 percent above the 1967 peak.

The reason was that Israel's need for money again became the emotional centerpiece of the annual UJA/federation campaign, reversing the trend of the preceding fifteen years. In the early postwar period the realization of what had happened to European Jewry and the excitement over the creation of a Jewish state had given UJA first claim on the dollars raised in the joint campaign; but that emotional high could not be sustained. During the 1950s and early 1960s, therefore, local agencies retained a steadily increasing share of the funds raised in the annual joint campaigns. This was partly to make up for the backlog

* The records kept by UJA and the Council of Jewish Federations, as well as by most local federations, make it impossible to determine the dimensions of the increase in the number of contributors nationwide.

of spending that had had to be deferred during the depression and war years and partly to meet the need for new facilities and programs generated by the mass movement of Jews to the suburbs and, as time went on, to the Sun Belt. Thus UJA's share of the annual campaign fell from 75–80 percent in 1946–48 to 47 percent in 1966.

For all the cooperation between them, there is in fact an inevitable tension between the UJA on one side and the CJF and local federations on the other. The UJA's role, after all, is to be the principal advocate as well as fund-raiser for overseas Jewry, in general, and, since 1948, for Israel, in particular.* UJA sets the overall theme for each year's joint campaign, and it takes large contributors to Israel on UJA missions, flies Israelis to the United States to speak at fund-raising events, supplies local federations with advertising and public relations, and works with them to improve their fund-raising capabilities; but it is the federations that actually raise the bulk of the money UJA receives. (UJA raises funds directly only in communities without a federation or in the handful of cities, such as New York, that until recently did not have a joint UJA/federation campaign.) Each year, therefore, UJA must negotiate separately with each federation to determine its share of that year's receipts.† Negotiations can be tense, for, in addition to their fund-raising role for UJA, the federations serve as spokesmen for the needs of the old people's homes, hospitals, community centers, family service agencies, and other local institutions they support and to whom they ultimately are accountable.

It would be a mistake, however, to overstate the conflict. Today, in contrast to the situation a generation or two ago, most federation

* The conflict within UJA between the Joint Distribution Committee and the United Israel Appeal, as the United Palestine Appeal was renamed, disappeared in the early 1950s. Indeed, JDC assumed responsibility for assisting elderly and handicapped immigrants to Israel.

† The percentage allocation is not the only matter that has to be negotiated. There always is a question, for example, as to whether UJA's share applies to pledges or to actual receipts (or, in official jargon, before or after "shrinkage"); some people take years to redeem their pledges, and some never pay at all or pay only a portion. If UJA is allocated 60 percent of pledges, therefore, it may receive only 55 percent of actual receipts. There are disagreements too over the form the UJA allocation takes. Wealthy contributors may make their payments in the form of property, such as real estate, jewelry, or paintings, but in a soft market the property may bring less than the value at which it had been appraised for purposes of the gift. Thus federations may keep all their cash receipts and give the UJA its share in property—a technique that again reduces UJA's actual take. When interest rates are high, moreover, federations may delay transmitting cash to UJA in order to increase their interest income.

officials are fervently committed to Israel's well-being; whatever differences they may have with UJA (I will discuss those differences in the next section) disappear when Israel is attacked, as it was in 1967. Although all the funds contributed to the 1967 Israel Emergency Fund went directly to UJA, the federations pitched in as if it were another joint campaign. The same technique was used, in fact, in subsequent campaigns: to increase contributions to UJA without cutting into the funds available for local needs, contributors were asked to make a second gift, to what became an annual Israel Emergency Fund drive, over and above their donation to the joint campaign.

When the Yom Kippur War broke out in October of 1973, therefore, American Jews were even more conditioned to give than they had been in 1967; $300 million was collected in the first three weeks, and by the time the campaign had ended, in 1974, $670 million had been raised, $505 million of it for UJA. (Israel received another $204 million through sales of Israel bonds.) As in 1967, the bulk of the funds came from large donors; there were three gifts of $5 million each—the largest previous contribution had been $3 million—and well over forty gifts of one million dollars or more.

To try to maintain the emotional commitment to Israel of large contributors after the 1967 and 1973 wars had ended, UJA, in cooperation with local federations, greatly expanded the number of people going to Israel on carefully planned "missions." Henry Montor had originated the idea in 1948 when he chartered a TWA plane, with the UJA "Star of Hope," as he called it, painted on the side, to take thirty-five communal leaders on a four-week mission—first to Europe to see the displaced persons camps where concentration-camp victims were still languishing, and then to Israel to see the absorption process first-hand and hear Israeli leaders describe the new country's needs. On their return the emotionally charged leaders spearheaded the campaign, speaking to groups and soliciting funds from other communities as well as their own.*

The emotions unleashed by the Six-Day War, along with the development of the jet plane, which cut travel time, enabled the UJA to

* Convinced by Israeli Prime Minister David Ben-Gurion that the necessary funds could be raised only if wealthy non-Zionists were attracted to the cause, Montor, who directed the United Palestine Appeal as well as the UJA, also ousted the Zionist leaders who had controlled the UPA from its inception, replacing them with wealthy federation leaders from around the country. (Ben-Gurion, who was at odds with American Zionist leaders, such as Rabbi Abba Hillel Silver, on a number of points, effectively removed them from positions of influence by this move, thereby giving him direct access to the large contributors whom he wanted to cultivate.)

expand the number of missions. In 1968 more than 2000 "key leaders" traveled to Israel, at their own expense, on various UJA missions—up from 140 four years earlier; by 1980 the number exceeded 4600.

The missions serve a number of purposes. For one thing, they provide great psychic rewards: hobnobbing with the Israeli prime minister at cocktails or dinner, meeting cabinet officers and generals, being briefed on Israel's security (or economic or foreign policy) problems by intelligence officers or officials from the defense or foreign ministries, and so on: "It's a real ego trip," one participant told me.

They also serve as a stimulus to future contributions as well as a reward for those made in the past, for they provide an intense emotional experience. "It's like spending ten days at a Moonie retreat," one leader told me with a laugh. The itinerary is designed to emphasize Israel's role as a refuge for persecuted Jews and a safeguard against future Holocausts; one by-product of the Six-Day War and of the Yom Kippur War of 1973 has been a growing preoccupation (some say obsession) on the part of American Jews with the Holocaust.*

In retrospect, it is not surprising that this preoccupation did not begin until after Israel's 1967 victory. The central message of Judaism, after all, is one of redemption—the conviction, in Abraham Joshua Heschel's words, "that evil is not the end, that evil is never the climax of history"; what made the Holocaust resonate so loudly in 1967 was precisely the fact that this time the catastrophe did not occur. Without Israel's victory, that is to say, the Holocaust might have been too dreadful to contemplate; with it Jews have been able to construct a new mythology, in which Israel serves as a symbol of redemption.

The UJA missions are designed to emphasize that mythic role. One of the focal points, therefore, is a visit to Yad Vashem, the memorial to the six million Jews killed in the Holocaust—an emotionally wrenching experience for any Jew but one made more intense by being part of a UJA group. (To vary the routine some missions now begin with a visit to Auschwitz and to the tiny and rapidly aging Jewish communities in Eastern Europe.)

The rest of the trip emphasizes Israel's role as a haven for persecuted Jews while reminding the visitors of the continuing threats to

* Jewish religious schools, which once ignored the Holocaust for fear that it would be too upsetting to young students, now make its study an important part of their curricula, and there are well over 700 courses on the history and literature of the Holocaust in secular American colleges and universities; these courses attract more students than any other Judaic studies. Most Jewish communities, moreover, now hold an annual service to commemorate the victims of the Holocaust, and a growing number are erecting public memorials, following the lead of the U.S. Holocaust Commission, which is creating a Holocaust Museum in Washington, D.C.

its security. Participants visit an absorption center, where new immigrants spend a few months learning Hebrew and preparing for life in Israel, and then a "settlement town," populated by recent immigrants. There will be a predawn visit to an army or air force base, complete with "confidential" briefing on Israel's security needs, followed by an inspection of the Golan Heights or some other border area, and a trip to the hills of Judaea, from which hostile guns could easily shell Jerusalem and Tel Aviv; a Sabbath service at the Western Wall; a visit to a kibbutz or agricultural station in the Negev; meetings with Israeli counterparts; and, in recent years, a candlelight ceremony on top of Masada, at which the participants renew their commitment to Jewish survival. The final night is often devoted to card-calling; those who go on a mission for the first time increase their pledges by an average of 50–60 percent—an increase that is likely to be parlayed when they solicit others on their return.

4

The Six-Day War affected more than fund raising; it profoundly influenced the way Jews felt—and still feel—about their Jewishness. Whether they contributed to the 1967 Israel Emergency Fund or not, it was the rare American Jew who did not share in the gloom in the weeks before the war or who did not feel a sense of exultation when Israel won its rapid and decisive victory.

One consequence was that concern for Israel became one of the principal means by which American Jews express their Jewish identity. By 1984, for example, at least two American Jewish adults in five had been to Israel at least once—up from 16 percent in 1970–71 and perhaps 5 percent before the Six-Day War. True enough, a trip to Israel is not in itself evidence of any deep commitment to the Jewish state; whether because they are more affluent or more cosmopolitan, Jews travel abroad more frequently than members of other ethnic groups—hence almost as many American Jews have been to Italy as to Israel. For some, however, especially those who have been there more than once, travel to Israel is an act of religious and communal identification; in fact, nearly one Jewish adult in five has visited Israel two or more times.

ITEM: The degree to which support for Israel has come to dominate American Jewish communal life is evident from the frequency with which communal leaders visit Israel. In his 1983 survey of American Jews, Steven M. Cohen queried a subsample of board members of The

American Jewish Committee, American Jewish Congress, B'nai B'rith, Anti-Defamation League, and UJA, only the last of which considers support for Israel its primary mission. Yet 94 percent of the board members had visited Israel at least once, and 78 percent had been there two or more times.

After 1967, moreover, a good many parents came to see a trip to Israel as an important element in their children's religious education. Thus the number of Jewish young people visiting Israel—the majority for a summer program but some for a semester or two of high school or college study—rose from less than 2000 a year before the Six-Day War to a peak of 16,000 in 1971. Student travel declined after the Yom Kippur War as a result of parental fears about their children's safety, a certain tarnishing of Israel's luster, and the impact of the recessions of the mid- and late 1970s, but the number has been growing again in the 1980s; all told, between 125,000 and 150,000 Jewish young people have spent a summer or longer in Israel since the end of the Six-Day War.

Travel aside, American Jews express warm and close feelings toward Israel. In Cohen's 1983 survey 78 percent of the respondents reported that "caring about Israel is a very important part of my being a Jew," and the same proportion agreed that "if Israel were destroyed, I would feel that I had suffered one of the greatest personal tragedies in my life." An even larger proportion (86 percent) described themselves as pro-Israel, with only 3 percent calling themselves anti-Israel and 6 percent neutral.

This concern for Israel manifests itself in other ways.

ITEM: More than nine Jews in ten (93 percent) say that they pay special attention to newspaper and magazine articles about Israel; three in four "often talk about Israel with friends and relatives"; and well over half (56 percent) consider themselves "very well-informed" about Israel.

The ties are more than sentimental: one Jew in three has relatives in Israel, and the same proportion report that they have personal friends there. Although there is considerable overlap between the two groups, it would appear that between 40 and 50 percent of American Jews have direct ties of either friendship or kinship with Israelis. (The proportion is far higher among communal leaders, 69 percent reporting that they had personal friends in Israel.)

This concern for Israel is part of a much broader revival of Jewishness that began during the Six-Day War. Jews who had thought that being Jewish did not matter—Jews who were proud of having outgrown the "parochialism" of their parents or grandparents—discovered in 1967 that Jewishness lay at the heart of their being. "One way or another the day always comes when you discover that you are a Jew, just as you discover that you are mortal," the Tunisian-born sociologist Albert Memmi wrote several years earlier, out of the pain of his experience as a supporter of North African revolutionary movements that turned on the Jews as soon as they came to power. "Sooner or later each Jew discovers his little Jew, the little Jews he sees around him and the *little Jew* who, according to other men, is within him. And that realization comes to him no matter what he is or what he thinks he has become and notwithstanding his pretenses, the masks he wears or even his profound metamorphosis [emphasis in original]."

For assimilated American Jews—indeed, for Jews the world over—that moment came in May and June of 1967. "I think it must have been this way for many of my generation, that the Israeli-Arab collision was a moment of truth," a young woman wrote in a letter to the editor of *The Village Voice*.

> For the first time in my grown-up life, I really understood what an enemy was. For the first time, I knew what it was to be us against the killers. Us. Two weeks ago, Israel was they; now Israel is we. . . . Something happened. I will never again be able to talk about how Judaism is only a religion, and isn't it too bad that there has to be such a thing as a Jewish state. I will never again say as I said two years ago: Yes, I feel sympathetic with Israel, but I would feel the same way if France were involved in this kind of a crisis. I will never kid myself that we are only the things we choose to be. Roots count.

Thus the Six-Day War was a watershed between two eras—one in which American Jews had tried to persuade themselves, as well as Gentiles, that they were just like everybody else, only more so, and a period in which they acknowledged, even celebrated, their distinctiveness. "This crisis has forcibly reminded many, perhaps most, American Jews that the posture and destiny of Jews in the world continue to be quite unique and that Israel is not a state like all other states," Arthur Hertzberg wrote a month after the war had ended. "The sense of belonging to the worldwide Jewish people, of which Israel is the center, is a religious sentiment, but it seems to persist even among Jews who regard themselves as secularists or atheists. There are no conventional Western theological terms with which to explain this . . ."

Explainable or not, identification with Israel was real. It also was a source of satisfaction and pride; having participated, so to speak, in the Jewish state's struggle to survive, Jews now exulted in her dramatic triumph. More than that: the military skill and daring Israel had displayed transformed the image of themselves American Jews had had. All Jews, it seemed, stood taller and walked straighter, wearing their Jewishness as a badge of honor rather than of embarrassment or shame. "No more does the Jew march to the ovens," a once completely assimilated resident of "Lakeville" told Marshall Sklare. Israel was "performing miracles," a phenomenon she experienced as "pure ecstasy." Her graduate-student son, who had hardly known he was Jewish, wrote of his new pride in being a Jew.

Gentiles too saw Jews in a new light. "Them's damn fightin' Jews," a South Georgia filling-station attendant told Eli Evans. "I always thought Jews were yaller, but those [Israeli] Jews, man, they're tough." This reversal of attitude was widespread; Sklare's respondents reported almost without exception that their stature had risen in the Gentile community. "You Hebes really taught those guys a lesson," one man's longtime business associate told him by way of compliment.

And yet the aftermath of the war left Jews—Jews everywhere—feeling less rather than more secure. If ordinary Americans (and ordinary people in other countries) admired the Israeli victory, most church leaders and a good many statesmen resented it. R. H. Edwin Espy, executive secretary of the National Council of Churches, had been scheduled to address a Jewish rally in Washington on June 8, but his talk was interrupted when news came of the cease-fire: lest anyone might think he had come to the rally to align the mainstream Protestant churches with Israel rather than with the Arabs who had threatened her destruction, his prepared text was published by the council. "Our hearts are filled with compassion and concern for the people of Israel and of all the Middle East," Espy wrote. "Our identification is not of course exclusively with any one community, one belligerent [sic], or one set of national aspirations. . . . Had we been invited to attend a corresponding meeting of the Arab community in the United States we would have been bound by our principles to bring the identical message—the plea for peace with justice and freedom which we derive from our Judeo-Christian heritage."

Less than a month later the National Council of Churches abandoned its pretense of neutrality and adopted a resolution that sharply criticized Israel's "territorial expansion by armed force" and "unilateral retention" of the territory it had occupied. The Council expressed particular disapproval of Israel's "unilateral annexation of the Jordanian portion of Jerusalem," urging "the establishment of an international presence" in the Holy City. But the so-called "Jordanian portion of Jerusalem" had become Jordanian through the same kind of "territorial expansion by armed force" that the National Council now deplored. The 1948 United Nations resolution ending the British mandate over

Palestine and dividing it into separate Jewish and Palestinian states had made Jerusalem an international city. In the war that followed Arab rejection of the U.N. resolution, Jordan had captured Jerusalem, along with the West Bank—the site of what was to have been the independent Palestinian state—and made it part of Jordan.

During the nineteen years of Jordanian rule, moreover, Jews had been denied access to the Old City, which contained the Western Wall, Temple Mount, and countless synagogues and cemeteries. The ancient and sacred graveyard on the Mount of Olives had been turned into a latrine for Jordanian troops, and all but one of the fifty synagogues in the Old City were destroyed. At no time during this period had the National Council of Churches or any other church body expressed or even hinted at disapproval of these actions, let alone called on Jordan to surrender control to some international body, as the NCC and the Vatican was now demanding. Nor did the National Council of Churches or Vatican statements take note of the well-advertised fact that before launching its preemptive strike Israel had assured Jordan's King Hussein that it had no designs on his territory and that it would not attack Jordan if the border remained quiet. Hussein's response was to shell Jerusalem and a number of other Israeli towns and villages, including the outskirts of Tel Aviv.

To Jews it appeared as though some monstrous double standard had come into play. Equally important, people they had thought of as allies seemed to turn on them; in the new Orwellian logic that suddenly governed Christian discourse, the victim became the aggressor by virtue of his refusal to play the role of victim. John Bennett, president of Union Theological Seminary, who before the war had signed a statement stating that "the people of Israel have the right to live and develop in tranquility and without fear," now denounced Israel for what he termed her "idolatry of the land." His predecessor, Henry P. Van Dusen, went further. "All persons who seek to view the Middle East problem with honesty and objectivity," he wrote in a letter to *The New York Times*, "stand aghast at Israel's onslaught, the most violent, ruthless (and successful) aggression since Hitler's blitzkrieg across Western Europe in the summer of 1940."

The message seemed clear. "The world begrudges Israel its victory," Elie Wiesel wrote in an angry essay. "Its lightning campaigns against four armies and some twenty nations were won too quickly and too spectacularly. . . . A victorious Israel does not conform to the image and destiny certain people want to assign to it. . . . They love the Jew only on the cross . . ."

An English journalist turned to satire to express the same view. "I have felt obliged to condemn your *unseemly haste* in opening hostilities

[and] your insistence on *winning* the war," he wrote in the London *Observer* in the form of a letter to "My dear Israel" from "Your affectionate Great-aunt Britain."

> To insist upon defeating your opponents is a discourtesy which they may find *very hard to forgive*. . . . What makes your behavior all the more perplexing is that when the war commenced you enjoyed the approval and sympathy of polite society as a whole. There you stood, surrounded on all sides by greatly superior hostile forces, whose proclaimed intention was to destroy you utterly. Everybody was *deeply touched!* . . . If things had gone badly, we had ships standing by which could have evacuated *several thousand* survivors—who would have had the *unreserved sympathy* of the entire world! . . . [Emphasis in original.]

It was, in fact, no laughing matter. After years of protesting that they were just like everybody else, only more so, Jews suddenly felt different—and terribly alone—for it was not only the churches that assigned to Israel the role of villain. Since the beginning of Emancipation, Jews had believed (correctly) that their enemies were largely on the right; suddenly they discovered that a good part of the left was arrayed against them, a change whose implications will be discussed in the last chapter. During its Labor Day meeting the National Conference on New Politics passed a resolution condemning "the imperialist Zionist war" and expressing sympathy for the "oppressed" Palestinian "victims." If some on the left tried to maintain a distinction between anti-Zionism and anti-Semitism, others dropped the pretense altogether, as witness this poem in a 1967 issue of the Black Panther journal:

We're gonna burn their towns and that ain't all
We're gonna piss upon the Wailing Wall
And then we'll get Kosygin and de Gaulle
That will be ecstasy, killing every Jew in Jewland.

Thus the experience of Jews during and after the war drove home to them their "overwhelming aloneness" and "peculiar *distinctiveness*," as Nathan Glazer put it, thereby justifying their "right to consider themselves specially threatened and specially worthy of whatever efforts were necessary for survival [emphasis in original]." That feeling deepened during the Yom Kippur War of October 1973, when Israel, taken unawares by the Arab attack on the holiest day of the year, received support only from the United States. Nor was the sense of siege lifted by Israel's victory, for it became increasingly clear that the Arab- and Soviet-led campaign against Israel involves far more than a disagreement over foreign or even domestic policy; it is an attempt to deny—indeed, to destroy—the legitimacy of the Jewish state, and thus of Jewish peoplehood. The campaign reached its nadir on November 10, 1975, when the United Nations General Assembly adopted its infamous resolution equating Zionism with racism—a resolution that served to convert Jews everywhere into at least nominal Zionists.

How much of a calumny that trendy Soviet/Third World notion is became clear in the fall and winter of 1984–85 when Israel airlifted 7500 Ethiopian Jews from the Sudan, to which they had fled, formally granting them citizenship (and Israeli identity cards) within twenty-four hours of their arrival. (Previously 5000 Ethiopian Jews had been brought to Israel over several years.) As Leon Wieseltier wrote in the *New Republic*, Operation Moses (the Israeli code name for the rescue operation) served to clarify the central meaning of Zionism: "there must exist a state for which Jews need no visas." The rescue operation revealed a central meaning of Jewish particularism as well: "for Jews, Jewish suffering is insufferable," and Jewish peoplehood transcends color and space as well as time.

In the process Operation Moses revealed the emptiness of the universalism that once had held many Jews in its thrall. "The community is not the only moral unit," Wieseltier wrote, "but it is a moral unit. Moreover, the alternative is never between helping your own and helping everybody. . . . In the real world, the position of the universalist usually comes to this: that nobody be saved unless everybody be saved. To be sure, it is neither easy nor enviable to choose from among the suffering. But practically speaking, there is no such thing as universalism. It is impossible to help everybody." That same lesson had been learned in 1973 and before that in 1967. Jews became particularists because so many of the universalists to whom they had looked for support turned out to be particularists themselves—only on the opposite side.

Nowhere was the rediscovery of Jewish particularism after the Six-Day War more striking than on college campuses, which previously had harbored the most universalist of Jews. Before 1967, for example, Jewish members of the Yale faculty had given a grand total of $200–$400 a year to the annual UJA drive on campus; by the third day of the Six-Day War they had contributed $10,000, and thirteen senior members of the medical school faculty were on their way to Israel to volunteer their services. In late May, moreover, a group of Cornell University professors had approached colleagues on other campuses, soliciting signatures for an ad supportive of Israel to appear in *The New York Times;* within three days they had collected 3700 names and enough money for a two-page ad. (An additional 1500 names came in after the ad had gone to press.) The intensity of the response persuaded the leaders of the group to create a permanent organization, American Professors for Peace in the Middle East.

For some on campus the rediscovery of particularism took other forms—specifically, the emergence of a "Jewish counterculture," as some called it, or "the Jewish students movement," as it was also called. The expulsion of whites from civil rights organizations such as SNCC a year or two earlier had persuaded some students and recent graduates to try to find specifically Jewish ways of expressing their liberal or radical political views; the search took on a new sense of urgency after the Six-Day War, when the New Left became a major forum for expressions of hostility to Israel.

Others set out on a spiritual rather (or more) than on a political quest, although the distinction between the two groups was never hard and fast. Alienated by the spiritual emptiness and intellectual vapidity, as they saw it, of the suburban synagogues and Jewish community centers in which they had been raised, they turned to Jewish tradition, as well as to the new, adversarial youth culture, to find ways of satisfying their hunger for a more intense and "authentic" religious experience.

The most characteristic expression of this spiritual hunger was the *havurah*, or religious fellowship, a group of ten to fifty (or, in a few instances, more) individuals and/or couples who met regularly for worship and study. The number involved never was very large; as William Novak, one of its leaders and its principal chronicler, once quipped, the entire Jewish counterculture contained no more than 144 people, all of whom were on a first-name basis. In fact, several thousand were caught up in the movement, and they included some of the brightest and most creative members of their generation; many have gone on to become distinguished scholars, writers, and "Jewish civil servants"—executives in Jewish communal agencies. The "new Jews," as they liked to be called, have had a profound impact on mainstream Conservative, Reconstructionist, and Reform Judaism through their insistence on "do it yourself Judaism" (a reaction against the previous generation's tendency to delegate Jewish study and practice to professionals), along with their egalitarianism (women played the same religious roles as men), liturgical experimentation, and their emphasis on study, especially of traditional texts.

The students made their presence felt in other ways. There was, for example, an explosion of Jewish student newspapers and magazines—2 in 1968, 23 in 1970, and 58 in 1972; the most important of them, the journal *Response*, is still published, albeit sporadically. For all the antipathy to institutions that the "new Jews" expressed, they were avid organization builders. The Jewish Students Press Service, the answer of the "new Jews" to the Establishment bias of the Jewish Telegraphic

Agency, still exists; the Student Struggle for Soviet Jewry forced that issue onto the agenda of the adult community; and until recently the North American Jewish Students Network was a fertile training ground for a new generation of Jewish leaders.

Having worried for years over the next generation's alienation from Judaism, the leaders of major communal organizations suddenly found themselves under attack for not being Jewish enough. The criticism came to a head in Boston in November 1969, eighteen months after the Six-Day War, when several hundred young activists threatened a sit-in at that year's General Assembly of the Council of Jewish Federations to dramatize their demand for a massive shift of philanthropic funds away from hospitals and other secular agencies and into support for programs of Jewish education and study.

The confrontation was averted when the CJF leaders agreed to permit a spokesman for the Concerned Jewish Students, as they called themselves, to address the General Assembly. "Knowing that we were given this opportunity only through threats of a disruption, you might dismiss us as children of our times, bored with the battle of the campus and looking for a new stage upon which to play our childish pranks," Hillel Levine, a Conservative rabbi and doctoral student in sociology at Harvard (he is now professor of religion and sociology at Boston University and chairman of its Judaic Studies Program) told the fifteen hundred delegates. "But we see ourselves as . . . children of timelessness. We see ourselves as Jews who know that when one has an urgent matter to bring to the attention of the community, even the reading of the Torah in the synagogue may be disrupted."

The "urgent matter" Levine wanted to bring to the delegates' attention was the belief of his group that "there was more to Judaism" than could be found in "the multimillion-dollar Jewish presences of suburbia." Specifically, he complained, Jewish education was the stepchild of the federations, whose priorities favored "a greater mobilization of resources to combat one crack-pot anti-Semite than to deal with the Jewish illiteracy of millions of Jews." "We want to build a Jewish community that is creative and not one that must concern itself with mere survival," Levine concluded. "We want to convert alienation into participation, acrimony into joy—the joy of being the possessors of a great legacy. . . . This renewal can be accomplished only through a massive rededication to Jewish study and meaningful Jewish existence."

If Levine's call for "a massive rededication to Jewish study" went unheeded, his plea for a change in communal priorities did not. The General Assembly delegates were taken aback by the activists' confrontational style—federations operate by consensus and place a heavy premium on avoiding conflict—but were pleased that the students cared so deeply about Jewish values. After a moment of silence there was loud applause. "It was as if the students found themselves prepared to knock down a door that was open to them," one delegate observed.

But not *too* open; CJF and local federation leaders were proud of their own accomplishments and therefore defensive about the students' critique of the way they and their institutions were functioning. They set out to co-opt the young activists, inviting them to be guests at the next GA and agreeing to a number of their demands. The Boston federation, for example, promptly increased its allocation to the local Hillel foundations and gave $40,000 to a new agency, Boston Student Projects, to fund projects outside the Hillel nexus; a number of other federations followed suit. The CJF itself encouraged federations to make grants to the Jewish Students Press Service and helped establish and fund the North American Jewish Student Appeal; it also created the short-lived Institute for Jewish Life to encourage innovative programs of Jewish education and culture. (Because the existence of the institute represented an implicit criticism of existing local and national agencies, it received neither the funds nor the autonomy it required to make a significant impact on Jewish life; it was quietly disbanded after four years of diminishing operations.)

In the long run, however, it was the federation officials who were co-opted, not the young activists; bit by bit, federations have increased the proportion of funds allocated to Jewish education and to other programs designed to enhance Jewish identification. What happened, in effect, was that the threat of demonstrations accelerated the transfer of power from an older generation of lay and professional federation leaders to a new generation with a different set of priorities.

In the past—the transformation occurred at different times in different communities—the philanthropic programs of federations were guided by considerations of noblesse oblige rather (or more) than by concern for Jewish continuity and survival. Despite their willingness to raise money for UJA, federation leaders of the old school tended to be highly assimilated Jews whose principal connection to Judaism was the obligation they felt to help Jews less fortunate than they; many were profoundly uncomfortable with any activity that smacked of being "too Jewish." As the historian Oscar Janowsky described them in 1948 in a report commissioned by the National Jewish Welfare Board, these leaders "equated Jewish learning and lore with fanaticism and ignorance . . . [and] regarded the abandonment of Jewish habits and ideas as prerequisite to cultured living."

ITEM: Nowhere was this more evident than in New York. Maurice Hexter, the federation's longtime administrative head (Willen was in charge of the campaign), complained of the trouble caused by "hyper-Jews," as he called them, who had wanted the federation to lend one million dollars to Israel in 1948 (the request was rejected) and to provide more support for Jewish education.

Although the New York federation was atypical in its refusal to raise funds for UJA—it was not until the Yom Kippur War that the federation agreed to a joint campaign—other federation leaders tended to share Hexter's distaste for "hyper-Jews."

ITEM: In the early 1960s a young Canadian social worker named Carmi Schwartz, who had applied for a staff position with a midwestern federation, was told that although he was eminently qualified on other grounds, the fact that he was Orthodox, and thus a strict Sabbath observer, made him ineligible. They had nothing against Orthodox Jews, the official emphasized, but the position for which Schwartz had applied would require him to work closely with the local Protestant and Catholic clergy, and Saturdays were the best time for that. One could not, after all, expect ministers to come to meetings on Sunday, for that was their Sabbath!

Today Carmi Schwartz is executive vice-president of the Council of Jewish Federations—the top staff position in the organization and one of the most important professional positions in Jewish communal life. The federation that turned him down has gained a national reputation for the imaginative programs it has developed to strengthen Jewish identity.

Similar changes are evident throughout the country. Younger lay and professional leaders are far more comfortable with their Jewishness; they are also more likely to see themselves as members of a group rather than as individuals who happen to be Jewish, and are therefore more willing to assert group interests.

ITEM: Los Angeles provides a case in point. The city used to be considered a Jewish wasteland; Orthodox Jews in the East joked that if a rabbi moved to Los Angeles, it meant that he had either one lung or two wives. For more than half a century the principal spokesman for Los Angeles Jewry was the late Edgar Magnin, rabbi of the affluent Wilshire Boulevard Temple. Magnin's own consciousness had been formed at a time when Jews were seen as an alien group, and the major concern of "the Cardinal," as he was called, seemed to be to demonstrate that Jews could be as patriotic as American Legionnaires and as decorous as upper-class Presbyterians. The lay leaders of the Jewish Federation-Council of Los Angeles were equally careful to avoid visible displays of their Jewishness. Until the middle or late 1970s, for example, the Federation-supported Cedars-Sinai Hospital refused to supply kosher food to observant patients; and although the hospital had a full-time Catholic chaplain on its staff, it had no rabbi.

The hospital has a rabbi now, along with a large kitchen, paid for with federation funds, that prepares kosher food, under rabbinic supervision, for those who want it. Even more striking, perhaps, the Jewish Federation-Council now begins its board meetings with a *d'var Torah*, or religious homily, and kosher food is served at all breakfast, lunch, or dinner meetings it sponsors. An entire division of the federation staff is charged with the responsibility of working with synagogues and other organizations to strengthen Jewish identity. Indeed, the former wasteland is now an important center of Jewish scholarship and learning.

Equally dramatic changes are evident at the national level, most notably at the CJF General Assembly. Until recently the GA was almost indistinguishable from a meeting of any other group of affluent Americans. When Carmi Schwartz attended his first GA in 1959, he discovered on his arrival that no provision had been made for delegates who observed the Jewish dietary laws. He called the director of the host federation to inquire where he might take his meals; the indifferent director offered no assistance. (Schwartz solved the problem on his own by calling the local Jewish home for the aged, which happily supplied kosher meals to Schwartz and a handful of other delegates whom he rounded up.) Today, by contrast, kosher food is available for any GA delegate who wants it, and official meals serve only kosher food.

The change is more than culinary; today there is no mistaking the fact that the GA is a Jewish event. Religious services are conducted each morning for those who wish to recite the daily prayers; on Saturday morning—once almost a normal working and meeting day for delegates—three services (Orthodox, Conservative, and Reform) are held, to provide for every taste, and they are preceded by half a dozen or so well-attended study groups. Friday nights are taken up with long Sabbath dinners at which the traditional prayers are chanted; before or after dinner small groups of delegates gather to sing *zemirot*, songs traditionally sung on the Sabbath. During the regular work week, moreover, meals at which official business is conducted begin with the *motzi*, or prayer over bread, and end with the chanting of the *birkat hamaazon*, or grace after meals—rituals few of the delegates observe in their own homes.*

* The latter practice dates back to 1970, when the young activists again threatened to disrupt the GA unless they were permitted to recite grace after the opening dinner; the dinner chairman, who was also the CJF president, rejected their request on the grounds that prayer was not on the

At first federation critics derided the significance of the change, seeing it as an ironic reversal of the nineteenth-century maxim, Be a Jew at home and a person in the streets. "These federation leaders may be Jews in public," one rabbi told me, "but they're goyim at home." In fact, federation leaders are increasingly Jewish at home as well as in public, for their public observances have insinuated themselves into their private lives. This is particularly evident among the 3000 or so twenty-five-to-forty-year-olds who pass through federation leadership development programs every two years. Although they are far from being models of religious piety—few American Jews are—a series of studies by Jonathan Woocher of Brandeis indicates that the young leaders are a good bit more observant than their age group as a whole; they are two to three times more likely to light Sabbath candles, belong to a synagogue and attend services with some regularity, fast on Yom Kippur, and so on. Also, as a group they are more observant than their parents were.

The result has been a shift in federation priorities. For one thing, the enormous growth of public support for nonprofit health and welfare programs made federation subventions less and less important to the operation of the Jewish-sponsored hospitals, child guidance clinics, family service agencies, and old-age homes that had been the primary concern of the older generation of federation leaders. Because of the strings attached to government funding, moreover, as well as the low level of poverty among American Jews, Jews came to represent a smaller and smaller proportion of the clientele these agencies served, and federation leaders began to question whether their limited funds might not be put to better use. (Although grants to hospitals provided a tiny proportion of the hospitals' operating budgets, they represented a large share of the federations' own allocations.) As federations came to see themselves as agencies serving the well-being and survival of the Jewish community, they began to apportion a larger share of their funds to programs concerned with Jewish education and identity.

5

The growing concern of the federations for Jewish continuity and survival, interestingly enough, has changed their relationship with UJA. For one thing, the debate over UJA's allocation no longer is a quarrel between "assimilationists" and "Jewish survivalists"; it is a dis-

---

agenda. The impasse was resolved when the dinner speaker, Elie Wiesel, persuaded the chairman to allow grace to be recited as a courtesy to him rather than as an agenda item or a submission to the activists' demand.

pute over how best to serve Jewish continuity and survival. Most UJA leaders, in fact, have served as federation presidents and/or campaign chairmen—hence they recognize the importance of supporting American Jewish institutions. But those whose primary commitment is to UJA believe that Israel's needs come first; federation leaders are devoted to Israel, but they attach a higher priority to programs designed to improve Jewish education, strengthen Jewish family life, and aid the elderly. (In the long run, they argue, Israel's well-being requires a healthy and vibrant American Jewish community.) The result has been a slow but steady decline in UJA's share of the annual joint campaign, from 70–75 percent before the Yom Kippur War to 55–60 percent in the 1980s.

The tension over allocations has been exacerbated by differences in organizational style—differences that are rooted in the ideological struggles of the late 1930s and 1940s and that for old-timers still carry a heavy emotional freight. "UJA has always been more than just a fund-raising organization," a longtime officer told me. "It's been the central address for the passionate exercise of Jewish feeling"—a passion he finds lacking in most federation leaders. To Irving Bernstein, its executive head from 1969 to 1983, UJA "is America's Jewish religion." In a secular society such as ours, Bernstein explains, American Jews practice Judaism "not by prayer, but through philanthropy."

To those caught up in the organization, in fact, UJA is the one true faith. One cannot attend a national UJA conference without being impressed with the emotional intensity the almost entirely male participants bring to their discussions of fund-raising techniques and results—and to their relationships with one another. Almost without exception, the men stepping down from one position or moving up to another hug and kiss each other on the podium, openly and without self-consciousness or embarrassment.

ITEM: "I love you, Herschel, I love you very much," Robert Loup, of Denver, told Herschel Blumberg in May 1982 when he replaced Blumberg as national campaign chairman.

This outpouring of emotion stems from the sense of transcendence UJA leaders derive from their identification with Israel, which they see as the center—for some, almost the totality—of Jewish life. Consciously or not, they accept the Israeli view that Israel is the only legitimate place for a Jew to be, and they feel guilty about continuing to live in the United States. Working for UJA assuages that guilt; it is a symbolic act of *aliyah* (literally, "ascent")—settling in Israel.

The intense feeling UJA evokes has been its greatest strength; those caught up in the movement (and it *is* a movement, not just an organization) give it extraordinary amounts of time as well as money. But that fervor has turned out to be a source of weakness as well. For one thing, making UJA "America's Jewish religion" meant deifying Israel; after Israel's invasion of Lebanon—indeed, after Menachem Begin's election as prime minister—a number of UJA supporters found that their god had been shattered. They were disillusioned too by the discovery that Israeli leaders were not ten-feet-tall mythic heroes but ordinary mortals with flaws common to most mortals.

Once that happened, fund raising became an irksome task rather than a holy obligation. "That's pretty dull stuff," one of the country's richest Jews told me by way of explaining why he no longer is active in UJA. "Nobody likes to fund-raise." He still gives UJA a large donation—although not as large as formerly—but he no longer plays an active role in soliciting others. He finds more satisfaction in being chairman of the federation-sponsored Jewish Community Relations Council in his city and involving himself in local and national politics, contributing to (and raising funds for) politicians sympathetic to Jewish concerns.

As a result, federations have been more successful than the UJA in attracting—and retaining—the best lay leaders. It is not simply that the federations are concerned with American Jewish life as well as with the needs of Israel and of overseas Jewry; they also offer lay leaders a larger and more interesting stage on which to exercise their talents. To serve on a federation board is to be involved not just with fund raising but with government relations, management, investments, and communal planning. (A federation's choice of location for a new Jewish community center, for example, may accelerate the movement of Jews away from an old area of settlement or slow (even reverse) the exodus.)

The "brain drain" away from UJA has been compounded by the extraordinary growth in U.S. governmental aid to Israel, which has made UJA's fund raising considerably less important to Israel's welfare. With military and economic assistance to Israel reaching $2.5 billion in fiscal 1985 (and perhaps as much as $4 billion in 1986), a single subcommittee vote on a single amendment to the foreign aid bill can add or subtract more money than UJA raises for Israel in an entire year (about $280 million in 1983).*

Because of that fact—and because politics is a lot more fun (and

* In 1983 the joint campaign raised a grand total of $584 million, of which UJA received $350 million. After deducting its own expenses, UJA allocated $280 million to the United Israel Appeal, $50 million to the Joint Distribution Committee, and the balance to agencies assisting Jewish immigrants to the United States.

certainly more glamorous) than fund raising—some of the wealthiest and most talented communal leaders have turned to political activity as the principal means of expressing their commitment to Israel. One beneficiary has been the American-Israel Public Affairs Committee, the principal domestic lobby for Israel, whose budget has risen from $280,000 in 1974 to $1.2 million in 1980 and $4 million in 1984. Once almost a one-man operation, AIPAC, as it is commonly known, now has a staff of 70, including 5 registered Congressional lobbyists and a much larger number of community organizers, who mobilize pro-Israel support around the country (AIPAC's 1984 national conference in Washington drew 800 delegates from 40 states, including Alaska and Hawaii.) When the foreign aid bill is being debated, therefore, or some other important issue is before the Congress, AIPAC supporters, most of them large contributors to House and Senate campaigns, call (or if the issue is important enough, visit) their senators or representatives. It is the rare state, moreover, in which Jews do not provide a significant proportion of the funds raised for political campaigns, through individual contributions and, in recent years, political action committees, or PACs, at least 54 of which concentrate on aiding candidates who are friendly to Israel and opposing those seen as hostile.

It is not only politics, however, that has drawn contributors away from UJA or, for that matter, from federations as well; almost every Jewish organization has been affected by the increased openness of American society. Until recently, for example, the boards of trustees of major art museums, opera companies, and symphony orchestras were almost as restricted as the town and country clubs to which their upper-class members belonged. They made little effort to solicit contributions from wealthy Jews for fear of having to open board membership to people with whom they would not feel comfortable.

As the costs of maintaining—and, in a good many cities, creating—a first-class cultural institution skyrocketed, the old WASP elite turned out to be an insufficient base; like the famous bank robber, Willy Sutton, a few unconventional leaders decided to go "where the money is." The change came first in Los Angeles, when Dorothy Chandler, wife of *Los Angeles Times* publisher Norman Chandler, whose sisters considered her an *arriviste*, decided to create an oasis in what had been a cultural desert. In saving the Hollywood Bowl from closing in 1951 Mrs. Chandler discovered, as David Halberstam has written, "that the good families of the old Los Angeles were either not interested in music or not easily separated from their money or, most likely, both." She put that lesson to work three years later when she began raising $18 million for a new music center; most of the money came from newly rich Jews in Beverly Hills and West Los Angeles. Because of that fact and because she was impressed by the intelligence and ability of some of the Jews who helped her in her campaign—"They were different from most of the people she had known, in the acuteness of their minds and their zest for life," Halberstam wrote—she and her husband began opening other doors to them—for example, the board of the California Institute of Technology, as well as those of the Symphony and the new Music Center.

In older cities it took longer for universities, museums, and other cultural institutions to open their boardrooms to Jews, but everywhere the change has come, and at an accelerating pace.

ITEM: In 1980 New York City's Metropolitan Museum of Art appointed Frederick P. Rose, chairman of Rose Associates and a former president of the New York federation, to its board; shortly after his election Rose secured a $10 million gift from his friend and fellow real estate developer Harold D. Uris. As a result, the museum decided on a new focus for its fund-raising drives. "Met Museum Aiming to Tap Real-Estate Industry," a *New York Times* headline read, using a new euphemism for "wealthy Jews."

Nor is the museum unique in that regard; Jews play an even more prominent role in the Lincoln Center for the Performing Arts, where Russian-born Martin E. Segal is chairman and George Weissman is vice-chairman. And in Baltimore, where the late Joseph Meyerhoff contributed well over half the $20 million cost of a new symphony hall, Miami, Atlanta, and a host of other cities, cultural institutions are increasingly dependent on Jewish support.

This has affected Jewish philanthropies not simply because of the money diverted to other causes but because membership on the board of UJA, CJF, or a local federation does not confer the same status as membership on the board of a museum, symphony, opera company, or elite university. "There's more *yikhus* [prestige] in being on the Met board than in being on ours, and a lot more social clout," a New York federation officer told me, referring to the difficulty the federation was having competing with groups such as the Metropolitan Opera Company.

But UJA has been hurt in another way as well. In the past the emotional intensity it evokes contributed to a certain administrative untidiness that irritated the "cooler" federation leaders, many of them lawyers and corporate executives, who place a heavy premium on managerial efficiency. To UJA leaders of the old school, *ruach*—fervent spirit—was the supreme value, and they saw it as almost antithetical to a concern with good management; one officeholder refers contemptuously to federation officials as "bureaucrats," people unduly concerned with details of management and planning. In choosing its executive heads, therefore, UJA until recently picked superb orators, whose principal role was to "rouse the troops"—to evoke the fervor that was thought necessary for effective fund raising—rather than to manage a large organization. "Irving [Bernstein] may not have been the world's best administrator," one of his supporters told me, "but he is a passionate human being; his gut feeling for Jewish continuity and survival found great resonance throughout the country."

In the late 1970s, however, the UJA's operating style began to come under fire from both within and without the organization. The UJA is a franchising operation, as Bernstein puts it, and the people who held the franchises—the federations—along with some mavericks within the UJA itself began to question the way the franchise was being run. What happened, in part, was that Israel lost some of its luster during the Yom Kippur War, when the godlike heroes turned out to have feet of clay; incipient disillusionment turned into outright disaffection after Menachem Begin became the Israeli prime minister—a response to what some thought of as his paranoid style as much as to his aggressive policies on the West Bank.

Equally important, a new generation of lay and professional leaders had begun to take over—men (women were still in the background) for whom the Holocaust and the creation of the Jewish state were historical events rather than the formative experiences of their lives and who therefore placed as high a priority on good management as they did on *ruach*. Members of this new generation began to question whether the money they were raising was being used in the most effective way. They complained about the organization's loose management practices, including an absence of modern financial controls and a failure to make adequate use of computers to keep records and to monitor the course of the campaign. But the most important lapse of all, in their estimation, was UJA's failure to exercise sufficient control over the way its money was being spent in Israel.

To understand this last complaint one needs to know something about the circuitous route the money follows from contributors to its final disbursement in Israel. As already noted, individuals make their contributions to their local federation's joint campaign. The federation in turn remits a portion of the total to UJA, which, after deducting its own expenses, transfers the balance to its constituent agencies, chiefly the Joint Distribution Committee and the United Israel Appeal. (A small amount goes to the Hebrew Immigrant Aid Society and one or two other agencies that assist Jewish immigrants to the United States.) The JDC operates its own welfare programs in Israel and in virtually every country in which there are Jews in need. The UIA, by contrast, is not an operating agency; it transmits the money it receives from UJA to the Jewish Agency in Jerusalem, specifying the purposes for which the funds may be used.*

And that is where the problems begin, for the Jewish Agency is an institution unlike any other. Established in 1922 by the League of Nations Mandate for Palestine, and reorganized in 1929 to encourage non-Zionist Jews to provide financial support for the creation of a Jewish homeland, the Jewish Agency was in effect a Jewish state before there was a Jewish state. Under the British Mandate the Jewish Agency was responsible for education and health and welfare services for the partially autonomous Jewish community in Palestine; during the struggle for freedom from British rule it served as an underground government as well. In a sense the Jewish Agency gave birth to the Jewish state, which in turn decided to use the agency as the institution through which Israeli and Diaspora Jews could deal with problems—in particular, the rescue of persecuted Jews and their resettlement in Israel—that, by mutual agreement, are the responsibility of the world Jewish community rather than of Israel alone. (The airlift rescue of Ethiopian Jewry is the latest in a long series of repatriations.)

The result is a hybrid—a quasi-private, quasi-public organization that is deeply embedded in Israeli and world Zionist politics and that exists, at least in part, because the U.S. tax laws deny tax exemption to contributions made to a foreign government.† Not surprisingly, the Jewish Agency, to put it as gently as possible, is anything but a model of efficiency, for successive Israeli governments have used some of its departments as political pork barrels. Others voice their criticism in blunter terms. "It is an endless sea of free junkets, waste, irrelevancy, and much else which is wrong," one critic argues; or as a senior UJA staff member told me in 1982, "The Agency is a quagmire of inefficiency, politics, and graft."

ITEM: Department heads and other senior executives have always been appointed because of their political affiliations, and although some, such

* To ensure that funds are not spent in ways forbidden by the Internal Revenue Code, UIA maintains an office in Israel to monitor Jewish Agency operations.

† Until its "reconstitution" in 1971 the Jewish Agency was a division of the World Zionist Organization. Although theoretically separate from the WZO, the latter appoints half the members of the Jewish Agency's assembly and board of governors and 7 of the 13 members of its controlling Executive; the two organizations share the same chairman, controller, treasurer, and director-general as well as a variety of services. (Diaspora fund-raising organizations appoint half the members of the assembly and board of governors and 6 of the 13 members of the Executive.)

as Raanan Weitz, the longtime head of the rural settlement department, are highly regarded, other departments have served as a means of rewarding the party faithful. Until recent budget cutbacks, the Jewish Agency owned more than 200 vehicles; department heads and other senior executives, who receive the same fringe benefits and pensions as Israeli cabinet ministers, had their own chauffeur-driven limousines, and expense accounts that encouraged long foreign trips. (Given a per diem allowance of $100, whether they stayed in a hotel or with relatives, friends, or local Jewish dignitaries—the most frequent arrangement—some department heads have spent as many as 105 days a year abroad, thereby effectively doubling their salaries.)

ITEM: Through long custom the Jewish Agency has appropriated funds for Israeli political parties, ostensibly to pay for their own "educational" and "social welfare" programs. Under an arrangement worked out in the early 1960s, when the IRS and the Senate Foreign Affairs Committee were investigating whether UJA contributions were being used for foreign political purposes, none of the funds coming from the United States are used for this purpose. But since other countries with large Jewish populations do not have restrictions of this sort, the agency has used contributions from Jews in Britain, South Africa, and other countries to continue its political grants, freeing UJA/UIA money for other programs.

Except when they were forced to come to terms with these problems under threat of losing UJA's tax exemption, the older generation of UJA and CJF leaders failed to take action. For them the existence of a Jewish state was a miracle, and they ignored its problems, preferring to "keep their eye on the larger picture," which meant deferring to Israeli leaders, whom, in any case, they viewed with awe. Flattered to be treated with respect, or even deference, by the prime minister and leading generals and cabinet ministers, they felt that questioning the Jewish Agency's expenditures would be a form of lese majesty.

One consequence was that the agency felt free to set its budget according to its definition of need rather than according to its receipts, borrowing in order to meet the difference. There were years, of course, when the procedure was essential in order to meet some emergency need, but in time the borrowing became routine. By 1981, when American representatives on the agency board belatedly forced the imposition of a statutory ceiling, the debt stood at $650 million, and annual interest charges were running to approximately $100 million. Since American contributions could not be used to underwrite the agency's political programs, the UJA, which provided 60 percent of the Jewish Agency's total budget, was paying 75 percent of the interest charges.

Afraid that contributors would rebel if they discovered that roughly 25 percent of their gifts to Israel were being used to service the agency's debt—"People think they're giving for programs, not interest," one UJA official told me—the American representatives on the Jewish Agency boards succeeded in 1981 in imposing a statutory debt ceiling, which has forced the agency to bring its budget in line with its receipts. Two years later, in what *The Jerusalem Post* called "the fund-raisers' revolt," the Diaspora members of the agency's board of governors ousted the head of its Aliyah department, turned down a Begin nominee for another high post, and at a board retreat at Caesarea, Israel, created a number of committees to study the agency's operations, thereby signaling their intent to make merit the chief criterion for office.

There has been another revolt, and this within the UJA itself, as a majority of its board came to feel that a new approach was needed. In the late fall of 1983 they reached into the federation world to find a new executive head, appointing Stanley Horowitz, the fifty-year-old executive director of the Cleveland federation, UJA's president and chief professional officer. The change was more than symbolic: Horowitz brought in senior executives from the business as well as the federation worlds.

Some UJA old-timers are unhappy with what they see as Horowitz's lack of passion—the mirror image, in their view, of his emphasis on modern management techniques, but Horowitz, in a rare show of passion, demurs. "You don't have to be a bad manager in order to have a big heart or a commitment to a big cause," he told me. "I reject the allegation that *ruach* and good management are mutually exclusive." Expectations have changed, Horowitz argues; a new generation of contributors wants "more than missionary zeal and technical expertise in running a dinner or mounting a mission to Israel." Contributors "expect good management on the part of their federations, and the federations expect it of UJA." The organization will have to meet those expectations, therefore, if it is to grow as Horowitz thinks it must: "In an age of well-educated, as well as committed, Jewish leaders, success is directly related to UJA's credibility, accountability, and knowledgeability, as well as its technical fund-raising skills."

To win back the confidence of the federations Horowitz has made UJA a leaner and more efficiently run operation, and he has involved federation, CJF, and other organization leaders, as well as UJA lay leaders, in a study of the UJA: the kind of organization it is, what it ought to be, and how any discrepancy between the two can be eliminated. In the past, Horowitz told me, "UJA had to go from crisis to crisis, and that made it impossible to take the time to define what it ought to be or to create an orderly, step-by-step process of change." He refused to discuss his own vision of what UJA should be, since the new Committee on Scope and Function is still at work; he is concerned that the "outside" members might feel they were being manipulated. It is "the process," Horowitz insists, that is crucial: if donors and federation and other communal leaders "see that the process is honest . . . if they believe that UJA really wants to reflect their views," they will come on board, for "we are still the biggest game in town"—the "best and biggest vehicle for expressing the Jewish philanthropic impulse." Whether Horowitz's assessment is correct or not remains to be seen.

CHAPTER SIX

LOOKING OUT THE WINDOW: THE RENEWAL OF AMERICAN JUDAISM

1

"We're the last generation with memory," a contemporary told me recently, explaining why he was so worried about the future of Judaism in America. For him, in fact, the Holocaust and the creation of the Jewish state were more than memories; they were the central experiences of his life. Those experiences, along with memories of his grandfather, who had been one of the great preachers of the Lower East Side, served to bind him to Jewishness in an irrevocable way. For his children and grandchildren, however, the Holocaust and Israel's formation are not memories but historical events, as remote in some ways as the destruction of the First Temple and the return from Babylonian exile 2500 years ago.

My friend's concern is real and cannot easily be dismissed. "Memory is among the most fragile and capricious of our faculties," the historian Yosef Yerushalmi has written, "yet the Hebrew Bible [has] no hesitation in commanding memory. Its injunctions to remember are unconditional, and even when not commanded, remembrance is always pivotal." Indeed, in its various declensions, the Hebrew verb *zakhar* (to remember) appears no fewer than 169 times in the Bible, with the obligation incumbent on both God and Israel. (In Israel's case it usually is accompanied by the complementary obligation not to forget.) The ritual of the Passover seder is designed to bring to life what Abraham Joshua Heschel called "the commandment of faith"—to "remember that ye were slaves in Egypt," and to "remember the day of your departure from the land of Egypt."

It is not surprising, therefore, that Jews of my generation talk, and worry, about the loss of memory. The novelist Anne Roiphe, once totally alienated from Judaism, gave the book describing her search for a way back to Judaism the title "Generation Without Memory." True enough, many Jews of my generation have enlarged their Passover ritual to include readings recalling the Holocaust and celebrating Israel's existence, but neither event can resonate for their children as it does for them.

It would be a mistake, however, to regard the loss of memory in negative terms alone. One reason Israel is central to the Jewish identity of older Jews, after all, is that it gives us a vicarious sense of potency and power. Israel's existence—most of all, perhaps, her military exploits—have transformed the way we see ourselves, because, as I discussed in Chapter Two, our consciousness was formed at a time when Jews lived in fear. Centuries of powerlessness, of survival through accommodation, had bred a distaste for physical combat and a tendency to shy away from confrontation. The self-image that resulted is parodied in Woody Allen's remark that at the interfaith summer camp he attended he was beaten up by kids of every race, religion, and national origin. For my generation, in fact, fear of Gentiles formed a staple subject of Jewish humor.

ITEM: From *The Big Book of Jewish Humor:* "Two Jews are walking through an anti-Semitic neighborhood one evening when they notice that they are being followed by a pair of hoodlums. 'Sam,' says his friend, 'we better get out of here. There are two of them and we're alone.' "

Young Jews have never known this kind of fear. For one thing, they have not experienced anti-Semitism—certainly not the physical kind that existed during my own childhood. Equally important, they are now sufficiently acculturated into American life to have acquired the athletic and other physical skills needed for peer acceptance during adolescence. As a result, there has been a dramatic change in the self-image of young Jews.

ITEM: In the 1980 American Council on Education survey of college freshmen, 42 percent of the Jewish students rated themselves above average in athletic ability—half again as many as had given themselves that rating just ten years earlier. Indeed, more Jewish than non-Jewish freshmen (42 percent as compared with 40 percent) now consider themselves "above average" in athletic ability—a reversal of the relationship that existed in 1970.

Never having known their parents' fear, young Jews do not need the vicarious sense of potency their parents derive from Israel's military accomplishments. As Jews, they may take pride in Israeli strength, but they are far less likely to turn Israelis into mythic heroes. Because they were not alive during the Holocaust, moreover, they do not share their parents' sense of guilt; and because they have never known a time when there was *not* a Jewish state, they take Israel's existence for granted in a way their parents never can; they see Israel as a fact—a flesh-and-blood state—rather than as a symbol or myth. For young Jews, therefore, the convenant is truly voluntary; they enjoy a freedom of choice that is not available to their parents, who are bound by guilt and other primordial ties.

Most important of all, young Jews do not see Jewishness as a burden, still less as an affliction. Having grown up in an almost completely open society, they are at home in America—and at ease with their Jewishness—in a way their parents can never be. I first appreciated the magnitude of the change some seventeen years ago when my wife and I celebrated our third son's tenth birthday by bringing him and his three brothers to Washington. A friend had arranged for the boys to meet then Vice-President Hubert Humphrey. A warm and gracious host, Mr. Humphrey brought us into the vice-president's ceremonial office, a cavernous room off the Senate chamber, which contained all the trophies he had accumulated in his lifetime of public service. While my wife and I chatted with the vice-president at one end of the room our son wandered off on his own. Suddenly, in the piercing tone of a thoroughly uninhibited ten-year-old, he called out to me from the other end of the room, "Hey, Dad, come look at the Torah in the showcase!" As I heard him I knew that with all the piety and ritual of my intensely Jewish upbringing, I could not have called out to my father that way if my life had depended on it. Had I been in that situation, I would have sidled up to my father, tugged at his coattails to get his attention, and given him the information in as inaudible a whisper as I could manage.

The total absence of inhibition my son displayed was not unique with him; it goes to the heart of the difference between the generations.

ITEM: "We were living in Miami Beach when Castro took over Cuba," Nathan Perlmutter, national director of the Anti-Defamation League, has written. "When the refugees began pouring into Miami, my daughter was thirteen years old and in junior high school. One dinner time, in response to my serviceable, if uninspired, parental conversation opener, 'How was school today?,' she replied that there were now over forty Cuban children in her school. 'Really?' 'Yes,' she answered, 'and they have such crazy names: Menendez, Morales, Gonzales.' She paused, and then added thoughtfully, 'But some of them have American names: Goldstein, Schwartz, Levy, Cohen.' " (The first wave of Cuban immigrants included a number of Jews, most of them refugees from Hitler's Europe who had settled in Havana when they could not gain entry to the United States.)

In short, the old burden has been lifted, and with it the self-consciousness, bordering on embarrassment, that Jewishness once entailed. The most striking evidence of this is the ease with which Jews now display their Jewishness in public. I described the rise of "public sector Judaism" in the last chapter, but it is evident as well in the facts that young Jews no longer feel obliged to anglicize their family names and that some have even reclaimed the names their parents or grandparents had abandoned. The best-known instance of this is the decision by novelist Irving Wallace's son, David, to revert to the surname Wallechinsky. Young Jews not only are keeping their own family names but a growing number are giving their children biblical or modern Hebrew first names instead of the "American" given names so popular a generation and two ago. My favorite example involves a college classmate who had changed his name from Isaacson to Iselin; his daughter, who is married to a young man named Tyler—himself the offspring of a mixed marriage—named their firstborn son Isaac in a deliberate attempt to recapture the family name.

This new attitude is significant, for names are a public as well as private expression of identity—a public expression, moreover, with enormous emotional resonance, for names have always played a powerful symbolic role in human consciousness. In the Bible, for example, the great moments in the lives of the patriarchs were almost always accompanied by a change in name: Abram to Abraham, Sarai to Sarah, and Jacob to Israel. The early Zionist settlers in Palestine displayed a similar "mania for renaming," as the Israeli journalist Amos Elon has called it. When a settler changed his name, say, from Gruen to Ben-

Gurion (son of a lion), as Israel's first prime minister did early in the century, or from Rachmilewitz to Onn (vigor), he was not simply Hebraizing a Russian-sounding name; the settler was, in Elon's formulation, "re-enacting a piece of primitive magic, reminiscent of the initiation rites of certain Australian tribes, in which boys receive new names at puberty and are then considered reborn as men."

In the United States today young Jews have no need to be reborn; nor are they at war with their parents, as earlier generations were. On the contrary, the distance that once separated one generation from the next is now largely closed; children no longer feel embarrassed by their parents' foreign accents and mannerisms, for the parents are now almost all native-born Americans, most of them college graduates with middle-class occupations. Thus a principal cause of earlier generations' flight from Jewishness has disappeared; young Jews wear their Jewishness with ease, whether they practice their religion or not.

There is another side to the coin, of course: that same ease means that young Jews can surrender their Jewishness without any struggle or trauma; they can simply drift away and disappear into the crowd, through apathy rather than deliberate choice. Some are doing precisely that; it would be feckless to pretend that all is for the best in this best of all possible Jewish worlds. Full acceptance also means that a significant minority of young Jews are marrying outside the faith, a phenomenon whose dimensions and consequences are discussed in detail in the next chapter.

The fact remains that the great majority of American Jews, young as well as old, are retaining their Jewish identity. As a group, in fact, young Jews are at least as committed to Jewishness as their elders; and among a small but significant minority, generational change now involves an intensification rather than diminution of Jewish religious, intellectual, and cultural life. Reading or listening to the gloomy forecasts that are a staple of American Jewish life, I am reminded of the advice a wise meteorologist once gave a young colleague: "Before committing your forecast to paper, look out the window." The Talmud makes a similar recommendation: before reaching a firm conclusion, it advises, "go and see what the people in the street are doing."

For nearly six years I have done precisely that: I have traveled the length and breadth of the American continent, talking to rabbis and congregants, communal leaders and followers, professors and students, cab drivers and corporate chief executives, teenagers and retirees, Orthodox Jews who pray three times a day and nonbelievers who never enter a synagogue or open a prayer book—in short, Jews of every age and rank and persuasion. I have read the literature and analyzed the data, and I have sat in on more meetings of more Jewish organizations than I care to total. The bottom line, as financial analysts like to put it, is that the end is *not* at hand, that Judaism is not about to disappear in the United States.

On the contrary, a major renewal of Jewish religious and cultural life is now under way, one that is likely to transform American Judaism. This is not to deny the existence of contrary trends; many young Jews who make no attempt to escape their Jewishness nonetheless see it as an irrelevant fact, one that has no impact on the way they live their lives. But if some are passively dropping out of Judaism, others are electing to come in—and when young Jews freely choose to be Jewish, they often do so with a seriousness, creativity, and élan that are wholly new to American Jewish life.

Religious renewal involves a number of separate if often overlapping trends. Some Jews who had appeared irretrievably lost to Judaism are finding their way back; others, who had never strayed, are intensifying their religious practice and commitment; still others are creating new ways of expressing their Jewishness, which is more important to them than they had thought. The openness of American society has created a whole new set of options for American Jews, who can now express their Jewishness in a wide variety of ways without surrendering their full participation in American life.

Until recently the greatest weakness of American Jewish life had been its intellectual dependence on the older centers of Jewish scholarship in Europe and, after World War II, in Israel. The faculties of rabbinic training schools were staffed almost entirely by European-born and -trained scholars, and until Brandeis University opened its doors in 1948, there were only two full-time professors of Jewish history and thought in secular American universities—Harry Austryn Wolfson at Harvard and Salo W. Baron at Columbia.

Today, in contrast, more than 300 American colleges and universities offer courses in Judaic studies; at least 40 have Judaic-studies majors, and 27 offer graduate programs at the master's and/or doctoral level. These courses and programs are staffed almost entirely by American-born and -trained scholars, who have already made major contributions to knowledge. Enrollments, moreover, are not limited to those who plan to specialize in Jewish studies; more undergraduates now study Jewish history, literature, language, and thought than are enrolled in courses in Greek and Latin. Nor are the programs confined to institutions with a particularly large proportion of Jewish students; there are important programs at such places as Duke University, in Durham, North Carolina, Ohio State University, the University of Minnesota, and Indiana University. In the 1983–84 academic year at Indiana, for example, 881 students were enrolled in the 32 courses that were offered; and Indiana University Press has become the most active publisher of books on Jewish life and thought. (Among the university presses that now have separate publishing programs in Judaic studies is the University of Alabama Press.)

The explosive growth in the number of Jewish-studies courses and programs is the result of a transformation in the way both Jews and Gentiles view Judaism. Jewish students used to shun any visible connection with Jewish tradition; they were in college, after all, to acquire the culture of the West, which meant—or so they and their mentors assumed—that they would have to shed the inferior culture and manners in which they had been raised. One of the axioms of academic life in Europe and the United States was that although Jews had a religion and a set of laws, they had no culture—at least none that any educated person needed to know anything about. In 1929, for example, when a gift from a Jewish alumnus enabled Columbia University to create a chair in Jewish history, literature, and institutions, it took forceful intervention by the university's president, Nicholas Murray Butler, to persuade the history department to accept Salo Baron on its faculty; the Jewish experience, the members argued, was not a fit subject for historians to study. (Baron himself was initially reluctant to accept the post. Who will take a doctorate in Jewish history? he recalls having thought.)

What is new, then, is not simply that Jewish students (and in some universities, non-Jewish students as well) are interested in learning more about Judaism—a fact that never ceases to amaze those who grew up in the 1920s or 1930s. More important, perhaps, a university curriculum, as Jacob Neusner suggests, is "an enormously effective symbolic statement about what matters and what does not." Specifically, the creation of Jewish-studies programs and departments, and the inclusion of courses about Jews and Judaism in departments of religion, sociology, and history constitutes a recognition that the Jewish experience is worth learning about. And recognition of Jewish studies as "part of the fabric of Western civilization," Gerson Cohen states, "marks a radical change in the place of the Jew in Western society."*

Interest in the Jewish experience extends far beyond the academy.

* The iconoclastic Neusner offers a partial dissent. "Jewish studies locate themselves in universities," he claims. "But they have yet to become part of universities," by which he means that too many Judaic-studies programs consist of random collections of courses taught by Jews for Jews for their own parochial purposes. Unless Judaic scholars put their work in the broader context of scholarly inquiry, Neusner argues—unless they speak to everyone in the university—"Jewish studies will pass from the scene." But a significant number of scholars are doing precisely that.

Consider, for example, the case of New York City's 92nd Street Y. Long known for its musical and cultural programs, the Y until recently provided relatively meager programs of specifically Jewish interest; today it is a major center for adult Jewish studies. In the first five years after John Ruskay, a young educator, assumed the post of education director in 1979, the number of Jewish programs quadrupled, and the number of people attending them increased fivefold; in the 1983–84 program year some 14,000 individuals attended the courses, lectures and lecture series, workshops, and films offered as part of the Y's Jewish Omnibus program.

The same kind of change is evident in the arts as well; the last decade has seen an explosive growth of interest in Jewish music.

ITEM: From a front-page story in the April 15, 1983, *Wall Street Journal,* datelined Poughkeepsie, New York:

> The joint is jumping. As the band cranks up the tempo, dozens of people break into an impromptu hora, the standard circle dance for countless Jewish weddings. Others kick their legs in the style of the Mexican hat dance. Still others simply run in place to the beat . . . while the rest of the 400 concert goers clap to the music.
>
> The agent of all this pandemonium is a young group with the unlikely name Kapelye, Yiddish for "the band." Kapelye plays klezmer music, and klezmer is hot. . . . "Klezmer knocks everybody's socks off," says Garrison Keillor, host of the radio comedy and folk show "A Prairie Home Companion."
>
> Until recently, klezmer was little more than a historical footnote—the music of Jews from Eastern Europe and immigrant neighborhoods in the U.S. But now, a dozen young klezmer revival bands are drawing enthusiastic audiences in cities such as Boston, New York, San Francisco, Providence, and Cincinnati. Although few of klezmer's fans understand the music's Yiddish lyrics and even fewer know the right dance steps, they are embracing klezmer for its unusual mixture of foot-stomping energy and piercing soulfulness. . . .
>
> Despite their differences [in background], the musicians tell strikingly similar stories of how they rediscovered klezmer. Most are nonreligious Jews who were looking for a music that expressed their heritage and had a beat that moved them. "As soon as I heard the music I knew that was it," says 30-year-old Lev Lieberman, leader of Klezmorim, a band in Berkeley, Calif.

The klezmer revival is significant because it is not simply a turn toward nostalgia or a search for a romanticized past that never was.

"We're not playing it as part of 'roots,' " Lieberman says, "We're simply playing a fascinating kind of music to the highest professional standards." (Since Lieberman cofounded the Klezmorim in 1975 the group has performed in twenty-eight states, including a sold-out concert in New York City's Carnegie Hall.) Indeed, the last ten years have seen the emergence of "a new Jewish music," as critic Neil Riesner calls it. "Like most things Jewish nowadays, it is not entirely new," Riesner writes, "It is the old, seen and heard with fresh eyes and ears—partly a revival of folk music around the world and throughout the ages and partly a reflection of American Jewry's new-found maturity." Most klezmer groups integrate elements of jazz and the blues with their "Jewish soul music," as they like to call klezmer, while others, such as the Fabrengen Fiddlers, of Washington, D.C., combine klezmer and Hasidic music with bluegrass and country music.

The emergence of a new Jewish music is part of a much broader upsurge of activity across the whole spectrum of the arts. There are at least ten theater groups across the country, for example, that perform both old and new works with Jewish themes, and there are annual Jewish arts festivals in Boston and Washington, D.C., among other cities. The eight-year-old Martin Steinberg Center for the Arts, an American Jewish Congress affiliate established to encourage activity in the Jewish arts, now publishes a quarterly newsletter so that interested parties can keep abreast of what is happening. One of the most striking changes, perhaps, has been the emergence of a group of successful novelists and short-story writers, such as Cynthia Ozick, Mark Helperin, Jay Neugeboren, and Johanna Kaplan, for whom Judaism and Jewishness are not material for satire but an intrinsic part of the air their fictional characters breathe.

What is happening, says Richard Siegel, who directs programs in the arts for the National Foundation for Jewish Culture, is that the third generation is trying to recapture what the second generation had tried to forget, just as historian Marcus Hansen had predicted. "We now have a group of people who are . . . well integrated within the surrounding culture and who have no bones to pick with their Jewish baggage," Siegel explains. One reason is that the gulf that once separated the generations has been largely closed; both parents and children are likely to be American-born, and both inhabit the same cultural milieu. In 1980, for example, three Jewish high school students in five had at least one parent who had a college degree; and since the overwhelming majority of Jewish students come from middle-class backgrounds, "making it" no longer involves estrangement from one's parents. Whatever tensions there may be between the generations, moreover, children no longer are ashamed of their parents because they are "Jewish" rather than "American." As a result, the principal cause of the flight from Jewishness by earlier generations has been removed. Having gained the acceptance that earlier generations craved, contemporary Jews are comfortable enough with their Jewishness to express it publicly through literature, music, dance, theater, and a variety of other art forms.

2

The growth in public expressions of Jewishness has its counterparts in the private sphere, and for the same reasons. Consider, for example, the profound change in the attitudes of American Jews toward Christmas and Chanukah. For American Jews, Christmas used to be the most awkward season of the year. From January until Thanksgiving, Jews might have been able to persuade themselves that they were just like everyone else, except that they observed (or more often did *not* observe) the Sabbath on Saturday instead of on Sunday; but from Thanksgiving until New Year's Day the pretense fell apart, for the world suddenly became Christian. The omnipresence of Christmas trees and decorations in homes and public places; the ubiquitous Santa Clauses in department stores and on street corners; the public school pageants and carol recitals; the manger scenes in front of churches and, often, City Hall; the genuine warmth that normally reticent people displayed; and, most of all, the kindly strangers asking young children what they hoped Santa would bring them—all these normal manifestations of the Christmas spirit served to remind Jews of how different they really were.

In an age in which to be different was to feel inferior, Christmas came to be seen as a Jewish problem as well as a Christian holiday. "While the awkwardness with which they once again confront Christmas is not the most desperate problem faced by American Jews," a young scholar wrote in 1954, "it yields to few in complexity." Such were the complexities, in fact, that Jewish families did not merely see Christmas as a problem; they felt the need to have a *policy* toward it. For example:

• Should children sing religious Christmas carols in school? Should they *pretend* to sing? Or should their parents ask that the youngsters be excused from participating?

• Should Jewish families acknowledge Christmas in some form—say, by sending Christmas cards—or should they try to ignore it? If they send Christmas cards, should the cards go to Gentile friends only or to Jewish friends as well?

• Should the family go beyond acknowledgment and actually *celebrate* Christmas, and if so, how? Should family members exchange gifts, and if so, what kind? Should the children be permitted (encouraged?) to hang Christmas stockings? And what about Santa Claus: should children's gifts be attributed to him or should they come directly from parents and grandparents?

• These questions were resolved relatively easily, compared to the great symbolic issue of the Christmas tree. Families had to decide whether or not to have a tree, and if so, how large it should be and how it should be decorated—specifically, whether it should have a star on top, and if so, what kind—the conventional five-pointed star or a six-pointed Jewish star?

For all the variations in the Christmas "policies" Jew adopted, they tended to fall into one of three groups. Among Orthodox Jews, insulated against the larger society, Chanukah remained what it had always been—a minor festival in the Jewish calendar. (Unlike the major holidays, work is not prohibited on the first or last days of Chanukah, nor is there an elaborate synagogue liturgy.) A much larger group, eager to acculturate without becoming fully assimilated, tried to hold their children's allegiance to Judaism by turning Chanukah into a major holiday. Chanukah was "better than Christmas," children were told, because they received eight gifts—one on each of the eight nights of the festival—instead of only one. But parents who made this argument usually did so without conviction and without persuading their children. The pull of Jewish tradition was sufficiently strong, in any case, so that Chanukah never really became a major holiday—certainly not an occasion on which the extended family gathered, as was the case with Passover; but the pull of Christmas was so strong that many families continued to be ambivalent about their choice.

For a significant number of Jews, however, substituting Christmas for Chanukah was an important step on the road to becoming fully American; most members of "Our Crowd" adopted Christmas as their holiday early in the century. Christmas played an important symbolic role for upwardly mobile Eastern European Jews as well; as Anne Roiphe has put it, "Christmas is a kind of checking point where one can stop and view oneself on the assimilation route." Roiphe's mother, whose Polish-born father had founded the firm that manufactures Van Heusen shirts, had been eager to have a Christmas tree during her own childhood. She "described to me how at Christmastime she would stare at all the store windows on upper Broadway, at the gentle, glowing lights of the Christmas tree, and how she wanted that tree in her home, bright and covered with tinsel and sparkling cotton at the base," Roiphe has written. But her mother's parents, who remained moderately observant Jews despite their wealth, would not consider it. When she was first married, therefore, Roiphe's mother had trouble deciding what her "Christmas policy" should be.

The question was resolved by Roiphe's German governess when Roiphe was born on December 25; it became customary for the entire extended family to gather for a combined Christmas-birthday dinner. "We exchanged presents under the tree, extra ones for me because it was my birthday," Roiphe recalls. "My birthday cake was always decorated with red and green. My mother, who may have experienced some guilt over the first tree, threw herself into the Christmas spirit with all her unused energy. On the dining table we had wreaths and reindeer pulling little carts. We had ice cream molds in the shape of Santa Claus and Christmas bells. We had holly on the mantel and mistletoe hung from the chandelier. . . ." "We [are] American," her mother explained when family members objected, "and Christmas . . . is an American holiday!"

Until a few years ago that was how Anne Roiphe and her family saw it too. In fact, in 1978, Roiphe wrote an article for *The New York Times Magazine* entitled "Christmas Comes to a Jewish Home," in which she described the Roiphe family's observance of Christmas. The article was greeted by an avalanche of angry, often hostile, letters from Jewish readers. The mail came from close friends as well as from strangers; almost everyone who wrote was enraged that Roiphe appeared to be recommending her assimilated life style to others.

It is a sign of the times, and of the changing attitudes of American Jews toward "the assimilation parade," that the Roiphe family now celebrates Chanukah with an elaborate party and exchange of gifts, lighting candles on a beautiful menorah that Anne Roiphe's children helped her select. The change had its origin in her 1978 article. Taken aback by the reaction, Roiphe spent the next few years exploring Judaism and her attitudes and relationship to it.

It was a profitable exploration. Roiphe discovered that there was considerably more to Judaism than "the thin, watered-down Jewishness" she had experienced as a child. To her surprise she found that she felt a close connection, even attachment, to Jewish tradition, and she came to see her Thanksgiving and Christmas celebrations as "eclectic, thin, without magic or the density of time." Roiphe's attachment is cultural, not religious; there is much about Judaism that she finds hard to accept and some things she rejects outright. But the attachment is real, and her searching goes on, guided by "a renewed or new connection to Jewishness, an amazed connection that supersedes all my ambivalences and doubts." "Taken all together," she has written, "the nationhood is a landscape of incredible grandeur, and the culture itself, the more one knows of it, well, the more it shines with radiance."

Anne Roiphe's experience is worth recounting because it exemplifies an important trend, in which lighting Chanukah candles increases, generation by generation, among secular as well as religious Jews.

ITEM: A distinguished publisher grew up in a completely assimilated home in which Christmas rather than Chanukah was celebrated. As is customary in this heavily Jewish industry, he used to give an annual Christmas party for literary agents, authors, and other publishers. He still gives the party, but since 1979 or 1980 it has been a Chanukah party, with a menorah on the mantel and potato *latkes* (pancakes), the traditional Chanukah food, among the hors d'oeuvres. A small change, perhaps, but one with important symbolic overtones.

This kind of change first became evident in the 1950s when, as we saw in the last chapter, Jews who had left their "urban shtetls" for predominantly Gentile suburbs began to worry about whether their children would remain Jews. Studying the relatively assimilated Jews of "Lakeville" in 1957–58, Marshall Sklare discovered to his surprise that lighting Chanukah candles–a ceremony that occupies a fairly low place in the hierarchy of religious obligations–had become the single most widely observed ritual. Two Jews in three lit Chanukah candles; the only other ritual observed by a majority of Lakeville residents–three in five–was attending a Passover seder. Comparing Lakeville Jews' ritual observances with those of their parents, Sklare found an increase from one generation to the next in the proportion lighting Chanukah candles and only a slight decline in the number attending a seder; with every other ritual–observing the dietary laws, lighting Sabbath candles, fasting on Yom Kippur, and so on–the pattern was the reverse–there were precipitous declines from the parental to the next generation.

Although this pattern of observance was hard to understand from a traditional religious standpoint, Sklare pointed out, it made perfect sense from a sociological perspective. The decisions of Lakeville Jews concerning which rituals to observe were the result of two quite contrary pulls: their desire to remain Jews and their desire to be at home in American culture. Thus the most popular rituals, Sklare suggested, were those that met five criteria: they can be redefined in contemporary terms; they do not require social isolation or a distinctive life-style; they provide a Jewish alternative to a widely observed Christian holiday; they do not have to be performed with great frequency; and they are centered on the children.

Chanukah and Passover meet these criteria perfectly. They are child-centered festivals—Passover intrinsically so and Chanukah through a long process of adaptation to American life. Unlike the Sabbath, moreover, Passover and Chanukah need be observed only once a year instead of once a week; and unlike the dietary laws, they do not require a distinctive life-style, nor do they impose any barriers to easy social relations with non-Jews. On the contrary, acculturated Jews increasingly invite Gentile friends to their seder services, and an interfaith seder the Sunday before Passover has become commonplace in many communities. By downplaying the traditional emphasis on God's benevolence and miraculous intervention and emphasizing instead the struggle for religious and political freedom, American Jews have turned Chanukah and Passover into holidays that subtly underscore their Americanness as well as their Jewishness.

ITEM: The racks of Chanukah cards one now sees in greeting-card stores in most large cities provide clear evidence of how American that holiday has become. "You know it's Hanukkah," Snoopy says on the cover of one popular card, "when the 'Fiddler on the Roof' comes down your chimney." We would have flinched at such a card when I was young—if, indeed, we could have conceived of venturing into a store to buy a Chanukah card at all; it was not until after World War II that manufacturers saw a potential market and began turning out Chanukah cards in sizable numbers. Now one can even buy a "Chanukah stocking"—a blue-and-white sock sprinkled with six-pointed stars.

It is not surprising, therefore, that observance of Chanukah and Passover have become the principal means by which American Jews affirm their Jewishness.

ITEM: According to Steven M. Cohen's annual surveys of American Jewish attitudes and behavior, nearly nine Jews in ten report that they attend a seder, either at home or elsewhere. Jews in their twenties and thirties are more likely to attend a seder than those in their sixties.

ITEM: More than three American Jews in four now light Chanukah candles—a number well above the level of a generation or two ago. Lighting Chanukah candles is more frequent now in every age group than it had been in the parental generation, with the largest discrepancy reported by Jews in their twenties and thirties.

Chanukah has become more popular, interestingly enough, despite a small increase in the number of Jews who celebrate Christmas.* For some American Jews, it would appear, having a tree is no longer a mark of detachment from Jewish life. Witness the fact that 12 percent of the Jewish communal leaders whom Cohen surveyed in 1983—board members of the United Jewish Appeal, B'nai B'rith, American Jewish Committee, Anti-Defamation League, and American Jewish Congress—have Christmas trees; yet 94 percent of the leaders had been to Israel at least once, and 78 percent had been there two or more times—proportions far above those in the Jewish population at large. (The communal leaders were also more likely to light Sabbath candles, attend a Seder, light Chanukah candles, and observe most other rituals.)

Some critics of American Jewish life dismiss the growth in observance of Chanukah and Passover as a trivialization of Jewish tradition. Many of those who light Chanukah candles, they point out, do not recite (or know) the blessings and prayers that are supposed to accompany the ceremony, and many a Passover seder is little more than a particularly warm family dinner party at which matzoh-ball soup is served and a prayer or two recited.

The observations are true enough; they also happen to be beside the point, for they reflect a profound misunderstanding of the nature of the change that has occurred. For many American Jews, attending a seder or lighting Chanukah candles is an ethnic far more than a religious act; it is a way of asserting cultural and national identity rather than of obeying God's law. To paraphrase Samuel Johnson's famous quip about the vaudeville dog that walks on two legs, what is remarkable is not that American Jews perform the rituals badly but that they perform them at all. Despite the frequent forecasts of Judaism's imminent demise, secular Jews are turning to religious rituals to affirm their Jewish identity.

It is historically appropriate to use Chanukah in this fashion; the triumph that Chanukah celebrates, after all, was that of Jewish particularists over Jewish universalists—a victory of those who were determined to maintain a separate Jewish identity over those who wanted

* According to Cohen's 1984 survey, 12 percent of American Jews now have Christmas trees, compared to 11 percent ten years earlier; 9 percent reported that their parents had had trees. Younger Jews are more likely to have trees than their elders, a difference attributable to their higher rate of intermarriage. It is not surprising that this should be so; for born Christians, after all, Christmas is filled with childhood memories and inextricably tied to present as well as past relations with parents, grandparents, and siblings.

Jews to disappear into the universal and highly accepting culture of Hellenism.* To be sure, Purim would be even more appropriate: it commemorates the triumph of a highly acculturated community of Diaspora Jews rather than of a faction within ancient Palestine; and secular American Jews are likely to be more comfortable with the Book of Esther, which never mentions the name of God, than with the religious zealotry of the Maccabees. But there is no Christian or secular American holiday in February to which Purim can be a Jewish counterpart; hence the festival is largely ignored by secular Jews. (In Israel, in contrast, it is more widely observed than Chanukah.)

It is even more fitting that attendance at a seder has become almost universal. Passover has always been the most popular Jewish holiday—and not only because it is so inextricably bound up with home and family.† The child-centeredness of the seder is not an accident, still less a modern interpolation. As I have said, it is the means of carrying out the biblical injunction that lies at the heart of Passover and, indeed, of Judaism itself: to remember Egyptian slavery and the Exodus and to transmit that memory from one generation to the next. To attend a Passover seder, therefore, no matter how watered down it may be, is to keep that memory alive and thus to affirm the desirability, as well as mystery, of Jewish survival.

What survey data do not show, moreover, is the seriousness with which a growing number of Jews take the responsibility of keeping the memory alive.

ITEM: As a child Eugene Eidenberg, senior vice-president of MCI, occasionally attended a seder in other people's homes but never in his own; his father, who had grown up on the Lower East Side, spent his adult life trying to escape his Jewishness. As a result, Eidenberg told me, "the content of the Haggadah [the text of the seder service] did not register on me until I was a father myself and began presiding over my own seders. I had to think about what it meant and signified—what knowledge had to be passed on from one generation to another." Now, he says, the seder is the most important evening of the year, but "in a secular more than a religious sense." Eidenberg, his two teen-

* As the historian Elias Bickerman has demonstrated, the Maccabean uprising was directed less against the Hellenistic rulers of the Jews than against the Hellenist sympathizers among them—those who wanted to eliminate the laws and rituals that had kept the Jews a distinct religioethnic group within the Hellenistic world.

† The seder is conducted at home, not the synagogue, and the elaborate meal is an intrinsic part of the religious service, rather than a diversion from it; making food part of the ceremony is a way of underscoring the Jewish view that one cannot liberate the soul without first liberating the body.

age sons, and their guests spend much of the evening talking about "the meaning of freedom and bondage, of responsibilities and opportunities, and the obligations of justice. These values are so important," Eidenberg adds, "that they *have* to be conveyed."

It is not only parents, moreover, who think about what Passover signifies; one of the most striking changes is recent years is the growing tendency for young single Jews to join with friends to hold their own seder—in some cases a traditional one, in others an "alternative," or "freedom," seder.

ITEM: "What do unaffiliated Jews do if they feel Jewish but don't feel they belong?" a woman in her early thirties asked me in a letter describing her own complex mixture of alienation and commitment. "The 'Freedom Seder' I attended," she wrote, "was loosely organized and alternated between following the seder format and being a free-flowing 'be-in,' complete with poetry and singing, some story-telling and political discussion, and a pot-luck dinner that was strictly vegetarian but hardly kosher (someone brought homemade brownies for dessert). About 30 people were present, scattered on the floor and furniture of a small living room in Queens." The group used a Haggadah published by New Jewish Agenda, an organization created by radicals who wanted a Jewish context within which to express their political views—still another indication of the eagerness of young Jews to affirm their Jewishness in one form or another.

But if the growth in observance of Chanukah and Passover provides clear evidence that American Jews are determined to remain Jews, it says relatively little about their interest in being what Jacob Neusner calls "Judaists"—practitioners of the Jewish religion. For, as I have argued, many of those who light Chanukah candles or attend seders do so for ethnic and cultural rather than religious reasons. Those who worry about the future of Judaism, as opposed to Jewishness, point to survey data indicating a steady erosion of religious commitment. Whatever the indicator—whether it is lighting Sabbath candles, observing the dietary laws, fasting on Yom Kippur, belonging to a synagogue, or attending services with some regularity—there *seems* to be a steady decline from older to younger people and from one generation to the next.

My accent is on "seems," for when the data are examined more closely, the trends prove to be different and far more complex than they appear. What is at issue, after all, is not whether American Jews are as religiously committed as they might be or as an observer might wish they were. As we have seen, American Jews never have been noted for their religiosity; despite the widespread assumption that the present represents a fall from grace, the American Jewish community of the first half of this century was a religious wasteland.

The question, then, is not whether American Jews are observant, according to some absolute scale; it is whether an inexorable erosion is going on, whereby each generation is less observant than the preceding one, as straight-line theory would lead one to expect. The answer is that it is not. True enough, there *had* been a generation-by-generation decline in observance of certain rituals as second- and third-generation Jews struggled to shed their image of being an alien, unassimilable group, but now that American Jews are accepted as fully American, that erosion is a thing of the past.

Consider, for example, the 1965 and 1975 Boston demographic surveys that I used in Chapter Four to illustrate the generation-by-generation shift from business to the professions. At first glance the Boston data seem to confirm the gloomiest prognostications about Judaism's disappearance: observance of most rituals declines steadily from one generation to the next. But simple generation-by-generation comparisons provide a misleading picture because they fail to take account of differences in age, and thus of stages in the life cycle, from one generation to the next. Third- and fourth-generation Jews, that is to say, are much younger than members of the first and second generations; in 1975 the median age of third- and fourth-generation Boston Jews was thirty-two and twenty-seven, respectively, compared to seventy-one and fifty-two for members of the first and second generations. Young Jews *are* less observant than their elders—not because they are young, however, but because a far larger proportion of them are single or childless, and in every age group single people and childless couples are less likely to belong to a synagogue or to observe religious rituals—other than lighting Chanukah candles or attending Passover seders—than those who have school-age children. (The same pattern, interestingly enough, is characteristic among American Christians as well.)

In his analysis of the Boston data, therefore, Steven M. Cohen analyzed the generational data separately for each age group, thereby reducing the distortions due to differences in the life cycle. The results are striking. When the purview is limited to the first three generations, straight-line theory seems to be vindicated: there is a steady decline in traditional observances, such as lighting Sabbath candles and keeping the dietary laws, and an increase in behaviors associated with integration into American society, such as membership in nonsectarian organizations and contributions to both Jewish and non-Jewish charitable causes.

When one looks at the youngest members of the third and fourth generations, however—those under the age of forty—it is apparent that the erosion not only has run its course but that the fourth generation is somewhat *more* observant than the third! Specifically, young fourth-generation Jews are more likely to light Sabbath candles, fast on Yom Kippur, belong to a synagogue, and attend services with some regularity than third-generation Jews in the same age group. These increases in religious commitment, interestingly enough, did not result from self-ghettoization on the part of fourth-generation Jews; there was, in fact, a sharp increase in the proportion belonging to nonsectarian organizations.

But what about now? The second Boston survey, after all, was taken ten years ago; perhaps religious observance has fallen off since then. Since 1979, however, demographic surveys have been completed in metropolitan areas that include more than 60 percent of the American Jewish population; those surveys confirm the turnaround shown in the Boston studies.

In his analysis of data from a 1981 survey of the New York metropolitan area, for example, Cohen studied the ways in which marriage and child rearing affected ritual observance, Jewish communal activity, and friendship patterns; I am indebted to him for sharing his findings with me before publication.* What appears to be a rapid decline in religious observance and communal affiliation as one goes down the age scale turns out to be a by-product of the fact that Jews today are marrying and having children at a later age than in the past. Postponement of the age of marriage creates the illusion of a decline in observance, because, as I have already mentioned, single Jews rarely join a synagogue or other Jewish organization, nor do they observe many rituals other than those connected with Chanukah and Passover. Observances and affiliation rates increase, however, when Jews marry; they take a sharp jump when children are born and another jump when children reach school age, as does the proportion having all or mostly Jews as close friends.

By analyzing the way in which the ritual observances and com-

* The ritual observances reported on included attending a seder, lighting Chanukah candles, attending synagogue services on the High Holidays, lighting Sabbath candles, "making Friday night special," observing the dietary laws at home, and refraining from handling money on the Sabbath; an index of religiosity was constructed according to the number of rituals observed. A second index of communal activity was built on four behaviors: belong to a synagogue, belonging to another Jewish organization, contributing at least $100 to Jewish charitable causes, and reading a Jewish newspaper. Intragroup friendship patterns were analyzed according to the proportion of respondent's three closest friends who were Jewish.

munal activities of married couples with school-age children vary from one age group to another, Cohen was able to separate the effects of age from those of differences in the life cycle. Young (twenty-five-to-thirty-four-year-old) couples with school-age children report slightly lower levels of communal involvement but significantly higher levels of ritual observance than do older (fifty-five-to-sixty-four-year-old) couples. To simplify the analysis Cohen divided the respondents into four groups according to the number of rituals they observed; nearly twice as many young couples were categorized as *frum* (the highest level of observance) and fewer than half as many were classified as nonobservant (the lowest level).

But what about those who are still single or childless? One cannot assume automatically that when they do have children they will be as religiously committed as their peers now are, since those who marry and have children at a young age come from somewhat more traditional backgrounds than those who do not. Cohen's analysis, however, indicates that any reduction in overall religiosity will be modest; in both the twenty-five-to-thirty-four and the thirty-five-to-forty-four age groups, single people and childless couples were *more* observant than their parents. Since the reverse was true for the older age groups, it would appear that the generation-to-generation decline in observance came to an end some twenty years ago.

3

The "most significant religious reality among American Jews," Nathan Glazer wrote nearly thirty years ago in his now classic *American Judaism*, was something that had *not* happened: American Jews had not stopped being Jewish. Because of that fact, he explained, even the most superficial manifestations of Jewishness contained the potential for religious renewal: American Jews may be "as ignorant of Judaism as a Hottentot," but their stubborn insistence on remaining Jews "means that the Jewish religious tradition is not just a subject for scholars but is capable now and then of finding expression in life. And even if it finds no expression in one generation or another, the commitment to remain related to it still exists. *Dead in one, two or three generations, it may come to life in the fourth* [emphasis added]."

It was a remarkably prescient observation, for this is precisely what is happening now. All over the United States one can see a return to Judaism on the part of third-, fourth-, and even fifth-generation Jews, who, a few years ago, had appeared to be irretrievably lost to Jewish life. Consider the route traveled by Paul Cowan, a staff writer for *The Village Voice* and fifth-generation scion of a highly assimilated American Jewish family. If one were to draw up a list of American Jews least likely to become religiously observant, Cowan would be near the top, for he was raised, as he says, as "a Jewish WASP." At twenty-one, beginning a climb that led to the presidency of CBS-TV, Paul's father, Louis, had changed his name from Cohen to Cowan and cut himself off from his family and his religion; amputating his past seemed to be the price of acceptance. The flight from Judaism had begun even earlier on Paul Cowan's mother's side; Polly Cowan had been raised as a Christian Scientist, her parents having adopted that faith in 1910. And so Polly and Lou Cowan and their four children observed no Jewish holidays or rituals; they celebrated Christmas in an elaborate way, gathered each year for an Easter dinner of ham and sweet potatoes, never entered a synagogue, and knew almost no one who did. When Paul was ready for high school the Cowans enrolled him in Choate, an elite Episcopalian prep school with compulsory daily chapel, so that he would feel at ease in the upper-class world in which they hoped he would travel.

Instead Paul Cowan has embraced the cohesive, communal Judaism his father had abandoned and his mother had never known. The transformation began when he and his wife, Rachel, decided "to make sure that our own children wouldn't grow up to be as ignorant and confused as we." Convinced that they would be uncomfortable in a conventional synagogue setting, the Cowans and some like-minded friends asked members of the New York Havurah, a Jewish religious fellowship with roots in both Jewish tradition and the American counterculture, to set up a school for their children. The Havurah agreed, on condition that the parents participate and not merely drop off the children at the school. In the spring of 1975, a year after the school had started, Paul and Rachel Cowan and their children lit Sabbath candles and recited the prayers over wine and bread for the first time in any of their lives.

By fall the Friday night ritual had become one of the anchors around which the family's lives were organized. In the cosmopolitan circle in which Paul and Rachel Cowan traveled, the combination of women's liberation, the sexual revolution, and the growing emphasis on "personal fulfillment" had begun to shatter the norms of adult behavior. To the Cowan children, then five and seven, who saw friends being abandoned as their parents' marriages fell apart, the world was becoming an unstable and frightening place. Thus the Sabbath, with its tranquil rituals and its assurance that parents and children would be together, without any distractions, on the same night each week, became an important source of comfort and stability.

But Judaism is a communal, not just an individual or family religion; in Judaism, community plays the role that in Christianity is occupied by God's grace. It is the community that "touches and moves people and brings them back to the faith," Glazer explains. "And the return to faith, which in Christianity means the acceptance of beliefs . . . in Judaism means the return to the community, which is made holy because it lives under God's law."

Sudden tragedy brought the Cowans into contact with Judaism as a holy community. At 3:00 A.M. one November morning in 1976 two New York City policemen rang their doorbell to tell them that Paul's parents had died at home in a fire. In the days that followed they found themselves supported and comforted by the community that had formed, almost invisibly, around the Havurah school. For the most part, Cowan recalls, his journalist and "movement" friends did not know how to respond to his grief; they were so uncomfortable with death and mourning that they made *him* uncomfortable, treating him as though he were the carrier of some dread disease. The members of the Havurah community, in contrast, knew exactly what to do, for they were familiar with traditional Jewish rituals of mourning. "They helped Rachel's mother cook and take care of the kids as if these were routine matters of communal responsibility," Cowan has written. "They treated us like mourners, not victims," thereby "letting our grief ebb and flow."

When the period of mourning was over, Cowan went to see Joseph Singer, a Hasidic rabbi and social worker on the Lower East Side, in search of a story his father had once urged him to pursue—or so he thought at the time. In fact, as he came to understand later, he was in search of some deeper meaning for his life, some way of exorcising his grief and coming to terms with his tragedy. And so the sixty-two-year-old European-born rabbi, tenth-generation descendant of the founder of Hasidism, became the fifth-generation American journalist's teacher and friend.

More than that, Rabbi Singer became a powerful force in Cowan's life. Accompanying the rabbi on his endless rounds—to comfort the sick and lonely, to find an apartment for the homeless, to purchase a comfortable mattress that an emotionally disturbed woman insisted was the only thing that would ease her distress (he was not sure that the mattress itself mattered, Rabbi Singer told Cowan, but he was certain that the woman needed to know that someone was concerned about her), to perform any number of other good deeds—Cowan was reminded of the emphasis on doing good that had attracted him to the New Left in the early and mid-1960s. But whereas the impulse to perform good deeds had evaporated among the members of the New

Left, Cowan realized, it was firmly woven into the fabric of Rabbi Singer's faith, and so was "far more durable than anything I had found in the secular world. Moreover, he helped me get outside myself and my grief and feel that all of us . . . were part of something—call it a tradition or a faith—that was bigger and more mysterious than ourselves."

Despite occasional fantasies of becoming Orthodox and moving to the Lower East Side, Cowan had no real desire to abandon his own world and submerge himself in Rabbi Singer's; instead he began taking parts of that world home with him, gradually adapting them, as best he could, to the world in which he lived. As a result, he has managed to find community and faith without abandoning his identity as an acculturated American; he has joined his new Jewish identity to his old American one, so that he now sees the world through two sets of eyes.

For all the idiosyncratic nature of Cowan's background, there is nothing idiosyncratic about his decision to become a practicing Jew. He is not even unique in his own family. His sister, Holly Schulman of Washington, D.C., now keeps a kosher home and belongs to a Conservative synagogue; she learned Hebrew so that she could chant the Haftorah (the Prophetic portion read in synagogue each Sabbath morning) on a Saturday morning in 1982 when she celebrated the bat mitzvah she had not had as a child.

And countless others are finding their own routes back to Judaism; wherever I have gone I have met men and women who are more observant than their parents had been or whose children are more observant than they are.

ITEM: A Des Moines, Iowa, insurance executive grew up in a small town sixty miles away, in which his was the only Jewish family. He attended a Methodist Sunday school until he was fifteen, when his concerned parents moved to Des Moines and joined the Reform temple so that he could be with other Jewish children. The executive's wife, who had a Jewish mother and Christian father, raised their children as Christian Scientists; one child continues in that faith, but the other is now an observant Conservative Jew who sends his own children to a Conservative-sponsored "day school."

ITEM: At breakfast in Houston, before a meeting of the American Jewish Committee's National Executive Committee that I was about to address, I chatted with the man seated to my left, a midwestern industrialist who is active in Jewish communal and philanthropic affairs but religiously nonobservant; his synagogue-going is limited to an occasional appearance at High Holy Day services at the Reform temple to which he belongs. In the manner of men our age, we talked about our children. His older son, he told me, has no Jewish involvement whatsoever, but his younger child recently transferred from Dartmouth (my acquaintance's alma mater) to Yale so that he could observe the dietary laws, a semester spent in Israel having turned him into an observant Jew.

This *baal teshuvah* phenomenon, as it is called (literally translated from the Hebrew, "the one who repents"–who returns to Judaism), is broader and deeper than most observers have recognized. The term is often used to refer to young people, many of them alumni of the counterculture, who have dropped out of mainstream American life to join Hasidic or other right-wing Orthodox sects. But although the return to Orthodoxy is important in its own right, it is only a small part of a broader and deeper trend.

The only way to comprehend the phenomenon, in fact, is to use the definition suggested by Charles Liebman of Bar-Ilan University: a *baal teshuvah* is anyone of college age or older who is more observant than his or her parents, teachers, or childhood friends would have predicted. Under this definition the number of *baalei teshuvah* (plural, or BTs, as they sometimes are called), is substantial. I have met them in every part of the country–men and women of every age and from every kind of background who are more religiously observant than they had been five or ten or twenty years before; many are also more observant than their parents had been. The specific reasons for returning to Judaism vary from person to person, as do the routes the returnees have followed, the particular forms their new-found observance takes, and the intensity and seriousness with which they approach their religion.

And yet as Carl Scheingold, director of the National Havurah Committee, discovered in a study of Jewish religious renewal that he conducted for The American Jewish Committee, certain common threads run through almost all the stories.* The most important is a search for meaning and purpose, a realization (sometimes conscious and sometimes not, sometimes before the fact and sometimes after) that full immersion in American secular life does not answer the ultimate questions of meaning, that life is fuller and richer when people attach themselves to something larger than themselves. It is not only

* I am indebted to Dr. Scheingold for sharing the full and unpublished draft of his study with me; a briefer version of the manuscript was published by The American Jewish Committee under the title *New Pockets of Jewish Energy*. (The portrait of Professor X beginning on the next page is drawn in part from Scheingold's manuscript and in part from my own conversations with X.)

Jews, of course, who are engaged in this kind of search; it is going on among Americans of every religious background. As Professor Robert N. Bellah of Berkeley, a leading sociologist of religion, explains, "There is a reaction against extreme individualism and self . . . a search for roots with a capital R, which takes people back to religion."

Nowhere is the change more evident (or more unexpected) than on college and university campuses, which have long been havens for religious skeptics. Religion was on the defensive when he arrived at Harvard a quarter of a century ago, Rabbi Ben-Zion Gold, director of the Harvard-Radcliffe Hillel, observes. "But people lost confidence in progress, in the social engineering they thought would usher in the Golden Age. This punctured the self-confidence of the academy's priests." The sociologist Daniel Bell of Harvard makes the same point: "The exhaustion of modernism, the aridity of Communist life, the tedium of the unrestrained self . . . all indicate that a long era is coming to a close"—an era in which intellectuals viewed religion as superstition. That view "makes little sense today," Bell argues. Every generation has to struggle with "the existential questions"—questions about the meaning of life and death, tragedy and obligation. And we have come to recognize that "the most coherent responses, historically the most potent responses," are the ones that religion provides. And so the theologian Harvey Cox of Harvard Divinity School, who twenty years ago argued that religion was "disappearing forever," now speaks of the "tremendous resurgence of religious interest" on college campuses.

The turn to religion on the part of Jewish professors is all the more striking in view of the self-hatred with which Jewish intellectuals have been afflicted for so long. As we saw in the first half of the book, "making it" in the world of high culture seemed to require abandonment of one's Jewishness. "Here I am, finally, out in the big world, a Jewish boy in fifth-century Athens," a Harvard Law School professor recalls having felt twenty years ago when he entered Harvard College. To Professor X, as I will call him (he prefers to remain anonymous), Judaism seemed "pale and inadequate" compared to "the world of Harvard—the world of universal, cosmopolitan culture" that he entered twenty years ago. True enough, immersing himself in that culture involved no great loss for X; his Jewish identity and knowledge were both rather meager, for he had grown up in a socialist, rabidly antireligious home in which no Jewish holidays were celebrated.

Professor X's relation to Judaism began to change in the mid-seventies. Having established himself professionally, this son of a cab driver-turned-milkman was less in awe of "the world of Harvard" than he had been at the start of his career, and his opposition to American involvement in Vietnam had led to a growing disillusionment with the universal, cosmopolitan culture he had admired and which Harvard seemed to embody. "Rationalism was tottering; the 'best and the brightest' didn't know their spiritual asses from their elbows," he says. "Fifth-century Athens had disappointed me terribly."

While this was happening, the oldest of X's three children was approaching adolescence. Eager to connect her to Judaism in a way that made sense to him—his own bar mitzvah had helped alienate him from Judaism—he enrolled her in an afternoon religious school affiliated with Harvard. He also visited Israel with a group of other academics on a trip sponsored by The American Jewish Committee. Examining the issues of Jewish identity with a group of people who were his intellectual peers, he gained a new sense of "the plausibility of religion" and a consequent desire to find a link to Jewish tradition.

The question was: How? The answer was not evident at first, since X had an aversion to ritual and prayer, which he considered servile and unthinking, and felt an even greater antipathy to what he calls "the typical suburban temple." After his return from Israel he attended High Holiday services at Harvard for the first time. Although he enjoyed the services, he was not moved by them; he still felt uncomfortable with the religious aspect of Judaism. A year or two later, however, he attended a bar mitzvah at the Harvard Worship and Study Group, whose members, most of them Harvard faculty members and graduate students, worship together on the Harvard campus each Saturday morning.* "Incredibly turned on" by the group—"they are a collection of serious people struggling to make meaning out of Judaism"—X began attending Saturday morning services on a regular basis. The group provided a comfortable, nonthreatening environment; instead of feeling embarrassed by his ignorance, as he might have been in a conventional synagogue, X felt free to proceed at his own pace.

The result has been an increasingly intense and meaningful involvement with Judaism. "Humanism does not seem to be the source of values for me that it once was," X explains, "and I've turned to the Jewish tradition as an alternative." What attracts him is precisely "the experience of particularity" that once had repelled him—the "concrete root" of the tradition "and its history and its suffering and its pain and the fact that for some weird reasons I am here to continue it." Not that he has suspended his disbelief. On the contrary, prayer still is "a difficult issue" for him; he continues to see many rituals as "hollow and empty" and to view much of Jewish law as "fundamentally alien

* Rabbi Ben-Zion Gold, the Harvard Hillel director, helped organize the group and is a regular participant, but he avoids any formal leadership role; the egalitarian services are run entirely by the members.

to [his] sensibilities." He would like to believe in God but remains a nonbeliever.

Now, however, X is a committed and observant nonbeliever, who speaks of "the evocative power of ritual" while wondering what he means by the phrase and who describes communal prayer as "an intense spiritual experience" while professing his atheism. This kind of mixture of skepticism and doubt is typical of intellectuals who have turned to religion in recent years. "I can't say to you I believe in God," the psychiatrist Robert Coles, who has played a significant role in the Christian revival at Harvard, told Fran Schumer, author of a *New York Times Magazine* article on the return to religion on college campuses. "There are moments when I do stop and pray to God. But if you ask me who that God is or what kind of image He has, my mind boggles. I'm confused, perplexed, confounded. But I refuse to let that confusion be the dominant force in my life."

Professor X feels the same way. He is intellectually and emotionally engaged by Judaism—by the intellectual depth embodied in the structure of the Sabbath liturgy, the nuances of feeling and meaning that different ways of reciting a particular prayer can impart, and the complex relationship between ritual and belief. Having always thought that one had to believe in God before performing any rituals, he is fascinated by the traditional Jewish notion that the relationship runs the other way—that behavior precedes belief, that one begins with ritual and moves on from there. He wonders whether his observance of ritual can be sustained without the belief he does not (or does not yet) have, but he is "prepared to see what happens." What was happening when I checked on his progress last was that religious observance was falling into place as "part of a more elaborate whole"—the result, as he put it, of "a normalization of my Jewishness." Thus his interest in Israel had grown—he had spent six weeks teaching in Israel under the Fulbright exchange program—and he had become an informal adviser to Jewish students at Harvard Law School. He is still uncertain about a number of aspects of his Jewish identity, but he feels that the outcome is not in doubt, for, as he told me, "the core has been secured."

It is being secured for a great many once highly assimilated Jews. For philosophy professor Hilary Putnam the first experience with "transcendence"—the sense of "belonging to a group larger than oneself"—came from involvement in radical political action during the 1960s; he was a member of the Progressive Labor Party, the extremist offshoot of the radical Students for a Democratic Society. But the turn to violence disillusioned Putnam. "It was a painful experience," he says, to discover that people on the left were as willing as those on the right to accept torture and murder as a political weapon. "I grew weary of people with political panaceas." Today he is an observant Conservative Jew who attends services regularly with his wife and family. "I recognized that I was, by nature, a religious person," he explains, and concluded that he "should no longer fight this, but accept it." It is the sense of belonging to something larger than himself that is the primary appeal. "Whatever one's image of God, there is a notion in religious thought of an obligation very far from one's own vanity," he says. "I try to think about the question of service now, service to the culture."

For Michael Medved of Santa Monica, California, an ebullient thirty-eight-year-old author and screenwriter, Judaism is a total way of life, the particulars of which are determined by the requirements of traditional Jewish law; he is a devoutly Orthodox Jew. That was not the way the San Diego-born and -bred Medved had been raised. "I majored in spitball-throwing," he says of his years in the afternoon religious school to which his outwardly assimilated parents sent him—for nostalgic reasons rather than religious commitment. (Their primary commitment seemed to be to liberal politics of the Henry Wallace variety.) After his bar mitzvah Medved abandoned his tenuous connection to Judaism. In college in the late 1960s, he wrote in *What Really Happened to the Class of '65*, he "was looking for roots, for a sense of belonging," and thought he had found it in the New England WASP tradition he encountered at Yale. "I loved the pomp, the pretensions, the Gothic entryways, the fireplace in my dorm room, the civility of the dining hall."

He also loved a woman from an upper-class Protestant background and planned to marry her. When her parents reluctantly agreed to the match—"You Jewish men never get drunk and never beat their wives," they told Medved—he returned to California to get what he assumed would be the blessing of his liberal, open-minded parents. Instead they responded with outraged anger. "They threatened that they'd never see my wife or their grandchildren," Medved recalls. "We didn't speak for six months." Medved postponed the wedding and used the time to read as much about Judaism as he could. "I had grown up worshiping my father; I thought he was the most brilliant man I knew," Medved told me. "When he reacted the way he did, I decided I had to find out what it was that he found so precious in Judaism; I figured there had to be something there that I didn't understand." His readings were "a major revelation for me," Medved says. "I discovered that Judaism is more than just a nostalgic ache or a remembrance of Yiddish phrases; it is a way of life"—one that challenged the very basis of the free-flowing life he had been leading.

And so his journey began. Back in California in the spring of 1971, Medved began lighting Sabbath candles and praying each morning, wearing *tefillin* (phylacteries), although, as he told me, he could barely read the Hebrew prayers. A year later he began observing the dietary laws at home, and the next year he experimented with observing the Sabbath by refraining from driving—a major change in life-style in Southern California. In 1978 Medved, by then a devout Orthodox Jew, and Daniel Lapin, an Orthodox rabbi with whom he had begun studying the year before, organized the Pacific Jewish Center—"the only community of bohemian Orthodox Jews in the world," one wag called it, referring to the offbeat backgrounds and occupations of the young men and women who were attracted to it. When I visited the community in 1979 it had eighty members, one of them Medved's divorced father, David, a physics professor at UCLA. Most, however, were young singles, many of them alumni of one or another of the many cults and communes that then existed in Southern California. "In a way, we are just another manifestation of the impulse behind the cults," Lapin told a reporter in 1980. "But we offer something far more wholesome."*

Today, the Pacific Jewish Center has nearly three hundred members, two thirds of them married couples, most with young children. "We sometimes call it the Prolific Jewish Center," Medved told me. The bohemian flavor has diminished as the onetime hippies have settled into conventional life-styles, but it is not what one would call a typical Orthodox community. Virtually everyone there is a *baal teshuvah*, and a large proportion of the still young members work as screenwriters, television and film producers, Hollywood agents, talk-show hosts, psychiatrists, and psychoanalysts—occupations not typical of Orthodox Jews. Turnover is fairly high: some cannot accept the system of beliefs, others find the demands of Orthodox law incompatible with their

* There was a decided cultlike atmosphere to the *shiur* (study group) I attended in 1979. It was evident in the authoritarian manner in which Rabbi Lapin conducted the "discussion" and, even more, in the sheeplike way in which the forty-five or fifty participants accepted his pronouncements as if they were profound and revealed truths. They were not. To someone familiar with the rabbinic commentaries on the biblical passage under discussion—Abraham's argument with God over the latter's proposed destruction of Sodom and Gomorrah—Lapin's comments seemed banal as well as unpleasantly chauvinistic. Yet no one in this group of seemingly bright, articulate young men and women questioned or challenged anything Lapin said, even when he was denigrating Christianity in what I found to be a crude and offensive way. "They don't want to be bothered any more," an Orthodox rabbi friend explained to me. "They are running away from complexity."

careers or private lives, still others pass through the community on their way to a far more rigid, fundamentalist Orthodoxy.

Like most Orthodox Jews, those who remain are firmly rooted in an intimate, close-knit community. Because of the requirements of Orthodox law—riding and handling money on the Sabbath are prohibited—members live close to the synagogue and thus to one another. And the prohibition against the use of electricity, as well as against work, on the Sabbath means a twenty-four-hour respite from the distractions of the world each week, thereby providing a period in which families and friends can renew their relationships.

It is not only Californians, however, who feel a hunger for community, nor is it only Orthodox Jews who seek the intimacy that comes from membership in a close-knit group. Sometimes the search is explicit, but many do not recognize their hunger until it has been satisfied—until they have discovered what membership in an organic community can mean in their lives. "Through all of our work," Leonard Fein and his colleagues wrote toward the end of their study of Reform congregants and congregations, "no single conclusion registers so strongly as our sense that there is, among the people we have come to know, a powerful, perhaps even desperate, longing for community, a longing that is, apparently, not adequately addressed by any of the relevant institutions in most people's lives." The Jews in question rarely spoke of their longing. "The need for community is so strong, and the prospect of community so weak," Fein concluded, "that people are reluctant to acknowledge the need." Thus some Jews find community accidentally; others find it as a by-product of their search for some connection with Judaism or Jewish peoplehood; still others seek it directly.

ITEM: "I had a need for something Jewish in my life," a member of the Havurah of South Florida told me, a need he had been unable to meet. Having grown up in the intimate atmosphere of the Havana Jewish community, he was turned off by what he felt was the coldness and impersonality of the huge temples he encountered in Miami. When the Havurah was started in 1980 he began attending a monthly study group and was drawn to it by the warmth he encountered. "I love the idea of this being a group where you can achieve closeness and sharing among people of a wide age range."

Community serves another function as well. Many if not most of those who return to Judaism are uncomfortable with their ignorance of the language, prayers, rituals, and procedures—so much so that they often refrain from attending a synagogue service for fear of being embarrassed and are reluctant to ask questions or to voice uncertainties and doubts. As we saw in Professor X's case, it is reassuring to meet others as ignorant as oneself who are also exploring their relation to Judaism. It is also comforting to meet intellectual or social peers who can serve as Jewish role models and who are willing to share their knowledge and experience without making the newcomers feel diminished.

Support is needed too in order to overcome the alienation from Judaism that most returning Jews have experienced—an alienation that can be intense. When he surveyed the people attending the Jewish Omnibus programs of the 92nd Street Y in 1980, John Ruskay discovered that 60 percent were not affiliated with a synagogue or other Jewish institution, and most of those who gave a reason for their lack of affiliation attributed it to what Ruskay calls "powerful negative memories—real or alleged—of what had been done to them by the Jewish institutions they had been affiliated with in the past." For many the most negative memory of all was the primitive nature of the theology offered to answer (or suppress) their youthful questions and doubts; having rejected the theology, they felt obliged to reject Judaism as well, for they had never been taught that Judaism offers multiple routes to religious expression. As a result, Ruskay established a program called "Connect," designed to help unaffiliated Jews learn about those routes and thereby find their way back to Judaism.

The return to Judaism rarely is the result of any peak experience, or rebirth, to use Christian terminology. In most instances it is a gradual process, albeit one that often is accelerated by some fortuitous event—attending a bar mitzvah, as in Professor X's case; spending a Sabbath with friends or even with new acquaintances; hearing a lecture or going on a weekend retreat sponsored by a Jewish organization; attending Sabbath services with some regularity during the year preceding a child's bar or bat mitzvah.

ITEM: For a midwestern couple I will call the Schwartzes (they prefer to be anonymous) the accelerating factor was their Reform temple's requirement that they attend Sabbath services before their son could become bar mitzvah. Until then the fact that Dan and Myra Schwartz were Jewish had had no discernible effect on their lives; but when their children were born they decided, in the vague fashion of many American Jews, that they "wanted the children to know they were Jewish." Thus the Schwartzes joined a nearby temple, attended High Holy Day services, and, at the appropriate time, enrolled the children in the religious school of the temple, which held classes two afternoons a week as well as on Sunday. Required to attend Sabbath services before their older son's bar mitzvah, they discovered after a while that they enjoyed the respite it provided and were stimulated by the way the rabbi connected Jewish tradition to the pressing issues of the day. They now observe the Sabbath on Friday nights—lighting candles, chanting kiddush (the prayer over the wine), and eating a leisurely meal with their sons before attending the temple service. Moreover, Myra Schwartz has enticed several other women with similar backgrounds to join her in a course of study leading to their belated bat mitzvahs—a phenomenon one now encounters in a great many Reform and Conservative congregations.

ITEM: Before she was married, says Malka Drucker, a California author, she believed that "ritual was for ignorant people or hypocrites. All one needed to be a good Jew was to be a good person." Having grown up "thinking that *Shabbat* and *kashrut* were part of some ancient time," it was difficult for her at first to adjust to her husband's observances. "I liked to do things when I felt like it," she writes, and not at set times. But before long Friday night "became our time to reach one another again after the long week." Even so, she was uncomfortable in synagogue until she attended Sabbath morning services at Valley Beth Shalom, a Conservative congregation in the San Fernando Valley. It was a revelation. "Rabbi [Harold] Schulweis talked about the Torah the way my English professors talked about Shakespeare—with wit, drama, and respect," Drucker explains. She began attending regularly and came to see the synagogue as more than an intellectually exciting classroom. "One day tears came to my eyes when the Torah was returned to the ark. It was no longer just intellectual nourishment; it had finally become my tree of life. A few weeks later, I began to call myself by my Hebrew name, Malka."

As Malka Drucker's story reveals, a charismatic rabbi or teacher often plays a crucial role in people's return to Judaism. The growing availability of such people is one of the factors that make the return to Judaism more than a passing fad. That was not the case a generation ago. "If Judaism is to have any vitality in the United States," Nathan Glazer wrote, "it will be by virtue of examples of Jewish lives that are meaningful." Role models were crucial, he said, because "the abstract demand to seek faith, to find God, tends to find little answer among Jews, and . . . concrete examples of Jewish living must be given before religion has an impact on their lives."

One of the strengths of the current religious renewal is the abundance of such "concrete examples of Jewish living"—in particular, examples of people who have been able to combine participation in American society with a rich Jewish life. Role models of a more traditional sort—the scholar or the *tzaddik* (righteous person) living in an entirely Jewish world—have always been present; what had been in short supply were men and women whose Jewish commitments were played out on a larger stage. The late Abraham Joshua Heschel was one such person; he influenced an entire generation before his death in December 1972.

Rabbi Irving Greenberg, president of the National Jewish Resource Center and a "postmodern Orthodox rabbi," as he likes to call himself, is another. In Washington, D.C., Des Moines, Iowa, Houston, San Diego—almost everywhere I have gone—I have met men and women who have either returned to Judaism or greatly intensified their observance as a result of workshops and weekend retreats that Greenberg has run, usually for the Young Leadership divisions of the United Jewish Appeal and the various local federations. A Harvard Ph.D. in history, Orthodox rabbi, participant in ecumenical dialogues, and husband of a leading Jewish feminist (Blu Greenberg is a major figure within the Jewish women's movement and its principal spokesperson in the Orthodox community), "Yitz" Greenberg, as almost everyone calls him, is living proof that one can be fully Jewish and fully American. The six-foot-six Greenberg is a dynamic speaker as well, with a rare ability to explain the reasons behind the traditional Jewish way of life. "In a way Jews have become evangelicals," he explains. They need to be; in an open society such as ours "all religions have to broadcast their message," for "if they don't, they get nowhere."

In fact, Greenberg is one of a growing number of "guru rebbes," as they have been called, who, in greater or lesser degree, devote themselves to religious "outreach" to unaffiliated and/or alienated Jews. Jonathan Omer-Man, a British-born *baal teshuvah* who lived in Israel for eighteen years, now works for the Los Angeles Hillel Council as a full-time "religious counselor" to "young Jews who are having difficulties integrating their religious feelings within Judaism." Much of the time he meets people over coffee at a local McDonald's because "it's neutral ground." "The people I deal with," he explains, "feel uneasy in a Jewish setting" because "they are bright, and they have been talked down to." A key part of his job, he feels, is to help established Jewish institutions understand their failures and change themselves so that they can attract some of the people who have been turned off by them.

Harold Schulweis is trying to do precisely that within his own congregation. When he moved to Los Angeles' San Fernando Valley, he told me, he realized that he "was dealing with a new kind of Jew"—men and women so consumed by their own problems that they were unable to commit themselves to anything larger than themselves. "This is not because they are selfish," Schulweis insists, but because "they are bleeding from hurts to which the synagogue pays no attention"—marital discord and divorce, abandonment, alcoholism and drug abuse, career problems, difficulties in parent-child relationships, and so on. "Instead of blaming them," he says, "we have to meet them where they are and try to deal with their problems."

To do so Schulweis has turned his synagogue into a counseling center. "It seemed wrong that I always had to send people away to a specialist," he told me, and even wronger that "the 'community of care' existed *outside* the synagogue." Enlisting the aid of psychiatrists, psychologists, and social workers, he set up a program to train congregants and other interested people in counseling and crisis-intervention techniques and to give them some knowledge of the ways in which Judaism relates to individual and family problems. The fifty or so paraprofessionals, each supervised by a social worker or psychologist, are housed in a wing constructed for that purpose, and see a hundred or more people a week. "The synagogue has established itself as a caring institution," Schulweis told me with evident pride.

He has changed the synagogue in other ways as well. Borrowing the most inspired innovation of the Jewish counterculture, he has adapted the idea of the *havurah* to the needs of a middle-aged, suburban congregation. The result has been the creation of *havurot* (plural), usually involving ten individuals and/or families, within the synagogue itself, to provide a more intimate and less threatening setting for religious observance as well as a system of mutual support in time of need. In the fall of 1984 there were more than 60 *havurot*, involving a third to a half of the congregation's 1700 family units. (Some *havurot* are little more than coffee klatches, while others are intensely involved in study or ritual practice.)

The success of the paracounseling program has led Schulweis to extend the idea to his religious role as well; he has trained a group of congregants to serve as pararabbis. "There are paramedics and paralegals; rabbis need help as much as lawyers and doctors do," he says. Equally important, "Jews need other Jews to be Jewish, far more than they need books or courses." Thus the twenty-five to thirty pararabbis meet with newlyweds, prospective parents, bar and bat mitzvah youngsters and their parents, and other congregants to help them understand the whys and hows of Jewish ritual and expression.

4

The renewal of American Judaism is not confined to lapsed Jews who are now returning; on the contrary, there is an intensification of religious interest and activity on the part of Jews who never strayed. The distinction between those who have returned and those who have always been religious is not always clear-cut; what matters, in any case, is that large numbers of Jews are now more observant than they had been. The change is most striking, perhaps, in the Orthodox community, which shows a vitality few had anticipated a generation ago, but the intensification or religious observance is evident across the whole denominational spectrum.

Consider, for example, the interest in Judaism that some college students now display. True, religious observance is more the exception on campus than the rule; the college years, after all, are a time for questioning and often temporarily abandoning old values and identities and for "trying on" new ones. And yet there are a number of colleges—UCLA, the University of Chicago, Harvard, Brandeis, Princeton, and Columbia are particularly striking examples—that have a vibrant Jewish religious and cultural life. For those who grew up in the thirties, forties, and fifties the change is astounding.

During my undergraduate and graduate years at Columbia, for example, there was a single Adviser to Jewish Students, a rabbi whose principal responsibility was to help Jewish students cope with the problems their Jewishness often entailed; if he conducted Sabbath or other services for Jewish students, the memory escapes me. Today, in contrast, Columbia's Jewish Office is staffed by two Jewish chaplains and an administrative assistant; three services are conducted on Friday evening and two on Saturday morning, and students who want kosher food and/or a Jewish ambience can choose between two off-campus residences. Moreover, the Council of Jewish Organizations, a union of some fifteen student groups, includes a monthly Jewish student newspaper, a Jewish theater group, two Zionist organizations, and a Sabbath Meals Committee, among others. Most impressive of all, perhaps, are the extracurricular Jewish-studies courses sponsored by the Jewish Office; a recent bulletin offered twelve courses, ranging from introductory and intermediate classes in Hebrew to an advanced Talmud study group.

ITEM: The change at Harvard is even more dramatic: as Henry Rosovsky, who was the dean, noted in his 1979 address dedicating the new Hillel building, Hillel had moved "from the periphery of the campus to its very center." The physical move has had its behavioral counterpart. When Ben-Zion Gold became the Hillel rabbi twenty-five years ago, there was a Conservative service on Friday night that attracted no more than 20 students and an Orthodox service on Saturday morning that attracted 40 to 50; there were no Reform services at all.

Today there are five worship groups, three of which meet on Saturday morning; between 300 and 400 students and faculty attend each week—a fivefold increase.

This kind of religious ferment, to repeat, is still more the exception than the rule and is testimony, in part, to the imagination and character of the Hillel rabbis on the campuses in question. Religious activity on campus is a reflection too of the religious environments from which the students come and of the harmony that exists between them and their parents. "The students are far closer to their parents than they imagine they are," Rabbi Gold told me. Certainly they are less rebellious and more conventional than the students of the 1960s; in an age in which one of Princeton's eating clubs offers kosher meals, students can retain their Jewishness without any psychic or social cost. One unfortunate by-product of this harmony is an absence of the creativity that was the hallmark of the Jewish counterculture described in the last chapter.

The erstwhile rebels, meanwhile, continue to make their presence felt. The old communitarian emphasis has largely disappeared as the founders have married, born children, and become immersed in their careers, but the *havurot* remain. There are at least 300 throughout the country and perhaps as many as 500. (Most are groups of 10 to 20 individuals or couples, but some have memberships of 60 or more.) New *havurot* continue to be formed—but by Jews in their thirties and early forties rather than by members of the next generation.

New or old, *havurot* continue to display most of the characteristics that distinguished them from conventional synagogue life. Specifically, they continue to be distinguished by their emphasis on celebration and joy (most *havurah* members reject the obsession with Jewish persecution and suffering that characterized their own religious upbringing); their insistence on equality of the sexes (women play the same religious roles as men) and on lay participation (members conduct religious services themselves, refusing to delegate religious worship or practice to rabbis and cantors); the importance they attach to study, especially of traditional texts; their experimentation with liturgy; and the worship style they have developed, which combines the warmth and fervor of Hasidism with the informality of American youth culture.

Whether the *havurot* are a passing fad, as their main-line critics have maintained, or a permanent entry in Jewish life remains to be seen; it was not until 1969, after all, that the first *havurah* came into being. But permanent or not, the *havurot* already have exerted a profound influence on Reform, Conservative, and Reconstructionist synagogues; witness the number of congregations, such as Valley Beth Shalom, that are now creating *havurot* of their own. Estimates of the number of synagogue *havurot* run as high as three thousand. One can see the influence of the *havurah* movement too in the number of congregations, especially Reform congregations, that are adopting elements of the *havurah* worship style.

The reason, quite simply, is that some of the impulses that led to the creation of the *havurah* movement are felt throughout the organized religious community. Among Reform Jews, for example, one can see a notable return to traditional rituals, ceremonies, and forms of worship.

ITEM: The headline on the front-page article of the September 30–October 5, 1984, issue of *Our Town*, a weekly newspaper serving Manhattan's fashionable Upper East Side, read "The New Year's call for renewal." The article that followed, written by Harvey M. Tattlebaum, rabbi of Temple Shaaray Tefila, a Reform congregation in the neighborhood, concluded with an invitation "to join us on Rosh Hashanah afternoon for our 'Tashlich' service (casting away of our sins) at the East River at about 81st Street (Finley Walk) at 3:00 P.M. New breath is infused into an ancient ritual. The Shofar is blown, songs are sung, prayers are intoned. It has become our Synagogue's Rosh Hashanah 'happening' by the waters."

The article leaped off the page, because this is precisely the kind of ritual that used to be anathema to Reform Jews, who emphasized the rational and rejected anything that appeared "unscientific" or incompatible with modern thought. Tashlich is an ancient folk ritual in which one throws bread crumbs into a body of flowing water to symbolize the casting away of one's sins and the hope for purification. When I was young, acculturated Orthodox Jews as well as Reform and Conservative Jews had abandoned the ritual, for it carried too many overtones of Eastern European folk superstition.* But American Jews no longer worry about appearing modern and up to date, and Tashlich is coming into favor again. When I took a late afternoon stroll along the East River this past Rosh Hashanah afternoon, I passed four separate groups performing the ritual, ranging from the smartly dressed members of Shaaray Tefila to a group of Hasidim in their traditional garb.

Cleveland's Fairmount Temple provides another example of the return to tradition within the Reform movement. Until recently this

* Tashlich is, in fact, a folk custom and not a ceremony required by Jewish law. Indeed, rabbinic authorities tried to suppress the ritual precisely because of its superstitious overlay; but, as happened with a number of other rituals, the folk tradition prevailed.

huge congregation (2300 families) was one of the prototypes of "high church" German Reform Judaism: services were conducted almost entirely in English, with music performed by a large choir; there was no cantor—the office was abandoned in the 1870s as too "Oriental"—and no congregational singing, except, perhaps, for an occasional English hymn; rabbis were bareheaded and wore ministerial robes; and the bar mitzvah ceremony was strongly discouraged, when it was not forbidden.

Today the senior rabbi, Arthur Lelyveld, wears a *kippah* (skullcap) and *tallit* (prayer shawl), as do a number of congregants; there is a cantor, who encourages the congregants to join her in singing the prayers; and thirteen-year-olds celebrate their bar and bat mitzvahs (an average of two a week) by chanting part of the weekly Torah portion to the traditional melody. Some congregants are even building their own sukkah (a thatched hut used for meals during the festival of Sukkot, which begins five days after Yom Kippur). What surprises him, Lelyveld told me, is not that his congregants have shown resistance to this return to tradition but that they are so willing to participate; even the old-timers "see the need for a warmer, more affirmative expression of Jewishness."

Nor are these isolated examples. As Rabbi Alexander Schindler, president of the (Reform) Union of American Hebrew Congregations (UAHC), told me, "The movement that used to be hyperrational now recognizes that it is important to feel, not just to think." In Schindler's judgment, the movement toward greater traditionalism and toward what he calls "a more participatory religious life,"—active participation in worship by the laity—is "irreversible." Publication of a new Reform prayer book in 1975 reflected but also greatly accelerated, this trend, for the new prayer book gives far more prominence to Hebrew prayers.

The change in the Reform rabbinate is also contributing to the return to tradition. In the past, Reform rabbis tended to be lapsed Orthodox or Conservative Jews, and they often felt the need to prove—to themselves, if not necessarily to others—that they had abandoned the shackles of the tradition against which they had rebelled. But the men and women who have entered the rabbinate in the last ten or fifteen years are almost all products of the Reform movement, particularly its youth groups and summer camps, and they do not feel the need to prove how "modern" they are. Having grown up in an open society, they are comfortable with their Jewishness; having spent part of their rabbinic training in Israel, they are usually fluent in Hebrew and often far more traditional in their personal observances than their elders. Some, in fact, are as meticulous in their observance of the Sabbath and the dietary laws as most Conservative (and many Orthodox) rabbis.

The growth in the number of women cantors is having a similar effect. Because they are more accepted than women rabbis, the cantors feel freer to be themselves; there is, after all, a long association of women with music, and besides, a cantor is less of an authority figure than the rabbi. Lacking any female role models, many women rabbis try to imitate their male peers, thereby repressing their warmth and expressiveness. Women cantors, in contrast, tend to put their expressiveness to work for them, imparting a warmth and informality that Reform services previously had lacked.

What happens to Reform Judaism is important, because it may soon replace the Conservative movement as the largest denomination. At the time of the 1971 National Jewish Population Survey, for example, nearly half the second-generation Jews identified themselves as Conservative, compared to fewer than a third classifying themselves as Reform. Among third-generation Jews, however, Reform had a slight plurality—41 percent compared with 40 percent. (The Orthodox proportion dropped from 11 to 3 percent.) More recent studies of individual metropolitan areas indicate that the shift to Reform continues in the fourth generation.

Many of those who identify themselves as Reform Jews do so, however, only in a nominal way, without joining a congregation; others join but observe little and rarely attend religious services. Having permitted Reform Judaism to be defined as the denomination of those who observe nothing, Reform leaders are now trying to bring their followers back to more traditional observance. It is not easy for them to do so, because of the emphasis Reform Judaism places on individual autonomy. As "the leaders of liberal Judaism, we cannot command, we can only convince," Rabbi Schindler told the UAHC convention delegates in 1983. "We lead not by precept but by example. The task of self-renewal, therefore, must begin with us."

Within the Orthodox community, on the other hand, leaders are running as fast as they can to catch up with the growing religiosity of their rank and file. The dramatic resurgence that Orthodoxy is enjoying is not the result of any increase in numbers; there is, at most, a stabilization of numbers after three quarters of a century of steady decline.* The vitality that Orthodoxy displays is due instead to the fact

* That stability is the net effect of contrary trends in different communities. In much of the country the number of Orthodox Jews continues to decline, generation by generation. That decline has been offset, however, by small increases in major centers of Orthodox life, such as New York, Baltimore,

that the "nonobservant Orthodox"—Jews who belonged to Orthodox congregations out of nostalgia or habit and who once constituted a majority of the membership—have dropped out of Orthodoxy, leaving an increasingly committed core of true believers.

Those who continue to practice Orthodoxy, therefore, now do so with far greater intensity and commitment than was the case in the recent (or even distant) past, observing rituals that had been widely ignored in this country a generation ago. There is an equally striking tendency to follow the strictest rather than the most lenient interpretation of each of the many laws Orthodox Jews are expected to observe. Rabbinic authorities have always differed in their interpretations and explications of religious law; today, it sometimes seems, only the strictest interpretation has any credence. For many Orthodox Jews, for example, it is no longer enough for a restaurant to be kosher; it has to be *glatt* kosher—an additional requirement that is entirely extralegal. And the movement toward the strictest and most rigid interpretation of Jewish law—"the *Chumrah*-[stringency] of-the-Month Club," one critic calls it—is being led by the young rather than the old.

This change is not primarily the result of a return to Orthodoxy on the part of third- and fourth-generation Eastern European Jews; it is a phenomenon of the second generation—the second generation of an entirely different immigrant stream. There are exceptions, of course, such as Michael Medved and his community in Venice, California, but most young Orthodox Jews today are the children of the half million or so Jews who came to the United States just before, during, and after World War II. In the almost exclusively Orthodox Boro Park section of Brooklyn, for example, only 10 percent of the Jews are third-generation, and in Flatbush, which contains another large Orthodox enclave, the proportion is 21 percent. In both Manhattan's Upper East Side and the North Shore of Long Island, in contrast—areas with relatively small Orthodox communities—54 percent of the Jews are members of the third generation.

A number of factors explain why the new immigrants were better able to retain their Orthodoxy than their predecessors. To begin with, the World War II immigrants came to a different America from the one in which their predecessors had settled. It was a far more open society, one that was more hospitable to religious and ethnic differences, in which children (and their parents) therefore felt less pressure to discard immigrant ways. They also felt less need to do so. By the early postwar period the five-day week was becoming standard; that in turn

---

and Cleveland, and by the creation of new Orthodox communities in metropolitan areas such as Los Angeles, Detroit, Washington, D.C., and Miami.

eliminated the enormous penalty that earlier generations had had to pay for observing the Jewish Sabbath.

If the United States was different, so too were the immigrants themselves. As a group they were far more observant than the Jews who came during the late nineteenth and early twentieth centuries; they also were more committed to maintaining their Orthodoxy and more experienced at doing so in a modern, Western society. To oversimplify just a bit, the earlier immigrants had had to make two separate adjustments when they arrived: first to the modern world, and then to American culture. The later immigrants, however, had already come to terms with modernity in Europe. (Hasidic Jews had done so in their own way by keeping contact with the outside world to an absolute minimum.) Thus the new immigrants had only one adjustment to make—to American culture.

There was another difference, as well. During the era of mass immigration, Orthodox Jews had come without their rabbis—certainly without rabbis of distinction and standing; to move to the United States, as we have seen, was to defy rabbinic injunctions. The World War II immigrants, by contrast, were often led, and sometimes preceded, by their rabbis, some of whom were charismatic leaders. Determined to keep their followers within the Orthodox fold, the rabbis made a deliberate decision to forgo the construction of new synagogues (any building can be used for prayer) or other luxuries and to concentrate their energies and resources on a single goal: the intensive Jewish education of the next generation. Scornful of American Orthodoxy, they proceeded to create their own advanced yeshivas (rabbinic training schools), which turned out a cadre of right-wing Orthodox teachers. They then built a large network of day schools and yeshivas, so that the teachers could be employed and the children could be educated without being exposed to the secular culture of the public schools.

The growth in the number of day schools and in the number of students enrolled has transformed American Orthodoxy: there now is an entire generation of youngsters who are Judaically better educated than their parents. And because they have been taught by graduates of the right-wing yeshivas, they often are more observant than their parents. This intensification has come about, moreover, with parental encouragement. Within the Orthodox community the traditional desire of parents that their children should be "better" than they are has shifted from the socioeconomic to the religious sphere. In part because the parents have been so financially successful themselves, they seem eager for their children to be "frummer" (more observant) and better educated than they.

The result is a second generation unlike any that American Judaism has seen before: corporate lawyers and accountants, biologists and chemists, doctors and medical school professors, academicians, and successful businessmen who are also yeshiva graduates (often with rabbinic ordination) and who remain devoutly Orthodox. A number of large New York law firms now have lunchtime Talmud study groups, and the kosher restaurants in midtown Manhattan are filled at lunchtime with businessmen and professionals, who have their choice of kosher French, Chinese, or traditional Jewish food.

Whether the third and fourth generations will remain Orthodox remains to be seen. It is hard to know how durable the insulation against secular culture will prove to be—in particular, whether the growing affluence and acculturation of Orthodox Jews will turn out to be a mixed blessing. On the one hand, affluence undoubtedly makes it easier to remain Orthodox; *glatt* kosher pizza parlors and hamburger joints enable Boro Park teenagers to imitate the eating habits of the other members of American youth culture, and kosher camping trips and cross-country tours permit them to enjoy pleasures previously available only to less devout members of the upper middle class. At the same time their parents take all-kosher package vacations in Europe, Mexico, and the Caribbean. These "cultural amalgamations," as Egon Mayer calls them in his study of the Boro Park Orthodox community, help reduce the dissonance between Orthodox Jewish and secular American cultures, but they do so at a price: the absorption of secular values into the religious domain. In subtle and not so subtle ways, *glatt* kosher pizza parlors, vacations in Acapulco, and teenage camping trips serve to legitimate the contemporary emphasis on individual autonomy, self-fulfillment, and the pursuit of pleasure. "The focus on self-realization and personal pleasure," Mayer says, "is a profound and chronic deviation from a religious system that emphasizes obligation to God and community."

5

In the long run the energy being released by the Jewish women's movement is likely to provide the most important source of religious renewal. Until recently, after all, Judaism had been the product not of the Jewish people but of the half of it that was male. The exclusion of women from Jewish religious life and learning, Cynthia Ozick has written, involved "a loss numerically greater than a hundred pogroms," and was "culturally and intellectually more debilitating than a century of autos-da-fé."

The loss was all the greater for being so completely thoughtless.

Sitting in the women's section of a Jerusalem synagogue one Friday evening, Blu Greenberg recalls, she noticed that the congregational prayer book opened with an introduction explaining the laws governing the *tefillin* (phylacteries) that traditional Jewish men put on at morning prayers; as the prayer book put it, "Every single Jew is required to put on tefillin each weekday." "At first I was stunned," Greenberg writes. "How progressive, I thought, to find such a siddur [prayer book] in an Orthodox synagogue! Then I noticed the publisher's date: 1905. In 1905 siddur compilers spoke the language of the community: every single Jew, the whole community, the entire spiritual congregation. But—I checked myself—it all refers only to men. Quietly, unself-consciously, with one stroke of the pen, the complete class of Jewish women simply was excised."

At the time, Greenberg adds, she was not troubled by that excision: "My newly raised consciousness was no match for layer upon layer of conditioning." And besides, she told herself, "This was 1975 and things were changing." They were not changing nearly as rapidly, however, as Blu Greenberg's consciousness.

ITEM: The time is four years later, the setting Greenberg's own modern Orthodox congregation during the services for Simchat Torah, the festival celebrating the completion of the annual Torah-reading cycle and the commencement of the new one; the center point of the service is the *hakafah* ceremony, in which every male member of the congregation makes a circuit of the congregation carrying a Torah scroll. It is a joyous, often almost raucous ceremony in which children are encouraged to participate. "At one point the noise level reaches a new high," Greenberg writes. "The rabbi pounds on the podium. 'Let us have silence here. We won't complete the service until every single person here has had a *hakafah.*' For a fleeting moment I find my husband's eye across the partition. He smiles. He knows."

Cynthia Ozick speaks of the same kind of experience. "In the world at large I call myself, and am called, a Jew," she has written. "But when, on the Sabbath, I sit among women in my traditional shul and the rabbi speaks the word 'Jew,' I can be sure that he is not referring to me. For him, 'Jew' means 'male Jew.' . . . My own synagogue is the only place in the world where I am not named Jew."

The most important fact about American Judaism, and the most favorable omen for its future, is that women as talented as Greenberg and Ozick have not turned away from Judaism. On the contrary, a group of highly talented writers, scholars, and activists, as well as a good many housewives, "professional volunteers," and women with conventional occupations are struggling to reconcile their commitment to equality for women with their commitment to Judaism. Some have never strayed from religious observance, whether of the Orthodox, Conservative, Reconstructionist, or Reform variety; others have been drawn to Judaism *because* of their feminism.

ITEM: "I had never considered myself religious. I am a daughter of the secular city," Betty Friedan has written. "For me as for other Jewish feminists, religion perpetuated the patriarchal tradition that denied women access to Judaism's most sacred rituals and enshrined them within the strict confines of their biological role. But when women like me broke through to our authentic personhood as women, we also found the strength to dig deep into ourselves on other levels."

For some time, Friedan continues, "[I had been] uncomfortable . . . with my conventional sophistication about religion. I was, in effect, denying the great questions of beginning, end and purpose, which are the substance of every religion. Now, with a sense of confidence born of the woman's movement, I and many other feminists found we could embrace our authentic Jewishness in a new way."

Attending an American Jewish Congress conference on women's rights in Jerusalem in the summer of 1984, Friedan found that "in some strange and wonderful way, my feminism and my Judaism were converging." That convergence reached its peak at the conference when, for the first time in her life, Friedan was invited to help form a *minyan* (the quorum of ten) for morning prayers. "It moves me very much, in that small hotel room, to watch young Naamah Kelman, an American-born Israeli, daughter of 13 generations of rabbis, in her white prayer shawl, leading us in the ancient rituals only men have been allowed to perform," Friedan wrote in *The New York Times Magazine*. "And tears came to my eyes as I join the young women in prayer: 'Blessed are You, O God, who has made me free. Blessed are You, O God, who has made me Jewish! Blessed are You, O God, who has made me in Your image."

One of the most striking manifestations of change has been the emergence of women's prayer groups among Orthodox women in cities as diverse as San Francisco, Berkeley, Los Angeles, Boston, Teaneck (New Jersey), Great Neck (New York), and New York City. Nor are the groups limited to younger women.

ITEM: From the second article in a six-part 1984 Associated Press series on American Jews, datelined San Francisco: "Eva Oles, an Orthodox Jew, does not drive on Sabbath. So at least once a month, the 59-year-old woman walks to services—a hike of six miles up and down San Francisco's hills.

"She need not go so far to find an ordinary Orthodox synagogue. But there, Mrs. Oles would have to sit in an area reserved for women, behind a curtain. She could not climb the pulpit and read from the Torah, like a man.

" 'I've always felt that I was as good a Jew as a man,' said Mrs. Oles."

In New York, which contains more than half the Orthodox population of the country, there are a growing number of Orthodox women's prayer groups. The most significant, perhaps, is a three-year-old women's *davening* (praying) group in the Flatbush section of Brooklyn, one of the most traditional Orthodox communities in New York. The thirty or so members are so devout that they refuse to call the group a *minyan*—a term that would imply acceptance of the notion that they are qualified to conduct a regular service. Determined to live according to Halachah (Jewish law), which holds that only men can comprise a *minyan*, the women do not recite any of the prayers that can be recited only when a *minyan* is present. Even so, they have been sharply criticized by local rabbis; indeed, the principal right-wing Orthodox organization issued a proclamation declaring that participation was forbidden.

The women meet nonetheless; since the summer of 1984 they have a Torah scroll of their own, donated by one of the members, New York City councilwoman Susan Alter. "They're afraid of what it looks like," says Rivkeh Haut, a founder of the group, referring to the rabbis who oppose its existence. (Haut teaches Talmud to the group's members.) "They're afraid we're feminists and that soon we'll want to come into the shul and want *aliyahs* there [calls to the reading of the Torah] and women rabbis."

"I'm sorry, I can't help what it looks like," Haut adds. "If we wanted [*aliyahs* or women rabbis] we could go to Conservative shuls. We're doing this precisely because we want to remain within Halachah," and because they are determined, as Haut puts it, "to have a physical closeness to the *Sefer Torah* [Torah scroll] that is impossible in an Orthodox shul." The first time she was called up to the Torah, councilwoman Alter says, echoing Betty Friedan's response, "it was very emotional. What to a little boy is nothing was to a grown woman a very emotional, moving experience."

And so it is that significant numbers of Jewish women are now insisting on being included as full members of the Jewish people; they are demanding equal access to the roles from which they have traditionally been barred—as teachers and scholars, religious and communal leaders, and participants in congregational worship. The result has been the release of an extraordinary burst of energy and talent, much like that accompanying the entry of Jewish male writers and scholars into the American scene after World War II.

Jewish religious and communal life will never be the same again. Some Orthodox thinkers, for example, believe that the way in which Orthodoxy responds to the women's movement will determine its future course. With the shift to the right over the last quarter century, Rabbi Moshe Adler, former Hillel director at the University of Minnesota, has argued, Orthodox Judaism "has turned itself into a garrison state," and the women's movement can be the catalyst that enables it to find its way out. To Adler the issue is clear: whether Orthodoxy will be simply "a form of scoring celestial brownie-points" or a means of acquiring "heightened spiritual awareness," of demonstrating "justice and compassion in the way [one] lives" his or her daily life.

Whatever its impact on Orthodoxy turns out to be, the women's movement already has had a profound effect on Reform, Reconstructionist, and Conservative Judaism. Since 1972, when Rabbi Sally Priesand became the first woman ordained as a rabbi in the United States, the Reform and Reconstructionist rabbinic colleges have ordained well over a hundred women rabbis. The number is growing rapidly; in recent years 40–50 percent of the students entering the two institutions have been women. And in September 1984 eighteen women entered the rabbinic training program at the Jewish Theological Seminary of America after a long and bitter fight over ordination of women as Conservative rabbis.

The Seminary's decision to ordain women as Conservative rabbis is a major turning point in the evolution of American Judaism. So long as women rabbis were confined to the Reform and Reconstructionist movements, they lacked a certain legitimacy; Reform Judaism, after all, has never accepted the authority of Jewish law, and Reconstructionism is still a small splinter group. But despite the growth of the Reform movement, Conservative Judaism is still the largest denomination. More important, it not only accepts the authority of Jewish tradition but lays claim to being its most authentic contemporary form—a claim that Orthodoxy heatedly denies. At the very least, therefore, the ordination of women as Conservative rabbis will make it impossible to avoid consideration of the complex problems that feminism raises for Jewish theology, liturgy and worship, and ritual practice.

The decision has other implications as well. Conservative Judaism may be revitalized by the infusion of female energy, talent, and sensibility; it has been floundering for a long time as a result of its own indecision about change. But the movement may also be fractured if members of its right wing, who bitterly oppose ordination of women, decide to join the Orthodox camp; for the moment, at least, they prefer to continue their losing fight within the Conservative movement. What does seem certain, however, is that ordination of women will significantly widen the division between the Orthodox community and everyone else, if for no other reason than that it almost inevitably commits the Conservative movement to make more radical changes in the near future.*

One important symbolic change—the creation of new religious rituals to celebrate the birth of a daughter—is being accepted fairly readily. Understandably so; few Jewish rituals have been so sacred as *brit milah*, the religious ceremony accompanying the ritual circumcision performed on male children on the eighth day after birth to symbolize in physical form their entry into the covenant. The absence of any comparable ceremony for girls involves a religious anomaly, for the Bible explicitly declares that the covenant at Sinai included women as well as men. Hence a growing number of young Jews, including Orthodox Jews, are developing their own rituals and ceremonies in order to give the birth of a daughter the same religious significance that the birth of a son has always entailed.

But Jewish feminists are demanding more than equality—more, that is, than the right to assume the roles, rituals, and symbols previously limited to men. They are seeking something larger and more profound: the incorporation of women's experiences and sensibilities into the corpus of Jewish religious thought and experience. "There is another pole to Jewish feminism," Paula Hyman, dean of the Jewish Theological Seminary's undergraduate College of Jewish Studies, argues, "and that is the assertion of our uniqueness, of our distinctiveness. We seek to develop our own spirituality and our own Jewish identity." More than that, feminists are trying to reinterpret the Jewish past from a woman's perspective—"as a resource for all Jews," Hyman explains, not just for women. "We want to contribute our insights and our experience to the heritage of the Jewish people." That contribution is likely to transform American Judaism in ways that cannot be anticipated.

* The really sticky issue, as far as Halachah is concerned, is not the ordination of women—that can be justified fairly easily—but the fact that women, along with children and the mentally impaired, may not serve as witnesses—to a wedding ceremony, for example, or in a court of Jewish law. The Conservative movement has avoided that issue so far; it will have to confront it once women are serving as rabbis.

6

When I began my research in the summer of 1979, most observers doubted that a return to Judaism was under way; by 1984, articles describing the return had become almost commonplace. What is at issue now is not the *existence* of a religious revival but its nature and significance. Students of the phenomenon disagree over how many people are involved, how durable the return is likely to be, and what it portends for the future of Judaism in the United States.

Some Orthodox thinkers, for example, have criticized the triumphalist mood with which their colleagues have greeted the *baal teshuvah* phenomenon. In a controversial article in *Jewish Life*, Rabbi Ralph Pelcovitz called attention to "the dangers as well as the opportunities which this movement presents to the Jewish community in general and to the Orthodox community in particular." Those who have had contact with Orthodox *baalei teshuvah*, Pelcovitz wrote, "can attest to the mercurial moods of some of these penitents and the ever-present danger of their leaving us as suddenly and abruptly as they arrived." Pelcovitz attributed this instability to the fact that many Orthodox *baalei teshuvah* "are not necessarily attracted to Judaism *per se:* they are young men and women who have found their lives devoid of values and lacking direction. Some have been with cults, others with drugs; they seek a safe harbor as well as some meaning and purpose for their lives. They are easily attracted to a religious leader who possesses a charismatic personality to whom they can cling and lean upon as a pillar of strength and support which they so desperately need." The same need that brings these troubled youths back to Orthodoxy, Pelcovitz suggested, drives many of them away. "The attrition rate is not documented," he writes, "but one gets the feeling that it is substantial."

By and large, however, the instability of which Pelcovitz speaks is characteristic only of those who are attracted to fundamentalist Orthodox sects. Among most of the people involved in Jewish renewal, as Carl Scheingold has documented, the religious impulse does not grow out of any sense of personal inadequacy or failure. "This surprising flowering of unorthodox Judaism," Sara Bershtel and Allen Graubard wrote in the summer 1982 issue of *Dissent*, "must be seen against the backdrop of the highly successful integration of Jews into American life."*

* The fact that this socialist journal published a serious evaluation of the Jewish revival is itself testimony to the breadth and depth of the phenomenon, as is the fact that *Dissent* is edited by two intensely committed Jews,

That same fact, however, leads Bershtel and Graubard to question the staying power and significance of the movement. "Do these activities really hold out hope for the revitalization of Judaism?" they ask, after describing a number of examples of what they call "active Judaism." Their answer is no: "The richness of the revival gives a misleading basis for hopes of glowing reconstruction, and . . . the resurgence of interest in practical Judaism is a problematic phenomenon, expressive of the very forces of dissolution it seeks to combat."

For all its apparent vigor, Bershtel and Graubard submit, the revival is ephemeral, because it is "expressive of dilemmas of modernity rather than of Judaism, of questions and discontents, yearnings and confusions that characterize thoughtful individuals today, whatever their cultural, religious, ethnic, or political allegiance. The various forms of new Jewish activity suggest origins traceable to ideals of social justice, to assertions of ethnic pride, to the questions evoked by family and parenthood, to the healing function of ritual in giving fragmented lives a longed-for sense of ceremony and significance, to that most contemporary desire to feel better, more existentially at ease."

In their view, the essence of the problem—the reason Jewish renewal will not last—is that it is the product of individual choice rather than a response to communal or divine demands. The Jews in question select only those parts of the tradition that are meaningful to them; their Judaism is "a self-conscious recreation . . . of tradition, theology, and ritual by individuals for themselves, in response to contemporary values, anxieties, and aspirations." Indeed, "the willing of meaning by individuals who believe that such commitments must be *chosen* is the distinguishing mark of this revival [emphasis in original]." The emphasis on individual choice makes the revival fragile, Bershtel and Graubard believe, for "if the form of Jewish commitment one has chosen at present does not satisfy one's emotional or spiritual needs next year, then one must move on—perhaps to a universalist politics or to a new version of Eastern mysticism or whatever."

Bershtel and Graubard have correctly described the distinguishing mark of the current religious revival. It is not coincidental, for example, that the most important literary creation of the *havurah* generation is *The Jewish Catalog*. First published in 1973, its three volumes have sold over 500,000 copies—more than any book, other than Bible translations, published in the Jewish Publication Society's ninety-seven-year history. *The Jewish Catalog*'s subtitle—"A Do-It-Yourself Kit"—reflects the *havurah* movement's emphasis on individual autonomy.

Irving Howe, of the City University of New York, and Michael Walzer, of the Institute for Advanced Studies, in Princeton.

The size of the audience the books have attracted makes it clear that large numbers of American Jews are comfortable with the approach to Judaism that they represent. As the Reform theologian Eugene Borowitz points out, their content is heavily ritualistic and highly traditional; the authors are at great pains to show the beauty and meaning inherent in rituals and observances that liberal Jews had long considered archaic or even primitive. And yet the *form* of the books, Borowitz adds, is anything but traditional. Previous generations turned to the *Shulchan Aruch* (literally, "the set [or ordered] table")—a compendium of Jewish religious laws—to learn what was required of them. In contrast, the new guide to Jewish practice is called a catalog, and a catalog, as Borowitz points out, "is a book you look through, in order to pick and choose what you will order." "We have become a cafeteria people," Borowitz concludes, "and each of us is on his or her own individual diet."

This emphasis on individual autonomy—on finding an approach to Judaism that has meaning for oneself—is the greatest *strength* of the current Jewish renewal movement, not its fatal flaw. Indeed, no religious revival that denied the centrality of will and choice would have any chance of survival; for the critical fact about modernity, as we have seen, is that it brings about "a near-inconceivable expansion of the area of human life open to choices." By shattering the traditional order, the scientific, technological, intellectual, and political revolutions of modernity have made every aspect of life subject to human volition. As Peter Berger puts it, "What previously was fate now becomes a set of choices . . . Destiny is transformed into decision."

The need to choose in turn means that "the modern individual must stop and pause where premodern men could act in unreflective spontaneity." "Quite simply," Berger states, "the modern individual must engage in more deliberate thinking—*not* because he is more intelligent, *not* because he is on some sort of higher level of consciousness, *but* because his social situation forces him to this. . . . Ordinary, everyday life is full of choices, from the most trivial choices between competing consumer commodities to far-reaching alternatives in life-style [emphasis in original]."

One consequence is a heavy emphasis on the subjective self. When destiny is transformed into decision, the answers to the fundamental questions of human existence no longer are provided automatically by the place in society into which each person is born. Since people need answers in order to function, they are forced to turn inward—to evaluate each option by how it looks, or feels, to *them.* "Fate does not require reflection," Berger explains; but "the individual who is compelled to make choices is also compelled to stop and think. The more choices, the more reflection. The individual who reflects inevitably becomes more conscious of himself . . . he turns his attention from the objectively given outside world to his own subjectivity." Indeed, concern with self—the belief that reality is a function of individual experience—lies at the heart of modern consciousness.

This is as true of religion as it is of every other aspect of life. Certainly some contemporary individuals inherit their faith and never question it, just as there were people before the modern period who were racked by religious doubts; both groups are exceptions to the rule. As Berger observes: "In premodern situations there is a world of religious certainty, occasionally ruptured by heretical deviations. By contrast, the modern situation is a world of religious uncertainty, occasionally staved off by more or less precarious constructions of religious affirmation . . . modernity creates a new situation in which picking and choosing becomes an imperative."

When Bershtel and Graubard complain, therefore, that "one can choose anything, whatever one was last year, or yesterday," they are simply describing the objective situation in which everybody, Jews and Christians alike, now find themselves. Freedom of choice is the prerogative even of Orthodox Jews, notwithstanding the fact that many, perhaps most, act as if there were no choice. Orthodox Jews, that is to say, submit to communal or family demands and follow what they believe to be God's laws; but that submission is in itself an act of choice. Orthodox Jews are able to maintain their Orthodoxy, in fact, by "compartmentalizing Judaism," as Charles Liebman puts it—by viewing their Jewish and their non-Jewish lives as if they were completely separate spheres and by making a virtue of the inconsistency between the two world views they are forced to maintain.

Even in the seemingly closed communities that Orthodox Jews have created in certain neighborhoods of Brooklyn, Baltimore, Cleveland, and Detroit, significant numbers of Jews choose their own approach to Judaism. If it appears otherwise, it is only because the monolithic nature of these communities forces those who choose a different approach to leave. "Among the dozens of boys and girls who were my own classmates in the yeshivas Toras Emes and Kamenitz, and who were my peers and friends in such organizations as the Young Israel, the 'Y,' and the Agudah, several became reputable rabbis, Talmudic scholars, or traditional housewives," Egon Mayer wrote in *From Suburb to Shtetl*, his sociological analysis of the Orthodox community of Boro Park, in which he was raised. "But I know a great many more who became doctors, lawyers, college professors, psychologists, editors, and executives. Many of the latter have become Orthodox *by their own definition of the term*," Mayer adds, "but all have left the

Boro Park community and settled in communities where religious demands do not have as easy and direct access to their private life as is the case in Boro Park [emphasis added]."

It is not surprising, therefore, that the Jewish renewal movement is self-centered, in the literal and nonpejorative sense of the term. Nor is it purely coincidental that the most influential Jewish theologians of our time—Franz Rosenzweig, Martin Buber, Abraham Joshua Heschel, Mordecai M. Kaplan, Joseph Baer Soloveitchik—have been concerned, in ways their predecessors were not, with problems of individual meaning and faith. To be sure, Buber, who defined the central religious experience as the relationship between I and Thou—between the solitary individual and God—has been attacked in traditionalist Jewish circles as more Christian than Jewish.

But no one questions the Jewish authenticity of Rabbi Joseph Baer Soloveitchik, the most respected Orthodox theologian and Talmudist of our age. Although the *Rav* (the teacher par excellence), as he is known, is a stern traditionalist whose approach to Jewish law is at the opposite pole from Buber's, he is equally concerned with the individual's relationship to God. "The one consistent element in Soloveitchik's thought," David Singer and Moshe Sokol have written, "is his preoccupation with a religious problematic uniquely his own." Thus Soloveitchik's magisterial essay "The Lonely Man of Faith" is an explication of his personal theology—or, as he puts it, an analysis of "the great dilemma confronting contemporary man of faith," a dilemma whose nature "can be stated in a three-word sentence. I am lonely."

The "I" of whom Soloveitchik speaks is himself: "It is not the plan of this paper to discuss the millennium-old problem of faith and reason," he wrote in the opening paragraph. "I want instead to focus on a human life situation in which the man of faith as an individual concrete being, with his cares and hopes, concerns and needs, joys and sad moments, is entangled. Therefore whatever I am going to say here has been derived not from philosophical dialectics, abstract speculation, or detached impersonal reflections, *but from actual situations and experiences with which I have been confronted.*"

Even Soloveitchik, in short, is searching for a Judaism that responds to his personal needs. True, his solution is to submit humbly to God's will, as expressed in Halachah—to establish a "covenantal relationship" with God and thereby with his fellow human beings. But not all Jews can make that leap of faith, nor can they simply disregard modern biblical scholarship, as Soloveitchik does. If the starting point for contemporary theology is the "actual situations and experiences" with which each individual has been confronted, there are bound to be almost as many theologies as there are situations and experiences.

This degree of pluralism involves certain risks, of course. The emphasis on self can slide all too easily into narcissism—a worship of the self that Judaism can see only as another form of idolatry. Among those recently returned to Judaism, moreover, as well as among the members of the *havurah* community, there is another danger, which might be termed idolatry of the group—a preoccupation with the specialness of one's own small community that inhibits or even precludes concern with the larger Jewish community or with individuals outside the group. Because finding like-minded, compatible peers plays such an important role in overcoming the alienation from Judaism of returning Jews, there is a tendency to equate the group with Judaism itself. "I can't imagine *davening* [praying] with any other group" and "I couldn't be comfortable anywhere else" are frequently heard remarks, and *havurah* members are sometimes unwittingly cold, even rejecting, to newcomers who are not at their particular stage of Jewish development.

Although the problem of individual and group narcissism is real, it is kept in check by young Jews' growing self-consciousness about it and by their deepening concern with Jewish peoplehood. There is an increasing recognition among liberal Jews, moreover, that they must find some way to reconcile their insistence on personal autonomy with traditional Jewish notions of authority—of externally given *mitzvot*, or commandments. There are almost as many approaches to reconciliation as there are "new Jews," but there is a wide agreement on several key points: it is essential to define what is authentic (or authoritative) in Judaism; authenticity involves some notion of *mitzvot*—of externally given rules; and that definition of the rules cannot be left entirely to individual preference or choice. Even the most latitudinarian Jews, Carl Scheingold reports, see Judaism "not just as large, but as larger than themselves—not just as something positive and rich, but as a tradition that commands respect and elicits feelings of awe." The result is a tendency to penetrate more deeply into the tradition—to be respectful of traditional laws, whether one accepts them or not—and to feel an obligation to base decisions about what to observe on substantive knowledge.

"What we need more than ever, or at least as much as ever," Franz Rosenzweig, one of the principal architects of modern Jewish renewal, wrote some sixty years ago, "are human beings—Jewish human beings." The Jewishness of which he spoke, Rosenzweig added, "can be grasped through neither the writing nor reading of books. . . . It is only lived." What makes the current Jewish renewal so significant is precisely the fact that it is not just being talked or written about; it is being lived.

CHAPTER SEVEN

JEWS BY CHOICE

1

"I have good news and bad news," I told a lecture audience in the fall of 1980, eighteen months into my research on this book. "The good news is that a major revitalization of Jewish religious and cultural life is under way; the bad news is that there may not be enough Jews left to sustain it." The combination of a high and rising intermarriage rate and a low and falling birthrate, I explained, seemed to portend a significant reduction in the size of the American Jewish population.

After five and a half years of further research I have an additional piece of good news to report—that my bad news was wrong. Specifically, the Jewish birthrate is higher than I had thought—high enough, in fact, to keep the Jewish population at about its current size; and the intermarriage rate is lower and its consequences less adverse to Jewish continuity than I had assumed. It seems unlikely, in fact, that intermarriage will lead to more than a slight reduction in the number of Jews, and it could bring about an increase.

To argue that American Jewry is not at demographic risk is to run against the grain. Leonard Fein, who shares my view, doubts "that there's a Jew left anywhere in America who doesn't believe that the number of Jews is shrinking as a consequence of assimilation, a low birth rate and intermarriage." It would be hard not to believe that the number of Jews is shrinking, given the doomsday forecasts that Jews are regularly bombarded with. A "disaster is in the making," Elihu Bergman, then assistant director of the Harvard Center for Population Studies, wrote in 1977 in a dire forecast cited in Chapter Five. "When the United States celebrates its Tricentennial in 2076, the American Jewish community is likely to number no more than 944,000 persons, and conceivably as few as 10,420."

Despite the fact that these projections were based on wildly improbable assumptions—one distinguished demographer calls them "demographic nonsense"—Bergman's dour view of the American Jewish future has been accepted as if it were carved in stone, and contrary views have been ignored or dismissed. "I am unaware of any convincing refutation of [Bergman's] procedures or . . . conclusions," Professor Robert Gordis of the Jewish Theological Seminary of America has written, ignoring the fact that one of the demographers responsible for the projections Bergman used repudiated both the procedures and the conclusions in the same journal in which Bergman's and Gordis' articles appeared. But Gordis, who is certain that the "situation is . . . desperate," believes that "precise figures are not the issue," since "the trend is indisputable." But precise figures are precisely the issue: without them we cannot know the trend, which, as we will see, is quite different from what Gordis assumes.

To reject Gordis' assessment of the demographic outlook, it should be noted, is not to dismiss the concern from which it stems. There have been times, of course, when expressions of alarm about intermarriage had no basis in fact; "If nothing is done to prevent the tendency to intermarriage, Judaism can barely survive another century," Mordecai Kaplan wrote in 1934, when no more than 2 to 3 percent of American Jews were marrying outside the faith. Today, however, there are ample grounds for concern; although the precise level and trend of intermarriage are matters of dispute, as are its consequences for Jewish continuity, there is no gainsaying the fact that intermarriage did increase sharply during the 1960s and early 1970s.

The old fear of intermarriage has been joined to a new—one is tempted to say belated—concern over the Jewish birthrate. Thus Professor Gordis, who once had reassured American Jews that contraception was sanctioned by Jewish law, is now afraid that too many Jews are following his counsel. "If a Jew assimilates, there is always hope that he will return," he says, "but the child who is not born is lost forever." In Gordis' new view, Jewish survival in America is threatened by the number of children who are *not* being born, and he has called for an all-out campaign to persuade young Jews to have more children. "If we can sell toothpaste and elect presidents through public relations techniques," Gordis told a 1983 National Conference on Population Growth, called by the American Jewish Committee at his urging, "we can 'sell' a larger Jewish family."

As it happens, nothing is harder to "sell" than a larger family. Certainly the birthrate is not impervious to change; it fluctuates widely and often unpredictably—so much so, that changes frequently take demographers by surprise. But increases and decreases in fertility are not brought about by public relations campaigns; on the contrary, human beings stubbornly resist attempts to influence their decisions about family size, even when elaborate incentives are offered. For forty years, in fact, a succession of French governments have tried to increase the birthrate without effect, and Herculean efforts by several East European countries have been equally unsuccessful. As a Yiddish proverb reminds us, The mere existence of a problem is no proof of the existence of a solution.

That there is a problem cannot be denied, but it is an old problem, not a new one; Jews have had a lower birthrate than most other Americans for as long as they lived in the United States. Until recently, however, fertility did not seem to be a problem. The Jewish population grew because of the number of immigrants who came and because the new immigrants, most of whom were young, usually had a birthrate well above that of native-born Jews. The children of immigrants, however, quickly adapted to the lower American Jewish norm.

ITEM: My maternal grandparents had 9 children—more than the average for their generation, perhaps, but not an exceptional number by any means. But those 9 children, two of whom were childless, produced only 17 children among them, or an average of 1.9 children each. And even with the post-World War II baby boom, the members of my own generation averaged only 2 children each.

This tendency to see 2 children as the norm goes back to the turn of the century. In a Rhode Island census of 1905, for example—the only one to collect information on religion—native-born Jewish women averaged 2.3 children each, compared to 2.5 for native-born Protestants and 3.2 for native-born Catholics. As second- and third-generation Jews began to outnumber immigrants after World War I, the Jewish birthrate dropped precipitously; since then fertility has averaged 2.1 children per woman—that is, American Jews have had just enough children to reproduce themselves, but no more.

Even so, the fact that Jewish immigrants continued to come to the

United States made most Jews indifferent to the long-term consequences of the low birthrate; those who did express concern felt that they were whistling in the wind.* Now, however, immigration is declining and there is no new large-scale source in sight—hence future changes in the size of the Jewish population will be determined by what happens to the birthrate.

Suddenly the question of family size has acquired a prominent place on the Jewish communal agenda. In the wake of the Holocaust, in which one third of world Jewry was killed, some argue, it is incumbent on American Jews to do more than reproduce themselves; they should have enough children to ensure population growth. An increase in average family size would contribute to group self-interest as well, for if the American Jewish population fails to grow, Jews would become a steadily declining proportion of the total population, which might well reduce their political influence. Stability in overall numbers would also mean that elderly Jews would constitute a steadily increasing proportion of the Jewish population—a change that has begun already and that could put a strain on communal resources.

What gives the discussion its note of urgency—at times of near hysteria—is the belief that the birthrate has plummeted far below the replacement level and that a major reduction in numbers is inevitable. For a time it looked as though that was, in fact, what was happening. In the past, Jewish women had borne most of their children while they were in their twenties: half of all Jewish births, in fact, occurred to women between the ages of twenty-five and twenty-nine, with three quarters of the births coming before they turned thirty. During the 1960s and 1970s, however, this age group experienced a sharp decline in fertility. In 1973, for example, married Jewish women aged twenty-five to twenty-nine had averaged just under one child each, compared to 1.7 to 1.8 children for Protestant and Catholic women in the same age group. Although the Jewish twenty-five-to-twenty-nine-year-olds said that they expected to have a total of 2.1 children each by the time they had finished their child rearing, most demographers

* The sociologist Eric Rosenthal was the first to call attention to the long-term consequences of the Jewish birthrate. "In view of the low Jewish fertility rate," he wrote in the 1961 *American Jewish Year Book,* "the question must be raised whether past and current fertility levels are high enough to maintain the size of the Jewish population." Since then the *Year Book*'s coeditor, Milton Himmelfarb, has been ridiculing the involvement of American Jews in the Zero Population Growth movement and attacking rabbinic indifference to the Jewish birthrate. "When [the rabbis] do turn their attention to Jewish fertility," he wrote in 1963, "it is to invoke the support of Jewish tradition or law for birth control. . . . They must imagine that we are unrestrained breeders."

assumed that the women would fall short—far short—of their expectations.

Pessimism deepened, moreover, because of the high proportion of Jewish women who remained single and childless throughout their twenties. Although these trends were visible among all religious and ethnic groups, they were far more acute among Jewish women.

ITEM: In 1980 the American Council on Education conducted a national survey of adults who had been college freshmen nine years earlier and who were, therefore, in their mid- to late twenties. More than half the Jewish women, compared to only a third of the non-Jewish women, had never been married. The difference in fertility was even more striking: only 6 percent of the Jewish women had had a child at that point, compared to 28 percent of the non-Jewish women. Moreover, only three tenths of 1 percent of the Jewish women had had two or more children, compared to 11.4 percent of the non-Jewish women.

To a good many observers it looked as though the Jewish family—once a principal source of stability and strength—was on the skids. Some pointed the finger at the new sexual permissiveness, which made it acceptable for men and women to live together without benefit of matrimony. To be sure, this change was not limited to young Jews, but since Jews take a more liberal stance than other Americans on most social issues, it was not surprising that young Jews appeared to be in the vanguard on this one as well. In 1980, for example, some 71 percent of Jewish college freshmen, compared to 45 percent of non-Jews, agreed that "sex is OK if people like each other"; 63 percent of the Jewish freshmen, compared to 40 percent of the non-Jews, approved of living together before marriage.

To other observers the problem seemed to be a new spirit of narcissism, with its emphasis on self-fulfillment; still others thought a decline in fertility was an inevitable by-product of the change in the status of women, which was more pronounced among Jews than among other ethnic and religious groups. With more and more Jewish women going to college and graduate school and pursuing professional careers, the reasoning went, marriage and child rearing were bound to suffer.

Whatever the reasons, men and women were, in fact, postponing the age at which they married; this in turn raised the possibility that there might be a large group of permanently single people—a group that was being expanded still more by the growing frequency of divorce. And since many of those who did marry did not have their first child until they were in their thirties, most demographers assumed that they would have fewer children than if they had started their childbearing at the usual, younger, age. Thus the demographers projected a massive decline in Jewish fertility—from the old replacement level of 2.1 children per Jewish woman to an average of 1.5 to 1.7 children; some thought the fertility rate would drop as low as 1.2 children.

It has not happened that way. The postponement of the age at which Jews marry and bear children appears to be precisely that—a postponement of traditional family life, not an abandonment. Men and women are marrying at a later age than in the past, but they *are* marrying—and in proportions surprisingly close to those of the recent past, when marriage was almost universal for Jewish women. Specifically, demographic surveys conducted in a number of Jewish communities in the early 1980s indicate that by the time Jewish women reach the thirty-five-to-forty-four age bracket, 92 to 95 percent have been married—a figure only 3 to 6 percent below the proportion in 1970–71.*

Although women are having their first children at a considerably later age than in the past, they *are* having children—as many children, it would appear, as their grandmothers had, if slightly fewer than their mothers. What has changed, in other words, is the age at which Jewish women do their child-bearing, not the number of children they bear. Preliminary analysis of a demographic survey of the New York metropolitan area, which includes over 30 percent of American Jews, indicates that women in the thirty-five-to-forty-four age group have had an average of a little more than two children each—the same level that has prevailed for the last sixty-five years.

But what about the future? Will women now in their twenties and early thirties have as many children as those who are thirty-five to forty-four? Members of the latter group, after all, fall between two worlds. Those who were thirty-five to forty-four in 1981, when the New York survey was taken, grew up in the 1940s and 1950s when women's roles were just beginning to change. They have had less education than younger Jewish women, and fewer of them have followed full-time, let alone professional careers. Thus the fact that contemporary thirty-five-to-forty-four-year-olds are having about as many children as their age group had in the past does not necessarily mean that the next generation will do the same when they reach that age.

Certainly women in their twenties and early thirties live in a different world than those who are just ten or fifteen years older; their consciousness was formed during a period of extraordinary ferment and

* To be sure, there has been a huge increase in the number of Jewish singles. But that increase is due to the postponement of the age of marriage and the greater frequency of divorce, not to the emergence of a large group of permanently single Jews.

change. Indeed, a whole generation—an entire cohort, in the language of demographers—has had the experience of being trailblazers almost everywhere they went: in college and graduate school and in their subsequent careers as lawyers, doctors, scientists, academicians, business managers, and a host of other professional and managerial occupations in which women previously had been notable mainly by their absence. They were the first generation to compete with men on men's own turf; diapers and formulas must have looked like impossible drudgery compared to the excitement and glamour of their new careers—all the more so as these women came to realize how much their own mothers envied the seemingly limitless horizons that lay before them. While they were building their careers, therefore, many put the question of marriage or child rearing off to what, for a time at least, appeared to be the indefinite future.

As they enter their thirties, however, career women are finding that their perspective has changed, and in ways they had not—perhaps could not have—anticipated.

ITEM: "Until you have one, you have no idea the extraordinary pull a child exerts," says Charlene Barshefsky, a thirty-four-year-old partner at Steptoe & Johnson, a leading Washington, D.C., law firm, and the mother of a two-year-old child. "For years, I had absolutely no interest in children," she explains. "I was busy with my career, busy with my friends, and my life was very full." Barshefsky did not change her mind overnight: deciding to have children "was a very gradual process that started when I was about 30 or 31 and my friends started having babies."

What is happening, in part, is that a great many young female careerists are discovering that there is, indeed, a sense in which "anatomy is destiny." When they were in their twenties they were determined to prove that gender differences were irrelevant, but as they enter (or move through) their thirties, they recognize that the "biological clock" is ticking away and that, unlike men, women cannot defer parenting indefinitely. Having experienced so much, moreover, they are deciding that they do not want to miss what they suspect may be the ultimate experience of all. Some women become pregnant, in fact, less because they want a child than because they do not want to *not* have one; they fear that if they do not become pregnant while they are still able, they will regret their decision when the option no longer is available.

But the change is more profound than that; for women with professional careers, in particular—a group comprising half or more of younger Jewish women—what *Washington Post* columnist Judy Mann calls "the post-Superwoman syndrome" is coming into play. "At the beginning of the Superwoman era working wasn't so much a choice as a challenge," Mann has written. "Stories abounded about pregnant women working until the day before the baby was born, then returning to work full time in a matter of weeks. Superwoman was not about to be undermined by her biological destiny. . . . It was a necessary phase, one myth destroying another." In short, "women kicked over the pedestal and established their right to work if they wanted to." They also demonstrated their ability to perform as well as men.

Having done so, a great many women are discovering that the maternal experience means more to them than they had anticipated—more, even, than the career to which they once had given primary allegiance. "You know, I *enjoy* taking care of Jessica!" one new mother told me recently. "I'm surprised by how much fun it is; she changes every day." The mother is changing as well. She had returned to her full-time research job six weeks after her baby had been born, but three months later she decided that she did not want to work full time after all. Now she works three days a week—an arrangement that gives her the intellectual stimulation she cherishes without depriving her of the rewards that come from raising her child herself.

Others are making the same discovery.

ITEM: "I've moved to a slower track," a partner in a Chicago law firm told me. "After Jesse [her second child] was born. I found that I was not as committed to my career as I thought I was—or as I guess I had been." She has retained her partnership—the firm is reluctant to lose someone with her ability—but she now works four days a week instead of the five-bordering-on-seven that she used to put in, and she does little traveling except for one-day or occasional overnight trips.

This kind of choice is becoming more and more frequent.

ITEM: "I thought I could do absolutely everything; I had to admit I couldn't. Something had to give," says thirty-one-year-old Marge Helfet of San Francisco. After the birth of her second child Helfet gave up her position with the investment banking firm of Morgan Stanley & Company, whose San Francisco office she helped establish. "I figure there are four parts to every marriage: your career, your husband's career, your married life, and your child's life," she explains. "And I figured out you could only do three at once."

For some career women, especially those whose husbands have well-paying jobs, child rearing represents a new career challenge: "It's the same as changing careers," one such mother explains. Most women, however, prefer—or need—to continue working. Some seek part-time jobs; so many women lawyers are in that category in Washington, D.C., in fact, that an employment agency—"the Kelly Girl for attorneys," its founder calls it—was established recently to bring them into contact with law firms seeking temporary or part-time legal assistance. Other women continue to work full time after their children are born but switch to less demanding jobs. Women lawyers, for example, may leave their firms for nine-to-five jobs with a government agency or the legal department of a bank or insurance company; some doctors give up private practice for positions on the staff of a health maintenance organization or corporate medical department.

What all this suggests, of course, is that the growing concentration of Jewish women in professional occupations need not bring about a decline in the birthrate. On the contrary, what evidence we have suggests that the reverse may actually occur. In his analysis of the 1975 Boston survey, which asked a detailed question about the anticipated family size, Calvin Goldscheider found that the most educated Jewish women also expected the largest families—2.5 children each, as compared to 2.2 for Jewish women as a whole. Women who worked, moreover, expected slightly larger families than those who were not in the labor force.*

Since it is impossible to predict human behavior with any degree of accuracy, surveys of expected family size provide the only clue to what women are apt to do. But how reliable is the clue? What is the likelihood that Jewish women will have as many children as they say they will have?

The question is anything but academic, for, as we will see in a moment, Jewish women consistently report that they expect to have, on average, a little more than two children each. Those who expect a significant reduction in family size dismiss the birth expectation surveys as unreliable. In a period of low or declining fertility, they argue, women will have fewer children than they expect, and when fertility is high or rising, women will exceed their expectations; women predict their births with reasonable accuracy only in periods when fertility is stable.

The demographers are wrong—wrong about women in general and even more so about Jewish women in particular.

ITEM: In a study of the annual population surveys of the Census Bureau for the period 1971–81, Martin O'Connell and Carolyn C. Rogers

* Jewish women are atypical in this regard. Among Boston Protestants and Catholics, women who work expect to have smaller families than those who are not in the labor force; expected family size also declines as the level of education increases.

found that although women who were single at the time of the first survey had fewer children than they expected, women who were already married predicted their family size with a high degree of accuracy.* Although births fell well below expectations during the first half of the decade, married women made up the difference in the second half; as a result, their completed family size was surprisingly close to what they had predicted. When married women fell short of their expectations, it was because of marital breakups, and although divorced women who remarried had almost as many children as they had expected, those who remained single (or separated) had considerably fewer than they had anticipated. But since the divorce rate for Jewish women is less than half that for non-Jews, and since Jewish divorcees remarry much more frequently, the margin of error in forecasting for married Jewish women is likely to be insignificant.

But what about single Jewish women, who report the same birth expectations as their married peers? Should their expectations be discounted?

The answer is no. The O'Connell–Rogers finding that single women had fewer births than they had expected was based on the experience of the entire cohort, without regard to differences in education, occupation, or religion. Other research—in particular, a longitudinal study of high school graduates by Ronald Rindfuss of the University of North Carolina's Population Center—has demonstrated that education has a powerful influence on the reliability of birth-expectation surveys. Specifically, the more education single women have, the more accurately they predict the number of children they will have. Among women with a college education, in fact, forecasting errors prove to be in the opposite direction: some of those who had expected to be childless ended up having one or more children. Since, as we have seen, the overwhelming majority of Jewish women now attend college, and a significant proportion go on to graduate or professional school, their predictions of family size are likely to be accurate, whether they are single or married.

One other factor accounts for the ability of Jewish women to predict the size of their families: they are, in Marshall Sklare's term, "contraceptive virtuosos." It is not simply that contraceptive use is more widespread among American Jews than among American Protestants or Catholics; Jews also are far more likely to use the most efficient contraceptive methods. The result is that Jews plan their pregnancies more

* This is not to suggest that every married woman has the number of children she expects; the overall accuracy of the surveys stems from the fact that forecasting errors offset one another.

precisely and more successfully than Protestants and Catholics and are therefore far more likely to have precisely the number of children they want. (One major national study found that only 3 percent of Jewish children were unwanted.)

Let us turn to the expectations data.

ITEM: In Philadelphia, which contains the third-largest Jewish community in the United States, married women below the age of thirty have already had 0.96 children each and expect another 1.4 children, for a total of 2.36 each—marginally higher than the figure for the thirty-to-thirty-nine-year-old group and well above the number that same age group reported a decade ago. Allowing for the fact that some of those who are now single will remain so, the fertility rate for twenty-to-twenty-nine-year-old Jewish women in Philadelphia will be at least 2.1 children.

ITEM: Much the same picture exists in Miami, which has the fourth-largest Jewish community: married women thirty-five years of age or younger expect to have 2.3 children each—marginally fewer than women in the thirty-five-to-forty-nine age group (the difference is too small to be statistically significant) but as many as the fifty-to-sixty-four age group have had and 16 percent more than women sixty-five and over had.

ITEM: In Milwaukee, whose Jewish community is shrinking in size because of out-migration, married women aged eighteen to twenty-nine expect to have 2.75 children each—15 percent more than the thirty-to-thirty-nine-year-old group. In Phoenix, which has experienced a huge influx of young Jews, eighteen-to-twenty-nine-year-olds expect only 2.1 children—but that is 16 percent higher than the expected family size in the thirty-to-thirty-nine-year-old group.

Surveys of single women, as well as surveys that include both single and married women, show the same expectations—a family size at or close to the replacement level.

ITEM: In a 1981–82 survey of 1200 Jewish students on fourteen college campuses, 41 percent of the students expected to have two children, 31 percent expected three children, and 18 percent expected four or more.

ITEM: According to the 1980 National Survey of High School Students, 37 percent of the Jewish students, compared to 32 percent of the nonminority whites, expected to have three or more children.

One might argue, of course, that high school and college students are too young to have realistic expectations of family size, but that is not the case. Calvin Goldscheider followed a large national sample of high school seniors for seven years after graduation—from 1972, when they were still in school, through 1979. On average, the Jews in the sample expected 2.2 children—almost the same number expected by nonminority white students. Admittedly, expectations fluctuated somewhat during the eight-year period, but the fluctuations were much smaller among Jews than among members of other groups; the number of births expected never dropped below two.* The fact that some Jews married during this period while others remained single did not alter their expectations; single and married Jews were remarkably consistent in expecting a little more than two children each.

In short, there is no convincing evidence to suggest any significant decline in fertility. For the birthrate to drop as low as 1.5 children per woman, for example, there would have to be a huge increase in the number of childless women as well as in the number of those having only a single child; yet survey after survey shows only a handful of Jews with those expectations. There is now a large body of data suggesting that the birthrate will remain at or close to the replacement level, and it is not beyond the boundaries of the possible to suggest that fertility might actually increase somewhat, for as they move through their child-rearing years, younger Jewish women could very well decide to have more children than they now plan.

2

But what about intermarriage? The note of urgency that Robert Gordis and others express when talking about fertility arises from their belief that a birthrate well above the replacement level is needed to compensate for large population losses brought about by intermarriage. "Obviously the low fertility rate among contemporary Jews is only one aspect of the threat to Jewish survival today," Gordis writes. "The hydra-headed monster of assimilation takes on many forms," the "most menacing" of which is intermarriage.

This view is widely shared; communal leaders differ only in the statistics they offer and the extravagance of the language they use in discussing the issue. Professor Gordis suggests that one Jew in three

* One reason the expectations of Jewish women were more consistent than those of Protestants or Catholics was that, as time went on, the Jews in the sample acquired considerably more education; but education alone did not account for the entire difference. Even when he controlled for education, Goldscheider found that Jews were more consistent—and more accurate—in predicting family size.

marries out; others put the intermarriage rate at levels ranging from 40 to upward of 60 percent. There is disagreement too over the dimensions of the losses attributable to intermarriage. In the opinion of Rabbi Sol Roth, a philosophy professor at Yeshiva University and former president of the (Orthodox) Rabbinical Council of America, intermarriage "is a holocaust of our own making"—a metaphor that implies the disappearance of at least one American Jew in three, and perhaps as many as two in three.

There is nothing new, of course, about such concern; Diaspora Jews have always seen intermarriage as the ultimate threat to Jewish survival. "Vastly outnumbered throughout most of their history by the dominant political and religious majorities among whom they lived, Jews have never been entirely free of the fear . . . that their sons and daughters would be swallowed up by the larger community," Yehuda Rosenman, of the American Jewish Committee, has written. "Intermarriage . . . has therefore been viewed as a perennial danger to Jewish viability and continuity. Ironically, this danger has always been greater when more direct threats to Jewish safety and security . . . were absent. . . . 'What centuries of persecution have been powerless to do,' wrote Lewis S. Benjamin, in 1907, in his book entitled *The Passing of the English Jew*, 'has been effected in a score of years by friendly intercourse.' "

In no country, of course, have Jews enjoyed such friendly intercourse as in the United States. During the eighteenth and early nineteenth centuries the tiny size of the Jewish community made Jewish-Christian marriages commonplace, especially in new areas of settlement, where Jewish men often had to choose between remaining single or marrying outside the faith. (Because men were more likely to migrate than women, every immigrant group initially experienced an imbalance between the number of men and women.) "In this country . . . the Jew, like every other citizen, is untramelled in his religious and civil rights; it is therefore a natural consequence that he should mingle and associate with persons of different religious beliefs," one Simeon Abrahams wrote in 1845. "But it is a great misfortune, and one which ought speedily to be remedied by the great body of Jews in the United States, that many of our people . . . become intermingled with the gentiles by marriage." To Rabbi David Einhorn, the intellectual leader of mid-nineteenth-century Reform Judaism, exogamy was more than just a misfortune: "Each intermarriage," he declared, "drives a nail in the coffin of Judaism."

For most of the twentieth century, however, intermarriage appeared to be a distant threat; warnings against it served more as ritual incantation designed to prevent the dread disease from striking than as a statement of genuine concern. Among first- and second-generation Eastern European Jews intermarriage was a rare event; between 1900 and 1940, as we have seen, no more than 2 to 3 percent of American Jews married people who had been Gentile at birth. And although intermarriage increased during the 1940s and 1950s to a level of 5 to 6 percent, it remained far below the 20 to 30 percent rate in other Diaspora communities. American Jews, as Calvin Goldscheider has put it, continued to provide "the classic illustration of voluntary group endogamy." "The prevailing attitude," Marshall Sklare complained in 1964, was "that the threat [of intermarriage] has been surprisingly well contained in America."

That attitude was changing even as Sklare wrote. He had detected the first signs of change, in fact, while studying the Jews of Lakeville in 1957–58. When asked whether they thought their child might marry a non-Jew, only 36 percent of the parents answered in the negative; 5 percent said yes, 29 percent said "possibly," and the remaining 29 percent were uncertain. Lakeville children, it would appear, already were inhabiting a more open and accepting world than the one in which their parents lived; with young Jews now socializing freely with their non-Jewish peers, one adult respondent told Sklare, intermarriage was "in the air." When he returned to Lakeville a decade later Sklare found that intermarriage was "an everyday occurrence." As a result, parental concern had shifted from how to prevent intermarriage to how to respond to it–in particular, how to respond "intelligently"–that is, so as not to alienate their child and his or her Gentile spouse.

It was, as they say, a changing world. Jews no longer were "guests" in someone else's country; they had become part of the "host" people. One measure of their acceptance was the transformation that occurred in Gentile attitudes toward marriages between Christians and Jews. Polls taken between 1940 and 1950 indicated that a clear majority of non-Jews disapproved of such marriages; by 1968 the proportion was down to 21 percent, and by 1983, 10 percent. The change was greatest, moreover, among younger Americans; in 1983, 87 percent of Americans below the age of thirty indicated approval of interfaith marriages, with only 4 percent disapproving. Clearly, Jews no longer were considered members of an alien, unassimilable group.

The shift in Jewish attitudes has been equally large. Asked how they would react to intermarriage on the part of their own child, only 25 percent of the adults responding to the 1965 survey of the Greater Boston Jewish community said they would be neutral or accept it. Just ten years later, however, the number taking that stand had grown nearly two and a half times, to 59 percent. The proportion indicating that they would discourage or strongly oppose such a marriage dropped by half, from 70 percent to 34 percent; among eighteen-to-twenty-nine-year-olds the proportion was only 16 percent, with 84 percent saying they would accept such a marriage or be neutral toward it. However much Jews may oppose intermarriage in principle, in short, they accept it in practice.

In the open society that America has become, Jews and Gentiles have closer and more frequent contact with one another than in the past. There is, in fact, no end to the ways in which Jews and Gentiles now meet—in school, on the job, at cocktail parties, jogging, sitting on the front stoop of the house in which both live, and in a host of other casual and serendipitous settings.* Since the choice of marriage partners is strongly influenced by "propinquity," as sociologists call it, marriages between Jews and Gentiles have become more common.

How rapidly intermarriage has increased, however, and how high it now is depend in part on how you define it and in part on whom you ask. To avoid confusion, let me deal first with the question of definition. From the standpoint of Jewish law, the term "intermarriage" refers only to a marriage between a Jew and someone who is not Jewish at the time the wedding occurs. A marriage between a born Jew and someone who previously had converted to Judaism is no different from a marriage between two born Jews, since both law and tradition forbid making any distinction—in particular, any invidious distinction—between those who were born Jewish and those who have chosen to become Jews.

That is not the way the term is used in ordinary conversation. Because of a deep-rooted suspicion of Gentiles in general, and converts in particular, most Jews use "intermarriage" as synonymous with "exogamy"—that is, marriage between a born Jew and someone who had been Gentile at birth, whether or not that person has converted to Judaism. Most sociologists follow the same practice, not because of prejudice against converts but because judgments about the consequences of intermarriage for Jewish continuity depend in good measure on judgments about the proportion of born-Gentile spouses who convert to Judaism either before or after their marriages to born Jews. In the discussion that follows, therefore, I will use the terms "intermarriage" and on occasion "out-marriage" to refer to marriages between born Jews and born Gentiles. Marriages in which the born-Gentile partner

* Orthodox Jews are an important exception. In part because of a deliberate desire to avoid intermarriage but largely as a result of the requirements of their own religious life-style, most Orthodox Jews live in an almost entirely Jewish—indeed, in an almost entirely Orthodox—ambience. In keeping with the old saw that you cannot marry someone you have not met, intermarriage is rare among Orthodox Jews, although it *is* increasing.

has converted to Judaism will be referred to as "conversionary marriages," and marriages in which the Gentile partner has not converted to Judaism will be called "mixed marriages."

Let us turn, then, to the questions at hand: how much intermarriage is there, and how much of a threat to Jewish survival does this pose? Unfortunately, the entire discussion of intermarriage has been built on an erroneous statistical base—one, as we shall see, that grossly exaggerates its frequency. Because judgments about the consequences of intermarriage are influenced so heavily by assumptions about its level and trend, it is necessary to understand what the figures really are and why they have been so widely misunderstood. (To enable lay readers to follow the discussion with ease, I have relegated technical matters either to footnotes or to the Notes on Sources in the back of the book.)

Because the U.S. Census Bureau does not ask questions about religion, information about intermarriage or any other aspect of Jewish life can come only from demographic and public-opinion surveys. But because Jews are such a small proportion of the U.S. population, surveys of the population at large rarely include enough Jews to permit any reliable conclusions to be drawn. What information we have, therefore, comes almost entirely from surveys of individual Jewish communities and from the 1971 National Jewish Population Survey (NJPS), the first (and still the largest) attempt to survey the American Jewish population as a whole.

It is the NJPS, sad to say, that is the source of the misunderstanding. In what he called a "first report" of the NJPS findings in the 1973 *American Jewish Year Book*, Fred Massarik, the scientific director of the study, provided intermarriage rates (the proportion of Jews marrying someone who had been Gentile at birth) for each five-year period since the turn of the century. According to these figures, the rate jumped from 5.9 percent in 1956–60 to 17.4 percent in 1960–65 and to a staggering 31.7 percent in 1966–71. This last statistic, indicating more than a fivefold increase in just ten years, sent shock waves through the organized Jewish community.

Understandably so; the statistic seemed to come with all the authority contemporary social scientists can muster. As Massarik wrote in his introduction to the report, the NJPS was "a sampling survey based on accepted principles of scientific sample selection." There was no reason, therefore, to attach particular significance to the cautionary note with which he concluded his introduction: the data presented in the article were offered simply as "first facts."

Unfortunately, it is the "first facts" that have stayed in people's minds and not the second and third "facts," which prove to be different—sometimes radically different—from the first ones.* The most detailed studies of the NJPS intermarriage data have been made by Bernard Lazerwitz, the demographer who was in charge of the NJPS sampling procedures and who therefore knows the weaknesses of the survey better than anyone else. In Lazerwitz's opinion, the tiny size of the intermarriage sample (344 respondents in all) means that a decade is the shortest period for which reliable data can be assembled. Statistics for time spans as brief as five years simply cannot be trusted; the intermarriage rate for 1966–71, for example, was based on only 83 cases nationwide. With so few cases, the margin of error is too great, and the peculiar weighting system that had to be used to move from the sample to the total Jewish population makes it possible for errors to be magnified as much as fivefold when using intermarriage figures for a five-year period.† Hence Lazerwitz urged Massarik and the CJF not to use the 32 percent intermarriage rate for 1966–71. His protest was ignored.

In the series of papers he has written on intermarriage and its effects on Jewish continuity, therefore, Lazerwitz has disregarded Massarik's figure. The statistics he provides—derived from the same raw data Massarik used—indicate that although there was a break in trend during the 1960s, intermarriage increased more slowly and reached a lower level than Massarik's paper or the CJF publications imply: in 1971, 14 percent of married Jews below the age of thirty-five were married to people who had been Gentile at birth. Whether because his papers have appeared in scholarly journals or because American Jews prefer to believe the worst about themselves—the Jews, Abba Eban has quipped, "are a people that can't take yes for an answer"—Lazerwitz's views have been generally ignored.

* The Council of Jewish Federations, which sponsored the NJPS, has published only a few meager reports of selected findings. The task of analysis has been left to a handful of sociologists and demographers who have had access to the raw data and who have reported their findings for the most part in scholarly journals and unpublished doctoral dissertations.

† In demographic surveys the weights are normally derived from detailed knowledge of the size and composition of the population being studied; because the decennial census does not ask any questions about religion, that information was lacking when NJPS was launched. Thus the social scientists who designed the survey were caught in a peculiar bind: the NJPS was intended to discover precisely the kind of information they needed in order to design the survey. This meant that the researchers had to base the weights on arbitrary assumptions, using whatever information was available. The task was complicated still more by the fact that midway through the field interviews the size of the remaining sample was cut in half. (Costs were running far ahead of the budget.) As a result, the margin of error is larger than in most demographic surveys.

They should not be, for it is apparent that Massarik's and Lazerwitz's statistics cannot both be correct. Most of those who married for the first time during the 1960s would have been younger than thirty-five in 1971; and most married Jews who were thirty-four or younger in 1971 must have gotten married during the preceding decade. Thus the two sets of statistics—Massarik's figure for the number of intermarriages contracted between 1961 and 1971 and Lazerwitz's figure for the number of Jews below the age of thirty-five who were intermarried in 1971—are simply different ways of measuring essentially the same phenomenon. Since the statistics came from the same raw survey data, they should have been in at least rough agreement; instead there is a large discrepancy.

Which statistic is correct?

When the evidence is weighed, it is clear that the lower figure is the correct one. The interesting question, in fact, is not why the 32 percent statistic should be disregarded but why it has been embraced so avidly. Statistics, after all, are a representation of reality, not reality itself—and statistics indicating more than a fivefold increase in intermarriage in just ten years defy belief. Human beings do not normally alter their behavior that rapidly, especially in so crucial—and sacred—an area of life as marriage.

If a change of that magnitude had been under way, moreover, the Jewish community would have been in a state of panic, even hysteria; parents, after all, do not need a national demographic survey to tell them that their children are marrying non-Jews. No such panic ensued. There was a brief flurry of excitement in 1964 when *Look* described the increase in intermarriage in an article with the sensational title "The Vanishing American Jew," but the excitement died down fairly quickly, and the discussion that followed was generally calm and measured. Writing on the subject in 1970, in fact, Marshall Sklare again complained that "despite the gravity of the problem, the Jewish community . . . has devoted little attention to the matter." Indeed, it was not until publication of Massarik's 32 percent figure in 1973 that the discussion of intermarriage acquired the urgency it now has.

There are empirical as well as purely logical reasons for disregarding the 32 percent figure: it is contradicted by other survey data for the same period. The most compelling data come from a survey by the National Opinion Research Center, one of the most respected academic polling organizations in the country. In 1961 NORC, as the center is commonly called, began a long-term study of some 40,000 men and women who had been graduated from college that year: in 1964, when well over half the Jewish respondents were married, the out-marriage rate was 12 percent—well below Massarik's 17 percent intermarriage rate for 1961–65. Because intermarriage undoubtedly was higher among college graduates than among Jews who did not go to college, a group that at the time comprised nearly a third of Jewish men and well over half the young Jewish women, the intermarriage rate among young Jews as a whole must have been lower than the NORC figure—say, 9 to 10 percent. Since intermarriage undoubtedly was increasing during the latter 1960s, a rise to Lazerwitz's figure of 14 percent in 1971 seems eminently plausible. But the NORC finding clearly is incompatible with Massarik's 32 percent rate for 1966–71. And the NORC figure carries considerably more weight than one derived from NJPS.*

Moreover, the 1965 and 1975 demographic surveys of the Greater Boston Jewish population—the sixth-largest in the country—provide further confirmation of the NORC and Lazerwitz-NJPS figures. Although Boston cannot be used as a surrogate for American Jewry as a whole, "the temper of its Jewish life," Marshall Sklare suggested at the time, "approximates that of the giant communities where the majority of American Jews live." The 1965 survey, Sklare continued, provided "perhaps the best guide to the current intermarriage situation."

Best guide or not, the value of the 1965 survey was greatly enhanced by the fact that it was repeated ten years later. Until recently the two Boston surveys provided the only direct measure of the trend in intermarriage in the United States—and they indicated a rate of increase far below that implied by the Massarik figure.

ITEM: In 1965, 11.1 percent of Boston Jews aged thirty or younger had married people who had not been Jewish at birth—a figure consistent with the NORC figure for 1964. (Surveys of other eastern cities which were taken during the 1960s—Providence, Rhode Island, in 1963, Camden, New Jersey, in 1964, and Springfield, Massachusetts, in 1966—showed even lower rates.) Intermarriage increased over the next decade, to be sure, but it did not go through the roof. By 1975, 15.3 percent of the thirty-and-under group had married born non-Jews; in the thirty-one-to-forty age group the rate was 12.4 percent. Both figures, of course, are consistent with Lazerwitz's NJPS figure for 1971.

* Because the universe that was studied was a random sample of 40,000 college graduates from all three faiths, and because questions about religion were a minor part of a questionnaire concerned with other issues, the NORC survey was able to capture born Jews who no longer considered themselves Jewish and who therefore excluded themselves from the NJPS sample. Since religious dropouts intermarry far more often than those who identify themselves as Jews, the NORC survey was less likely than NJPS to understate the number of intermarriages taking place.

Let us agree, then, that the 14 percent intermarriage rate for 1971 (for Jews thirty-four years of age and younger) is the best measure we have and turn to the real issues: how much has intermarriage increased since 1971, and, to the extent to which one can see ahead, what is likely to happen in the near future? And what are the consequences of intermarriage for Jewish continuity and survival?

When I began my research in 1979 these were open and in large measure unanswerable questions, for there was a terrible dearth of information. That is true no longer; since 1979, demographic surveys, most of them well designed and administered, have been conducted in fifteen Jewish communities–metropolitan areas that include nearly 65 percent of the American Jewish population.* (A number of other surveys were conducted in this period, but they did not include questions about intermarriage.)

Only one survey, that of the Washington, D.C., metropolitan area, the seventh-largest Jewish community in the country, provided direct information on the trend as well as the current level. (The Jewish Community Council of Greater Washington had sponsored a survey in 1956, using an analogous if somewhat less sophisticated sampling technique.) Over the twenty-seven-year period 1956–83 the mixed-marriage rate (the proportion of Jews married to people who were not Jewish at the time the survey was taken) increased 127 percent. (Taking the view that marriages between born Jews and born Gentiles who have converted to Judaism are in-marriages, the Washington surveys collected data only on mixed marriages.) This is a considerable rise, to be sure, but it is far less than is usually assumed; in the youngest cohort–those under thirty-five years of age–the mixed-marriage rate in 1983 was 21.5 percent. (If 25 percent of born-Gentile spouses had converted to Judaism either before or after their marriages–a generous estimate–the intermarriage rate in that age group would be 27 percent, well below the Massarik figure for 1966–71.)

* The analysis that follows would not have been possible without assistance from the scholars and federation officials responsible for a number of the surveys. My greatest debt by far is to Steven M. Cohen and Bruce A. Phillips, who provided me with large amounts of unpublished data, including innumerable special tabulations, from the surveys of the New York (Cohen) and Los Angeles, Denver, Phoenix, and Milwaukee (Phillips) metropolitan areas. I am deeply indebted as well to Barry Schrage (Cleveland, Richmond, and Pittsburgh), William Yancey (Philadelphia), and Gary Tobin and Barbara Shamir (St. Louis). I also benefited greatly from Steven Cohen's comments on successive drafts of this chapter as well as from Calvin Goldscheider's and Bernard Lazerwitz's comments. I take full responsibility, however, for any errors of fact or judgment.

There is always a risk, of course, in inferring national trends from data for a single metropolitan area—all the more so because there are such large differences in the frequency of intermarriage from one part of the country to another. Specifically, intermarriage rates are far higher in the West than in the East and Midwest, so much so, that we almost seem to be talking about two separate phenomena. In Denver and Phoenix, for example, well over half the married Jews below the age of thirty—57 percent in one, 58 percent in the other—have married born Gentiles; in Los Angeles in 1979 the figure was 39 percent. By contrast, in the New York metropolitan area, the figure was only 13 percent; although the rate was somewhat higher in most other eastern and midwestern cities—14 percent in St. Louis, 20 percent in Chicago, and 24 percent in Philadelphia and Cleveland—it was still far below the figures in the West.* (The one exception is Milwaukee, which reported an intermarriage rate of 45 percent.)

These regional differences are of long standing; in the 1964 NORC survey the rate was more than two and a half times higher in the West than in the Northeast or the South. Despite the move to the Sun Belt, however, the great majority of American Jews continue to live in metropolitan areas with relatively low intermarriage rates; for all their rapid growth, communities such as Denver and Phoenix contain only a minute proportion of the total Jewish population. Indeed, a single New York City neighborhood, such as Manhattan's Upper West Side or the Forest Hills–Rego Park section of Queens, has half again as many Jews as Denver or Phoenix; the Flatbush neighborhood of Brooklyn has 20 percent *more* Jews than the two Sun Belt cities combined.

To estimate the intermarriage rate for the country as a whole, therefore, I have weighted the figures for each of the recently surveyed metropolitan areas by the proportion of the total Jewish population they contain; including Boston, which I estimated by extrapolating the 1965–75 trend, the sixteen cities contain 64 percent of

* The intermarriage rates I am using all refer to the proportion of individual Jews who marry born Gentiles. In some surveys intermarriage rates are reported in a different way—as the proportion of *marriages* in which one partner is a born Gentile. When the intermarriage rate is reported this way, it is always higher than when the rate refers to the number of individuals who have married out. To understand why this is so, assume a Jewish community consisting of two men and a woman. If the woman marries one of the men, and the other man marries a born Gentile, half the marriages would be considered intermarriages, whereas only one third of the Jews have married out. Failure to distinguish between these two ways of reporting the data is a major source of confusion.

American Jewry. Because regional differences are so large, I estimated the rate in each remaining metropolitan area and/or section of the country, using the rate from the surveyed city it resembled most closely, and weighted the figures accordingly. When in doubt I chose to err on the high side; to reduce the chance of error still more, I used a range for most areas. Adding them together yields the intermarriage rate for the country as a whole. (The procedure is described in greater detail in the Notes on Sources for this chapter.)

For the youngest cohort—Jews below the age of thirty or thirty-five—the intermarriage rate in 1981, the year in which most of the surveys were taken, was no less than 22 percent and no more than 27 percent. Because these figures are so much lower than those used by even optimistic students of intermarriage, I recalculated the 1981 rate, using a different approach—one that gives more weight to the Denver, Phoenix, and Los Angeles figures. The rate came out to 24 percent—the midpoint between the high and low figures derived by my first method! In short, roughly one Jew in four now marries someone who had been Gentile at birth.

This figure, it should be understood, is not carved in granite; it is simply the best estimate available of the frequency of intermarriage. The emphasis should be on "estimate," for there is some measure of understatement in any intermarriage rate based on survey data. The reason, quite simply, is that there is no way to obtain a completely representative sample of the American Jewish population.

ITEM: Because participation is voluntary, Jews who no longer identify themselves as Jews or for whom Jewishness is unimportant are less likely to be willing to take the time to fill out a questionnaire or answer a telephone interviewer's lengthy questions. Yet these same people are more likely to have married out.

ITEM: Some survey techniques are likely to miss Jews, particularly Jewish women, who have married out. In order to hold down costs, for example, a number of communities derive their sample by using a list of distinctive Jewish names. Although the approach provides a sample that is representative of the entire Jewish community in most respects, it inevitably misses many Jewish women who are married to born-Gentile men—whether the husband has converted to Judaism or not—for the husbands are likely to have distinctively Gentile, not Jewish, surnames. And when the sample is drawn from the names of people who appear on the mailing lists of local federations, synagogues, and other Jewish organizations, they inevitably exclude people who have no communal affiliation at all.

There is no way of knowing precisely how large the understatement is, but it is not likely to exceed 10 to 15 percent. In all probability, moreover, the understatement is smaller now than it was a generation or two ago. This is true in part because assimilating Jews feel less need to deny or escape their Jewishness and in part because the sampling technique used in a number of the recent surveys is more likely to include marginally identified Jews, especially those living outside the principal areas of Jewish concentration.* All told, the surveys provide a reasonably reliable if rough approximation of the frequency of intermarriage.

Taking 24 percent as the figure for 1981, therefore, it would appear that intermarriage grew by one percentage point a year in the ten years following 1971. If that rate of increase has continued, the intermarriage rate today would be around 28 percent—double what it had been in 1971 but well below the 40 to 60 percent rates now being cited. In fact, there is reason to believe that the increase has about run its course and that it may stabilize around the current level.

It is even possible that intermarriage may decline somewhat over the next decade or two. The most important single component of the rise over the last fifteen or twenty years has been the geometric increase in intermarriage on the part of Jewish women, who make up 40 to 45 percent of the total today, compared to one quarter, or at most one third, a generation ago. In the next decade or two there is likely to be a reduction in the number of Jewish women who marry out.

To understand why this is apt to happen, we need to examine the reasons for the recent increase, which came about through the conjuncture of a number of demographic and cultural changes. Specifically, women who are in their thirties and early forties today were the products of the post-World War II "baby boom." Because women usually marry men several years their senior—the difference used to average four years—and because the birthrate was catastrophically low during the 1930s and early 1940s, the women in this cohort faced a severe shortage of Jewish men of the "correct" marriageable age. This demographic quirk was exacerbated by two cultural changes. As homosexuals came out of the closet (homosexuality is far more prevalent

* These surveys used, in whole or in part, a technique called random-digit dialing, in which a computer generates a random sample of telephone numbers. Each number is called, and the person answering is asked whether there is someone Jewish living in that household. If the answer is no, the caller says thank you and hangs up; if the answer is yes, arrangements are made for the full telephone interview. By using the telephone and the computer it is possible to construct the Jewish sample from a random sample of the population as a whole—which would be far too expensive in the traditional door-to-door canvassing.

among men than among women), a number of men who in the past would have gotten married chose to remain single; and a growing number of Jewish men married non-Jewish women. The result was that Jewish women who did not marry Jewish men at the conventional age of first marriage faced a number of options: they could postpone the age at which they married; they could marry someone closer to their own age (the age difference between husbands and wives dropped by half); they could remain single; or they could marry a non-Jew.

While all this was happening women were undergoing a revolution in their status, and Jewish women more so than most; not surprisingly, therefore, they chose all four options, including marriage to non-Jewish men. In the past, intermarriage had been rarer among Jewish women than Jewish men because women had been kept much closer to home and under much tighter social controls. In the 1960s, however, Jewish women began to be emancipated in a social if not necessarily religious sense; they began attending out-of-town colleges and pursuing professional careers almost to the same extent as men.

That change is now largely if not yet entirely completed; and over the next decade there will be a surplus rather than a shortage of Jewish men of marriageable age, which means that a larger proportion of Jewish women are likely to marry within the faith. In Canada, where statistics on mixed marriages are available on an annual basis from government sources, the proportion of Jewish women marrying non-Jews has dropped already. This decline may be offset, of course, by an increase in the number of Jewish men who marry out; but since men are freer to postpone the age of marriage—for them the biological clock does not start ticking for several more decades—the net effect is likely to be some small reduction in intermarriage and perhaps a lengthening of the age difference between brides and grooms.

3

When, as often happens, a fellow Jew tells Rachel Cowan, a New York photographer and writer, that she doesn't *look* Jewish, Cowan responds, "Funny how Jewish looks these days, isn't it?" Her riposte is meant to relieve the awkwardness that an insensitive if innocent remark creates, as well as to diffuse her annoyance at being labeled an outsider, but it reflects an important new social and religious reality as well. Far from being "a holocaust of our own making," to use Sol Roth's unfortunate metaphor, intermarriage may actually increase the number of Jews and provide a much-needed spiritual boost as well; in the process it can change "how Jewish looks."

Consider Rachel Cowan herself. The descendant of English Protestants who settled in New England in the seventeenth century, she is now a deeply observant Jew who has served as program director of Ansche Chesed, a once declining one hundred and forty-year-old Conservative congregation that has become a center of Jewish life on Manhattan's Upper West Side. This is not what any sentient observer would have predicted twenty years ago when Rachel Brown and Paul Cowan were married in a nonsectarian ceremony conducted by a Protestant minister. As we saw in the last chapter, Paul Cowan himself seemed lost to Judaism. His meager Jewish consciousness stemmed mainly from the anti-Semitism he had experienced at Choate, the Episcopal prep school to which his parents had sent him. In any event, the civil rights and antiwar movements seemed to provide all the religion Paul or Rachel Cowan felt they needed.

In the early 1970s, however, that secular faith seemed wanting. Moved by Israel's isolation during the 1973 Yom Kippur War and upset by the indifference (or hostility) to Israel so many of their "movement" friends displayed, the Cowans helped organize a once-a-week school to give their children a Jewish identity. They found themselves drawn to the Jewish rituals they learned through their involvement in the school and began to introduce them into their own home. By the mid-seventies Rachel—along with Paul—was beginning to live the life of an observant Jew, but the thought of conversion had not entered her mind. She was afraid that conversion would cut her off from the family she loved and the tradition that had shaped her, and besides, "conversion seemed like a statement that who I was was not adequate."

The sudden death of her husband's parents forced a confrontation with mortality that got Rachel Cowan thinking about the role of religion in her life, and she found that worshiping as a Jew "released something inside" that enabled her to feel a faith whose intensity was startling. A sympathetic rabbi persuaded her that conversion was analogous to marriage: "You are joined to a new community, but you bring to the union the strengths and values that have been your foundation all your life."

In the fall of 1979, therefore, Rachel Cowan began the process that culminated a year later in her formal conversion to Judaism, under the auspices of a *Beth Din* (rabbinic court) headed by Rabbi Wolfe Kelman, executive vice-president of the Rabbinical Assembly of America, the professional organization of Conservative rabbis. Had she become a Jew before her marriage, Cowan believes, she "would have missed a long struggle to discover what really attracted me to Judaism.

I might never have learned that being Jewish was something important to me, and not just another way of being a good wife and mother."

True, one swallow does not a summer make, or, as the Yiddish proverb has it, " 'For example' is no proof." It would be disingenuous, in fact, to suggest that the Cowans are representative of intermarried couples in general, but it would be grossly misleading to conclude that they are sui generis. On the contrary, a significant minority of born-Gentile spouses–approximately 20 percent–convert to Judaism, and although the level of commitment varies from person to person, as it does among born Jews, those who convert to Judaism are, on average, more religiously observant than the average born Jew. One measure of their seriousness is the fact that most "Jews by choice," as they prefer to be called, resent being referred to as converts. As Dr. Sandra Shachar, a St. Louis psychologist, has written, "No one converts to Judaism to become a convert; one converts to Judaism to become a Jew."

In doing so, Jews by choice often contribute a spirituality and piety, and a seriousness about questions of faith, that are rare among born Jews, who tend to be uncomfortable when talking about God. In a sense, intermarriage involves an exchange of population: although some marginal Jews do drop out (usually without converting to Christianity), they are replaced, so to speak, by Christians who choose to become Jews. The result is what Milton Himmelfarb calls a positive balance of trade. "Our imports," he says, "are better than our exports."

It is more complicated still. The fact that a born-Gentile spouse chooses not to convert to Judaism does not necessarily mean that the Jewish spouse becomes an "export" or that the Gentile spouse is hostile to Judaism. As a group, Jews in mixed marriages are more committed to their Jewish identity than their mates are to their religious or ethnic backgrounds; the Jewish spouses are also more concerned with transmitting their religious identity to their children. This is particularly true of Jewish women who are married to Gentile men–a radical change from the situation a generation or two ago. In the past, intermarriage was so deviant an act for Jewish women that those who did marry out were usually lost to Judaism. But now that intermarriage is almost as frequent among women as among men, Jewish women who marry out are likely to hold onto their Jewish identity–all the more so, because conversion to Judaism is so much less frequent among men than among women.

Gender differences aside, many Gentile spouses are attracted to Judaism, but are hesitant about converting. Some, like Rachel Cowan, are concerned about losing their own identities. Others fear that their parents may regard conversion to Judaism as a rejection of them; it is not only Jewish parents, after all, who find intermarriage problematical. Because conversion is an intrinsically religious act, moreover, people who have abandoned their own faith often are reluctant to adopt another—particularly when they discover that their Jewish in-laws who are so insistent on their becoming Jews do not practice Judaism themselves. "I didn't see any need to undergo conversion in order to become a 'cardiac Jew,' " one such person told me.*

The result is that some Gentile spouses who are reluctant to convert to Judaism identify themselves as Jews nonetheless, in much the same way that secular born Jews do. They are, so to speak, Jewish fellow travelers; as the sociologist Egon Mayer puts it, they are willing to join the Jewish community of *fate*, but not the community of *faith*—"to associate themselves with the social and cultural fate of the Jewish people, but not with the religious faith of Judaism." Still others associate themselves with the community of faith as well, albeit without undergoing formal conversion; there is hardly a Reform congregation in the country that does not have many such members, and their number is growing in Conservative congregations as well.

Even so, the notion that intermarriage means the inevitable loss of the Jewish partner is hard to shake, for it is rooted in the long association of intermarriage with apostasy and self-hatred. In Europe until the nineteenth—in some countries the twentieth—century, a Jew and Christian could not marry unless one partner converted to the other's religion, a requirement that in practice meant that the Jew became a Christian. For socially ambitious Jews intermarriage and baptism were two sides of the same "ticket of admission" to the larger culture. This was less true of the United States, where civil marriage was an option from the start; in the eighteenth and early nineteenth centuries, in fact, intermarried couples often were accepted and, indeed, integrated into the Jewish community. But with the rise of anti-Semitism in the late nineteenth and early twentieth centuries, intermarriage became associated, if not with apostasy as such, then with a desire to shake off the burden of Jewishness.

Among American Jews of Eastern European origin, in particular, intermarriage was a deviant act, one that often involved a break with parents and separation from the Jewish community. As recently as twenty years ago, according to the 1964 NORC survey, Jews who married out had much poorer relationships with their parents than those who married other Jews; not surprisingly, the estrangement was

* "Cardiac Jews" is a term of derision that rabbis and others use to refer to Jews who assure them that they have no need to observe any rituals or give to charity because they "feel their Jewishness in their hearts."

greater among women than among men. Jews who married out were also four to five times more likely to describe themselves as "unconventional" or "rebellious."*

This no longer is the case, except perhaps in the Orthodox community, where intermarriage continues to be a relatively rare and therefore deviant act. This is not to suggest that home background is irrelevant: although the difference is narrower now than it had been even a decade ago, intermarriage still is more frequent among Jews who grew up in nonobservant or assimilated homes than among those who come from traditional, albeit non-Orthodox, backgrounds. "My father's only Jewish characteristic was paranoia," one young man told me.

Today, moreover, Jews who marry out do not appear to be rebelling against their parents, nor are they acting out some other primal struggle—no more so, at least, than Jews who marry other Jews; for Jewishness no longer is a burden, and intermarriage has lost its aura of deviance. As we have seen, even parents who are anguished by a child's intermarriage now accept it in order to retain their relationship with their child—which in turn makes it possible for exogamous Jews to maintain their membership in the Jewish community.

Over the last twenty years, in fact, acceptance of intermarriage has transformed its meaning and thereby its consequences. Specifically, a decision to marry a non-Jew no longer is a decision to leave the Jewish community; as Marshall Sklare has put it, "The Jew who intermarries . . . generally does so because he wishes to *marry* rather than because he wishes to intermarry." There may well be some Jews who deliberately set out to find Gentile spouses, but this was not the case with any of the men and women I interviewed. Although some had dated Gentiles in college or afterward, most had assumed (if they thought about it at all) that their spouses would be Jewish—until they found themselves falling in love with the non-Jews they ultimately married.

ITEM: Nancy Ludmerer, an attorney, grew up in a Conservative congregation in Queens. If she showed any deviant tendencies as a child, it was that she was more religiously observant than her parents. She began observing the dietary laws six months before her bat mitzvah and continued her Hebrew education through high school, taking courses at the Jewish Theological Seminary of America and serving in the

* Exogamous Catholics and Protestants, by contrast, were no more rebellious or unconventional than those who married within their faiths, nor did they have worse relationships with their parents; it was only among Jews that intermarriage was a deviant act.

Leadership Training Program of the Conservative movement. Ludmerer met her husband, Geoffrey Peppiatt, in the fall of 1979 when they attended the same Washington, D.C., cocktail party. She was serving as a legal intern at the National Endowment for the Arts, and the British-born Peppiatt, who is a physicist, was on the staff of the British Embassy. They were married four and a half years later, six months after Peppiatt had converted to Judaism; they light candles and chant *kiddush* (the prayer over wine) at home each Friday night before attending Sabbath services at the Reform synagogue they joined after his conversion. ("I'd prefer a Conservative service," Ludmerer told me, "but Geoff is comfortable here, and since becoming a Reform Jew was an enormous change for him and only a slight one for me, it's a reasonable compromise.")

ITEM: "I'm shocked that I married a Gentile," Susan Kander, a young playwright, told me. Throughout her childhood she had rebelled against her highly assimilated upbringing, surreptitiously studying Hebrew (the Kansas City Reform temple to which her parents belonged held Sabbath services in English on Sunday morning), and lighting Chanukah candles behind the closed door of her bedroom. She met her husband, Warren Ashworth, while visiting her closest friend, who was a classmate of his at architecture school. Having grown up in a completely areligious (if nominally Protestant) home in which religion was viewed as a crutch, Ashworth feels that it would be synthetic for him to convert to Judaism himself, but he has agreed that their children (when they have them) will be raised as Jews. Kander is determined that this will not be left to chance. When I interviewed her in the summer of 1984 she was enrolled in an adult bat mitzvah course at the Reform congregation to which she and her husband belong. "My kids will be Jewish anyway, so they had better be prepared to defend themselves," she told me. "And with a last name like Ashworth, it will take a lot of work on my part to make Jewishness real to them."

It is the children, of course, who are the key to Jewish continuity. Whether they will be Jews or not depends on a host of factors. When the born-Gentile partner converts to Judaism, for example, the children almost always are raised as Jews; if there is a difference between these families and those in which both parents are born Jews, it is that the former are more likely to light Sabbath candles, belong to a synagogue, and attend services with some frequency.

Even where there is no conversion, however, mixed-married couples often raise their children as Jews, especially when it is the wife who is Jewish; this is true among women from highly assimilated backgrounds as well as those who come from religious homes.

ITEM: "I didn't think that being Jewish mattered to me at all—until the children were born," a Detroit architect told me. She had had a Christmas tree at home, and except for attending a seder at her grandparents' home—a practice she had abandoned when she went away to college—Judaism had played no role in her life at all, nor did she give it any thought at the time she was married. "The difference in religion between Pete and me seemed irrelevant," she told me. "We always spent Christmas at Pete's parents' home on the lake in Wisconsin, but I never thought of it as anything but a family gathering until Andy was born. I suddenly discovered that I wanted him to regard himself as a Jew and that that wouldn't happen if I didn't do something about his upbringing." Now this woman lights Chanukah candles each year and attends a seder, with her two young children, at the home of friends. "The fact that I'm married to a non-Jew makes me far more conscious of my Jewishness than I think I would have been if I had married a Jew from a background like mine."

Many young women feel the same way. In his analysis of the New York demographic survey, Steven Cohen found that in mixed marriages involving a Jewish wife and Gentile husband, three couples in four are raising or plan to raise their children as Jews. When the mixed marriage involves a Jewish husband, the ratio is only one in three; it takes a strong Jewish identification to offset the tendency for children to be raised in their mother's religion.

What is the net effect of these permutations? What proportion of the children are being raised as Jews?

To listen to the current discussion one would think that any ratio short of 100 percent spelled disaster. It does not. To assess the impact of intermarriage, one has to start with a simple but crucial mathematical truism: *If half the children of intermarriages are raised as Jews, there will be no net reduction in the number of Jews, no matter how high the intermarriage rate is.** It is this truism, of course, that

* By way of illustration, let us assume a Jewish community consisting of six people—three men and three women. If the Jews marry one another and have two children per couple, they will produce a total of six Jewish children. If, instead, four of the Jews marry one another and two marry non-Jews—an intermarriage rate of one third—and the birthrate remains the same, the in-married couples will have four children, and the out-married couples four; if half the latter are raised as Jews, there again will be six Jewish children.

Assume now that only two of the Jews marry each other and that four marry non-Jews—an intermarriage rate of two thirds. There now will be a makes it possible for intermarriage to expand as well as contract the number of Jews.

What does the evidence show?

The most striking finding—one that emerges from every study—is that the critical factor in determining whether or not children of intermarriages are raised as Jews is whether or not the born-Gentile partner converts to Judaism. In his analysis of the National Jewish Population Survey, for example, Bernard Lazerwitz found enormous differences between the Jewish religious observances of "conversionary couples"—31 percent of the total—and those in mixed marriages. When the born-Gentile spouse had converted to Judaism the couple was more likely to light Sabbath candles, attend a Passover seder, and belong to a synagogue than the average in-married couple. Equally important, conversionary couples were twice as likely as mixed-married couples to raise their children as Jews. Since the former group expected to have 70 percent more children than the latter, the net effect was that half the children born to intermarried couples were (or were going to be) raised as Jews—a finding that meant that intermarriage was a "wash"—that is, it had no effect at all on the number of Jews.

In a 1982 study made for the American Jewish Committee, in which he queried 117 grown children—aged sixteen to forty-six—of intermarried couples, Egon Mayer found that conversion of the born-Gentile parent played an even larger role in children's Jewishness; 84 percent of the children of conversionary marriages considered themselves Jews, compared to only 24 percent of the offspring of mixed marriages. Moreover, 70 percent of the former group, compared to 18 percent of the latter, reported that "being Jewish is very important to me." Fully 85 percent of the children of conversionary marriages, but only 20 percent of those born to mixed-married couples, had received a Jewish education. Of the 37 respondents who were married, 92 percent of the children of mixed-married couples, compared to 36 percent of the offspring of conversionary marriages, had married non-Jews.

Mayer's study generally has been interpreted as showing that the consequences of intermarriage are disastrous as far as Jewish continuity is concerned. The study shows nothing of the sort. It is true that Mayer's data do suggest that most of the children of mixed marriages will be lost to Judaism—a conclusion I will soon question—but

---

total of ten children—two from the in-married couple and eight from the out-married couples. If half the latter group are raised as Jews, the number of Jewish children remains the same—six.

the overall findings are consistent with Lazerwitz's analysis of the NJPS data. If the fertility difference that Lazerwitz found between conversionary and mixed-married couples still obtains—and a number of recent demographic surveys of metropolitan areas indicate that it does—no fewer than 44 percent of the children, and perhaps as many as 53 percent, would consider themselves Jews.*

At worst, therefore, Mayer's study indicates only a slight reduction in the number of Jews as a result of intermarriage, and there are solid grounds for thinking that the outcome will be more favorable in the future than it has been in the past. Because the phenomenon is so new—a significant proportion of intermarried couples are still childless or in the early stages of child rearing—and because intermarriage has such a different meaning now than it had twenty, not to say thirty or fifty years ago, Mayer's study tells us more about the past than about the future consequences of intermarriage in general and mixed marriages in particular.

Specifically, the youngest children Mayer surveyed were the offspring of marriages that had occurred before 1964—before intermarriage was as widely accepted and intermarried couples as warmly welcomed by the Jewish community as is now the case. The oldest "children" in the sample were born to parents who had intermarried in the early 1930s, when intermarriage was a highly deviant act. Thus the parents of the group Mayer surveyed, particularly those involved in mixed marriages, were far more likely to be separated, and in many cases alienated from the Jewish community, as well as from their own parents, than is the case among couples who marry out today. Thus the children were less likely to have developed positive feelings about Judaism or Jewish identity.†

The point is that the growing acceptance of intermarriage makes it much easier for mixed-married couples to be integrated into the Jewish community and thus to identify themselves as Jews; this in turn

* The difference stems from the fact that in his original study of the parents Mayer found that 22 percent of the born-Gentile spouses had converted to Judaism; in the follow-up study of the children the proportion was 36 percent.

† There were other flaws in Mayer's study as well: his sample was not representative; and because of the small number of people surveyed, he was unable to control for age or stage in the life cycle. As we saw in the last chapter, however, there are profound changes in religious observance, affiliation with synagogues and other Jewish organizations, and almost every other measure of Jewish identity as people move through the life cycle—for example, married couples with children are far more "Jewish" than singles or childless couples with the same background. And as we will see, these differences are even larger for intermarried than for in-married couples.

makes it much more likely that mixed-married couples will raise their children as Jews. To say this, of course, is to do no more than speculate about the future; the best we can do is gauge the future consequences of current behavior. In the case of childless couples or those with infants, moreover, judgments about the future are necessarily dependent on what the couples say they plan to do about their children's religious and ethnic upbringing; whether they will carry out their plans remains to be seen.

With these qualifications in mind, let us consider some new evidence. Using data from the 1981 demographic survey of the New York metropolitan area, Steven M. Cohen has made the most thoroughgoing (and by far the most sophisticated) assessment of the ways in which intermarriage affects the Jewish identification of both outmarrying Jews and their children. In making his assessment Cohen tried to distinguish between the impact of intermarriage per se and that of other factors affecting Jewish continuity, such as the nature of the Jewish spouse's upbringing. Some Jews who come from highly assimilated homes may abandon their Jewishness or raise their children without any religion, whether they marry Gentiles or other assimilated Jews.

Cohen also took account of each couple's age and stage in the life cycle, for among *all* couples—those involved in in-marriages, conversionary marriages, and mixed marriages—participation in home rituals and synagogue life increases when children are born and takes a sharp jump when the youngsters reach school age; the largest increase of all, interestingly enough, occurs among mixed-married couples.

The New York-area couples fell into three main groups:

- At one end of the spectrum are marriages in which the born-Gentile partner has converted to Judaism; virtually all their children will be raised as Jews.

- At the other end of the spectrum are couples in which a highly assimilated Jew—usually the husband—is married to a non-Jew who retains his or her religion. By and large, the children of these marriages are *not* raised as Jews—at least not as actively identified Jews.

- In the middle is the largest and by far the most critical group, one that, on the whole, did not exist a generation ago: mixed-married couples in which the Jewish spouse (in most instances, the wife) retains a strong Jewish identification. Because this last phenomenon is so new, studies of intermarriages that occurred a generation or two ago tell us relatively little about how the next generation of children will be raised. And because most such couples are either childless or in the early stages of child rearing, judgments about the Jewishness of the next generation necessarily are based on what the couples themselves say about their child-rearing plans.

If they follow through on those plans—if mixed-married couples raise their children as they say they will—intermarriage would lead not to a reduction in the number of Jews but to a gain of more than 40 percent! It is possible, of course, perhaps even probable, that raising a Jewish child in a mixed household will prove to be more difficult than either the Jewish or Gentile spouse anticipates—hence the effort may be abandoned or youngsters may grow up with only a nominal Jewish identity and attachment. If that were to happen to half the families in the middle group, Cohen calculated—an unlikely eventuality in his view—there would be a 13 percent reduction in the number of actively committed Jews.

The most probable outcome is something in between these two extremes: a modest increase in the number of Jews. Some Jewishly committed spouses undoubtedly will find it too hard to raise a Jewish child in an interfaith household, but some now Gentile spouses will decide to become Jews. Although most Jews by choice convert to Judaism before they marry, that is not the only time conversions can or do occur; a significant minority of those who become Jews—the proportion may be as high as one in three—make the choice *after* they have been married for some time.

Pregnancy, for example, can be a powerful impetus to conversion, for it raises in concrete and urgent terms the question of how the difference in religious backgrounds will affect the children and the way in which they are reared.

ITEM: Before she was married fourteen years ago "the thought of conversion seemed absurd to me," Carol Levithan told me. Raised as a Methodist, she was a nonbeliever when she met her husband, Jack Levithan (they both taught at the same school). But five years after their marriage, when they were planning a family, Carol Levithan "realized that it meant a great deal to Jack that the children be Jewish, while it meant nothing to me that they be Methodists." Nor was it just a matter of deferring to her husband's wishes; "the practicalities," as she calls them, pointed to the need to raise the children as Jews. "Obviously the kids would be identified as Jews because of their last name," she explains, "so why not give them the good parts of being Jewish," as well as the exposure to anti-Semitism that their Jewish identity may entail? And besides, she adds, "I didn't want them to have *nothing*." By that time, moreover, Carol Levithan had begun to find Judaism attractive; she had enjoyed attending the Passover seder at Jack's grandparents' home, and when his grandfather died, she was profoundly moved by the warmth and dignity of the funeral and "the humaneness" of the postfuneral ritual in which the mourners were surrounded by friends and family for an entire week to cushion the pain and help them come to terms with their grief. While trying to become pregnant, therefore, Carol Levithan began a formal course of study that resulted in her conversion to Judaism shortly before the birth of her first child.

For Carol and Jack Levithan conversion was the beginning of a process that led to their becoming active as well as observant Jews who rarely miss a Sabbath morning service. He is now chairperson of the membership committee and she of the religious school committee in their Reconstructionist congregation. "I used to feel that there were such gaps in my knowledge that I could never pass," she told me, "but I don't feel that way anymore." With good reason; hearing her chant the Haftorah (the weekly Prophetic portion) or lead part of the Shacharit (early morning) service on Rosh Hashanah and Yom Kippur, a stranger would assume that she had grown up in an observant Jewish home.

The desire to avoid religious dissonance in the home is, in fact, one of the most frequently cited reasons for converting to Judaism.

ITEM: "Jason needs something to grab onto; he needs an identity," Dianna Viner told me, explaining why she had arranged for her son to be converted to Judaism before his circumcision. Although she had been thinking of becoming a Jew herself, she resisted the idea for several years because of her hurt over her in-laws' rejection of her—a rejection she feels was based more on her race (she is a light-skinned black woman) than on her religion. "I didn't want them to think I was doing this for them," she told me. When I spoke to her in the summer of 1984, Dianna Viner was expecting her second child and had begun a course of study preparatory to becoming a Jew. "I decided that it was important for the family to be all of one faith," she told me. "There will be enough problems for my children without there being a difference of religion too."

ITEM: For Dr. Janet Gold, a West Coast hematologist, it was her stepdaughter's impending bat mitzvah, five years after her marriage, that made her think about becoming a Jew.* "I wanted to make a Jewish home," she told me. "I felt my stepdaughter should have a

* To protect her privacy I have, at her request, changed this woman's name and some of the details of her life.

clear and undiluted identity." Dr. Gold herself had grown up in the heart of the Bible Belt and had remained an active church member throughout her college years. In medical school, however, she began to lose her own faith, and she found herself powerfully drawn to the Jews she met, for the first time, as classmates and teachers. "I admired their warmth and expressiveness," she told me, "and their positive approach to intellectual inquiry. There was a joy in living I had never seen before."

Her admiration grew during her years as a resident in hematology, a field in which Jewish doctors predominate, and she suspected that she would end up marrying a Jew. But since the man she did marry had only a nominal attachment to Judaism, the question of conversion did not arise before her wedding. Five years later, however, her husband's daughter, who had come to live with them, was enrolled in a Reform religious school to prepare for her bat mitzvah. Because the congregation required bar and bat mitzvah candidates and their parents to attend Sabbath services as part of the preparation, Dr. Gold began going to services too and found that she enjoyed them greatly—so much so, in fact, that she continued to attend after the bat mitzvah. A few months later she began taking courses in Judaism and Jewish history before beginning the course of study that led to her conversion.

These same considerations lead many Gentile spouses to convert to Judaism before their marriage.

ITEM: "I've known a lot of products of Protestant-Catholic and Protestant-Jewish mixed marriages, and every one of them is maladjusted," Ginger Ignatoff, a former executive with the United Presbyterian Church, told me, "so I felt the parents *had* to have the same faith. When it became clear to me that I'd like to spend the rest of my life with Elisha, I decided that either we would have to live together without marriage or children or I would have to become a Jew; my faith wasn't strong enough any longer for me to ask him to become a Presbyterian." She began studying Judaism in 1979 and converted a year later in a traditional ceremony held several months before their wedding.

It is not only a concern about the children that leads Gentile partners to convert to Judaism; the impetus often comes from a desire to please the Jewish mate, who may be reluctant to get married unless the Gentile is willing to become a Jew.

ITEM: Richard Wilson, a manager and agent for musicians and other entertainers, told me, "I had very little information about Judaism; I hadn't known many Jews before I moved to New York." (Raised on a wheat farm in the state of Washington, Wilson spent his undergraduate years at the University of Idaho; he studied music in Munich and Vienna before completing his graduate work in music at the University of Washington.) "But I knew the difference in religion was a problem for Jean," Wilson added. "Although she never said it in so many words, the message was clear: she wouldn't marry me if I did not convert." Having abandoned his Lutheran faith before he finished high school—"Once I left home I never went to church again"—he felt open to the possibility of becoming a Jew and was converted in the fall of 1982, a few months before his wedding to Jean Miller.

In general, the seriousness with which the Jewish partner takes his or her Jewishness has a great deal to do with determining whether or not the Gentile spouse converts to Judaism. Prospective converts are not likely to stay the course, however, unless Judaism becomes important to them in its own right; a desire to please one's Jewish spouse (or in some cases, in-laws) is not a strong enough reed on which to build a new religious and ethnic identity. "Over and over again, we were informed that one should convert for oneself" and not simply to please the Jewish spouse or in-laws, Steven Huberman has written in *New Jews: The Dynamics of Religious Conversion*, a study of Boston-area converts to Reform Judaism.* Marrying a Jew "is not an adequate reason for conversion," the respondents told Huberman. "There must be a stronger and higher commitment. To do it to please is a poor reason and not a lasting one. Don't do it for any reason unless it is what *you* want to do [emphasis in original]."

Conversion, it should be noted, is two to three times more frequent among born-Gentile wives than among husbands. Some men who might otherwise convert are deterred by the fact that traditional Jewish law requires a male convert to undergo ritual circumcision or, in the case of those who have had surgical circumcision, the drawing of a symbolic drop of blood. But fear of circumcision is not the major deterrent. Wives are also more willing than husbands to convert in Protestant-Catholic marriages; the reason can be traced to traditional sex roles—in particular, the male assumption that the wife will

* Huberman's primary sample consisted of all those who had completed the Union of American Hebrew Congregation's "Introduction to Judaism" course in the Greater Boston area in the years 1970–76, a group that can be presumed to represent the majority of converts to Reform Judaism in that period; 85 percent of the graduates returned the questionnaire. Depth interviews were conducted with a subsample in the summer of 1978; Huberman also sat in on a five-month session of the course as well as a discussion group for prospective converts and their fiancé(e)s and/or spouses.

assume the husband's identity. Women, after all, have usually abandoned their own surnames in favor of their husbands', and, as we have seen, a name is a powerful symbol of identity. For men, therefore, changing their religion may appear to be surrender of a traditional male prerogative; for women it has been part of a larger pattern of accommodation.*

There is a further complication. In Jewish-Christian marriages the male reluctance to convert has been strengthened by the traditional Jewish view that the child's religious status is determined by the mother's religion rather than the father's. Knowing that his children will be considered Jewish whether he converts or not, a Gentile husband may see no particular reason to become a Jew himself, whereas Gentile wives may wish to convert in order to ensure their children's status as Jews. In the last few years, however, the Reform and Reconstructionist rabbinic organizations have urged abandonment of the traditional emphasis on matrilineal descent, arguing that the offspring of any Jewish parent, whether mother or father, should be considered Jewish if the child is raised as a Jew and affirms his or her own Jewishness. (In most Reform and some Reconstructionist congregations mixed-married couples are accepted as members.) Some critics fear that changing the laws governing personal status may reduce the parental incentive to convert to Judaism; although the fear is understandable, there is no evidence to support or refute it.

In fact, born-Gentile spouses convert to Judaism for a variety of reasons in addition to their concern for their children or their desire to please their Jewish mates. For some it is the realization that marrying or even dating a Jew involves them, however tangentially, in the Jewish fate. "I have read a lot of history," one Los Angeles Jew by choice told Rabbi Harold Schulweis, "and I decided that I would rather that I and my children be identified with the persecuted than with the persecutors; Jews stand for something."

ITEM: Deborah Beveppo Hirsch of Savannah, Georgia, a receptionist in the city's Visitors Bureau, hardly had been aware of Jews or Judaism until she encountered nasty anti-Semitism on the part of her college classmates when she began dating her future husband. After their marriage the couple settled in Chickamauga, a tiny Georgia town in which her husband was the only Jew—a fact that made him interested

* Today, of course, a growing number of women retain their own names when they marry—a clear assertion of their determination to retain their own identities. Whether this will mean that husbands will be more willing to adopt the religions of their wives or that wives will be less willing to adopt the religions of their husbands remains to be seen.

in his Jewishness for the first time. Because of their discomfort in Chickamauga, the couple began spending weekends in Chattanooga, a hundred miles away, where at first they went to synagogue on Saturday and church on Sunday. Never completely comfortable with her Catholicism, Deborah Hirsch found herself drawn to Judaism because of the direct relationship between worshiper and God, and she began taking instruction from the rabbi of the Reform temple they attended. After her conversion the Hirsches moved to Savannah to find a more hospitable environment. They are active members of Congregation Mikve Israel, a 250-year-old Reform congregation.

For other Gentile partners, identification with Jewish history leads to a determination to raise their children as Jews, even when they do not convert to Judaism themselves.

ITEM: When she was first married, Zahava Jacobson (a pseudonym) has written, her husband "wasn't sure he wanted his children to be brought up as Jews. This was a bone of contention between us." After a great deal of discussion, however, Jacobson's husband read some of the literature of the Holocaust; the "description of Jewish suffering and losses had a powerful impact on him. He told me, 'I don't want to take away more people from the Jewish people by having my children born of a Jewish woman but not raised as Jews. I want my children to be part of the chain of Jewish history.'" As a result, the couple belong to a Reform temple and light candles on Friday night; the older son celebrated his bar mitzvah in New York and again in Israel, where Jacobson was raised.

Often, too, there is a gradual development of interest in and commitment to Judaism. "I can't put my finger on when it began," one Jew by choice told me, "or even how it evolved." For others the "it" may evolve as a by-product of being caught up in a Jewish social or religious milieu.

ITEM: When he married his Orthodox-raised wife fifteen years ago, Robert Junghandel of Westbury, Long Island, was attracted by the direct relationship between worshiper and God that he discovered in Judaism; his own once active Lutheran faith had been waning. He rejected the idea of converting to Judaism, however, because of his hurt over his Orthodox Jewish in-laws' rejection of him—a rejection he now understands. By the time the couple moved to Long Island several years later their hurts were beginning to heal. Since she knew no one in her community, Phyllis Junghandel joined a Reform congregation out of a desire to make friends; she was also prompted by a renewed interest in Judaism. Attending synagogue services with her from time to time and participating in the temple's social life, Junghandel again found himself attracted to Judaism. "The more I read, the more deeply I felt that [conversion] was the right thing to do and the right way to live my life." In 1981, after an extended course of study, Junghandel was converted to Judaism in the traditional manner, with ritual circumcision, immersion in a *mikveh* (ritual bath), and examination by a Beth Din. Afterward he and his wife were remarried in a Jewish religious ceremony.

There are times, of course, when conversion is an empty shell, undertaken to placate in-laws who demand a Jewish wedding but who are indifferent to the spiritual life of the Jew-to-be. But this seems to be rarer than it used to be, if only because parents are more accepting of mixed marriages. Most conversions come after a serious course of study—three to four months at the minimum and often a year or more—with individual or group counseling sessions, in which the prospective Jew by choice is encouraged to articulate the uncertainties and doubts that inevitably arise.

ITEM: For Richard Wilson the course involved "incredible ups and downs"—"downs" that for a time threatened his relationship with his fiancée, Jean Miller. "My old subconscious prejudices came rising to the surface," Wilson told me, prejudices he had forgotten he had once had. "Knowing that everyone was watching my reactions," Wilson explained, "terms I hadn't used since childhood came bubbling up—and my own fears as well"—in particular, the fear of being rejected by the woman he loved. (Miller experienced the same fear and the same revelation about her own feelings: "I discovered anti-Christian prejudices in myself that I hadn't known I had," she told me.) The fears were allayed, however, and their relationship proved strong enough to withstand the strains. Biweekly counseling sessions with Rabbi Helene Ferris, the rabbi who was supervising his conversion, helped Wilson exorcise the remnants of anti-Semitism left over from his childhood. At his conversion ceremony in 1982, conducted as part of the weekly Sabbath service, he chanted the weekly Torah portion and spoke to the congregation about his newfound love of Judaism.

Today Wilson and his wife live in an almost entirely Jewish social ambience, and he worries about how to protect his daughter from the anti-Semitism she may encounter. "We've found that we are more comfortable with people who are like us," Wilson told me by way of explaining why their closest friends are almost all Jewish. In this regard Wilson and Miller are typical of "conversionary couples" in general; in the New York metropolitan area, for example, nine such couples in ten reported that most or all of their closest friends were Jews, a figure only marginally below that reported by in-married couples.

It requires time, of course, for new Jews to take their Jewishness for granted. "I'm always looking over my shoulder, wondering if people accept me," Wilson says, reflecting a common concern. As is true of most recent converts, his insecurity is heightened when he overhears remarks about "goyim" or when people comment that Wilson is not a Jewish name. (He responds to the latter remark by saying that his mother was Jewish. "It avoids the hassle of explaining the whole thing," he told me. "My life is not a political forum.")

Because of the "anti-goyism" ingrained in so many older Jews, full acceptance can be a long time in coming; insensitive remarks and thoughtless attempts at humor can make the most profoundly observant Jews feel like second-class citizens. "Not bad for a shiksa," a former president of her congregation told Carol Levithan after she had chanted the Haftorah on Yom Kippur in flawless Hebrew and with perfect command of the *trop*, or traditional melody.

The greater frequency of intermarriage is chipping away at this kind of provincialism. After her conversion and marriage, for example, Mary Lynn Kotz and her husband worked as journalists in Des Moines, Iowa, "where we were strangers to the Jewish community. But not for long," she has written. "A couple from Temple B'nai Jeshurun gave a dinner party for us, and invited six other couples. For the next six Saturday nights, each of those couples entertained us, introducing us to still more of their friends. At the end of two months, we were part of the Des Moines Jewish community."

Recognizing the insecurities to which newly converted Jews are prone, the Task Force on Reform Jewish Outreach of the Union of American Hebrew Congregations now sponsors workshops and weekend retreats before major holidays; the programs serve as a support system for recent converts and their spouses as well as a means of familiarizing them with Jewish rituals and observances. In some cities—Los Angeles is the most notable example—the Jewish federation now sponsors programs designed to help integrate Jews by choice into the larger Jewish community.

The most important single factor making for acceptance, however, is the prominent role that Jews by choice are beginning to play in synagogue life, especially in Reform congregations, which attract the majority of Jews by choice. One reason for this affinity is the fact that intermarriage is more frequent among Reform than among Conservative or Orthodox Jews; another is that the Reform movement makes fewer demands on would-be converts. But because the movement has a far more active outreach program than the other denominations, people interested in becoming Jews gravitate toward Reform conversion programs even when their Jewish fiancé(e)s or spouses come from a Conservative or Orthodox background. A 1982 demographic survey of the St. Louis Jewish community, for example, found that two thirds of those who had converted to Judaism had done so under Reform auspices. In his study of alumni of the Boston Reform conversion program, moreover, Steven Huberman found that only 40 percent of the born-Jewish spouses had been Reform Jews at the time the born-Gentile spouse enrolled in the program; half were Conservative Jews, and one in ten reported an Orthodox identification. When Huberman queried the group, however, 85 percent of the couples identified themselves as Reform Jews.

The choice of conversion program in turn strongly influences future affiliation. The intensity of the conversion process often creates a powerful bond between rabbi and convert; when the conversion ceremony takes place in synagogue, there is a bond between the convert and the congregation as well. That bond aside, Jews by choice often feel more comfortable in a Reform than in a Conservative or Orthodox congregation. Many of the people I interviewed had attended services at a number of congregations and had spoken to a number of rabbis before deciding on a Reform conversion.

For the Reform movement, certainly, the infusion of new Jews is a clear spiritual plus. In Boston, for example, Reform Jews by choice are a good bit more observant than born Jews who identify themselves as Reform. They are far more likely to belong to a synagogue (57 percent, compared to 39 percent among born Jews), to light Sabbath candles (49 percent, versus 30 percent), and to fast on Yom Kippur (67 percent, compared to 47 percent); the differences are greatest, moreover, among Jews in their twenties. Jews by choice are also more likely to attend Sabbath services, and they are more involved in synagogue life.

Although no survey of converts to other denominations has been conducted, the same phenomenon can be observed in Conservative and Reconstructionist congregations. "There is hardly a rabbi I meet who doesn't tell me that one of the most involved members of his congregation is a convert," says Rabbi Wolfe Kelman, longtime executive vice-president of the Rabbinical Assembly, the professional organization of Conservative rabbis. Certainly this is the case in my own Reconstructionist congregation, in which a number of Jews by choice play leading roles.

Denominational preferences aside, converts to Judaism show high levels of religious observance and synagogue affiliation. In his analysis of the demographic survey of the New York metropolitan area Steven M. Cohen categorized Jews into four groups according to the number of religious rituals they observed. Although fewer conversionary than in-married couples were classified as "frum"—meticulously observant of Jewish law—a much larger proportion—52 percent, compared to 34 percent—fell into the next category, which Cohen called "traditional." All told, 57 percent of conversionary couples, compared to 50 percent of in-married couples, were classified as "frum" or "traditional" Jews.

It is not hard to understand why Jews by choice are somewhat more ritually observant than born Jews and more likely to belong to a synagogue and to attend services with some regularity. For one thing, many Jews by choice had been raised to see church attendance as the sine qua non of religious identification, hence they take it for granted that they will go to synagogue with some regularity.

ITEM: "It has taken Elisha a long time to get used to going to shul," Ginger Ignatoff told me. "It was easy for me because I used to go to church every Sunday when I was growing up, but he had hardly set foot in a synagogue." In fact, Elisha Ignatoff had grown up in a profoundly Jewish but intensely antireligious household. His grandfather, David Ignatoff, had been a distinguished Yiddish poet, and his father, who worked for a national Jewish communal organization, refused to enter a synagogue. "My father-in-law used to joke that his worst fear had come true: his son had married a *frumme*" [a woman who is *frum*] Ginger says. "But he came to understand that I couldn't go through the process of conversion in order to become a secular Jew; he accepted my need to be a religious Jew if I was going to be a Jew at all." In the process Elisha Ignatoff has become a religious Jew himself.

Equally important, Jews by choice find it easier to feel Jewish in the religious than in the ethnic sense, hence they turn to religious observance rather than to communal activity to validate their identity as Jews; for recent converts, in particular, synagogue membership is evidence of their membership in the Jewish community. "I feel like I'm in limbo—not really belonging anywhere. But I'm willing to recognize it will take time," one of Huberman's informants told him. "I can't *feel* Jewish, because my ancestors weren't Jewish. My ancestors didn't light *Shabbes* candles. Slowly, I will be able to be comfortable with being a Jewish person. Maybe when my child is 13 years old and having a bar mitzvah, I'll feel like a Jew. And when my beard becomes gray, maybe I'll even look like a Jew."

Years after their conversion, in fact, Jews by choice are likely to be more comfortable—and to feel more accepted—in religious than in communal settings. "There is an ethnic factor you can never fully replicate," one deeply observant Jew told me. "I'm completely comfortable in shul, but I don't think I could ever get involved with UJA or Hadassah; there's an in groupiness that makes me feel like an outsider." Not surprisingly, membership in communal organizations is substantially lower among Jews by choice than among born Jews.

The fact that Jews by choice define their Jewishness in religious far more than in ethnic terms does not mean that they feel alienated from Jewish life; the point, rather, is that becoming a Jew is a long-term process. "I didn't *feel* Jewish until much later," says Lydia Kukoff of Los Angeles, a leader in the Reform movement's Outreach program and coauthor of its text for conversion classes. "I had to build a Jewish past for myself; this didn't happen overnight." "I end up at the same point that Joe does," one woman told me in discussing her attitude toward Israel. "But for me it is an intellectual process, whereas for him it is purely visceral."

Virtually every Jew by choice to whom I spoke told me that conversion involves a transformation in identity. "All of a sudden you feel labeled and vulnerable," a Denver convert told me. "The biggest adjustment I had to make," a Los Angeles woman said, "was going from being part of the majority to being part of a minority." A New Yorker put it more graphically: "I feel much more of that 'When will those goyim get me?' syndrome than I had expected."

Lacking the family memories and associations that lie at the heart of the Jewishness of many born Jews, Jews by choice cannot take their Jewishness for granted—at least not in the first years after conversion. Many compensate by taking greater pains with ritual observance and by continuing their studies of Judaism; as a result, Jews by choice often know more about Judaism than their spouses do and are more observant as well. At times this can put a certain strain on the relationship, with the born Jew feeling that his or her spouse is "overdoing" religion, or turning into a zealot. More often than not, however, it makes the born-Jewish spouse more observant than he or she had been. "What we are seeing is Jews converting to Judaism," says Rabbi Mark Loeb of Baltimore.

ITEM: When her first child was born, Sharon Lieberman has written, she and her husband, Dale Good, "immediately did as parents what we never did as a couple: We began celebrating Shabbat and we joined a liberal Conservative synagogue. We prepare [their son] Aaron and ourselves for each Jewish observance with stacks of books. Dale has begun teaching Aaron Hebrew letters and words. In fact, Dale is teaching himself Hebrew from a series of programmed texts and now knows more about Jewish law and liturgy than I do. . . . So now I wonder if, ironically, I will transmit the smaller part of my son's Jewish identity, the part he may come to regard as less valuable than his father's contribution." In view of her own casual approach to Jewishness, in fact, Lieberman believes that "Aaron will be a conscious, deliberate Jew *because* of his parents' intermarriage [emphasis in original]."

4

Clearly, American Jews have entered new and uncharted territory, in which the terrain is as treacherous as it is unfamiliar. Not surprisingly, they disagree over what course to steer. The most controversial route is that proposed by Rabbi Alexander Schindler, president of the [Reform] Union of American Hebrew Congregations, who has called on American Jews "to face reality"—to accept the fact that a high rate of intermarriage is inevitable in an open society. The appropriate stance, Schindler argues, is "to reject intermarriage but to accept the intermarried—to reach out to our children, to try to make them part of Jewish life rather than to sit *shiva* [mourn] over them." Hence he has called for an extensive program of outreach whose goals "are clear and simple: to make sure that the majority of interfaith marriages will result in the conversion of the non-Jewish partner to Judaism; and that the majority of the children issuing from such marriages will be reared as Jews."

Schindler's call is controversial, for it runs up against a widespread belief among Jews that proselytizing is "un-Jewish"—that Judaism is opposed to evangelical activity of any sort, and that rabbis are supposed to discourage prospective converts, especially those whose interest in Judaism stems from their intention to marry a Jew. The reverse may be closer to the truth.* For most of their history, in fact, Jews have actively sought converts; estimates of the number converted to Judaism during the late Hellenistic and early Roman period, when Jewish evangelism was at an all-time peak, run as high as six million.

* True, the Talmud says that one should push away prospective converts with the left hand—but it adds that one should draw them closer with the right. As commentators have pointed out, the right hand is stronger than the left, thus drawing them near is expected to prevail. Elsewhere, moreover, the Talmud declares that "God exiled Israel among the Gentiles with no other object than that converts should be added unto them."

When Christianity became the state religion of the Roman Empire, seeking and accepting converts to Judaism became a capital offense, both for the Christians who converted and the Jews who received them. Even so, Jews continued to proselytize until the end of the Middle Ages; although the massacres that accompanied the Crusades served to cool the missionary ardor of Jews, it was not until the sixteenth century that they abandoned their evangelical position altogether. Forced into ghettos, Jews turned their backs on the outside world, persuading themselves that conversion not only was undesirable but was contrary to Jewish tradition. "What our enemies once forced on us to abase and diminish us," Milton Himmelfarb wryly notes, was "taken to be alone authentically Jewish."

But American Jews inhabit a different universe. "We live in America today," Schindler points out. "No repressive laws restrain us. The fear of persecution no longer inhibits us. There is no earthly reason now why we cannot reassume our ancient vocation and open our arms wide to all newcomers." Others are beginning to share the same view. Recognizing "that Jewish attitudes toward conversion have varied with the periods and the circumstances," Rabbi Emanuel Rackman, president of Israel's Bar-Ilan University and one of the intellectual leaders of "modern Orthodoxy" in both Israel and the United States, has urged Jews to "reconsider their pristine hostility" to converts. In the recent past, Rackman argues, Jews' "aversion to conversion and converts" was an effective barrier against intermarriage—"not always, but often enough." That no longer is the case: "To stem the tide of intermarriage today our present attitude is as helpful as aspirin is for cancer. . . . our chances for avoiding astronomical losses in our Jewish population are much better if we think positively about conversion and warmly integrate the convert."

Thinking positively about conversion means acknowledging that a desire to marry a Jew and to raise one's children as Jews is sufficient grounds for converting to Judaism. "Even in Talmudic times, conversion was seen primarily as an act of joining the Jewish people, becoming part of the Jewish national destiny," another Orthodox scholar, Rabbi Marc D. Angel of New York's Congregation Shearith Israel, has written. Since "a non-Jew who wants to marry someone Jewish and to raise Jewish children has opted to become part of our people, even though the commitment to our religion may be less than perfect," it should be possible for Orthodox rabbis to recognize the validity of Reform, Conservative, and Reconstructionist conversions—which many Orthodox rabbis do not now do. "It will not be easy for Orthodox and non-Orthodox to come to an agreement on this issue," Angel adds. "There is a great deal of pride at stake. But if we do not come to an agreement we will cause the Jewish people to be senselessly divided."

Whether agreement is possible is another question. Because of the turn toward fundamentalism within Orthodoxy itself, Orthodox rabbis who try to find some common ground with Reform or Conservative rabbis put their own status at jeopardy. This, certainly, was the case in Denver, where Orthodox, Conservative, and Reform rabbis had agreed upon a conversion procedure that met the requirements of traditional Jewish law. The modest experiment was scuttled when the Rabbinical Council of America—the organization of modern Orthodox rabbis—censured the three Orthodox rabbis who had participated. "Denver was one more instance of the Orthodox inability to cooperate with us on religious questions, so long as they are asked to recognize the legitimacy of another point of view," Dr. Gerson Cohen, chancellor of the [Conservative] Jewish Theological Seminary of America angrily commented. Or as one dissenting Orthodox rabbi sadly noted, "the Orthodox definition of 'Jewish unity' is 'Do it our way.' "

And conversion procedures are simply the tip of the iceberg that divides Orthodox from non-Orthodox Jews. Implicit in Marc Angel's call for unity, for example, is the assumption that conversion will occur *before* marriage, but as we have seen, a significant minority of Jews by choice do not convert to Judaism until *after* marriage—in some cases, long after. The question, then, is how to respond to intermarried couples in which the born-Gentile spouse has not—or not yet—converted to Judaism. The Orthodox answer is clear and uncompromising. Although there are a few dissenting voices, the official position of the Orthodox rabbinate is that synagogue membership should be denied to the Jewish as well as the non-Jewish partner in a mixed marriage.* Some would go even further: one prominent Orthodox leader has called for "the elimination from leadership roles in Jewish public life" of anyone married to a non-Jew.

In the opinion of most Reform and Reconstructionist and a growing number of Conservative rabbis, that approach is both insensitive and unproductive. "I wonder what the evidence is that harshness leads to better results than kindness, consideration, and friendliness," asks Rabbi Seymour Siegel, chairman of the Department of Philosophies of Judaism of the Jewish Theological Seminary of America. "Is it clear that we will benefit if we cut off the non-Jew from everything

* The intensity of the Orthodox rabbinate's feelings is evident in the fact that expulsion from synagogue membership is reserved solely for those who marry non-Jews; someone convicted of a criminal offense may remain a member in good standing.

communally Jewish?" Siegel's answer is in the negative. Jewish law is a means to an end, he argues, not an end in itself. "As the history of halakha shows, so shiningly clear, halakha is changed in light of the ends." Since the end in this instance is to convert non-Jewish spouses to Judaism, Siegel reasons, and since circumstances vary widely from individual to individual, "the halakha in this very difficult situation" should be to leave it up to each individual rabbi "to decide what kind of action will likely lead to conversion of spouses and/or children."

This, in effect, is what the Reform rabbinate has already done. Since they do not feel bound by Jewish law, as Conservative rabbis do, most Reform rabbis and congregations now welcome mixed-married couples and their children, in the hope that acceptance will lead to conversion of the Gentile spouse. Equally important, and far more controversial, there is a growing recognition that, for all the reasons discussed above, many Gentile spouses will not convert to Judaism. The Reform outreach program would welcome these spouses too, along with their Jewish partners—in part out of simple courtesy and in part with the hope that they will decide to identify with the Jewish people, if not the Jewish religion, and therefore raise their children as Jews. As Schindler puts it, "We must remove the 'not-wanted' signs from our synagogues, and from our hearts."

The fact that the signs are being removed has given rise to the bitterest and most divisive controversy of all—that over the religious status of children born to mixed-married couples involving a Jewish father and Gentile mother. According to traditional Jewish law, children born to a Jewish mother and Gentile father are Jews, whereas the unconverted offspring of a Gentile mother and Jewish father are not, no matter how the children are raised or what their Jewish commitments may be; Jewishness can be transmitted from one generation to the next through the maternal line alone.

From a Reform perspective, however, what matters is not the religious identity of the mother but the way in which the child is raised. "It can no longer be assumed *a priori* that the child of a Jewish mother will be Jewish any more than [that] the child of a non-Jewish mother will not be," the Central Conference of American Rabbis (CCAR) declared in March 1983 in a resolution stating that the criteria for determining the religious identity of children of mixed marriages should be the same, whether the Jewish parent is the mother or the father. Specifically, the Conference declared, "the child of one Jewish parent is under the presumption of Jewish descent. This presumption of the Jewish status of the offspring of any mixed marriage is to be established through appropriate and timely public and formal acts of identification with the Jewish faith and people." These "acts of identification," the rabbis went on to explain, "will include entry into the covenant [circumcision], acquisition of a Hebrew name, Torah study, bar/bat mitzvah and Kabbalat Torah [confirmation]."

The resolution unleashed a fire storm of criticism. Calling it "an act of schismatic heresy that would destroy the unity of the Jewish people," Rabbi Gilbert Klaperman, the incumbent president of the [Orthodox] Rabbinical Council of America, appointed a committee to determine whether the organization should sever its relations with Reform Judaism—for example, by withdrawing from the Synagogue Council of America and other interdenominational Jewish organizations. More temperate Orthodox, Conservative, and Reform critics expressed regret that the Reform rabbinate had acted unilaterally in so crucial an area of Jewish law and life, and fear that the action would cause an irreparable breach between Reform and traditional Jews.* "Unless action for unity is started soon," Dr. Irving Greenberg, president of the National Jewish Resource Center, warns, "Jews will be engaged in a religious civil war within a generation."

The intensity of the reaction was puzzling, not because of the content of the CCAR resolution but because it contained so little that was new. The Reform rabbinate's break with the traditional definition of Jewishness had occurred in 1909, when the CCAR *Rabbi's Manual* declared that if a child of a Jewish father and Gentile mother received a Jewish education, he or she was to be considered a Jew; and the CCAR formally reaffirmed its acceptance of patrilineal descent in 1947 and again in 1961. In large measure, therefore, the 1983 resolution was simply a recodification of long-standing Reform practice. It broke new ground only to the extent of making the Reform criteria more stringent than they had been—for example, it added new requirements, such as "entry into the covenant, acquisition of a Hebrew name, Torah study, [and] bar/bat mitzvah"—and applying them to children of a Jewish mother and non-Jewish father.†

The outcry is comprehensible, therefore, only if one recognizes

* In the opinion of Professor Jacob J. Petuchowski of Hebrew Union College in Cincinnati, the leading Reform opponent of the resolution, Jews have been able to maintain themselves as a cohesive, worldwide community because of "the universal acceptance of the laws of personal status" and the consequent "ability to recognize one another as Jews." By changing those laws unilaterally, Petuchowski fears, Reform Judaism may become a separate sect.

† The Reconstructionist movement adopted comparable resolutions in 1968, 1979, and 1984; because of the small size of the movement, the resolutions have drawn little attention.

that the 1983 resolution was a political as well as religious document. To say this is not to denigrate the motives of those who wrote or voted for the resolution, which was the product of years of study and debate. It is simply to acknowledge that the resolution was the product of other factors as well, the most important being the bitterness Reform rabbis feel over the increasingly strident attacks of the Orthodox rabbinate on their legitimacy, attacks that many felt had eliminated the possibility of agreement between the two groups. "The Orthodox will never agree to anything we do, so we might as well go ahead and do it," one rabbi who voted for the resolution explained. "If it is unity the Orthodox want, let them not look upon us with disdain," Rabbi Joseph Glaser, executive vice-president of the CCAR, declared. "They have cut us loose and do not accept our conversions. . . . Admittedly, our plan has imperfections, but life is not perfect and we have to do the best we can to meet the challenges of our time."

The Conservative movement faces the same challenges, and in time it is likely to follow the Reform and Reconstructionist lead. It has not done so yet, in part because of a reluctance to break with tradition and in part because it has been consumed by a heated debate over the ordination of women as rabbis, a debate that almost split the movement in two. That issue has now been resolved; as we have seen, women were admitted to the Jewish Theological Seminary's rabbinic training program in September 1984, and in February 1985 the Rabbinical Assembly, the Conservative rabbinic group, voted to accept graduates of the program as members.

It will be increasingly difficult, therefore, for the Conservative rabbinate to avoid coming to terms with the issues raised in the CCAR resolution. The questions being put to the Committee on Jewish Law and Standards of the Rabbinical Assembly make it clear that Conservative congregations contain a growing number of mixed-married couples, including many involving a Jewish father and Gentile mother. The fact that such couples are members of Conservative congregations is evidence in itself of their desire to raise their children as Jews. As the number of such children grows, the Conservative rabbinate will have to decide whether to accept them as Jews or to deny their Jewishness, with all the bitterness and heartache such an act would entail.

The decision will not be easy. Conservative rabbis are committed to uphold the sanctity of Jewish law; but they are also committed to the view that Jewish law changes—has always changed—in response to the needs of the time. "We of the Conservative movement are convinced that no faith ought to depend on a willful refusal to face facts," Rabbi Jacob Agus of Baltimore, one of the movement's elder statesmen has written. "In the perspective of history, it is clear that whenever possible, rabbis and lay leaders acted in concert to meet the challenges of the day." In the America of the 1980s no challenge is more urgent or more important than that posed by the willingness of mixed-married couples to raise their children as Jews.

PART THREE

Notes on the Future

CHAPTER EIGHT

"IF THEY'RE EVER GOING TO GET US, THEY'RE GOING TO GET US NOW."

1

"You now have in the United States the most affluent group of Jews that ever existed," the manager of a Jewish political action committee, or PAC, told a *Wall Street Journal* reporter in February of 1985. "If they're ever going to get us, they're going to get us now."

It would be hard to imagine a more succinct statement of the ambivalence American Jews feel about themselves and their position in American society. On the one hand, there is pride in achievement and enough confidence to play an increasingly conspicuous role in the political process. (Between the 1982 and 1984 congressional elections the number of Jewish PACs doubled, as did their contributions to the candidates they supported.) On the other hand, there is the suspicion that "they" (and no Jew needs to be told who "they" are) may be out "to get us."

This fear is widespread. More than three quarters of those responding to Steven M. Cohen's 1984 Survey of American Jews agreed that "anti-Semitism in America may, in the future, become a serious problem for American Jews." Moreover, nearly half the respondents rejected the notion that "anti-Semitism in America is currently not a serious problem for American Jews"; two in five agreed. True enough, Jewish communal leaders are more relaxed than members of the rank and file; in Cohen's 1983 survey nearly two thirds of the leaders felt that anti-Semitism was *not* currently a serious problem. And yet a visceral distrust of non-Jews remains even among Jews whose achievements have catapulted them into the ranks of the American elite.

ITEM: "Most non-Jews are anti-Semitic," the managing editor of a major eastern newspaper told me. "The only question is how deep you have to stick the needle in before you hit it."

ITEM: "Jews are at peace in this community; it is a very comfortable place for Jews to live," the chief editorial writer for a leading midwestern newspaper told me during lunch at the city's most prestigious dining club. Even so, Jews continue to lead their social lives almost exclusively with other Jews. "I guess we feel a little more comfortable, a little more secure with each other," the journalist explained. Despite the absence of anti-Semitism in recent years, he added, "we wonder what they are thinking—and what they are saying—behind closed doors."

At times he thinks he knows. Along with everyone else I interviewed in that particular city, the editor recalled an incident in 1961 when members of the most exclusive country club voted down the admission of two Jews. The club reversed itself in 1964 after the newspaper publisher and the presidents of several large corporations had resigned from the club and stopped holding corporate social functions there. But fifteen years later my friend—himself a member of the country club—doubted that Jews were really welcome there. "I suspect that the secret ballot in 1961 is more indicative of how upper-class Gentiles *really* feel about Jews than the current policy," he told me.

Fear of anti-Semitism is based on more than ancient memories. It is renewed at regular intervals by manifestations of anti-Semitism at home and abroad—synagogue bombings in Paris and Brussels, machine-gun and hand-grenade attacks on worshipers at synagogues in Rome and Vienna, acts of vandalism against American synagogues and Jewish religious schools, the venom spewed forth by Arab delegates to the United Nations or by Black Muslim leader Louis Farrakhan.

Equally important, anti-Semitism is not experienced at second or third remove; surprisingly large numbers of American Jews—40 percent of twenty-one-to-thirty-five-year-olds in St. Louis and 46 percent in Washington, D.C.—report that they have had a direct, personal experience of anti-Semitism in the last twelve months. It is true that the incidents—most of them occurring in business and in informal social situations—appear to have been mild; only 7 percent of the St. Louis respondents and 11 percent of those in Washington say they have experienced "a great deal" of anti-Semitism in their lives. Even so, the proportions are far higher than one would have expected, given the steady decline in anti-Semitism since the end of World War II.

It is possible, of course, that the respondents are misinterpreting their experiences—that, expecting anti-Semitism, they find it where it does not exist, interpreting an unprejudiced rebuff as an instance of anti-Semitism. American Jews do, in fact, exaggerate the amount of anti-Semitism that exists. A 1981 study found that three Jews in four believed that the majority of non-Jews think that "Jews have too much power in the business world"; only one non-Jew in three expressed that view. Similarly, a clear majority (55 percent) of Jews thought that non-Jews see them as trying to "push in where they are not wanted," whereas only 16 percent of non-Jews articulated that belief. But if hypersensitivity were the primary explanation of the current findings, one would expect older Jews to report more anti-Semitism than those below the age of thirty-five; the former, after all, have far more reason to see anti-Semites lurking under every bed. In fact, the reverse was the case; only 7 percent of Jews sixty-five and older, compared to 40–46 percent of those under thirty-five, reported that they had experienced anti-Semitism in the past year.

One can understand these responses, it seems to me, only as a paradoxical by-product of young Jews' full integration into American society. Older Jews, who live in a predominantly (and in many cases, entirely) Jewish world, have little contact with Gentiles and so have little current experience of anti-Semitism.* Younger Jews, on the other hand, have daily contact with non-Jews in their business, professional, and, to a lesser degree, their social lives; the result has been a quantum leap in the number of instances in which anti-Semitism may be expressed—or inferred.

In fact, what Jews take to be an expression of anti-Semitism frequently is not that at all; misunderstandings arise because group stereotypes, and the language that surrounds them, persist long after the anti-Semitic attitudes that engendered them have been abandoned.

* The past is something else again. When asked how much anti-Semitism they had experienced over the course of their lives, far larger proportions of older than of younger Jews reported that they had experienced a "great deal" of anti-Semitism.

ITEM: "The U.S. government will never be as quick as Israel to retaliate against terrorism because the United States is not an Old Testament society that believes in an 'eye for an eye,' " a "senior White House official" told reporters at a November 1984 briefing. "We have a New Testament in this country." To Jews it was an odious comparison, one that was all too reminiscent of the theological claims—"the teaching of contempt," as a Catholic scholar has called it—on which fifteen hundred years of Christian anti-Semitism had been built, and Jewish defense organizations responded accordingly. In fact, the official in question, later identified as Robert C. McFarlane, the President's Assistant for National Security Affairs, is one of Israel's principal advocates within the Reagan administration. "He doesn't have an anti-Semitic bone in his body," one of the most knowledgeable Jews in Washington told me. A longtime proponent of a firmer American response to terrorist attacks, McFarlane had simply used an all-too-familiar idiom to express the notion "that the Israeli government had the support of their people to respond quickly to terrorist acts," whereas the American government was finding it hard to build a consensus.

ITEM: "You are one of the senators who receives a large amount of Jewish contributions, and you have been undeviating in your support [for Israel]," Fred Graham of CBS told Alan Cranston, on *Face the Nation* when Cranston was a candidate for the Democratic presidential nomination. Then came the question: "Now, don't you think that raises the question whether you can be unswervingly for American interests when so much of your financial support comes from Jewish sources?" To many Jews, including some who are highly critical of Israeli policy, Graham was not simply asking whether Cranston would be too obligated to Jewish contributors to make up his own mind on U.S. foreign policy in the Middle East; by implying that there was an inherent conflict between accepting contributions from Jews and serving the national interest, Graham seemed to be reading Jews out of the political process. That, apparently, was not what Graham had had in mind. "It was the kind of 'tough' question reporters love to ask," one of Graham's Jewish colleagues told me. "Fred is not an anti-Semite." But it was also the kind of question that makes Jews suspect that to members of the majority they are still outsiders.

There are times, of course, when the intent is less innocent, but even the best intentioned and most worldly people may give offense without realizing it. It would be surprising if it were otherwise; Jewish-Gentile relations were strained for so long and negative stereotypes were so deeply ingrained that it is difficult for Jew or Gentile to escape them altogether. (As we saw in Chapter Two, Jews are no freer from the virus of "anti-goyism" than Gentiles are from anti-Semitism.) The result, in any event, is that despite the insignificance of the anti-Semitism that remains, it continues to shape the way in which American Jews see themselves and the world in which they live.

But what about the future?

When I began my research in the summer of 1979, and for several years thereafter, there was wide concern that American Jews had reached or perhaps even passed the peak of their influence—that American society was likely to be considerably less hospitable to Jews in the future than it had been in the past, and that an erosion in the position of Jews in American society might get under way soon, if it had not started already. This view was a response to the worldwide energy shortage, which seemed to threaten Jews in a number of ways.

To begin with, the energy shortage had vastly increased the power of OPEC members, such as Saudi Arabia, Iraq, Iran, and the smaller Gulf states, which controlled a large part of the supply of oil and which were also deeply hostile to Jews and Judaism as well as to Israel. With oil prices increasing twelvefold—from $3 a barrel in 1973 to $36 in 1980—the Gulf states were piling up enormous financial surpluses, "draining the world of its wealth," as *Business Week* put it in 1979. "Just as the U.S. and the West lost control of energy in the 1970s," the magazine added, "so too are they in danger of losing control over the world's flow of capital and wealth in the 1980s."

European countries, more dependent than most on Middle East oil, began to curry favor with the Arab states; this in turn meant lessening opposition to (and at times outright support for) the Arab-Soviet campaign to exclude Israel from the company of nations. In principle, of course, anti-Zionism is not necessarily synonymous with anti-Semitism; in practice the distinction becomes meaningless. After the 1975 United Nations resolution equating Zionism with racism, for example, Jewish students at several British universities were denied the right to participate in university functions on the grounds that their Jewish Students Union was a Zionist entity and therefore racist by definition. In France, Italy, Belgium, and Austria the pretense was dropped altogether; hostility to Israel was expressed through terrorist acts directed against Jews as Jews—against synagogue worshipers, students at Jewish schools, even patrons of a Jewish restaurant. These acts of terror seemed to provide an ominous signal of what *could* happen in the United States.

To be sure, the United States remained friendly to Israel and continued to provide it with military and economic aid, but the energy shortage seemed to lend credence to those who had always argued that American strategic interests lay with the Arabs rather than with Israel and who now suggested that American friendship for Israel was a luxury the United States no longer could afford. (To antagonize the Arab states, the argument ran, was to risk not only another cutoff of oil but the withdrawal of their financial surpluses, most of which had been invested in the United States.) During the last two years of the Carter and the first two years of the Reagan administrations, therefore, there was a decided tilt toward the Arabs, and it looked as though for the first time American Jews might find themselves in the position French and British Jews have long occupied—that of deep and lasting opposition to their own government's foreign policy.

To some thoughtful Jewish leaders, such as Philip Klutznick, a former president of the World Jewish Congress and Secretary of Commerce in the Carter administration, the most ominous symptom was the subtlest of all. As a result of the energy shortage, which led to a fivefold increase in energy costs, Klutznick told me, the United States had entered a period of major economic and strategic decline. Indeed, Carter's foreign policy was designed to reduce the nation's global commitments to a level compatible with its declining capabilities. Since, to paraphrase the late Charles "Engine" Wilson, what's good for the United States has always been good for the Jews, Klutznick's assessment was bad news indeed. A weaker America was bound to mean a weaker Israel, and a weaker American Jewish community as well. If nothing else, a long period of American economic and political decline would pit one group against another—the classic breeding ground for political anti-Semitism.

In the late seventies and early eighties, moreover, a new nastiness did seem to be in the air. "Toward the end of lunch in a crowded East Side restaurant last week, a woman at the next table said that the Jews had gone too far and taken too much and it was about time that somebody presented them with the bill," Lewis H. Lapham, editor in chief of *Harper's Magazine*, wrote in a 1981 newspaper column. "Her companions wished her to speak more softly. No, she said, she didn't care who was listening, and she didn't mind saying that she hoped she was around to enjoy the grand dispossession."

Nor was that the only such incident Lapham reported. "Later that same day at a fund-raising dinner to honor a Jewish politician, a broker up from Wall Street, slightly drunk and gesturing indignantly with his cigar, asked another of the candidate's friends if he knew of a private boys' school in the city that hadn't been turned into a yeshiva."

Two offensive remarks do not constitute a trend, Lapham argued, and yet it seemed to him that the inhibitions against expressing anti-

Semitic sentiments were weaker than they had been. "As recently as a year ago," he wrote, "the lady in the restaurant might have taken the trouble to lower her voice, and the broker would have been more careful to dissemble his envy." "I'm not saying that anti-Semitism is more pronounced than it was a few years ago," Lapham told me several weeks later, "but people—some people, at any rate—are feeling freer to give voice to it. I simply would not have heard that remark five years ago." And Lapham was not alone in reporting this kind of change; directors of two large corporations, an executive of a major business group, and a prominent Lutheran minister all told me that they were beginning to hear anti-Semitic jokes and remarks in board meetings and social settings, remarks that they too were convinced they would not have heard a few years earlier.

It was more worrisome than that, for the increase in social anti-Semitism seemed to have its counterpart in the political sphere. During most of his term as president, Jews had been troubled by Jimmy Carter's failure to disavow his brother's anti-Semitic vulgarisms; as one White House aide cogently remarked, "American Jews look at Billy as Jimmy Carter's id." That feeling seemed to be confirmed by Carter's behavior after Andrew Young's August 1979 "resignation" as ambassador to the United Nations. When black leaders blamed American Jews for Young's dismissal in an unprecedented outburst of anti-Semitic vituperation, Carter sailed the Mississippi, kissing babies at each stop but refusing to comment on the Young affair. It was not until four weeks later that Carter acknowledged that Jewish leaders had urged him to keep Young in his post. To many, myself included, it looked as though the president had tacitly encouraged the black-Jewish confrontation in order to counteract the growing black disaffection with his domestic policies.*

Two years later things seemed to have gone from bad to worse. "I saw something that I never thought I would encounter in my life," Democratic Senator Daniel Patrick Moynihan of New York remarked in the fall of 1981. "I saw the threat of anti-Semitism used for political objectives." Moynihan was referring to the tactics the Reagan administration and its allies had employed to win Senate approval of the sale of AWAC planes to Saudi Arabia. Reluctant to rest the case for the sale on its merits—the House had voted it down by an overwhelming margin, and the press was almost unanimously opposed—

* In doing so Carter was adapting an old southern technique whereby the white ruling class had kept itself in power for generations: pitting poor whites against blacks. At the time, the play seemed to work; black criticism of Carter stopped abruptly after Young's resignation as black leaders concentrated their fire on Israel and on American Jews.

Fred Dutton, the Saudis' chief congressional lobbyist, managed to define the controversy as a test of "Jewish power." Echoing the Saudi charge that American Jews, and through them Israel, controlled American foreign policy in the Middle East, Dutton told members of the Senate over and over again that the complicated issue before them involved a simple choice of "Begin or Reagan." In the weeks before the vote, moreover, administration supporters echoed this view. "We can't let the Jews win this one," Gerald Ford told the senators he was lobbying—and suggested that it was improper, even disloyal, for American Jews to oppose the sale.

The president did his part to create the same impression. "It is not the business of other nations to make American foreign policy," Reagan declared in a prepared statement read at the beginning of his October 1, 1981, press conference. "The President did not quite say, 'Choose Begin or Reagan,' or accuse the opponents of his AWACs deal of putting Israel's interests ahead of America's," the *Washington Post,* a frequent and severe critic of Israeli policy, commented editorially the next day. "But those are the repugnant implications of his prepared statement . . . [This] ill-tempered, premeditated remark was a crude effort to blame the 'Israeli lobby' for the likely defeat of a mismanaged venture."

The uneasiness of American Jewish leaders was heightened, moreover, when the president dissembled with them at a meeting after the Senate had approved the AWACs sale. Reagan professed surprise that anyone had thought he was criticizing Israel; his press conference statement had been aimed at Saudi Arabian interference in American foreign policy, he insisted, not at Israel. In fact, Prince Bandar bin Sultan, the Saudi Arabian prince who oversaw the Saudi lobbying effort, had sat in on administration strategy sessions at the president's invitation. (On the day of the Senate vote Dutton and Prince Bandar continued their lobbying efforts from offices in Senate Majority Leader Howard Baker's own suite, just off the Senate rotunda.)

All told, the AWACs affair seemed to be a turning point for American Jews. "For the first time since World War II," Milton Ellerin, director of the American Jewish Committee's Trends Analysis division, wrote in a low-keyed memorandum, "an American President, some ranking officials of his administration, U.S. Senators, and other prominent political figures, regardless of intent or design, had cast aspersions on the loyalty of American Jews for exercising their right to make their views known on a public issue." Indeed, some longtime critics of American Jews' preoccupation with anti-Semitism concluded that "a new anti-Semitism" had arisen. He had always believed that "we have exaggerated the importance of anti-Semitism," Leonard Fein wrote shortly after the AWACs vote. "Until now. Today, I no longer quarrel with those who insist that we face no more serious problem than anti-Semitism in the United States."

2

The fears turned out to be groundless. As I finish this chapter in March of 1985, in fact, it is hard to recall the level of anxiety that prevailed just three years earlier. What has changed is less the mood itself—it will be a long time before American Jews are willing to drop their guard—than the objective situation in which they now find themselves. Specifically, the principal threat to Jewish security has been dissipated. The energy crisis is over; prices have come down by a third or more as the shortage of oil has turned into a worldwide glut. Indeed, some of those who once predicted steadily increasing energy costs now worry about the consequences of a collapse in world oil prices!

What happened, in essence, was that the market worked. Like most cartels, OPEC was too greedy; the policies it followed planted the seeds of its own destruction. Specifically, the extraordinary increase in oil prices that OPEC engineered led to drastic and almost certainly permanent changes in both the demand for energy and its supply.

It took a while, however, for these changes to take effect—or to be noticed. The United States had been in shock during the 1970s, because its economy had been built on cheap energy. Gasoline was so cheap, for example, both absolutely and relative to prices in Europe and Japan, that motorists had been wholly uninterested in fuel economy; auto manufacturers, therefore, had had little incentive to spend money developing fuel-efficient cars. The same was true of energy consumption within industry itself; even industries that used large amounts of energy, such as steel and paper manufacturing, saw no need to economize on energy, because it was so cheap, relative to every other resource. Indeed, productivity was higher in the United States than elsewhere precisely because producers had such a strong incentive to substitute energy for labor.

OPEC changed all that. The combination of scarcity and high prices forced producers and consumers to find ways of cutting down on energy use. Since the first oil boycott in 1973, in fact, there has been a 20 percent reduction in the amount of energy consumed per dollar of gross national product—a far greater decline than anyone had thought possible. The high price of oil also increased the use of coal and other fuels that could be substituted for oil, thereby reducing demand for oil even more. Moreover, the heavy capital costs of converting to other fuels and of changing production methods to conserve energy make it unlikely that either consumers or business firms will return to their former profligate ways. Today's Cadillacs, for example, get considerably more miles per gallon than the Chevrolets of ten years ago, so that even if Americans started buying Cadillacs instead of Chevrolets, gasoline consumption would not return to its former level. And much the same is true in every other sector of the economy.

The high price of oil made it profitable to develop large new oil fields in Mexico, the North Sea, Alaska, and elsewhere, as well as to increase production in old fields. The result has been a huge increase in the supply of oil and a corresponding reduction in OPEC's share, which has fallen by half—from two thirds of world production to less than one third. Thus the ability of the Gulf states to disrupt supplies or to control prices has virtually disappeared; indeed, the Iraq-Iran war, which has caused sharp cutbacks in output in those two countries—reductions that once would have caused an international crisis—has had no effect at all on oil supplies or prices.

Thus there no longer is any strategic reason for the United States to be obsequious to Saudi Arabia or the other Arab nations; by the fall of 1982 the Reagan administration had come around to the view that "they need us a lot more than we need them." As indeed they did; Saudi oil revenues, which had reached $113 billion in 1981, dropped to $47 billion two years later, causing major cutbacks in spending on the kingdom's development plans. Although United States-Saudi relations remain close, there is growing recognition that Saudi Arabia has been a far less reliable ally than its American supporters had expected or promised—that, indeed, it has obstructed American objectives far more often than it has supported them.

For all the lip service paid to the notion that solving the Arab-Israeli conflict is the key to peace in the Middle East, it has become increasingly evident that this is not the case. The fratricidal conflict within Lebanon, the seemingly endless war between Iran and Iraq, the tension between Libya and Egypt and Libya and the Sudan, the Syrian threats against Jordan, the conflict between North and South Yemen, the warfare in the southwest Sahara between Algerian- and Moroccan-backed forces—none of these has anything at all to do with Palestinian claims or Israeli policy; the region would be in turmoil even if Israel did not exist. Nor is a reduction in American support for Israel the prerequisite for close relations with the oil-producing states that proponents have claimed—witness the fact that in 1984 Iraq, the most intransigent of the so-called "rejectionist states," resumed diplomatic relations with the United States without getting the reduction it had demanded ever since it broke off relations in 1967.

The result is that U.S. policy has tilted back toward Israel. American-Israeli relations are closer now than they have been for a number of years; a November 1983 agreement on "strategic cooperation" between the United States and Israel gave formal recognition to the fact that American aid to Israel reflects that country's strategic importance to the United States and not simply the influence of the pro-Israel lobby. Since public opinion tends to follow the president's lead, support for Israel is high, with five times as many Americans expressing sympathy for Israel as for the Arabs. To be sure, tensions between Israel and the United States are bound to arise from time to time; although the strategic interests of the two countries are close, they are not always identical–and even when they are, there may be disagreements over tactics. But as things now stand, a serious rupture between the two countries seems highly unlikely.

Nor is there any "new anti-Semitism" or any significant increase in the old. The nastiness of 1978–82 disappeared with remarkable speed, for the American public refused to pick up on the hints that were dropped during the AWACs debate; public-opinion polls showed no change in Gentile attitudes toward Jews. Moreover, the Reagan administration found that even a subtle use of anti-Semitism backfired; the Congress responded angrily, and the president was roundly condemned by the press for his press conference barb at Israel and, indirectly, at American Jews.

The reason, quite simply, is that the American consensus forbids the use of anti-Semitism in the political arena–not because of philo-Semitism (although its importance should not be underestimated) but because anti-Semitism would unravel the fabric of American political and social life. A multiethnic, multireligious society cannot permit anti-Semitism, or group prejudice of any sort, to intrude in its public life. "If they go after the Jews now," members of other groups reason, "they may come after us next." Ronald Reagan seems to have learned that lesson well. Since the AWACs affair, he has leaned over backward to avoid any hint of attack on Israel or on American Jews' political activities on Israel's behalf, notwithstanding several sharp disagreements with Israel during the latter part of Menachem Begin's tenure as prime minister.*

* Former Texas Governor John Connally learned the lesson the hard way during his 1979 campaign to secure the Republican nomination for president. He had been considered the leading candidate until he made a speech in which he tried to capitalize on black-Jewish tensions, as well as on unrest over the gasoline shortage, which he blamed on Israel. The United States,

Given the long history of anti-Semitism, as well as Jews' continued experience of it on the personal level, it would be feckless to argue that "it can't happen here." The relevant question, however, is not can it but *will* it happen here, and the answer to that is a resounding no, barring changes so massive that American democracy itself is threatened. Certainly a residue of anti-Semitism remains, but it declines from one generation to the next, with one exception, which I will discuss on the next page.

The experience of the last fifteen years, moreover, indicates that American resistance to anti-Semitism is far stronger than anyone had realized. On a number of occasions the classic conditions for anti-Semitism seemed to be present, and observers quite reasonably predicted a significant increase; none of those predictions was realized.

ITEM: Reasoning from Germany's experience after its defeat in World War I, a number of German-Jewish intellectuals expected the American defeat in Vietnam to produce an anti-Semitic backlash; Americans would want a scapegoat, they thought, and the Jews would be it. No such backlash occurred.

ITEM: When the Arabs imposed an embargo on oil shipments during the 1973 Yom Kippur War, American Jewish leaders were fearful that Israel—and, by extension, American Jews—would be blamed. But as public opinion surveys demonstrated, Americans overwhelmingly put the onus on the Arabs.

ITEM: Later in the seventies, when gasoline had to be rationed and Americans were forced to wait on hour-long lines, Jewish leaders again expected that anti-Semitism would increase. It did not.

ITEM: During Begin's latter tenure as prime minister there were recurrent fears that distaste for his bombastic style would spill over into dislike of Israel and of American Jews. Americans showed a remarkable ability to distinguish between Begin, whom they disliked, and Israel, which they continued to support.

Most significant of all, perhaps, there has been no discernible backlash against American Jews for their increasingly visible lobbying on Israel's behalf. Few charges worry Jews more than the allegation that

---

Connally declared, must "now" base its foreign policy on "American interests"—a clear implication that until then American interests had been subverted. ("I did not . . . as is customary for presidential candidates," Connally bragged, "take all my cues on Israel from the Israeli embassy and 'lobby.' ") His candidacy collapsed immediately, for it marked him as a regional candidate, willing to pit one group against another, rather than as someone able to harmonize group interests.

they are more loyal to Israel than to the United States. In 1979 some 29 percent of Americans agreed with that proposition; the number has fluctuated from year to year—it rose after the AWACs debate and again after Israel's invasion of Lebanon—but in the more benign atmosphere prevailing in 1984 the proportion dropped to 25 percent, the lowest since the question was first asked. Only 8 percent of Americans, moreover, believe that Jews have "too much power in the United States"—another ancient fear; by contrast, 50 percent of Americans believe that business corporations, labor unions, and the news media have too much power, 30 percent list "Arab interests," and 13 percent name blacks.

There is one exception to this string of good news. While anti-Semitism has been falling among white Americans, it has increased somewhat among blacks. When the last comprehensive survey was taken in 1981, proportionately twice as many blacks as whites displayed significant prejudice against Jews, and fewer than half as many were classified as unprejudiced. The problem is less the level of anti-Semitism, however, than its composition. In the population at large, younger people are considerably less anti-Semitic than their elders, and anti-Semitism declines sharply as education increases: college graduates are far less prejudiced than people with a high school education or less.

Among black Americans the reverse is true: younger blacks are more anti-Semitic than older blacks, and those with higher educations are more anti-Semitic than those with less, with black leaders the most anti-Semitic of all. In a 1978 survey of attitudes toward blacks and Jews, pollster Louis Harris included a subsample of fifty-three "national black leaders"; the latter showed levels of anti-Semitism nearly twice as high as those of all blacks taken together. As public opinion analyst William Schneider commented, "This is not the anti-Semitism of ignorance or religious bigotry; it is the anti-Semitism of political conflict and confrontation."

This concentration of anti-Semitism among the best-educated and most affluent members of the black community found expression in Jesse Jackson's anti-Semitic utterances during his 1984 campaign for the Democratic presidential nomination and in the scurrilous speeches of his supporter Louis Farrakhan, who repeatedly called Judaism a "gutter religion." The most striking—and frightening—evidence of black anti-Semitism, however, came from a *Los Angeles Times* poll of black delegates to the 1984 Democratic convention: three quarters of the delegates committed to Jackson and nearly half of those committed to Mondale said that they saw no reason to disassociate themselves from any of Farrakhan's views.

There is nothing new about black anti-Semitism as such; it is embedded in the Protestant tradition blacks share with their fellow white southerners. "All of us black people who lived in the neighborhood hated Jews, not because they exploited us, but because we had been taught at home and in Sunday school that Jews were 'Christ-killers,' " the late Richard Wright wrote in 1945, describing his childhood in a small southern town. "With the Jews thus singled out for us, we made them fair game for ridicule," chanting anti-Semitic ditties they barely understood. "Our mothers and parents generally approved, either actively or passively. To hold an attitude of antagonism or distrust toward Jews was bred in us from childhood; it was not merely racial prejudice, it was part of our cultural heritage." It was so much a part, in fact, that before America's entry into World War II much of the black press favored Hitler because of his anti-Semitism.

Not that Jews are immune to prejudice themselves; as white Americans they have absorbed the racism endemic to American society. "I was walking along a street near my house, and had to pass a small grocery store located in our neighborhood," the late Horace Mann Bond wrote, describing an incident that occurred in 1916, when he was twelve. "There was a small boy—perhaps six years old—looking through the picket fence that surrounded the store. As I passed he began to chant: 'Nigger, nigger, nigger, nigger.' . . . And my response still surprises me; I retorted to the boy, 'You Christ-killer!' "

But black anti-Semitism is not just a mirror image of Jewish racism. There is a lack of symmetry in the relationship between blacks and Jews that gives black anti-Semitism a distinctive and troublesome cast. Whereas Jewish leaders are considerably *less* racist (and considerably more sympathetic to black aspirations) than the rank and file, the opposite, as we have seen, is true of the black community.

Nor is black anti-Semitism simply an instance of Christian folk anti-Semitism or of black animosity to whites as a whole. "The tension between Negroes and Jews contains an element not characteristic of Negro-Gentile tensions," James Baldwin wrote in 1948, "an element which accounts in some measure for the Negroes' tendency to castigate the Jew verbally more often than the Gentile, and which might lead one to the conclusion that, of all white people on the face of the earth, it is the Jew whom the Negro hates the most."

That, of course, was precisely the impression that Jackson, Farrakhan and company created during the 1984 presidential campaign and that a good many black leaders and spokesmen created five years earlier, after Carter's firing of Andrew Young. It is the impression that black activists continue to create on college campuses and at meetings of black professional groups. The fact that anti-Semitism is so much more intense among black college students and younger professionals is evidence that what we are seeing today is not just a continuation (or revival) of the old folk anti-Semitism.

It is, in fact, a new anti-Semitism, at least for the United States. The old folk anti-Semitism is there, of course, as is what social scientists call "objective anti-semitism"—anti-Semitism that arises from real conflicts of interest between Jews and members of other groups. Some part of the anti-Semitism now being manifested reflects the fact that many upwardly mobile blacks have chosen occupational lines, such as teaching, social work, law, and medicine, that Jews had entered a generation earlier—a choice that has led to conflict over criteria for admission to colleges and professional schools and for appointment and promotion to supervisory jobs.* But this is only a part of black anti-Semitism, and a small part at that. If black anti-Semitism were primarily a response to conflicts of interest between blacks and Jews, one would expect to find the same hostility directed against members of other ethnic groups with whom blacks are colliding—the Irish, who have controlled the New York City police department, or the Italians, who control the sanitation department. This is not the case.

What we are seeing instead is a classic instance of "subjective" (or "abstract") anti-Semitism, to use the scholarly terms—hatred directed not against the flesh-and-blood Jews with whom blacks may be in conflict (although such conflicts provide a pretext) but against the abstract idea of the conspiratorial Jew.

ITEM: "The key question before us as representatives of the Black community in America," Black leaders declared on August 22, 1979, in what one of them called "our declaration of independence," is the "extent to which the successful demand for the resignation of Andrew Young has in fact further damaged an already unhappy relationship between American Jewish organizational spokesmen and the rank and file and the leadership of American Blacks." The "successful demand" had been made by precisely one Jewish spokesman—the head of a minor organization; the heads of every major Jewish organization had either kept silent or urged the administration to retain Young. In fact, it was Secretary of State Cyrus Vance who forced Young's resignation

* There is an old view that black anti-Semitism is a result of blacks' having so often met Jews as merchants and landlords. But the Jew whom Richard Wright and his childhood friend hated as a Christ-killer was a merchant almost as poor as the blacks among whom he lived. (Far from exploiting blacks, Jewish merchants in the South were the only whites willing to do business with them.) In a city such as Detroit, moreover, the merchants in black neighborhoods are far more likely to be Palestinians than Jews—which has not deterred black Detroit congressmen from supporting the PLO.

when he told the president he could not continue to serve if Young remained in his U.N. post.

ITEM: That it is the abstract rather than the flesh-and-blood Jew who concerns him is evident from Jesse Jackson's congenital inability to distinguish Jews from Gentiles. "I have seen very few Jewish reporters that have the capacity to be objective about Arab affairs," Jackson told a press conference after returning from a trip to the Middle East. One of the reporters he cited was David Shipler, then *The New York Times* Jerusalem correspondent, who happens to be Gentile. Six years earlier Jackson had blamed President Nixon's insensitivity to the poor on his top advisers, "four out of five of [whom] are German Jews." The "German Jews" he singled out for particular mention were John D. Ehrlichman and H. R. Haldeman!

If this were all, black anti-Semitism might be a cause for concern but not for real anxiety. Unfortunately it is not all. Since 1967 black anti-Semitism has taken a new and dangerous turn: consciously or not, a significant number of black civil rights spokesmen, political leaders, and intellectuals have adopted the political anti-Semitism that has become a central part of the ideology of the left throughout the world. The first person to do so explicitly was the writer Harold Cruse, whose widely hailed volume *The Crisis of the Negro Intellectual* was published before the Six-Day War. Cruse attacked black intellectuals in general and James Baldwin in particular for failing to recognize that their principal enemy was the Jew. "It would not be correct to call Baldwin a Jew-lover," Cruse wrote; "it is that Baldwin simply loves everybody. More exactly, he fits the category of apologist for the Jews."

Baldwin has come a long way since then. "The state of Israel was not created for the salvation of the Jews," he wrote a month after Young's resignation; "it was created for the salvation of the Western interests." Baldwin's thesis is central to the ideology of the left as it has developed since 1967. Couched in the trendy rhetoric of so-called "Third World politics," the new view is that the nation state no longer is the primary arena for the class struggle. There is instead a worldwide struggle between have and have-not nations, with Israel being the prime symbol of the former.

Having been "created for the salvation of the Western interests," that is to say, Israel exists only to serve those interests, and American Jews exist only to serve Israeli interests—hence the tendency to use "Zionist" and "Jew" interchangeably as pejorative terms. As Cruse put it in 1967, Jews "function in America as an organic part of the distant nation state—a state that is the prime example of colonialism, racism, and imperialism." That same view was expressed in 1979 by Joel Dreyfuss, a writer of Haitian and Jewish ancestry. "The resignation of Andrew Young is a metaphor for a struggle between competing ethnic groups, for relationships between the haves and the have-nots here and elsewhere," Dreyfuss wrote. "*The conflict between blacks and Jews reflects the fact that these two groups have made their alliances with opposing camps in an international struggle for power* [emphasis added]."

It is not hard to understand the appeal this view has for some black leaders and their younger followers—and, judging by their activities on college campuses, for young Hispanics as well.* It makes them feel that they no longer are a minority—that they are instead part of a worldwide majority composed of people of color. Equally important, so far as black civil rights and political leaders are concerned, "Third World politics" provides the race issue that has been lacking since the legislative victories of the 1960s. It has been difficult to construct a distinctively black agenda on domestic policy, since the issues that affect blacks the most—economic growth, unemployment, welfare reform, and so on—are not susceptible to discussion in purely racial terms.

Hence Jesse Jackson's 1984 campaign emphasis on foreign policy—not previously a major black concern—which flowed out of his Third World view of "colonialism" and "imperialism" as the principal enemy. ("The industrial powers purposefully and consciously structured their relations with weaker societies," Jackson explained in Havana, in ways "that benefited the powerful at the expense of the powerless.") Jackson's anti-Semitism, therefore, was of a piece with his support for the PLO and for Syria's Assad, his praise for Castro as standing "on a moral higher ground," his attack on the Panama Canal as "a badge of disgrace" for the United States, and his reference to the "moral appeal" of the Sandinistas, who had put Nicaragua "back on the road to democracy."

What makes this kind of rhetoric (and thinking) dangerous is not just that it represents the first systematic use of anti-Semitism as a political device but that it could become the dominant foreign policy view within the Democratic party. One of the ways in which the United States continues to be different is that, unlike other democratic societies, ideology has played little role in political life; as a result, the United States has escaped the factional politics in which extremism is bred. The two major parties have been characterized instead by coali-

* Because of the difficulties involved in constructing a representative sample of the various Hispanic groups, there are no survey data on Hispanic attitudes.

tion politics, whereby they have been forced to harmonize the separate and sometimes conflicting views of a variety of interest groups. As a result, the Democratic party has been (and continues to be) the principal means through which Jews have developed coalitions with other groups.

Until recently much the same had been true of Jews in other countries. In the nineteenth and most of the twentieth century the primary obstacle to full participation in political and social life came from the distaste for Jews on the part of the old elites. Although the left was hardly immune to anti-Jewish prejudice—a powerful strain of anti-Semitism has run through socialist thought since its beginning—effective political anti-Semitism was, to all intents and purposes, a phenomenon of the right.

That is true no longer. The Soviet Union, which now imprisons Jews for the crime of teaching Hebrew, is the world's largest supplier of anti-Semitic propaganda, and with the help of its mostly leftist Third World allies, it has turned the United Nations into a forum for the dissemination of the oldest anti-Semitic canards. There has been a change, meanwhile, within much of the democratic West: "the conservative Establishment" is now largely pro-Israel and philo-Semitic, while the left has become strongly anti-Israel and, as a result, anti-Semitic. "Fringe neo-Nazi groups notwithstanding," the Australian sociologist W. D. Rubinstein argues, "significant anti-Semitism is now almost exclusively a left wing rather than a right wing phenomenon."

Rubinstein's generalization is far too sweeping. True enough, Jerry Falwell and most other national leaders of the Christian right in the United States have condemned anti-Semitism and have taken a strongly pro-Israel position. Some of their followers, however, have been less scrupulous: in at least three 1984 congressional races, right-wing Christian groups made overt use of anti-Semitism in an effort to unseat Jewish incumbents.

ITEM: "I'm sure that you recognize the need for Christian leadership in the U.S. Congress," the campaign manager for a Minnesota Republican candidate wrote in a letter sent to district voters; the campaign against the incumbent, he added, was "part of the great cause, furthering God's kingdom on earth." "These people vote almost 100% of the time," a Florida group wrote to voters in its district. "It remains to be seen whether we Christians, when offered a genuine champion, will do all we can to deliver the same turnout."

In France, which has the second-largest Western Jewish community, the socialist government of François Mitterrand is far friendlier to Israel than its conservative predecessors had been. Indeed, the government of Giscard d'Estaing included a number of members of the so-called New Right—a group whose anti-Semitic views are indistinguishable from those of the old right, though couched in far more polished and sophisticated language. The Holocaust did not put an end to French right-wing anti-Semitism, one observer has commented, it merely set higher standards for its expression.

There is enough truth in Rubinstein's position, however, and in similar arguments advanced in this country by Irving Kristol, Nathan Perlmutter, and Lucy Dawidowicz, among others, that it cannot be dismissed out of hand. Certainly it applies to Britain and Australia, where the combination of hostility on the left and hospitality on the right has persuaded Jews to move, en masse, into the conservative parties.

For a time it looked as though American Jews would follow suit. In 1980 only 45 percent of American Jews voted for Jimmy Carter—the lowest Jewish vote for a Democratic candidate since Franklin D. Roosevelt brought Jews firmly into the Democratic fold; 15 percent of Jews voted for John Anderson in 1980, and 39 percent for Ronald Reagan—a statistic that many took as evidence that the half-century love affair of the Jews with the Democratic party was waning and that a rightward shift was in process. After the 1984 Democratic convention refused to pass a resolution condemning anti-Semitism for fear of offending Jesse Jackson, conservative Jews and non-Jews alike predicted mass Jewish defections to the Republican party. Nor was this mere wishful thinking. In Steven M. Cohen's 1984 National Survey of American Jews, which was taken between April and August of that year, 39 percent of the respondents indicated that they had voted for Reagan in 1980; but when asked whom, in retrospect, they would have preferred to have seen elected, 53 percent chose Reagan. Thus a Jewish Republican majority did seem to be in the offing.

3

It did not happen that way. Exit polls taken the day of the election indicated that no more than 35 percent of American Jews, and perhaps as few as 31 percent, had voted for Reagan; the Jewish vote for Mondale was put at 65–69 percent. Some of the Democratic votes came from normally Democratic Jews who had voted for Anderson in 1980, but analysis of the polls indicated that between 25 and 35 percent of the Jews who had voted for Reagan in 1980 switched to Mondale in 1984.

At first Jewish Republicans denied these findings. They offered their own exit poll, which indicated that 41 percent of the Jewish vote had gone to Reagan, and they claimed that the newspaper and TV network exit polls were biased, that Orthodox and other conservative Jews were underrepresented. "I cannot see any way that Reagan could have gotten less than 40 percent," Ben Waldman, director of the National Jewish Coalition for Reagan-Bush, declared. "The numbers that the networks were reporting . . . were far below what we knew in our hearts to be true." "They have a lot of explaining to do," one of his Democratic counterparts acidly replied.

The explanation did not wash; the president's own pollster, Richard Wirthlin, put the Jewish vote for Reagan at 34 percent—just one point above the average of the four leading exit polls. And William Schneider of the American Enterprise Institute, one of the most respected public-opinion analysts, pointed out that if the Jewish Republican criticisms were correct, the exit polls must have understated the Jewish vote for Reagan in 1980 as well, since they used the same techniques. Whatever polls one uses, therefore (and Schneider considers the network exit polls to be more reliable than the one commissioned by Waldman), the Jewish vote for Reagan was lower in 1984 than in 1980. The decline was all the more striking in view of the fact that the only other group that gave fewer votes to Reagan in 1984 than in 1980 were the unemployed. In 1984, moreover, proportionately more Jews than Hispanics voted for Mondale; only blacks gave him a greater proportion of their vote.

To some Jewish conservatives the lopsided vote for Mondale was evidence of myopia at best and self-hatred at worst. In a bitter lecture delivered four weeks later the historian Lucy Dawidowicz accused Jews who had voted for Mondale of having "voted with the opposition, as it were—with those groups in America who have little stake in the country's future, with groups who are not our allies but our enemies." Indeed, Jews who voted for Mondale "voted for the party with a direct line to the PLO through Jesse Jackson and Jack Odell [Jackson's chief foreign policy adviser]," and "put the marginal issue of prayer in the school ahead of Israel's survival."*

Dawidowicz's intemperate language aside, did Jews vote against

* Mrs. Dawidowicz apparently had second thoughts about her diatribe. In a far more temperate version of the speech published in *Commentary*, in which she offered a reasoned (and reasonable) argument on behalf of a Jewish shift to the right, Dawidowicz replaced the arguments quoted above with this statement: "The lopsided Jewish voting pattern resembled that of the blacks, the unemployed, and persons in households earning under $10,000 a year, even though Jews in no way resemble those groups or share their social and political interests."

their real group interests? That they voted against their *class* interest seems clear enough; people with comparable incomes, at any rate, voted for Reagan by margins of better than two to one. But American Jews have rarely voted their pocketbooks, for they rarely have defined their group interests in economic terms; political and social concerns have been far more important. When Jews pose that perennial question "Is it good for the Jews?," the subject is not taxes or government spending but Israel's well-being and security, or anti-Semitism, or the impact of school prayer or of affirmative-action quotas on Jewish security in the United States. These, in fact, are the grounds on which Irving Kristol and Lucy Dawidowicz have built their case for a Jewish shift to the Republican party.

Why, then, did Jews vote as they did? In William Schneider's opinion there are two reasons: "One is Walter Mondale. The other is Ronald Reagan." Jewish voters tend to be traditional Democrats, Schneider explains, "and Mondale, the 'son of Hubert,' is exactly the kind of traditional Democrat they feel comfortable with." The long Jewish allegiance to the Democratic party, that is to say, is more visceral than ideological; Jews feel far more comfortable—far more at home—in the Democratic than in the Republican party.

The reasons are rooted in Jews' continuing, if vestigial, sense of marginality. For all their affluence and achievements, Jews are not (or not yet) part of the middle- and upper-class social world to which the majority of Republican leaders belong. In most cities "five-o'clock shadow," as it is called, still governs social relations between Jews and Gentiles; however much they may mix during the working day, Jews and Gentiles generally go their separate ways when the workday is over. And, as we have seen, even when Jews are admitted to once restricted clubs, they continue to socialize with other Jews for fear of being rejected.

The Democratic party, in contrast, with its traditional hospitality to non-WASP ethnic groups, is far more *haimish* (warm and informal), to use the Yiddish term. And as Leo Rosten points out, Jews place a high value on being *haimish*. It would be hard to exaggerate the significance of this fact; because of it, sophisticated Jews often voted for Mondale despite major differences with his platform.

ITEM: A distinguished economist who strongly disagreed with Mondale's economic policies voted for him nonetheless. "I watched the conventions on television," he explained, "and the Republicans did not look like my kind of people." That same reaction led many Jews to vote for Carter in 1980 despite their dislike of him; "I'd rather live in a country governed by the faces I saw at the Democratic convention than by those I saw at the Republican convention," a well-known author told me.

Ronald Reagan contributed to this visceral reaction through his embrace of the Christian right—an embrace that more than offset Jews' fear of Jesse Jackson. In its exit poll, for example, ABC News asked people to check the one item that best described what they disliked about the candidate they voted against; 23 percent of the Jews, compared to 7 percent of the population at large, indicated that they voted against Reagan because he "mixes politics with religion." In another poll 78 percent of the Jews, compared to 46 percent of the national electorate, indicated an unfavorable opinion of the Reverend Jerry Falwell, the best-known leader of the Christian right. Indeed, more Jewish voters indicated an unfavorable opinion of Falwell than of Jesse Jackson, and "the Falwell factor," as pollsters called it, cut deeper than "the Jackson factor." Whereas three Jewish Mondale voters in five were "strongly influenced" by Reagan's church-state views, only one Reagan voter in three said the same about Jesse Jackson's role in the Democratic campaign.

From a Jewish Republican standpoint the problem was one of timing. "Had Jesse Jackson and the Democratic Party's opportunistic insouciance been an autumn rather than a summer story, and the Separation of Church and State summer rather than autumn headlines," Nathan Perlmutter has written, "that 53 percent figure [the proportion of Jews saying that, in retrospect, they would have voted for Reagan in 1980] would likely have been a more nearly realized omen." But "Jesse Jackson's summer antics, and Mondale's glazed view of them, cooled in November's memory." Perlmutter has a point. In the spring and summer, when Cohen's 1984 National Survey of American Jews was taken, 74 percent of American Jews thought that Jesse Jackson was anti-Semitic; by election day, according to the *Los Angeles Times* exit poll, the proportion holding an unfavorable opinion of Jackson (and viewing someone as anti-Semitic is about as unfavorable as a Jew can get) had dropped to 58 percent.

But fickle memories and accidents of timing tell us why fear of Jackson faded, not why fear of Falwell loomed so large. "American Jews, so many of whose parents and grandparents fled religious persecution, have more in common with each other in their shared wariness of True Believers than they do in their modes of religious observance," Perlmutter explains. "No matter that some who invoked 'Christian' values in their political rhetoric intended it as a synonym for uncontroversial moral values, it was heard by many Jews as the language of separatism." Because in the past anti-Semitism had been "propounded by religious zealots in the accents of Christian conceit, large numbers of Jews reacted tropistically"—that is, with a Pavlovian-like response to a stimulus devoid of its original referents; "in their polling booths, they fled." In this instance, Perlmutter seems to be saying, Jews voted as they did because their memories were too long!

Clearly something is missing. An explanation that holds on the one hand that Jews were too forgetful and on the other that they were too committed to atavistic memories cannot be the entire story. To explain the Jewish vote that way is to misconstrue what happened and thus to make more difficult a badly needed reformulation of Jewish views on church-state matters.

Why, then, did the church-state issue cut so deeply?

For the members of my generation, certainly, it was not memories of the Cossacks, still less of the Inquisition, that led so many of us to vote Democratic; it was the memory of the United States of our own childhood. Specifically, it was the recollection of a United States that was, indeed, a Christian society—more precisely, perhaps, a white Protestant society. It was a society, moreover, in which the omnipresent Christian symbols—the prayers we recited in school, the New Testament lessons that were read to us, the Christian hymns and carols we sang (who were the "they," we wondered, in "They nailed Him to the cross"), the crèches on public property—drove home to us that we were, indeed, "guests," or strangers, in someone else's country. It was, in short, as I described in Chapter Two, a world in which religious and ethnic differences were frowned upon, a world in which the editors of *Fortune* could doubt that "this eternal stranger" could be absorbed into American society, because, as they put it, even the most assimilated Jews were "still subtly but recognizably different."

For many Jews, therefore, "separation of church and state" is not (certainly not merely) a constitutional issue; it is a metaphor for religious and cultural pluralism, for a society in which Christian symbols and rhetoric are sufficiently muted for Jews to be accepted as full and equal members. When leaders of the Christian right talk about "Christianizing America," therefore, Jews hear it as a call to return to the time when Jews were tolerated rather than accepted. And when a pastor delivering an invocation at the Republican convention called the Republicans "the "Prayer Party," or the president called those who differ with him on church-state matters "intolerant of religion," a great many Jews concluded that their old suspicion of the Republican party was correct—that a country governed by a Democratic administration was, indeed, more likely to be hospitable to Jews than one governed by Republicans.

It is more complicated still. Support for separation of church and state is part of a larger set of attitudes often referred to as "cultural liberalism." A more accurate term, the political scientists Seymour Martin Lipset and Earl Raab suggest, would be "cultural tolerance." American Jews are committed to cultural tolerance because of their belief—one firmly rooted in history—that Jews are safe only in a society acceptant of a wide range of attitudes and behaviors, as well as a diversity of religious and ethnic groups. It is this belief, for example, not approval of homosexuality, that leads an overwhelming majority of American Jews to endorse "gay rights" and to take a liberal stance on most other so-called "social issues."

It is this belief too, and not any commitment to "secular humanism," still less to pornography, abortion, or other fundamentalist targets, that makes many Jews feel threatened by the Christian right. When Jerry Falwell calls the American Civil Liberties Union "the single most destructive threat to our traditional American way of life," for example, and refers to its leaders as "thugs," liberal Jews shiver—less because they are enamored of the ACLU than because Falwell's strident language seems to bespeak intolerance (and, if he were to gain power, repression) of unpopular points of view.

There is ample precedent in American history for this fear. "Committed to the principle of religious freedom and the voluntary method," the church historian Robert T. Handy has written, "the leaders of the thrust to make America Christian usually failed to sense how coercive their efforts appeared to those who did not share their premises. It was hard for them not to view their opponents as agents of evil, for they were convinced that they were unequivocally on the side of the good." And as Lipset and Raab explain, "Jews can reasonably feel threatened by a climate of factional politics in which deadly political extremism is bred."

The extremism, it must be confessed, is not limited to one side; nor is the strident language. "It is no coincidence that the rise of right-wing Christian fundamentalism has been accompanied by the most serious outbreak of anti-Semitism in America since World War II," Rabbi Alexander Schindler—normally one of the most thoughtful and soft-spoken of men—told the trustees of the Union of American Hebrew Congregations shortly after the 1980 election. "I do not say that the Jerry Falwells are deliberately fomenting anti-Jewish sentiments and violence," Schindler added. "But I do say that their preachments have that effect . . . there should be no surprise when synagogues are destroyed by arson and Jewish families are terrorized in their homes."

It was not Rabbi Schindler's proudest moment. For one thing, the "outbreak of anti-Semitism" to which he referred—a sudden increase in acts of vandalism against synagogues and other Jewish institutions—was cause for concern but not for alarm. Most of it consisted of petty acts of vandalism by unorganized young people of high school age; none of it could be attributed to increased political activity by right-wing fundamentalists. There are more than enough grounds for disagreeing with the agenda of the Christian right without accusing its leaders of anti-Semitism—which Falwell, in particular, has taken great pains to avoid.

Curiously, this fact has escaped the notice of most American Jews.

ITEM: In Steven M. Cohen's 1984 National Survey of American Jews respondents were asked whether "most," "many," "some," or "few" members of each of a number of groups were anti-Semitic; 46 percent indicated their belief that "most" or "many" fundamentalist Protestants are anti-Semitic—the highest level of anti-Semitism attributed to any group except blacks.

There was a time when this perception may have been valid; a 1964 survey did indicate that Protestant fundamentalists were more anti-Semitic than Catholics and "mainstream" Protestants.* But this is not the case now; a 1981 survey indicated only slight differences in the level of anti-Semitism expressed by fundamentalists and by other Christians. One reason the difference has narrowed is that the educational gap between fundamentalists and nonfundamentalists has also narrowed. A more important reason would appear to be the admiration for Israel that has emerged since 1967, especially in the South, where fundamentalists are most heavily concentrated.

Despite their deep attachment to Israel, American Jews are blissfully unaware of this change and of the strongly pro-Israel stand that Falwell and most other evangelical and fundamentalist Protestant leaders have taken.

ITEM: In his 1983 survey Cohen asked respondents whether each of a number of groups was "generally friendly, mixed or neutral, or generally unfriendly to Israel." By subtracting the proportion who answered "generally unfriendly" from the proportion saying "generally friendly," he constructed an index by which we can compare the way in which different groups are perceived. Democrats were considered the most friendly to Israel, with a rating of plus 60; blacks, rated minus 41, were seen as the most hostile. Evangelical Protestants ranked near the bottom of the list with a rating of only plus 3—even

* I have written "may have been" rather than "were" because serious questions have been raised about the validity of the 1964 survey that indicated that fundamentalists were more anti-Semitic than other groups.

lower than mainstream Protestants, most of whose national bodies have taken strongly anti-Israel stands since 1967!

Jewish communal leaders, by contrast, who were queried separately in 1983, were well aware of the Evangelicals' pro-Israel stance, giving them a rating of plus 63. (The leaders were more accurate than the rank and file in all their assessments.) Not surprisingly, the heads of some Zionist and Orthodox groups have embraced Falwell; others—at the American Jewish Committee and the Anti-Defamation League—have tried to steer a middle course, working with evangelical and fundamentalist leaders on matters pertaining to Israel and to Jewish-Christian relations while opposing them on school prayer and other social issues.

Most liberal Jewish leaders, however, have been reluctant to enter an alliance with the Christian right, even on Israel, and have kept their distance—and their suspicions. Fundamentalist support of Israel is unreliable, they argue—perhaps even undesirable—because it stems from fundamentalist theology—that is, the belief that restoration of the Jews to the Holy Land is the precursor of the Second Coming of Christ and thus to the Jews' ultimate acceptance of and conversion to Christianity.

It is a puzzling position for Jews to take; as Irving Kristol rightly notes, "It is their theology, but our Israel." More to the point, perhaps, distaste for mainstream Protestants' theologically-based animus toward Israel has not kept Jewish organizations from working with them on domestic issues; nor has black anti-Semitism prevented Jews from seeking—and gaining—the support of black congressmen when aid to Israel is up for a vote. Just how counterproductive the liberal Jewish position is can be seen, Kristol argues, "by asking the question: how significant would it be for American Jews if the Moral Majority were *anti*-Israel? The answer is easy and inescapable: it would be of major significance. Indeed, it would be generally regarded by Jews as a very alarming matter." "Today, the fundamentalists are on our side," Oscar Cohen, a retired Anti-Defamation League executive, remarks, "but if Jews work hard enough at it, they won't be."

4

None of this means that Jews should abandon the Democratic party and move, en masse, to the right. It is certainly true that support from the Moral Majority and other fundamentalist groups is important to Israel's well-being, as is support from liberal and moderate Republicans; the strength of the close ties between Israel and the United States is a function of the bipartisan backing those ties receive.

But if right-wing support for Israel is necessary, it hardly is sufficient; indeed, too much reliance on fundamentalist support could backfire, leading to an eventual and serious reduction in U.S. aid to Israel. Most of the liberal senators and representatives who have been placed on right-wing "hit lists" have been strong supporters of Israel, and some who have been elected in their stead have been equally strong opponents. Indeed, the darling of the Christian right is North Carolina Senator Jesse Helms, who is generally regarded as Israel's most implacable Senate foe—so much so that some of the most conservative Jewish Republicans contributed to the campaign of Governor Jim Hunt, Helms's unsuccessful opponent in the 1984 election. And although it would be a mistake to put too much weight on how people voted on the 1981 AWACs sale to Saudi Arabia—it is politically costly for Republican senators to oppose a Republican president, especially one who has put his prestige on the line—the fact remains that, almost without exception, senators sympathetic to the Christian right voted for the sale, whereas the congressional black delegation voted solidly against it.

This last fact is relevant in other ways. Kristol and Dawidowicz urge Jews to move to the right not only to gain the Moral Majority's support for Israel but because—so they argue—black anti-Semitism has made the Democratic party hostile (indeed, dangerous) to Jewish interests.

They are wrong. What is extraordinary, given the rise in black anti-Semitism described above, is that the black-Jewish congressional coalition has remained strong, as have the alliances with black mayors such as Thomas Bradley in Los Angeles and W. Wilson Goode in Philadelphia. There are exceptions, of course, such as Detroit congressmen John Conyers and George Crockett, who are active PLO supporters. But most successful black politicians recognize that they need coalitions with Jews if they are to achieve their own goals—and black voters show remarkably little interest in the pro-PLO antics of some of their leaders. The most striking illustration of this fact came in Berkeley, California, where in the 1984 presidential primary, black voters resoundingly voted for Jesse Jackson and against "Proposition E," which would have called upon the president to reduce American aid to Israel by an "amount equal to . . . what Israel spends annually on settlements in the occupied territories" of the West Bank, Gaza Strip, and Golan Heights. Indeed, the vote against the measure was only marginally lower in black precincts than it was in white neighborhoods.

This is not to deny the real threat posed by Jackson and his supporters; it is precisely *because* of that threat that it would be harmful for Jews to abandon the Democratic party. As W. D. Rubinstein acknowledges, one of the ways in which the United States is different from other democratic countries is that the ideological left has never played a significant role in American politics; unlike the British Labour party, for example, the Democratic party has actively avoided ideology in favor of pragmatic coalition politics.

Until now. What makes Jackson dangerous is not that he is likely to gain control of the party but that, through a coalition with other radical and dissident groups, he may push the party into an ideological, Third World stance on foreign policy. Jews are not alone in seeking to prevent this kind of change, but given their prominence in Democratic party organization and finances, their presence may be crucial in holding the party to its traditional anti-Communist views. For Jews to abandon the Democratic party, therefore, is to run the risk that it will go the way of the British and Australian Labour parties—a change that would be disastrous to Jewish interests.

There are other reasons as well for remaining Democrats. If the absence of a strong ideological left makes the United States different, the presence of a great many religious, ethnic, and racial groups, living in relative harmony with one another, makes it unique. (The English, who once spoke derisively of American racism, have discovered how difficult harmonious race relations can be.) It is that harmony, moreover, that permits American Jews to be as secure as they are; nothing would be more threatening to Jewish security than governmental policies that create or contribute to intergroup tensions. This, and not aid to Israel, is the real reason Jews seek to maintain—or restore—a close working relationship with black Americans. It is also why most Jewish neoconservatives—intellectuals such as Seymour Martin Lipset, Earl Raab, Nathan Glazer, Ben Wattenberg, and Daniel Bell—remain firmly committed to the Hubert Humphrey–"Scoop" Jackson wing of the Democratic party; for the Democratic domestic agenda is far more likely than the Republican agenda to maintain that harmony.

So is the Democratic commitment to separation of church and state. True, the danger from the right is not nearly as great as liberal Jewish rhetoric sometimes implies; exposure to the national scene is likely to temper the language and perhaps even the positions presented by fundamentalist leaders. That fundamentalist leaders can and do become sensitized to Jewish concerns is evident from the experience of the Reverend Bailey Smith, former president of the Southern Baptist Convention. "It is interesting, at great political rallies, how you have a Protestant to pray, a Catholic to pray, and then you have a Jew to pray," Smith declared at a widely publicized briefing for evangelicals during the 1980 presidential campaign. "With all due respect to those dear people," Smith continued, "God Almighty does not hear the prayer of a Jew. For how in the world can God hear the prayer of a Jew, or how in the world can God hear the prayer of a man who says that Jesus Christ is not the true Messiah? That is blasphemy."

Coming from a religiously homogeneous community of thirty thousand, Smith was mystified by the storm of criticism that greeted his remark. It was, after all, a simple statement of religious belief; as he explained the next day, "No prayer gets through that is not prayed through Jesus Christ." To Smith, moreover, there was nothing anti-Semitic about his statement. "I am pro-Jew. I believe they are God's special people," he declared; but special or not, "Without Jesus Christ they are lost."

What was noteworthy about Bailey Smith was not the view he expressed—it is widely shared—but the fact that he expressed it in public. Someone more familiar with the rules of religious discourse in the United States would have avoided such a straightforward claim in a meeting covered by the national press and graced by the presence of the Republican candidate for president. To avoid public statements of one's belief when that belief may give offense to others is an expression not of hypocrisy but of civility. The fundamental tenet of American civil (or public) religion—"the religion of civility," as John Murray Cuddihy calls it—is a willingness to surrender in public the claims one makes in private, in order to avoid offending members of other faiths.* To be "religiously sensitive to religious differences," Cuddihy writes—to be aware of how one's own religious claims appear to others—"is to practice the religion of civility." The "fear of offending against its canons," he adds, "makes cowards of us all."

It also makes Americans of us all. Specifically, what makes American pluralism work—what enables us to maintain a sense of national unity while preserving our religious differences—is that people who believe (indeed, people who *know*) that theirs is the only true religion act as if they accepted the legitimacy of other religions. As the Jesuit theologian John Courtney Murray, the foremost Catholic exponent of religious pluralism, expressed the paradox: "Religious pluralism is against the will of God. But it is the human condition; it is written

* Claims of possessing the exclusive route to God are not unique with Protestant fundamentalists. As Lucy Dawidowicz points out, Jewish fundamentalists claim the same knowledge of what God will and will not hear. Each year, a week or two before Rosh Hashanah, the chief rabbi of Jerusalem warns that city's residents that God will not hear the shofar (ram's horn) if it is blown in a Conservative synagogue. And in this country no less an authority than Rabbi Joseph B. Soleveitchik has declared in effect that God will not hear the prayers of any Jew who worships in a synagogue in which men and women sit together.

into the script of human history." However much Americans may believe that theirs is the only route to God, therefore, they have learned to behave as if members of every other religion have equal access to Him. And in religious matters, as the historian Martin Marty has put it, we are "a nation of behavers" rather than of believers.

We are also a nation of fast learners; for that reason, and because he is a warm and decent man, it did not take long for Bailey Smith to be inducted into the religion of civility. Three months after his controversial statement Smith and some colleagues met with officials of the Anti-Defamation League at the League's headquarters in New York. "The Rev. Smith expressed deep regret for any hurt to the Jewish community and stands with them for an American pluralistic society and against anti-Semitism," a joint press release declared. "He also said that if he had to do it over, knowing how it would be misinterpreted, he would not have made those statements. He said he has distinctive theological beliefs that he cannot compromise, but he stands with the Jewish community for total religious liberty."

Bailey Smith stands with the Jewish community in support of Israel as well, having visited that country in the company of Anti-Defamation League officials. "He is a genuine friend of Israel *and* of the Jewish people," Rabbi Yechiel Eckstein, former codirector of interreligious affairs for the ADL has written. "And while he might still maintain that God does not answer the prayers of those who do not call out to Him through Jesus . . . I believe him when he says that he would 'go to the death for the right of Jews to pray as they wish' [emphasis in original]."

In the absolutist position Jewish liberals take on church-state issues, moreover, they sometimes sound as extreme (and at times as intolerant) as the fundamentalists they oppose. One reason is a failure to distinguish the general question of the relation between religion and politics from the specific questions involved in the debate over abortion, school prayer, and other church-state issues—a failure to recognize that Ronald Reagan was right when he said that religion and politics are inseparable and wrong when he advocated a return to school prayer. There is, in fact, no way of preventing people's religious commitments from influencing their political views; nor would it be desirable if it could be done.

The result is a double standard that infuriates people on the right—and in the center as well. Specifically, liberals who hailed Martin Luther King as a moral leader and marveled at his use of biblical language—liberals who applaud the Catholic bishops for their stand on nuclear disarmament or on the government's role in relieving poverty—reject, *on principle*, the right of the bishops to oppose abortion or Falwell's right to advocate school prayer. In doing so they sometimes sound as coercive as the fundamentalists they oppose—witness the warnings to New York's Bishop O'Connor that his attacks on Geraldine Ferraro might cause a rise in anti-Catholic prejudice. In presenting their own views, moreover, liberal "separationists" come through all too often as intolerant—indeed, derogatory—of their opponents' religious beliefs. Witness Norman Lear's sarcastic references to Ronald Reagan as the nation's "Evangelist-in-Chief" and his ridiculing of Reagan's apparent fundamentalist beliefs.

ITEM: From a letter by Norman Lear soliciting contributions for the Action Fund of People for the American Way: "You can hear the 'Evangelist-in-Chief' in him at work in the administration's 'good vs. evil' foreign policy. And in his *alarming* statement . . . that 'within the covers of that single Book [the Bible] are *all* the answers to all the problems that face us today . . .' *It is worrisome indeed that the 'Evangelist-in-Chief' 's ultra-fundamentalist theology may affect this nation's nuclear arms policies* [emphasis in original]." But so far as I am aware, Lear has not condemned the nuclear arms policy proposed by the Catholic bishops—a policy equally dependent on a particular theology.

The rules of civility, in short, apply to both sides. It merely blurs the issue, moreover, when liberals claim, as Lear does, that their goal is to prevent "the mixture of religion and politics." Like it or not, they are inescapably mixed. What is really at issue, as the Lutheran theologian Richard John Neuhaus argues, is whether we can devise ways of mixing religion and politics that will strengthen rather than weaken our pluralistic society.

Unfortunately, the approach Neuhaus himself proposes would have the opposite effect, for once again it would make Jews strangers in their own land. In attacking the concept (and to his view, reality) of "the naked public square," as he calls it—a politics devoid of religious values—Neuhaus poses a false dichotomy: that the choice is between a wholly secular society, in which there is no transcendent basis for moral values, and an explicitly Christian society. It is "obvious," he writes, "that this is, as the Supreme Court said in 1931, a Christian people," and "that this fact ought, somehow, to make a difference. It is not an embarrassment to be denied or disguised."

But those are not the only choices. "There is a clear distinction to be drawn between 'God' and 'Jesus' in our public affairs," the conservative columnist James J. Kilpatrick wrote in criticizing a 1984 Supreme Court decision permitting the erection of a crèche on public property. "Every religion, so far as I know, acknowledges a god," Kilpatrick continued, but "the birth of Jesus . . . is an article of peculiarly Christian faith. . . . Our government must not be hostile to religion . . . But [it] has no business promoting the divinity of Jesus Christ. The government's business is to govern, and to leave religion to the churches, the temples, and to the people themselves."

Kilpatrick's position leaves ample room for disagreement. He believes, for example, that the courts should permit "voluntary prayers" in public schools. But because children are so much more susceptible than adults to ridicule or coercion, voluntary school prayer seems to me to be more threatening to religious pluralism than a crèche in a public park. Disagreements over school prayer or other church-state issues need not be divisive, however, if conservatives like Kilpatrick set the terms of the debate.

5

To sum up, then: American Jews are secure—secure enough, in fact, to risk displeasing a second-term Republican president by remaining liberal Democrats. If there is a danger, it comes from within—from a new parochialism that leads many communal leaders to turn inward and focus exclusively on Jewish concerns. The principal manifestation of this "ominous 'narrowing' within Jewish life," as Lipset and Rabb call it, is the growth of a new and aggressive brand of single-interest politics. Most Jewish PACs, for example, distribute their funds to congressional candidates according to a single criterion: support (in many cases, unconditional support) for Israel.

What is at issue, let it be understood, is not particularism versus universalism; it is how best to serve particularist Jewish interests in the United States of the 1980s. Exclusive preoccupation with Israel, or with a narrowly defined Jewish agenda, constitutes a kind of self-ghettoization of Jewish public life, one that runs a real risk of sacrificing long-run support for short-run gains. The reason, Lipset and Rabb explain, is that the political influence of Jews has stemmed in large measure from their active involvement in business, professional, and communal associations. "By dint of this activity," they write, "Jewish individuals have become 'influentials' in the general community," and "as a *consequence,* have become *political* influentials" as well [emphasis in original].

It is the "networks" that grow out of becoming an "influential"—the friendships and associations with others that Jews gain through their involvement in non-Jewish organizations and causes—that form the basis of the coalitions on which Jewish interests depend. Jewish political power, to put it differently, is generated when Jews are concerned not only with the Jewish agenda itself but with the larger issues of American political and communal life. For Jews to withdraw from those concerns and focus on their own agenda alone is to risk—almost to guarantee—a serious reduction in political influence.

Let me end, as I began, on a personal note. Before the twelve spies set out on their trip to survey the Promised Land, a rabbinic legend tells us, Moses instructed them on how they should proceed and, more important, on what they should look for. "Look about carefully what manner of land it is, for some lands produce strong people and some weak," he told the spies. "If you find the inhabitants dwelling in open places, then know that they are mighty warriors, and have no fear of hostile attack. If, however, they live in fortified places, they are weaklings and, in their fear of strangers, seek shelter behind their walls."

The future of American Judaism will ultimately depend on the ability of my fellow Jews to discern what manner of land it is in which we dwell. The choice is clear: whether, through fear of strangers, we live like weaklings behind walls of our own construction or whether we have the courage to live like mighty warriors in this great open place we call the United States.

AFTERWORD

"Speaking Truth to Power"

In one of the most widely reproduced photographs of the Holocaust, taken the day the slave labor camp at Buchenwald was liberated in 1945, twenty-four skeletal figures, lying in cage-like bunks, stare at the camera. Forty years later, in a White House ceremony carried live by every TV network, the president of the United States presented the Congressional Gold Medal of Achievement, the highest honor the American government can give a civilian, to one of the survivors in that photograph, the writer/lecturer/teacher Elie Wiesel. When he came to the podium to accept, the still-gaunt Wiesel, now fifty-seven, did something virtually unheard of in American life: he "spoke truth to power," as Jewish tradition demands, firmly but respectfully chiding the president for his planned trip to the military cemetery in Bitburg, Germany, which contains the graves of forty-seven members of the Waffen SS. "That place, Mr. President, is not your place. Your place is with the victims of the SS," Wiesel told the president, urging him "to do something else, to find another way, another site." As *Newsweek* commented, it "was surely one of the more remarkable moments in the annals of the White House."

It was surely the most remarkable moment in the annals of American Jewry—so much so that I felt impelled to add this epilogue after the rest of the book had gone to press. "Think of the cabinet members over the decades who—after resigning over a policy dispute—have stood before the cameras and announced that they were leaving government because of their health or their desire to practice law," the journalist M. J. Rosenberg suggested, delineating what it was that made the moment unique. "Think of all the people who, determined to address a president on a moral issue, backed off as the aura of the White House stifled their protest." Because of that aura, some of the most prominent Jewish political and communal leaders pressured Wiesel to back off. "Never criticize the *poritz* [czar]," some told him, in the traditional Eastern European Jewish formulation. Others urged silence on political grounds: "We have a long agenda," they explained. Important items on it—in particular, an additional $1.5 billion in U.S. aid to Israel—might be jeopardized. "And besides," they added, the old fear showing, "we have to live with Reagan for another three and a half years."

Wiesel held firm. "I understood that we would have to mend fences after the Bitburg visit," he told me three weeks later. "But not before. Compromise was impossible; Jewish dignity was at stake." At stake too was the meaning—indeed, the very memory—of the Holocaust, to which Wiesel has devoted his adult life. Nor could a confrontation with the president himself be avoided: this was no decision made by others, to which he had passively consented. On the contrary, Mr. Reagan's explanations of his itinerary had been more offensive than the trip itself.

ITEM: The German people have "a guilt feeling that's been imposed on them, and I think it's unnecessary," Reagan told his March 21 press conference, in defense of his decision not to visit the Dachau concentration camp as expected. He went on to say that he was not interested in "reawakening the memories and so forth."

ITEM: On April 18, Holocaust Remembrance Day, the president defended his trip to Bitburg by arguing that the soldiers who died serving the Nazi regime "were victims, just as surely as the victims in the concentration camps," an argument he repeated to a second audience. Twelve days later he insisted that "it is morally right to do what I am doing."

Not since the Six-Day War have American Jews felt so assaulted—or so determined to speak out. Even those leaders who had urged silence on Wiesel felt obliged to criticize the president, and some of Reagan's most ardent supporters made passionate public attacks. At a luncheon meeting of the Conference of Presidents of Major Jewish

Organizations, at which its chairman, Kenneth Bialkin, explained that his criticism of the president was made more in sorrow than in anger, the principal speaker, *Commentary* editor Norman Podhoretz, began by saying that he spoke in anger, *not* in sorrow, for this was no casual or minor error on the president's part. "What makes the Bitburg incident so serious," Podhoretz later wrote in his syndicated newspaper column, "is that it undermines the very foundation on which Mr. Reagan's foreign policy . . . has hitherto stood: the idea that there is something special, something unique, about totalitarian states. . . . By proposing to lay a wreath at a military cemetery in which Nazi stormtroopers lie buried, Mr. Reagan is for all practical purposes treating Nazi Germany as though it had indeed been just one ordinary nation at war with other ordinary nations."

Jewish dignity was upheld. After the White House ceremony, in fact, almost every reporter and editorial writer commented on Wiesel's respectful tone and gentle manner and the graciousness with which, in *Time*'s phrase, he "lectured [the president] on morality while a national television audience looked on." Wiesel expressed his gratitude to the United States "for having offered us haven and refuge" and paid tribute to "the freest nation in the world, the moral nation." He expressed admiration for the president, as well, and thanked him for his support of Israel and his efforts on behalf of imprisoned Soviet Jews. Wiesel continued: "But, Mr. President, I wouldn't be the person I am, and you wouldn't respect me for what I am, if I were not to tell you also of the sadness that is in my heart. . . . The issue here is not politics, but good and evil. And we must never confuse them."

Ironically, the Reagan administration's inability to understand that distinction led it into what Representative Vin Weber, a leading Congressional conservative, called "an obvious political disaster—the Watergate of symbolism." Although Reagan's own aides defended him and insisted that the Teflon surrounding the president had not been penetrated, those more concerned about the future of the Republican party worried that the party had been tarred with the brush of anti-Semitism and that it might forfeit any chance of gaining Jewish votes in 1988. Weber explained his concern:

> We have had a tremendous chance to move the Jewish community. The Jews had provided most of the talent, brainpower and money for the Democratic party. Many Jews were prepared to vote for Reagan . . . But the Democrats succeeded [in 1984] in making Jerry Falwell and the religious right a centerpiece issue. A lot of Jewish voters got the uneasy feeling that there is a growing anti-Semitic force within the Republican party. I don't believe that's true, but I under-

stand that concern. Then comes Bitburg, many candlepower greater than the Falwell issue.

Presidential pollster Richard Wirthlin expressed the same fear. Mr. Reagan's visit to Bitburg had evoked emotions "stronger than we are able to measure in survey research," he remarked a few days after the president's return—emotions that "go far beyond [questions of] simple political support. I think it has created an emotional tearing that will have some consequences . . . the Jewish community has been strongly alienated . . ." So much so, in fact, that some Republicans worried that their party might abandon any effort to woo the Jews, considering it a lost cause. After Bitburg it may well be.

To their credit, a great many politicians were concerned with more than just the political fallout. "It was a moral disaster," Representative Weber said. "We were shocked that that was not the feeling at the White House." The "we" was more than editorial: in the House of Representatives, 84 Republicans, many of them closely aligned with the president, joined 173 Democrats in a letter urging West German Chancellor Helmut Kohl to give the president a graceful way out by withdrawing his invitation to visit Bitburg. Even more striking, 82 of the 100 members of the Senate, including Republican Majority Leader Robert Dole, voted for a resolution urging the president to bypass Bitburg and "visit a symbol of German democracy" instead.

It was a classic example of American pluralism at work, for members of Congress were not the only ones to respond in this way; there was a similar reaction from the press, the American Legion, and leaders of some religious and ethnic groups. True, at least one Jewish communal leader who actively protested the Bitburg visit was troubled that many Christian leaders did not respond until they were asked; in lending their names to a protest, he told me, the Christians in question seemed to feel that "they were paying off a debt, not addressing a moral issue of concern to them." But as David Gordis, executive vice president of the American Jewish Committee, observed, "Having insisted that the Holocaust was a uniquely Jewish event, we should not be surprised when others do not see it as their issue." And if the church response was not all that Jews might have wished, the Congressional and mass media response was. Indeed, the press was almost unanimous in condemning Reagan's moral obtuseness and the shallowness of his view of history, as well as of morality.

In short, the Reagan administration discovered that even an inadvertent display of insensitivity to Jewish sensibilities carried a heavy price. And it *was* inadvertent; Reagan's intention was not to slight Jews but to pay off a political debt to Chancellor Kohl by helping him with conservative elements in his own party. Neither the president nor his aides had any conception of the anger—and anguish—their decision would cause American Jews in general, and survivors of the Holocaust in particular.

The White House fell into a trap of its own devising because it is out of touch with the changes of the past few decades, whereby the United States has become a genuinely multi-ethnic, multi-racial, and multi-religious society. Indeed, Ronald Reagan is the first president since Herbert Hoover who has not had a Jew as a member of his inner circle, either as a friend and/or political confidant or as a ranking member of the White House staff. Since the day Reagan took office, in fact, no Jew—none, that is to say, who acknowledges his Jewishness (or as an old Washington hand puts it, "no one who would show up at Bill Safire's annual Yom Kippur 'break the fast' party")—has had direct access to the president on matters of this sort. Not even the frustrated leaders of the Jewish Republican Caucus have been able to establish any direct relation with him.

It is not because of anti-Semitism. On the contrary, the administration has been unusually responsive to Jewish concerns, not out of benevolence, to be sure, but because such responsiveness serves its own anti-Soviet stance. Whatever the reasons, however, the administration has provided more aid to Israel than any of its predecessors and has formally acknowledged that that aid stems not from Jewish political power but from Israel's strategic importance to the United States; and it has brought considerable pressure on the Soviet Union to release Jewish "prisoners of conscience" and permit the emigration of Russian Jews. (The administration also played a key role in the rescue of Ethiopian Jewry, but the unsung hero of that episode would appear to be Secretary of State George Shultz.) Nor are Jews absent from other government agencies; both Alexander Haig and George Shultz appointed Jews to high State Department posts. The fact remains that, except in minor posts, there are no Jews in the White House. Nor are there any non-Jewish advisers—men such as Joseph Califano or LBJ adviser John Roche—who are attuned to Jewish sensibilities. "The people around Reagan simply do not know many Jews and they seem to be uncomfortable when Jews are around," a prominent Jewish Republican told me. "I think they are as uncomfortable with me as I am with them," the head of a major Jewish organization told me.

The result was that no one was in a position to counsel the president against the Bitburg visit before he had put his prestige on the line, as Stuart Eizenstat would have done during the Carter administration, Leonard Garment under Nixon, or any of a number of people who were close to Gerald Ford and Lyndon Johnson. Nor was there anyone who could interpret the Jewish reaction and help White House officials understand why it was so intense; hence the administration violated what one Democrat called the first rule of politics: when you find yourself in a hole, stop digging. As an administration official from elsewhere in the government observed, there was a complete "lack of understanding about what this cemetery visit really means to Jews."

For the same reason, there was no one to advise the administration against compounding the problem by adding a visit to Bergen-Belsen to the president's schedule, as if the decision to go to Bitburg, and thus to honor Nazi criminals, was simply an awkward bit of scheduling whose harm could be undone by a political balancing act. As *Washington Post* columnist Richard Cohen wrote:

> The issue then became not one of justice or morality, of remembering history and learning from it, of honoring the survivors and their constant pain, but of numbers and alliances—NATO and Star Wars and Pershing missiles. In a way, this was an echo of the very mentality that is associated with the Holocaust itself—a hierarchy of heartless priorities where always there was something more important than the fate of Jews being killed by Nazis, something, that is, more important than morality itself.

In Germany, the consequences appeared to be everything that Jews had feared; former Nazis, at any rate, took the president's visit to Bitburg as a signal that they had been rehabilitated.

ITEM (From a *New York Times* dispatch, published three days before the Reagan visit): "They stood relaxed, shaking hands, introducing wives, these men of Germany's dark past, looking forward to a three-day meeting that began here today.

"The Hotel Krone . . . where about 250 veterans of the Waffen SS Death's Head Division have gathered, is closed to outsiders. But the veterans, in the loden coats of postwar German prosperity, are more relaxed, less defensive.

"Long the pariahs of West German society for their record of atrocity and brutality during the Third Reich, this year they are returning reporters' telephone calls, and talking, quietly, assuredly. . . . Conversations with the veterans leave no doubt that President Reagan's insistence on going to Bitburg . . . has made them feel better about their role in history. . . . 'It took a long time,' an SS veteran said, 'but this shows we were soldiers, just like the others.' "

ITEM: Visiting the Bitburg cemetery the day after the president and Chancellor Kohl had placed wreaths of reconciliation in front of its chapel, Marvin Kalb reported this scene:

> Six feet to the left of the President's wreath stood an equally impressive one. Across its banner: "To the Waffen SS who fell at Leningrad." No more than a foot to the right of the Chancellor's was another wreath: "For the fallen comrades of the Waffen SS." These two wreaths had been placed in the chapel, out of sight, hours before the president arrived. They were restored to their original places of honor only hours after he left.

Nor were the wreaths the only signs Kalb found that the old Germany was alive and well. "We Germans had been cooperating very well," one Bitburg resident told Kalb, "until the Jews began to make trouble." And his was not an isolated voice. "A number of leading West German politicians and professors—several close to Kohl—think anti-Semitism was on the rise even before Bitburg," Kalb wrote. " 'The Jews were getting too impertinent,' one politician said. . . . 'We've listened to them much too long. It's enough.' "

The reaction in the United States was something else again. True, Elie Wiesel received some virulent hate mail, as did Henry Siegman, executive director of the American Jewish Congress, who led a group to Munich to pay tribute to the graves of the heroes of the anti-Nazi White Rose movement. But a certain amount of hate mail was to be expected, since, as we have seen, there is a residue of anti-Semitism in the United States. "We get that kind of mail every time we burp," an executive of the Anti-Defamation League told me—that is, every time Jews (or the ADL) occupy a prominent place in the news. During and after Bitburg, however, the volume of such mail was no larger and its tone no worse than the norm, nor was there any increase in anti-Semitic incidents or acts of vandalism. "I expected a lot of anti-Semitism," the official told me, "but we're not seeing it." Indeed, reports from the League's thirty offices showed "nothing significant."

In fact, nothing could be more significant than the absence of any significant upturn in anti-Semitism. Not that Bitburg was entirely free of cost; if nothing else, it revealed how vast a gulf still separates the Jewish and non-Jewish world views. But if Gentiles did not always understand why Jews reacted with such intensity—as we have seen, memory plays a different role in Judaism than in Christianity—a large majority supported their right to protest, and roughly half the population opposed the president's visit. For all the pain it brought, therefore, the Bitburg incident demonstrated that for American Jews, the United States is now home as well as haven; once characterized as "eternal strangers," Jews are now natives, free to assert their pain and anger—able and willing to "speak truth to power."

NOTES ON SOURCES

Chapter One
Introduction: The Great Transformation

23
"For the Jew": Mordecai M. Kaplan, *Judaism as a Civilization* (Philadelphia and New York: Jewish Publication Society of America/Reconstructionist Press, 1981), pp. 13–14.
24
"It is seduction": Leonard J. Fein, "The Jewish Community of the 1980s," *Journal of Jewish Communal Studies*, Vol. LVII, No. 1 (Fall 1980), pp. 9–16.

"The central issue": Jacob Neusner, *Stranger at Home* (Chicago: Univ. of Chicago Press, 1981), p. 30.
27
"act of saying I": Quoted in Charles E. Silberman, *Criminal Violence, Criminal Justice* (New York: Random House, 1978), p. ix.

"if you get the right [words]": Tom Stoppard, *The Real Thing* (London and Boston: Faber & Faber, 1983), p. 54.

Chapter Two
". . . and Some Are Born Jews"

28
"To be a Jew": Muriel Rukeyser, *Breaking Open: New Poems by Muriel Rukeyser* (New York: Random House, 1973), p. 62.

"Before the beginning": Mordecai M. Kaplan, *Judaism as a Civilization* (Philadelphia and New York: Jewish Publication Society of America/Reconstructionist Press, 1981), p. 3.

"being Jewish was": Henry Morgenthau III, "The Ways We Were," *Moment,* Vol. 7, No. 4 (April 1982), p. 19.

29

the tenor Jan Peerce: Alan Levy, *Bluebird of Happiness* (New York: Harper & Row, 1976), quoted in Charles S. Liebman, "The Religious Life of American Jewry," in Marshall Sklare, ed., *Understanding American Jewry* (New Brunswick, N.J.: Transaction Books/Brandeis Univ. Center for Modern Jewish Studies, 1982), p. 101.

30

"The Jews are probably": Maurice Samuel, *Jews on Approval* (New York: Liveright, 1932), pp. 9–10.

"There are certain problems of life": Harry Austryn Wolfson, *Escaping Judaism,* Menorah Society Pamphlet No. 2 (New York: Menorah Press, 1922), pp. 1, 50–51.

31ff.

On Heine and the origins of Jewish self-hatred, see Milton Himmelfarb, *The Jews of Modernity* (Philadelphia: Jewish Publication Society of America, 1973), and S. S. Prawer, *Heine's Jewish Comedy* (New York: Oxford Univ. Press, 1983).

For most of its history: See Jacob Katz, *Exclusiveness and Tolerance* (New York: Schocken Books, 1975), and *Out of the Ghetto* (New York: Schocken Books, 1978); H. H. Ben-Sasson, "The Middle Ages," in Ben-Sasson, ed., *A History of the Jewish People* (Cambridge, Mass.: Harvard Univ. Press, 1976).

32

The Metz contest: Arthur Hertzberg, *The French Enlightenment and the Jews* (New York: Columbia Univ. Press, 1968), pp. 328–338.

"implacable enemies": Ibid., p. 329.

"Let us concede": Christian Wilhelm von Dohm, "Concerning the Amelioration of the Civil Status of the Jews," in Paul R. Mendes-Flohr and Jehuda Reinharz, eds., *The Jew in the Modern World* (New York: Oxford Univ. Press, 1980), pp. 27–34.

33

"a nasal duck-like quack": Quoted in Gerson D. Cohen, "State of World Jewry Address," 92nd Street YM–YWHA, 1982, mimeo, p. 33.

"An intellectual who is": Himmelfarb, *The Jews of Modernity*, p. 23.

"I lack the strength": Quoted in Amity Shlaes, "A Life of the Poet as Kibitzer" (review of S. S. Prawer, *Heine's Jewish Comedy*), in *The Wall Street Journal,* Jan. 19, 1984.

"the baptismal certificate": Mendes-Flohr and Reinharz, eds., *The Jew in the Modern World,* pp. 223–224.

Abraham Mendelssohn, in Himmelfarb, *The Jews of Modernity*, p. 28. See also Mendes-Flohr and Reinharz, pp. 222–223.

34

"it was better to be": Himmelfarb, *The Jews of Modernity*, p. 43.

"little stepfather land": Shlaes, "A Life of the Poet as Kibitzer."

Schleiermacher's warning: Katz, *Out of the Ghetto*, p. 123.

35

"Having love": Quoted in John Murray Cuddihy, *The Ordeal of Civility* (New York: Basic Books, 1974), p. 14; Helene Deutsch anecdote, Cuddihy, p. 23.

"The politeness which I practice": Sigmund Freud, *The Interpretation of Dreams,* quoted in Cuddihy, p. 17.

36

"A Galician Jew": Sigmund Freud, *Jokes and Their Relation to the Unconscious* (New York: W. W. Norton, 1960), pp. 80–81. See also Theodor Reik, *Jewish Wit* (New York: Gamut Press, 1962), p. 58, and Cuddihy, pp. 21–22.

"an avenue of flight": Jean-Paul Sartre, *Anti-Semite and Jew* (New York: Schocken Books, 1948), pp. 110–111.

37

"Do you know how it feels": Mendes-Flohr and Reinharz, eds., *The Jew in the Modern World*, p. 237.

"It is there all the time": Quoted in Jacob Neusner, *Stranger at Home* (Chicago: Univ. of Chicago Press, 1981), p. 54.

Over the preceding 2500 years: Gerson D. Cohen, "The Blessing of Assimilation in Jewish History," commencement address, Hebrew Teachers College, Boston, June 1966. See also Yehezkel Kaufman, "The Biblical Age," Ralph Marcus, "The Hellenistic Age," Gerson D. Cohen, "The Talmudic Age," and Abraham Halkin, "The Judeo-Islamic Age," in, resp., Leo W. Schwarz, *Great Ages and Ideas of the Jewish People* (New York: Modern Library, 1956); Salo Wittmayer Baron, *A Social and Religious History of the Jews*, 2d ed., rev. and enl. (New York and Philadelphia: Columbia Univ. Press and Jewish Publication Society of America, 1952), esp. Vol. 1, Chap. 1; Jacob Neusner, *Stranger at Home,* Chaps. 2 and 3; Neusner, ed., *Take Judaism, for Example* (Chicago and London: Univ. of Chicago Press, 1983). I am indebted to my former research associate Professor Shulamit Magnus, of the Reconstructionist Rabbinical College, for her insightful research memoranda and for helping to guide me through the historical literature.

38

"all that is new": Charles Liebman, "Religion and the Chaos of Modernity: The Case of Contemporary Judaism," in Neusner, ed., *Take Judaism, for Example,* esp. pp. 150 ff. On the Orthodox, Reform, and Zionist responses, see also Neusner, *Between Time and Eternity: The Essentials of Judaism* (Encino and Belmont, Cal.: Dickenson Publishing Co., 1975), Chap. 3. On the Zionist response, see Arthur Hertzberg, Introduction, in Hertzberg, ed., *The Zionist Idea* (New York: Atheneum–Temple Books, 1979), pp. 16–100.

"The Judaism of the Galut": Jacob Klatzkin, "Boundaries," in Hertzberg, ed., *The Zionist Idea*, p. 322.

"We have no history": Haim Hazaz, "The Sermon," in James A. Michener, ed., *First Fruits* (Philadelphia: Jewish Publication Society of America, 1973), p. 142.

39

"Was the Jew": Joseph Hayyim Brenner, "Self-Criticism," in Hertzberg, ed., *The Zionist Idea,* p. 311.

Samson Raphael Hirsch: Quoted in Neusner, *Between Time and Eternity,* pp. 142–144.

"To the Jews as a nation": The Count of Clermont-Tonnerre, during the French National Assembly debate over the eligibility of Jews for citizenship, quoted in Mendes-Flohr and Reinharz, eds., *The Jew in the Modern World,* p. 104.

40

"When they crossed the Atlantic": Seymour Martin Lipset, *The First New Nation* (New York: W. W. Norton, 1979), Chap. 4. See also Alexis de Tocqueville, *Democracy in America* (New York: Vintage Books, 1961), esp. Vol. I, pp. 310–326; Abraham J. Karp, *Haven and Home* (New York: Schocken Books, 1985), and *Golden Door to America* (New York: Penguin Books, 1977); Arthur A. Goren, *The American Jews* (Cambridge, Mass.: Belknap Press of Harvard Univ. Press, 1982); Henry L. Feingold, *Zion in America* (New York: Hippocrene Books, 1974), Chap. 2. I am indebted to Professor Abraham Karp for sharing the manuscript of *Haven and Home* with me before publication.

". . . the rabbi of the Jews": Goren, *The American Jews,* p. 17.

"You cannot know": Letter from Rebecca Samuel of Petersburg, Va., in Karp, *Golden Door to America,* p. 26.

41

"The citizens of": Washington's reply to the Hebrew Congregation in Newport, R.I., in Joseph L. Blau and Salo W. Baron, eds., *The Jews of the United States, 1790–1840: A Documentary History* (New York: Columbia Univ. Press, 1969), Vol. 1, p. 8.

"Acceptance was made easier": On the early Jewish settlers, see Marc D. Angel, "The Sephardim of the United States: An Exploratory Study," *American Jewish Year Book,* Vol. 74 (1973), pp. 80–84; Nathan Glazer, *American Judaism,* 2d ed., rev. (Chicago and London: Univ. of Chicago Press, 1972), Chap. 2, and "Social Characteristics of American Jews, 1654–1954," *American Jewish Year Book,* Vol. 56 (1955), pp. 3–6; Bernard D. Weinryb, "Jewish Immigration and Accommodation to America," in Marshall Sklare, ed., *The Jews* (Glencoe, Ill.: The Free Press, 1958), pp. 4–22; Henry L. Feingold, *A Midrash on American Jewish History* (Albany: State Univ. of New York Press, 1892), Chap. 1, and *Zion in America,* Chaps. 1–3; Karp, *Haven and Home,* Chaps. 1–2; Leon A. Jick, *The Americanization of the Synagogue, 1820–1870* (Hanover, N.H.: Brandeis Univ. Press/Univ. Press of New England, 1976), Chap. 1.

"are not identifiable by their beards": Jick, *The Americanization of the Synagogue,* p. 7.

42

All this changed: On German Jewish immigration, see Bernard D. Weinryb, "The German Jewish Immigrants to America (A Critical Evaluation)," in Eric E. Hirshler, ed., *Jews from Germany in the United States* (New York: Farrar, Straus & Cudahy, 1955); Jacob Lestschinsky, "Jewish Migrations,

1840–1946," in Louis Finkelstein, ed., *The Jews* (Philadelphia: Jewish Publication Society of America, 1949), Vol. IV, Chap. 32; Glazer, *American Judaism*, Chap. 3; Goren, *The American Jews*, pp. 21–36; Jick, *The Americanization of the Synagogue, 1820–1870;* Karp, *Haven and Home*, Chap. 3, and *Golden Door to America*, Chap. 2; Naomi W. Cohen, *Encounter with Emancipation: The German Jews in the United States, 1830–1914* (Philadelphia: Jewish Publication Society of America, 1984). For population statistics, see Calvin Goldscheider, "Demography of Jewish Americans: Research Findings, Issues, and Challenges," in Marshall Sklare, ed., *Understanding American Jewry* (New Brunswick, N.J.: Transaction Books, 1982), Chap. 1; Sidney Goldstein, "Jews in the United States: Perspectives from Demography," *American Jewish Year Book*, Vol. 81 (1981).

43

"Situated as our Congregation is": Jick, *The Americanization of the Synagogue*, p. 29.

"Blows passed": Isaac Mayer Wise, *Reminiscences*, quoted in Feingold, *Zion in America*, p. 107.

"The Jew must become an American": Quoted in Jick, *The Americanization of the Synagogue*, pp. 155–156.

44

"It is hard": Karp, *Golden Door to America*, pp. 54–57; Jick, *Americanization of the Synagogue*, pp. 34–36.

"How wonderfully . . . conditions have changed": Jick, *Americanization of the Synagogue*, pp. 40–41.

By 1860: Karp, *Haven and Home*, Chap. 3.

. . . after the Civil War: Glazer, "Social Characteristics of American Jews, 1654–1954," pp. 9–10; John Higham, *Send These to Me: Jews and Other Immigrants in Urban America* (New York: Atheneum, 1975), esp. Chaps. 7 and 8; Stephen Birmingham, "*Our Crowd*" (New York: Pocket Books–Wallaby Books, 1977).

45

Wise and his friend: Jick, *Americanization of the Synagogue*, p. 178.

"Everywhere there were signs": Clifton E. Olmstead, *History of Religion in the United States* (Englewood Cliffs, N.J.: Prentice-Hall, 1960), p. 447, quoted in Jick, pp. 178–179.

"The honor of Judaism": Jick, *The Americanization of the Synagogue*, p. 180.

There was even more grandeur: Ibid., p. 179.

46

In one congregation after another: Ibid., Chaps. 10 and 11. See also Sefton D. Temkin, "A Century of Reform Judaism in America," *American Jewish Year Book*, Vol. 74 (1973), pp. 3–76; Glazer, *American Judaism*, Chap. 3; Joseph L. Blau, *Judaism in America* (Chicago and London: Univ. of Chicago Press, 1976), Chaps. 2 and 3; Feingold, *Zion in America*, Chap. 7.

The "*trefa* banquet": John J. Appel, "The *Trefa* Banquet," *Commentary* (Feb. 1966), pp. 75–78.

47
"In most large cities": Isaac Leeser, "Renewed Illiberality," *The Occident*, Vol. 23, No. 7 (Oct. 1865), p. 319.

"Second Battle of Saratoga": Birmingham, *"Our Crowd,"* pp. 158–167.
48
Austin Corbin: New York *Herald*, July 22, 1879, rptd. in Michael Selzer, ed., *"Kike!"* (New York: World Publishing–Meridian Books, 1972), pp. 55–58.

Henry Adams: W. C. Ford, ed., *Letters of Henry Adams, 1892–1918*, rptd. in Selzer, ed., *"Kike!,"* pp. 54–55 and 80–83.

For population and immigration statistics, see citations for pp. 41ff. above. On Eastern European Jewish immigration, see Simon Kuznets, "Immigration of Russian Jews to the United States: Background and Structure," *Perspectives in American History*, Vol. IX (1975), pp. 35–124; Eli M. Lederhendler, "Jewish Immigration to America and Revisionist Historiography: A Decade of New Perspectives," *YIVO Annual of Jewish Social Science*, Vol. XVIII, pp. 391–410; Jonathan Frankel, "The Crisis of 1881–82 as a Turning Point in Modern Jewish History," in David Berger, ed., *The Legacy of Jewish Immigration: 1881 and Its Impact* (New York: Brooklyn College Press, 1983); Lucy S. Dawidowicz, *On Equal Terms* (New York: Holt, Rinehart & Winston, 1982).
49
"America was in everybody's mouth": Mary Antin, *From Plotzk to Boston* (1899), quoted in Irving Howe, *World of Our Fathers* (New York and London: Harcourt Brace Jovanovich, 1976), p. 27.

Too poor even to become peddlers: Glazer, "Social Characteristics of American Jews, 1654–1954," p. 12. See also Thomas Kessner, *The Golden Door* (New York: Oxford Univ. Press, 1977); Moses Rischin, *The Promised City* (Cambridge, Mass.: Harvard Univ. Press, 1977).

"I suppose there are": William Dean Howells, *Impressions and Experiences* (1896), rptd. in Milton Hindus, ed., *The Old East Side* (Philadelphia: Jewish Publication Society of America, 1969), p. 57.

"Nowhere in the world": Jacob A. Riis, *How the Other Half Lives*, American Century Series (New York: Sagamore Press, 1957), p. 77.
50
"a frightening apparition": Glazer, *American Judaism*, p. 66.
51
"It was a second birth": Abraham Cahan, *The Rise of David Levinsky* (New York: Harper Torchbooks, 1960), p. 97.

the Eastern European Jews: Glazer, "Social Characteristics of American Jews," pp. 10–20; Kessner, *The Golden Door*, esp. Chaps. 3, 4, 5; Stephan Thernstrom, *The Other Bostonians* (Cambridge, Mass.: Harvard Univ. Press, 1973), Chap. 7.

Ivy League colleges: Marcia Graham Synnott, *The Half-Opened Door* (Westport, Conn.: Greenwood Press Contributions in American History, No. 80); Oliver B. Pollak, "Anti-Semitism, the Harvard Plan, and the Roots of Reverse Discrimination," *Jewish Social Studies*, Vol. XLV, No. 2 (Spring 1983), pp. 113–120; Stephen Steinberg, *The Academic Melting Pot* (New York: McGraw-Hill, 1974), esp. Chaps. 1–4, and *The Ethnic Myth* (New York: Atheneum, 1981), esp. Chap. 9.

"Oh, Harvard's run": Steinberg, *The Academic Melting Pot*, pp. 16–17.

52

"One of the commonest references": Frederick P. Keppel, *Columbia* (New York: Oxford Univ. Press, 1914), quoted in Norman Podhoretz, *Making It* (New York: Random House, 1967), pp. 46–47.

the proportion of Jews enrolled: Steinberg, *The Ethnic Myth*, p. 237.

"We must put a ban on the Jews": Synnott, *The Half-Opened Door*, pp. 17, 15.

53

various tests of "character": Synnott, *The Half-Opened Door*, pp. 17–19.

Fn.: Leon J. Kamin, "The Politics of IQ," in Paul L. Houts, ed., *The Myth of Measurability* (New York: Hart Publishing Co., 1977), p. 55.

54

Charles Eliot . . . had welcomed Jews: Henry Rosovsky, "Then and Now: The Jewish Experience at Harvard," *Moment*, Vol. 5, No. 6 (June 1980), pp. 20–28. See also Synnott, *The Half-Opened Door*, Chap. 2.

That was precisely the problem: Pollak, "Antisemitism, the Harvard Plan, and the Roots of Reverse Discrimination," pp. 113–122; Synnott, *The Half-Opened Door*, Chaps. 3–4; Steinberg, *The Ethnic Myth*, pp. 238–246, and *The Academic Melting Pot*, pp. 21–31.

55

the editors of *Fortune:* The editors of *Fortune*, *Jews in America* (New York: Random House, 1936).

56

"The practices of the Orthodox Jewish faith": J. F. Brown, "The Origin of the Anti-Semitic Attitude," in Isacque Graeber and Steuart Henderson Britt, eds., *Jews in a Gentile World* (New York: Macmillan, 1942), Chap. 5.

Talcott Parsons of Harvard: Talcott Parsons, "The Sociology of Modern Anti-Semitism," ibid., Chap. 4, esp. pp. 115, 120–121.

57

a public-opinion survey: Charles Herbert Stember, "The Recent History of Public Attitudes," in Charles Herbert Stember et al., *Jews in the Mind of America* (New York: Basic Books, 1966).

58

The sociologist Robert K. Merton: Robert K. Merton, "The Self-Fulfilling Prophecy," *The Antioch Review* (Summer 1948), rptd. in Merton, enl. ed. *Social Theory and Social Structure* (New York: The Free Press, 1968), pp. 475–490.

59

Rabbi Irving Greenberg: Interview, Feb. 12, 1980.

"I know I look like a rabbi": Interview, June 11, 1979.

Anglicizing one's name: J. Alvin Kugelmass, "Name-Changing—And What It Gets You," *Commentary* (Aug. 1952), pp. 145–150. See also Werner

Cohn, "The Name Changers," *Forum on the Jewish People, Zionism and Israel,* No. 50 (Winter 1983/84), pp. 65–71.

60

Name changes: Richard Siegel and Carl Rheins, eds., *The Jewish Almanac* (New York: Bantam Books, 1980), pp. 14–16. On Jews in Hollywood, see Larry L. May and Elaine Tyler May, "Why Jewish Movie Moguls: An Exploration in American Culture," *American Jewish History*, Vol. LXXII, No. 1 (Sept. 1982), pp. 6–25; Sarah Blacker Cohen, ed., *From Hester Street to Hollywood* (Bloomington: Indiana Univ. Press, 1983); Stephen J. Whitfield, "The Enchantment of Comedy," in Whitfield, *Voices of Jacob, Hands of Esau* (Archon Books, 1984). I am indebted to Mordecai Newman and Robin Reif for their research on the role of Jews in the entertainment industries.

61

"One of the longest journeys": Norman Podhoretz, *Making It*, pp. 3–4.

"The demand being made on me": Ibid., pp. 49–50.

62

"We soon got the idea": Leonard Covello, *The Heart Is the Teacher* (New York: McGraw-Hill, 1958).

"a persistent torment": Joseph Proskauer, *A Segment of My Time* (New York: Farrar, Straus & Giroux, 1950), pp. 12–13.

"an interesting little man": Joseph P. Lash, *Eleanor and Franklin* (New York: W. W. Norton, 1971), p. 214.

"a self-torturing and prophylactic pleasure": Quoted in Gabriele Annan, "The Defrocked Romantic," *The New York Review of Books*, Vol. XXXI, No. 2, Feb. 16, 1984, p. 13.

63

Lippmann's "conflict with Jewry": Stephen J. Whitfield, "From Publick Occurrences to Pseudo-Events: Journalists and Their Critics," *American Jewish History*, Vol. LXXII, No. 1 (Sept. 1982), p. 65.

"I do not regard the Jews": Quoted in Ronald Steel, *Walter Lippmann and the American Century* (New York: Vintage Books, 1981), p. 194.

"Harvard, with the prejudices of": Ibid., p. 195.

Lippmann avoided identification: Ibid., Chaps. 1 and 15.

For his seventieth birthday: Whitfield, "From Publick Occurrences to Pseudo-Events," p. 62.

64

"The Jews are fairly distinct": Walter Lippmann, "Public Opinion and the American Jew," *American Hebrew* (Spring 1922), quoted in Steel, *Walter Lippmann and the American Century*, p. 191.

"By satisfying the lust of the Nazis": Steel, p. 330.

Robert Moses: Robert A. Caro, *The Power Broker* (New York: Vintage Books, 1975), p. 411.

65

Arthur Krock: David Halberstam, *The Powers That Be* (New York: Knopf, 1979), p. 217.

David Lawrence: Interview with Richard Clurman, July 13, 1983.

65ff.

Bernard Berenson: Michael Fixler, "Bernard Berenson of Butremanz," *Commentary* (Aug. 1963), pp. 135–143; David Landes, "On Being Bernard Berenson," *Moment*, Vol. 5, No. 9 (Oct. 1980), pp. 27–35; Meryle Secrest, *Being Bernard Berenson* (New York: Penguin Books, 1979), esp. Chaps. 2–3, 16–17.

66

"No people on earth": "Under Forty: A Symposium on American Literature and the Younger Generation of American Jews," *Contemporary Jewish Record* (Feb. 1944), pp. 3–36 (Greenberg, pp. 32–34; Kronenberger, pp. 20–23; Trilling, pp. 15–17).

"I am nothing": "A Symposium: Jewishness and the Younger Intellectuals," *Commentary* (April 1961), pp. 306–359 (Aronowitz, pp. 313–314; Epstein, pp. 319–320).

67

"at times I seem": Secrest, *Being Bernard Berenson*, p. 356.

"drop the mask of being *goyim*": Ibid., pp. 358, 395.

68

The year after his graduation: Ibid., pp. 49–53.

"A day scarcely passes": Ibid., p. 357.

in deference to Jewish tradition: Ibid., p. 396.

"If you refuse": See note, p. 28.

69

A Jew converts: William Novak and Moshe Waldoks, eds., *The Big Book of Jewish Humor* (New York: Harper & Row, 1981), p. 94.

"For a colonized people": John Murray Cuddihy, *No Offense: Civil Religion and Protestant Taste* (New York: Seabury Press–Crossroad Books, 1978), pp. 78–79.

Three Jews: Novak and Waldoks, eds., *The Big Book of Jewish Humor*, p. 95.

70

Judaism defines itself: See, for example, Charles Liebman, *The Ambivalent American Jew* (Philadelphia: Jewish Publication Society of America, 1973), Chaps. 1–3. See also Jacob Neusner, *Between Time and Eternity: The Essentials of Judaism* and *The Way of Torah* (North Scituate, Mass.: Duxbury Press, 1979); Arthur Hertzberg, *Being Jewish in America* (New York: Schocken Books, 1979), esp. Chaps. 3, 19, and 24; Eugene Borowitz, *The Mask Jews Wear* (New York: Simon & Schuster, 1973), esp. Chap. 6.

"what was decision": Borowitz, *The Mask Jews Wear*, p. 112.

71

Converts to Judaism: See, for example, Marc D. Angel, "A Fresh Look at Conversion," *Midstream* (Oct. 1983), pp. 35–38; Liebman, *The Ambivalent American Jew*, pp. 6–7.

"I've always considered myself a Jew": John Vinocur, "A Most Special Cardinal," *The New York Times Magazine*, March 20, 1983, pp. 29 ff.

In their study of "religious drop-outs": David Caplovitz and Fred Sherrow, *The Religious Drop-Outs* (Beverly Hills, Cal.: Sage Publications, 1977), esp. Chaps. 7 and 8.

73

"Today most Jews": Saul Friedlander, *When Memory Comes* (New York: Farrar, Straus & Giroux, 1979), p. 29.

"The Egyptians, the Babylonians": Mark Twain, "Concerning the Jews," *Harper's* (Sept. 1897), rptd. in Twain, *In Defense of Harriet Shelley and Other Essays* (New York: Harper & Row), p. 25.

historians such as Arnold Toynbee: See Arnold Toynbee, *A Study of History* (New York and London: Oxford Univ. Press; abridged ed., 1947).

75

"Food is always good": Mark Zborowski and Elizabeth Herzog, *Life Is with People* (New York: Schocken Books, 1967), pp. 372–373.

"Judaism has always been": Leon Wieseltier, review of Irving Howe, *World of Our Fathers*, in *The New York Review of Books*, Vol. 23, No. 12, July 15, 1976, p. 28, quoted in John Murray Cuddihy, *No Offense*, p. 102.

"It seems impossible": J. L. Talmon, *The Unique and the Universal* (London: Secker & Warburg, 1965), p. 69.

"I was always an unbeliever": Sigmund Freud, "On Being of the B'nai B'rith: An Address to the Society in Vienna," *Commentary* (March 1946), pp. 23–24. See also Freud's introduction to the Hebrew edition of *Totem and Taboo*, quoted in Paul R. Mendes-Flohr, "Sentiment, Memory and Vision: Between Existentialism and Zionism," *Forum on the Jewish People, Zionism and Israel*, No. 48 (Spring 1983), p. 54.

76

"To be a Jew": Borowitz, *The Mask Jews Wear*, p. 130.

"I walk with this sign": Daniel Bell, "Reflections on Jewish Identity," *Commentary* (June 1961), p. 477, rptd. in Peter I. Rose, ed., *The Ghetto and Beyond* (New York: Random House, 1969), p. 475.

In one recent survey: Steven Martin Cohen, "The 1981–1982 National Survey of American Jews," *American Jewish Year Book*, Vol. 83 (1983), p. 92. In his 1984 survey Cohen asked respondents to indicate how many of their "three closest friends" were Jewish; 56 percent indicated that all three were Jewish, and 22 percent that two of the three were Jewish (Cohen, *The Political Attitudes of American Jews, 1984* [New York: American Jewish Committee], mimeo, p. 5 of tables).

"Each Jew knows": Milton Himmelfarb, *The Jews of Modernity*, p. 359.

77

"Judaism should have fallen away": Henry Siegman, "A Decade of Catholic-Jewish Relations–A Reassessment," *Journal of Ecumenical Studies*, Vol. 15, No. 2 (Spring 1978), p. 245.

"the Jews have been around all along": Paul M. van Buren, *Discerning the Way* (New York: Seabury Press–Crossroad Books, 1980), p. 42.

"the one designated in the Scriptures": Ibid., p. 32.

Christians "have been called": Ibid., p. 44.

78
"God's stake in human history": Abraham Joshua Heschel, *The Earth Is the Lord's* (Cleveland and New York: World Publishing Company–Meridian Books, 1963), p. 109.

"I thought to be a Jew": Herbert Gold, *My Last Two Thousand Years* (1972), rptd. in Daniel Walden, ed., *On Being Jewish* (Greenwich, Conn.: Fawcett Publications–Premier Books, 1974), pp. 455–466.

"Whatever most diaspora Jews believe": Richard L. Rubenstein, "Homeland and Holocaust," quoted in Glazer, *American Judaism*, p. 184.

the experience of exile and persecution: See Arnold Eisen, *The Chosen People in America* (Bloomington: Indiana Univ. Press, 1983), Chap. 2, esp. pp. 12–22; Jacob Katz, *Exclusiveness and Tolerance* (New York: Schocken Books, 1962), Chap. 2; "Chosen People," *Encyclopedia Judaica* (Jerusalem and New York: Keter Publishing House and Macmillan, 1971), Vol. 5, pp. 498–502.

79
The balance was altered: Katz, *Exclusiveness and Tolerance*, Chap. 12.

"The more the Jew": *Encyclopedia Judaica*, Vol. 5, p. 501.

"a distasteful secular version": Ismar Schorsch, "The Holocaust and Jewish Survival," *Midstream*, Vol. XVIII, No. 1 (Jan. 1981), pp. 38–42.

Their religious leaders: See Eisen, *The Chosen People in America*.

80
"It seems to be the will of God": "A Conversation with Dr. Abraham Joshua Heschel," on *The Eternal Light* (TV program). Mimeo transcript of NBC/TV Network presentation, Feb. 4, 1973, p. 13.

"We Jews have a remarkable history": Ira Eisenstein, *What Can a Modern Jew Believe* (New York: Reconstructionist Press, n.d.), p. 10, quoted in Charles S. Liebman, "Reconstructionism in American Jewish Life," *American Jewish Year Book*, Vol. 71 (1970), p. 21.

"Can't you grasp something": Philip Roth, *Portnoy's Complaint* (New York: Random House, 1969), pp. 75–76.

"The outrage, the disgust": Ibid., p. 56.

81
"a certain comic detachment": Ibid., pp. 55–56.

"no body of law": Remarks at "Second Dialogue in Israel," *Congress Bi-weekly*, Vol. 30, No. 12, Sept. 16, 1963, p. 21.

"this almost unique desire for survival": Marshall Sklare, *Conservative Judaism*, new, augmented ed. (New York: Schocken Books, 1972), p. 34.

Chapter Three
"*A Guy Named Shapiro*"

82
only 2.5 percent: See U. O. Schmelz and Sergio DellaPergola, "The Demographic Consequences of U.S. Jewish Population Trends," *American Jewish Year Book*, Vol. 83 (1983), pp. 143–144.

83

"a significant residue of anti-Semitism": See *The American Jewish Committee's January 1984 Poll: A Research Note from the American Jewish Committee's Information and Research Services* (New York: American Jewish Committee, n.d.), mimeo; *The Study of Attitudes Concerning the American Jewish Community* (Princeton, N.J.: Gallup Organization, Sept. 1979); Geraldine Rosenfield, "The Polls: Attitudes Toward American Jews," *Public Opinion Quarterly*, Vol. 46 (Fall 1982), pp. 431–443; Nathan and Ruth Ann Perlmutter, *The Real Anti-Semitism in America* (New York: Arbor House, 1982); *Anti-Semitism in the United States* (New York: Yankelovich, Skelly and White), a report prepared for The American Jewish Committee (July 1981), mimeo; William Schneider, *Anti-Semitism and Israel: A Report on American Public Opinion,* report to American Jewish Committee (Dec. 1978), and *Update Data on Anti-Semitism and Jewish Attitudes*, Schneider's memorandum of March 6, 1979, to Milton Himmelfarb of American Jewish Committee, mimeo; among others.

Gerard Swope: David Loth, *Swope of G.E.* (New York: Simon & Schuster, 1958); *Current Biography* (New York: H. W. Wilson, 1941), pp. 848–849; E. J. Kahn, Jr., *The World of Swope* (New York: Simon & Schuster), Chap. 21.

Philip Sporn: Undated tape-recorded interview, William E. Wiener Oral History Library of The American Jewish Committee; obituary, *The New York Times*, Jan. 24, 1978.

83ff.

Irving Shapiro's appointment: Peter Vanderwicken, "Irving Shapiro Takes Charge at Du Pont," *Fortune* (Jan. 1974), pp. 79–81, 152, 154, 156; Tamar Lewin, "Irving S. Shapiro, Attorney at Law," *The New York Times*, Aug. 8, 1982, pp. F1, F15; my interview with Irving Shapiro, Aug. 3, 1983; *American Jewish Biographies* (New York: Facts on File–Lakeville Press Books, 1982), p. 397; *Who's Who in America,* 42d ed. (Chicago: Marquis Who's Who, 1982–83), p. 449; Fred W. Friendly, *Minnesota Rag* (New York: Vintage Books, 1981), Chap. 4.

85

Minneapolis was considered the most anti-Semitic city: Daniel J. Elazar, *Community and Polity* (Philadelphia: Jewish Publication Society of America, 1976), p. 57. See also Judith R. Kramer and Seymour Leventman, *Children of the Gilded Ghetto* (New Haven: Yale Univ. Press, 1961), pp. 43–44.

88

In their 1982 study: Richard L. Zweigenhaft and G. William Domhoff, *Jews in the Protestant Establishment* (New York: Praeger, 1982), esp. Chap. 2.

89

"Jews go where": Steven Silberman telephone interview with Walter Shorenstein, June 23, 1983; Richard Behar with Jeff Bloch, "The 400 Richest People in America," *Forbes*, special issue, Oct. 1, 1984, pp. 108, 112.

"Corporate life is Mickey Mouse": Steven Silberman interview with Bernard Mendik, Aug. 2, 1983.

"I was supposed to be a doctor": My interviews with Av Westin, July 29 and Aug. 11, 1983.

"Elegant manners and fine breeding": Interview with Daniel Rose, June 21, 1983.

90

"son of an immigrant delicatessen owner": Myra Alperson interview with Morris Tanenbaum, Jan. 24, 1984.

the most likely person: "4 Senior Officers Shifted at A.T.&T.," *The New York Times*, Jan. 17, 1985, p. D2.

"I wasn't offered any jobs": Jeremy Bernstein, "Physicist," *The New Yorker*, Oct. 13, 1975, p. 56.

Tanenbaum's mother: Alperson interview with Tanenbaum.

91

Philip Sporn: Tape-recorded interview, Wiener Oral History Library of AJC.

when Emanuel Piore received: Interview with Emanuel Piore, June 30, 1983.

"As far as I can judge": Alperson interview with Tanenbaum. See also profile of Tanenbaun in AT&T Communications, *Quest*, No. 1 (1983), pp. 6–9.

92

"forty-nine year-old Gerald Greenwald": Myra Alperson interview with Greenwald, April 3, 1984; John Holusha, "Lee Iacocca's Heir Apparent," *The New York Times*, June 14, 1984.

the anti-Semitic activities [of] Henry Ford, Sr.,: Judd L. Teller, *Strangers and Natives* (New York: Delacorte Press, 1968), pp. 102–103; Michael N. Dobkowski, *The Tarnished Dream* (Westport, Conn: Greenwood Press, 1981), pp. 97–102; Robert Singerman, "The American Career of the *Protocols of the Elders of Zion*," *American Jewish History*, Vol. LXXI, No. 1 (Sept. 1981), pp. 48–78; Naomi W. Cohen, *Not Free to Desist* (Philadelphia: Jewish Publication Society of America, 1972), pp. 129–137.

"Jerry has the talent": Lee Iacocca with William Novak, *Iacocca* (New York: Bantam Books, 1984), pp. 168–169.

93

"I find it . . . hard to believe": Ibid., p. 15.

"one of those guys": Ibid., p. 176.

Reuben Mark: *The New York Times*, March 9, 1984; *Who's Who in America*, 42nd ed., 1982–83, v. 2.

"a fantastic overdevelopment": Sir Isaiah Berlin, *Jewish Slavery and Emancipation*, Herzl Institute Pamphlet No. 18 (New York: Herzl Press, 1961), p. 15.

94

"the farther you get from headquarters": Alperson interview with Greenwald.

"Tom Watson, Jr.": My interviews with Piore, June 30 and July 7, 1983.

Fn.: Interview with Piore, July 7, 1983.

a sample of . . . Harvard Business School alumni: Richard L. Zweigenhaft,

Who Gets to the Top? Executive Suite Discrimination in the Eighties (New York: The American Jewish Committee, 1984), pp. 9–19.

95

"People who deliver": Ibid., p. 19.

"Brilliant intellectual powers": Paul Hoffman, *Lions of the Eighties* (Garden City, N.Y.: Doubleday, 1982), p. 11. See also Robert T. Swaine, *The Cravath Firm and Its Predecessors*, Chap. 7, rptd. in James B. Stewart, *The Partners* (New York: Simon & Schuster, 1983), Appendix 2.

"I do not want anybody": Jerrold Auerbach, "From Rags to Robes: The Legal Profession, Social Mobility and the American Jewish Experience," *American Jewish Historical Quarterly*, Vol. LXVI, No. 4 (Dec. 1976), p. 259.

96

"whose gestures are unwholesome": Ibid., pp. 161–162.

In the spring of 1936: Ibid., pp. 252, 267.

"What can I tell you?": Interview with Joseph Flom, May 24, 1983.

Flom earns: *The American Lawyer's Guide to Law Firms* (New York: AmLaw Publishing Corp., 1981), p. 731.

largely dominated by Jewish lawyers: Interview with Steven Brill, editor in chief, *The American Lawyer*, Jan. 20, 1982; not-for-attribution interview with head of corporate department of major law firm, Dec. 4, 1984.

Something similar happened: Auerbach, "From Rags to Robes," pp. 271–273.

97

had flocked to Washington: Ibid., pp. 272–273; Leonard Dinnerstein, "Jews and the New Deal," *American Jewish History*, Vol. LXXII, No. 4 (June 1983), pp. 461–476; John Brooks, "Advocate," profile of Simon Rifkind, Esq., *The New Yorker*, May 23, 1983.

lawyer-client relations: See, for example, James B. Stewart, "Major Banks Loosen Links to Law Firms, Use In-House Counsel," *The Wall Street Journal*, April 26, 1984, pp. 31, 40; Tamar Lewin, "A Gentlemanly Profession Enters a Tough New Era," *The New York Times*, Jan. 16, 1983, sec. C, pp. 1, 10; James B. Stewart, "A Blue-Chip Law Firm Comes on Hard Times After a Coup d'Etat," *The Wall Street Journal*, Nov. 18, 1983, pp. 1, 20.

98

"Dartmouth is a Christian college": Lawrence Bloomgarden, "Our Changing Elite Colleges," *Commentary* (Feb. 1960), p. 152, quoted in Seymour Martin Lipset and Everett Carll Ladd, Jr., "Jewish Academics in the United States: Their Achievements, Culture and Politics," *American Jewish Year Book* (1971), p. 90.

"Jewish representation in the academic field": Talcott Parsons, "The Sociology of Modern Anti-Semitism," Isacque Graeber and Steuart Henderson Britt, eds., *Jews In a Gentile World* (New York: Macmillan, 1942), p. 112.

"Anti-Semitism was unbelievably rife": Jeremy Bernstein, "Physicist," *The New Yorker*, Oct. 13, 1975, pp. 86, 94.

"When I decided to go": Lionel Trilling, "Young in the Thirties," *Commentary* (May 1966), p. 47. On Trilling's experience at Columbia, see also

Diana Trilling, "Lionel Trilling: A Jew at Columbia," *Commentary* (March 1979), pp. 40–46; Edward Alexander, "Lionel Trilling," *Midstream* (March 1983), pp. 48–57; and Eleanor Grumet, "The Apprenticeship of Lionel Trilling," *Prooftexts*, Vol. 4, No. 2 (May 1984), pp. 153–173.

99

"Jews comprised 9 percent": Lipset and Ladd, "Jewish Academics in the United States," and Lipset and Ladd, "The Changing Social Origins of American Academics," in Robert K. Merton, James S. Colemand, and Peter H. Rossi, eds., *Qualitative and Quantitative Social Research* (New York: The Free Press, 1979), pp. 319–338.

"It is almost impossible": Richard L. Rubenstein, "The Protestant Establishment and the Jews," in Rubenstein, *After Auschwitz* (Indianapolis and New York: Bobbs-Merrill, 1966), Chap. 9.

"in his annual report": Quoted in Rubenstein, *After Auschwitz*, p. 156.

the grandson of a distinguished Reform rabbi: Dates from *Who's Who in America*, 42nd ed., 1982–83.

100

"I have known people": Interview with Henry Rosovsky, Jan. 24, 1983.

carrying a Torah scroll: Description of procession in Martin Peretz, "Cambridge Diarist: Marks of Identity," *The New Republic*, Oct. 22, 1984, p. 50. Rosovsky's speech in Henry Rosovsky, "Then and Now: The Jewish Experience at Harvard," *Moment*, Vol. 5, No. 6 (June 1980), pp. 20, 23–24, 27–28.

101

The trustees of Yale: Interview with Rosovsky, Jan. 24, 1983.

In the Ninety-third Congress: Stephen D. Isaacs, *Jews and American Politics* (Garden City, N.Y.: Doubleday, 1974), p. 231.

102

When he left the White House: Ibid., pp. 198–199.

"Anti-semitism is not a problem": Interview with Senator Metzenbaum, March 12, 1980; Isaacs, *Jews and American Politics*, pp. 208–209.

"I have encountered": Interview with Senator Levin, Jan. 27, 1984.

103

"Voters do not tolerate": Steven Silberman interview with Representative Gejdenson, July 26, 1983.

a qualified Jew for president: Milton Himmelfarb, " 'Would you vote for a Jew for President?' " (New York: The American Jewish Committee, n.d.), a research note from the Information and Research Services of AJC, mimeo.

A California poll: *San Francisco Chronicle*, Oct. 14, 1982, p. 1.

In the Ninety-ninth Congress: David Friedman, "Jews in Congress," *The Jewish Week*, Nov. 16, 1984.

"The wraps are coming off": Interview with Representative Barney Frank, *Moment*, Vol. 8, No. 5 (May 1983), pp. 13–17.

"People my age": Interview with Representative Frost, March 13, 1980.

104

Jews such as Samuel Rosenman: Henry L. Feingold, "'Courage First and Intelligence Second': The American Jewish Secular Elite, Roosevelt and the Failure to Rescue," *American Jewish History*, Vol. LXXII, No. 4 (June 1983), pp. 424–460, and *The Politics of Rescue* (New York: Holocaust Library, 1970). See also David S. Wyman, *The Abandonment of the Jews* (New York: Pantheon Books, 1984). Rosenman quote in A. J. Sherman's review of Wyman, *The Abandonment of the Jews*, in *The New York Times Book Review*, Dec. 16, 1984, p. 16. On Sol Bloom, see excerpts from Breckinridge Long diaries in Feingold, *The Politics of Rescue.*

Stuart Eizenstat always left the office: Interview with Eizenstat, Aug. 2, 1983, and conversations with other members of the White House staff.

105

"People are very accepting": Interview with Frank, *Moment* (May 1983).

"It would be counterproductive": My interview with Metzenbaum, March 12, 1980.

"If you're a black congressman": Steven Silberman interview with Gejdenson, July 26, 1983.

"I did not grow up in fear": Interview with S. Ariel Weiss, Aug. 3, 1983.

106

Tisch's son Andrew: Interview with Lawrence and Wilma Tisch, April 26, 1983; Behar with Bloch, "The 400 Richest People in America," p. 88.

his Gentile golfing companions: Interview with Sidney Gruson, May 6, 1983.

watering hole of the rich: Suzanne Garment, "Discrimination Puts On a New Face in Palm Beach," *The Wall Street Journal*, Feb. 10, 1984, Op Ed page.

107

"a group of upper-class WASPs": Interview with Richard Ravitch, June 21, 1983.

"The discrimination that remains": Interview with Irving Shapiro, Aug. 3, 1983.

after reaching a historic peak: Charles Herbert Stember, "The Recent History of Public Attitudes," in Stember et al., *Jews in the Mind of America* (New York: Basic Books, 1966), Part One. See also Leonard Dinnerstein, "Anti-Semitism Exposed and Attacked," *American Jewish History*, Vol. LXXI, No. 1 (Sept. 1981), pp. 134–149.

108

Americans have always been: Interview with Professor John F. Wilson of Princeton, Oct. 24, 1980. See John F. Wilson, *Public Religion in American Culture* (Philadelphia: Temple Univ. Press, 1979); Abraham J. Karp, *Haven and Home* (New York: Schocken Books, 1985) and "Ideology as Strategy in Jewish Group Survival in America," unpub. mimeo; Will Herberg, *Protestant-Catholic-Jew* (Garden City, N.Y.: Doubleday, 1955).

"religious pluralism is": Herberg, *Protestant-Catholic-Jew*, pp. 98-99.

109

In 1940: Stember, *Jews in the Mind of America*, p. 54.

by 1981: Gallup poll, April 16, 1981.

except among black Americans: Schneider, *Anti-Semitism and Israel: A Report on American Public Opinion* and *Update Data on Anti-Semitism and Jewish Attitudes;* Yankelovich, Skelly and White, *Anti-Semitism in the United States*, Vol. I, pp. 25–26 and Vol. II, pp. 31–48; Harold E. Quinley and Charles Y. Glock, *Anti-Semitism in America* (New York: The Free Press, 1979), Chap. 4.

13 percent of the female respondents: Zweigenhaft, *Who Gets to the Top?*, pp. 20–21.

110

"the Jews no longer stand out": Talcott Parsons, "Postscript to 'The Sociology of Modern Anti-Semitism,'" *Contemporary Jewry*, Vol. 5, No. 1 (Spring/Summer 1980), p. 34.

When he returned: Stephen S. Hall, "Italian-Americans Coming into Their Own," *The New York Times Magazine*, May 15, 1983.

"The change is more than cosmetic": Interview with Angelo Costanza, April 1, 1984.

111

a "dumb wop": Iacocca with Novak, *Iacocca*, pp. 14–15.

"a high squeaky voice": Hall, "Italian-Americans Coming into Their Own."

Governor Mario Cuomo: Ken Auletta, "Governor," *The New Yorker*, April 9, 1984, pp. 57–58; Hall, "Italian-Americans Coming into Their Own," p. 28.

Nor could Iacocca escape: Iacocca with Novak, *Iacocca*, Chaps. 10–12.

112

"lacked grace": Ibid., p. 135.

The change was driven home: Hall, "Italian-Americans Coming into Their Own."

"the first new nation": Semour Martin Lipset, *The First New Nation* (New York: W. W. Norton, 1979).

as Toqueville pointed out: Alexis de Tocqueville, *Democracy in America* (New York: Vintage Books, 1954), Vol. I, pp. 314–326, Vol. II, pp. 21–29, 114–118. See also Lipset, *The First New Nation*, Chap. 4.

113

American identity has been inclusive: See Stephan Thernstrom, ed., *Harvard Encyclopedia of American Ethnic Groups* (Cambridge, Mass.: Belknap Press of Harvard Univ. Press, 1980): Philip Gleason, "American Identity and Americanization," pp. 31–58; Michael Walzer, "Pluralism: A Political Perspective," pp. 781–787; and Harold J. Abramson, "Assimilation and Pluralism," pp. 150–160. See also Lipset, *The First New Nation*, Chap. 2.

the war itself: Leonard Dinnerstein, "Anti-Semitism Exposed and Attacked," *American Jewish History*, Vol. LXXI, No. 1 (Sept. 1981), pp. 134–149.

114
the indignities visited on them: Charles E. Silberman, *Crisis in Black and White* (New York: Random House, 1964), pp. 60–64.

Fn.: *Encyclopedia Judaica*, Vol. 12, p. 406.

"The army gave me": Myra Alperson interview with Jerome Shapiro, Jan. 16, 1984.
115
Henry Kissinger had hoped: W. D. Rubinstein, *The Left, the Right, and the Jews* (London & Canberra: Croom Helm, 1982), p. 74, n. 42.

The women's movement: Betty Friedan, *The Feminine Mystique* (New York: Random House, 1963) and *It Changed My Life* (New York: Random House, 1976), pp. 8–16.

The economic boom: The editors of *Fortune*, *The Changing American Market* and *Markets of the Sixties* (New York: Harper & Row, 1954 and 1960, resp.).
116
"When you look at Harvard": Interview with Henry Rosovsky, Jan. 24, 1983.

Chapter Four
Horatio Alger and the Jews

117
12 percent of American Jews live in those . . . boroughs: For population of Brooklyn and Queens, see Paul Ritterband and Steven M. Cohen, "The Social Characteristics of the New York Area Jewish Community, 1981," *American Jewish Year Book*, Vol. 84 (1984), p. 140, Table 1.1; total U.S. Jewish population in U. O. Schmelz and Sergio DellaPergola, "The Demographic Consequences of U.S. Jewish Population Trends," *American Jewish Year Book*, Vol. 83 (1983), p. 143.
118
a significant minority: Evan A. Bayer and Gary A. Tobin, "Jewish Economic Dependency and Dislocation," statement of The American Jewish committee, submitted to the Subcommittee on Public Assistance and Unemployment Compensation, U.S. House of Representatives Committee on Ways and Means, Nov. 18, 1983, mimeo, p. 2.

fewer than one family in six: Jewish income figures from Steven M. Cohen, "The Political Attitudes of American Jews, 1984" (*The 1984 National Survey of American Jews*), a survey conducted for The American Jewish Committee, mimeo; non-Hispanic white income figures from *Statistical Abstract of the United States*.

Jews are better educated: Statistics on American Jews from Cohen's 1984 survey; on non-Hispanic whites from *Statistical Abstract*.

A 1980 national survey: James L. Peterson and Nicholas Zill, *American Jewish High School Students: A National Profile* (New York: The American Jewish Committee, 1984).

"It is doubtless true": Quoted in Henry Rosovsky, "Then and Now: The Jewish Experience at Harvard," *Moment*, Vol. 5, No. 6 (June 1980), p. 23.

119

"Nobody came to my office": Mark Singer, "God and Mentsch at Yale," *Moment*, Vol. 1, No. 2 (July/Aug. 1975), p. 29.

Jews made up 3.6 percent: David E. Drew and Melanie R. Williams, *After College: A Longitudinal Study of Jewish Adults* (technical report submitted to The American Jewish Committee) (Los Angeles: Higher Education Research Institute, 1982), p. 15.

Jewish students set: Drew and Williams, *After College;* David E. Drew, Margo R. King, and Gerald T. Richardson, *A Profile of the Jewish Freshman: 1980* (Los Angeles: Higher Education Research Institute, n.d.).

In the Boston metropolitan area: Calvin R. Goldscheider, *Jewish Continuity and Change: Emerging Patterns in America* (Bloomington: Indiana Univ. Press, 1985). See also Floyd J. Fowler, *1975 Community Survey: A Study of the Jewish Population of Greater Boston* (Boston: Combined Jewish Philanthropies of Greater Boston, 1977).

The proportion of Jews: *The Jewish Population of Rochester (Monroe County), New York* (Rochester: Jewish Community Federation of Rochester, N.Y., 1981); Nancy Hendrix, *A Demographic Study of the Jewish Community of Nashville and Middle Tennessee* (Nashville: Jewish Federation of Nashville and Middle Tennessee, 1982), mimeo; *Survey of Cleveland's Jewish Population, 1981*, Report No. 3 of the Population Research Committee (Cleveland: Jewish Community Federation of Cleveland, 1982); James McCann, *A Study of the Jewish Community in the Greater Seattle Area* (Seattle: Jewish Federation of Greater Seattle, 1979).

120

Men who were sixty: See note to p. 119. See also Steven M. Cohen, *American Modernity and Jewish Identity* (New York and London: Tavistock Publications, 1983), pp. 83–87.

121

The late Samuel J. Bernstein: Burton Bernstein, *Family Matters* (New York: Summit Books, 1982).

"The story of Jews in the South": Eli N. Evans, *The Provincials* (New York: Atheneum, 1973), p. 9.

Jews who were blue-collar workers: Goldscheider, *Jewish Continuity and Change.*

122

as recently as the mid-1970s: Peterson and Zill, *American Jewish High School Students*, p. 5.

Jewish women now show: Goldscheider, *Jewish Continuity and Change*, Chap. 8.

A 1982 survey in Cleveland: *Survey of Jewish 18-to-29-year-olds in Cleveland: Information for our Future*, Report No. 4 of the Population Research Committee (Cleveland: Jewish Community Federation of Cleveland, 1983), pp. 20–21.

123

a 1980 national survey: Drew, King, and Richardson, *A Profile of the Jewish Freshman: 1980*, p. 44.

two thirds of the Jewish girls: Peterson and Zill, *American Jewish High School Students*, p. 20.

124

educational opportunities were limited: Selma C. Berrol, "Education and Economic Mobility: The Jewish Experience in New York City, 1880–1929," *American Jewish Historical Quarterly* (March 1976), pp. 257–271, esp. pp. 259–261. See also Irving Howe, *World of Our Fathers* (New York: Harcourt Brace Jovanovich, 1976), pp. 271–278.

half the students applying: The editors of *Fortune*, *Jews in America* (New York: Random House, 1936), p. 70.

In Stamford, Connecticut: Samuel Koenig, "The Socioeconomic Structure of an American Jewish Community," in Isacque Graeber and Steuart Henderson Britt, *Jews in a Gentile World* (New York: Macmillan, 1942), p. 209, Table 2.

a lot more Jewish doctors today: For Boston: Goldscheider, *Jewish Continuity and Change*, Chap. 8; Minneapolis: Lois Geer, *The Jewish Community of Greater Minneapolis* (Minneapolis: Minneapolis Federation for Jewish Service, 1982), pp. 3–35, Table 3:25; St. Louis: Gary A. Tobin, *A Demographic and Attitudinal Study of the Jewish Community of St. Louis* (St. Louis: Jewish Federation of St. Louis, 1982), Table P65A.

Jews gravitated to medical education: Seymour Martin Lipset and Everett Carll Ladd, Jr., "Jewish Academics in the United States: Their Achievements, Culture, and Politics," *American Jewish Year Book*, Vol. 72 (1971), p. 95, Table 4.

125

"The rise in socio-economic status" Milton M. Gordon, *Assimilation in American Life* (New York: Oxford Univ. Press, 1964), p. 185.

Horatio Alger became: Stephen Birmingham, "*Our Crowd*" (New York: Pocket Books–Wallaby Books, 1977), pp. 250–251.

three out of five were blue-collar workers: Nathan Glazer, "Social Characteristics of American Jews, 1654–1954," *American Jewish Year Book*, Vol. 56 (1955), pp. 11 ff. See also Nathan Glazer, *American Judaism*, 2d ed. rev. (Chicago and London: Univ. of Chicago Press, 1972), Chap. 5.

Half or more of them: On Boston, see Stephan Thernstrom, *The Other Bostonians* (Cambridge, Mass.: Harvard Univ. Press, 1973), Chap. 6; on New York, see Deborah Dash Moore, *At Home in America* (New York: Columbia Univ. Press, 1981), Chap. 1.

Jewish immigrants "begin as helpers": Glazer, "Social Characteristics," p. 13.

126

When he arrived in New York: Bernstein, *Family Matters*, pp. 31–34.

When Louis Borgenicht: Irving Howe, *World of Our Fathers*, pp. 159–161.

"It puzzled me greatly": Alfred Kazin, *A Walker in the City* (New York: Grove Press, 1958), pp. 38–39.

127
In their eagerness to move up: See David Singer, "The Jewish Gangster: Crime as 'Unzer Shtik,'" *Judaism*, Vol. 23, No. 1 (Winter 1974), pp. 70–77; Arthur A. Goren, *New York Jews and the Quest for Community* (New York: Columbia Univ. Press, 1970), Chaps. 7–8; Albert Fried, *The Rise and Fall of the Jewish Gangster in America* (New York: Holt, Rinehart & Winston, 1980); Jenna Weissman Joselit, *Our Gang* (Bloomington: Indiana Univ. Press, 1983); Edward J. Bristow, *Prostitution and Prejudice* (New York: Schocken Books, 1982); David Singer, review of *Meyer Lansky: Mogul of the Mob*, by Dennis Eisenberg, Uri Dan, and Eli Landau, *The New Republic*, Jan. 19, 1980, pp. 36–38.

Jews were statistically underrepresented: Goren, *New York Jews and the Quest for Community*, p. 147.

a significant drop: Joselit, *Our Gang*, pp. 157–158.

Jews moved, en masse: Chicago data from Louis Wirth, *The Ghetto* (Chicago: Univ. of Chicago Press–Phoenix Books, 1956), p. 244; New York data from Moore, *At Home in America*, Chap. 2.

one felony arrest in four: Joselit, *Our Gang*, p. 158.

128
the legendary Arnold Rothstein: Leo Katcher, *The Big Bankroll: The Life and Times of Arnold Rothstein* (New York: Harper & Row, 1959); Joselit, *Our Gang*, Chap. 7; Fried, *The Rise and Fall of the Jewish Gangster in America*, esp. pp. 94–98.

Fn.: Rothstein was the model: Katcher, p. 8; Fried, p. 96, n.

"another Jewish boy": Howe, *World of Our Fathers*, p. 384.

There were many others: Fried, Chaps. 3–6; Joselit, Chaps. 5–8.

every bit as violent: Fried, pp. 102 ff.

129
Moses Annenberg laid the foundations: John Cooney, *The Annenbergs* (New York: Simon & Schuster, 1982), esp. pp. 1–80, 138–154; Fried, pp. 116–118.

"I always thought of Annenberg": Cooney, *The Annenbergs*, p. 52.

It was Meyer Lansky: Fried, Chap. 6; Dennis Eisenberg, Uri Dan, and Eli Landau, *Meyer Lansky: Mogul of the Mob* (London: Paddington Press, 1979); Hank Messick, *Lansky* (New York: Putnam's, 1971).

130
A few elderly figures from the past: Fried, pp. 281–286; Gregory Strichարchuk, "Teamsters' Presser May Be Charged by U.S. in Probe of 'Ghost' Workers," *The Wall Street Journal*, Oct. 10, 1983.

By the mid-1920s: Glazer, "Social Characteristics of American Jews, 1654–1954," *American Jewish Year Book*, Vol. 56 (1955), pp. 14–20; Moore, *At Home in America*, Chaps. 1–3; Jeffrey S. Gurock, *When Harlem Was Jewish, 1870–1930* (New York: Columbia Univ. Press, 1979), Chaps. 5–6; William Toll, *The Making of an Ethnic Middle Class* (Albany: State Univ.

of New York Press, 1982), Chap. 4; Leonard Bloom, "The Jews of Buna," in Graeber and Britt, eds., *Jews in a Gentile World*, pp. 180–199.

"Jewish youth is turning": Jacob Lestchinsky, "The Position of the Jews in the Economic Life of America," in Graeber and Britt, p. 413.

In Detroit in 1935: Lestchinsky, p. 414, Table 2; Glazer, "Social Characteristics of American Jews," pp. 21–23.

in Stamford, Connecticut: Samuel Koenig, "The Socioeconomic Structure of an American Jewish Community," in Graeber and Britt, pp. 207–216.

131

"The most striking fact": Talcott Parsons, "The Sociology of Modern Anti-Semitism," in Graeber and Britt, p. 113.

they were less traumatized: On the differences between Italian and Jewish immigrant adjustment, see Thomas Kessner, "The Selective Filter of Ethnicity," in David Berger, ed., *The Legacy of Jewish Migration: 1881 and Its Impact* (New York: Brooklyn College Press, 1983), pp. 169–185, and Kessner, *The Golden Door: Italian and Jewish Immigrant Mobility in New York City, 1880–1915* (New York: Oxford Univ. Press, 1977), esp. Chap. 2. See also Alice Kessler-Harris and Virginia Yans-McLaughlin, "European Immigrant Groups," in Thomas Sowell, ed., *Essays and Data on American Ethnic Groups* (Washington, D.C.: Urban Institute, 1978), pp. 107–137; Thomas Sowell, *Ethnic America* (New York: Basic Books, 1981), Chap. 5, esp. pp. 109–110; and Joseph J. Barton, *Peasants and Strangers* (Cambridge, Mass.: Harvard Univ. Press, 1975), Chap. 3.

Jews, on the other hand: Simon Kuznets, "The Immigration of Russian Jews to the United States: Background and Structure," *Perspectives in American History*, Vol. IX (1975), esp. pp. 47–48 and 94–100; Jacob Lestchinsky, "Jewish Migrations, 1840–1946," in Louis Finkelstein, ed., *The Jews* (Philadelphia: Jewish Publication Society of America, 1949), Vol. IV, pp. 1224–30; Kessner, "The Selective Filter of Ethnicity," p. 174; Howe, *World of Our Fathers*, pp. 57–63. For a somewhat contrary view, see Jonathan D. Sarna, "The Myth of No Return: Jewish Return Migration to Eastern Europe, 1881–1914," *American Jewish History*, Vol. LXXI, No. 2 (Dec. 1981), pp. 256–268. Sarna's argument that Jewish return migration was higher than has been assumed applies only to the period before the Kishinev pogrom of 1903.

"They pushed me": Howe, *World of Our Fathers*, p. 63.

a different set of aptitudes: Kuznets, "Immigration of Russian Jews to the United States," pp. 53–62, 72–82; Kessner, *The Golden Door*, Chap. 2, esp. pp. 32–39; Stephen Steinberg, *The Ethnic Myth* (New York: Atheneum, 1981), pp. 93–105; Moses Rischin, *The Promised City* (Cambridge, Mass.: Harvard Univ. Press, 1977), pp. 55–69.

132

There was another difference: Glazer, "Social Characteristics of American Jews," pp. 29–33.

"one tries his hand": Mark Zborowski and Elizabeth Herzog, *Life Is with People* (New York: Schocken Books, 1962), pp. 254–255.

133
"you never refuse a job": Ibid., p. 259.

the rush . . . to Brownsville: Moore, *At Home in America*, p. 40. On the growth in number of Jewish builders and developers, see Moore, pp. 39–58, and Gurock, *When Harlem Was Jewish*, pp. 45–49.

The founder of: Alan Tishman: Steven Silberman interview, July 13, 1983; my interviews with Jack Rudin, July 20, 1983, and Richard Ravitch, June 21, 1983.

by taking in boarders: Charlotte Baum, Paula Hyman, and Sonya Michel, *The Jewish Woman in America* (New York: New American Library–Plume Books, 1976), pp. 103–106.
134
"an abnormal hunger": Quoted in Theodore H. White, *In Search of History* (New York: Harper & Row, 1978), p. 14.

"stone poor": Ibid.

his family's escape: Jeremy Bernstein, "Allocating Sacrifice," *The New Yorker*, Jan. 24, 1983, p. 49; Cary Reich, *Financier* (New York: Morrow, 1983), pp. 225–226. See also Edward Jay Epstein, *The Rise and Fall of Diamonds* (New York: Simon & Schuster, 1982), pp. 76–79.

with his bags packed: Reich, *Financier*, p. 21.
135
"to make sure he could sell": Ibid., p. 63.

"Jews had to be smart": Richard Ravitch: my interview, June 21, 1983; Steven Silberman interviews with Walter Shorenstein, June 22, 1983; Alan Tishman, July 13, 1983; and Bernard Mendik, Aug. 2, 1983.

his first piece of property: Steven Silberman interview with Peter Feinberg, Aug. 4, 1983.
136
a developer has to see: Steven Silberman interview with Larry Silverstein, Aug. 2, 1983. See also Stephen Aris, *The Jews in Business* (London: Jonathan Cape, 1970), Chap. 9.

Melvin Simon of Indianapolis: "The 400 Richest People in America," *Forbes*, special issue, Oct. 1, 1984, p. 118; "The Richest People in America: The Forbes Four Hundred," *Forbes*, Sept. 13, 1982, p. 117.

"The Jews have shown": Quoted in Aris, *The Jews in Business*, p. 69.

a source of upward mobility: Glazer, "Social Characteristics of American Jews," pp. 21–22.
137
"Thrift is the watchword": Jacob Riis, *How the Other Half Lives* (New York: Sagamore Press, 1957), pp. 78–79.

As early as 1908: Glazer, "Social Characteristics of American Jews," p. 15.

"*a life lived in deferment*": Gershom Scholem, "Toward an Understanding of the Messianic Idea in Judaism," in Scholem, *The Messianic Idea in*

Judaism and Other Essays on Jewish Spirituality (New York: Schocken Books, 1971), p. 35. See also Glazer, "Social Characteristics of American Jews," p. 30; Fred L. Strodtbeck, "Family Interaction, Values, and Achievement," in Marshall Sklare, ed., *The Jews* (Glencoe, Ill.: The Free Press, 1958), esp. pp. 152, 154–157.

138

Jewish parents . . . have seen their children: Charles Liebman, *The Ambivalent American Jew* (Philadelphia: Jewish Publication Society of America, 1973), pp. 163–165; Zena Smith Blau, "The Strategy of the Jewish Mother," in Marshall Sklare, ed., *The Jew in American Society* (New York: Behrman House, 1974), pp. 167–187; Natalie F. Joffe, "The Dynamics of Benefice Among East European Jews," *Social Forces*, Vol. 27 (1948–49), pp. 238–247. See also Zborowski and Herzog, *Life Is with People*, pp. 308–329; Strodtbeck, "Family Interaction, Values, and Achievement," pp. 147–165.

"It was not for myself alone": Alfred Kazin, *A Walker in the City*, 1958, pp. 21–22.

"I'm what he lives for": Philip Roth, *Portnoy's Complaint* (New York: Random House, 1969), pp. 30, 5, 8.

"My father lived vicariously": Myra Alperson interview with Jerome Shapiro, Jan. 16, 1984.

"When I am not being punished": *Portnoy's Complaint*, p. 89.

"I was always asked": My interview with Av Westin, July 29, 1983.

'My God, those conversations': My interview with Eugene Eidenberg, Aug. 2, 1983.

139

Nobel Laureate Isidor Rabi: Francis Bello, "The Physicists," in the editors of *Fortune*, *Great American Scientists* (Englewood Cliffs, N.J.: Prentice-Hall, 1961), pp. 7–8, quoted in Stephen J. Whitfield, "Jews and Other Southerners," in Nathan M. Kaganoff and Melvin I. Urofsky, eds., "*Turn to the South*" (Charlottesville: Univ. of Virginia Pres, 1979), p. 79.

"I can't help it that": *Portnoy's Complaint*, pp. 89, 4.

"Jewish mothers seemed": Blau, "The Strategy of the Jewish Mother," pp. 167–187, esp. pp. 170 ff.

Gentiles reared in the Anglo-American tradition: Charles Liebman, *The Ambivalent American Jew*, pp. 163–164.

140

"Jewish mothers were demanding": Blau, "The Strategy of the Jewish Mother," in Sklare, ed., *The Jews in American Society*, p. 173.

his mother could not wait: My interview with Irving Shapiro, Aug. 3, 1983.

"At any signs": Blau, "The Strategy of the Jewish Mother," p. 173.

"What *was* it with these Jewish parents": *Portnoy's Complaint*, p. 119.

141

"Mother, I'm thirty-three!" *Portnoy's Complaint*, pp. 110, 107.

a significantly lower rate: Leo Srole and Anita K. Fischer, eds., *Mental Health in the Metropolis*, rev. and enl. (New York: New York Univ. Press, 1978), Chap. 19; Jerome K. Myers and Bertram H. Roberts, "Some Relationships Between Religion, Ethnic Origin and Mental Illness," in Marshall Sklare, ed., *The Jews*, pp. 551–559.

"a survival-insurance process": Srole and Fischer, eds., *Mental Health in the Metropolis*, p. 424.

Jews consult psychiatrists: Ibid., pp. 421–422.

the much-maligned Jewish mother: Blau, "The Strategy of the Jewish Mother," pp. 183–187.

"a Jewish man": *Portnoy's Complaint*, p. 111.

Jewish college students show: Drew and Williams, *After College: A Longitudinal Study of Jewish Adults*, pp. 39–40; Drew, King, and Richardson, *A Profile of the Jewish College Freshman: 1980*, p. 36; Geraldine Rosenfield, *Jewish College Freshmen: An Analysis of Three Studies* (New York: The American Jewish Committee, 1984), p. 7.

142

these data contradict: Rosenfield, *Jewish College Freshmen*, p. 8.

in Rhode Island: Calvin Goldscheider, "Residential Concentration, Migration, and Jewish continuity," paper presented at conference on Jewish Settlement and Community in the Modern Western World, Center for Jewish Studies, Graduate Center of the City Univ. of New York, March 21–23, 1983, pp. 3–4.

in Cleveland: *Survey of Cleveland's Jewish Population, 1981*, pp. 26–29.

a college away from home: Drew, King, and Richardson, *A Profile of the Jewish Freshman: 1980*, p. 35.

giving almost always flows: Natalie F. Joffe, "The Dynamics of Benefice Among East European Jews," pp. 238–247, esp. pp. 240–242. For a seventeenth-century formulation of this view, see the parable of the birds in *The Memoirs of Gluckel of Hameln*, trans. Marvin Lowenthal (New York: Schocken Books, 1977), pp. 2–3.

not peculiar to: Joffe, "The Dynamics of Benefice," p. 242; Barbara Myerhoff, *Number Our Days* (New York: Dutton), 1978.

143

people listed in . . . *Who's Who:* Stanley Lieberson and Donna K. Carter, "Making It in America: Differences Between Eminent Blacks and White Ethnic Groups," *American Sociological Review*, Vol. 44, No. 3 (June 1979) p. 349, Table 1.

leaders in some eight fields: Richard D. Alba and Gwen Moore, "Ethnicity in the American Elite," *American Sociological Review*, Vol. 47, No. 3 (June 1982), pp. 373–383, esp. pp. 376–378 and Table 1.

some 23 percent of the people: My analysis of "The 400 Richest People in America," *Forbes*, 1984.

* Fn.: W. D. Rubinstein, *The Left, the Right, and the Jews* (London & Canberra: Croom Helm, 1982), pp. 61–64.

† Fn.: My analyses of the 1982 and 1983 *Forbes* 400 List.

144

a group of leading intellectuals: Charles Kadushin, *The American Intellectual Elite* (Boston: Little, Brown, 1974), esp. pp. 19, 23–24, 28–32.

Jews constituted 10 percent: Seymour Martin Lipset and Everett Carll Ladd, Jr., "The Changing Social Origins of American Academics," in Robert K. Merton, James S. Coleman, and Peter H. Rossi, eds., *Qualitative and Quantitative Social Research* (New York: The Free Press, 1979), p. 326. (I am indebted to Professor Lipset for sharing the typescript of an earlier and longer draft with me. Data on proportions of each religion teaching at top-ranked institutions are from the earlier draft.) See also Stephen Steinberg, *The Academic Melting Pot,* (New York: McGraw-Hill, 1974), Chaps. 5–6.

"Jewish professors are also far more likely": My analysis of data in Seymour Martin Lipset and Everett Carll Ladd, Jr., "Jewish Academics in the United States: Their Achievements, Culture, and Politics," p. 101, Table 7.

145

an industry that was: The editors of *Fortune, Jews in America,* pp. 57–58.

30 percent of American Nobel laureates: My updating of data in Harriet Zuckerman, *Scientific Elite: Nobel Laureates in the United States* (New York: Columbia Univ. Press, 1977), esp. p. 68. See also Charles Singer, "Science and Judaism," in Louis Finkelstein, ed., *The Jews* (New York: Schocken Books, 1971), Vol. III, Chap. 7; Lewis Feuer, *The Scientific Intellectual* (New York: Basic Books, 1963), pp. 123–128; Ernest van den Haag, *The Jewish Mystique* (New York: Stein & Day, 1977), pp. 22–23.

(In Great Britain . . .): Rubinstein, *The Left, the Right, and the Jews,* pp. 63–64.

It is a fact: Thorstein Veblen, "The Intellectual Preeminence of the Jews," *The Political Science Quarterly,* Vol. XXXIV (March 1919), rptd. in Veblen, *Essays in Our Changing Order,* pp. 221, 223–224.

Few Jews were attracted: Interview with Dr. Emanuel Piore, June 30, 1983, and analysis of changing membership roster of National Academy of Science.

"only when the gifted Jew": Veblen, pp. 225–227, 229–230.

146

"it is by loss of allegiance": Veblen, p. 226.

Nobel laureate such as: Elizabeth Stone, "A Mme. Curie from the Bronx," *The New York Times Magazine,* April 9, 1978.

"professors are . . . more likely: Cohen, *American Modernity and Jewish Identity,* pp. 90–92 and Table 4(5).

the role Jews play: I am indebted to Mordecai Newman and Robin Reif for their research on the role of Jews in the entertainment industries.

147

The Broadway musical: Stanley Green, *The World of Musical Comedy* (New York: Ziff-Davis Publishing Co., 1960); memoranda from Robin Reif, and her interviews with Deena Rosenberg, Nahma Sandrow, Dorothy Rodgers, and William Hammerstein.

Cole Porter . . . was powerfully drawn: Richard Rodgers, *Musical Stages* (New York: Random House, 1975), p. 88.

The motion picture industry: Lary L. May and Elaine Tyler May, "Why Jewish Movie Moguls: An Exploration in American Culture," *American Jewish History*, Vol. LXXII, No. 1 (Sept. 1982), pp. 6–25; the editors of *Fortune*, *Jews in America*, pp. 59–62; Stanley Rothman and S. Robert Lichter, "What Are Movie-Makers Made Of?" *Public Opinion*, Vol. 6, No. 6 (Dec./Jan. 1984), pp. 14–18; Linda S. Lichter, S. Robert Lichter, and Stanley Rothman, "Hollywood and America: The Odd Couple," *Public Opinion*, Vol. 5, No. 6 (Dec./Jan. 1983), pp. 54–58. Mordecai Newman: interviews with Patricia Ehrens, David McClintock, Jeremy Zimmer, Budd Schulberg, Mel Shavelson, Len Hill, and Paul Klein, among others.

Fn: E. Anthony Rotundo, "Jews and Rock and Roll: A Study in Cultural Contrast," *American Jewish History*, Vol. LXXII, No. 1 (Sept. 1982), pp. 82–107.

Berlin likens the Jews: Isaiah Berlin, *Jewish Slavery and Emancipation*, Herzl Institute Pamphlet No. 18 (New York: Herzl Press, 1961), pp. 7–12, 15.

148

To increase his understanding: May and May, "Why Jewish Movie Moguls," pp. 11–12.

The Jews who built: Ibid., pp. 6–25.

149

obsessed with Jewish "domination": See Stephen J. Whitfield, "The American Jew as Journalist," forthcoming. (I am indebted to Professor Whitfield for sharing his manuscript with me before publication.)

Henry Adams was "clean daft": John Higham. *Send These to Me* (New York: Atheneum, 1975), p. 183.

Henry Ford was equally daft: Whitfield, "The American Jew as Journalist."

Spiro Agnew complained: Ibid. Jesse Jackson: Interview on *60 Minutes*, Sept. 16, 1979; see also "Jackson and the Jews," *The New Republic*, March 19, 1984, p. 9.

General George Brown: Stephen J. Whitfield, "From Publik Occurrences to Pseudo-Events: Journalists and Their Critics," in Whitfield, *Voices of Jacob, Hands of Esau* (Hamden, Conn.: Archon Books, 1984), p. 182.

150

"Granted the great power": The editors of *Fortune*, *Jews in America*, pp. 61–62.

When Leo Rosten surveyed: Leo Rosten, *The Washington Correspondents* (New York: Harcourt, Brace, 1937).

"a scruffy occupation": Steven Silberman interview with Reuven Frank, Aug. 4, 1983.

"Going into journalism": My interview with Richard Clurman, July 13, 1983.

journalism was not a profession: Interview with Edward Jay Epstein, July 20, 1983; Joseph Kraft, "The Imperial Media," *Commentary*, Vol. 71, No. 5 (May 1981), pp. 36, 38.

Ben Hecht and Charles MacArthur's 1930 hit: *The Front Page* (New York: Covici, Friede, 1940), p. 1.

151

"My parents told me": Steven Silberman interview with Mel Elfin, July 28, 1983.

his family begged him: My interview with Av Westin, July 29, 1983.

"My Nathan is in the pen line": Interview with Richard Clurman, July 13, 1983.

"the best generation of all": Quoted in Kraft, "The Imperial Media," p. 36.

"among the principal beneficiaries": Ibid., pp. 36–37.

152

The catalyst for this change: See, for example, David Halberstam, *The Powers That Be* (New York: Random House, 1979), pp. 38–44, 68–76, and Theodore H. White, *In Search of History* (New York: Harper & Row, 1978), Chaps. 2–6, esp. pp. 83–85, 102–131.

The number of reporters: White, *In Search of History*, p. 103.

journalism was transformed: Kraft, "The Imperial Media," p. 37.

the emergence of the television networks: Edward Jay Epstein, *News from Nowhere* (New York: Random House, 1973) and *Between Fact and Fiction* (New York: Vintage Books, 1975); my interview with Epstein, July 20, 1983.

a little less than 6 percent: Data from national survey of U.S. journalists by David H. Weaver, Richard G. Gray, and G. Cleveland Wilhoit of Indiana University School of Journalism.

25 to 30 percent of the media elite: S. Robert Lichter and Stanley Rothman, "Media and Business Elites," *Public Opinion*, Vol. 4, No. 5 (Oct./Nov. 1981), p. 43; 1971 figures from Richard D. Alba and Gwen Moore, "Ethnicity in the American Elite," *American Sociological Review*, Vol. 47 (June 1982), p. 377, Table 1.

it was harder for Jews: Gay Talese, *The Kingdom and the Power* (New York: World Publishing, 1969), pp. 58–61, 91–95, 115–116, 168–170; Harrison E. Salisbury, *Without Fear or Favor* (New York: Ballantine Books, 1980), pp. 28–30, 401–403; David Halberstam, *The Powers That Be* (New York: Random House, 1979), pp. 208–209, 213–218.

"put a Jew in the showcase": Halberstam, *The Powers That Be*, pp. 216–217.

"Dad was more concerned": My interview with Arthur Ochs Sulzberger,

June 23, 1983. See also Stephen D. Isaacs, *Jews in American Politics* (Garden City, N.Y.: Doubleday 1974), pp. 47–48.

"comfortable in his own skin": Not-for-attribution interviews, spring of 1983.

Fn.: Talese, *The Power and the Glory*, p. 60.

The Wall Street Journal: Bob Kuttner, "Up The Wall Street Journal," *The New Republic*, April 16, 1984, pp. 15–21.

154

the producers who decide: Epstein, *News from Nowhere;* my interview with Epstein, July 20, 1983; my interviews with Av Westin, July 29 and Aug. 11, 1983. See also Av Westin, *Newswatch* (New York: Simon & Schuster, 1982), esp. Chap. 2.

"Jews are foreign correspondents": Steven Silberman, interview with Richard Cohen, July 26, 1983.

"One thing happened to me": Steven Silberman interview with Hal Bruno, July 29, 1983.

"Journalism had great appeal": My interview with Max Frankel, April 27, 1983.

"The great and near-great": Steven Silberman interview with Mel Elfin, July 28, 1983.

155

"*Yikhus*, *tzedakah*, and a yenta quality": Ibid.

"history on the run": Steven Silberman interview with Richard Cohen, July 26, 1983.

"I am not a distant spectator": Steven Silberman interview with Lawrence Meyer, July 25, 1983.

entry was so easy: Steven Silberman interview with Professor Penn Kimball, Graduate School of Journalism, Columbia University, July 13, 1983.

"You can't say no": Steven Silberman interview with Marvin Kalb, July 24, 1983.

"TV had a tough time": Steven Silberman interview with Reuven Frank, Aug. 4, 1983.

the enormous size and weight: Westin, *Newswatch*, Chap. 1.

"No one would be hired today": Steven Silberman interview with Reuven Frank, Aug. 4, 1983.

156

"I was the first kid": My interview with Av Westin, July 29, 1983.

Don Hewitt, who took charge: Westin, *Newswatch*, pp. 32–34.

"When I started": My interview with Av Westin, Aug. 11, 1983.

CHAPTER FIVE
"I had not known how deeply Jewish I was."

160
one respondent in ten: National Jewish Population Study, *Jewish Identity* (New York: Council of Jewish Federations and Welfare Funds, 1974), p. 15, Table 13–2.

few American Jews believe: Ibid., p. 14, Table 12. See also Marshall Sklare, *Jewish Identity on the Suburban Frontier*, 2d ed. (Chicago: Univ. of Chicago Press, 1979), Chap. 3; the editors of *Commentary*, *The Condition of Jewish Belief* (New York: Macmillan, 1966). The symposium appeared originally in *Commentary* (Aug. 1966).

On the contrary, most Jews: See, for example, Steven M. Cohen, *American Modernity and Jewish Identity* (New York and London: Tavistock Publications, 1983), Chaps. 3–4.

The essence of modernity: Peter L. Berger, *The Heretical Imperative* (Garden City, N.Y.: Anchor Press/Doubleday, 1979), Chap. 1, esp. pp. 3 and 28.

Judaism more so than most: Ibid., pp. 29–31.

161
"It was, indeed": Louis Ginzberg, *The Legends of the Jews* (Philadelphia: Jewish Publication Society of America, 1968), Vol. III, pp. 92–93, and Vol. VI, p. 36, n. 202.

A "disaster is in the making": Elihu Bergman, "The American Jewish Population Erosion," *Midstream* (Oct. 1977), pp. 9–19.

disavowed his forecast: Samuel S. Lieberman and Morton Weinfeld, "Demographic Trends and Jewish Survival," *Midstream* (Nov. 1978), pp. 9–19.

Fn.: Robert Gordis, " 'Be Fruitful and Multiply'–Biography of a Mitzvah," *Midstream* (Aug./Sept. 1982), p. 25.

162
"The world makes many images": Simon Rawidowicz, "Israel: The Ever-Dying People," in Rawidowicz, *Studies in Jewish Thought* (Philadelphia: Jewish Publication Society of America), Chap. 4, esp. pp. 210–211.

"no catastrophe": Ibid., p. 221.

163
"With every day that passes": Jacob Katz, *Out of the Ghetto* (New York: Schocken Books, 1973), p. 134.

"The grandfather believes": Annie Kriegel, "Generational Difference: The History of an Idea," *Daedalus*, Vol. 107, No. 4 (Fall 1978), p. 34.

"a synagogue will not be found": Leon A. Jick, *The Americanization of the Synagogue, 1820–1870* (Hanover, N.H.: Brandeis Univ. Press/Univ. Press of New England, 1976), p. 3.

"increased the Jewish population": Nathan Glazer, "Social Characteristics of American Jews, 1654–1954," *American Jewish Year Book*, Vol. 56 (1955), p. 6.

"Synagogues are springing up": Jick, *The Americanization of the Synagogue*, p. 43.

"Within fifty years": Article by W. M. Rosenblatt in *The Galaxy*, quoted in Abraham J. Karp, *Ideology as Strategy in Jewish Group Survival in America* (Rochester: Univ. of Rochester, n.d.), pp. 22–23.

"Since the downfall": Eulogy at the funeral of Rabbi Abraham Rice, quoted in David Ellenson, "A Jewish Legal Decision by Rabbi Bernard Illowy of New Orleans and Its Discussion in Nineteenth-Century Europe," *American Jewish History*, Vol. LXIX, No. 2, Dec. 1979), p. 178. (I am indebted to Dr. Steve J. Zipperstein, now of Oxford University, for his research on the history and current state of Orthodox Judaism in the United States.)

164

"You sit back": Sermon (delivered on April 24, 1910), in Arthur A. Goren, ed., *Dissenter in Zion* (Cambridge, Mass.: Harvard Univ. Press, 1982), pp. 110, 107.

"A prominent Christian lawyer": Ibid., pp. 113, 107.

English sermons: Aaron Rothkoff, *Bernard Revel* (Philadelphia: Jewish Publication Society of America, 1972), p. 16.

"Three generations rejoiced": Deborah Dash Moore, *At Home in America* (New York: Columbia Univ. Press, 1981), p. 10.

165

"For all that we are": Leonard Fein, "The Jewish Community of the 1980s," *Journal of Jewish Communal Service*, Vol. LVII, No. 1 (Fall 1980), p. 12.

first- and second-generation Norwegian: Nathan Glazer, *American Judaism*, 2d ed. (Chicago: Univ. of Chicago Press, 1972), pp. 4–10; Charles S. Liebman, *The Ambivalent American Jew* (Philadelphia: Jewish Publication Society of America, 1973), Chap. 1.

"a generational clock": Arthur Hertzberg, "The Emancipation: A Reassessment After Two Centuries," *Modern Judaism*, Vol. 1, No. 1 (May 1981), pp. 46–53, esp. p. 48.

166

"will the Jews continue to exist": Arthur Hertzberg, *Being Jewish in America* (New York: Schocken Books, 1979), pp. 82, 85.

In his enormously influential book: Will Herberg, *Protestant-Catholic-Jew* (Garden City, N.Y.: Doubleday, 1955), esp. Chaps. 3, 8.

"straight-line theory": The term was coined by Neil C. Sandberg in his *Ethnic Identity and Assimilation: The Polish-American Community* (New York: Praeger, 1974).

167

ethnicity was alive: Nathan Glazer and Daniel P. Moynihan, *Beyond the Melting Pot* (Cambridge, Mass.: MIT Press and Harvard Univ. Press, 1963). (The quotation is on p. xcvii of the second edition.) See also Glazer and Moynihan, introduction to the second edition, esp. pp. xxxi–xlii, lxxvi–xci.

a new appreciation: See, for example, Andrew M. Greeley, *Ethnicity in the United States* (New York: John Wiley, 1974); Talcott Parsons, "Some

Theoretical Considerations on the Nature and Trends of Change of Ethnicity," in Nathan Glazer and Daniel P. Moynihan, eds., *Ethnicity* (Cambridge, Mass.: Harvard Univ. Press, 1975); Gerald D. Suttles, *The Social Order of the Slum* (Chicago and London: Univ. of Chicago Press, 1968); Harold R. Isaacs, *Idols of the Tribe* (New York: Harper & Row, 1975); Michael Novak, *The Unmeltable Ethnics* (New York: Macmillan, 1971); William Yancey, Eugene P. Ericksen, and Richard N. Juliani, "Emergent Ethnicity: A Review and Reformulation," *American Sociological Review,* Vol. 41, No. 3 (June 1976), pp. 391–403; William Yancey, Eugene P. Ericksen and George Leon, "The Structure of Pluralism: 'We're All Italian Around Here. Aren't We, Mrs. O'Brien?,' " paper presented at the SUNY-Albany conference "Ethnicity and Race in the Last Quarter of the Twentieth Century," April 6–7, 1984.

A principal weakness: Herbert J. Gans, "Symbolic Ethnicity: The Future of Ethnic Groups and Cultures in America," in Herbert J. Gans, Nathan Glazer, Joseph R. Gusfield, and Christopher Jencks, eds., *On the Making of Americans: Essays in Honor of David Riesman* (Philadelphia: Univ. of Pennsylvania Press, 1979), p. 195. On Gans's advocacy of straight-line theory, see Gans, "Ethnicity, Acculturation and Assimilation," foreword to Neil Sandberg, *Ethnic Identity and Assimilation* (New York: Praeger, 1974).

ethnicity may remain: Gans, *Symbolic Ethnicity,* pp. 193–220, esp. pp. 200 ff.

168

Instead of returning: Ibid., pp. 204 ff.

The Talmud: Jacob Neusner, *Stranger at Home* (Chicago: Univ. of Chicago Press, 1981), pp. 35–39. See also Gerson D. Cohen, "The Talmudic Age," in Leo W. Schwarz, ed., *Great Ages and Ideas of the Jewish People* (New York: Modern Library, 1956), Chap. 7.

Samuel . . . was noted for: *Encyclopedia Judaica,* Vol. 14, pp. 786–788.

"Moses Maimonides": Isadore Twersky, Introduction to Twersky, ed., *A Maimonides Reader* (New York: Behrman House, 1972), pp. 1–29; *Encyclopedia Judaica,* Vol. 11, pp. 754–764, 777–780.

169

the history of Judaism: Neusner, *Stranger at Home,* p. 50.

over the long sweep: Gerson D. Cohen, "The Blessing of Assimilation in Jewish History," commencement address, Hebrew Teachers College, June 1966.

immigrants were less observant: Charles S. Liebman, "Orthodoxy in American Jewish Life," *American Jewish Year Book,* Vol. 66 (1965), pp. 27–30; David Singer, "David Levinsky's Fall: A Note on the Liebman Thesis," *American Quarterly,* Vol. XIX, No. 4 (Winter 1967), pp. 696–706.

170

"To America!": Abraham Cahan, *The Rise of David Levinsky* (New York: Harper & Row–Torchbooks, 1960), p. 61.

"My former interest": Ibid., p. 59.

"socialism, Zionism": Nathan Glazer, *American Judaism,* pp. 65–66.

David Toback: Carole Malkin, *The Journeys of David Toback* (New York: Schocken Books, 1981).

"It was as though": Cahan, *The Rise of David Levinsky*, pp. 101, 93.

171

"all that is new": Charles Liebman, "Religion and the Chaos of Modernity," in Jacob Neusner, ed., *Take Judaism, for Example* (Chicago: Univ. of Chicago Press, 1983), esp. p. 151.

if they dropped one practice: Glazer, *American Judaism*, pp. 69–70.

Orthodoxy "is absolutely inflexible": Cahan, *The Rise of David Levinsky*, p. 110.

"Jews lost their faith": Glazer, *American Judaism*, pp. 69–70.

172

only 25 percent: Ibid., pp. 72–73.

Twenty-five years later: Ibid., p. 86.

a 1935 survey: Ibid., p. 85.

Today, by comparison: Steven M. Cohen, Shelley Tenenbaum, and Paul Ritterband, "Age and Life Cycle Differences in Jewish Identification," Report No. 4 (New York: Greater New York Jewish Population Study, 1983), mimeo, Table 1. See also Calvin Goldscheider, *Jewish Continuity and Change: Emerging Patterns in America* (Bloomington: Indiana Univ. Press, 1985).

relation between religion and ethnicity: Charles S. Liebman, *The Ambivalent American Jew* (Philadelphia: Jewish Publication Society of America, 1973), pp. 9–15.

in 1917, for example: Arthur A. Goren, *New York Jews and the Quest for Community* (New York: Columbia Univ. Press, 1970), p. 78. See also Irving Howe, *World of Our Fathers* (New York: Harcourt Brace Jovanovich, 1976), pp. 190–199; Kate Simon, *Bronx Primitive* (New York: Harper & Row–Colophon Books, 1983).

173

the immigrants formed: Charles S. Liebman, "Orthodoxy in American Jewish Life," pp. 27–28.

"In the communal life": Howe, *World of Our Fathers*, p. 190.

Even the anti-religious: Ibid., p. 191.

"Although my parents": Vivian Gornick, "There Is No More Community," *InterChange*, Vol. 2, No. 8 (April 1977), p. 4.

174

"It was in the very nature": Ibid., p. 5.

"At the age of five": Howe, *World of Our Fathers*, pp. 274–275.

"Back in my freshman year": Philip Roth, *Portnoy's Complaint* (New York: Random House, 1969), p. 9.

175

"often in later years": Norman Podhoretz, *Making It* (New York: Random House, 1967), p. 25.

"The father had pride": Anne Roiphe, *Generation Without Memory* (New York: Linden Press/Simon & Schuster, 1981), p. 167.

"The second-generation community": Judith R. Kramer and Seymour Leventman, *Jews of the Gilded Ghetto* (New Haven: Yale Univ. Press, 1961), p. 11.

In 1920: Deborah Dash Moore, *At Home in America*, p. 30.

176

"Participation in the myriad aspects": Ibid., p. 4.

synagogues went up as well: Ibid., Chap. 5.

"one could live a": Nathan Glazer, *American Judaism*, p. 118.

177

Gentiles were usually different: Marshall Sklare, *Conservative Judaism*, enl. ed. (New York: Schocken Books, 1972), p. 67; Glazer, *American Judaism*, pp. 118–119; Harry Gersh, "The New Suburbanites of the '50's, Jewish Division," *Commentary* (March 1954), pp. 209–221.

"Italians were really": Kate Simon, *Bronx Primitive* (New York: Harper & Row–Colophon Books, 1983), p. 94.

Jews felt awkward: Herbert J. Gans, "The Origin and Growth of a Jewish Community in the Suburbs: A Study of the Jews of Park Forest," in Marshall Sklare, ed., *The Jews* (Glencoe, Ill.: The Free Press, 1958), pp. 205–248. See also Gans, "American Jewry: Present and Future," *Commentary* (May 1956), pp. 422–430, and "The Future of American Jewry, Part II," *Commentary* (June 1956), pp. 555–563; Morris Freedman, "New Jewish Community in Formation," *Commentary* (Jan. 1955), pp. 36–47; Harry Gersh, "The New Suburbanites of the '50's, Jewish Division," *Commentary* (March 1954), pp. 209–221; Evelyn N. Rossman, "The Community and I," *Commentary* (Nov. 1954), pp. 393–405; Marshall Sklare, *Jewish Identity on the Suburban Frontier*, 2d ed. (Chicago: Univ. of Chicago Press, 1979), esp. Chap. 1; Benjamin B. Ringer, *The Edge of Friendliness* (New York: Basic Books, 1967), esp. Chaps. 1–5.

"sticking out": Gans, "The Origin and Growth of a Jewish Community in the Suburbs," p. 243.

"The synagogue symbolizes": Gersh, "The New Suburbanites of the '50's, Jewish Division," p. 217.

178

"In moving from city": Ibid., pp. 217–218.

"We need a synagogue": Gans, "The Origin and Growth of a Jewish Community," p. 224.

In the 1920s: Sklare, *Jewish Identity on the Suburban Frontier*, pp. 351, 357.

In the early 1960s: Ibid., pp. 354–358.

179

"Unlike sections of Nassau": Freedman, "New Jewish Community in Formation," p. 36.

"When your street": Gersh, "The New Suburbanites," p. 220.

In Park Forest in the early 1950s: Gans, "The Origin and Growth of a Jewish Community," p. 236.

180

"Most parents' knowledge": Gersh, "The New Suburbanites," p. 220.

they turned to rabbis: Glazer, *American Judaism,* pp. 111–113, 118–125; Gans, "The Origin and Growth of a Jewish Community," pp. 214–226; Gersh, "The New Suburbanites," pp. 220–221; Sklare, *Jewish Identity on the Suburban Frontier,* Chaps. 3, 9.

"Intellectually, many of us": Gersh, "The New Suburbanites," p. 220.

The most popular rituals: Sklare, *Jewish Identity on the Suburban Frontier,* pp. 49–59; Gans, "The Origin and Growth of a Jewish Community," pp. 219–221.

"re-created for the children": Glazer, *American Judaism,* p. 122.

181

the ultimate vindication: Ibid., pp. 125–126.

"a Copernican revolution": Mordecai M. Kaplan, *Judaism as a Civilization* (Philadelphia and New York: Jewish Publication Society of America/Reconstructionist Press, 1981), p. xiv.

"And if these forms": Glazer, *American Judaism,* p. 125.

it would be hard to exaggerate: See Glazer, *American Judaism,* p. 151; Hertzberg, *Being Jewish in America,* pp. 210–220; Marshall Sklare, "Lakeville and Israel: The Six-Day War and Its Aftermath," *Midstream* (Oct. 1968), pp. 3–21, rptd. in Sklare, ed., *American Jews: A Reader* (New York: Behrman House, 1983), pp. 413–439; Milton Himmelfarb, "The 1967 War," in Himmelfarb, *The Jews of Modernity* (Philadelphia: Jewish Publication Society of America, 1973), pp. 343–360; Lucy Dawidowicz, "American Public Opinion," *American Jewish Year Book,* Vol. 69 (1968), pp. 198–229.

Chronology of events leading to Six-Day War: *Encyclopedia Judaica,* Vol. 14, pp. 1624–28, and Nadav Safran, *Israel: The Embattled Ally* (Cambridge, Mass.: Belknap Press of Harvard Univ. Press, 1978), Chap. 21, esp. pp. 388–390. For a detailed history, see Theodore Draper, *Israel and World Politics* (New York: Viking Press, 1968), esp. pp. 41–136.

182

the churches themselves: My own notes and recollections of the period. See also Dawidowicz, "American Public Opinion," p. 218; Hertzberg, *Being Jewish in America,* pp. 216–217.

Jews had paid little attention: Deborah E. Lipstadt, "The Holocaust: Symbol and 'Myth' in American Jewish Life," *Forum on the Jewish People, Zionism and Israel,* No. 40 (Winter 1980/81), pp. 73–88; Glazer, *American Judaism,* 1st ed., 1957, p. 114; 2d ed., rev., 1972, pp. 155–156, 169–186.

183

Before Elie Wiesel's *Night:* Data from Georges Borchard Agency, July 31, 1984.

When *Commentary* conducted: Symposium in the Aug. 1966 *Commentary,* rptd. by the editors of *Commentary* as *The Condition of Jewish Belief* (New York: Macmillan, 1969).

"anxiety and tension were commonplace": Dawidowicz, "American Public Opinion," pp. 204–205.

"In those days": Abraham Joshua Heschel, *Israel: An Echo of Eternity* (New York: Farrar, Straus & Giroux, 1969), pp. 197, 198, 199.

184

"I must confess surprise": Glazer, *American Judaism*, p. 178.

"As soon as the Arab armies": Arthur Hertzberg, "Israel and American Jewry," *Commentary* (Aug. 1967), rptd. in Hertzberg, *Being Jewish in America*, p. 210.

one of the gloomiest predictions: Hertzberg, "The Present Casts a Deep Shadow," *Jewish Heritage*, Vol. 6, No. 3 (Winter 1963–64), rptd. in *Being Jewish in America*, p. 85.

Commentary's editors: *The Condition of Jewish Belief*.

185

"The two greatest events": Glazer, *American Judaism*, 1st ed., p. 114.

threw caution to the wind: Dawidowicz, "American Public Opinion," p. 204.

"We lost our cool": Leonard Fein, "Israel's Crisis: Its Effect on the American Jewish Community and Its Implications for Jewish Communal Service," *Journal of Jewish Communal Service*, Vol. 45 (Fall 1968), p. 14, quoted in Marc Lee Raphael, *A History of the United Jewish Appeal, 1939–1982*, Brown Judaic Series 34 (Scholars Press, 1982), p. 84.

"It seemed as if": Dawidowicz, "American Public Opinion," p. 206.

Between May 22 and June 10: Hertzberg, *Being Jewish in America*, p. 211; Raphael, *A History of the United Jewish Appeal*, p. 77.

for the year as a whole: Abraham J. Karp, *To Give Life* (New York: Schocken Books, 1981), p. 145; Charles S. Liebman, *The Ambivalent American Jew* (Philadelphia: Jewish Publication Society of America, 1973), p. 91, Table 4.1.

"The UJA didn't raise money": Raphael, *A History of the United Jewish Appeal*, p. 77.

an . . . effective fund-raising apparatus: Ibid., Chaps. 1–2; Karp, *To Give Life*, Chaps. 9–10; Milton Goldin, *Why They Give* (New York: Macmillan, 1976), Chaps. 5–6; Joseph J. Schwartz and Beatrice I. Vulcan, "Overseas Aid," and Abraham G. Duker, "The Problems of Coordination and Unity," in Oscar I. Janowsky, ed., *The American Jew: A Reappraisal* (Philadelphia: Jewish Publication Society of America, 1967), Chaps. 9, 11.

187

the UJA became a powerful force: Raphael, *A History of the UJA*, Chaps. 3–4; Karp, Chaps. 11–13.

188

"The American Red Cross and United Way": Red Cross figure from Goldin, *Why They Give*, p. 173; United Way figure supplied by United Way, Arlington, Va. (April 10, 1985, phone conversation with Pat McClenic).

To raise these sums: Raphael, Chaps. 3–5, esp. pp. 21–22; Karp, pp. 87–89. On Baruch and Swope, see also E. J. Kahn, Jr., *The World of Swope* (New York: Simon & Schuster), pp. 436–437, and James Grant, *Bernard Baruch* (New York: Simon & Schuster, 1983), p. 287.

To understand this approach: See, for example, Allan Lehman, "Tzedakah: Traditions," in Sharon Strassfeld and Michael Strassfeld, eds., *The Third Jewish Catalog* (Philadelphia: Jewish Publication Society of America, 1980), pp. 12–19, and Jacob Neusner, *Tzedakah* (Chappaqua, N.Y.: Rossel Books, 1982), esp. Chaps. 1–4.

189

Fn.: Moses Maimonides, *Mishne Torah*, 9:1–3, trans. David Alschuler in Neusner, *Tzedakah*, pp. 93–94.

The solution: On Willen's role, see Goldin, *Why They Give*, pp. 177–179.

190

On Henry Montor's role, see Raphael, *A History of the UJA*, Chaps. 3–5.

191

"The more you know about your customer": "Aryeh Nesher, Solicitor General," *Moment*, Vol. 2, No. 8 (June 1977), pp. 28–30, 60–62.

invited to a "parlor meeting": Bram Goldsmith, "Parlor Meetings," in Marc Lee Raphael, ed., *Understanding Jewish Philanthropy* (New York: Ktav Publishing Co., 1979), pp. 103–108.

192

the UJA's Young Leadership Cabinet: Gary Rosenblatt, "The Youngers of Zion," *Moment*, Vol. 2, No. 8 (June 1977), pp. 37–40, 66–70. See also Jonathan Woocher, *The 1980 United Jewish Appeal Young Leadership Cabinet: A Profile*, n.d.), mimeo.

some 3000 to 3500 twenty-five-to-forty-year-olds: Interview with Ted Comet, Council of Jewish Federations, Dec. 7, 1984, and with Jonathan Woocher, Dec. 7, 1984.

193

The Cleveland federation: Interview with Henry Zucker, Oct. 18, 1982; interview with Barry Schrage, assistant director Jewish Community Federation of Cleveland, Jan. 29, 1985.

In January 1984: *Jewish Telegraphic Agency Daily News Bulletin*, Jan. 24, 1985, p. 3.

30 to 40 percent of all households: My estimate, based on a variety of sources. In Steven M. Cohen's 1981–82 National Survey of American Jews, for example, 49 percent of the respondents reported that they contribute every year to UJA/federation (*American Jewish Year Book*, Vol. 83 [1983], p. 92, table), and in his 1983 National Survey, 34 percent reported that they contributed $100 or more in the preceding twelve months. (*A Study of Giving Patterns to the United Jewish Appeal*, conducted for UJA by Yankelovich, Skelly and White, Inc. [1981, mimeo], estimates that 50 percent contribute.) Demographic surveys of individual metropolitan areas, in which reports of contributions have been compared with federation records, indicate significant overreporting—most of it, however, on the part of small contributors; Cohen estimates that 75 percent of those who reported

a $100 gift actually gave that amount, which means that 25 percent of household heads contributed $100 or more. Data on differences among cities are based on demographic surveys and/or reports from the federations in question.

194

"In every city": Interview with Henry Zucker, Oct. 18, 1982.

1 percent of the donors: *A Study of Giving Patterns to the United Jewish Appeal.* Similar estimates in Goldin, *Why They Give*, and Raphael, *A History of the UJA*. See also Melvyn Bloom, "The Missing $500,000,000," *Moment*, Vol. 2, No. 8 (June 1977), pp. 30–35.

Sklare returned to "Lakeville": Sklare, "Lakeville and Israel: The Six-Day War and Its Aftermath," pp. 3–21.

195

In New York, where: Interview with Ernest Michel, UJA of Greater New York, Jan. 11, 1985. Los Angeles data: interview with Morris Sherman, Jewish Federation Council of Greater Los Angeles, Jan. 29, 1985. Cleveland data: interview with Barry Schrage, Cleveland Jewish Community Federation, Jan. 10, 1985.

In New York the first: Raphael, *A History of the UJA*, p. 142, Table 8.1. In Columbus, Ohio: Ibid., p. 143, Table 8.2.

For the country as a whole: S. P. Goldberg, "Jewish Communal Services: Programs and Finances," *American Jewish Year Book*, Vol. 73, rptd. in Daniel Elazar, *Community and Polity* (Philadelphia, Jewish Publication Society of America, 1976), p. 297, Table 24.

196

On UJA–Federation relations: conversations with lay and professional leaders at 1979, 1982, and 1983 General Assemblies and 1982 national UJA conference.

197

When the Yom Kippur War broke out: Elazar, *Community and Polity*, Appendix A.

Henry Montor had originated the idea: Raphael, *A History of the UJA*, pp. 34–35.

Fn.: Raphael, pp. 35–37; Goldin, *Why They Give*, pp. 184–186.

198

UJA missions: Raphael, p. 114.

"evil is not the end": Abraham Joshua Heschel, *The Prophets* (Philadelphia: Jewish Publication Society of America, 1962), p. 284.

199

two American adults in five: Steven M. Cohen, *The 1984 National Survey of American Jews* (New York: The American Jewish Committee, 1985) and "What American Jews Believe," *Moment*, Vol. 7, No. 7 (July–Aug. 1982), p. 26.

200

94 percent of the board members: Steven M. Cohen, *Attitudes of American Jews Toward Israel and Israelis: The 1983 National Survey of American Jews and Jewish Communal Leaders* (New York: Institute on American

Jewish-Israeli Relations, The American Jewish committee, 1984), p. 7, Table 3.

the number of Jewish young people: Data from Donald Adelman, American Zionist Youth Foundation (interview Dec. 11, 1984).

warm and close feelings toward Israel: Data from *The 1983 National Survey of American Jews and Jewish Communal Leaders.*

201

"One way or another": Albert Memmi, *Portrait of a Jew* (New York: Viking Press, 1971), pp. 25–26.

I think it must have been this way: Nancy Weber, "The Truth of Tears," *The Village Voice*, June 15, 1967, quoted in Dawidowicz, "American Public Opinion," p. 211.

"This crisis has": Arthur Hertzberg, "Israel and American Jewry," *Commentary* (Aug. 1967), in Hertzberg, *Being Jewish in America*, pp. 218–219.

202

"No more does the Jew": Sklare, "Lakeville and Israel: The Six-Day War and Its Aftermath," pp. 11–12.

"Them's damn fightin' Jews": Eli N. Evans, *The Provincials* (New York: Atheneum, 1973), p. 108.

their stature had risen: Sklare, "Lakeville and Israel," p. 15.

R. H. Edwin Espy: Dawidowicz, "American Public Opinion," p. 219.

Less than a month later: Ibid.

203

During the nineteen years of Jordanian rule: Alan M. Tigay, ed., *Myths and Facts, 1980* (Washington, D.C.: Near East Report, 1980), pp. 172–173.
"idolatry of the land": The Reverend William Harter, "American Protestants and Israel," address to Anti-Defamation League, Nov. 17, 1978.

"All persons who seek": Henry P. Van Dusen, letter to the editor, *The New York Times*, July 7, 1967, quoted in Dawidowicz, "American Public Opinion," p. 221.

"The world begrudges Israel": Elie Wiesel, *One Generation After* (New York: Random House, 1970), p. 132.

"I have felt obliged": Milton Himmelfarb, *The Jews of Modernity*, p. 353.

204

National Conference on New Politics: Dawidowicz, American Public Opinion," pp. 228–229.

their "overwhelming aloneness": Glazer, *American Judaism*, 2d ed., rev., p. 171.

205

As Leon Wieseltier wrote: Leon Wieseltier, "Brothers and Keepers," *The New Republic*, Feb. 11, 1985, pp. 21–23.

on college campuses: Dawidowicz, "American Public Opinion," pp. 216–218.

206

the emergence of a "Jewish counterculture": Bill Novak, "The Making of a Jewish Counter-Culture," in Jacob Neusner, ed., *Contemporary Judaic Fellowship in Theory and Practice* (New York: Ktav Publishing Co., 1972), Chap. 9. See also *Response*, Vol. VI, No. 3 (Fall 1972): Bill Novak, "Jewish Survival and the New Priorities," pp. 5–13; Richard L. Narva, "The Still-born Revolution? Reforming the Philanthropies," pp. 15–22; and "The Jewish Students Movement: Four Viewpoints," pp. 23–33. See also James A. Sleeper and Alan L. Mintz, eds., *The New Jews* (New York: Vintage Books, 1971).

The most characteristic expression: Stephen C. Lerner, "The *Havurot*"; Arthur Green, "*Havurat Shalom:* A Proposal" and "Some Liturgical Notes from *Havurat Shalom*"; Bill Novak, "The *Havurah* in New York City: Some Notes on the First Year" and "Havurat Shalom: A Personal Account"—all in Neusner, ed., *Contemporary Judaic Fellowship in Theory and Practice*, Chaps. 8, 10, 11, 12, and 21.

The students made their presence felt: "The Jewish Students Movement: Four Viewpoints," pp. 23–33.

207

The criticism came to a head: The most detailed account is in Gary Rosenblatt, "The Life and Death of a Dream," *Baltimore Jewish Times*, Nov. 7, 1980, pp. 43–45. See also Narva, "The Stillborn Revolution? Reforming the Philanthropies," in *Response*, Vol. VI, no. 3, Fall 1972, pp. 15–22, and Elazar, *Community and Polity*, pp. 224–225. (My account is based also on conversations with Steven Shaw and Hillel Levine.)

"Knowing that we were given": Hillel Levine, "To Share a Vision," *Response*, Vol. III, No. 3 (Winter 1969–70), pp. 3–10.

208

Oscar Janowsky described them: Oscar I. Janowsky, *The JWB Survey* (New York: Dial Press, 1948), p. 241.

209

the trouble caused by "hyper-Jews": Charles S. Liebman, "Leadership and Decision-Making in a Jewish Federation: The New York Federation of Jewish Philanthropies," *American Jewish Year Book*, Vol. 79 (1979), pp. 23–24.

In the early 1960s: Interview with Carmi Schwartz, Feb. 5, 1980, and Oct. 22, 1982.

210

Cedars-Sinai Hospital refused: Interview with Rabbi Maurice Lamm, June 11, 1979.

The hospital has a rabbi now: Ibid.

no provision had been made: Interview with Carmi Schwartz, Feb. 5, 1980.

The change is more than culinary: My observations at 1979, 1982, and 1983 General Assemblies.

Fn. 12: Conversation with Elie Wiesel, fall of 1979. See also Elazar, *Community and Polity*, pp. 324–325.

211
This is particularly evident: Jonathan S. Woocher, "The 'Civil Judaism' of Communal Leaders," *American Jewish Year Book,* Vol. 81 (1981), pp. 149–169, and "'Jewish Survivalism' as Communal Ideology: An Empirical Assessment, *Journal of Jewish Communal Service,* Vol. LVII, No. 4 (Summer 1981), pp. 291–303. See also Deborah E. Lipstadt, "From Noblesse Oblige to Personal Redemption: The Changing Profile and Agenda of American Jewish Leaders," *Modern Judaism,* Vol. 4, No. 3 (Oct. 1984), pp. 295–309; Elazar, *Community and Polity* (Philadelphia: Jewish Publication Society of America, 1976), Chaps. 9–10; Charles S. Liebman, "Leadership and Decision-Making in a Jewish Federation: The New York Federation of Jewish Philanthropies," pp. 3–76, esp. pp. 20–34, 60–72.

a shift in federation priorities: Conversations with federation executives in New York, Cleveland, Miami, Houston, San Diego, Los Angeles, Baltimore, Des Moines, and San Francisco, among others. In New York City, for example, federation grants to hospitals have declined from 40 percent in the early 1950s to under 10 percent in 1984.

212
a slow but steady decline: Raphael, *A History of the UJA,* p. 96. (Raphael estimates a reduction of 2.5 percentage points a year.) Recent data from UJA. (Percentages are approximate because of inconsistencies in the way data are reported.)

"UJA has always been": Not-for-attribution interview with UJA officer, Jan. 21, 1985.

UJA "is America's Jewish religion": Raphael, *A History of the UJA,* p. 115. Mr. Bernstein expressed the same view in my interviews with him on May 7, 1980, and May 25, 1982.

a national UJA conference: My notes on the annual meeting of UJA's National Campaign Policy Board in Washington, D.C., May 20–21, 1982.

213
"That's pretty dull stuff": Not-for-attribution interview, April 26, 1983.

U.S. governmental aid to Israel: See, for example, Robert S. Greenberger, "Israel Secretly Requests $12 Billion in Aid From U.S. for 3 Years," *The Wall Street Journal,* Jan. 24, 1985, p. 60.

a single subcommittee vote: Interview with Kenneth Wollack, former chief congressional lobbyist for American–Israel Public Affairs Committee (AIPAC), March 10, 1980. Interview with I. L. Kenen (former director AIPAC), March 10, 1980.

One beneficiary has been: Budget and staff data from Thomas Dine, Feb. 5, 1985; other information from AIPAC staff member, Feb. 6, 1985.

at least 54 of which: "Study Finds Pro-Israeli PAC's Active in '84 Races," *The New York Times,* Aug. 16, 1984.

The change came first in Los Angeles: David Halberstam, *The Powers That Be* (New York: Random House, 1979), pp. 274–275.

215
New York City's Metropolitan Museum of Art: Grace Glueck, "Met Mu-

seum Aiming to Tap Real-Estate Industry," *The New York Times*, Nov. 9, 1981.

Jews play: On Baltimore: interview with Dr. Louis Kaplan, April 1, 1981; Elsa A. Solender, "Joseph Meyerhoff: The Man and 'His' Hall," *Baltimore Jewish Times*, July 9, 1982; and obituary for Meyerhoff in *The New York Times*, Feb. 4, 1985. On Miami: interview with Brenda Shapiro, Jan. 19, 1981.

This has affected Jewish philanthropies: Interview with Carmi Schwartz, Feb. 6, 1985.

"There's more *yikhus*": Not-for-attribution interview, Aug. 25, 1983.

To UJA leaders of the old school: Not-for-attribution interviews in June 1982 and Jan. 1985. On oratorical ability of UJA leaders: letter from Jonathan Woocher, Sept. 16, 1982.

216

"Irving may not have been": Interview, Jan. 21, 1985.

In the late 1970s: Raphael, *A History of the UJA*, p. 102; not-for-attribution interviews, May 20, 1982, Jan. 21, 1985, Feb. 2, 1985, and undated notes of conversations with UJA lay leaders.

217

On the Jewish Agency: Charles S. Liebman, *Pressure Without Sanctions* (Rutherford: Fairleigh Dickinson Univ. Press, 1977), Chap. 6; Ernest Stock, "The Reconstitution of the Jewish Agency: A Political Analysis," *American Jewish Year Book* Vol. 71 (1972); *The Jewish Agency for Israel: A Brief Description*, United Jewish Appeal (n.d.)

anything but a model: Marvin Schick, "Has the Time Come to Scrap the Jewish Agency?" *Long Island Jewish World*, July 22–28, 1983, p. 5; not-for-attribution interview with UJA executive, March 29, 1982. See also Eliezer Jaffe, "A price of politics," *The Jerusalem Post*, June 26–July 2, 1983, and "Wanted: A New Agency," *Moment* (April 1983), pp. 62–63; Robert E. Loup, "No, Dr. Jaffe," *Moment* (June 1983), pp. 61–63; Charles Hoffman, "Five-Star Heresy," *The Jerusalem Post*, Dec. 25–31, 1983, p. 11; Judy Siegel-Itzkovich, "The Fund-Raisers' Revolt," *The Jerusalem Post*, Nov. 6–12, 1893.

218

funds for Israeli political parties: Raphael, *A History of the UJA*, pp. 74–76; Loup, "No, Dr. Jaffe," p. 61; Goldin, *Why They Give*, pp. 201–202.

leaders failed to take action: Liebman, *Pressure Without Sanctions*, pp. 192–194.

the debt stood at $650 million: Not-for-attribution interview with UJA executive, March 29, 1982; reports on Jewish Agency debt at UJA National Campaign Policy Board, May 20–21, 1982; Jaffe, "A price of politics."

219

"people think they're giving for programs": Not-for-attribution interview, March 29, 1982.

"the fund-raisers' revolt": Judy Siegel-Itzkovich, "The Fund-Raisers' Revolt."

There has been another revolt: Not-for-attribution interviews Jan. 21 and Feb. 2, 1985.

"You don't have to be a bad manager": Interview with Stanley Horowitz, Jan. 25, 1985.

Chapter Six
Looking Out the Window: The Renewal of American Judaism

221
"Memory is among the most fragile": Yosef Hayim Yerushalmi, *Zakhor* (Seattle: Univ. of Washington Press, 1982), p. 5.
222
"the commandment of faith": Abraham Joshua Heschel, *Israel* (New York: Farrar, Straus & Giroux, 1969), p. 200.

"Generation Without Memory": Anne Roiphe, *Generation Without Memory* (New York: Linden Press/Simon & Schuster, 1981).

"Two Jews are walking": William Novak and Moshe Waldoks, eds., *The Big Book of Jewish Humor* (New York: Harper & Row, 1981), p. 62.
223
42 percent of the Jewish students: Geraldine Rosenfield, *Jewish College Freshmen: An Analysis of Three Studies* (New York: The American Jewish Committee, 1984), p. 7, Table 6.
224
"We were living in Miami": Nathan Perlmutter, *Bias and Reflections* (New York: Arbor House, 1972).

names are a public: See, for example, Harold R. Isaacs, *Idols of the Tribe* (New York: Harper & Row, 1975), Chap. 5.

"a mania for renaming": Amos Elon, *The Israelis* (New York: Holt, Rinehart & Winston, 1971), p. 125.
225
the great majority of American Jews: The thesis will be demonstrated in the remainder of this chapter.

others are electing to come in: For individual instances, see Paul Cowan, *An Orphan in History* (Garden City, N.Y.: Doubleday, 1982) and Anne Roiphe, *Generation Without Memory*. For analyses of one or another aspect of the religious revitalization, see Carl Scheingold, *New Pockets of Jewish Energy* (New York: The American Jewish Committee, 1982); Gerald Bubis and Harry Wasserman with Alan Lert, *Synagogue Havurot* (Washington, D.C.: Univ. Press of America, 1983); Eugene Borowitz, *The Mask Jews Wear*, updated version (Port Washington, N.Y.: *Sh'ma*, 1980), pp. 215–235; James A. Sleeper and Alan L. Mintz, eds., *The New Jews* (New York: Vintage Books, 1971); Gerson D. Cohen, "State of World Jewry Address, 1982" (New York: 92nd Street YM-YWHA, 1983); Jonathan D. Sarna, "The Great American Jewish Awakening," *Midstream* (Oct. 1982), pp. 30–34; Sara Bershtel and Allen Graubard, "The Jewish Revival: A New Saving Remnant?" *Dissent* (Summer 1982), pp. 314–319; Natalie

Gittelson, "American Jews Rediscover Orthodoxy," *The New York Times Magazine*, Sept. 30, 1984, pp. 41 ff.; Fran Schumer, "A Return to Religion," *The New York Times Magazine*, April 15, 1984, pp. 90 ff. For statistical evidence, see Steven M. Cohen, Shelley Tenenbaum, and Paul Ritterband, "Age Cohort and Lifecycle Differences in Jewish Identification" (New York: The Greater New York Jewish Population Study, 1984), mimeo, and Calvin Goldscheider, *Jewish Continuity and Change: Emerging Paterns in America* (Bloomington: Indiana Univ. Press, 1985).

more than 300 American colleges: Data from reports of the Association for Jewish Studies. See also Cohen, "State of World Jewry Address, 1982."

important programs at such places: Jacob Neusner, "Judaic Studies at Universities," lecture presented at Duke Univ., Sept. 19, 1984. Data on Indiana Univ. from 1984 newsletter of Jewish Studies Program, Indiana Univ.

227

a transformation in the way: Cohen, "State of World Jewry Address, 1982."

it took forceful intervention: Estelle Gilson, "A Book Contract" (interview with Sal W. Baron), *Columbia* (Nov. 1982), pp. 9–10.

a university curriculum: Jacob Neusner, *Professors or Curators? Universities or Museums? The Case of Jewish Studies* (Columbus, Ohio: Melton Center for Jewish Studies, Ohio State Univ., 1983), p. 2.

recognition of Jewish studies: Cohen, "State of World Jewry Address, 1982."

Fn.: Neusner, *Professors or Curators?*, pp. 1–14.

228

Data on 92nd Street Y: Letter from John Ruskay, Sept. 19, 1984.

"The joint is jumping": Bob Davis, "Lively and Soulful, Old Klezmer Music Undergoes a Revival," *The Wall Street Journal*, April 15, 1983, pp. 1, 20.

229

"We're not playing it": Neil Riesner, "The New-Old Jewish Music," *Hadassah Magazine* (June–July 1983), p. 17.

"Like most things Jewish nowadays": Ibid., p. 16.

part of a much broader upsurge: Anita Diamant, "Jewish Renaissance," *The Boston Phoenix*, March 23, 1982, Sec. 2. See also articles in *National Jewish Arts Newsletter*, pub. by Martin Steinberg Center of American Jewish Congress, and *Jewish Cultural News*, pub. by National Foundation for Jewish Culture.

"We now have a group": Riesner, "The New-Old Jewish Music," p. 17.

three Jewish high school students in five: James L. Peterson and Nicholas Zill, *American Jewish High School Students* (New York: The American Jewish Committee, 1984), p. 6, Table 1. On the overall reduction of the gulf between generations, see Goldscheider, *Jewish Continuity and Change: Emerging Patterns in America.*

230

"While the awkwardness": Melvin Landsberg, "That Christmas Problem,"

Commentary (Dec. 1954), p. 558. See also Judith R. Kramer and Seymour Leventman, *Children of the Gilded Ghetto* (New Haven: Yale Univ. Press, 1961), pp. 92–94.

231

"Christmas is a kind of checking": Anne Roiphe, *Generation Without Memory*, pp. 206–207.

232

the article was greeted: Ibid., pp. 125–126.

now celebrates Chanukah: Interview with Anne Roiphe, July 11, 1984.

It was a profitable exploration: Roiphe, *Generation Without Memory*, esp. pp. 214, 185, 213.

233

the single most widely observed ritual: Marshall Sklare, *Jewish Identity on the Suburban Frontier*, 2d ed. (Chicago: Univ. of Chicago Press, 1979), Chap. 3, esp. pp. 52–56.

it made perfect sense: Sklare, *Jewish Identity on the Suburban Frontier*, pp. 57–59.

234

According to Steven M. Cohen's annual surveys: Steven M. Cohen, "The 1981–1982 National Survey of American Jews," *American Jewish Yearbook*, Vol. 83 (1983), pp. 89–110, esp. pp. 91–92, Table 1, and p. 94, Table 2; Cohen, *Attitudes of American Jews Toward Israel and Israelis: The 1983 National Survey of American Jews and Jewish Communal Leaders* (New York: The American Jewish Committee, 1983), p. 35. (Because of differences in the samples, the precise proportions vary slightly from year to year.)

235

despite a small increase: Steven M. Cohen, *The Political Attitudes of American Jews: The 1984 National Survey of American Jews* (New York: The American Jewish Committee, 1984), pp. 5–6, Tables.

Fn.: Ibid., plus conversation with Steven Cohen, Aug. 18, 1984.

Jewish communal leaders: Cohen, *The 1983 National Survey of American Jews and Jewish Communal Leaders*, esp. Tables 3, 5, and 12.

the triumph that Chanukah celebrates: Elias Bickerman, *From Ezra to the Last of the Maccabees* (New York: Schocken Books, 1974), pp. 93–135; Theodore H. Gaster, *Festivals of the Jewish Year* (New York: Morrow Quill Paperbacks, 1978), Chap. 11.

236

Fn.: Bickerman, *From Ezra to the Last of the Maccabees*, esp. pp. 102–111.

Purim would be even more: Irving Greenberg, *Guide to Purim* (New York: National Jewish Resource Center, 1978).

Passover always has been: A complete bibliography would require almost a volume of its own. For some recent descriptions and explanations, see Irving Greenberg, *Guide to Passover* (New York: National Jewish Resource Center); Michael Strassfeld, *The Jewish Holidays* (New York: Harper & Row, 1985); Arthur Waskow, *Seasons of Our Joy* (New York: Bantam Books,

1982); and Ruth Gruber Fredman, *The Passover Seder* (Philadelphia: Univ. of Pennsylvania Press, 1981).

As a child: Interview with Eugene Eidenberg, Aug. 2, 1983.

237

"What do unaffiliated Jews do . . . ?": Letter from Myra Alperson, n.d.

238

the 1965 and 1975 Boston demographic surveys: Steven M. Cohen, *American Modernity and Jewish Identity* (New York and London: Tavistock Publications, 1983), Chap. 3, esp. pp. 54–57, tables 3.1, 3.2, and 3.3.

239

the youngest members: Ibid., p. 57, Table 3.3.

What appears to be: Cohen, Tenenbaum, and Ritterband, "Age Cohort and Life-cycle Differences in Jewish Identification."

240

The "most significant religious reality": Nathan Glazer, *American Judaism*, 2d ed., rev. (Chicago: Univ. of Chicago Press, 1972), pp. 141–144.

Paul Cowan, a staff writer: Paul Cowan, *An Orphan in History* (Garden City, N.Y.: Doubleday, 1982). See also Charles E. Silberman, "Living in 1982 and 5743," review of Cowan's book, *The New York Times Book Review*, Oct. 10, 1982, pp. 13, 23.

242

community plays the role: Glazer, *American Judaism*, p. 148.

243

He is not even unique: Conversation with Paul Cowan, Nov. 1, 1982.

A Des Moines, Iowa, insurance executive: Interview, Dec. 11, 1979.

At breakfast in Houston: Nov. 1981.

244

the definition suggested by: Charles S. Liebman, "The Religious Life of American Jewry," in Marshall Sklare, ed., *Understanding American Jewry* (New Brunswick, N.J.: Transaction Books, 1982), p. 117.

certain common threads: Carl Scheingold, *New Pockets of Jewish Energy* (New York: The American Jewish Committee, 1982), pp. 21–27. I am indebted to Dr. Scheingold for permitting me to read his much longer original draft in typescript.

245

"There is a reaction against": quoted in Fran Schumer, "A Return to Religion," p. 90.

Religion was on the defensive: Ibid., p. 92.

"The exhaustion of modernism": Ibid., p. 98.

the "tremendous resurgence": Ibid., p. 90.

"a Jewish boy in fifth-century Athens": Scheingold, *New Pockets of Jewish Energy*, p. 3. My portrait of Professor X is drawn from the original version of Scheingold's monograph and from my interview with Professor X on Jan. 24, 1983.

247

"I can't say to you": Schumer, "A Return to Religion," p. 98.

the first experience with "transcendence": Ibid., p. 93.

248

For Michael Medved: Profile of Medved and the Pacific Jewish Center from my interviews with Medved on June 11, 1979, and Oct. 28, 1984, and speech by Medved, Nov. 13, 1982. See also Paul Cowan, "A Renaissance in Venice," *Jewish Living* (March/April 1980), pp. 52–58. On other members of the community, see Arlene and Howard Eisenberg, "We Found God Again," *Woman's Day*, April 24, 1984, pp. 95, 98–99.

250

"Through all of our work": Leonard J. Fein et al., *Reform Is a Verb* (New York: Union of American Hebrew Congregations, 1972), p. 140.

"I had a need": Evening meeting of Havurah of South Florida, Jan. 21, 1981. See also Mitchell Chefitz, "The Havurah of South Florida," *Raayanot*, Vol. 3, No. 3 (Summer 1983), pp. 14–18.

251

60 percent were not affiliated: John Ruskay, "The Challenge of Outreach: Examining a Living Model," *The Melton Journal*, No. 18 (Summer 1984), pp. 19–20.

The return to Judaism: Scheingold, *New Pockets of Jewish Energy*, original draft.

For a midwestern couple: Conversation at dinner party, Dec. 1979.

252

"ritual was for ignorant people": Malka Drucker, "Accommodating to an Intramarriage," *Sh'ma*, Jan. 20, 1984, pp. 46–47.

"If Judaism is to have": Glazer, *American Judaism*, p. 150.

253

"Jews have become evangelicals": Kenneth A. Briggs, "Jewish Leaders Strive to Rouse the Uncommitted," *The New York Times*, Aug. 22, 1982, p. B1.

a British-born *baal teshuvah:* Gary Rosenblatt, "Reaching Out to the Unaffiliated," *Baltimore Jewish Times*, July 15, 1983; Arthur Kurzweil, "The God Talk of Jonathan Omer-Man," *The Jewish Monthly* (Jan. 1982).

Harold Schulweis is: My interviews with Rabbi Schulweis, June 11, 1979, and Oct. 30, 1984.

255

Hillel had moved: Henry Rosovsky, "Then and Now: The Jewish Experience at Harvard," *Moment*, Vol. 5, No. 6 (June 1980), pp. 20, 23–24, 27–28.

When Ben-Zion Gold became: Interview with Rabbi Gold, Jan. 24, 1983.

256

There are at least 300: Interview with Carl Scheingold, director National Havurah Committee, Oct. 31, 1984.

257

estimates of the number of synagogue havurot: Ibid.

Cleveland's Fairmount Temple: Interviews with Rabbi Arthur Lelyveld and Cantor Sarah Sagar, Oct. 19, 1982.

258

"The movement that used to be": Interview with Rabbi Alexander Schindler, Nov. 4, 1982.

"the men and women who have entered: Ibid.

259

nearly half the second-generation Jews: Bernard Lazerwitz, "Past and Future Trends in the Size of American Jewish Denominations," *Journal of Reform Judaism,* Vol. XXXVI, No. 3 (Summer 1979), pp. 77–82.

"we cannot command": Alexander Schindler, presidential address, 57th General Assembly, Union of American Hebrew Congregations, Nov. 10–15, 1983.

not the result of any increase: Until quite recently survey data had shown dramatic generation-by-generation declines in the number of Orthodox Jews. See, for example, Lazerwitz, "Past and Future Trends in the Size of American Jewish Denominations," and Calvin Goldscheider, *Jewish Continuity and Change: Emerging Patterns in America.* More recent demographic surveys indicate that the decline has ended.

"The vitality . . . is due: Charles S. Liebman, "Orthodox Judaism Today," *Midstream,* Vol. XXV, No. 7 (Aug./Sept. 1979), pp. 19–26; interview with Rabbi Irving Greenberg, Feb. 13, 1980.

260

In the almost exclusively Orthodox Boro Park: Steven M. Cohen and Paul Ritterband, "Generational Changes in Jewish Identification: Decline, Stability, or Historical Variation?"–to appear in Cohen and Ritterband, *Family, Community and Identity: The Jews of Greater New York,* forthcoming. See also Cohen, "Archtypical Jewish Neighborhoods: Traditional, Ethnic, Suburban and Cosmopolitan Areas in New York," Greater New York Jewish Population Study (March 1983), mimeo, Table 4.

261

During the era of mass immigration: Charles S. Liebman, "Orthodoxy in American Jewish Life," *American Jewish Year Book,* Vol. 66 (1965), pp. 27–30.

The World War II immigrants: Ibid., pp. 67–75. See also Liebman, "A Sociological Analysis of Contemporary Orthodoxy," *Judaism,* Vol. 13, No. 3 (Summer 1964), pp. 285–304, and "Left and Right in American Orthodoxy," *Judaism,* Vol. 15, No. 1 (Winter 1966), pp. 102–107.

262

These "cultural amalgamations": Egon Mayer, *From Suburb to Shtetl* (Philadelphia: Temple Univ. Press, 1979), Chap. 6, esp. pp. 139–142.

"a loss numerically greater": Cynthia Ozick, "Notes Toward Finding the Right Question," *Lilith,* No. 6 (1979), p. 25.

263

Sitting in the women's section: Blu Greenberg, *On Women and Judaism* (Philadelphia: Jewish Publication Society of America, 1981), p. 76.

The time is four years later: Ibid., pp. 76–77.

"In the world at large": Ozick, "Notes Toward Finding the Right Question," p. 21.

a group of highly talented writers: See, for example, Susannah Heschel, ed., *On Being a Jewish Feminist* (New York: Schocken Books, 1983); Elizabeth Koltun, ed., *The Jewish Woman: New Perspectives* (New York: Schocken Books, 1976); Susan Weidman Schneider, *Jewish and Female* (New York: Simon & Schuster, 1984); *On Our Journey: A Creative Shabbat Service* (San Diego: Woman's Institute for Continuing Jewish Education, 1984); *The Role of Women in Jewish Religious Life: A Decade of Change, 1972–1982* (New York: The American Jewish Committee, n.d.), mimeo, among others.

264

"I had never considered myself": Betty Friedan, "Women on the Firing Line," *The New York Times Magazine*, Oct. 28, 1984.

the emergence of women's prayer groups: See, for example, Diana Katcher Bletter, "Women of Spirit," *Hadassah Magazine* (June-July 1984), and citations in following notes.

"Eva Oles, an Orthodox Jew": Jerry Schwartz, "Women Emerging as Force in U.S. Judaism," *Staten Island Advance*, May 21, 1984.

265

a three-year-old women's *davening* group: Larry Cohler, "Women's Davening Group Comes into Its Own, Despite Criticism," *Long Island Jewish World*, July 13–19, 1984. See also Charles Austin, "Orthodox Jewish Women Push Role in Prayer," *The New York Times*, June 6, 1983.

266

"turned itself into a garrison state": Moshe Adler, "Faith and Fear," *Moment*, Vol. 3, No. 9, Sept. 1978, pp. 33–35.

267

to celebrate the birth of a daughter": See, for example, Daniel I. Leifer and Myra Leifer, "On the Birth of a Daughter," in Elizabeth Koltun, ed., *The Jewish Woman*, pp. 21–30; Toby Fishbein Reifman, ed., *Blessing the Birth of a Daughter: Jewish Naming Ceremonies for Girls* (Englewood, N.J.: Ezrat Nashim/T. Reifman, 1978); *Birth Ceremonies* (New York: Jewish Women's Resource Center, 1981); Sharon Strassfeld and Michael Strassfeld, eds., *The Second Jewish Catalog* (Philadelphia: Jewish Publication Society of America, 1976), pp. 30–37; Gary and Sheila Rubin, "Preserving Tradition by Expanding It: Creation of Our Simchat Bat," *Response*, Nos. 41–42, pp. 61–68.

"There is another pole": Lecture by Dr. Paula Hyman at 92nd Street YM-YWHA, March 16, 1982.

268

"the dangers as well as the opportunities": Ralph Pelcovitz, "The Teshuva Phenomenon: The Other Side of the Coin," *Jewish Life* (Fall 1980), pp. 15–21.

Among most of the people: Scheingold, *New Pockets of Jewish Energy*.

"This surprising flowering": Sara Bershtel and Allen Graubard, "The Jewish Revival: A New Saving Remnant?" *Dissent* (Summer 1982), pp. 314–319. See also Jonathan D. Sarna, "The Great American Jewish Awakening," pp. 30–34.

269

Jewish Catalog sales figures from Bernard Levinson, Jewish Publication Society.

270
As the Reform theologian Eugene Borowitz: Lecture by Dr. Borowitz at 92nd Street Y, Feb. 23, 1981.

"a near-inconceivable expansion": Peter L. Berger, *The Heretical Imperative* (Garden City, N.Y.: Anchor Books/Doubleday, 1979), p. 3.

"What previously was fate": Ibid., p. 16.

"Quite simply": Ibid., p. 20.

"Fate does not require reflection": Ibid., p. 22.
271
"In pre-modern situations": Ibid., p. 28.

"Orthodox Jews are able to maintain: Charles S. Liebman, "Orthodox Judaism Today," pp. 23–24.

"Among the dozens of boys and girls": Egon Mayer, *From Suburb to Shtetl*, Philadelphia: Temple University Press, 1979, p. 142.
272
"The one consistent element": David Singer and Moshe Sokol, "Joseph Soloveitchik: Lonely Man of Faith," *Modern Judaism*, Vol. 2, No. 3 (Oct. 1982), p. 229.

"the great dilemma": Joseph B. Soloveitchik, "The Lonely Man of Faith," *Tradition*, Vol. 7, No. 2 (Summer 1965), p. 9.

"I am lonely": Ibid., p. 6.

"It is not the plan": Ibid., p. 5.
273
a wide agreement on several key points: Scheingold, *New Pockets of Jewish Energy*. See also the respect for tradition expressed in all three volumes of *The Jewish Catalog* and the Reform rabbinate's attempt to reconcile authority with individual autonomy in the Central Conference of American Rabbis' "Centennial Perspective," reproduced and annotated in Eugene B. Borowitz, *Reform Judaism Today* (New York: Behrman House, 1978).

"What we need: Franz Rosenzweig, "On Being a Jewish Person," in Nahum N. Glatzer, ed., *Franz Rosenzweig* (New York: Schocken Books, 1953), pp. 214, 216.

Chapter Seven
Jews by Choice

274
"I have good news and bad news": Lecture at 92nd Street YM–YWHA, Nov. 13, 1980.

Leonard Fein . . . doubts: "Jews, More or Less: Interview with Steven M. Cohen and Calvin Goldscheider," *Moment* (Sept. 1984), p. 41.
275
"A disaster is in the making": Elihu Bergman, "The American Jewish Population Erosion," *Midstream* (Oct. 1977), pp. 19, 1.

"I am unaware of any . . . refutation": Robert Gordis, "'Be Fruitful and Multiply'–Biography of a Mitzvah," *Midstream* (Aug./Sept. 1982), pp. 25, 28.

repudiated both the procedures and the conclusions: Samuel S. Lieberman and Morton Weinfeld, "Demographic Trends and Jewish Survival," *Midstream* (Nov. 1978), pp. 9–19, esp. p. 19, n. 1.

"If nothing is done": Mordecai M. Kaplan, *Judaism as a Civilization* (Philadelphia and New York: Jewish Publication Society of America/Reconstructionist Press, 1981), p. 417. Data on intermarriage rate in 1930s from Fred Massarik and Alvin Chenkin, "United States National Jewish Population Study: A First Report," *American Jewish Year Book*, Vol. 73 (1973), p. 295, Table 1.

"If a Jew assimilates": Robert Gordis, in *National Conference on Jewish Population Growth: Summary of Proceedings* (New York: The American Jewish Committee, 1984), pp. 1, 3.

276

For forty years: Sheila B. Kamerman, "Jews and Other People: An Agenda for Research on Families and Family Policy," in Marshall Sklare, ed., *Understanding American Jewry* (New Brunswick, N.J.: Transaction Press, 1982), p. 152.

Jews have had a lower birthrate: Sidney Goldstein, "Jews in the United States: Perspectives from Demography," *American Jewish Year Book* (1981), pp. 6–13. See also Calvin Goldscheider, "Demography of Jewish Americans: Research Findings, Issues, and Challenges," in Sklare, *Understanding American Jewry*, pp. 7–12, 24–27.

277

those who did express concern: Conversation with Milton Himmelfarb, Jan. 30, 1985.

Fn.: Eric Rosenthal, "Jewish Fertility in the United States," *American Jewish Year Book* (1961), p. 25; Milton Himmelfarb, "The Vanishing Jew," *Commentary* (Sept. 1963), rptd. in Himmelfarb, *The Jews of Modernity* (Philadelphia: Jewish Publication Society of America, 1973), pp. 121–122.

Jewish women had borne: Goldstein, "Jews in the United States: Perspectives from Demography," p. 14.

During the 1960s and 1970s, however: Ibid., p. 19, Table 4. See also William D. Mosher and Gerry E. Henderson, "Religious Affiliation and the Fertility of Married Couples," *Journal of Marriage and the Family* (Aug. 1984), pp. 671–677; U. O. Schmelz and Sergio DellaPergola, "The Demographic Consequences of U.S. Jewish Population Trends," *American Jewish Year Book*, Vol. 83 (1983), pp. 153–161.

278

More than half the Jewish women: David E. Drew and Melanie R. Williams, *After College: A Longitudinal Study of Jewish Adults*, a technical report submitted to The American Jewish Committee (Los Angeles: Higher Education Research Institute, 1982), p. 44.

71 percent of Jewish college freshmen: David E. Drew, Margo R. King,

and Gerald T. Richardson, *A Profile of the Jewish Freshman: 1980* (Los Angeles: Higher Education Research Institute, n.d.), p. 62.

postponing the age at which they married: See references, p. 277.

279

the demographers projected a massive decline: Schmelz and DellaPergola, "The Demographic Consequences of U.S. Jewish Population Trends," pp. 153–161; Lieberman and Weinfeld, "Demographic Trends and Jewish Survival," p. 11.

It has not happened that way: I am deeply indebted to a number of scholars who provided invaluable guidance in the rest of this section. Calvin Goldscheider suggested major lines of inquiry, patiently answered innumerable questions, and guided me to crucial sources. Steven M. Cohen and Paul Ritterband provided unpublished data from their demographic study of the New York metropolitan area, William Yancey from the Philadelphia study, and Bruce Phillips from surveys of the Los Angeles, Denver, Phoenix, and Milwaukee Jewish communities. Sergio DellaPergola offered useful comments on an earlier draft of the chapter, and he and Morton Weinfeld provided data from the most recent Canadian census. In addition, William Mosher and Martin O'Connell provided crucial information on the usefulness of surveys of birth expectations.

Men and women are marrying: Recent data from demographic surveys of the Cleveland, Denver, Miami, Milwaukee, Minneapolis, Phoenix, Rochester, N.Y., and Washington, D.C., metropolitan areas. In the Washington, D.C., metropolitan area, for example, which usually is thought of as having a particularly large population of single women, 7.1 percent of Jewish women in the thirty-five-to-forty-four age group have never been married. (The 1971 figure is from Schmelz and DellaPergola, "The Demographic Consequences of U.S. Jewish Population Trends," p. 155, Table 7.)

Preliminary analysis of a demographic survey: Conversation with Dr. Paul Ritterband, Feb. 22, 1985. See also Steven M. Cohen, "Vitality and Resilience in the American Jewish Family Today," paper delivered at First International Symposium on the Jewish Family, Tel Aviv Univ., May 28, 1984, mimeo; Steven M. Cohen and Calvin Goldscheider, "Jews, More or Less," *Moment*, p. 41.

280

"Until you have one": Sandra G. Boodman, "The New Baby Boom," *The Washington Post*, Aug. 27, 1984.

281

"the post-Superwoman syndrome": Judy Mann, "Choices," *The Washington Post*, Sept. 12, 1984.

"You know, I enjoy taking care": Dinner party conversation, Jan. 28, 1984.

"I've moved to a slower track": Interview, June 13, 1984.

"I thought I could do . . . everything": "At Home by Choice," *Newsweek*, Sept. 10, 1984, p. 18.

282

an employment agency: "New Businesses Helping to Bring Up '80s Babies," *The Washington Post*, Aug. 27, 1984.

the most educated Jewish women: Calvin Goldscheider, *Jewish Continuity and Change: Emerging Patterns in America* (Bloomington: Indiana Univ. Press, 1985).

Those who expect a significant reduction: Interview with Sergio DellaPergola, Jerusalem, Nov. 21, 1984.

the annual population surveys: Martin O'Connell and Carolyn C. Rogers, "Assessing Cohort Birth Expectations Data from the Current Population Survey, 1971–1981," *Demography*, Vol. 20, No. 3 (Aug. 1983), pp. 369–384, and interview with Martin O'Connell, Feb. 22, 1985.

283

education has a powerful influence: Ronald Rindfuss, "Social and Demographic Aspects of Delayed Child-Bearing," final report submitted to National Institute of Child Health and Human Development, Sept. 14, 1984; conversation with Martin O'Connell, Feb. 22, 1985.

contraceptive use is more widespread: William D. Mosher and Calvin Goldscheider, "Contraceptive Patterns of Religious and Racial Groups in the United States, 1955–76: Convergence and Distinctiveness," *Studies in Family Planning*, Vol. 15, No. 3 (May/June 1984), pp. 101–111; Calvin Goldscheider, "Contraceptive Use Among American Jewish Families," in U. O. Schmelz, P. Glikson, and S. DellaPergola, *Papers in Jewish Demography 1981* (Jerusalem: Institute of Contemporary Jewry, Hebrew Univ. of Jerusalem, 1983), pp. 239–256.

284

only 3 percent . . . were unwanted: Goldstein, "Jews in the United States: Perspectives from Demography," p. 13.

In Philadelphia: Data from Dr. William Yancey, director of the Philadelphia demographic study, Sept. 5, 1984.

much the same picture exists in Miami: Ira M. Sheskin, *The Greater Miami Jewish Population Study*, Dec. 1, 1982, mimeo, p. 94.

Milwaukee and Phoenix data: Special tabulations provided by Dr. Bruce Phillips.

a survey of 1200 Jewish students: Rela Geffen Monson, *Jewish Campus Life* (New York: The American Jewish Committee, 1984), p. 20.

37 percent of the Jewish students: James L. Peterson and Nicholas Zill, *American Jewish High School Students* (New York: The American Jewish Committee, 1984), p. 8, Table 2.

285

a large national sample of high school seniors: Data from Calvin Goldscheider in interviews, Dec. 21, 1984, and Feb. 21, 1985.

"The hydra-headed monster": Robert Gordis, "Be Fruitful and Multiply," *Midstream*, p. 26.

one Jew in three: Ibid.

286

others put the intermarriage rate at: *The New York Times* has formally declared the intermarriage rate to be 40 percent; the Lubavitcher Youth

Organization uses the figure of 50 percent in its mailings; figures of 60–70 percent appear with some frequency in the Jewish press.

"a holocaust of our own making": Richard Yaffe, "Intermarriage abettors should be ousted from leadership, Roth urges," *The Jewish Week*, June 29–July 6, 1980, p. 2.

"Vastly outnumbered": Yehuda Rosenman, introduction to Egon Mayer and Carl Scheingold, *Intermarriage and the Jewish Future* (New York: The American Jewish Committee, 1979), p. 1.

"In this country": *The Occident* (March 1845).

"a nail in the coffin": Marshall Sklare, "Intermarriage and Jewish Survival," *Commentary* (March, 1970), p. 55.

287

although intermarriage increased: Fred Massarik and Alvin Chenkin, "United States National Jewish Population Study: A First Report," *American Jewish Year Book*, Vol. 73 (1973), p. 295, Table 1.

"the classic illustration": Calvin Goldscheider, "Demography of Jewish Americans," in Sklare, ed., *Understanding American Jewry*, New Brunswick, N.J.: Transaction Books, 1983), p. 36.

"The prevailing attitude": Marshall Sklare, "Intermarriage and the Jewish Future," *Commentary* (April 1964), p. 46. See also the view expressed by Robert Gordis that intermarriage is "part of the price that modern Jewry must pay for freedom and equality in an open society," in Gordis, *Judaism in a Christian World* (New York, 1966), p. 186.

the first signs of change: Marshall Sklare and Joseph Greenblum, *Jewish Identity on the Suburban Frontier*, 2d ed. (Chicago: Univ. of Chicago Press, 1979), pp. 306–320.

intermarriage was "an everyday occurrence": Sklare, "Intermarriage and Jewish Survival," p. 53.

the transformation . . . in Gentile attitudes: For 1940 to 1950, see Charles Herbert Stember, "The Recent History of Public Attitudes," in Stember et al., eds, *Jews in the Mind of America* (New York: Basic Books, 1966), pp. 104–107. For 1968 and subsequent years, see *The Gallup Report*, Report No. 213 (June 1983), p. 9.

The shift in Jewish attitudes: Floyd J. Fowler, *1975 Community Survey* (Boston: Combined Jewish Philanthropies of Greater Boston, 1977), p. 67, Table 5.17. Analysis of differences among age groups in Goldscheider, *Jewish Continuity and Change.*

289

In what he called a: Massarik and Chenkin, "The United States National Jewish Population Study: A First Report," p. 295, Table 1. (The section on intermarriage was written by Massarik.)

"based on accepted principles": Ibid., p. 264. (The introduction was written by Massarik.)

offered simply as "first facts": Ibid., p. 266.

290

In Lazerwitz's opinion: Dov (Bernard) Lazerwitz, "Current Jewish Intermarriages in the United States," *Papers in Jewish Demography 1977* (Jerusalem: Institute of Contemporary Jewry, Hebrew Univ. of Jerusalem, 1980), pp. 103–114; interview with Lazerwitz, Aug. 21, 1984; letter from Lazerwitz, Dec. 4, 1984.

based on only 83 cases: Lazerwitz, "Current Jewish Intermarriages in the United States," p. 106, n. 4.

"Lazerwitz urged Massarik: Letter from Lazerwitz, Dec. 4, 1984.

14 percent of married Jews: Ibid., pp. 105–106. See also Bernard Lazerwitz, "Jewish-Christian Marriages and Conversions," *Jewish Social Studies*, Vol. XLIV, No. 1 (Winter 1981), pp. 31–46, esp. pp. 33–34.

"a people that can't take yes": Quoted by Leonard Fein in *Moment* (Sept. 1984), p. 45.

291

statistics . . . defy belief: In their own analysis of the NJPS intermarriage data, U. O. Schmelz and Sergio DellaPergola have corrected Massarik's figures, raising the statistic for 1956–60 to 6.6 percent and lowering the 1965–71 figure to 29.2 percent (Schmelz and DellaPergola, "The Demographic Consequences of U.S. Jewish Population Trends," p. 162, Table 10).

a brief flurry of excitement: Thomas B. Morgan, "The Vanishing American Jew," *Look*, May 5, 1964. On the reaction, see Sklare, "Intermarriage and Jewish Survival," p. 52.

"has devoted little attention": Ibid.

The most compelling data: Fred Solomon Sherrow, "Patterns of Religious Intermarriage Among American College Graduates," unpubl. Ph.D. diss. Columbia Univ., 1971 (Ann Arbor, Mich.: Univ. Microfilms, 1972).

the out-marriage rate was 12 percent: Ibid., p. 38, Table 2.9. On the proportion of Jews married, see p. 8; on the size of the sample (n. 9) see Chap. 1, esp. p. 8, n. 5. On college attendance, see Steven M. Cohen, *American Modernity and Jewish Identity* (New York: Tavistock Publications, 1983), p. 81, Table 4(1).

292

"the temper of its Jewish life": Sklare, "Intermarriage and Jewish Survival," p. 51.

In 1965, 11.1 percent: Morris Axelrod, Floyd J. Fowler, and Arnold Gurin, *A Community Survey for Long-Range Planning* (Boston: Combined Jewish Philanthropies of Greater Boston, 1977), p. 169, Table 15.2 (data presented are for couples; I have converted them to individual rates); 1975 data from Fowler, *1975 Community Survey*, p. 67, Table 5.16.

Surveys of other eastern cities: Marshall Sklare, *America's Jews* (New York: Random House, 1971), p. 187.

293

in fifteen Jewish communities: New York, Los Angeles, Chicago, Miami, Philadelphia, Washington, D.C., Denver, Phoenix, Milwaukee, Cleveland, St. Louis, Kansas City, Minneapolis, Richmond, Va., and Pittsburgh. (Surveys were conducted in a number of other cities—for example, Tampa, Fla., Nashville, Tenn., Rochester, N.Y., and Seattle—but questions about intermarriage were not asked.)

the mixed-marriage rate . . . increased 127 percent: Joseph Waksberg, Janet Greenblatt, and Gary A. Tobin, *A Demographic Study of the Jewish Community of Greater Washington, 1983,* June 1984 draft, p. 6-6.

in the youngest cohort: Ibid., p. 6-11, Table 6-4.

294

In Denver and Phoenix: *The Denver Jewish Population Study, 1981* (Denver: Allied Jewish Federation of Denver, 1982), p. 45, Table 23 (couple rates were converted to individual rates); *The Greater Phoenix Jewish Population Study* (Phoenix: Jewish Federation of Greater Phoenix, 1984), p. 10, Table I-8a.

in Los Angeles: Special tabulation provided by Bruce A. Phillips.

In the New York metropolitan area: Steven M. Cohen and Paul Ritterband, "Jewish Intermarriage in the New York Area: Recent Rates, Parental Background, and Some Consequences for Jewish Identification," Greater New York Jewish Population Study (June 1984), mimeo. (The paper will appear as Chap. 9 in Paul Ritterband and Steven M. Cohen, *Family, Community, and Identity: The Jews of Greater New York,* forthcoming.)

the rate was somewhat higher in: St. Louis: Gary A. Tobin, *1982 Demographic and Attitudinal Study of the Jewish Community of St. Louis* (St. Louis: Jewish Federation of St. Louis, 1982), p. 233, Table P16S by MA1; Chicago: *Metropolitan Chicago Jewish Population, 1981,* preliminary tables (Chicago: Jewish Federation of Metropolitan Chicago), April 18, 1984, mimeo, p. 16; Philadelphia data from Dr. William Yancey; Cleveland: *Survey of Cleveland's Jewish Population, 1981,* Report No. 3 of the Population Research Committee (Cleveland: Jewish Community Federation of Cleveland, 1982), p. 47, Chart 24; Milwaukee: Bruce A. Phillips and Eve Weinberg, *The Milwaukee Jewish Population: Report of a Survey* (Chicago: Policy Research Corp., 1984), p. B-8, Table B-4.

These regional differences: Sherrow, "Patterns of Religious Intermarriage Among College Graduates," p. 103, Table 4.1.

a single New York City neighborhood: Paul Ritterband and Steven M. Cohen, "The Jewish Population of Greater New York: Estimates of Households and Individuals for Eight Counties and Selected Neighborhoods," 1981 Greater New York Jewish Population Study, Report No. 1 (March 1982), mimeo. (There were 64,309 Jews on the Upper West Side, 55,822 in Forest Hills–Rego Park, and 102,707 in Flatbush in 1981, compared to 42,600 in Denver and 43,100 in Phoenix.)

To estimate the intermarriage rate: In order of size, the metropolitan areas are New York (the five boroughs of New York City plus Westchester, Nassau, and Suffolk counties), Los Angeles, Philadelphia, Chicago, Miami, Boston, Washington, D.C., Cleveland, St. Louis, Pittsburgh, Phoenix, Denver, Minneapolis, Kansas City, and Richmond, Va.

From a purely scientific standpoint my approach leaves much to be desired. Some surveys are more inclusive than others, and the figures are not always reported in the same way; when intermarriage statistics were presented for couples rather than for individuals, I converted the couple rates to individual rates. Moreover, different communities used different age breaks—for example, some reported figures for the eighteen-to-twenty-nine and thirty-to-thirty-nine age groups, others for Jews below the age of thirty-five; still others reported figures according to the five- or ten-year period in which marriages had taken place, in which cases I used data from the most recent five- or ten-year period. Some surveys were made as long ago as 1979 and others as recently as 1983, although the bulk of the figures are for 1981. There is reason to believe, however, that any resulting errors (and some are inevitable) cancel each other out.

The metropolitan areas listed above include 64 percent of the American Jewish population. Another 18 percent live in metropolitan areas that resemble one or more of the areas in which surveys have been conducted. In the great majority of cases I assigned a high and low figure: for example, I assumed that the intermarriage rate in San Diego, San Francisco, and San Jose would be no lower than that in Los Angeles and no higher than the rate in Denver or Phoenix, or that the rate in Bergen and Essex counties—New Jersey suburbs of New York City—would be no lower than the rate for the New York metropolitan area and no higher than that in Philadelphia. For a few cities closely resembling one of the surveyed cities I assigned a single rate: for example, I assumed that the rate in Detroit was identical to that in Cleveland. For each metropolitan area the intermarriage rate was weighted by that area's share of the total U.S. Jewish population.

The remaining 18 percent of American Jews are scattered in smaller cities and suburban areas. I divided them between sections of the country that historically have had high intermarriage rates and those that can be presumed to resemble the average of the rest of the country. For the former I assumed that the Los Angeles rate would be the low and the Phoenix-Denver figure the high; for the rest of the country I used the low and high average figures for the country as a whole. Both areas were weighted by the populations they contain.

Here are the figures themselves.

METROPOLITAN AREA	WEIGHT	INTERMARRIAGE RATE	WEIGHTED RATE
New York	.30	12.5	3.75
Los Angeles	.0874	39.1	3.42
Chicago	.043	20.5	0.88
Miami	.043	12.1	0.52
Philadelphia	.052	23.8	1.24
Boston	.03	20.3	0.61
Washington, D.C.	.028	26.3	0.74
Denver	.007	56.7	0.40
Phoenix	.006	57.6	0.35
Milwaukee	.004	45	0.18
Cleveland	.012	24.4	0.29
St. Louis	.009	14.3	0.13
Kansas City[1]	.003	14–33	0.04–0.1
Minneapolis	.004	18	0.07

METROPOLITAN AREA	WEIGHT	INTERMARRIAGE RATE	WEIGHTED RATE
Pittsburgh[1]	.008	15.3	0.12
Richmond	.001	48	0.048
Subtotal	.637		12.79–13.37
ESTIMATES			
California cities[2]	.024	39–57	0.94–1.37
Connecticut cities[3]	.01	12.5–24	0.24–0.45
Ft. Lauderdale	.014	25–39	0.35–0.55
Hollywood, Fla.	.01	12.1	0.12
Palm Beach	.008	12.1–25	0.10–0.2
Atlanta	.006	24.4–45	0.15–0.27
Baltimore	.016	12.5–23.8	0.2–0.38
Detroit	.012	24.4	0.29
Bergen/Essex	.034	12.5–25	0.42–0.85
Upstate N.Y.[4]	.01	24.4–45	0.24–0.45
Rockland	.004	25	0.1
Ohio cities[5]	.006	24.4–45	0.15–0.27
Bucks County	.004	25	0.1
Memphis	.002	12.5–24.4	0.02–0.05
Houston	.002	39	0.08
Dallas	.004	24.4–39	0.10–0.16
Seattle	.003	12.5	0.04
Subtotal	.169		3.64–5.73
Subtotal	.805		16.43–19.1
Rest of U.S.[6]			
a)	.088	39.1–57.6	3.44–5.07
b)	.107	19.7–23.0	2.10–2.46
Grand Total			*21.97–26.63*

[1] *In the Pittsburgh and Kansas City surveys, parents were asked about the marriages of their grown children, whether or not the children lived in those cities or elsewhere; the intermarriage figures derived in this manner were significantly higher—33 percent in Kansas City and 49 percent in Pittsburgh, indicating that intermarriage was far more frequent among children who moved away from their hometowns. Because the Kansas City survey was taken in 1976, well before the other surveys, I have used the higher as well as the lower intermarriage rates. I have not done so in the case of Pittsburgh, on the assumption that the higher intermarriage rate among young people who migrate is reflected in the intermarriage rates in cities with high rates of in-migration, such as Los Angeles, Denver, Phoenix, and Richmond. Because of its small population, however, inclusion of the higher Pittsburgh figure would not alter the totals to any noticeable degree.*

[2] *San Diego, San Francisco, San Jose.*

[3] *Hartford, Bridgeport, New Haven.*

[4] *Buffalo, Rochester, Albany area.*

[5] *Cincinnati and Columbus.*

[6] *I have divided the rest of the country into two parts. Some 45 percent live in areas that can be presumed to have intermarriage rates at the high end of the scale: for example, the Far West, small cities and towns in the South and Midwest, and larger southern and midwestern cities, such as New Orleans and Des Moines, that have small Jewish communities. (The proportion is*

295

I recalculated the 1981 rate: Instead of assigning an intermarriage rate to metropolitan areas that have not been studied, I used only the survey data themselves. Since the New York metropolitan area is atypical in many ways—the size of the Jewish "marriage market," as sociologists call it, is vastly larger than elsewhere, and there is a higher proportion of Orthodox Jews—I assumed that the rest of the country resembled the surveyed areas, excluding New York. Instead of weighting each city's intermarriage rate by its share of the population, I took a simple arithmetical average of the reported intermarriage rates—a procedure that gives far more weight to the high Denver-Phoenix figures. The procedure yields a 29 percent intermarriage rate for the 70 percent of the country outside New York; including the latter, the national figure is 24 percent.

Using a more precise but less inclusive approach than mine, Bernard Lazerwitz has come up with precisely the same rate of increase. In his analysis Lazerwitz compared the recent survey data for New York, Miami, Los Angeles, Cleveland, and Chicago with the 1971 intermarriage rates for those metropolitan areas, drawn from the NJPS raw data. (He selected those metropolitan areas because they were the only recently surveyed cities for which reliable data were available from the NJPS.) Converting the changes in each city to annual rates of increase, he then extrapolated from the date of the survey to 1984 (Bernard Lazerwitz, "Trends in National Jewish Identification Indicators: 1971–1984," mimeo).

there is some measure of understatement: See Bernard Lazerwitz, "Jewish-Christian Marriages and Conversions," p. 45, nn. 10 and 11, and pp. 45–46, n. 12. See also Bernard Lazerwitz, "An Estimate of a Rare Population Group: The U.S. Jewish Population," *Demography*, Vol. 15, No. 3 (Aug. 1978), pp. 389–394; and Lazerwitz, "The Sample Design of the National Jewish Population Survey" (New York: Council of Jewish Federations, n.d.).

a list of distinctive Jewish names: On the general reliability as well as the drawbacks of the distinctive Jewish name approach, see Harold S. Himmelfarb, R. Michael Loar, and Susan H. Mott, "Sampling by Ethnic Surnames: The Case of American Jews," *Public Opinion Quarterly*, Vol. 47, No. 2 (Summer 1983), pp. 247–260, esp. pp. 250–251.

296

not likely to exceed 10 to 15 percent: That judgment is based on the analysis of Jewish "apostasy" during the early 1960s in David Caplovitz and Fred Sherrow, *The Religious Drop-Outs* (Beverly Hills, Cal.: Sage Publications, 1977). Among Jewish college graduates "apostasy"—no longer identifying as a Jew—peaked at 13 percent during the respondents' senior year in college; three years later nearly half the former apostates again identified themselves as Jews. (Some 4 percent of those who had identified as Jews as seniors no longer did so three years later; the net effect was a decline from 13 percent to 11 percent.)

---

closer to 40 percent, but I prefer to err on the high side.) I have assigned the Los Angeles-Phoenix range to this part of the population and have assumed that the intermarriage rate for the other 55 percent is the average for the rest of the country.

women . . . faced a severe shortage of Jewish men: U. O. Schmelz and Sergio DellaPergola, "The Demographic Consequences of U.S. Jewish Population Trends," pp. 148–151.

297

a surplus rather than a shortage: Ibid., pp. 150–151, esp. p. 150, Table 5.

the proportion . . . has dropped already: Data from 1978 to 1982 supplied by Professor Morton Weinfeld of McGill Univ., updating table in M. Weinfeld, W. Shaffir, and I. Cotler, *The Canadian Jewish Mosaic* (New York: John Wiley, 1981), p. 369.

a fellow Jew tells Rachel Cowan: Paul and Rachel Cowan, "Our People," *Moment* (March 1983), p. 30.

298

Consider Rachel Cowan herself: Portrait drawn from Rachel Cowan's statement in the note above and in Susan Weidman Schneider, *Jewish and Female* (New York: Simon & Schuster, 1984), pp. 347–351; Paul Cowan's account in Paul Cowan, *An Orphan in History* (New York: Doubleday, 1982) and my interview with Rachel and Paul Cowan, July 19, 1984. See also Doug Chandler, "Jews by Choice," *Long Island Jewish World*, April 23–29, 1982; Adam Snitzer, "It's Hard to Be a 'Real Jew,'" *The Jewish Week*, Oct. 19, 1984.

she "would have missed a long struggle": Schneider, *Jewish and Female*, p. 347.

299

"No one converts to . . . become a convert: Sandra Ariela Shachar, "Jew—Not Convert," *Moment* (Dec. 1979), p. 64.

"Our imports are better than our exports" Milton Himmelfarb, *The Jews of Modernity*, p. 123.

Jews . . . are more committed to their Jewish identity: According to the National Jewish Population Survey, 27 percent of the born-Gentile wives had converted to Judaism, but 46 percent identified themselves as Jewish; only 2.5 percent of the born-Gentile husbands had converted, but 44 percent identified as Jewish (Massarik and Chenkin, "United States National Jewish Population Study: A First Report," p. 296, Tables 2 and 297, Table 3). Confirmation comes from Fred Sherrow's analysis of the NORC sample. In marriages involving Protestant men and Jewish women, the Protestant community suffered a loss of 58 percent; when Jewish men married Protestant women, the loss to the Jewish community was less than 16 percent. Much the same applied to Jewish-Catholic marriages (Sherrow, "Patterns of Religious Intermarriage Among American College Graduates," pp. 72–77).

Egon Mayer's 1976–77 study of intermarried couples—the only recent study of the religious identification of Gentile as well as Jewish spouses in mixed marriages—also indicates large declines in the proportion of Gentile spouses who continue to identify themselves as Christians. Whereas 30 percent of the nonconverted Gentile spouses had considered themselves Catholic before their marriages, only 10 percent did so at the time of the study; the corresponding drop for Protestants was from 45 to 26 percent. By contrast, two thirds of the Jewish spouses in mixed marriages still thought of themselves as Jews.

(Mayer and Sheingold, *Intermarriage and the Jewish Future*, p. 16, esp. Table 9). See also Mayer, *Patterns of Intermarriage Among American Jews: Varieties, Uniformities, Dilemmas, and Prospects*, report to The American Jewish Committee (Aug. 1978), mimeo, Chaps. 4 and 5.

Unfortunately Mayer's study is marred by a sample that is unrepresentative in a number of respects. Even so, analogous findings may be inferred from Lazerwitz's analyses of the NJPS data, and they are explicit in Steven M. Cohen's analysis of the effects of mixed marriages on the Jewish identification of the Jewish partners and their children in New York and in Bruce Phillips' analysis of the way in which children of mixed marriages are being raised in Los Angeles, Denver, Milwaukee, and Phoenix. See Cohen and Ritterband, "Jewish Intermarriage in the New York Area: Recent Rates, Parental Background, and Some Consequences for Jewish Identification," to appear in their forthcoming book *Family, Community, and Identity: The Jews of Greater New York*, and Bruce A. Phillips, "Intermarriage, Fertility, and Jewish Survival: New Evidence from the Eighties," to appear in *Contemporary Jewry Annual*, Vol. 8, forthcoming.

This is particularly true of Jewish women: See especially Cohen and Ritterband, "Jewish Intermarriage in the New York Area," Lazerwitz, "Current Jewish Intermarriages in the United States," in *Papers in Jewish Demography*, esp. Table 2, and Lazerwitz, "Jewish-Christian Marriages and Conversions," in *Jewish Social Studies*, Vol. XLIV, No. 1, Winter 1981, p. 43.

300

"I didn't see any need": Interview, Aug. 10, 1984.

"the Jewish community of *fate*, but not . . . of *faith*": Egon Mayer, "Intermarriage Among American Jews: Consequences, Prospects, and Policies" (New York: National Jewish Resource Center, Policy Studies 1979), p. 8.

a Jew and Christian could not marry: See, for example, Marsha L. Rozenblitt, *The Jews of Vienna 1867–1914* (Albany: State Univ. of New York Press, 1983), pp. 128–130.

much poorer relationships with their parents: Sherrow, "Patterns of Religious Intermarriage Among College Graduates, pp. 123–125, esp. p. 124, Table 4.9, and pp. 129–131, esp. p. 130, Table 4-12.

301

"unconventional" or "rebellious": Sherrow, pp. 137–140.

"My father's only Jewish characteristic": Interview, Aug. 9, 1984.

"the Jew who intermarries" Marshall Sklare, *America's Jews*, p. 201.

Nancy Ludmerer: Interview, Aug. 14, 1984.

302

Susan Kander: Interview, Aug. 15, 1984.

When the born-Gentile partner converts: For supporting data from the surveys of Denver, Los Angeles, Milwaukee, and Phoenix, see Bruce A. Phillips, "Intermarriage, Fertility, and Jewish Survival: New Evidence from the Eighties," forthcoming in Vol. 8 of *Contemporary Jewry Annual*. For the New York metropolitan area, see Cohen and Ritterband, "Jewish Intermarriage in the New York Area," to appear in *Family, Community, and Identity*, their forthcoming book. See also Egon Mayer, *Children of Intermarriage* (New York: The American Jewish Committee, 1983), p. 7, Table 1, and Lazerwitz, "Jewish-Christian Marriages and Conversions," p. 37.

the former are more likely to light: Lazerwitz, "Jewish-Christian Marriages and Conversion," p. 36, Table 2; Lazerwitz, "Current Jewish Intermarriages in the United States," p. 106, Table 2; Steven Huberman, *New Jews: The Dynamics of Religious Conversion* (New York: Union of American Hebrew Congregations, 1979), pp. 20–24. See also Cohen and Ritterband, "Jewish Intermarriage in the New York Area," Table 9-3.

mixed-married couples often raise: On the large differential between Jewish women and Jewish men in mixed marriages, see Cohen and Ritterband, "Jewish Intermarriages in the New York Area," esp. p. 28.

303

"I didn't think": Interview, Jan. 23, 1984.

in mixed marriages involving: Cohen and Ritterband, "Jewish Intermarriages in the New York Area," esp. pp. 27–31.

304

The most striking finding: See sources cited in notes for page 302, above.

70 percent more children: Lazerwitz, "Jewish-Christian Marriages and Conversions," pp. 37–38. Bruce Phillips' analysis of data from the Denver, Milwaukee, and Phoenix surveys leads to the conclusion that the fertility difference between conversionary and mixed-married couples has apparently continued into the 1980s.

In a 1982 study: Mayer, *Children of Intermarriage*.

conversion . . . played an even larger role: Ibid., p. 7, Table 1.

"being Jewish is very important": Ibid., p. 12, Table 5.

had received a Jewish education: Ibid., p. 19, Table 12.

respondents who were married: on p. ix.

305

the offspring of marriages: If each person in Mayer's sample had been born two years after his or her parents' marriage, the parents of the sixteen-year-olds would have been married in 1964, and the parents of the forty-six-year-olds in 1934. If the children were born later in their parents' marriages, the latter would have taken place even earlier.

Second fn.: The sample was derived by asking respondents to Mayer's 1976–77 study to provide addresses for their grown children. The original sample had a number of serious flaws. For one thing, it was not random: potential respondents were identified by members of eight American Jewish Committee chapters; since the Jewish spouses were known as Jewish, the most assimilated intermarried couples undoubtedly were underrepresented. The refusal rate (the proportion of couples contacted who declined to participate) was high—50 percent for half the sample, 25 percent for the remainder. The final sample interviewed was unrepresentative in other respects: it was considerably older, on average, than intermarried couples as a group; it was wealthier; and it contained an unusually high proportion of born-Gentile husbands who had converted to Judaism. These sampling problems were compounded in Mayer's study of the children. The refusal rate exceeded 70 percent; children of conversionary couples were overrepresented, and children of mixed marriages underrepresented. Because of the small size of the sample, the margin of error is unusually large—that is, differences of less than 15 percentage points are not statistically significant. Because of the small sample and large margin of error, moreover, Mayer did not control for age or stage in the life cycle—a flaw that makes it difficult to interpret many of the answers. Also, when reporting measures of Jewish identification, Mayer failed to compare the answers with those derived from studies of children of in-married couples, thereby exaggerating the significance of the low level of observance and identification reported.

306

The New York-area couples: Cohen and Ritterband, "Jewish Intermarriage in the New York Area."

307

"the thought of conversion seemed absurd": Interview, Aug. 9, 1984.

308

"Jason needs something": Interview, Aug. 14, 1984.

For Dr. Janet Gold: Interview, Aug. 12, 1984.

309

"I've known a lot of products": Interview, Aug. 10, 1984.

"I had very little information": Interview, Aug. 15, 1984.

310

"Over and over again": Huberman, *New Jews: The Dynamics of Religious Conversion*, pp. 17–18.

two to three times more frequent: In Huberman's sample 66 percent were women, 34 percent men (pp. 11–12). The proportion of women is even higher in most surveys that have yielded data on conversion.

311

On male reluctance to convert, see Huberman, p. 12.

"I have read a lot of history": Harold Schulweis, "The Proselyte Within Us," tape of sermon delivered Sept. 8, 1983.

Deborah Beveppo Hirsch: Interview, June 1, 1982.

312

When she was first married: "Raising Kids Jewish in a Mixed Marriage," *Lilith*, No. 11 (Fall/Winter 1983), pp. 28–29.

When he married his Orthodox-raised wife: Chandler, "Jews by Choice," *Long Island Jewish World.*

313

For Richard Wilson: Interview, Aug. 15, 1984.

Nine such couples in ten: Cohen and Ritterband, "Jewish Intermarriage in the New York Area."

314
Mary Lynn Kotz and her husband: Mary Lynn Kotz, "Jewish Is Becoming," *Moment* (June 1981), pp. 19–31, 34.
315
two thirds of those who had converted: Gary A. Tobin, *1982 Demographic and Attitudinal Study of the St. Louis Jewish Population*, p. 115, Table P19. (The table indicates that 84 percent of the respondents who converted did so under Reform auspices; the comparable figure for wives of respondents was 50 percent: averaging the two yields gives the two-thirds figure.)

Steven Huberman found: Huberman, *New Jews: The Dynamics of Religious Conversion*, pp. 29–30, esp. p. 30, Table V-17.

a good bit more observant: Ibid., pp. 20–24.

"There is hardly a rabbi I meet": Interview with Wolfe Kelman, Aug. 11, 1982.
316
Cohen categorized Jews into four groups: Cohen and Ritterband, "Jewish Intermarriage in the New York Area."

"It has taken Elisha": Interview, Aug. 10, 1984.

"I feel like I'm in limbo": Steven Huberman, "From Christianity to Judaism: Religion Changers in American Society," *Conservative Judaism*, Vol. 36, No. 1 (Fall 1982), p. 26.
317
"There is an ethnic factor": Interview, Aug. 9, 1984.

membership in communal organizations is . . . lower: See, for example, Huberman, *New Jews*, pp. 24–25; Cohen and Ritterband, "Jewish Intermarriage in the New York Area"; Lazerwitz, "Jewish-Christian Marriages and Conversions," p. 36, Table 2.

"I didn't feel Jewish": Gary Rosenblatt, "Opening the Door to Converts," *Baltimore Jewish Times*, Nov. 26, 1982, p. 48. See also Lydia Kukoff, *Choosing Judaism* (New York: Union of American Hebrew Congregations, 1981), esp. Chap. 2.

"I end up at the same point": Interview, Aug. 8, 1984.

"All of a sudden": Interview, Aug. 12, 1984.

"The biggest adjustment": Interview, May 15, 1983.

"I feel much more": Interview, Aug. 10, 1984.

"What we are seeing": Gary Rosenblatt, "Opening the Door to Converts," p. 49.

When her first child was born: "Raising Kids Jewish in a Mixed Marriage," *Lilith*, Issue 11, pp. 27–28.
318
"to face reality": Alexander Schindler, address to UAHC board of trustees, Dec. 2, 1978; interview with Rabbi Schindler, Nov. 4, 1982.

goals "are clear and simple": Schindler, presidential address to 57th General Assembly, Union of American Hebrew Congregations, Nov. 10, 1983.

318

For most of their history: Milton Himmelfarb, "A Time for Jewish Activism," *Congress Monthly* (Nov. 1979), pp. 12–14; Himmelfarb, *The Jews of Modernity*, pp. 120–124; "Proselytes," *Encyclopedia Judaica* (Jerusalem and New York: Keter Publishing House/Macmillan, 1971) Vol. 13, pp. 1182–93; Salo Wittmayer Baron, *A Social and Religious History of the Jews*, 2d ed., rev. and enl. (New York and Philadelphia: Columbia Univ. Press/Jewish Publication Society of America, 1952), Vol. 1, pp. 172–179, Vol. 2, pp. 147–150; Jacob Katz, *Exclusiveness and Tolerance* (New York: Schocken Books, 1962), Chap. 6; Shaye J. D. Cohen, "Conversion to Judaism in Historical Perspective: From Biblical History to Postbiblical Judaism," and Michael Panitz, "Conversion to Judaism in the Middle Ages: Historic Patterns and New Scenarios," in *Conservative Judaism*, Vol. XXXVI, No. 4 (Summer 1983), pp. 31–46 and 46–56, resp.

319

"What our enemies forced on us": Himmelfarb, "A Time for Jewish Activism," p. 13.

"We live in America today." Schindler, address to UAHC board of trustees, Dec. 2, 1978.

"Jewish attitudes . . . have varied": Emanuel Rackman, "Converts May Be Key to Jewish Survival," *The Jewish Week*, Feb. 10, 1984, p. 27.

"Even in Talmudic times": Marc D. Angel, "A Fresh Look at Conversion," *Midstream* (Oct. 1983), pp. 35–38.

320

This . . . was the case in Denver: Kenneth A. Briggs, "Rabbis' Denver Project Fuels Fight on Converts," *The New York Times*, March 23, 1984, p. A14. See also Lawrence Grossman, "Intermarriage and the Jewish Community," *News and Views: Reports from the American Jewish Committee*, Vol. 7, No. 2 (Winter 1985), p. 32E.

"Denver was one more instance": Briggs, "Rabbis' Denver Project Fuels Fight on Converts."

"the Orthodox definition": Rabbi Irving Greenberg, at American Jewish Congress Seminar on Patrilineal Descent, Jan. 11, 1984.

synagogue membership should be denied: Rabbi Benjamin Walfish, executive vice-president Rabbinical Council of America, quoted in Richard Yaffe, "Orthodox Head Warns Against Isolating Jew Due to Intermarriage, *The Jewish Week*, week of July 12, 1981. For a contrary view by Rabbi Walter S. Wurzburger, see the same issue of *The Jewish Week* (a report of his address as president of the RCA).

"the elimination from leadership roles": Yaffe, "Intermarriage abettors should be ousted from leadership, Roth urges," *The Jewish Week*, p. 2.

"I wonder what the evidence is": Seymour Siegel, "Comments on the Statement '*Keruv* and the Status of Intermarried Families' by J. Roth and D. Gordis," *Conservative Judaism*, Vol. XXXV, No. 4 (Summer 1982), pp. 56–58.

321

"We must remove the 'not-wanted' signs": Schindler, address to UAHC board of trustees, Dec. 2, 1978.

children born to a Jewish mother: The definitive history of the laws governing the status of children of mixed marriages is Shaye J. D. Cohen's "The Origins of the Matrilineal Principle in Rabbinic Law," paper delivered at 1983 meeting of the Society of Biblical Literature, to be published. A shorter version of the paper was published as "The Matrilineal Principle in Historical Perspective," *Judaism*, Vol. 34, No. 1 (Winter 1985), pp. 9–13. (I am indebted to Professor Cohen for sharing a copy of the original manuscript in typescript.) For the full range of views on the subject, see "The Issue of Patrilineal Descent–A Symposium," in the aforementioned issue of *Judaism.*

"It can no longer be assumed": Resolution adopted by Central Conference of American Rabbis, March 15, 1983, as printed in *Reform Judaism* (Spring/Summer 1983), p. 16.

322

"an act of schismatic heresy": Quoted in Eleanor Lester, "Jewish Birthright: Reform, Orthodox at Impasse," *Philadelphia Jewish Exponent*, Aug. 12, 1983 (rptd. from *The Jewish Week*).

"Unless action for unity is started": Quoted in Briggs, "Rabbis' Denver Project Fuels Fight on Converts," p. A14.

The Reform rabbinate's break: Irving Greenberg, paper at American Jewish Congress Seminar on Patrilineal Descent; text of the CCAR resolution of March 15, 1983.

First fn.: Jacob J. Petuchowski, "Toward Sectarianism," *Moment* (Sept. 1983), pp. 34–36.

Second fn.: Text of Federation of Reconstructionist Congregations and Havurot, resolution on Intermarriage as passed at 24th Annual Convention, June 16, 1984; Richard A. Hirsch, "Jewish Identity and Patrilineal Descent: Some Second Thoughts," *Raayonot*, Vol. 4, No. 1 (Winter 1983), pp. 6–11; "Symposium: Reactions to the Reconstructionist Rabbinical Association's *Guidelines on Intermarriage*, in aforementioned issue of *Raayonot*, pp. 12–26.

323

"The Orthodox will never agree": Ian Blynn, "Local Rabbis Deal with the Issue: Who Is a Jew?" *Philadelphia Jewish Exponent*, Aug. 12, 1983.

"If it is unity": Eleanor Lester, "Jewish Birthright: Reform, Orthodox at Impasse."

"We of the Conservative movement": Jacob B. Agus, "The *Mizvah* of *Keruv*," *Conservative Judaism*, Vol. XXXV, No. 4 (Summer 1982), p. 37.

CHAPTER EIGHT
"If they're ever going to get us, they're going to get us now."

327

"You now have": John J. Failka and Brooks Jackson, "Jewish PACs Emerge as a Powerful Force in U.S. Election Races," *The Wall Street Journal*, Feb. 26, 1985, p. 16.

more than three quarters of those: Steven M. Cohen, *The 1984 National Survey of American Jews: Political and Social Outlooks* (New York: The American Jewish Committee, 1984), p. 29, Table 6.

328

Jewish communal leaders are more relaxed: Steven M. Cohen, *Attitudes of American Jews Toward Israel and Israelis: The 1983 National Survey of American Jews and Jewish Communal Leaders* (New York: The American Jewish Committee, 1983), p. 13, Table 6.

"Most non-Jews are anti-Semitic": Interview, March 21, 1982.

"Jews are at peace": Interview, Dec. 10, 1979.

329

a direct, personal experience: Gary A. Tobin, *A Demographic and Attitudinal Study of the Jewish Community of St. Louis* (St. Louis: Jewish Federation of St. Louis, 1982), p. 230, Table P8-M7, and p. 231, Table P8-M8; Joseph Waksberg, Janet Greenblatt, and Gary A. Tobin, *A Demographic Study of the Jewish Community of Greater Washington, 1983* (Bethesda, Md.: United Jewish Appeal Federation of Greater Washington, 1984), mimeo, pp. 12-4 to 12-6, Tables 12-1 to 12-3.

A 1981 study: *Anti-Semitism in the United States,* a report prepared for The American Jewish Committee (New York: Yankelovich, Skelly and White, 1981), Vol. II, p. 60.

the reverse was the case: See note for p. 329 above.

Fn.: Ibid.

330

"The U.S. Government will never be": Joseph Polakoff, "Reagan Aide Denies Bias in Comments," *The Jewish Week,* Dec. 14, 1984.

one of Israel's principal advocates: Not-for-attribution interview, March 4, 1985.

"You are one of the senators": *Face the Nation* (TV program) April 1, 1984, quoted in *Near East Report,* April 20, 1984, p. 64.

"the kind of 'tough' question": Not-for-attribution interview with CBS-TV correspondent, March 5, 1985.

331

With oil prices increasing twelvefold: Eliyahu Kanovsky, "Mideast Oil–The Iran-Iraq War," *Energy Information Service,* Vol. VI, Issue 1 (New York: The American Jewish Committee), Aug. 8, 1984, p. 2.

"draining the world of its wealth": *Business Week,* Nov. 19, 1979, quoted ibid.

Jewish students at several British universities: Irwin Cotler, "The Jewish Condition in the 1980s–A Global View," paper delivered at the General Assembly of the Council of Jewish Federations, Nov. 14–18, 1979, p. 5.

332

To some thoughtful Jewish leaders: Interview with Philip Klutznick, May 19, 1980.

"Toward the end of lunch": Lewis H. Lapham, "The Rising Voice of Intolerance," *The Washington Post,* Dec. 5, 1981.

333

"I'm not saying": Interview with Lewis Lapham, Jan. 27, 1982.

"as Jimmy Carter's id": quoted in Martin Schram, "President Ends His Silence," *The Washington Post,* Dec. 25, 1979, p. A4.

black leaders blamed American Jews: For text of the statement, see *The Amsterdam News,* Aug. 27, 1979. See also Thomas A. Johnson, "Black Leaders Air Grievances on Jews," *The New York Times,* Aug. 23, 1979; Roger Wilkins, "Black Leaders' Meeting: 'Watershed' Effort for Unanimity," *The New York Times,* Aug. 24, 1979. For my view at the time, see Silberman, "Jesse and the Jews," *The New Republic,* Dec. 29, 1979, pp. 12–14.

Carter sailed the Mississippi: See, for example, Bill Peterson and Martin Schram, "No Room for Controversy Aboard Political-Image Steamboat," *The Washington Post,* Aug. 26, 1979, p. A2; "Riverboat Gambol," editorial, *The Washington Post,* Aug. 22, 1979; "Who Did Andrew Young In, and Why?" editorial, *The New York Times,* Aug. 26, 1979; "Now It's Carter's Lie," editorial, *The New Republic,* Sept. 15, 1979.

not until four weeks later: Edward Cowan, "President Asserts Jewish Leaders Did Not Pressure Him to Dismiss Young," *The New York Times,* Sept. 24, 1979.

"I saw something I never thought I would encounter": Letter from Senator Moynihan to his constituents, quoted in Wolf Blitzer, "An Anti-Jewish Lobby Emerges," *The Jerusalem Post,* Jan. 17–23, 1982.

334

a test of "Jewish power": Paul Taylor, "Lobbying on AWACs," *The Washington Post,* Sept. 28, 1981, p. A4. The most comprehensive accounts of the lobbying on both sides are contained in Taylor, "Lobbying on AWACs"; Aaron Rosenbaum, "The AWACs Aftermath," *Moment* (Dec. 1981), pp. 13–22, 57–58; Milton Ellerin, "The AWACs Debate: Is There An Anti-Semitic Fallout?" (New York: The American Jewish Committee), Feb. 17, 1982; Albert R. Hunt, "How Pressure, Pleas and Horse-Trading Won AWACs for Reagan," *The Wall Street Journal,* Oct. 29, 1981; and Thomas Edsall, "Conservatives, Corporations Aided AWACs," *The Washington Post,* Nov. 1, 1981.

"we can't let the Jews win": Rosenbaum, "The AWACs Aftermath," p. 21; Ellerin, "The AWACs Debate: Is There an Anti-Semitic Fallout," p. 10.

"The President did not quite say": "Mr. Reagan Blames Mr. Begin," editorial, *The Washington Post,* Oct. 4, 1981.

The uneasiness of . . . Jewish leaders was heightened: Not-for-attribution interviews with two of those present at the meeting. See also David Friedman, "Reagan Makes Major Effort to Allay Fears in Jewish Community in the Aftermath of Debate on AWACs Sale," *JTA Daily Bulletin,* Nov. 23, 1981.

Prince Bandar bin Sultan . . . had sat in: Paul Taylor, "Lobbying on AWACs." See also *Middle East Policy Survey,* No. 40, Sept. 25, 1981.

(On the day of the Senate vote . . .): Rosenbaum, "The AWACs Aftermath," p. 57.

"For the first time since World War II": Ellerin, "The AWACs Debate," p. 10. For a similar view, see Stephen S. Rosenfeld, "Dateline Washington: Anti-Semitism and U.S. Foreign Policy," *Foreign Policy*, No. 47 (Summer 1982), pp. 172–183.

"a new anti-Semitism" had arisen: Leonard Fein, "Notes on the New Anti-Semitism," *Moment* (Dec. 1981), p. 61.

335

The energy crisis is over: See, for example, Youssef M. Ibrahim, "Crumbling Cartel: OPEC's Old Iron Grip on World's Oil Prices Becomes Ever Weaker," *The Wall Street Journal*, Jan. 11, 1985. See also in The American Jewish Committee's *Energy Information Service:* Arnold E. Safer, "The Oil Glut: Private vs. Public Sector Impacts," Vol. VII, Issue 1, Jan. 25, 1985; Eliyahu Kanovsky, "The Diminishing Importance of Middle East Oil: Its Future Implications," Vol. IV, Issue 4, Aug. 4, 1982, and Kanofsky, "Mideast Oil—The Iran-Iraq War," Vol. VI, Issue 1, Aug. 8, 1984. See also in *Petro-Impact:* "OPEC: Ten Years Later," Vol. 6, No. 3 (Sept.-Oct. 1983), and "The End of the Oil Weapon," Vol. 5, No. 3 (Nov. 1982).

"worry about . . . a collapse in world oil prices: Charles Krauthammer, "The Oil Bust Panic," *The New Republic*, Feb. 21, 1983; William M. Brown, "Why We Must Keep Oil Prices High," *The Washington Post*, Feb. 14, 1982, pp. C1, C3.

a 20 percent reduction: Steven J. Marcus, "Conservation in Industry," *The New York Times*, Sept. 30, 1983.

increased the use of coal and other fuels: Douglas Martin, "Role of Oil Is Diminished," *The New York Times*, Sept. 30, 1983.

336

large new oilfields: Ibid., plus references for p. 335.

"they need us a lot more": *The Wall Street Journal*, Oct. 1, 1982, quoted in "The End of the Oil Weapon," *Petro-Impact.*

Saudi oil revenues: Ibrahim, "Crumbling Cartel: OPEC's Old Iron Grip on World Oil Prices Becomes Ever Weaker."

Iraq . . . resumed diplomatic relations: On the significance of that resumption, see Jim Hoagland, "A New Ballgame in the Mideast," *The Washington Post*, Dec. 2, 1984, p. D5. See also Robert L. Bartley, "Arab States Hum a Moderate Mideast Melody," *The Wall Street Journal*, Dec. 11, 1984.

337

U.S. policy has tilted back: George E. Gruen, "A Brief Survey of U.S.-Israel Relations" (New York: The American Jewish Committee), mimeo, Oct. 22, 1984. On the significance of the strategic cooperation agreement, see *Middle East Policy Survey*, No. 92, Nov. 25, 1983, and No. 93, Dec. 9, 1983.

support for Israel is high: In a January 1984 Roper poll, in which respondents were asked, "In the Mideast stiuation, are your sympathies more with Israel or more with the Arab nations?" 44 percent answered Israel, compared with 8 percent indicating the Arab nations. (See "The American Jewish Committee's January 1984 Poll," A Research Note from The American Jewish Committee's Information and Research Services, Table III-A.)

Since 1967 the difference has averaged slightly more than five to one; see Steven J. Rosen and Yosef I. Abramowitz, *How Americans Feel About Israel,* AIPAC Papers on U.S.-Israel Relations: 10 (Washington, D.C.: American Israel Public Affairs Committee, 1984), p. 6.

the American public refused : Asked whether they agreed or disagreed with the statement "Most American Jews are more loyal to Israel than to the United States," 34 percent indicated agreement in Nov. 1981–up from 29 percent in Oct. 1980 but the same level as in April 1980; by January 1984 the proportion agreeing was down to 25 percent ("The American Jewish Committee's January 1984 Poll," Table 1-A). The 1984 poll was taken by Roper, the earlier ones by Gallup.

Fn.: Bernard Weinraub, "Connally Urges Israelis to Leave Occupied Lands," *The New York Times,* Oct. 12, 1979, p. 1; "Merchants of Myth," editorial in *The New York Times,* Oct. 21, 1979, p. E20; George F. Will, "Dear John," *The Washington Post,* Nov. 8, 1979, p. A19.

338

Americans . . . put the onus on the Arabs: Immediately after the embargo, the proportion indicating that their sympathies were more with Israel than with the Arabs rose from 44 percent to 56 percent, returning to the previous level in 1975. (Summary of survey data in Rosen and Abramowitz, *How Americans Feel About Israel,* p. 6.) Other survey data showing the same picture, ibid., p. 33. See also William Schneider, "Anti-Semitism and Israel: A Report on American Public Opinion," unpub. report to the American Jewish Committee, Dec. 1979, and Schneider, "Update Data on Anti-Semitism and Jewish Attitudes," memorandum to Milton Himmelfarb, The American Jewish Committee, March 6, 1979, mimeo; William C. Adams, "Middle East Meets West: Surveying American Attitudes," *Public Opinion,* Vol. 5, No. 2 (April/May 1982), pp. 51–55.

"Later in the seventies: See citations immediately above.

During Begin's latter tenure: Adams, "Middle East Meets West: Surveying American Attitudes." pp. 53–54.

339

the proportion dropped to 25 percent: "The American Jewish Committee's January 1984 Poll," Table 1-A.

Only 8 percent . . . believe: Ibid., Table II-A.

proportionately twice as many blacks: *Anti-Semitism in the United States,* report to The American Jewish Committee by Yankelovich, Skelly and White (1981), Vol. II, pp. 31–48, esp. pp. 34 and 40, tables.

younger blacks are more anti-Semitic: William Schneider, "Update Data on Anti-Semitism and Jewish Attitudes," esp. p. 5 (The Harris survey, conducted for The National Council of Christians and Jews, included a sample of 732 blacks and 1,673 whites.) For earlier data, see Gary T. Marx, *Protest and Prejudice* (New York: Harper & Row, 1967), p. 146, Table 84.

"a gutter religion": See, for example, report by E. R. Shipp in *The New York Times,* June 29, 1984, with transcription of tape of speech in which Farrakhan first used the term. On Farrakhan's past history of anti-Semitism, see Milton Ellerin, "Minister Louis Farrakhan, Leader of the Nation of Islam," confidential background memorandum, The American Jewish Committee, May 1, 1984, and *Louis Farrakhan,* ADL Facts, Vol. 29, No. 1, (New York: Anti-Defamation League, Spring 1984).

a *Los Angeles Times* poll: George Skelton, "Jackson Delegates Favor Farrakhan, Survey Finds," *Los Angeles Times,* July 16, 1984.

340

"All of us black people": Richard Wright, *Black Boy* (New York: Harper & Row, 1945), pp. 53–54.

"I was walking along a street": Quoted in Silberman, "Jesse and the Jews," p. 12.

"The tension between Negroes and Jews": James Baldwin, "The Harlem Ghetto," *Commentary* (Feb. 1948), pp. 165–170.

341

"objective anti-Semitism": The distinction between objective and subjective anti-Semitism was originated by Eva Reichmann in her history of Nazi anti-Semitism (Eva G. Reichmann, *Hostages of Civilization* [Boston: Beacon Press, 1951]). For application of the concept to American history, see Seymour Martin Lipset and Earl Raab, *The Politics of Unreason,* 2d ed. (Chicago: Univ. of Chicago Press, 1978), pp. 157–84.

Fn.: On Jewish merchants in the South, see John Dollard, *Caste and Class in a Southern Town* (Garden City, N.Y.: Doubleday Anchor Books, 1949).

"The key question before us": *The Amsterdam News,* Aug. 27, 1979.

precisely one Jewish spokesman: Richard Yaffe, "11 top national Jewish organizations vow not to stop aiding Blacks," *The Jewish Week,* week of Sept. 2, 1979, p. 2. (According to Yaffe's account, Rabbi Joseph Sternstein, president of the American Zionist Federation, the one Jewish leader who called for Young's resignation, did so without consulting the members of his board. On the role of other Jewish organizations, see my interviews at the time with Henry Siegman, executive director of the American Jewish Congress, and Nathan Perlmutter, national director of the Anti-Defamation League. See also Nathan Perlmutter and Ruth Ann Perlmutter, *The Real Anti-Semitism in America* [New York: Arbor House, 1982], Chap. 8. On Oct. 17, 1979—two months after his resignation—Young told reporters that Jewish members of the White House staff urged him *not* to resign [*JTA Daily News Bulletin,* Oct. 18, 1979, p. 3].)

it was Secretary of State Cyrus Vance: William Safire, "Of Blacks and Jews," *The New York Times,* Sept. 27, 1979.

342

Jackson's . . . inability to distinguish Jews from Gentiles: Memorandum from Nathan Perlmutter to Anti-Defamation League National Executive Committee, Oct. 6, 1983, pp. 8–9.

"It would not be correct to call Baldwin": Harold Cruse, *The Crisis of the Negro Intellectual* (New York: Morrow, 1967), p. 482.

"The state of Israel": James Baldwin, "Open Letter to the Born Again," *The Nation,* Sept. 29, 1979, p. 264.

343
"The resignation of Andrew Young": Front-page article in *The Village Voice,* Aug. 27, 1979.

"The industrial powers": Speech by Jackson at Havana Univ., quoted in Robert W. Merry, "Jesse Jackson's Third World Fandango," *The Wall Street Journal,* July 3, 1984. Other Jackson quotes from same articles.

ideology has played little role: See, for example, Seymour Martin Lipset, *The First New Nation* (New York: W. W. Norton, 1979), Chap. 9.

344
There has been a change: W. D. Rubinstein, *The Left, the Right, and the Jews* (London & Canberra: Croom Helm, 1982), Chap. 3. See also Irving Kristol, "The Political Dilemma of American Jews," *Commentary* (July 1984), pp. 23–29, and Lucy Dawidowicz, "Politics, the Jews, & the '84 Election," *Commentary* (Feb. 1985), pp. 25–30.

"I'm sure that you recognize": M. J. Rosenberg, "Light vs. Darkness," *Near East Report,* Sept. 24, 1984, p. 160.

"These people vote": Ibid. In the third race, against Representative Howard Wolpe of Michigan, Representative Mark D. Siljander sent a letter urging local ministers to "send another Christian to Congress" ("Campaign Notes," *The New York Times,* Oct. 20, 1984).

government of François Mitterrand is far friendlier: See, for example, statement by Theo Klein, president of the Representative Council of French Jewry (CRIF) that Mitterrand is "the best President French Jewry has ever had or is likely to have," in *JTA Daily News Bulletin,* March 8, 1985, p. 3.

the government of Giscard: "French Jewry Since the War," research memorandum from Shulamit Magnus, Feb. 1982. See also interview with Bernard Henri-Levy on *Sixty Minutes* (TV program), April 26, 1981, and Henry H. Weinberg, "Facing the Left and the Right in France," *Midstream* (March 1985), pp. 3–6. For a view contrary to Henri-Levy's, see Michael R. Marrus, "French Antisemitism in the 1980s," *Patterns of Prejudice,* Vol. 17, No. 2 (April 1983), pp. 3–20.

345
similar arguments advanced . . . by: See Irving Kristol, "The Political Dilemma of American Jews," pp. 23–29, and Kristol's reply to critics, *Commentary* (Oct. 1984), pp. 14–17; Lucy Dawidowicz, "Politics, the Jews & the '84 Election," *Commentary* (Feb. 1985), pp. 25–30; Nathan Perlmutter and Ruth Ann Perlmutter, *The Real Anti-Semitism in America.* See also Murray Friedman, *The Utopian Dilemma: American Jews and Public Policy,* to be published. (I am grateful to Mr. Friedman for sharing his manuscript with me before publication.)

only 45 percent: William Schneider, "The Jewish Vote in 1984: Elements in a Controversy," *Public Opinion,* Vol. 7, No. 6 (Dec./Jan. 1985), p. 58.

53 percent chose Reagan: Cohen, *The 1984 National Survey of American Jews* (answers to Questions 85 and 86).

no more than 35 percent: Schneider, "The Jewish Vote in 1984: Elements in a Controversy," pp. 18–19, 58; Seymour Martin Lipset and Earl Raab,

"The American Jews, the 1984 Elections, and Beyond," *The Tocqueville Review*, Vol. 6, No. 2 (1984). ABC News put the vote at 31 percent, the *Los Angeles Times* at 32 percent, the CBS News/New York Times poll at 33 percent, and NBC News at 35 percent. An exit poll conducted by The American Jewish Congress put the Jewish Republican vote at 27 percent; I have disregarded the figure because the sample was clearly unrepresentative. (Only 27 percent of the people surveyed had voted for Reagan in 1980; the figure is so far below that of every other exit poll in 1980 as to call the entire survey into question.)

between 25 and 35 percent . . . switched: Schneider, "The Jewish Vote in 1984," p. 58.

Jewish Republicans denied: David Silverberg, "GOP Disputes Jewish Vote for Mondale," *Washington Jewish Week*, November 15, 1984. See also Walter Goodman, " '84 Poll Results Disputed by Jews," *The New York Times*, Dec. 18, 1984, p. B14; and Walter Ruby, "Network poll findings are disputed by JCRC, Coalition," *Long Island Jewish World*, Nov. 16–22, 1984, p. 3.

346

the president's own pollster: "Moving Right Along? Campaign '84's Lessons for 1988: An interview with Peter Hart and Richard Wirthlin," *Public Opinion* (Dec./Jan. 1985), p. 61.

William Schneider . . . pointed out: Schneider, "The Jewish Vote in 1984," pp. 18–19, 58. See also Adam Clymner and Warren Mitofsky, letter to the editor of *The New Republic*, Feb. 4, 1985, p. 42.

In a bitter lecture: Lucy Dawidowicz, address, "State of World Jewry," 92nd Street YM–YWHA, Dec. 2, 1984. Quotations are from my tape recording of the lecture.

Fn.: Comparison is with Dawidowicz, "Politics, the Jews & the '84 Election," p. 29.

347

they voted against their *class* interest: Lipset and Raab, "The American Jews, the 1984 Elections, and Beyond," p. 402.

there are two reasons: Schneider, "The Jewish Vote in 1984," pp. 19, 58. See also Lipset and Raab, "The American Jews, the 1984 Elections, and Beyond," pp. 401–419, and Earl Raab and Seymour Martin Lipset, *The Political Future of American Jews* (New York: American Jewish Congress, 1985).

Jews place a high value: Leo Rosten, *The Joys of Yiddish* (New York: McGraw-Hill, 1968), p. 148.

348

ABC News asked people: Lipset and Raab, "The American Jews, the 1984 Elections, and Beyond," p. 406.

78 percent of the Jews: Ibid., and Schneider, "The Jewish Vote in 1984," p. 58.

three Jewish Mondale voters in five: Schneider, "The Jewish Vote in 1984," p. 58.

"Had Jesse Jackson": *This World*, no. 10 (Winter 1985), p. 16. I am indebted to Mr. Perlmutter for sharing a copy with me before publication.

In the spring and summer: Cohen, *The 1984 National Survey of American Jews*, Question 87.

by election day: Schneider, "The Jewish Vote in 1984," p. 58.

"have more in common": Perlmutter, in *This World* (Winter 1985), p. 16.

349

talk about "Christianizing America": "We are talking about Christianizing America," Paul Weyrich, organizer of the Committee for the Survival of a Free Congress, has said (quoted in *Moment*, Nov. 1984, p. 33).

"the Prayer Party": The Reverend E. V. Hill, quoted in James R. Dickenson, "Religion Is Powerful GOP Theme," *The Washington Post*, Aug. 24, 1984, p. A8.

"intolerant of religion": "Voters Found Uneasy Over Religion as Issue," *The New York Times*, Sept. 19, 1984, p. B9.

350

A more accurate term: Raab and Lipset, *The Political Future of American Jews*, p. 13.

It is this belief: See analysis of answers in Cohen, *The 1984 National Survey of American Jews*, pp. 14–17.

"the single most destructive threat": Norman Lear, "People vs. Falwell," *Moment* (Nov. 1984), p. 32. Falwell referred to ACLU leaders as "thugs" in a speech in Memphis on Feb. 14, 1985, reported in John Beifuss, "Falwell's Cup Runneth Over," *The Memphis Commercial Appeal*, Feb. 15, 1985, p. B1.

"Committed to the principle": Robert T. Handy, *A Christian America* (New York: Oxford Univ. Press, 1981), p. viii.

"Jews can reasonably feel threatened": Raab and Lipset, *The Political Future of American Jews*, p. 8.

"It is no coincidence": Quoted in *The National Agenda-I: The Evangelical Right* (New York: American Jewish Congress, Feb. 1981), p. 8.

351

petty acts of vandalism: Nathan Perlmutter and Ruth Ann Perlmutter, *The Real Anti-Semitism in America*, Chap. 9.

none of it could be attributed: Of the 377 acts of anti-Semitic vandalism reported to the Anti-Defamation League in 1980, two thirds occurred in four states–New York, California, New Jersey, and Massachusetts–not generally thought of as fundamentalist strongholds. There were 15 acts of vandalism reported in the entire South–4 percent of the national total. In 1981, when the total jumped sharply, the South accounted for 3 percent (statistics from *Anti-Semitic Acts: A Problem of National Concern* [New York: Anti-Defamation League of B'nai B'rith, n.d.]).

46 percent indicated: *The 1984 National Survey of American Jews*, p. 31, Table 7. When the answers are tabulated separately, the results are even

more striking: 19 percent thought that "most" fundamentalist Protestants were anti-Semitic, compared to 17 percent holding that opinion about blacks and 11 percent about Mainstream Protestants (answers to questions 55, 61, and 62).

There was a time: Charles Y. Glock and Rodney Stark, *Christian Beliefs and Anti-Semitism* (New York: Harper & Row, 1966), Chap. 7, esp. p. 129, Table 48, and Harold E. Quinley and Charles Y. Glock, *Anti-Semitism in America* (New York: The Free Press, 1979), Chap. 6.

Fn.: Scholarly reviewers argued that Glock and Stark had used a poor definition of anti-Semitism and an inadequate questionnaire and had also disregarded earlier research (interview with Geraldine Rosenfield, The American Jewish Committee, March 14, 1985). Their organizing hypothesis had been that orthodox religious beliefs were associated with anti-Semitism; for a different (and, in my judgment, far more sophisticated) view of the relation between Christian beliefs and anti-Semitism, see Bernhard E. Olson, *Faith and Prejudice* (New Haven: Yale Univ. Press, 1963), esp. Chaps. 2, 3, and 8.

a 1981 survey indicated: *Anti-Semitism in the United States,* a report to The American Jewish Committee by Yankelovich, Skelly and White, Vol. II, pp. 124, 127–30. The most important finding was that whatever difference in anti-Semitism remained between fundamentalists and other Christians disappears when one controls for education, race, and age.

a more important reason: William Schneider, *Anti-Semitism and Israel: A Report on American Public Opinion,* report to The American Jewish Committee, Dec. 1978.

Cohen asked respondents: Cohen, *Attitudes of American Jews Toward Israel and Israelis: The 1983 National Survey of American Jews and Jewish Communal Leaders,* p. 15, Table 7.

352

Jewish communal leaders: Ibid.

"It is their theology": Kristol, response to critics in *Commentary,* p. 16.

"how significant would it be": Kristol, The Political Dilemma of American Jews," *Commentary,* p. 25.

353

Israel's most implacable Senate foe: See, for example, Rosenbaum, "The AWACs Aftermath," p. 21. This is also the consensus of all the Jewish "Washington hands" with whom I have spoken. On contributions to the Hunt campaign, conversation with fund-raiser, Oct. 21, 1984.

almost without exception: Of the 28 senators generally regarded as comprising the New Right bloc, 26 voted for the sale; by contrast, 16 of the 17 black members of the House of Representatives voted against the sale. See Leonard Fein, "Notes on the New Anti-Semitism," p. 63.

The most striking illustration: Edwin Epstein and Earl Raab, "The Foreign Policy of Berkeley, California," *Moment* (Sept. 1984), pp. 17–21; Earl Raab, "Jackson's Role in the Democratic Party," *Sh'ma,* Oct. 19, 1984, pp. 144–155.

354
As W. D. Rubinstein acknowledges: W. D. Rubinstein, *The Left, the Right, and the Jews*, p. 139.

most Jewish neoconservatives: Seymour Martin Lipset, "Jews Are Still Liberals and Proud of It," *The Washington Post*, Dec. 30, 1984, pp. C1–2.

"It is interesting": "Baptist Leader Insists He Is 'Pro-Jew,' " *The Washington Post*, Sept. 18, 1980, p. A17.
355
it is widely shared: See, for example, 'The Evangels [sic] and the Jews," *Time*, Nov. 10, 1980, p. 76.

a willingness to surrender: See John Murray Cuddihy, *No Offense: Civil Religion and Protestant Taste* (New York: Seabury Press, 1978). The quote is on p. 8.

"Religious pluralism is against": Ibid., Chap. 4.
356
"The Rev. Smith expressed": Anti-Defamation League Press Release, Dec. 18, 1980.

He stands with the Jewish community: Memorandum to Anti-Defamation League National Commission, Dec. 22, 1981. See also Joseph Aaron, "Bailey Smith's Change of Heart," *Baltimore Jewish Times*, Nov. 27, 1981.

"He is a genuine friend": Yechiel Eckstein, *Understanding Evangelicals: A Guide for the Jewish Community* (New York: National Jewish Resource Center, 1984), p. 28.
357
"the 'Evangelist-in-Chief' ": Undated mass mailing from Norman Lear, Feb.-March 1985, p. 2.

"the mixture of religion and politics": Lear, "People vs. Falwell," *Moment*, p. 30.

What is really at issue: Richard John Neuhaus, *The Naked Public Square* (Grand Rapids, Mich.: William B. Eerdmans Publishing Co., 1984).

It is "obvious": Ibid., pp. 81–82.

"There is a clear distinction": James J. Kilpatrick, "A U.S. Crèche? No," *The Washington Post*, Nov. 30, 1984.
358
this "ominous 'narrowing' within": Raab and Lipset, *The Political Future of American Jews*, pp. 19–21.

the political influence of Jews: Ibid., pp. 2–21.

"By dint of this activity": Ibid., p. 7.
359
"Look about carefully": Louis Ginzberg, *Legends of the Jews* (Philadelphia: Jewish Publication Society of America, 1968), Vol. III, pp. 266–267.

INDEX